TRANSCENDENTAL WORDPLAY

Transcendental WORDPLAY

America's
Romantic Punsters
and
the Search for the
Language of Nature

MICHAEL WEST

Ohio University Press
ATHENS

Ohio University Press, Athens, Ohio 45701

Printed in the United States of America

Ohio University Press books are printed on acid-free paper ⊖™

09 08 07 06 05 04 03 02 01 00   5 4 3 2 1

Jacket illustration: Rufus Blanchard, *The Grammatical Tree* (New York: Colton, ca. 1853). Courtesy of the American Antiquarian Society.

Library of Congress Cataloging-in-Publication Data

West, Michael, 1937–
    Transcendental wordplay : America's romantic punsters and the search for the language of nature / Michael West.
        p. cm.
    Includes bibliographical references (p.) and index.
    ISBN 0-8214-1324-4 (cloth : acid-free paper)
    1. American literature—19th century—History and criticism.
2. Puns and punning in literature. 3. Thoreau, Henry David, 1817–1862—Knowledge—Language and languages. 4. American wit and humor—History and criticism. 5. English language—United States—Rhetoric. 6. English language—19th century—Rhetoric. 7. Transcendentalism (New England) 8. Romanticism—United States. 9. Nature in literature. 10. Play on words.
    I. Title

PS217.P85 W47 2000
808'.042'097309034—dc21
                                                    99-089320

For Gram, Roy Stibbs, and Mrs. Calabash

wherever she may be

Contents

Illustrations ix

Preface: Punsters, Philosophers, Philologues,
Pedagogues, and Other *Grammatis Personae* xi

Acknowledgments xix

Abbreviated References xxiii

1. Spellers, Punsters, and Spread-Eagle Linguistics — 1
From Every Mountainside Let Fredish Ring 1 / Webster's Speller Casts a Spell—
and Breeds Rebellion 3 / Lexicographers, Journalists, and the Roots of Our Jocular
Slang 10 / Gentlemen Punsters Off on a Spree 14 / Professional Jesters and the
Wordplay of "Jest Plain Folks" 19 / Further Etiology of America's Punning
Epidemic 23

2. Enlightened Europeans, Romantic Americans: Origins
of Our Transcendental Quest for the Language of Nature — 27
Dreaming Philosophical Dreams about a Language of Nature 27 / How Enlightened French Savants Enlighten Thoreau's Wordplay 32 / Volatile Words: The
Ironic Materialism of Tooke's Diverting Etymologies 42 / Scottish Commonsense
Philosophy of Language Charms American Colleges 46 / The Birth of Comedy
from the Spirit of Philology—Romantic Irony Germinates in Germany 50 / Moon-
shine in Vermont: Coleridge as America's First Punning Transcendental Sage 57

3. Parsing the Language of Nature — 68
Murray's Grammar and the Mania for Etymological Parsing 68 / The Lurking
Transcendentalism of William Cardell's "Philosophic Parsing" 72 / Sherman's
Attack on Cardell: Grammar Enters Politics—and Vice Versa 79 / Unequivocal
Eminence Achieved!!! The Language of Nature Mechanized!!! 91 / Brown's
English Syntax Institution and the Peripatetic Tradition, 1836–1856 102

4. Antebellum America Goes Gaga over Grammar — 110
The Heirs of Cardell, Legal and Illegal 110 / Beautiful Dreamers: Philosophical
Grammarians and Their Homespun Hermeneutics 120 / Thoreau and the Educa-
tional Establishment 125 Verbal Fever Rages on the Ohio—and Elsewhere 130

5. Copyrighting Etymological Ecstasy — 141
Pop Philology: The Vogue of American Etymological Manuals 141 / Native
Roots—Walt Whitman and America's Anglo-Saxon Zealots 147 / *The Scholar's
Companion* (1836) Becomes the Businessman's Friend 155 / Treasuries of Words:
From Roget to John Williams of Lancaster, Ohio 159 / Picking Flowers from
Florilegia—Thoreau and the Etymological Entertainers 163 / Three Ramblers
among Words—Whitman, Thoreau, and William Swinton 171

6. Thoreau and the Life of Words — 183
Sporting with Etymological Metaphysics on a Sandbank 183 / *Walden*'s Dirty
Language and Walter Whiter's Geocentric Etymology 189 / Thoreau's Hydraulic

Psychology of Humor 196 / Elizabethans, Indians, and Animated Nature-Writing 200 / Making Prose Spring from the Earth 206 / Getting the Point of Thoreau's Puns 211

7. The Ironic Drift in Antebellum Language Philosophy   219
Alexander Bryan Johnson: Utica's Philosophical Emperor of Empiricism 219 / Ironing Out Utica's Antinomies with Irony 227 / Rational Theology and Its Discontents 238 / From Paradigm to Paradox: Horace Bushnell Shakes Up American Protestantism 242

8. Go Slow—Man Thinking   251
Emerson Whips Words Until the Silence *Reverberates* 251 / Exploding the Correspondence Theory of *Nature* (1836) 259 / The Playthings in the Playhouse of the Children 268 / The Inarticulacy of Old Man Eloquent 276 / Man Thinking about American Scholars 283

9. Wordplay, Romantic Irony, and the Forms of Antebellum Fiction 291
Irving's Bawdy Double Entendres 291 / Leatherstocking and the Languages of Nature 296 / The Gothic Grotesquerie of Poe's Grinning Skull 303 / The Spell of a Scarlet Letter 315 / The Whale's Tale and Other Literary Flukes 323

10. Savoring the Wiles of Words   334
Dickinson's Love Affair with Dictionaries 334 / A Punning Humorist Grows Up in Amherst 344 / The Paradoxical Power of Webster's Primal Words 354 / Little Emily's Romantic Ironies 362

11. Whitman's Experiments with Language   370
The Allure of Native American Names 370 / Body Language and the Adamic Mystique of Voice 376 / The Mock Epic of the Elastic Self 385 / Ebbing Afflatus—and Unspeakable Ironies 393

12. Thoreau and the Sounds of Silence   402
Harvard Harkens to the Music of a Sphere 402 / A Mediocre Lecturer Flirts with Acoustic Mysticism 406 / Floating from Concord to the Heart of Silence 411 / Unraveling the Rhetoric of *Walden*'s "Reading" 417 / The Social Reverberations of *Walden*'s "Sounds" 421

13. *Walden*'s Antic Dialectic between Self and Society   427
Fusing Polarities with Coleridgean Imagination 427 / The Duplicity of Solitude 430 / Clowning for Visitors 433 / Bean-Field or Battlefield? 437 / A World Reintegrated in Transcendental Sport 440

14. Scatology and Eschatology: The Heroic Dimensions of
Thoreau's Wordplay   445
Thoreau's Excremental Cosmology 445 / Men, Women, and the Pollution of Sympathy 454 / Ascetic Heroism against Dirt, Disease, and Death 460 / Heroic Language Games: Romantic Irony, Art, and the Play of Life 466 / Concluding Unscientific Postscript 478

Notes 481
Index 507

Illustrations

Fig. 1. Noah Webster, *Elementary Spelling Book* (1829; Claremont, N.H.: Ide, 1843), frontispiece. Courtesy, Nietz Textbook Collection, University of Pittsburgh Library System. / 6

Fig. 2. Noah Webster, *Elementary Spelling Book* (1829; New York: American Book Co., 1908), frontispiece. Courtesy, Nietz Textbook Collection, University of Pittsburgh Library System. / 7

Fig. 3. B. D. Emerson, *National Spelling Book* (ca. 1828), frontispiece. Courtesy, Nietz Textbook Collection, University of Pittsburgh Library System. / 8

Fig. 4. Antoine Court de Gébelin, *Origine du langage et de l'écriture* (1774), Table 4. Courtesy, Annenberg Rare Book and Manuscript Library, University of Pennsylvania. / 36

Fig. 5. Antoine Court de Gébelin, *Origine du langage et de l'écriture* (1774), Table 5. Courtesy, Annenberg Rare Book and Manuscript Library, University of Pennsylvania. / 37

Fig. 6. James Brown, *The American System of English Syntax* (Philadelphia: Blackmarr, 1837). Courtesy, Nietz Textbook Collection, University of Pittsburgh Library System. / 98

Fig. 7. James Brown, *The American System of English Syntax* (Philadelphia: Blackmarr, 1837). Courtesy, Nietz Textbook Collection, University of Pittsburgh Library System. / 99

Fig. 8. Smith B. Goodenow, "map of etymology city," *New England Grammar* (1839; Boston: Lewis & Sampson, 1843), reproduced from the original textbook held in the Historical Textbooks Collection, Monroe C. Gutman Library Special Collections, Harvard Graduate School of Education. / 133

Fig. 9. Rufus Blanchard, *The Grammatical Tree* (New York: Colton, ca. 1853). Courtesy, American Antiquarian Society. / 138

Fig. 10. Christopher Pearse Cranch, "becoming a transparent eyeball . . ." fMS Am 1506, by permission of the Houghton Library, Harvard University. / 275

Fig. 11. Christopher Pearse Cranch, "I expand . . ." MS Am 1505, by permission of the Houghton Library, Harvard University. / 276

Fig. 12. Jonathan Barber, *A Practical Treatise of Gesture* (1829; Cambridge, Mass.: Hilliard & Brown, 1831), Plate III. Courtesy, Haverford College Library. / 405

Preface

Punsters, Philosophers, Philologues, Pedagogues, and Other *Grammatis Personae*

Tons of puns—that's what this book contains. Fair warning! If you don't think puns are fun, close it now. What made puns a nineteenth-century art form relished by ordinary folk and cultivated with genius in the literature of the American Renaissance? This study of America's punsters in their heyday tries to explain the appeal of a form of joking that more sedate ages like ours mistrust. As a popular nineteenth-century pastime punning drew energy from the ways in which the nation's classrooms taught English—that is, as if it were Latin. Fortunately, there is more to be said for such teaching than one might suppose. Most of our leading authors were punsters, and all of them registered the impact of punning and philology. Indeed, the larger literary forms that the American Romantics evolved resemble puns in many ways. By midcentury the United States had produced a distinctive brand of American humor, British critics conceded. From Irving to Whitman the major figures of the American Renaissance were humorists—though to make that claim good one must understand how their humor embraced the somber and the savage, the tragic and the terrifying. Puns do just that, as Freud famously suggested. So did nineteenth-century sages like Friedrich Schlegel, who dubbed the stance linked to punning Romantic irony. Sparked by a philological and philosophical struggle with language, Romantic irony more than anything else is the trait that makes our antebellum American authors Romantics.

Like the emerging field of biology from which it borrowed much, eighteenth- and nineteenth-century philology struggled to classify a chaotic mass of data—all the world's known languages. By the later nineteenth century that effort had produced modern linguistic science, which in our day continues to make exciting progress toward that goal. History is written by the victors, however, and the annals of comparative philology are no exception. At the end of the eighteeenth century Sir William Jones glimpsed the shadowy outlines of Indo-European. But another half-century and more went by before the implications of his hypothesis were generally understood. While the brothers Grimm clarified the laws of phonological change in that linguistic family, a host of lesser scholars noted resemblances among languages and puzzled how to account for them. Modern linguistics defined itself by rejecting the dream of discovering the origin of language that animated Romantic philology. Even today the legitimacy of such a project triggers strenuous intradisciplinary debate. Small wonder that the minor philologists who embarked on this quest have been sidelined to historical obscurity as cranks, visionaries, and religious fundamentalists.

Yet they defined the popular understanding of language in antebellum America. Advanced continental philology was terra incognita to most American scholars; indeed, it scarcely penetrated British intellectual circles before midcentury. When our country's dynamic provincials demanded literary and linguistic sophistication, educators then as now responded with authoritarian bromides, provocative insights, garbled half-truths, and arrant nonsense. The taxonomic zeal of Romantic philology was replicated on a humbler scale in the schoolroom conception of grammar. But while schoolrooms taught parsing, they also sparked nationwide punning. Intertwined with the era's educational rituals, puns both satisfied and undermined our rhetoricians' attempt via etymology to find "the language of nature." Jacksonian democracy struck perceptive observers like Tocqueville as an exciting but hazardous orgy of rootlessness, so it is perhaps not surprising that as hordes of Americans trekked westward, their schoolbooks were intensely preoccupied with verbal roots.

Just as puns bubbled up from the Republic's classrooms, so writers tried to harness our naive fascination with the embryonic science of linguistics. Marking his reading copy with special symbols to regulate the voice, Thomas Jefferson had tried to ensure that our Declaration of Independence evoked what pre-Romantic rhetoricians saw as the archetypal language of nature. To understand classic American literature properly we need to know the bizarre philological traditions that shaped the Romantic era's assumptions about language. Much like critical "theory" today, Romantic philology was a passionate, prejudiced, and often preposterous enterprise. But it fanned more curiosity about foreign languages and the ancient, hidden meanings of words than the average American today possesses. Victorian pedagogy bred credulous readers but not lazy ones. *Walden* was aimed at a national audience habituated to etymological speculation. The search for a primal language lurking beneath all natural languages provided American authors with something like a secret language. It encodes their meanings. To fathom them we must decipher it.

Household names for the most part, the writers whom I have chosen to treat at length will startle few except academics mired in debates over canonicity. I plead guilty to a rather traditional hierarchy of literary merit. But the intellectual milieu to which I trace their achievements should prove more surprising. Historians commonly talk of Transcendentalism as an idealistic reform movement bred in the rarefied atmosphere of Boston Unitarianism, often mocked by New York literati like Poe and Melville. But on the lecture circuit Emerson was welcomed as an apostle of enlightenment in states where Unitarianism never penetrated, for Americans across the country had been prepared by village grammarians to entertain novel ideas about language as a gateway to spiritual uplift. New England Transcendentalism witnessed one of the more sophisticated ebullitions of a nationwide ferment of linguistic speculation that might be called "transcendental." Boston's was in some respects merely an elite response to a grass-roots movement already sweeping the hinterlands.

In upstate New York the enterprising Joseph Smith founded a religion in the 1820s by supposedly unearthing buried golden plates invisible to all but him. From their hieroglyphical characters he then "translated" the Book of Mormon. His converts craved philological testimony to the genuineness of the "reformed Egyptian" script on Smith's jealously guarded plates. His first backer mortgaged his farm in the cause only after traveling to New York City to consult authorities about the sample characters that Smith cribbed from philological works, then grudgingly doled out as proof. When skeptics claimed that the name *Mormon* came from a Greek word denoting a particularly hideous baboon, the prophet reassured the faithful of Nauvoo with inspired etymology: "There was no Greek or Latin upon the plates from which I, through the grace of God, translated the Book of Mormon. . . . We say from the Saxon, *good*; the Dane, *god*; the Goth, *goda*; the German, *gut*; the Dutch, *goed*; the Latin, *bonus*; the Greek, *kalos*; the Hebrew, *tob*; and the Egyptian, *mon*. Hence, with the addition of *more*, or the contraction *mor*, we have the word Mormon; which means, literally, *more good*."[1]

Transcendentalism sought to appease the same naive hunger for esoteric roots that the prophet fed so lavishly by the banks of the Mississippi. Digging for treasure buried in the ground was a craze that claimed thousands, but digging for treasures buried in words was a fad that swayed millions. Bogus etymology enjoyed a vogue much like phrenology. It flourished across the nation in hamlet after hamlet, where schoolteachers tantalized pupils with derivations both dazzling and dubious. Scores of these hitherto unsung pedagogues shaped America's sense of the transcendent possibilities of language study in a way that this book hopes to spotlight, to emulate, and perhaps even modestly to revive.

They might be styled Transcendentalists-in-waiting. Likewise, the Romantic authors they inspired—even those who, like Poe, Hawthorne, and Melville, rather mistrusted Emerson—share overlapping concerns with the New England movement that might loosely be called "transcendental." In that sense they are all transcendental punsters, transcendental with a small *t*.

Though Emerson, Poe, Hawthorne, Whitman, and Dickinson all drew on philology for inspiration, Thoreau did more than any other American—indeed, more than almost any writer one can think of—to evolve from etymology a punning style that could dramatize his deepest convictions. Romantic theories of language must often strike us as absurd, and part of Thoreau's genius was the sure instinct that led him to milk them for laughter. As the best linguist and best punster among the era's major literary figures, he receives the most attention in this study. How this Concord ne'er-do-well turned himself into a legend, known to millions around the world who have never read his books and revered with religious intensity by some who have, is a complicated story. I do not pretend to have done it full justice; but I hope that my treatment of him as a witty moralist, satirist, and social critic will make those unsympathetic to the man as well as his more sentimental devotees look again at the actual words of *Walden*, the main literary monument to the era's eccentric etymological speculation. Seduced by the Romantic mantic, too many miss the antic in the mantic.

Yet perhaps his devotees are right to revere the man more than his works. By their Orphic, prophetic stance the works court that response. Emerson, Poe, Melville, Whitman, and Dickinson likewise cultivated Orphic mannerisms to produce writing that apes the status of Scripture, yet all professed discontent with the result of these efforts to embody their visions in words. Like their Romantic irony, their interest in philology was part of the armory of the Victorian sage. For cultivating that pose deftly each writer has been accorded near cult status by disciples ranging from Baudelaire, who canonized Poe as a saint of Satanism, to those modern feminists who worry the curators at Harvard's Houghton Library by their evident desire simply to fondle fragile Dickinson memorabilia as talismans.

However naive, this hagiographic impulse strikes me as healthier than current academic sloganizing proclaiming "the death of the author." With notable frankness, all the major writers of the period asked for the imaginative cooperation of readers in interpreting their texts. They cultivated oracular styles to enlist their audiences in the process of making meaning from mystery. Alas, in current academic discourse veneration of the authorless text too often does less to empower the reader than to apotheosize the critic. Altogether it seems best to admit that this book, at least, has an author, who has not yet been deconstructed but resides in Pittsburgh, Pennsylvania. This book is not simply the product of a creative interaction between the Zeitgeist and you, gentle reader. It is my barbaric yawp. Call me Ishkabibble, there's a whale out there somewhere—scout this book as a hideous and intolerable allegory if inclined. My views—my personal prejudices if you wish—pervade the volume, usually with fair warning. They may prove hard to get rid of. However disgruntling to deconstructionists, this would hardly have perturbed Thoreau, who felt that "the researcher is more memorable than the researched" (*PJ*, 1:414). My main concern is with what American authors wrote and how wordplay invites us to read it. But I hope I have not forgotten that *they* wrote it, difficult though that distinction is to maintain at times.

To keep this distinction vivid my remarks about their writing are seasoned with observations about their lives and characters. If not sages, they were intriguing people living during an era that seems familiar yet was stranger than we imagine. Five of the nine major writers this book treats, for example, have been diagnosed as manic-depressives; four have been claimed as homosexuals. One need not endorse all these judgments to conclude that our schoolroom classics were a more peculiar lot than most suppose. I have no desire to argue that because Washington Irving never married and hung around with known homosexuals in Britain, therefore we should imagine that Rip Van Winkle's twenty years away from home were spent haunting gay bars in New York City. These authors speak to us despite history and through history. But if their personalities do not crudely explain their literary works, neither is biography irrelevant to understanding what they wrote, for ideally that means understanding all the reasons why they wrote as they did. This book falls well short of that ideal. But intelligent readers have far more tact in this respect than academic criticism sometimes credits them with.

Like my definition of Transcendentalism, my definition of wordplay is intuitive and expansive. Readers should expect no elaborate rhetorical classification of puns. Many have been attempted, and some will be noted in passing, but no taxonomy has gained widespread currency. "A classification of the types of linguistic deviation and incongruity would be hard to achieve, for probably all types of language structure have been used as the basis of an effect at one time or another," observes the *Cambridge Encyclopedia of Language*. Though riddles might seem a childish enthusiasm, defining them with linguistic rigor is scarcely child's play. "A satisfactory definition encompassing the whole of the genre is difficult to achieve because riddles come in several linguistic forms and are used for a variety of purposes," laments the *Encyclopedia*. "It is also not easy to draw a clear distinction between riddles and other kinds of linguistic game, such as puns, and 'catch' questions."[2] Philosophers, to be sure, have rushed in where linguists fear to tread, so those who do wish a philosophy of punning may find their needs amply served by current deconstructive criticism. Jacques Derrida, for example, construes all puns as playful evasions of logic. But without wishing to deride Derrida, puns strike me as resisting his formulations just as vigorously as they resist "logocentricity."[3] Where cultural or psychological patterns mark punning, I have highlighted them. But a big book devoted to puns runs enough risk of becoming unreadable without trying to cram every crazy example of wordplay into a single theoretical straitjacket.

My hope is that this book can be read with pleasure and profit by people who recoil from most academic literary criticism. I too mistrust it, rest assured. What I have to say may interest ordinary readers amused by puns, riddles, acrostics, anagrams, dirty jokes, and other forms of wordplay. A hearty welcome to anyone curious about what the origins of words have to teach us, about the links between language study and literature, about the intellectual pretensions of America's English teachers and how good writers learn to transcend their lessons.

As a child in the 1950s, for several summers I spent time at a gemütlich resort on Lake Michigan. After summering there for thirty years, my Ohio grandparents had achieved the dignity of elder statesmen, with rights to the best cottage. But many other guests were veterans of long standing. After lunch my grandparents took naps. Then in midafternoon it was time for amateur philology. Under the aegis of my grandmother, who had been a high school teacher of French and German, anagrams spilled out on a table. The jazzy elaboration of Scrabble was not unknown, but its souped-up scoring displeased local cognoscenti. Like baseball fans who scorn professional football and basketball, anagrammarians cherished the older word game as a finer and purer test of skill. Down from the shelf came the big *Webster's,* and combat was joined. Half a dozen white-haired midwestern ladies, who had honed their vocabularies all morning doing diagramless crossword puzzles, conducted a politely cutthroat seminar in the transmogrification of words. Rummy or reading claimed the men, but some did not disdain to kibitz on the anagram game, smugly suggesting opportunities missed by the players or veiling their wisdom behind clouds of cigar smoke. Time hung heavier than the cicadas during those long afternoons, heavier than the wet bathing suits festooning the veranda—so an excursion to the dictionary was always a welcome diversion even when the needs of the game did not require it. In this bevy of amateur philologists my grandmother was a rara avis in being a college graduate, but all these good people assumed that the derivations of words were fascinating.

So I found them when I gained my entrée to the game by discreetly identifying anagrams for Mrs. Histed, a stalwart Christian Scientist who shunned spectacles, with the result that she sometimes confused *N*'s and *Z*'s. And so I find them still. This book's words all derive from those long-ago afternoons, in the conviction that today as in the nineteenth century many ordinary Americans like to have fun with the esoteric roots of their language. If none of those white-haired midwestern word sharks (rest their souls) would take pleasure reading what follows, then I have sadly abused their indulgent tutelage.

Acknowledgments

If this long book has had a long gestation, part of the reason has been my desire to produce something as substantial as the indebtedness I have accumulated in writing it. However futile that wish, it is a pleasure at last to record my gratitude to all who have supported me throughout a project that has taken more time than I ever anticipated when I set out three decades ago to write a brief note explicating an unnoticed pun in *Walden*.

Fellowships from the Wesleyan Center for the Humanities and the American Council of Learned Societies gave me leisure to hone my thoughts about Thoreau's wordplay when I was under the illusion that it could be largely isolated from its cultural context. The American Antiquarian Society, the Newberry Library, and (in conjunction with the National Endowment for the Humanities) the Huntington Library obliged me with further fellowships that enabled me to spend 1985-86 exploring their collections of textbooks and linguistic scholarship undergirding the wordplay of all the American Romantics. The University of Edinburgh's Institute for Advanced Study in the Humanities awarded me an Honorary Fellowship that helped me flesh out the roles played by Coleridge and the thinkers of the Scottish Enlightenment. Librarians at the University of Virginia, the University of Pennsylvania, the Library Company of Philadelphia, the Haverford College Library, and the Schmulowitz Collection of Wit and Humor at the San Francisco Public Library have been obliging beyond the call of duty.

Harvard University has unparalleled resources for the study of American Transcendentalism. I am thankful that in 1849 Thoreau made such a pest of himself that President Jared Sparks authorized alumni who were not ministers to borrow from the library, for I have regularly availed myself of that invaluable privilege. The University of Pittsburgh has accommodated me with leaves, summer research fellowships, and a grant in support of expenses. Pitt's splendid John A. Nietz Old Textbook Collection is a boon to anyone investigating the history of American education, and its curator Charles Aston has been helpful throughout. Many chapters were first typed by the staff of Pitt's English Department, and I am especially grateful to Patricia Renkiewicz for shouldering this task with unfailing cheerfulness.

Several colleagues at Pitt have done yeoman duty in reading and criticizing earlier versions of this manuscript, among them Richard Tobias,

William Searle, and Timothy Ziaukas, while other colleagues have been an indispensable stimulus to my imagination. Thomas Philbrick's advice helped me shape the book more satisfactorily. By bending "an old man's eagle eye" on my drafts Robert Gale spared me the need to join Yeats in wishing for one of my own. Hans Aarsleff of Princeton University criticized early drafts of two chapters so acutely they shrank into one. David Sonstroem of the University of Connecticut offered wise counsel and reassurance when it was sorely needed; so too did Robert Grudin of the University of Oregon. Many former students served as captive audiences for various chapters, and two in particular provided extraordinarily thoughtful critiques of the entire manuscript; Molly Lundquist's and Michael Gionfriddo's detailed marginalia taught me at least as much as I ever taught them. The editorial expertise of my brother Anthony West and the legal expertise of the late Robert Robinson have both left their mark on these pages, while the hospitality of Anne Brainerd made possible extended summer forays into Widener Library. My sister-in-law Diane Cloutier West guided my fledgling steps in Wordperfect. My colleague David Brumble laughed at my puns, contributed a few of his own, and gave this techno-peasant the unstinting benefit of his computer sophistication.

Anonymous publisher's readers and the staff of Ohio University Press made helpful suggestions. One was to reduce the bulk of my footnotes, which were much more extensive in an earlier draft. Because of limited space, many works that corroborate my thinking must go unacknowledged except for this general statement of indebtedness. Scholars whose work is uncited should not conclude that it was unread, and I trust the scholarly community at large can gauge the extent of my originality.

Without the help of all those named above this book would be distinctly weaker. But since I have not always heeded their advice, none of them should be blamed for whatever faults remain.

A version of the second section of chapter 2 appeared in *English Literary History* 51 (1984): 747-70 as "Thoreau and the Language Theories of the French Enlightenment," and versions of other sections elsewhere were published in *PMLA, ESQ, Harvard Library Bulletin,* and *Teaching Thoreau's* Walden *and Other Works.* I am grateful for permission to reprint, and especially grateful to the DeGolyer Institute at Southern Methodist University for awarding my *Southwest Review* essay "Spellers and Punsters" the 1987 DeGolyer Prize in American Studies.

It remains to thank my wife, Deborah, and my daughter, Alexandra, for putting up with a husband and father who was often transcendentally abstracted. Without their tolerant and generous support this book would not exist. They also serve who only stand and wait, not least by reminding an academic author that for very good reason ordinary readers may not share all his intellectual obsessions.

Were I to enumerate all the ways in which they and others helped me imagine this book, the result would be a rather boring memoir, ranging from friends, relatives, and former teachers through public figures, colleagues, and scholars here unnamed. The dedication must stand as my imperfect effort to thank all those who helped shape my way of thinking about literature and American culture.

Abbreviated References

Standard Editions

James Fenimore Cooper, *Writings,* ed. James Franklin Beard et al. (Albany: State University of New York Press, 1980-). The Leatherstocking Tales are cited from this edition.

Emily Dickinson, *Letters,* ed. Thomas H. Johnson (Cambridge, Mass.: Harvard University Press, 1958-65), 3 vols.

———, *Poems,* ed. Thomas H. Johnson (Cambridge, Mass.: Harvard University Press, 1963), 3 vols. Poems are cited by number in this edition; otherwise citations refer to *Letters.*

Ralph Waldo Emerson, *Collected Works,* ed. Alfred R. Ferguson et al. (Cambridge, Mass.: Harvard University Press, 1971-). Hereafter *CW.*

———, *Journals and Miscellaneous Notebooks,* ed. William H. Gilman et al. (Cambridge, Mass.: Harvard University Press, 1960-82), 16 vols. Hereafter *JMN*; alternate readings and editorial markings silently omitted.

———, *Complete Works,* ed. James Elliot Cabot (Cambridge, Mass.: Riverside, 1883-95), 12 vols. Hereafter *W.*

Nathaniel Hawthorne, *Works,* ed. William Charvat et al. (Columbus: Ohio State University Press, 1962-88), 20 vols.

Washington Irving, *Complete Works,* ed. Henry A. Pochman et al. (Madison, Wisc., and Boston: University of Wisconsin Press and Twayne Publishers, 1969-91).

Herman Melville, *Writings,* ed. Harrison Hayford et al. (Evanston, Ill.: Northwestern University Press, 1968-91).

Edgar Allan Poe, *Collected Works,* ed. Thomas Ollive Mabbot (Cambridge, Mass.: Harvard University Press, 1969-78), 3 vols. Hereafter *Works.*

———, *Essays and Reviews,* ed. G. R. Thompson (New York: Library of America, 1984).

———, *Letters,* ed. John Ward Ostrom (Cambridge, Mass.: Harvard University Press, 1948), 2 vols.

Henry David Thoreau, *Writings,* ed. Bradford Torrey (Boston: Houghton Mifflin, 1906), 20 vols. Hereafter *W.*

———, *Writings,* ed. Walter Harding et al. (Princeton: Princeton University Press, 1971-). Whenever possible Thoreau's Journal is cited by date, with entries before 27 April 1852 referring to the

Princeton edition (otherwise *PJ*). *Walden, The Maine Woods, Reform Papers, Early Essays and Miscellanies, A Week on the Concord and Merrimack Rivers,* and *Cape Cod* are also cited from the Princeton edition.

Walt Whitman, *Collected Writings,* ed. Gay Wilson Allen et al. (New York: New York University Press, 1961–84). *Leaves of Grass* (*LG* and *Variorum*), *Notebooks and Unpublished Prose Manuscripts* (*NB*), *Daybooks and Notebooks* (*DBN*), *Correspondence,* and *Prose Works 1892* are cited from this edition.

Journals and Annuals

AL	*American Literature*
AN&Q	*American Notes and Queries*
AQ	*American Quarterly*
ATQ	*American Transcendental Quarterly*
BNYPL	*Bulletin of the New York Public Library*
ESQ	*ESQ: A Journal of the American Renaissance*
HLQ	*Huntington Library Quarterly*
JEGP	*Journal of English and Germanic Philology*
JHI	*Journal of the History of Ideas*
MLQ	*Modern Language Quarterly*
MP	*Modern Philology*
NEQ	*New England Quarterly*
PQ	*Philological Quarterly*
SAR	*Studies in the American Renaissance*
SP	*Studies in Philology*
TJQ	*Thoreau Journal Quarterly*
TSB	*Thoreau Society Bulletin*
WWQR	*Walt Whitman Quarterly Review*
WWR	*Walt Whitman Review*

TRANSCENDENTAL WORDPLAY

1/

Spellers, Punsters, and Spread-Eagle Linguistics

> The secret source of Humor itself is not joy but sorrow. There is no humor in Heaven.
> — Mark Twain, *Pudd'nhead Wilson's New Calendar*

From Every Mountainside Let Fredish Ring

In the early nineteenth century the supposed royalist undertow of the King's English troubled many Americans. In Anglophobic fits, Hebrew, Greek, French, and Algonquin were each reputedly proposed for adoption as the official language in which the infant republic could "lisp the praise of liberty."[1] Connecticut's Roger Sherman was rumored to have quashed one such proposal with the observation that linguistic patriots might find it more convenient to keep their language as it was and make the English speak Greek. Apocryphal though they may have been, such anecdotes expressed a widespread aspiration. Boston's *North American Review* waged a vigorous campaign for a native style and a national literature. Samuel Latham Mitchill wanted to rechristen the country Fredonia and dreamed of speaking Fredish with his fellow Fredes. A few hamlets across the country memorialize his idea, but the Marx Brothers still spoke fractured English in the Fredonia where they set *Duck Soup*. When in the 1840s the Transcendentalist F. H. Hedge regretfully equated "the English language" with "the English mind," he was only echoing the complaint of Walter Channing's "Essay on American Language and Literature" (1815).[2] Depressed by the spectacle of a linguistic influence so despotic that American English seemed unlikely ever to express "our intellectual vigor and originality," Channing had patriotically hoped for a distinctive literary dialect capable of rendering national idiosyncrasies: "I mean a peculiar language."[3]

James Ruggles undertook to furnish his countrymen with a very peculiar language. No mere national dialect could satisfy his dreams; he proposed a universal language employing Latin roots. That method "of obtaining radical words is, undoubtedly, better than . . . analysis [of ideas], which would have given sounds entirely arbitrary, having no relation to the ideas expressed by them; whereas by taking the roots of a language once actually spoken, such a relation may often be traced; it being admitted that the first principles of every tongue must have their foundation in nature."[4] Founding his system on Latin preserved its links to the language of nature, which figured in his vocabulary as *nat. Nav, nas, nan,* and *nal* denoted respectively ship, nose, dwarf, and canal. The naturalness of his artificial language was compromised by his odd orthography, however. Though in his pages the classically educated can quickly recognize *merd* (dung) and *ming* (urine), neither mind (*mcns*) nor maturity (*mqts*) is so evident. The words of Rugglese seem further estranged from nature by an elaborate system of terminal inflections. To show its literary charms Ruggles translated into his artful terms an extract on autumn. "Viszpxns langzdxr hcktyonpxs skriptzport spegszbxr felhxr" (p. 159). What tongue could render more expressively the sentiment of the English original—"The powers of language are unequal to the description of this happy season!"

Ruggles solicited subscriptions and pestered various luminaries for endorsements. President John Quincy Adams replied wearily on 27 July 1827:

> Sir:—I return herewith, conformably to your request, the Plan of a Universal Language, which was enclosed with your letter of 28th May. An opinion, long since formed, unfavorable to all projects of this character, has perhaps influenced that formed with regard to yours. From the examination, necessarily superficial, which I have been able to give to it, I consider it creditable to your ingenuity,
>
> Respectfully, your fellow citizen

Attorney General William Wirt was hardly warmer, but the postmaster general seemed intrigued. His subordinate C. K. Gardner, also at work on a universal language, was deputed to explain why Ruggles's plan was too remote from nature. Gardner offered a list of improvements that might constitute "the foundation of a *perfect* language" (pp. 178-79). These tepid tributes daunted Ruggles, but in 1829 he published them together with his magnum opus—also his *opus solum*—dedicated despairingly to Congress. He consoled himself for the failure he foresaw by reflecting on his manifold disadvantages isolated in Cincinnati, Ohio, "the want of sources of knowledge in relation to the subject, the want of time for uninterrupted study . . . and indeed, the want of almost every thing . . . as well as a deficiency of abilities" (p. iii). Sadly, the oblivion or contempt that he anticipated has prevailed even in quarters predisposed to sympathy: his work remains unknown to historians of the international language movement. But in combining features of the a priori philosophical languages like that of Bishop Wilkins and the a posteriori simplified languages like

Esperanto, this Ohioan's is arguably the first mixed universal language, with fifty years' priority over Johann Schleyer's Volapuk, hitherto deemed the earliest such hybrid.⁵ Ruggles should be remembered as a characteristic specimen of the age. In an era busy building turnpikes, canals, and railroads, his artificial language of nature promoted a key goal of national policy: improved communication. This first American universal language appeared the same year as the first American locomotive.

Despite their fervent desire for a native patois, linguistic patriots were generally concerned that the emerging American language be a purified improvement of the mother tongue and not a transatlantic corruption. Insisting that neology be "judicious," Thomas Jefferson exemplified such abstemious innovation by apparently coining the term *neology* itself. When Noah Webster became one of the first to call for the establishment of the federal Constitution, he was already knee-deep in linguistic projects. In a New York procession held in 1788 to urge ratification of the Constitution, Webster's Philological Society vied with the floats of other tradespeople by parading a scroll gloriously inscribed "Federal Language." Ostentatiously toting a volume by John Horne Tooke, the marching book-lovers reveled in an elaborate coat of arms designed by Webster. According to his description, it featured a flag "embellished with the Genius of America . . . her right hand pointing to the Philological Society, and in her left, a standard, with a pendant, inscribed with the word, Constitution."⁶ These verbal icons have proved as ephemeral as the ten-foot federal loaf displayed by four master bakers in a wagon. But Webster's *American Spelling Book* of 1783 was a more durable testament of his linguistic patriotism.

Webster's Speller Casts a Spell—and Breeds Rebellion

Earlier educators viewed spelling as a humble incidental study. But at the beginning of the nineteenth century it blossomed into the central linguistic skill. The craze for correct spelling bred scads of textbooks, with zealous schooling backed by extracurricular activity. Edward Eggleston wryly recalled instruction on the Indiana frontier of the 1840s:

> There is a solemn conviction that the chief end of man is to learn to spell. . . . It often happens that the pupil does not know the meaning of a single word in the lesson. That is of no consequence. What do you want to know the meaning of a word for? Words were made to be spelled, and men were created that they might spell them. Hence the necessity of sending a pupil through the spelling book five times before you allow him to begin to read, or indeed to do anything else. Hence the necessity of those long spelling classes at the close of each forenoon and afternoon-session of the school, to stand at the head of which is the cherished ambition of every scholar.

> Hence, too, the necessity of devoting the whole of the afternoon session of each Friday to a "Spelling Match." In fact, spelling is the national game in Hoopole County. Baseball and croquet matches are as unknown as Olympian chariot races. Spelling and shucking are the only public competitions.[7]

The community ritual celebrating such training was of course the evening spelling bee, staged with much the same fervor now devoted to high school basketball games. The whole district participated, each family contributing a candle. These soirées piquantly blended socializing and superstition, romance and self-improvement. The rivalry could be keen. Horace Greeley wept bitterly the only time he was ever defeated. But team format muted individual competitiveness, and the champions emerged as standard-bearers for community norms imperiled by the irregularity of the English language. Eggleston's village squire, who referees the match, rhapsodizes about its significance in religious terms: "I put the spellin'-book prepared by the great Daniel Webster alongside the Bible. I do, raley. I think I may put it ahead of the Bible. For if it weren't fer spellin'-books and sich occasions as these, where would the Bible be?" Many an American hamlet shared the squire's faith that "spelling is the cornerstone, the grand underlying subterfuge of a good eddication" (p. 48).

In its various revisions Noah Webster's blue-backed speller sold some seventy-five million copies throughout the nineteenth century. Championing orthographic reforms—sometimes successfully, sometimes not—it became perhaps the world's best-seller after the Bible. Webster never quite realized his youthful dream of differentiating our spelling sharply enough to require all British books to be reset for the American market, thus protecting our nascent printing and publishing industry. But after years of agitating for national copyright laws to protect his interest in the speller, this canny Yankee triumphed at last. Probably no scholar has ever served God, country, and Mammon with more unabashed self-assurance. When the Appleton firm acquired the copyright at midcentury, one large rotary press was consecrated to printing nothing else. It ran round the clock year after year until it wore out in service—and then it was replaced.

Webster's format stamped itself on our national consciousness. At first he had classified words by the number of syllables and the principles of pronunciation involved, so that learning to spell was always cloudily equated not only with learning to read but with learning to speak. Gradually, however, he began to experiment with novel material "intended to exhibit the manner in which derivative words, and the variations of nouns, adjectives, and verbs are formed. . . . The examples of derivation will accustom youth to observe the manner, in which various branches spring from one radical word, and thus lead their minds to some knowledge of the formation of the language, and the manner in which syllables are added or prefixed to vary the sense of words."[8] But he remained largely committed to a classification independent of meaning. "It is useful to teach children the significations of words as soon as they can comprehend them," he admitted in his last major revision of the speller, "but the understanding can hardly keep pace with the memory, and the minds of children may well be employed in learning to spell and pronounce words, whose signification is not within the reach of their capacities: for what they do not clearly understand at first, they will understand as their capacities are enlarged."[9]

Despite this unpromising pedagogy, the capacities of many students were enlarged, as the flowering of American literary culture at midcentury might suggest. But we must make a conscious effort to reimagine the attitude toward language inculcated by such texts. The interpolated readings were skimpy. Tables of words were paramount. "No man may put off the law of God," read the first sentence upon which students were turned loose. But that divine law itself was put off till the middle of the book, and the student was not allowed to frolic in any prose at all, however pietistic, until he had been drilled relentlessly in long lists of three- and four-syllable words like *alcoran, parallax, sumptuary, apostacy,* and *empyreal.*

The process was laughably inadequate for fostering mass literacy. Weaker students boggled at mastering written English on these terms. As the century wore on, educators grew uneasy about relying so much on the rote recitation of unmeaning words. Demands to revamp English orthography from scratch merged with the reformist babble of antebellum culture. Cincinnati spawned the crusading *Type of the Times: A Journal of the Writing and Spelling Reform Devoted to All True Interests of the Human Race.* In the 1840s Horace Mann campaigned as secretary of the Massachusetts Board of Education against Webster's alphabetic/phonetic approach. He sought to replace it with the "word method" that he found in use throughout Britain and Europe. But the public would not have it. Mann was assailed as unpatriotic for upholding European schools as models for Americans. Throughout the century Webster reigned supreme if not unchallenged.

Why? Whitman spoke for the baffled minority when he declared, "The spelling of words is subordinate. Morbidness for nice spelling, and tenacity for or against some one letter or so, means dandyism and impotence in literature."[10] Yet Webster's speller charged language with peculiar potency. Absorbing vocabulary must have exhilarated some, for spelling drill invested the acquisition of words with an aura of incantation. Deprived of any semantic function, written words first impressed children as darkly mysterious phonetic formulas, to be savored syllabically, reverentially pronounced, and related to other words if possible by similar sounds. "Bare lists of words are found suggestive, to an imaginative and excited mind," proclaimed Emerson in "The Poet" (*CW*, 3:11). By rationalizing such lists Webster helped ensure that for imaginative souls spelling once again cast a spell.

Indeed, Webster half-wittingly recreated for American schools the *rite de passage* long associated with a classical education. For centuries Western civilization had turned privileged youths over to tribal elders, who secluded them from the opposite sex and punished them harshly while inculcating esoteric languages encoding the society's central myths—heroic and religious. Rationalized as "mental discipline," the difficulties and mysteries of Greek and Latin kept their study a male puberty rite long after the knowledge to which the learned languages gave access had been absorbed by the vernaculars.[11] By insulating English orthography from the spoken and written vernacular while ostensibly making it the gateway to both that and the classics, Webster helped ensure that children learning their own language would still grapple with esoteric words as an initiation to adulthood.

The disciplinary link with classical pedagogy was clearly suggested in the frontispiece to the *Elementary Spelling Book* of 1829, where a barefoot urchin implausibly rigged out in a tunic—Huck Finn in classical drag—recoils in awe from the temple of Fame and Knowledge looming like some second-rate statehouse in our hinterlands. A sandaled goddess draws the unnerved tyro forward by an exceedingly limp wrist (see fig. 1). One nostalgic survivor of the speller spoke for many in recalling "that wonderful picture of Minerva, the Goddess of

This Spelling Book is almost universally used throughout the United States, the sale of it being *one million* copies per annum !!!

Fig. 1. Noah Webster, *Elementary Spelling Book* (1829; Claremont, N.H.: Ide, 1843), frontispiece. Courtesy, Nietz Textbook Collection, University of Pittsburgh Library System.

Fig. 2. Noah Webster, *Elementary Spelling Book* (1829; New York: American Book Co., 1908), frontispiece. Courtesy, Nietz Textbook Collection, University of Pittsburgh Library System.

Wisdom, with her lofty and dignified cap (I suppose it was she, though when a boy it bewildered me not a little). . . . It was a picture which I have pored over for hours on the school bench, wondering how those rocks and precipices would ever be surmounted which stood so gloomily in the way of the coveted journey."[12] After midcentury, later editions tried to mitigate juvenile fears by altering the plate slightly, making the student a tender androgyne while providing a path of neatly laid steps through the rocky terrain (see fig. 2). Indeed, to *apprehend* words properly was to be *apprehensive* about them, for their occult power made them hard to grasp, even dangerous. The legend beneath the frontispiece urged arduous effort until "the youth, from lisping A, B, C, / Attains, at length, a Master's high degree." All education not only began by mastering English spelling but was analogized to it. The painful labor involved loomed as a test of manhood, a trial by endurance. The ultimate reward for suffering stoically was an M.A. degree like Noah Webster's, signifying both American adulthood and admission to the penetralia of the learned languages. The alphabet was followed by tables of nonsense syllables, so that a child's first lesson

involved intoning such phrases as "Fe fi fo fu" (p. 28). Any sensitive ear could hear the ominous chant of a giant who smelled the blood of an English major. If the youth lisping his A, B, C enunciated these runes as abracadabra, such a talisman would stand him in good stead on his perilous but vital quest for linguistic manhood. The frightening frequency of failure was graphically represented in the frontispiece of B. D. Emerson's *National Spelling Book* (1828), where a dutiful boy and girl aglow with knowledge mount toward matrimony and apparent sainthood in a nimbus while three weeping miscreants gnash their teeth in the purgatory of protracted illiteracy (see fig. 3).

When the American Adam awoke to literary consciousness in the verdant garden of the Republic, its schools thus encouraged him to utter his first written words in a spirit of quasi-magical naming. Emerson gave this idea classic expression when he defined the Poet as "the Namer, or Language-maker, naming things sometimes after their appearance, sometimes after their essence, and giving to every one its own name and not another's, thereby rejoicing the intellect, which delights in detachment or boundary" (*CW,* 3:18). No writer did more than Whitman to realize the Emersonian program of the poet as Primal Namer, who conjures the world around him into being with the word. For all his distrust of nice spelling, Whitman's gargantuan catalogs of the world simply reflect and expand the catalogs of words beloved by nineteenth-century spellers. Cataloging is verbal, not visual activity. Whitman's omnivorousness is fundamentally linguistic, as he well knew; for he completes his meditation on spelling in *The American Primer* by conceding that "of course the great writers must have digested all these things,—passed lexicons, etymologies, orthographies, through them and extracted the nutriment." Webster would not have regarded being excreted by Whitman as a compliment; his pet project had been a Bowdlerized Bible (1833) expurgating such indiscreet terms as *dung* and *womb*. Being absorbed into the body of Whitman's democratic chants would have pleased the old man still less, for he renounced the Jeffersonian fervors of his youth and became a sour conservative. Still, *Leaves of Grass* is an oblique tribute to Webster. Twentieth-century America has found more effective ways to teach spelling, but none has produced for American poetry a primal namer to match Whitman.

To be sure, the overtly moral atmosphere of Webster's speller is rather suffocating. Weighty with prophetic pessimism, the first monosyllabic sentences come largely from the Psalms. The tyro reader deciphers oracles with an impressive aura of brooding Calvinist sacrality: "There is none that doeth good; no, not one." But after forty gloomy counsels of this ilk a note of special pleading makes itself felt in the moral advice that children are asked to spell out: "When good boys and girls are at school, they will mind their books, and try to learn to spell and read well, and not play in the time of school." The brooding prophet turns into a querulous pedagogue, who seems to have trouble controlling his class. Recreation outside school is also suspect: "Play not with bad boys; use no ill words at play; spend your time well; live in peace and shun all strife. This is the way to make good men love you, and save your soul from pain and woe" (pp. 57–58). Of course, the more Webster insists on his earnest vision of the good child, who "will comb his hair and make haste to school . . . not play by the way, as bad boys do," the more he reveals that children's impulse to play could not be suppressed. Despite the affecting fable of poor Tray, a dog who fell in with a surly mastiff of the wrong sort, then was ill-treated for being found in bad company, many students continued to risk eternal pain and woe by lagging to school, fighting with their fellows, whispering ill words, and amusing themselves in any way possible to relieve the tedious solemnity.

Catering to the desire for comic relief, there flourished a genre of humorous books like *A was an archer, or, A new amusing alphabet for children* (Newark, N.J., 1836). These ranged from genuine primers to risqué adult satire: "A is the artful devices he uses, / B is the Blush as she gently refuses . . . / Y is the yearning for more every day, / Z is the zeal that they carry away."[13] The finest comic alphabets were British. Aimed at adults, however, these did little to vent the rebellious impulses of American youth.

But Webster's solemn speller did offer one avenue for amusement. A student who persevered to the end might be saved from terminal boredom by Table LIII, "Words of the same sound, but different in spelling and signification." How many young minds scanned this five-page list of common homonyms and thought that they must *groan* till they're *grown?* Such crude schoolyard witticisms resurface in every age, but they had a special tang while we conned Webster's phonetic speller in pursuit of mass literacy. In "Puns and Punsters" for *Putnam's Magazine* (January 1854) A. S. Hill defended clever wordplay as sophisticated humor. The puerile bad puns that many relished he traced to "constant perusal of . . . those parts of the spelling book where words of a similar sound congregate" (3, No. 13, 106).

Juvenile punsters could even invoke the blue-backed speller's moral authority for such playfulness. Considering the joyless sense of duty that permeates the book, it is all the more surprising when its concluding moral catechism ends with the question, "Is cheerfulness a virtue?" Webster's answer is a brisk affirmation: "It doubtless is, and a moral duty to practice it." But America's schoolmaster came to literary maturity in the ambience of the Hartford Wits. True, his moralized cheerfulness seems scarcely spontaneous. Instead, the calculating jolliness that he recommends makes him one of our earlier apostles of positive thinking. "Cheerfulness is a great preservative of health, over which it is our duty to watch with care," he urged. "Besides, a cheerful man will do more business, and do it better, than a melancholy one." The Gay Nineties drummer poring over a jestbook to chat up customers was once a tyke poring over Webster's speller and coining faintly rebellious puns.

Lexicographers, Journalists, and the Roots of Our Jocular Slang

Drummers sold Webster's speller by the case to country stores, but his great *American Dictionary* (1828) was not so lucrative at first. But it was a *succès d'estime* from the beginning. Commercial success would follow. Sold in effect as a small encyclopedia, the book was an authority for millions, including some who marched to the beat of rather different drummers. Emily Dickinson called the 1844 edition her only companion. Thoreau owned the revised 1848 edition but also consulted the 1828 folio.

Like his spellers, Webster's dictionary assumed that the language needed to be rescued from contemporary speakers in the British Isles. Their faddish pronunciations corrupted the genius of the tongue, Webster argued, whereas American speech adhered more faithfully to original standard English. To support this contention he evolved his own ramshackle theory of linguistic development. The Introduction proudly blazoned it forth as his greatest accomplishment. Most of his predecessors except for the unreliable Horne Tooke he dismissed with contempt. In analyzing English historically, Webster dallied like Tooke with Anglo-Saxon, but he was also eager to trace its roots to the Middle East—especially to "the Chaldee." Though Babylonian is a Semitic tongue unrelated to the Indo-European family, bumptious ignorance led Webster to treat it as the source of English. With the dictionaries for twenty languages from Europe and western Asia ranged around his horseshoe-shaped lexicographer's table, he became convinced of their underlying affinities while ignoring the continental scholarship that was demonstrating the real nature of Indo-European. Thus though the word *woodchuck* represents a genuinely indigenous contribution to our speech, deriving from Algonquin vocabulary, Webster doggedly ran it to ground in the Persian term for swine. Thoreau gravely copied down this misinformation: "According to Webster, in Welsh a hare is furz or gorse-cat. Also, Chuk, a word used in calling swine. It is the original name of that animal, which our ancestors brought with them from Persia, where it is still in use. Pers. *chuk,* etc. Sans. *sugara.* Our ancestors while in England adopted the Welsh *hwc,* hog; but chuck is retained in our popular name of woodchuck, that is, wood-hog" (5 Feb. 1855).

Though this derivation of the woodchuck would eventually be chucked, the words for swine are indeed cognate in Indo-European. However flawed his etymologies, Webster could rightly claim a genuine advance over Johnson's dictionary in this area. Such lexicographical niceties were exhaustively publicized through commercial rivalry with Joseph Emerson Worcester's dictionaries. In advertising campaigns worthy of Barnum, the Merriam-Webster *New American Dictionary* (1847) vied with Worcester's *Universal Dictionary* (1846) for the endorsements of luminaries and for the lucrative trade that followed legal or educational adoption. The so-called War of the Dictionaries presaged the War between the States, for as Merriam-Webster publicity sedulously implied, Worcester's definitions of some words betrayed abolitionist bias. In the emerging United States, with an essentially stipulative and statutory government that Alexis de Tocqueville characterized as a "legal fiction," dictionaries became a peculiar focus of cultural concern. Washington Irving satirically defined the country as a "pure unadulterated LOGOCRACY or government of words" (6:142–43). Worcester rightly noted that "the Americans have formed their language more from books, and less from oral speech than the English; and they are more in the habit of having recourse to a dictionary for instruction respecting the pronunciation and use of words." Though our squabbling over these linguistic totems remains acerb, it reached its zenith during the War of the Dictionaries. In Dr. Oliver Wendell Holmes's phrase, it was "a disguised rivalry of cities, colleges, and especially publishers," who for business reasons dramatized lexicography as the arena of class and regional conflict.[14]

Worcester's abolitionism and his Anglophiliac conservatism long made his judicious dictionary the favorite with Boston literati. "Etymologies are not the most important part of a good working dictionary," harrumphed James Russell Lowell. "The writers who have wielded our mother-tongue with the greatest mastery . . . did not stay their pens to ask what idea the radicals of those words may possibly have conveyed to the mind of a brick-layer going up from Padanaram to seek work on the Tower of Babel."[15] But Webster's flair for succinct and apt definition equaled Worcester's. By the time that the editors of Webster's *International Dictionary* (1864) silently repudiated the bulk of old Noah's etymological bizarreries for advanced continental scholarship, a nation avid for self-improvement had been taught to view Webster as the arbiter of proper usage. A Merriam-Webster dictionary became not so much the subject of impassioned debate as its indispensable starting point.

Webster justly claimed that his dictionaries contained more American usages than competing lexicons. But his treatment of our linguistic innovations left much to be desired. He could speculate about the Asiatic origin of *Yankee:* "The word Yankee claims a very honorable parentage; for it is the precise title assumed by the celebrated Mongolian Khan, Jenghis; and in our dialect, his titles literally translated, would be, Yankee King, that is, *Warlike Chief.*"[16] Whatever its puzzling origins, one may safely assert that New England was not settled by Yankee Doodle Khans. Webster retracted this dandy conjecture before it disfigured the pages of his great *American Dictionary* (1828), but much remained to amuse the sophisticated, mislead the gullible, and inspire the imaginative.

To do justice to such terms, John Bartlett published his *Dictionary of Americanisms* (1848). Yet he was concerned to show that most New England colloquialisms "derived directly from Great Britain; and . . . are now provincial in those parts from which the early colonists emigrated."[17] Providing the American patois with a British pedigree gratified many riled by British complaints about our barbarisms. But other readers of Bartlett's *Dictionary* were disappointed. "It is too late to be studying Hebrew," opined Thoreau, whose shelves were graced by a copy of Bartlett's. "It is more important to understand even the slang of today" (*W,* 5:223). Like Bartlett, he noted that the expressions of early Elizabethan writers "you now hear only in kitchens and barrooms," where people "speak like men who have backs and stomachs and bowels, with all the advantages and disadvantages that attach to them" (9 Jan. 1855). But Thoreau also relished American speech for its idiosyncrasies. "We must look to the West for the growth of a new literature," he felt. "Already there is more language there, which is the growth of the soil, than here; good Greekish words . . . 'diggings,' for instance. If you analyze a Greek word you will not get anything simpler, truer, more poetical; and many others, also, which now look so ram-like and colloquial when printed, another generation will cherish and affect as genuine American and standard."[18]

Bartlett encouraged a new generation of word-connoisseurs to found *American Notes and Queries* for collecting "*American Idioms, cant phrases, new vulgar expressions.*"[19] "What a pity that we cannot curse & swear in good society," Emerson exclaimed in the privacy of his journal. "Cannot the stinging dialect of the sailors be domesticated? It is the best rhetoric and for a hundred occasions those forbidden words are the only good ones" (*JMN,* 7:524). Whitman too relished "the blab of the pave" and dreamed of an emerging nation where "oaths, quarrels, hiccup'd songs, smutty expressions . . . do not offend" (*LG,* pp. 36, 195). Despite a prim streak, Thoreau likewise could toy with the notion of addressing "a sonnet, genial and affectionate, to prophane swearing," in the conviction that "the utterer of oaths must have honeyed lips, and be another Attic bee after a fashion" (15 June 1840). It was the creativeness of cussing that he valued. Whereas Bartlett rejoiced most when he could show that Americanisms had been legally imported and custom-duty paid, Thoreau could whimsically contemplate "a tariff on words, on language, for the encouragement of home manufactures," exclaiming, "Have we not the genius to coin our own?" (16 Oct. 1859).

Indeed we had. Nothing better reveals the linguistic effervescence of the American Renaissance than the word *okay.* Naturalized in hundreds of languages around the world, it is probably our chief contribution to international speech. To say OK is now okay, but when Thoreau graduated from Harvard in 1837 the word did not exist. Three years later it was nationally familiar, though for decades both Webster and Bartlett failed to include it. It began as a faddish joke in a society addicted to humorous wordplay involving spelling.

Newspapers consumed filler material voraciously. To provide it editors churned out humorous squibs of all kinds. "Why is Noah Webster, of Dictionary notoriety, like the D—l? D'ye give it up? Because he takes you (u) from our Saviour."[20] Bound together by a network of complimentary exchanges, the editorial confraternity was given to cliquish professional joshing. About 1825 the New York journalist George Arnold launched the national vogue for comic cacography with misspelled epistles from a yokel named Joe Strickland. The late 1830s also saw a vogue for elaborate jocular abbreviations. Newspaper columns were suddenly sprinkled with mysterious acronyms that other editors and the public had to demonstrate their cleverness by figuring out. These journalistic fads were flourishing lustily in Boston when the Anti-Bell-Ringing Society (generally called the A.B.R.S.) was founded there on 26 October 1838, to contest a municipal ordinance prohibiting the ringing of dinner bells. That November the A.B.R.S. brought suit in police court to dramatize the ludicrousness of the law. Under such officers as its Lord High Chancellor and Keeper of the Society's Conscience the A.B.R.S. met to listen to mock dignitaries like the "professor of Bell-ocution," "the benign Reliever of the Bell-y-ache," and the "Pacificator of Canadian Re-bells." At the first anniversary dinner they raised their glasses to toast "the ladies—the only belles the members of this society will ever ring."[21]

The expression O.K. developed in that group of sportive sparks to abbreviate the comically misspelled catch-phrase *oll korrect*. Their doings were wittily reported in the *Boston Morning Post*. But until the phrase leapfrogged to New York via journalistic exchanges it was only one of many ephemeral slang expressions like O.W. (for "oll wright"). Originating in the mock-populist antics of Boston bluebloods, O.K. lost its aristocratic taint by entering politics. In the 1840 campaign Tammany rowdies picked it up to ballyhoo Martin Van Buren, popularly known as Old Kinderhook from his birthplace in that Hudson River village. Bandied back and forth by Whigs and Democrats, who churned out jocular explanations of the abbreviation by the score, the word swept the country and then the world.

It captivated Thoreau too. "They do not make them so now," his Concord tailoress gravely replied when he asked for pants cut to his specifications. She spoke "as if she quoted the Fates!" Thoreau found himself "wondering who they are & where *they* live. It is some Oak Hall O Call—OK all correct establishment which she knows but I do not. Oliver Cromwell—I emphasize & in imagination italicize each word separately of that sentence to come at the meaning of it" (*PJ* 3:63). Fashionable dress he firmly rejected, but with the era's linguistic fads his facile parroting suggests a certain sneaking fascination.

Gentlemen Punsters Off on a Spree

The ebullience that spawned such slang provoked other humorous neologisms. "Among the new words which have been coined within the few past years, none have had greater runs than . . . absquatalized," proclaimed the *New Orleans Weekly Picayune* in 1839. Jocular coinages like *blustrification, dumfungled, brassfaceitiveness,* and *goshbustifiedly* suggest the high jinks of professional wordsmiths as much as the oral creativity of the folk. Typical of such badinage was the *Rhode Island Republican*'s injunction that "Brother Greene, of the Post, will please to consider *hisself exflunctified.*" Thus the *Boston Courier* applauded the *Vandalia Free Press* for enriching the American vocabulary with the term *intipsicated.*[22]

Popularized by Charles Dickens, the Wellerism throve in the United States. "Stirring times, as the hasty pudding said to the pudding-stick"—that wisecrack epitomizes the linguistic ferment of America's Golden Age. One scholar notes that as they became a chief component of newspaper filler in the American Renaissance, "puns and word play reached a frantic virtuosity which must be read to be believed."[23] In this environment the conundrum flourished, sometimes bawdily. "What is the difference between this 'ere novel of Mr. Dickens and the hiring of a young woman as a wet nurse?" asked the *San Francisco Golden Era.* "Why, one is the *Tale of Two Cities,* and the other is the *sale of* —— ——."[24]

For such comic material newspaper editors drew not only on their own teeming brains but on the various publications that sprang up to cater exclusively to the public taste for horseplay. In 1831 Charles Ellins published *The American Comic Almanac,* and continued it annually until 1846. By 1860 more than thirty comic almanacs had appeared in Massachusetts alone, under different names and imprints, including *Crockett's Awl-Man-Axe, Sam Slick's All-My-Nick,* and *Komical Comic All-I-Make.* As these forced and pointless titles suggest, their punning was not very elegant. Yet they enjoyed wide circulation. In these cheap thirty-six-page comic books, with their grotesque and crudely drawn illustrations, puns were occasional bubbles bursting from a swamp of often cruel physical humor. "Why is that child falling from its mother's nipple into a shark's mouth like a certain fish swallowed?" asked *Fisher's Comic Almanac* (Boston: Fisher, 1844). Answer: "Because it's a gone sucker" (sig. A4v). Even in almanacs with a Yankee theme the emphasis on violence and sexuality is startling. Less dour than commonly supposed, the New England yeoman who bought them was rough but not stuffy, crude but no prude.

Puns proliferated in the buckram-bound jestbooks that editors plundered for their filler material. Though sometimes also styled almanacs, these collections of jokes were genuine books that cultivated verbal wit more than the brief, paper-backed almanacs where jokes supplemented astronomical tables. Their prefaces usually genuflect to intellectual standards by treating the pun as a lower form of humor while striving to justify it. "Laugh and grow Fat" was the jestbooks' motto. Jokes could stave off death, they professed, for so long as we could chuckle, we would never die unless it were of laughter. "There is no wisdom more profound than that which develops itself by our risible faculties," proclaimed *The American Comic Almanac* (Boston: Allen, 1835). "I feel an antipathy towards a whale, because it has a tendency to blubber" (p. 2). Strike through the mask, and beneath this genial rationale lurk the same brutal preoccupations that characterize the cheap paper pamphlets. Its jokes appealed to an audience for whom sudden death was common and feared. Hostility was a driving force in this humor. The compiler's jocular antipathy to whales and crybabies was writ large in the lives of many New England sailors. His pun on *blubber* is a verbal harpoon. If Ahab glanced at a jestbook, it would have resembled this one. And what the maimed captain of the *Pequod* or his first mate might have scorned to read, Stubb, Flask, and the crew would have relished.

Such anthologies were not exclusively lowbrow in their appeal. Thus *The Humorist's Own Book* (Philadelphia: Key & Biddle, 1834) retails an anecdote about "a man who . . . proposed to write an Etymological Dictionary of the English language. Being asked what he understood the word *pathology* to mean, he answered . . . 'Why, the art of *road-making*, to be sure'" (p. 187). Readers expected to enjoy this joke not only knew the meaning of the word *pathology*—for which the anecdote gives no explanation—many apparently had some sense of its Greek root. Today people are amused when bartenders style themselves professors of *mixology*. But even sophisticates cannot tell whether this mock-pompous commercial coinage involves linguistic miscegenation. As a matter of fact, *mixo-* is a perfectly good Greek root like *-logy*, whereas the neologism *television*, which raises few hackles, is actually the mongrel offspring of Greek and Latin roots—*proculvision* would have been of purer blood.

Punning was pandemic when E. Gunnison purchased a standing ad in the *Concord Freeman* for 15 March 1846 headed "To Dye, or Not to Dye." In it this village cleaner informed customers that "he is yet alive, though often dyeing! and is ready to dye for anyone who may need his services in the DYEING ART." Tradesmen and advertisers have long cherished puns—witness slogans in today's yellow pages. But gentry joined democratically in the game. Thoreau's boon companion Ellery Channing was an inveterate punster, whose blue blood sometimes expressed itself in blue humor. Dr. Oliver Wendell Holmes, the very model of a Boston patrician, cracked off-color jokes for his medical students. Beginning his lecture on the female genitalia by blandly observing, "My subject this

afternoon is one with which I trust you young gentlemen are not familiar," he went on to compare the birth canal to an express company,
"Because they both contract to make / Delivery of freight."[25] Our era
furnishes fewer such virtuoso displays of the punster's art, nor do our
critical theories do much to discriminate levels of punning. Victorian
America at least felt the need for critical discrimination. "We can see
whence the notion has arisen that any one can make puns, and that
brainless men are the most likely to make them," A. S. Hill conceded in
his *Putnam's Magazine* essay on punning. "But we must not forget that
it is one thing to pun and quite another to pun well" (3, No. 13, 106).

Reviewing the claims made for puns, however, Willis Gaylord Clark
echoed Lamb in arguing that "the *worst* are the *best*. The most far-
fetched are certainly the most unexpected and consequently the most
humorous." Whereas the Autocrat of the Breakfast Table became Boston's paragon of finesse in this popular art, Washington Irving remained
the beau ideal of Knickerbocker wits like Clark. Philadelphians were
once the most atrocious punsters in the Union, Clark granted. But by
1835 "they have the name only, which, however, has attained such an
altitude, that they sleep on their laurels."[26] New York's taste for literary
froth let punning flourish, perhaps all too readily. In Manhattan's more
frivolous society the pun never developed the intellectual weight that
New England gravity forced upon it.

Dr. Holmes was the Brahmins' punster *sans peur et sans reproche,*
but he chivalrously acknowledged one peer—Thomas Gold Appleton,
the first man in Boston to cultivate a mustache. Politely declining to
swell his ample inheritance by hard labor, this genial bon vivant set
about living on it tastefully. "All good Bostonians expected when they
died to go to Paris," he declared, so he divided his time between Europe
and New England. As a gentlemanly amateur he painted, patronized the
arts, wrote travel sketches and light essays. He was a fixture of Newport
summer society, a prototype of the gentlemen in Henry James's novels
whose sophistication expresses itself tiresomely in arch wordplay. Yet he
never forfeited the respect of Boston's cultural luminaries. He was Longfellow's devoted brother-in-law and neighbor. Emerson thought it
supremely desirable that he meet with the Town and Country Club. This
bachelor was indeed a clubbable soul. When Harvard classmates wanted
to form a society to meet once a decade, he suggested calling the club
"*Boors drinking,* after Teniers." Like a proper Boston gentleman he had
been grounded in the classics, but at George Bancroft's progressive
Round Hill School in Northampton. His letters home to his father were
at first so poorly spelled as to earn the eleven-year-old schoolboy a

paternal rebuke. But Round Hill's training was thorough, and Appleton *père* was soon reassured to learn that his irrepressible son was "dashing on in Homer at the rate of eleven knots an hour,—blinding Miss Polly Phemus, sacking cities, falling in love with goddesses."[27]

To foster nature study the school rented a smack for fishing expeditions. One catch in particular impressed the young Appleton, as he later recalled. "One waggish creature made himself into a ball when pummeled, and emitted ejaculations like grunts, which convinced everyone that if not one of the happiest, he was certainly one of the most humorous of dying fishes." The schoolboys were encouraged to moralize the event, but Appleton finally did so less like a good Unitarian than like a Transcendentalist:

> Perhaps it was the Deity's intention that we should think him funny . . . even in death, rather than, like the boys in model story books, profit by the occasion, and drop a sympathetic tear. This element of fun, in the works of God, is one which Religion has accepted with Reluctance. . . .
> On conversing once with our great naturalist upon these elements of humor in the works of God, the many animal conditions of our own lives, the many queer, prodigious growths he has made,—the living puns, for such they really seem to be, with a laugh the Great Agassiz said he hoped to write, yet, a work to bear the title, "Dieu comme Farceur."[28]

This jovial dilettante retained the vestiges of Puritan conscience, so his freakish humor remained tinged with gravity. At the end of his life he grew hard of hearing. "It may be only wax in your ears," speculated a lady consolingly. Appleton knew the Almighty Punster too well to believe that. "Ah, my dear!" he replied, "I fear it is not wax but wane" (*Life*, p. 345).

The *New York Literary Gazette* dramatized the clash between rival schools of punning through a scene set in the dining room of a packet bound from New York to Boston:

> "Your friend," said a young chap, who sat next Ned W——, and whose crows-feet discovered him to be a Junior of Harvard—"your friend is a man of the *homines gravis* class," looking full at my swimming plate. "A pun, a pun," exclaimed I, "who made it—was it yon *puny* cur?" "*Cur punis.*" "How dare you!" "Adair, sir, Charles Adair, Jun." "Scandalous! 'tis *too* much by the twins," said I, making an attempt to damp his ardour by thrusting him with his own weapon. "I thought so *before*," echoed this mirror of punning chivalry, . . . "My friend there," said Adair, "is a little humorous, but—" "Undoubtedly the effect of butter," interrupted an M.D. who until then had been too busily engaged in discussion of the eatables. "So" —"Very sore," retorted the invincible. "You're a wit," sighed the man of physic. "Not a *whit*—" was the ready answer. . . . "Is this,"

thought I, "Can this be any thing belonging to that Alma Mater, which was once so proud of her poorest sons, and to whom I still look back with fond filial remembrance? . . . May I not meet the crows-feet on many such!" The good doctor was likewise an alumnus.[29]

Such tedious, mechanical raillery was very much to New York's taste. But the contest is dominated by Harvard graduates, with young Adair, putative class of 1827 (Tom Appleton was '31), easily besting two elder alumni and cowing a table of New Yorkers into silence by punning atrociously not only in English but in Latin (*gravis* = gravies, etc.). Here we see gentlemen infusing learning into a popular oral art form so that—in the words of A. S. Hill—they "may make puns and after sufficient explanation convulse the ladies" (106). As piping hot oral repartee such banter might have some smack to it. Served up coldly in print it tends to congeal on the plate, for much less skill is required to write like this than to talk like this.

Professional Jesters and the Wordplay of "Jest Plain Folks"

The fluid distinction between oral and literary punning is important. Brilliant puns may stale on the page unless the context of an anecdote clearly indicates their role as oral repartee. Many jestbook anecdotes do just that. Perhaps the most successful attribute so-called bons mots to historical personages. One enjoys a witty remark attributed to the jestbook hero Frederick the Great, even if apocryphally, more than in the mouth of a fictional character created for the occasion. Historical context lets one reimagine the pun as a flash of living wit rather than a readily calculated literary witticism. The jokes peddled in almanacs were not meant just to be read. Like the era's popular comic songs, jestbooks were often bought by people who hoped to reintroduce their favorite jokes into speech by telling them in company. That fine raconteur Abraham Lincoln claimed that he never invented a joke. The scores of comic anthologies are in a sense anthologies of comic scores.

As the century wore on, the pun lost its roots in oral discourse—to its detriment. After the Civil War comedians in the line of Artemus Ward whipped up a frenzy of dialect humor, cacography, and wordplay. But platform antics that were funny viva voce were either not readily transcribed to print—or too readily transcribed. The problems involved are foreshadowed in an anecdote of Mrs. Partington. In this New England widow the Boston journalist B. P. Shillaber sketched an American Mrs. Malaprop. She was a comic creation of considerable merit and influence, a prototype for Tom Sawyer's Aunt Polly. With her nephew Ike she delighted audiences in the 1850s:

"There was a cereous accident happened down here, just now, aunt," said Ike, running in hastily.

"Dear me!" cried Mrs. Partington, dropping her knitting work and starting from her seat in great alarm; "what upon airth was it, Isaac? Was anybody killed, or had their legs and limbs broke, or what?"

"O," replied he, giving his top a tremendous twirl, that sent it round among the chairs at a great rate; "O, no! 't was only a man capsized a box of candles, that's all."

The old lady looked at Ike reproachfully. He will break her heart one of these days. Her mind, at the first alarm, had flown among her balsams, and bandages . . . and to be thus lowered down from her hope of usefulness was too bad. But Ike went out with his top, laughing all the while, and the old lady subsided into the old arm-chair, and went on with her knitting.[30]

The strength of the sketch lies in its ironic portrait of an old woman famous for making Ike warm the water before drowning kittens. Here she is so good-natured, so proud of her huswifery (and so bored), that she innocently wishes someone harm. It breaks her heart to learn that everyone is safe, so that she cannot unbosom herself and show off her medicine chest. Telling details of dialect and setting lend the scene verisimilitude and eke out the pawky rendition of character. But the excuse for the anecdote is the pun on *cereous* (*waxen/grave*). Ike's perpetrating such a pun strains credibility. Moreover, we feel that Mrs. Partington, who cannot understand it at all, would do more than look reproachfully at a scamp who seems to her simply to have lied. Here the author's hand obtrudes to violate characters' speech and behavior, and the anecdote rings false.

To the extent that Ike's pun is credible, we must imagine that young scapegrace diligently conning Webster's lists of strange polysyllables. As his use of *capsized* suggests, midcentury American schooling has given him a better vocabulary than his aging aunt. The punning mania to which the jestbooks testify was a reaction to American spelling pedagogy. "Why is imprisonment like a person eating dinner in the rail cars," *Fisher's Comic Almanac* (1844) queried its readers, then tickled them by explaining, "Because its in-cars-a ration, (incarceration)" (sig. Br). Such jokes pleased an audience relentlessly drilled in dividing words syllabically, then spelling them by sounding them out. Conundrums do not strike us as sophisticated humor, but we have not been trained to regard spelling as the quintessence of the intellectual enterprise. The man-about-Gotham delighted in spelling squibs that would scarcely make the *New Yorker* today: "There is in Webster's old spelling-book a spelling and defining lesson of words of four syllables. A friend mentions a ludicrous mistake made by a district school-boy in the country, in the exercises of this lesson. One of the words happened to be '*Acephalous*: without a head.' It was divided as usual into its separate syllables, connected by a hyphen (which 'joins words or syllables, as sea-water!') which probably led the boy to give a new word and a new definition: '*Ikun* do it,' and he did; '*A-c-e-p-h, cef,* ACEPH—*a louse without a head!*'"[31]

Apocryphal, maybe—but such blunders were doubtless common. Whether or not this hapless offspring of the American peasantry persevered in his education, he probably learned to vent his anger at the clerisy through such popular abbreviations as "A.B.—Apt to Blunder," "LL.D.—Licensed to Lie Damnably," or "M.D.—Maker of Dead Men."[32] In *Broad Grins* (New York: Dick & Fitzgerald, ca. 1850), the pseudonymous Pickle the Younger told this typical joke: "A teacher, one day endeavoring to make a pupil understand the nature and application of a passive verb, said—A passive verb is expressive of the nature of receiving an action, as, Peter is beaten: now, what did Peter do? The boy, pausing a moment, with the gravest countenance imaginable, replied— Well, I don't know; I s'pose he *hollered*" (p. 10). Holler Peter did, and his yell resounds in the jestbooks—the docile rebellion of a people who found it hard to take their schooling quite as passively as their teachers wished.

Philander Q. Z. Doesticks whimsically reveals how the nirvana of the nation's professional humorists was dreamed up in grammar school while sweating over columns of impenetrable words. Wordplay will make him either celebrated or notorious, he avers:

> Through an accidental rip in the curtain of futurity, I have caught a glimpse of the Goddess of Fame. I have heard her sing out from her rather elevated position for me to come up and take a "hasty plate" of glory; and I have not the heart to refuse the request of such a good-looking female, preferred in such elegant language. I am going to shin up the slippery rope leading to her aerial temple (for accurate dimensions and appearance, see engraving in the Old Elementary Spelling Book), for the purpose of taking a hand in the game of literary renown, trusting that Nature has given me trumps enough to make the "game," and that Fortune will deal me all "the honors."[33]

Renown did indeed come to him. After the Civil War many of his Phunny Phellows became even more popular with their pun-a-minute books and lectures. Like the audience that relished their verbal antics, these jesters paid ambivalent tribute to Webster's misconceived but powerful pedagogy. In assaulting Fame's temple Doesticks seems a dutiful pupil, but his metaphor also suggests that he is treading in the footsteps of Jack the Giant-Killer.

All their whimsicality scarcely concealed the aggressive animus underlying the jest. "A pun does not commonly justify a blow in return," argued Oliver Wendell Holmes, but it "is *prima facie* an insult to the person you are talking with. It implies utter indifference to or sublime contempt for his remarks, no matter how serious."[34] Among the belligerent punsters of the American Renaissance none was more feared than the journalist George Prentice. Editing the *Louisville Daily Journal* with dash from 1830 to 1858, Prentice wielded the pun as a weapon on behalf of the Whigs. He could parry opponents' rhetoric with lethal effect. "The 'Richmond Enquirer' calls us 'a miserable calumniator,'" Prentice noted. "He, on the contrary, is a first-rate one. Practice makes perfect."[35] Deft puns were weapons in a journalistic world where editors still challenged one another to pistols. "James Ray and John Parr have started a locofoco paper in Maine, called the 'Democrat,'" Prentice observed. "Parr, in all that pertains to decency, is below zero; and Ray is below Parr."[36] After three decades of such verbal dueling Prentice collected his best ripostes in a volume. His publisher insisted on the title of *Prenticeana* (1860), so well-known had his name become.

According to Oliver Wendell Holmes, the appeal of such punning insults lay precisely in their capacity to break social taboos with impunity. "Homicide and verbicide—that is, violent treatment of a word with fatal results to its legitimate meaning, which is its life—are alike forbidden," he claimed. "Manslaughter, which is the meaning of the one, is the same as man's laughter, which is the end of the other." Thanks to tart epigrams, Prentice gained enough practice in editorial rencontres to become known as "the best pistol shot in Kentucky."[37] Rival editors who attempted to retaliate in kind were no match for his punning barbs. "Messrs. Bell and Topp, of the 'N.C. Gazette,' say that 'Prentices are made to serve masters.' Well, Bells were made to be hung, and Topps to be whipped" (in Piatt, p. xxi). When a Southern paper denounced the Northern Democrats as "a wishy-washy party," the *Journal* gleefully pounced on the item. "They are no doubt a wishy party," Prentice allowed, "but there's precious little of the washy about them." With such bons mots he terrorized Democratic editors, who reportedly "trickled with the cold sweats of apprehension and shook in their boots in anticipation of the hour when the mail would bring the Journal to their sanctums." When the Civil War broke out, the *Louisville Journal* was instrumental in keeping Kentucky in the Union camp. A grateful Lincoln made Prentice a key adviser.

"Louisville is situated on the South bank of the Ohio River, at the Falls," observed a New York newspaper, "but it is significant for nothing except the place where the *Louisville Journal* is published" (in Scrugham, pp. 23-25). The paper became the country's leading Whig organ. At times half the visitors in town seemed to be victims of Prentice's wit seeking to call the editor out. To "the miserable code" of dueling he had a principled aversion. But scruples about premeditated killing did not dampen his zest for spontaneous encounters. Receiving an insulting card from an editor during the turmoil of a Know-Nothing campaign, he replied, "Tell Mr. Hughes I will be down as soon as I load my pistols."[38] When another editor fired at him without warning and wounded him near the heart, he threw his assailant to the ground. A sympathetic bystander handed Prentice a knife. "Kill him! kill him!" shouted the crowd. But Prentice loosened his hold. "I cannot kill a disarmed and helpless man," he explained (Piatt, p. xv). The editor of the *Louisville Courier*, Reuben Durrett, ran a paragraph intimating that Prentice fell in the Ohio River while drunk. Prentice did not deny the truth of the story but demanded its cancellation. It ran again. Prentice and Durrett exchanged shots, the police intervened, and each editor, honor satisfied, had a ball extracted from his hide.

In old age Prentice could not remember how often he had been shot or his life despaired of. During his last decades he suffered from the occupational malady known as *chorea scriptorum*. It obliged him to dictate longer editorials to a secretary. With painful effort, however, he still wrote paragraphs and brief notes, often grasping the pen in his left hand. Penning his punning left-handedly only made it more sinister. With the sure touch of a master polemicist he kept detonating the squibs that made him famous as the peer of such British punsters as Charles Lamb, Sydney Smith, and Douglas Jerrold. His conversation was unimpressive. Witty company only made him seem boring and awkward. He chiseled his quips from the written language that he learned as a farmboy preparing for college by memorizing Lindley Murray's grammar in a week and reciting the twelfth book of the *Aeneid* as a half-day's lesson. "I want an *e*," he muttered on his deathbed—then, "I want an *i*" (Piatt, p. xli). Still dreaming of honing his spelling, the pugnacious old punster died.

Further Etiology of America's Punning Epidemic

It was not just elegant whimsy that led Dr. Holmes to find laughter in slaughter. His own chronic wordplay was a relief from the strains of medical practice. In the period's discussions of humor no theme is more stressed than its role in fighting sickness. "Many people laboring under depressed spirits fly immediately to a physician, or resort to divers quack medicines, to cure that which might be remedied by a hearty laugh," opined Dr. William Valentine. "When a person laughs, every organ in the human system is thrown into action, and produces an excitement conducive to health."[39] This comedian cultivated the role of mock-physician in such books as *A Budget of Wit and Humor; or Morsels of Mirth for the Melancholy: A Certain Cure for "the Blues," and All Other Serious Complaints* (1849). Most jestbooks espouse the conviction rooted in traditional humor physiology that jokes worked like pills to purge melancholy. The therapeutic value of humor was such a stock notion that medical advertisers capitalized on it. Bristol's Sarsaparilla Company of Boston issued *Bristol's Free Almanac* in 1844, the first of myriad patent medicine almanacs.

To be sure, the jestbooks' professions of a public health mission must be taken with many a grain of salt. Mingled among them, however, were grains of truth. In *Laughable Anecdotes* (Frankfort, Ky.: Kentuckian, 1832) the pseudonymous Lunenburg G. Abernethy related this story: "A young physician being requested to give the origin and meaning of the word consumption, went on to say that the word was composed of three other words, viz: 'con, sum, and shun.' 'Con,' said he, 'means the complaint is constant to the patient; sum means that some persons have the complaint, and shun means, shun it if you can'" (p. 21). Tuberculosis was pandemic in nineteenth-century America, feared more than cancer or AIDS today. Its menace was magnified by faulty medical diagnoses ascribing half all adult deaths to this plague. Baffled by the disease, even sophisticated physicians could do little to stem its ravages. And as the anecdote hints, Kentucky medicos were not very sophisticated.

On one point medical wisdom and popular folklore agreed. However desperate a consumptive's plight, despair only aggravated the disease that was killing him. If to laugh and grow fat were beyond hope, at least one might laugh and waste away a little more slowly. Like the gallows humor of Abernethy's pun, the chipper wordplay of the jestbooks was often a way of tolerating the intolerable. As Henry James would suggest, for the American citizen of the 1830s life was often lived so bleakly that "it would be cruel, in this terrible denudation, to deny him the consolation of his national gift, that 'American humour' of which of late years we have heard so much." Deprived of most comforts of high civilization on Kentucky's dark and bloody ground, Lunenberg G. Abernethy's reader still knew, in James's fine phrase, "that a good deal remains; what it is that remains—that is his secret, his joke."[40]

The American abroad took his painful secret with him but was willing to share it. "Whatever is it that makes you Americans pun so dreadfully?" inquires an English hostess in a sketch by Tom Appleton. "I suppose it is your familiarity with percussion-caps and revolvers. . . . There was a man here from Philadelphia the other day who emptied all the chambers of his brain into mine, snapping such shots that I thought I should expire."[41]

Locating human life on the border between tragedy and comedy, Emerson found that the essence of all humor seems to be halfness—not the wholeness of nature revealed by reason. Arguing that the human form was a pledge of wholeness, he linked comedy to corporal injury and disease, since "a nail of pain and pleasure . . . fastens the body to the mind." Fractured expectations result in "violent convulsions of the face and sides." As for wordplay, "in all the parts of life, the occasion of laughter is some seeming, some keeping of the word to the ear and eye, whilst it is broken to the soul." Puns are crippled words. Like the jestbooks, Emerson stresses our need to guffaw. But in insisting that "we must learn by laughter, as well as by tears and terrors . . . explore the whole of nature," he almost inverts their emphasis on the therapeutic function of humor. His theory of the comic as maimed reality is grounded in a surprisingly bleak notion of metaphysical integrity:

> Mirth quickly becomes intemperate, and . . . some persons have been tick-led to death. The same scourge whips the joker and the enjoyer of the joke. When Carlini was convulsing Naples with laughter, a patient waited upon a physician in that city, to obtain some remedy for excessive melancholy, which was rapidly consuming his life. The physician endeavored to cheer his spirits, and advised him to go to the theatre and see Carlini. He replied, "I am Carlini."[42]

"Wherever you find Humor, you find Pathos close by its side," agreed the Boston critic E. P. Whipple.[43] Emily Dickinson put it even more starkly: "Mirth is the Mail of Anguish" (#165). Few Americans were better armored than the manic-depressive James Russell Lowell, whose feats in punning contests on summer porches delighted his wife. "Thackeray came at ten: Longfellow, Dana, Quincy, Estes, Howe, Felton, Fields and another," wrote the English poet A. H. Clough recalling one supper at Elmwood. "Puns chiefly."[44]

On the evening of 11 October 1861, a genteel assemblage flocked to Tremont Temple for what was billed as The Brains of Boston Conundrum Contest. Prizes had been offered for the best conundrums submitted by ladies and gentlemen. "Why is Mrs. Lincoln like Lazarus?" asked one entry in the distaff competition. "Because she reposes in Abraham's bosom."[45]

While the audience snickered over such witticisms, good Boston brains were soaking into the field at Bull Run. Unlike one biblical Lazarus, the boys who reposed there would not rise again in this life. Abraham's bosom was currently vexed because General George B. McClellan seemed in no hurry to retrieve the Union's fortunes in battle. Instead, Little Mac was predicting imminent assault upon Washington by Confederate hordes under General Robert E. Lee. Public confidence in the nation's leadership, both civil and military, was shaky. One Boston lady who visited McClellan's army that fall finally read a righteous sentence by its dim and flaring lamps. Julia Ward Howe jotted it down on U.S. Sanitary Commission letterhead. But what first struck her eye in the capital, adjoining Willard's Hotel where she lodged, was the grisly advertisement of a firm that embalmed and forwarded soldiers' corpses. Introduced to the president, she could not forget "the sad expression of Mr. Lincoln's deep blue eyes," for he was laboring "under a terrible pressure of doubt and anxiety."[46]

Not the least of his problems was how to pay for what he described as "this most uncivil war." His secretary of the treasury solemnly brought up the national debt. "Its great interest," replied Lincoln, "claims my most devout attention."[47] To the consternation of his cabinet, he was to open one meeting by reading at length from the drollery of Artemus Ward. "Gentlemen, why don't you laugh?" he finally asked. "If I did not laugh I should die, and you need this medicine as much as I do."[48] Then he turned to the major order of business: soliciting their advice about a proclamation that he proposed to issue concerning slavery.

During the bleak autumn of 1861 the brains of Boston churned out 1,301 conundrums for the contest at Tremont Temple. Gold watches went to the lady and gentleman who most deftly displayed the punster's frivolous art.

2 /

Enlightened Europeans, Romantic Americans
Origins of Our Transcendental Quest for the Language of Nature

> The classification of the constituents of a chaos—nothing less is here essayed.
>
> — Melville, *Moby-Dick,* chap. 32

Dreaming Philosophical Dreams about a Language of Nature

All languages permit wordplay and all cultures have indulged in it, but it flourished in the nineteenth century with special vigor. Education and the penny press created a mass audience that could relish malapropisms as well as commit them. The gentlemanly English cult of the pun, frowned upon by *The Spectator* but persisting throughout the eighteenth century as the lackluster efforts of the Scriblerians testify, flourished anew with such Romantic devotees as Lamb and Byron, was vitalized by Carlyle and mechanized by Hood. British and American punsters shared a common literary heritage reaching back through Milton to Shakespeare. In America, however, Romantic wordplay was distinctively energized by swirling currents of speculation stemming both from the mother country and the Continent.

Consider a rich but representative passage from *Walden*'s chapter "House-Warming":

> It would seem as if the very language of our parlors would lose all its nerve and degenerate into *palaver* wholly, our lives pass at such remoteness from its symbols, and its metaphors and tropes are necessarily so far fetched, through slides and dumb-waiters, as it were; in other words, the parlor is so far from the kitchen and workshop. The dinner even is only the parable of a dinner, commonly. As if only the savage dwelt near enough to Nature and Truth to borrow a trope from them. How can the scholar, who dwells away in the North West Territory or the Isle of Man, tell what is parliamentary in the kitchen?[1]

This passage criticizes Concord's social discourse for losing touch with reality. Crackling wordplay exemplifies the concretely rooted language that Thoreau craves. The slang term *palaver* is set against the genteel term *parlor* so that an alert reader can think about how both descend from the same French root, *parler,* to talk, as does the word *parliamentary.* How, Thoreau asks, can we truly understand these words if ignorant of their etymology? What does it tell us about Victorian culture that its houses contain a separate room crowded with conversation pieces and consecrated to "talking"? What might it tell us about modern American culture that its ranch houses contain a separate room dominated by a spectral TV set and dedicated to "living"? As Thoreau complains that our figurative language risks forgetting its origins, his own metaphor simultaneously literalizes the abstract meaning of the word *far-fetched,* just as we are invited to realize the radical irony of having the talking room serviced by a dumbwaiter. Whatever the lax gabble in the parlor, Thoreau's own language has certainly not lost its nerve. Indeed, some may think it has rather too much, for a contorted pun ridicules scholars as idlers (literally those who do no physical work, from the Greek *scholē,* leisure) who dwell on the Isle of Man—i.e., insist on an abstract conception of man artificially isolated from nature (*isola*ted = islanded, from Latin *insula,* isle).

Is such punning prose truly muscular or merely nervous? To anatomize its intellectual sinews properly we need to recapture the tradition of linguistic speculation that Thoreau inherited and in a sense perfected. While at work on *Walden* he confided to his journal that he "dreamed of" writing a book that would "return to the primitive analogical and derivative sources of words" (5 Sept. 1851). His ambition was hardly unique. "The connection between sign and thing signified has been so severed," complained the Boston man of letters E. P. Whipple in the year *Walden* appeared, that a philosopher's premises "might be afflicted with the confluent small-pox without his conclusion being in any danger of catching it."² As the apostle of representative government and religious toleration, John Locke remained America's philosopher par excellence well into the nineteenth century. His *Essay Concerning Human Understanding* (1690) famously insisted that words have no natural connection with the objects they denote but are only arbitrarily associated with them, deriving their force, like government, from a social contract. At the same time, however, his sensationalism led him to stress "how great a dependence our words have on common sensible ideas; . . . *Spirit,* in its primary signification, is breath; *angel,* a messenger: and I doubt not but, if we could trace them to their sources, we should find, in all languages, the names which stand for things that fall not under our senses to have had their first rise from sensible ideas." The result was ambivalence about the relation between language and physical reality, for by means of the dogma of sensationalism "we may give some kind of guess what kind of notions they were, and whence derived, which filled their minds who were the first beginners of languages, and how nature, even in the naming of things, unawares suggested to men the originals and principles of all their knowledge."[3]

Locke had a marked impact on philosophy of language in France. Reconstructing the genesis of speech became a European intellectual pastime. In his *Essai sur l'origine des connaissances humaines* (1746) Condillac rejected Locke's linguistic conventionalism and made the origin of language the cornerstone of his entire philosophy. A totally arbitrary language corresponding to no reality struck him as a gibberish that man could never have learned. Like Locke, he rejected innate ideas, but he postulated an innate language of gesture and facial expression, which he styled the language of action. Primitive man responded involuntarily with it to emotional stimuli like desire and pain. As men discovered the utility of this natural language, by analogy they evolved the more complex symbolic system of articulate speech. All signs are thus ultimately natural. But as language develops, arbitrary social agreement increasingly fixes the meanings of words while obscuring the radical physical analogies underlying them. If we could only recover a language based on true correspondences, Condillac was convinced, philosophical reasoning would proceed easily and naturally.

Accepting Locke's sensationalism, Berkeley challenged his doctrine of abstract general ideas as an improper reification of words. The multiple meanings of words led Berkeley to wonder whether the essence of language was really naming. Almost alone among philosophers before 1900 he grasped the limitations of a purely referential theory of meaning. He saw how this understanding could be put to good use in theology. Redirecting attention from individual words to the function of sentences, Berkeley thus concluded that "words may be significant, although they do not stand for ideas."[4] As Thoreau would echo this belief, "The words which express our faith and piety are not definite; yet they are significant and fragrant like frankincense to superior natures" (*Walden*, p. 325). Berkeley's empirical adherence to sensationalism drove him, by its own inner logic, into a paradoxical attitude toward language. Mistrusting it, he constantly urged readers to brush aside words as a web of illusions. By pure introspection, he claimed, even a speechless Solitary Man might "after long experience . . . know without words" (*Philosophical Commentaries*, I.71). But while he strove to tidy up philosophy by sweeping verbal language off into a corner, he tried to account for knowledge through the sensationalist doctrine of perception offered in *A New Theory of Vision* (1709). "The proper objects of Vision constitute the Universal Language of Nature," he concluded. "And the manner wherein they signify and mark out unto us the objects which are at a distance is the same with that of languages and signs of human appointment; which do not suggest the things signified by any likeness or identity of nature, but only by an habitual connexion that experience has made us to observe between them" (Sec. 147).

The notion of nature as a language was not novel, of course. It had been broached by the Neo-Platonists and Jacob Boehme, for example, and was to be employed by the Swedenborgians—all of whom were favorite authors of Emerson's. But no other philosopher made the concept so central as did Berkeley or developed it so ingeniously. As Berkeley dissolved existence into perception, vision and (to a lesser extent) sound could be regarded as the language of nature. Thus scientific observers like Newton "seem to be grammarians, and their art the grammar of Nature" (*Principles,* 1st ed., I.108). With this key analogy Berkeley pushed home his attack against Enlightenment scientists. They treated signs as causes, he argued, whereas their approach should be descriptive rather than explanatory, psychologically concrete rather than abstract. Like grammatical rules, scientific laws are valuable, but "a man may be well read in the language of Nature without understanding the grammar of it," since "two ways there are of learning a language, either by rule or by practice"—and the second generally produces better results. Grammarians' rules never match the native speaker's linguistic competency, so we should also be wary of relying naively on the scientific grammar of things (i.e., of phenomena). Berkeley's provocative linguistic analogy explains science as frankly teleological activity, meant to enhance either our appreciation of the creative wisdom or our practical comforts through technical progress. It was in this spirit that Thoreau commenced his career as a naturalist.[5] He could never have written his masterpiece without the conviction that "while we are confined to books, though the most select and classic, and read only particular written languages . . . we are in danger of forgetting the language which all things and events speak without metaphor, which alone is copious and standard" (*Walden,* p. 111). Like Berkeley, he believed that "the man of science, who is not seeking for expression but for a fact to be expressed merely, studies nature as a dead language" (10 May 1853).

With his doctrine of the Universal Language of Nature Berkeley was in a curious position. While he strenuously sought to banish language from the mansion of philosophy as an unwelcome intruder, that very effort compelled him to usher it in the front door as the guest of honor. His criticism of language led him to a deeper criticism of the sensationalist theory of cognition on which it was based. And his later work shows that empiricism needed neither Coleridge nor German idealism to develop a full-blown symbolic worldview. That was always latent in the empirical struggle with language, striving to emerge through its own inner dynamic. For Berkeley's philosophy culminates in the *Siris: A Chain of Philosophical Reflexions and Inquiries concerning the Virtues of Tar-Water and Divers Other Subjects* (1744). Berkeley was troubled throughout his life with gastrointestinal disorders, and his grand philosophic effort to dissolve all matter while stabilizing the flux of perception was seconded by practical researches for better laxatives and bowel coagulants. His American sojourn familiarized him with the folk remedy of water impregnated with pine pitch. He became convinced that he not only owed his own life to it but had discovered the universal panacea, "of so just a temperament as to be an enemy to all extremes. . . . I have known it correct costive habits in some, and the contrary habit in others" (Sec. 72). The therapeutic virtue of this decoction he derived from the sun, arguing that in the balsam of evergreens solar energy was chemically congealed. Tar he regarded as a concentrate of the "aether or pure invisible fire" which "seemeth no other than the vegetative soul or vital spirit of the world" (Sec. 152). As for the world itself, after ransacking ancient and modern authorities he concluded that "from all the various tones, actions, and passions of the universe, they supposed one symphony, one animal act and life to result" (Sec. 273). He thus endorses Pre-Socratic, Neo-Platonic, and Hermetic speculation about the *anima mundi,* from which "Nature seems to be not otherwise distinguished . . . than as life is from soul" (Sec. 278). The universe is one great living organism animated by a divine intellectual principle. Thoreau echoed this belief in *Walden*'s penultimate chapter: "The earth is not a mere fragment of dead history . . . but living poetry . . . not a fossil earth but a living earth; compared with whose great central life all animal and vegetable life is merely parasitic" (p. 309).

Berkeley's odd meditation on tar-water ends by urging the study of Plato as striking the proper balance between "the flowing philosophers, who held all things to be in a perpetual flux . . . and those others who maintained the universe to be fixed and immovable" (Sec. 348). Evidently Berkeley equated philosophic wisdom with good digestion, a golden mean between diarrhea and constipation. "The human mind is so much clogged and borne down by the strong and early impressions of sense" that he prescribes the Platonic ideal as its ideal tonic (Sec. 301). Only this can purge it of error yet permit it to extract intellectual nourishment from a world of appearances "fluent and changing without anything permanent in them" (Sec. 292). Purging the "idea" of sensationalist and psychological connotations, the *Siris* revived the Platonic doctrine of innate ideas. In Berkeley's final phase language emerged as his key concept. Both sensory and spiritual reality were converted into language; sensationalism yielded to a symbolic view of the world. What we take to be bodies and perceptions are better understood as the concrete sign language by which the Absolute converses with our finite spirit. Strenuously denied any role in metaphysical speculation, language finally resurfaced triumphantly as Berkeley's master model for metaphysical form.[6]

How Enlightened French Savants Enlighten Thoreau's Wordplay

"In all the dissertations—on language—men forget the language that is—that is really universal—the inexpressible meaning that is in all things & every where," complained the young Thoreau (23 Aug. 1845). He was familiar with Enlightenment speculation, when savants spawned such dissertations by the score. Like most other literate Americans he owned a copy of Hugh Blair's *Lectures on Rhetoric and Belles Lettres* (1783), a massively influential work that saw fifty American editions by 1865. In the two lectures "Rise and Progress of Language" Blair singled out the Frenchman Charles de Brosses as "the Author, who has carried his speculations on this subject the furthest."[7] Thoreau no doubt read the summary of de Brosses's theories with close attention. Very likely he accepted Blair's invitation to consult the two-volume *Traité mécanique de la formation des langues et des principes physiques de l'étymologie* (Paris: Saillant, 1765).

De Brosses sought to show that "the basis of universal language already exists" (1:xxii, my trans.). Downplaying Condillac's germinal language of action, he argued that names were first attached to things by a process neither arbitrary nor conventional but rather through "a true system of necessity determined by two causes. One is the formation of the vocal organs, which can only render certain sounds analogous to their structure; the other is the nature and property of the real objects that one wishes to name. This obliges us to use for their name sounds that portray them, to establish between the word and the thing a rapport by which the word can excite an idea of the thing" (1:xii–xiii). The result was a classic bow-wow theory, for according to De Brosses the essence of all language is onomatopoetic imitation. Since "there are few things that do not make noise," they acquired their original names as the cuckoo is called from its cry (1:7). This primary principle accounted for most names in aboriginal speech, De Brosses believed (without realizing that it left primitive man inhabiting a pastoral pandemonium fit to drown out the hubbub of Paris).

As for noiseless objects, "the organ assumes, as much as it can, the very appearance of the object that it wishes to paint with the voice: it gives a hollow sound if the object is hollow, or rough if the object is rough; so that the sound that results from the natural form and movement of the organ put in that state becomes the name of the object, a name that resembles it by the rough or hollow sound that the chosen pronunciation carries to the ear." Thus the voice employs organs that properly represent "either the thing or some quality or effect of the thing that it wishes to name" (1:8). De Brosses concludes that "there exists a primitive language, organic, physical, and necessary, common to the entire human race, which . . . constitutes the first foundation of the language of all countries; a foundation that the immense superstructure of accessories built upon it hardly lets one perceive" (1:14-15).

Devoting nearly a thousand pages to this theme, de Brosses was just erudite enough to make it plausible, for his knowledge of European languages let him buttress it with examples while his relative ignorance of non-Indo-European data left him serenely untroubled by doubts. He held that sounds have inherent semantic meanings. A rapid global survey of several score languages convinced him that similar labials and dentals were always used for the first childish words *Papa* and *Mama*. After this atypical paradigm case he confined himself largely to the Indo-European family, providing lengthy lists of European words supposedly explaining why N, the most liquid of letters, designates anything like *navis* that acts upon liquid; why FL naturally designates fluid motion in air, fire, or water; and why other phones and consonantal clusters like SL, SW, R, G, SR, H, S, and SM have various inherent meanings that form the basis of the primitive universal language.

Though many of his etymologies were erroneous, just as many were true and illuminating. What might Thoreau have learned from him? Consider again Thoreau's remarks on the language of our parlors at the beginning of this chapter. While sporting with the French root of *parlor, palaver,* and *parliamentary* to demonstrate that our words are fetched too far from the kitchen, he interjects, "The dinner even is only the parable of a dinner, commonly." Why this slightly strained locution? As de Brosses admirably explained, "the French *parler* and all its derivatives come from παραβολή and παραβαλλείν, words composed from the primitive βαλλω which itself derives from the root *Bal*, which has produced numerous other branches very distant from this one and itself has no connection of any kind with the idea expressed by the word *parler*"

(2:436-38). Even a good classical scholar might not recognize that *parler* and *parable* both derive from Greek *paraballein* = throw together, via medieval Latin *parabola* = discourse (cf. such Romance cognates as *palabra* and *parole*). Standard English dictionaries available to Thoreau traced our Romance derivatives to the French *parler,* then gave up the chase. That Thoreau could consciously exploit this recondite etymological connection corroborates the likelihood that he had read de Brosses; it certainly testifies to his interest in comparative philology.

When de Brosses derived *parler* from a primitive root BAL, he was relying on the work of his friend Antoine Court de Gébelin, Franklin's collaborator in publications urging American independence. Influenced reciprocally by de Brosses, Court de Gébelin conceived the ambitious plan of his *Monde primitif analisé et comparé avec le monde moderne.* Its prospectus appeared in 1773. He promised subscribers what we call an anthropological encyclopedia. All knowledge about primitive culture fell into two divisions: the first embraced words, while the second dealt with things. Envisioning etymology as the key to prehistory, he proposed first to elucidate the development of languages by composing an introductory treatise on the physical Principles of Language and Writing, a Universal Grammar, a Dictionary of the Primitive Language, and a bevy of comparative etymological dictionaries introducing his analysis of primitive arts, sciences, and folkways. Today his huge quartos seem artifacts more remote than the primitive world. Few read them now; indeed, few subscribers read them then. But one who did plunder this storehouse of misinformed wisdom was Thoreau. By happy coincidence there exists a holograph dated 14 November 1836 in which a young Harvard senior isolated in the primitive culture of Massachusetts records an encounter with the *Monde primitif* at the behest of his college debating society.

> A discussion having arisen in our famous club (Grex Epicuri, etc.— "quae vivit ut edet, non edit ut vivat,"), respecting the origin of the word *ballot,* some affirming that it was derived from the Greek, while others stopped short at the French *ballotte,* it was thought advisable to settle the question at once by a reference to suitable authorities.
>
> Bal was a Celtic monosyllable, and primitive and radical word, which signified the sun; and consequently, 1st. all that is beautiful and brilliant like the sun; 2ndly. all that is elevated; 3rdly. all that is round. Under each of these heads, this word has become the source of a multitude of words in the French language; being pronounced by different people, Bal, Bel, Bol, and with the lision of the vowel, Bla, Blo, etc.
>
> Hence result 10 branches derived from that single root, and from these a cinquantaine of divisions.
>
> Under the 1st branch are found the names of some plants and animals.

2nd Bel, meaning beauty.

3rd Bal, become Bla, the name of different colors,—of the words blanc, bleu, blond, blason, etc.

4th Bail, a name relating to power, to preservation and protection.

5th Bal, relating to elevation, whence Balcon, Balustrade.

6th Bal, signifying to protectect [*sic*] with an envelope, whence Bale, Baline, Baldaquin, etc.

7th Bal, relating to the physical action de s'elever en s'elançant; whence Bal, Balet, Balade, Baladoire, Baliste, etc.; whence also the Greeks have made βαλλω.

8th Bal, signifying greatness, whence Baleine, Bloc.

9th Bal, signifying rotundity; whence Bale, Balon, Balote, Boule, etc.

10 Some words compounded of Bal, joined to others.[8]

Thoreau has faithfully summarized the entry "Bal" in Court de Gébelin's *Dictionnaire étymologique François-Celte,* where philological insights jostle drastic oversimplifications. *Ballot* is indeed descended from an Indo-European root signifying rotundity (*bhel-*, blow, swell up), as the entry illuminatingly suggests; and that root might conceivably be connected to a similar root (*bhel-*, shine) reflected in Beltane, the Celtic May Day celebration. But possessing a fertile mind and few laws restricting phonetic development, Court de Gébelin expounded the various branches of this root, prolific enough in itself, with a veritably anagogic passion. He traced them all ultimately to one solar divinity together with the derivatives of several other distinct Indo-European roots (e.g., Bel = beauty from I.E. *deu-*, do, via Latin *bonus, bene;* Bal = envelope from I.E. *pel-*, skin; Bal = throw from I.E. *gwel-*, throw, via Greek *ballein, ballizein*, to throw, dance). Since in his view all languages were one, for lagniappe he also added unrelated Semitic derivatives like *balsamum*. But if his analogizing habit of mind often betrays him into howlers, it also scores enough real triumphs to dignify his naive methodology; for to one ignorant of the phonetic laws governing linguistic evolution in the Indo-European family, the conceptual analogies underlying his mistakes seem no more far-fetched than those underlying genuine and plausible derivations.

Brewed from equal parts of fantasy and insight, Court de Gébelin's etymologies were heady stuff for a young man with Thoreau's literary ambitions. If *parler* derives from the root *Bal* as De Brosses demonstrated, what then is the essence of our common *parlance?* In Court de Gébelin Thoreau found an authority for regarding speech itself as physical activity, a balancing act as it were, the beautiful jugglery of tossing words about, a form of verbal ballet. Since modern American education takes for granted a vital link between throwing the ball and throwing the bull, we tend to forget what foreign language study could mean to a

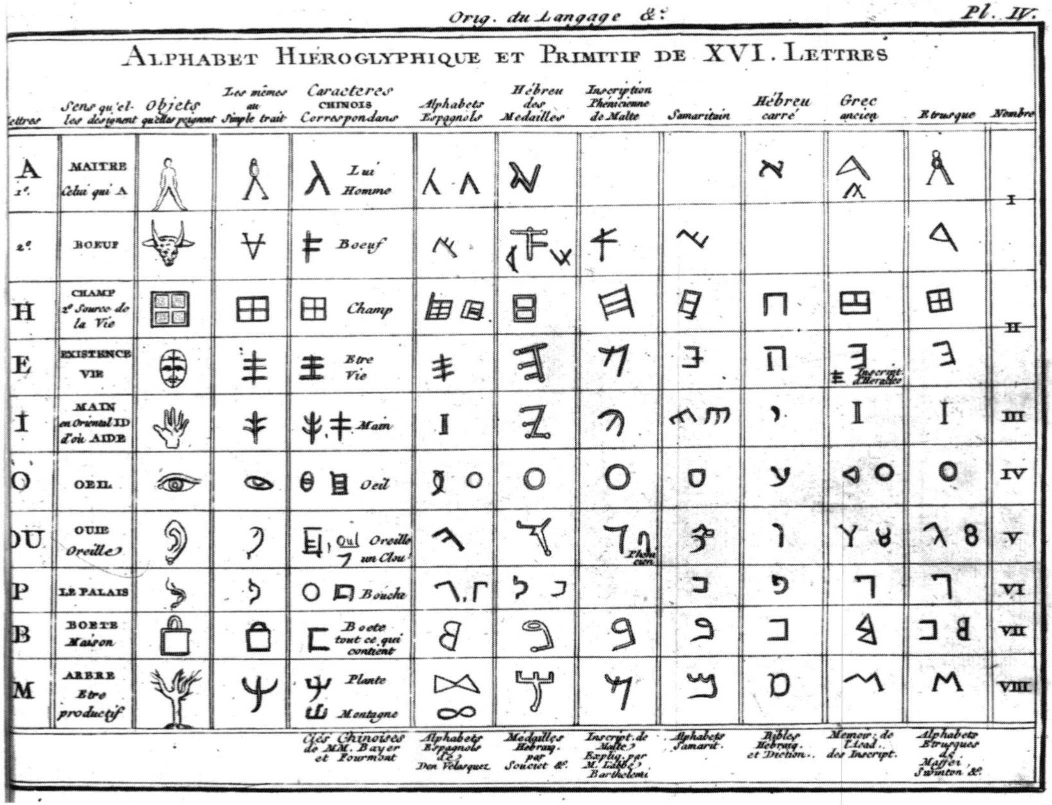

Pl. IV.

Orig. du Langage &:

ALPHABET HIÉROGLYPHIQUE ET PRIMITIF DE XVI. LETTRES

Fig. 4. Antoine Court de Gébelin, *Origine du langage et de l'écriture* (1774), Table 4. Courtesy, (Annenberg) Rare Book and Manuscript Library, University of Pennsylvania.

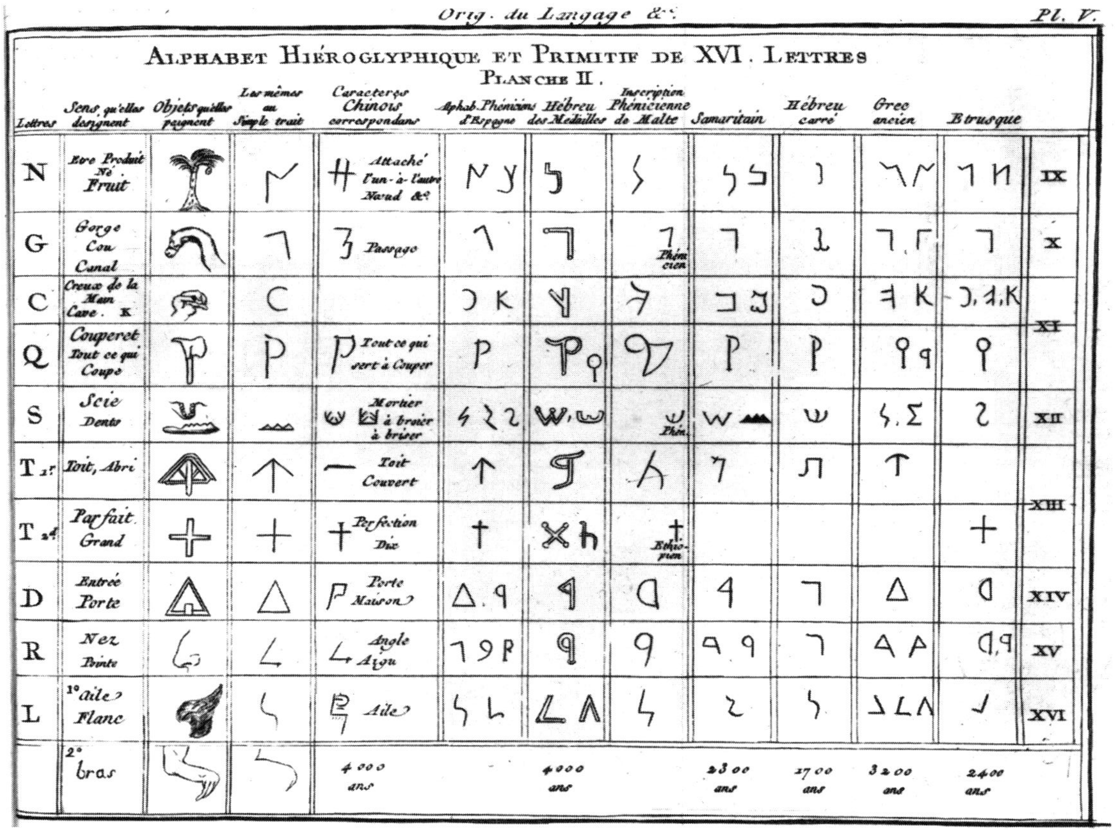

Fig. 5. Antoine Court de Gébelin, *Origine du langage et de l'écriture* (1774), Table 5. Courtesy, Annenberg Rare Book and Manuscript Library, University of Pennsylvania.

child of the Puritans in early Victorian Massachusetts. By speaking, a man might be performing an ecstatic dance to worship the sun.

What Thoreau imbibed from these pages was a paradoxical vision of primeval truths obvious to all yet somehow hidden. He certainly read more widely in Court de Gébelin than the dispute before his debating society demanded. As the young Harvard senior copied out, carefully though not without misspellings, "From the primitive word Ver, signifying water, (a monosylable [sic] frequently occurring in the names of rivers—as Var, Varine, Varna, Veresis, Vere, Vir, Vire) is derived the word verité; for as water, by reason of its transparency and limpidness, is the mirror of bodies—of physical êtres, so also is truth equally the mirror of ideas—of intellectual êtres, representing them in a manner faithful and clear, as the water does a physical body, Gebelin—Monde Primitif.—Dictionnaire Etymol. Francoise." Thoreau probably retained this mistaken belief years later when his chapter "The Ponds," that elaborate paean to their purity, made them the moral and symbolic center of his great book. "After all, man is the great poet, and not Homer," observed Thoreau in *A Week on the Concord and Merrimack Rivers,* "and our language itself . . . his work" (p. 95). Thus that book records an ecstatic moment when the poetic voyagers "are reminded by interior evidence of the permanence of universal laws." Contemplating the sunset limpidly reflected in the water, they transcend faith and faintly remembered knowledge in sublimer visions—"when we do not have to believe, but come into actual contact with Truth, and are related to her in the most direct and intimate way" (pp. 291-92). Paradoxically but understandably enough, the young writer who could cultivate such symbolic obliquity chose to "build my lodge on the southern slope of some hill, and there take the life the gods send me" (5 Apr. 1841). His life required "a greater baldness," greater perhaps than words themselves could afford: "I want a directer relation with the sun" (11 Apr. 1841).

Haunted like De Brosses by fancied correspondences between sounds and objects, Court de Gébelin extended this principle by showing how it shaped the sixteen written characters of the first primitive alphabet. In his view all letters were pictographs representing either a bodily organ somehow associated with the sound in his elaborate scheme or a symbolic object intimately related to the value of the sound (see figs. 4, 5). Thus the character M designating "in all languages the idea of Mother, of maternity, of a productive and fruitful being," was really a shorthand sketch of a tree, which primitive man had selected as the hieroglyph of these qualities (3:410, my trans.). "Talk of learning our letters and being literate!" exclaimed Thoreau. "Why the roots of our letters are things" (16 Oct.

1859). He shared the Romantic era's fascination with Egyptian hieroglyphics and was aware of Champollion's successful decipherment of them; but occult and garbled theories like Court de Gébelin's helped him imagine them as the radically physical basis of a primitive secret language that could serve as a model for concretizing stylistic innovations. "Shall I be indebted to another man's thought?" he asked himself while laboring over *Walden*. "Shall I not have words as fresh as my thoughts? A genuine thought can find expression if it have to invent hieroglyphics" (7 Sept. 1851).

Unfolding from its first sentence, where Thoreau explains that he "lived alone, in the woods . . . in a house which I had built myself, on the shore of Walden Pond" (p. 3), his great book seeks to develop the concept of "Economy." With its parodic balance sheets, his opening chapter sports with that title, tracing expenditures down to the half-penny. "I have always endeavored to acquire strict business habits," he proclaims, ironically determined to out-pennypinch the stingiest Yankee (p. 20). Of course, Thoreau dramatizes himself as a radical economist, not a devotee of the dismal science. He knows that etymologically *economy* signifies *the law of the house,* and he is determined to make his audience appreciate the root meaning of the term. Thus he quickly breaks down "the necessaries of life for man in this climate . . . under the several heads of Food, Shelter, Clothing, and Fuel." Amalgamating food with fuel and shelter with clothing, his narrative proceeds to prove that "the grand necessity, then, for our bodies, is to keep warm, to keep the vital heat in us" (pp. 12–13).

Throughout the chapter conceptual play conflates these four categories. From the Laplander's hide clothes and sleeping bag he modulates to the Indian's wigwam, reminding us that Adam and Eve "wore the bower before other clothes. Man wanted a home, a place of warmth, or comfort, first of physical warmth, then the warmth of the affections" (pp. 27–28). But believing that the phrase "domestic comforts . . . may have originally signified the satisfactions of the house more than of the family," Thoreau is inclined to view even affection as a luxury. Building his own house becomes a major symbol for doing what is radically necessary to sustain physical existence. He regrets that never in all his walks did he come across "a man engaged in so simple and natural an occupation." His critique of architecture insists that "the inhabitant, the indweller . . . build truly within and without, and let the ornaments take care of themselves" (pp. 45–48). By Anglicizing the term *inhabitant* with a Saxon neologism he stresses the way in which genuine architectural beauty grows "from within outward, out of the necessities and character of the indweller, who is the only builder,—out of some unconscious truthfulness, and nobleness, without ever a thought for the appearance and whatever additional beauty of this kind is destined to be produced will be preceded by a like unconscious beauty of life." The heart of his architectural doctrine is the rejection of a false classicism imposed from without, and this innovative epithet reproduces it linguistically. This is indeed beautiful prose, but its beauty is highly self-conscious.

Frank Lloyd Wright thought that Thoreau's observations were indispensable to the history of American architecture. But this native theory of architecture has one flying buttress in France. It is grounded in Thoreau's philological reading. In the *Grammaire universelle* Court de Gébelin had explained the origin of the primitive Verb EST, "the only one that exists." Onomatopoetically expressive of respiration, in his view "the word EST animates language . . . it is to words what life is to Beings." He felt there was no language on earth without derivatives of the primal copula denoting existence. He buttressed this view both on legitimate Indo-European cognates and on wilder parallels from Hebrew and Basque.

Moreover, according to Court de Gébelin the words for other basic necessities of human life flow directly from the verb *to exist.* From EST he derived the primitive word EIS, progenitor of the article, the numeral one, and a multitude of generic terms "signifying Man, he who is." Other derivatives of the primal verb were "ED, AID, AD, signifiant le lieu ou l'on EST, l'habitation." Here he ranged half a dozen European cognates of Latin *aedes* = edifice. Finally, the primal Verb begat

> ES, signifying, 1*. Heat, 2*. Food: And by these one preserves one's existence: Enormous families, which we could not trace in detail here, but to which belong these familiar words:
> EST, The quarter of the world from which comes the Sun, the Fire that lights and reanimates the Universe.
> VESTA, Goddess of Fire.
> ESSE, To eat, in Latin, in Greek, in Teutonic, &c.
> (*Monde primitif,* 2:179-82).

What Thoreau consulted was a linguistic cookbook with a radically simplified recipe for being. Court de Gébelin's anthropology envisioned the vital force embodying itself in primitive man. Concomitantly—by a process fusing linguistic, cultural, and biological evolution—man evolved means to heat, feed, and house himself. As our vocabulary allegedly testifies, all these physical activities remain the direct outgrowth of the same vital principle that both powers the universe and animates language as a whole. Linking food, fuel, and shelter like the Frenchman, Thoreau also seeks the unified basis of our physical being.

He was surely imaginative enough to extend Court de Gébelin's "enormous family" of words by independently linking it to VESTIS and hence to all terms for *vestments,* that is, clothing. For some time it has been recognized that Thoreau's mock-serious references to *capital* in "Economy" involve persistent etymological punning: "I determined to go into business at once, and not wait to acquire the usual capital, using such slender means as I had already got."[9] Thoreau's point, of course, is that he figured out how to realize his dreams not by relying on the usual financial capital (from Latin *caput*) but simply by using his *head.* But despite the example of Carlyle's clothing philosophy in *Sartor Resartus,* nobody has guessed just how radically Thoreau imagined his Transcendental theory of *investment.*

Thoreau's insistence that architectural ornament reflect the life of the indweller is not merely a piece of Transcendental symbolism. Behind this correspondential concern is an organic view of the universe buttressed on philology. "There is some of the same fitness in a man's building his own house that there is in a bird's building its own nest," he claims. He proceeds to link the instinct to construct honestly with "the poetic faculty" (fr. Greek *poiein,* to make). One suspects that he exercised his own poetic faculty on another list of Court de Gébelin's detailing various words for housing: "*Bat* in Persian, *beth* in Hebrew, in Sanskrit, &c., *both* in Irish, in Breton, *bod* in Teutonic, *bodde* in Flemish, *bwthe* in Gaelic, *buthe* in Scots, &c. are the same word, signifying always *ha*-BIT-*ation,* dwelling, house, &c. & thence BOUT*ique,* & the Italian *bottega,* an inn; likewise the English *a*-BOD-*e,* dwelling" (*Origine du langage,* p. 48). If the forms of man's housing spring ideally from his physical needs, then his proper *abode* seems naturally but an extension of his *body.* Vitruvius thought anatomy the architect's basic discipline, according to Emerson in "The Poet," and at its roots *Walden*'s theory of architecture is strikingly anthropomorphic: "It would be worth the while to build still more deliberately than I did, considering, for instance, what foundation a door, a window, cellar, a garret, have in the nature of man" (p. 45). As a good house *embodies* the spirit of its indweller, so the details of architecture are founded on the human frame: "This frame, so slightly clad, was a sort of crystallization around me, and reacted on the builder" (p. 85).

Poe, Hawthorne, and Melville all wrote works equating houses with human beings, but Thoreau's two paragraphs on architectural theory are the most dazzling display of analogical thinking and etymological wordplay. His confidence that "they can do without *architecture* who have no olives or wines in the cellar" depends on knowing that, as Court de Gébelin explained, a *cellar* is where things are con*cealed*. Thoreau needs no classical architecture (literally, arched vaults covering) because he has nothing to hide. He dismisses the American taste-maker Horatio Greenough (who argued that to be natural, houses should be painted in earth-toned colors) with the caustic remark, "Is he thinking of his last and narrow house?" According to Court de Gébelin, the primitive term HÊ or KHÉ was indeed the common ancestor of words for the earth like Greek *Gaia* and also of words denoting "habitation, house, place where one nourishes oneself or lives" (*Origine du langage,* p. 305). But like Thoreau he saw nothing somber in this since the same root supposedly gave birth to the Greek *gao,* to rejoice, and to such modern descendants as *gay.* "Better paint your house your own complexion; let it turn pale or blush for you," concludes Thoreau, adding mordantly, "When you have got my ornaments ready, I will wear them." Mockingly equating the gingerbread of American cottage architecture with costume jewelry, Thoreau gaily shifts back to the analogy of clothing. He ends his sparkling display of conceptual and verbal pyrotechnics by punningly threatening to traipse about in drag.

Volatile Words: The Ironic Materialism of Tooke's Diverting Etymologies

Ransacking other French lexicographers, Thoreau also drew upon the linguistic thought of philosophes like the Baron de Gérando, who called for a philosophical dictionary defining all our ideas by tracing them back historically and etymologically to the concepts that prevailed at the origin of speech. At Emerson's instigation Thoreau translated portions of Gérando's history of philosophy. Through Emerson he was familiar with Jacob Bryant's *Analysis of Ancient Mythology* (1774–76), perhaps the nearest thing to the *Monde primitif* that eighteenth-century England produced, while Bronson Alcott made him aware of James Harris's *Hermes* (1751), the influential tract on universal grammar. But for Thoreau as for other Americans, the most important linguistic authority of the British Enlightenment, once Webster had displaced Johnson's *Dictionary,* was John Horne Tooke's Επεα Πτεροεντα; *or, Diversions of Purley* (1786–1805). In later editions this curious philosophico-grammatical dialogue, prolonged over a thousand pages, dominated English philology (to its detriment) well into the nineteenth century. Grammarians like Harris flirted with innate ideas to establish the existence of intellectual powers independent of language. In his *Dissertation on Language* (1767) the economist Adam Smith had marveled that primitive man could invent prepositions, since they seemed to express abstract intellectual relations. Reasserting Locke's most radical implications, Tooke set out to show that such assumptions were unnecessary.

Championing an extreme nominalism, Tooke proclaimed as his cardinal principle "that the errors of Grammarians have arisen from supposing all words to be *immediately* either the signs of things or the signs of ideas; whereas in fact many words are merely *abbreviations* employed for dispatch, and are the signs of other words."[10] Locke's *Essay Concerning Human Understanding* should be rechristened an *Essay on Language,* for that is what human understanding boils down to: "The business of the mind, as far as it concerns Language, appears to me to be very simple. It extends no further than to receive impressions, that is, to have Sensations or Feelings. What are called its operations, are merely the operations of Language" (p. 25). Physical impressions bombard the cerebellum to produce sensational nouns while "the other Part of Speech, the *Verb,* must be accounted for from the necessary use of it in communication. It is in fact the communication itself: and therefore well denominated Ῥῆμα, Dictum. For the Verb is QUOD *loquimur;* the Noun, DE QUO" (p. 25).

Treating all other words as merely shorthand for these two fundamental parts of speech, Tooke sought to demonstrate etymologically how prepositions and conjunctions, for example, derived from verbs and nouns. To this task he brought a smattering of Anglo-Saxon and related Teutonic languages, among others. This knowledge often enabled him to derive English words more plausibly than had Johnson. Since few Englishmen were then able to contradict his scholarship in this area, his etymological authority long remained unchallenged. Thus discussing the preposition *through,* he cites relevant Germanic, Greek, and Persian cognates meaning *door,* concluding that "*Door* and *Thorough* have one and the same Gothic origin . . . mean one and the same thing; and are in fact one and the same word" (pp. 182–83). Characteristic was the wild leap from a perception of linguistic relationship (here genuine enough except when he saw further parallels in the Chaldean) to a flat assertion of semantic identity, so that Tooke could translate *the sun shines through the air* as "really meaning" *the sun shines, air being the door.* Also characteristic was the scatological imagination with which Tooke (was he Junius, some asked, the anonymous master of English invective?) proceeded to explain, "The Greeks abbreviated in the same manner as the English; and as we use *Thro* for *Thorough,* so they used θρα for θυρα. Thus we find Ουρηθρα, the Urethra, or urine passage, compounded of Ουρον and θυρα, and by abbreviation θρα" (p. 181n.). Explaining the urethra as a *pissport* might well have intrigued the young builder by Walden, who was considering "what foundation a door, a window, a cellar, a garret, have in the nature of man" (p. 45).

Deriving other prepositions from nouns, Tooke was on even shakier ground. "FROM means merely BEGINNING, and nothing else. It is simply the Anglo-Saxon and Gothic noun ᵮᚱᚾᛗ, Beginning, Origin, Source, Fountain, Author" (p. 184). With a confidence this speculation scarcely supports he denounced Samuel Johnson for enumerating twenty separate meanings of *from* when one would suffice. Nor was he able to derive all connectives from nouns so often as his sensationalist psychology really demanded. *With*, for example, he explained erroneously as the imperative of the Anglo-Saxon verb *withan,* to join. He argued further that *if, though*, and *unless* were really the imperative forms of the Anglo-Saxon verbs *gifan* = give, *tharfigan* = allow, and *onelesan* = dismiss. Though false, such etymologies had some plausibility. Since a Middle English form of *if* was *gif,* it did seem that *if I go* might be an abbreviation of *give* (that) *I go.* Tooke could triumphantly assume that he had reduced the logically abstruse conditional conjunction to a simple verbal imperative.

But a further problem remained, for as his readers finally realized, in Tooke's grammatical system the role of the verb itself remained ambiguous. All other parts of speech he derived easily enough from verbs and nouns; but unlike nouns, verbs, as a class of abstract actions, did not seem directly derivable from the physical world. Tooke never described the relation between his two fundamental grammatical categories nor explained which might have priority in the origin of language, though his interlocutors press him on this point. He often cited de Brosses with approval but always avoided treating the genesis of speech himself. After one thousand pages Tooke ended his second volume in 1805 by mocking Harris's account of the verb and promising to deal with it himself in a third volume that would "apply this system of Language to all the different systems of Metaphysical (i.e. verbal) Imposture" (p. 684). But the third volume never appeared, for shortly before his death in 1812 he threw into the fire the manuscript he had drafted to answer the nagging question with which he had concluded the second volume: "What is the *Verb?* What is that peculiar differential circumstance which, added to the definition of a *Noun,* constitutes the *Verb*" (p. 683).

Though his grammatical ambitions were frustrated, in pursuing them he compiled two tomes offering mostly fanciful etymologies for more than twenty-five hundred words, often illustrated with quotations from early English literature. Liberally seasoned with caustic wit, his observations urged a radically materialist viewpoint to debunk metaphysical pretensions. Thus he blandly quotes a sixteenth-century tract, "They say that this word HEUEN in the article of our foyth, ascendit ad coelos, signifieth no certain and determinate place," to illustrate his own etymological explanation: "HEAVEN-(subaud. some place, any place) *Heav-en* or *Heav-ed*" (pp. 353–54). Thoreau filed this away, for it reemerges in his journal describing a cheerful choir of crickets: "It is heaven where they are, and their dwelling need not be *heaved* up" (22 May 1854). One wonders what he made of Tooke's further prestidigitation with this verb, for the sage of Purley proceeded to assert that its other verbal forms each generated a string of common nouns: heaved = head, heaft = heft; hove = hoof, huff, hovel; hoved = hood, hat, hut; hoven = haven, oven. The physical and linguistic analogies seemed so obvious to Tooke that "if you should find some difficulties (I cannot think they will be great) to make out to your satisfaction the above derivations . . . it will be but a wholesome exercise; and I shall not stop now to assist in their elucidation; but will return to the word WRONG" (p. 369). That was, indeed, the appropriate conclusion to all the above etymologies.

Yet the *Diversions of Purley* could claim to have advanced Gérando's program. Subjecting words like *right, wrong, just, law, truth,* and *think* (methinks = it thingeth me) to his brand of reductive etymologizing, Tooke seemed to verge on a genetic account of the rise of moral consciousness. Thus Emerson relied on some of these examples to furbish out the section on "Language" in *Nature*. Likewise Thoreau developed a collegiate enthusiasm for Tooke, quoting him familiarly in his theme for 17 March 1837. As Hazlitt recognized, the *Diversions* appealed to many of its readers by seeming to proffer a model of linguistic analysis that was thoroughly scientific: "Mr. Tooke . . . treated words as the chemists do substances; he separated those which are compounded from those which are not decomposable."[11] Yet though the *Diversions* diverted Bentham and James Mill, who tried to absorb the work into their system, those Utilitarians mistook Mr. Tooke. For perhaps unknown to its author, at the core of the book there lurks an astonishing mysticism about language quite incompatible with Utilitarian rationalism. Tooke's doggedly reductive attack on the concept of mind just displaced most human mental faculties onto language, until it began to resemble a giant intellectual organism that not only grew and developed but could think for itself. His etymological theories endowed words with an occult semantic identity extending throughout history that somehow determined their meaning even for speakers ignorant of their roots. "A word is wiser than any man," the young Thoreau orotundly observed (27 July 1840). But an unwise man might take those words too literally.

Just how literally Tooke should be taken is open to question. "It may fairly be objected to him, that his conversation was hardly ever quite serious; and that what with paradox, and what with irony, it was not easy to get at his true meaning," remarked the *Quarterly Review*. Its reviewer admired his rich vein of humor but suspected deliberate mystification. "The truth seems to be, that he comforted himself for not having a larger share in the business of the world, by laughing at every body and every thing it contained. His skeptical disposition probably kept his mind unsettled upon many important facts as to which the generality of men entertain more fixed opinions, and he was therefore ready to espouse either side with equal zeal and equal insincerity, as accident or caprice inclined him at the moment."[12] In the controversies that swirled around his work from the beginning both friends and enemies became unbalanced. The dialogue form of the *Diversions* masked an irony that its philological disciples often ignored—and its philosophical opponents often emulated.

Scottish Commonsense Philosophy of Language Charms American Colleges

While Tooke encouraged skeptical radicalism, irony, and obsessive philological speculation sometimes blossoming into full-blown insanity, the Scottish commonsense philosophers offered American colleges a more palatable view of language. In the early nineteenth century they dominated our philosophic curricula. Like Condillac, the Scotsman Thomas Reid had argued against Locke's conventionalism and postulated an original language of gesture, the "language of nature." His compatriot Hugh Blair drew on Reid in composing his vastly influential *Rhetoric* (1783). After five introductory chapters on the pleasures of taste, Blair's two seminal lectures on the "Rise and Progress of Language" broached his "principal subject" (1:97). Summarizing and copiously citing Enlightenment speculation on the topic, Blair was convinced that, however barren intellectually, primitive language was preeminently natural and poetical. Like the Bible, American Indian languages are "full of figures; hyperbolical and picturesque in a high degree" (1:114). Indian chiefs and Old Testament prophets share a predilection for communicating by sweeping symbolic actions, and this primitive gestural language retains a vital role in oratorical discourse.

As for verbal language, Blair like Rousseau believed that "interjections, uttered in a strong and passionate manner, were, beyond doubt, the first elements or beginnings of speech." Tentatively disagreeing with Locke, he cites Plato's *Cratylus* to suggest that language may not be entirely arbitrary in its origin. But he concludes that a natural relation between words and objects obtains only in the most primitive speech. "Though in every Tongue, some remains of it . . . can be traced, it were utterly in vain to search for it throughout the whole construction of any modern Language" (1:102-6). From his copy of the *Rhetoric* Thoreau would have learned that primitive men are ruled by imagination and passion, so "their Language will necessarily partake of this character of their minds. They will be prone to exaggeration and hyperbole. They will describe everything with the strongest colours, and most vehement expressions; infinitely more than men living in the advanced and cultivated periods of Society" (1:113). In *Walden* he passionately proclaims, "I am convinced that I cannot exaggerate enough even to lay the foundation of a true expression" (p. 324). This hyperbolic credo in itself embodies the essence of primitive style as defined by Blair. And despite Blair's caution, the *Rhetoric* encouraged Thoreau to believe that an acute author seeking the most natural style might recapture occult correspondences prevailing at the origin of language. He knew that *exaggerate* comes from the Latin *agger,* which Court de Gébelin defined as either a ditch or a mound, since the term denotes the rampart thrown up around a camp with the earth from an encircling entrenchment. Thoreau asks us to grasp that exaggeration is literally construction work involving the physical excavation and filling necessary to lay a true foundation— whether for an expression or for a shanty beside Walden Pond.

Scottish commonsense philosophy was definitively formulated by Dugald Stewart, whose *Elements of the Philosophy of the Human Mind* (1792-1827) was the standard philosophical text at Thoreau's Harvard. That Thoreau had studied his copy carefully is evident from his college essays since several quote Stewart respectfully enough. More even than his master Reid, Stewart made language a central topic. Instead of extolling the language of nature, Stewart located the boundary between animal and rational precisely in our "capacity of Artificial Language, which none of the brutes possess even in the lowest degree."[13] He thus made articulate speech seem the quintessence of the human condition. Like Condorcet he thought its development boded infinite good for the future. "To how great a degree of perfection the intellectual and moral nature of man is capable of being raised by cultivation, it is difficult to conceive," he opined (2:66). Feats of highly trained child prodigies made this philosopher sanguine in the extreme about chances for improving the species. Stewart's vision of human perfectibility was congenial to Thoreau, as *Walden*'s climactic paean on that theme might suggest. Also congenial was Stewart's belief that vocational and intellectual specialization strengthened some faculties only at the expense of others. A well-balanced life, Stewart urged, was needed to preserve the mind's powers "in that just proportion to each other which constitutes the perfection of our intellectual nature" (2:31).

"It is wonderful how much pains has been taken to describe a flower's leaf—compared for instance with the care that is taken in describing a psychological fact," observed Thoreau. "Suppose as much ingenuity (perhaps it would be needless) in making a language to express the sentiments. . . . The precision and copiousness of botanical language applied to the description of moral qualities" (20 Aug. 1851). His belief that botany repays study if only as a linguistic discipline reflects Stewart's desire for "a reformation of the common language in most of the branches of science. How much such a reformation has effected in chemistry is well known; and it is evidently much more necessary in the philosophy of mind" (2:347).

In Stewart's *Elements* Thoreau also encountered a shrewd and authoritative criticism of the peculiar limitations of scientific language. The Scotsman could not share the enthusiasm of many Enlightenment thinkers for reformulating language along mathematical lines and so developing a moral calculus. According to Stewart, such speculation ignored a crucial linguistic distinction between mathematics and other disciplines.

> In the former science, where the use of an ambiguous word is impossible, it may be easily conceived how the solution of a problem may be reduced to something resembling the operation of a mill—the conditions of the problem, when once translated from the common language into that of algebra, disappearing entirely from the view; and the subsequent process being almost mechanically regulated by general rules, till the final result is obtained. In the latter, *the whole* of the words about which our reasonings are conversant, admit, more or less, of different shades of meaning; and it is only by considering attentively the relation in which they stand to the immediate context, that the precise idea of the author in any particular instance is to be ascertained. (3:106)

Even if moralists and politicians defined their terms as carefully as mathematicians, such a logical reform of language would probably prove "nearly as useless, in morals and politics, as the syllogistic art is acknowledged to be at present in the investigations of pure geometry" (3:111). Instead of hoping for an unequivocal moral calculus, philosophers should learn to reckon on nonscientific topics with the instrument now at their disposal—ordinary language.

And the essence of ordinary language Stewart located precisely in its ambiguity. The multivalence of our language means that "in following any train of reasoning beyond the circle of the mathematical sciences, the mind must necessarily carry on, along with the logical deduction expressed in words, another logical process of a far nicer and more difficult nature,—that of fixing, with a rapidity which escapes our memory, the precise sense of every word which is ambiguous, by the relation in which it stands to the general scope of the argument" (3:107). Intellectual progress results "rather in a more precise distinction and classification of the various meanings of words, than in a reduction of these meanings in point of number," so this hermeneutic approach to language is unlikely ever to be superseded by scientific advance. Indeed, "the intellectual superiority of one man above another, in all the different branches of moral and political philosophy will be found to depend chiefly on the success with which he has cultivated these *silent habits of inductive interpretation.*" As one scholar observes, in midwifing the newborn concept of linguistic form for philosophy Stewart provided a new semantic model. "Locke considered meaning as the product of the relationship between language and the mind of the speaker but Stewart (perhaps acting on hints found in Berkeley) sees meaning rather as a function of the relation between the utterance and the hearer. The mental component in this model is not the idea which precedes the word but the thought process which interprets it."[14] Insofar as Thoreau's style relies on puns and double entendres, he just highlights for the reader that aspect of verbal communication that Stewart taught him to regard as fundamental.

As a self-proclaimed nominalist Stewart stressed that "a talent for reasoning must consist, in a great measure, in a skillful use of language as an instrument of thought" (2:186). The *Elements* included a one-hundred-page chapter "Of Language," citing and summarizing the leading ideas of Condillac, de Brosses, Court de Gébelin, Adam Smith, Tooke, and others. "That these theories are altogether unfounded I am far from thinking; but I am fully convinced that they have been all carried too far, and that fancy or whim has had a large share in their formation," he wrote, after describing how in his *History of the European Languages* (1823) Alexander Murray traced their origin to nine primitive monosyllables: *ag, bag, dwag, gag, lag, mag, nag, rag,* and *swag* (4:76). Wary of drawing philosophical conclusions from such speculation, Stewart criticized what he called "etymological metaphysics." Do we really learn much about economics by deriving the Latin *pecunia* = money from the word for ox? Tooke and others he found guilty of "confounding the historical progress of an art with its theoretical principles when advanced to maturity" (5:166). Their philosophical materialism could be dispelled by more carefully considering the mind's tendency to borrow metaphors from the material world.

To prevent misleading analogies Stewart recommended "the only effectual remedy against this inconvenience;—to *vary,* from time to time, the metaphors we employ, so as to prevent any one of them from acquiring an undue ascendant over the others, either in our own minds, or in those of our readers" (5:173). The inherent imperfection of language requires this tactic, for "however full and circumstantial our statements may be, the words which we employ, if examined with accuracy, will be found to do nothing more than to suggest *hints* to our hearers, leaving by far the principal part of the process of interpretation to be performed by the Mind itself" (5:152). "I will only hint at some of the enterprises which I have cherished," observes Thoreau at the beginning of *Walden.* "In any weather, at any hour of the day or night, I have been anxious to improve the nick of time, and notch it on my stick too; to stand on the meeting of two eternities, the past and future, which is precisely the present moment; to toe that line" (pp. 16-17). Thoreau's insistence that the obliquity of language requires conscious interpretation by the reader, his carefully mixed metaphors illustrating the abstract notion of time present, his ultimately self-canceling verbal play with physical analogies (notching the nick of time) all reflect Stewart's teachings.

The Birth of Comedy from the Spirit of Philology—Romantic Irony Germinates in Germany

As eighteenth-century thinkers vainly pursued the primal word, they chipped away at the Enlightenment's confidence in the power of any language to describe the world accurately. Hence the irony suffusing Tookean speculation. On the Continent also linguistic thought tended toward irony. In cryptic essays and tracts like the *Kreuzzüge des Philologen* (1762) J. G. Hamann dramatized himself as "the Philologian" crusading against Enlightenment "philosophers" and their ideas about language. He shrewdly criticized Kant for ignoring the topic of language and philosophizing in a technical, abstract terminology that often violated the normal conditions for understanding human discourse. Oscillating between sarcastic eloquence and ironic obscurity, tinged with religious mysticism, and influential for the succeeding generation of German Romantics (even Kierkegaard was in his debt), Hamann's verbalism, as he termed his disorganized philosophy, pointed to the multivalence of ordinary language as a reservoir of spiritual truth. At the same time the stylistic opacities in which, like Carlyle, he delighted, forced his audience to become more consciously involved in the hermeneutic process. Lurking murkily in his work was the implication that Christianity could be refurbished were theology reconceived as the linguistic rules that govern talk about God.

In *Über den Ursprung der Sprache* (1772) Hamann's disciple Herder answered the question propounded by the Berlin Academy so as to mock both extreme positions and wound up doubting "that the origins of the first human language, even though it were Hebrew, can ever be completely elaborated."[15] This prize essay was promptly attacked by Hamann. Herder quickly reversed field, attacking his own essay anonymously in *Älteste Urkunde des Menschengeschlects* (1774-76). That work treated Genesis as a divinely inspired account revolving around a single primordial hieroglyph of seven letters, "Let there be light." Encouraging a vein of auroral mysticism that appealed to American Transcendentalists, Herder now claimed that every dawn recapitulates the Creation by reintroducing us to the universe that is God's silent, visible word. But just how serious was he in either work?

Romanticism questioned whether the world should be imagined in terms of Enlightenment fixities. With his evolutionary view of history, Herder (like Humboldt after him) saw language as process rather than result, *Werdendes* rather than *Gewordenes, energeia* rather than *ergon.* He articulated this view in organic metaphors. Yet he was troubled by the inadequacy of language, by the way it seems to limit man's ability to innovate, "ungedankte Dinge zu Denken, und ungesagte Worte zu Sprechen."[16] Though Kant had not worried about the problem of language, his resolute insistence on the limits of human knowledge left many followers in a quandary. They yearned to know the *Ding-an-sich,* yet Kant stood before the noumenal realm of pure being like an angel with a flaming sword, relegating them dourly to the finite, phenomenal realm of sensible knowledge. As the lesser German idealists turned Kant into cant, this problem perplexed a slew of able minds.

With the help of Fichte, Friedrich Schlegel blazed a trail around the lower slopes of the Kantian mountain that many nineteenth-century authors eagerly trod. His elder brother August hiked along with him, while Schiller, Bernhardi, Brentano, Novalis, Richter, and Tieck were among the talented troop who early seized alpenstocks and helped thrash out the theory of irony around the campfires of *Frühromantik.* Romantic irony was a novel theory in at least one sense, for Friedrich coined our term *Romantic* from the the Franco-German word *roman* meaning *novel,* the prose form that he thought epitomized a new age. Whether Romantic irony was as novel in other senses is still disputed, but the Schlegels' ideas were provocative and far-reaching. Unlike Kant they made language central to their philosophies. Indeed, the matrix of their thought was less philosophy than philology. Both brothers made important contributions to the first wave of European Sanskrit studies. These versatile men of letters became critics of the first rank because literary criticism promised, in Friedrich's words, "to put philosophy in touch with philology," from which it had much to learn.[17] A true critical philosophy, Fichte led him to surmise, might be grounded on the possibility that Kant's noumenal realm of pure being was neither so pure nor so unapproachable as many fancied. Do not imagine reality as a frozen order shrouded by the fogs around the snow-covered Kantian peak. If scaled in the sunlight, that would reveal no order but a teeming chaos of fiery volcanoes and lush valleys stretching to the horizon, unmappable because the landscape heaves and crumbles as one watches.

Thus in his early essay "On the Limits of the Beautiful" (1794) Friedrich laid down a dynamic view of the universe that was radically Romantic: "The most prominent characteristic of nature is an everflowing and exhaustless vital energy."[18] The famous antinomies that Kant thought demonstrated pure reason's inability to characterize the noumenal realm actually point toward the nature of the Absolute as self-contradictory. Kant wrongly assumed that the *Ding-an-sich* must be constituted on the Aristotelian principle of identity and contradiction whereas he should have consigned that firmly to the phenomenal realm with the rest of logic. If the Absolute resembles a Heraclitan flux, A can equal not-A, for in the process of becoming, everything is both itself and something else. Schlegel dubbed his infinite, fertile chaos *die Fülle,* the Abounding Fullness.

But could man glimpse the awesome beauty of the Infinite? No, Schiller reluctantly concluded in *Naive and Sentimental Poetry* (1795–96). But earlier his *Letters on the Aesthetic Education of Man* (1795) had suggested that man's conflicting desires for variety and permanence, for abundant sensual gratification and ideal rational order, could be satisfied through the *Spieltrieb,* the play impulse. Purposive but without a purpose, bound by rules but freely choosing them, temporary, dynamic, but creating an enduring pattern, our instinct for play is the pattern for aesthetic experience. Within the limits of the world only that promises to reconcile contending desires, make us free and fully human.

Die Fülle might seem even more forbidding than the Kantian *Ding-an-sich.* Philosophical theory could hardly approximate it, for our "inner happiness depends . . . on some such point of strength that must be left in the dark, but that nonetheless shores up and supports the whole burden, and would crumble the moment one subjected it to rational analysis."[19] Man's longing to merge with the generative chaos meant death and would end only with death. But Schlegel found salvation in the *Spieltrieb*. Infinity was a philosophical concept, but he longed for the *union* of finitude and infinity, of being and becoming. Philosophy could not supply that, he conceded, but perhaps poetry could. Mocking Enlightenment hopes for a universal philosophical language, he dreamed instead of *eine progressive Universalpoesie* that would subsume philosophy and lift it to a higher plane where the finite individual bard could participate in the ecstasy of chaos. Grandly conceived as the study of all language, criticism would winnow literature for the great "Romantic" artists of the past who provided the best models for the new Romantic language sketched by aesthetics. That would reconcile poetry and philosophy, the infinite and the finite, and perhaps even one finite individual with another.

In his theory of *eine progressive Universalpoesie* irony was crucial, for it mirrored the self-contradictory nature of the Abounding Fullness. Schlegel's concept of irony is hard to define, for he practiced what he preached, using this key term in deliberately confusing ways. Indeed, in the convoluted notion of "the Irony of Irony" his paradoxical masterpiece "Of Incomprehensibility" ironizes the notion of systematizing irony. Though Socrates was one of his heroes, few readers of Plato credit Socrates' feigned ignorance. Romantic irony denoted a different, more unsettling attitude than classical irony. Enlightenment ironists like Voltaire and Franklin usually assumed an understanding of words and ideas shared by an elite, at least, who could be relied on to gauge the satiric truths being inverted. But as language came to seem increasingly equivocal, that fostered a more radical and enveloping ironic sensibility. It sought less to correct social abuses than to keep the ironist afloat, like Melville's Ishmael, in a billowing, dynamic, paradoxical, and even menacing cosmos. Man yearns both for coherent order and for chaotic freedom, to become being and to be becoming (i.e., nonbeing). "Whatever does not annihilate itself," proclaimed Schlegel, "is not free and is worth nothing."[20] The Romantic ironist could achieve transcendence through an orgy of self-destructive recreation. Among the best models for this process are masterworks in which an intrusive narrator, an element of fantasy, or a jarring mixture of genres stresses the artificial, illusory nature of the artist's own achieved order, which is simultaneously created and destroyed. Ariosto, Cervantes, and Sterne loom large in the new Romantic canon. That began as a manifesto against classicism, but the Schlegels soon expanded their new canon until it included virtually all classical literature except tragedy, deftly reinterpreted through the flexible concept of irony.

"There are ancient and modern poems which breathe throughout and overall the divine breath of irony," Friedrich insisted. "There lives in them a true transcendental buffoonery. Inwardly, the mood which surveys all and which infinitely elevates itself over everything finite, including its own art, virtue, or generality; outwardly, in the realization of the mimic manner of an ordinary good Italian buffo."[21] The divine ironist, he might add, knows *ecstasy* (literally, *standing outside*). In such an ironic "high," being and becoming finally merge, and the Romantic artist cavorts joyously in the Abounding Fullness.

Was Schlegel inspired by *die Fülle* or simply full of it? To answer, one must distinguish his rickety religio-philosophical underpinning from his cultural and psychological acumen. Complex, multiform, and thereby powerful, his ambiguous notions of irony helped spark one of the most sweeping revolutions in taste that Western civilization has ever witnessed. And if irony was the soul of his poetics, the heart of Romantic irony was *wordplay*. Or something like that. "The poem is a higher or deeper self," he speculated at one point, and found a mathematical formula to prove "its body wordplay." Like poetry, puns defy translation. As one Delphic dictum put it, poetry originates in punning: "Die ursprüngliche Form der Poesie ist das Wortspiel; es giebt davon eine eigne Art für jede besondere Kunst?" (*KA*, 16:428). In speculating whether the principle of wordplay might not embrace all the arts Schlegel reveals just how ambitiously the German Romantics conceived of this figure. Like *die Ironie* and *der Witz*, *das Wortspiel* was a Protean critical concept, a pun in its own right. Early Romantic criticism often analogized it to other rhetorical tropes like metaphor, parallelism, antithesis, rime, musical form, and the allied figures of sound, so that "it is at times almost impossible to tell whether *Wortspiel* refers to the figure in specific—the pun—or to the generalized principles of *Wort-Spiel*." In this respect the early Romantics proudly exploited that property of the German language that lets one coin neologisms that retain their radical force. But the result also suggests how German philosophers have had to struggle to make their ideas precise. Evolving a conceptual vocabulary that is "an idiosyncratic system of etymologically interrelated terms," philosophy in Germany came to proceed "by way of definition, etymological explication, neology, and terminological recombination."[22] From Fichte, Schlegel, and Hegel through Kierkegaard, Nietzsche, and Heidigger, German idealism has produced more than its share of occult etymological sages, philosophical ironists, and system-builders prone to reify their own abstractions.

Much is at stake therefore in the early German Romantics' criticism of wordplay. The Jena circle delighted in puns. Schlegel's vivacious mistress Dorothea (later his wife) was a notable punstress. "Der Witz ist der Blitz," exclaimed Bernhardi when analyzing the topic.[23] In Schlegel's prose, puns indeed seem lightning flashes, often striking twice or more to illuminate the murk brilliantly for a few moments by linking the noumenal with the phenomenal (but also filling us with Romantic longing for the full light of day). In his scandalous novel *Lucinde* (1799) the Schlegelian lover wonders whether the union of male and female principles implies a marvelous allegory of full humanity, then concludes, "There's a deep, underlying meaning here, and what lies in it surely does not stand out so fast as I do when I lie under you" (German *unterliegen* = lie under/succumb to, *KA*, 5:13). Energized by the Abounding Fullness and the bouncy Dorothea, Schlegel ejaculated streams of sparkling aphorisms comparing wordplay and other sciences. The catalyst of *Universalchemie*, it might also prove "a logical and grammatical music, which must furnish fugues, fantasies (and sonatas)."[24] Or if *der Witz* was not *der Blitz,* then some wit might be mental shit: "Es giebt einen Witz der den Exkrementen des Geistes gleicht" (*LN*, p. 115).

His predilection for etymological wordplay provoked a dispute with Jean Paul Richter. In his *Vorschule der Aesthetik* (1804) that notable ironist distinguished wordplay exploring buried intellectual connections from homonymic puns relying solely on the haphazard association of sounds. Charles Lamb would happily proclaim that "the worst puns are the best," citing a porter carrying a rabbit down the street who was asked, "Is that thy own hare, or a wig?"[25] Likewise Richter gave the palm to such grotesque caprices, implicitly reserving the back of his hand for Schlegel's etymological wordplay. A homonymic pun especially charms us, Jean Paul suggested, because this "wild pairing without a priest" defies causality and stuns us with the power of "chance, which holds sway throughout the world, sporting with sounds and continents."[26] While Friedrich Schlegel preferred intellectually grounded etymological wordplay, his brother finally sided with Jean Paul in favor of homonymic punning because he wished to stress the phonological and musical basis of poetry.

Manifold and undogmatic, discussion of this rhetorical figure was insistently grounded in large philosophical principles like freedom and order, economy and abundance. Though Friedrich's Delphic punning was criticized as Transcendental egotism, he grandly identified wit with the principle of absolute sociability, "unbedingt geselliger Geist" (*KA*, 2:148). Lessing had contrasted the temporal organization of music and literature with the spatial organization of the plastic arts, which permitted simultaneous apperception. Schlegel wished to claim for literature the advantages of its sister arts: "In music there is only sequential variety, in the plastic arts only coexistent variety; in poetry both" (*KA*, 16:29). Puns suggest this by allowing two or more meanings to be apprehended simultaneously in one word. A votary of metaphor, Jean Paul questioned whether it was healthy for wordplay to divert attention from objects to their signs. But most early Romantics valued the pun precisely because it provoked transcendental reflection on the limits of linguistic understanding. Like Jean Paul, they suspected that the etymological connections for which they groped might often be bogus or tautological. But by flickering between the poles of semantic identity and sheer homonymy, this trope dramatized the unreliability of its own intuitions. On the rhetorical dueling ground puns thus remained the Romantic ironist's weapon of choice. Goethe, the master spirit of the age, was a masterful punster.

Byron, perhaps, hardly needed the theories of the Schlegels to intuit his way toward the punning style and ironic form of *Don Juan,* but for Carlyle the German influence was catalytic. Thanks partly to the Emersonian connection, the mock-Teutonic punning opacities of *Sartor Resartus* had a like catalytic impact in America before Carlyle was elevated to the status of a British sage. When German criticism reached America in translations, A. W. Schlegel's work was more influential than his younger brother's in popularizing Romantic irony. But Poe's *Tales of the Grotesque and Arabesque* (1839–40) never would have been so titled without Friedrich's seminal treatment of the Arabesque as artificiality, and Poe's entire oeuvre breathes a spirit of Romantic irony inspired by the arch archbishop of German Romanticism. A translation of Friedrich's *Lectures on the History of Literature, Ancient and Modern,* originally delivered in Vienna in 1812, appeared in Philadelphia within the decade; by the 1860s there were annotated school editions. But American youth did not need to slog through them to grasp the intellectual potency of wordplay. A. W. Schlegel's *A Course of Lectures on Dramatic Art and Literature* first appeared in English in 1815 and was reprinted frequently throughout the century. On the shelves of Emerson's library stood the translation by John Black (Philadelphia: Hogan, 1833). Shakespeare was the patron saint of Romantic wordplay, and A. W. Schlegel had labored with great success to preserve it in his standard German translations. From his *Lectures* an alert reader would learn how irony and ambiguity of intention overflowed in Shakespeare so that "he himself is not tied down by the subject represented, but soars freely above it; and that if he chose, he could unrelentingly annihilate the beautiful and irresistibly attractive scenes which his magic pen has produced." The attentive reader would also note that in using or avoiding wordplay, Shakespeare "must have been guided by the measure of the objects, and the different style in which they require to be treated, and have followed probably, as in everything else, principles which would bear a strict examination" (pp. 296-99). And A. W. Schlegel insisted that the Elizabethans' taste for punning was a hallmark of cultural sophistication. From his pages alone a thorough reader with a taste for puns might construct his own theory of Romantic irony. All the Transcendentalists worshiped Shakespeare—and one punning reader was indeed Thoreau.

Moonshine in Vermont: Coleridge as America's First Punning Transcendental Sage

The Vermont Transcendentalist James Marsh published his translation of Herder's *The Spirit of Hebrew Poetry* (Burlington, Vt.: Smith, 1833) as part of a campaign to heal the split between Congregational orthodoxy and Boston Unitarianism. Across Massachusetts feuding congregations had been embroiled in lawsuits over the ownership of church property and communion silver. Marsh hoped that both pious folk perplexed by biblical literalism and sophisticates scornful of biblical barbarism could learn from Herder to appreciate Scripture as literature inspired partly by a people's historical circumstances and conditioned by their language. In this epochal work Herder presented Hebrew as one of the eldest offspring of the primal *Ursprache*. The preeminently poetical energy of Scripture Herder grounded in the peculiar grammar of Hebrew, where "the verb is almost the whole of the language. In other words, every thing lives and acts. The nouns are derived from verbs, and in a certain sense are still verbs. They are as it were living beings, extracted and moulded, while their radical source itself was in a state of living energy." In some modern languages verbs and nouns remain closely related, which benefits English and German poetry. Hebrew is "an abyss of verbs, a sea of billows, where motion, action, rolls on without end" (1:29). Such a billowing, tempestuous language, one might suppose, could almost express *die Fülle,* the chaotic energy of the Romantic cosmos imagined by Schlegel.

The greater sonority of Hebrew (and Greek) Herder attributes to the Mediterranean climate's fostering passionate, orotund expression from the depths of the lungs. In their open-mouthed appreciation of the wonders among which they moved the Jews were thus ideally equipped to ingest and proclaim the world's glory. Barren in abstract terms, Hebrew abounds in sensuous synonyms denoting the same object in all its various sensory contexts. Like Blair's and Reid's romantic primitives, the Jews were so intimate with nature that surviving Hebrew writings contain more than 250 botanical terms. The spoken language was no doubt still richer. "Everything in it proclaims 'I live, and move, and act. The senses and the passions, not abstract reasoners and philosophers were my creators. Thus I am formed for poetry, nay my whole essence is poetry'" (1:30-34). Hebrew is even more fortunate poetically in its power of compression. Time is collapsed into one tense, for to poetry "all is present time." Living in the infancy of the human race, the Hebrews, "like children, aim to say the whole at once, and to express by a single sound, the person, number, tense, action and still more. . . . They express by a single word what we can express often only by five or more words." From the radical form for *he is gone* we can trace "a series of expressions signifying, loss, disappearance and death, vain purposes, and fruitless toil and trouble . . . and if you place yourself in the circumstances of the ancient herdsmen, in their wandering unsettled mode of life, the most distant derivative will still give back something of the original sound of the words, and of the original feeling." Resembling a collection of paintings, the Hebrew vocabulary is uniquely vital and concrete, each word resonating with overtones of meaning generated by derivation from powerful primal verbs. Thus, "though we should be convinced that it contained nothing remarkable, yet the language of nature in it . . . we must believe, for we feel it" (1:36-46).

Convinced that Hebrew words held multiple meanings in suspension, Herder admired Old Testament punning. "I must request beforehand, however, that the term 'pun' (wortspiel) may be omitted, and that we substitute the terms, verbal conceits, accordances of sound, paronomasia, &c," he cautioned. "By the first we understand usually the low art, which the English call the art of punning, and of the levity of which the Hebrews knew nothing." Samson's wordplay bespeaks a "sensuous age" bent on exercising its "childlike wit" in verbal conceits. Exulting over the mighty heap slain with the jawbone of an ass (*heap = ass* in Hebrew), Samson is a heroic punster. The bold locutions of this "punning hero" correspond naturally to his physical prowess in a warlike era that celebrated inventing or solving a good riddle as victories in intellectual combat. Herder wisely concludes that in an oral tradition "paronomasia is not so ridiculous a matter, as we are apt to infer from the place and character of such things in modern languages." Like verse and rhyme, verbal conceits based on echoing sounds then served to make traditional lore memorable. Herder himself thought it would be foolish "to imitate the taste of the Hebrew language in our own" (2:209-15). But from his pages an American author like Melville might well conclude that the primitive energy of our young country would sound its barbaric yawp in explosive puns. In *Israel Potter* he characterized the imprisoned Ethan Allen as a Herderesque jocular hero, a primitive Samson from Vermont. Certainly Duyckinck and the "Young America" crowd with whom Melville consorted in New York (zealous punsters all) were animated by such ideas when like Cornelius Mathews they called for a brawling national literature in comic form.[27] "A great cheerfulness have all great wits possessed," opined the young Thoreau in Herder's wake, "almost a prophane levity to such as understood them not" (15 Mar. 1841). One has not understood Thoreau here unless one knows his links to "Young America," knows he means not coffeehouse habitués but *magnanimous* heroes (the epic epithet comes from *magnus animus*, great wit). This aspiring artist was flexing his verbal sinews and flirting with the role of heroic joker.

To nudge natives of Brattleboro and Boston Brahmins toward common religious ground Marsh also tapped Coleridge, editing his *Aids to Reflection* in 1829 with a lengthy introduction aimed at reconciling the warring camps. His choice of peacemaker was apt, for Coleridge was a British Unitarian, a fervent Christian apologist, a disciple of German idealism, and the English Romantic who did the most to extend and transform Enlightenment speculation about language. He began as a vehement disciple of Tooke, whom he read in the 1790s. Tookean fancies like the derivation of *truth* from *troweth* fascinated him. He was soon sporting with etymological metaphysics as a master juggler in his own right: "Truth is implied in Words among the first Men. . . . Word, wahr, wehr—truth, troweth, throweth i.e. *hitteth = itteth* = it is *it.*"[28] In the first flush of enthusiasm for Hartleian associationism he urged his mentor Godwin to write a book on language. He himself wrote a callow ode hailing the Purleyan as the "Patriot and Sage! whose breeze-like Spirit first / The lazy mists of Pedantry dispers'd."[29] His son Hartley became a test case for studying a child's acquisition of language. As an educational reformer Coleridge wanted to supply boys with a philosophical grammar so they would "learn a language by learning its history, and would learn history by learning a language."[30] It would explain, for example, that the elaborate structure of Greek syntax reflected a society subordinating individuals to the whole, whereas short Teutonic sentences expressed the primacy of the individual. He felt that the greatest benefit a rich man could bestow on Britain and on mankind would be "a philosophical English Dictionary, with the Greek, Latin, German, French, Spanish and Italian synonyms, and its corresponding indices."[31] Patrons willing to fund his own lexicographical ambitions proved laggard or prudent (for he would never have completed such a project). But he was certainly one of the earliest proponents of what finally emerged as the *OED*.

As his thought matured, Coleridge grew discontented with Tooke's materialism. "He gives the accidental history of words, in which, though frequently right, he is also often mistaken," he decided. Tooke's Greek title EPEA PTEROENTA—the Homeric epithet "winged words"—might better be translated as "Hasty Words."[32] Grammarians and philosophers now seemed fundamentally wrong in assuming that words and syntax represent or directly correspond to things. "Words correspond to Thoughts; and the legitimate Order and Connection of words to the Laws of Thinking and to the Acts and Affections of the Thinker's mind."[33] As idealism displaced materialism in his philosophic affections he christened his second son Berkeley. The unlucky infant soon died, but Coleridge's respect for the bishop lingered on into his later Kantian phase. From Akenside, Berkeley, and Boehme he gleaned his ideas of nature as the language of God. Increasingly he tended to derive words from incorporeal verbs rather than from nouns, as Tooke had done. "A whole Essay might be written on the Danger of *thinking* without Images," the young Coleridge had enthused. But by 1817 he was counseling a disciple, "Habituate yourself to derive your illustrations from your consciousness inwardly, instead of from visual images—εἴδωλα" (in H. Jackson, p. 83). In this frame of mind he returned to thinking about things: "To think (Ding, denken; res, reor) is to *thing*ify. Thing = The *Ing*, a word . . . of all the Gothic Dialects, a somewhat set apart" (CL, 4:885). Here he twists the derivation that had propped Tooke's materialism until it attests instead to the mind's shaping power to create things.

Coleridge's esemplastic imagination created more than its share of philosophic ings. As his penchant for neologisms suggests, his imagination was incurably verbal. A complex ambivalence pervaded his view of etymology. To call etymology a science was a misnomer, he declared. Instead, "etymology is a *logy* which perishes from a plethora of probability."[34] Yet shaky though it was, he could not do without it. Like Tooke, whose indifference to syntax was monumental, authors had rejected "all the *cements* of language, so that a popular book is now a mere bag of marbles, i.e. aphorisms and epigrams on one subject" (CL, 4:885). Etymologic might yet provide a necessary connective principle for unifying style, thought, and literary works. In a wildly speculative note on the derivation of *eight*, Coleridge describes how he relied on free association between words as his main heuristic: "In writing these first

Ebullitions of Thought in words intended only for my own eyes, I purposely throw open all the doors, windows and inlets of my mind—come in what will, wafted from without by chance breezes, or attracted from within by the nucleal thought and the magnetic *aura* or Consequence" (in H. Jackson, p. 85).

Thus he long contemplated writing "An Apology for Paronomasy, alias Punning." He wanted to defend such turns of words "by proving that Language itself is formed upon associations of this kind, that possibly the sensus genericus of whole classes of words may be thus decyphered." Pointing to universal conceptual categories, puns might signpost Platonic ideas. "All men who possess at once active fancy, imagination, and a philosophical spirit, are prone to *Punning,* but with a presentiment that the Pun itself is the buffoon Brutus concealing Brutus, the consul," he grandly claimed. "A ridiculous likeness leads to the detection of a true analogy."[35] Scholastic logicians and schoolmasters were preeminently punsters because they had to attend to the primary sense of words, to the concrete image underlying all abstract derivatives. With relish he illustrated this by quoting a pedagogue's remark to a merchant, "I have indorsed your Bill, Sir!" after flogging his son William (*Marginalia,* 1:354).

Like so many of his projects, the Apology for Paronomasy apparently fizzled. Although he claimed at one point to have written it, inconsistency in his methods suggests that it was never fully formulated. But throughout his life "a punarhoea" flowed for kindred spirits like Lamb. Creating definitions carried him over the Brocken, and coining words (the reverse of the process of etymological analysis) was his constant delight. Etymology could lend itself to playfulness when he derived "erisypelas" from "Harry, sip the less" or "mulish" from the Latin *mulier* = woman (H. Jackson, pp. 78–85). But Coleridge was etymologist enough to know that such playfulness must end in *delusion.* He was painfully aware of his capacity for self-delusion. Understandably, he mistrusted his "disposition to catch fire by the very rapidity of my own motion, & to speak vehemently from mere verbal associations" (*CL,* 2:1000–01). Thus his marginalia are full of what their editor describes as "preposterous philological speculation driven to self-mocking extremes of grotesquerie" (1:lvii). The gleefulness of his wordplay can be deceptive. His puns are often efforts to exorcise through spasms of Romantic irony acute pangs of doubt.

Never reduced to clarity, Coleridge's doctrine of language must be quarried from hints and insights scattered throughout his voluminous writings. Its inconsistencies frustrated him and triggered further conjectures. During his life his habit of etymologizing tempted him into more materialistic speculation than he wished to publish when he set up as a Transcendental sage. Revering philology as "the most *human* practical and fructifying Form, and . . . the most popular *Disguise*, of Logic and Psychology—without which what is Man?" he was simultaneously driven to mock it: "The last 5 words I wrote with the line 'Without black velvet Breeches what is man?' running in my head."[36] Shared by similar European sages like Carlyle and Ruskin, De Maistre and Renan, Grundtvig and Müller, Jacob Grimm and Friedrich Schlegel, Coleridge's faith in philology was part of a Romantic reaction against Enlightenment skepticism and the French Revolution. Parlor etymology was for the Romantics much what popular science became for the Victorians. But for all his miscellaneous learning Coleridge remained an amateur philologist, whose contributions to scientific linguistics "are in the highest degree worthless."[37]

Coleridge believed that Indo-European languages stemmed from "one great Iapetic [i.e., Japhetic, from Noah's second son] original."[38] He sensed the importance of Sanskrit. But he was cloudy about the relation between the Romance and Teutonic families; moreover, he clung doggedly to belief in Hebrew as the divinely inspired primitive language of mankind. Despite his weaknesses as a philologist and a systematic philosopher he strove manfully to harness linguistics as the driving force for an idealistic critique of British empiricism. Grandiosely he projected an analysis of "the Laws by which language would polypize ad infinitum" as well as "a complete history of its original formation" (*UL*, 1:400). From his Hebrew studies Coleridge surmised that the most ancient languages consisted of very few categories and employed words of enormous semantic range. Indeed, he thought that the Hebrew consonants stood for immense but indistinct primal words that were *logoi*, participating in the reality they represented. Likewise, in the Oriental languages "the forms of connection are few and simple and express merely annexment and disjunction, not the niceties of cause and consequence, division and exception."[39] Such languages were ideally constituted to express man's primal unity of perception, his enviable oneness with his world.

The archetypal primal word was the form "I am." It was also the matrix of all thought in Coleridge's *Logic*, which in the eighteenth-century manner he tended to equate with grammar. But unlike Harris, who derived grammar from logic, Coleridge derives logic from grammar. Splitting into the polarized forces of verb and noun, and then into the other parts of speech, language has evolved historically toward clear and distinct discourse by individuating words and then connecting them syntactically: "The history of language is a process of one intelligent power dividing into two (verb and noun), then ever-dividing in the separative projection of desynonymization" (Havens, p. 173). Desynonymization fosters philosophy, which aims at translatability, unlike poetry, which strives for unique synthesis. Fortunately for poets, Coleridge envisions a third stage of linguistic evolution when they may help language recapture its primal unity. Despite its intellectual necessity, philosophy's analytic desynonymizing is not entirely healthy. In his *Notebooks* Coleridge speculated that "the too great Definiteness of Terms in any language may . . . consume too much of the vital and idea-creating force in distinct, clear, full made Images & so prevent originality—*original* thought as distinct from positive thought" (1:1017). Etymology could help recover the primal metaphoric unity of words, things, and thoughts that made the Divine *Fiat* at once speech, idea, and creation itself. He likes to trace multiple senses of words back to an original term charged with ambiguous meaning later differentiated. For him as for Stewart, all words in natural human language are inherently equivocal. He was poorly served by his organic cast of mind, which invites us to think of the Word as a kind of inspired jellyfish subdividing over millennia. Today desynonymization might better be imagined as a self-sustaining intellectual chain reaction. His mania for stipulative definition involves splitting atomic ideas, for meaning explodes from complex, powerful nuclear clusters of thought.

The heart of Coleridge's philosophy is an effort to unite the knower and the known, the mind and the world. In seeking to subvert the epistemological distinction between subject and object, he made ingenious use of etymological metaphysics. Everyone "who calls himself a Christian, holds himself to have a Soul as well as a Body. He distinguishes Mind from Matter, the *Subject* of his consciousness from the *Objects* of the same," he argued in the *Aids to Reflection* (1825). "But though *Subject* and *Substance* are words of kindred roots, nay little less than equivalent terms, yet never the less it is exclusively to sensible OBJECTS, to Bodies, to modifications of Matter, that he habitually attaches the attributes of reality, of substance."[40] If the appeal of such arguments is not to degenerate into intellectual sleight of hand, however, we need more explanation of what joins the two terms that desynonymization has seen fit to distinguish. Presumably they are not merely discrete concepts tied together by what Locke and Berkeley might dismiss as the cheat of words, nor are they grounded in some form of Platonic idea. So what originally linked *subject* and *substance,* or why is our association of them now cognitive?

To his credit, Coleridge tried to answer these questions. Unfortunately, his efforts to recruit help from Germany too often rely on similar argumentation. They seldom cohere beyond the level of suggestiveness.

His hermeneutic invokes the Kantian distinction between Reason and Understanding, but he often asserts this distinction just as baldly as he identifies *subject* and *substance*. When we are told that "the Understanding is that which *stands under* the phenomenon, and gives it objectivity," one may object that more than a pun is required to give objectivity to this circular hermeneutic for linguistic phenomena, that our normal understanding of *understanding* is being violated rather than clarified, that Coleridge is not interpreting language so much as reinterpreting it (*TT*, p. 36). In the last analysis Coleridge's Understanding seems simply a catch-all term for empiricism, which he fears but cannot entirely reject. Likewise, though his Reason supposedly incorporates the clearest of logical truths, elsewhere it is described as "a vague appetency toward something which the Mind incessantly hunts for . . . or the impulse which fills the young Poet's eye with tears, he knows not why."[41] Coleridgean Reason seems simply a slogan for whatever ideals or religious beliefs scientific empiricism fails to guarantee. The concept closely resembles Christian faith. Although Coleridge often invokes the distinction between Reason and Understanding as if he were relying on straightforward conceptual analysis, he is not. Losing its original rigor, in Coleridge's hands the dichotomy seeks to legitimize speculation about God that Kant had not included among the constitutive elements of knowledge. The result is an unsteady blend of philosophy and theosophy. "Christianity is not a Theory, or a Speculation, but a *Life*," Coleridge exclaims at one point in the *Aids* after posing the rhetorical question of how it is to be proved. "Not a *Philosophy* of Life, but a life and a living Process. . . . TRY IT" (p. 178). Had he held more steadily to this insight, he might not have been so provocative a religious apologist, but he would certainly have been a less exasperating one.

In apotheosizing the copula as the origin of language Coleridge developed a theme dear to idealism's heart. To counter Tooke's materialistic veneration of nouns, other turn-of-the-century thinkers based language on the verb, especially on the verb *to be* that Court de Gébelin had made a cornerstone of the *Monde primitif*.[42] In post-Kantian German philosophy the notion exfoliated luxuriantly. Coleridge welcomed it warmly enough to devote considerable space in the *Biographia Literaria* (1817) to expounding the first principle "SUM OR I AM" (1:83). But further reflection convinced him that German thinkers since Fichte erred radically "in deducing the whole Grammar of Philosophy and Religion from the Verb Substantive, Esse, *alone:* excluding (its coordinate) the auxiliary Verb, Habere. Our Father, that art—thine is the Kingdom and the Power and the Glory."[43] Thus in the *Aids* (1825) Coleridge also stresses the Bible's tendency to fuse *nomen* and *numen,* name and divine power. In the beginning was the Verb, perhaps, but a balanced idealism also needs as its complement the beatific noun. Exactly how the dialectic of verb and noun, mind and nature, derives from the great I AM's own self-consciousness Coleridge's prose envelops in obscurity, perhaps necessarily so.

Unlike some Romantics who revolted against the Lockean view of language (or against their misunderstanding of it), Coleridge did not seriously challenge the arbitrariness of words by positing a semantic phonetics or by dreaming of hieroglyphics. "The sound sun, or the figures *s, u, n* are pure arbitrary modes of recalling the objects, and for visual mere objects they are not only sufficient, but have infinite advantages from their nothingness *per se.*"[44] Whereas Harris had linked words to universal concepts, Coleridge located their power in the psychological process by which we interpret bundles of concepts yoked together by words that need not categorize the world in the same way. In most languages he saw harmony between terms for "operations of the mind and heart" but endless discrepancies between the names of things (*TT,* p. 75). His vision of harmony was hard-won and fitful. Deprecating the notion that there are niceties that language cannot convey because it is too abstract and general, he roundly declared: "There is nothing which, being equally known as any other thing, may not be conveyed by words with equal clearness. But the question . . . is, to whom?" (*AP,* p. 266). Of course, the question was also, "By whom?" He was reproached for obscurity, often with considerable justice. As poets he and Wordsworth might communicate to each other "What may be told, to the understanding mind / Revealable" (*PW,* 1:404). But even in such ideal circumstances qualifications suggest how limited and imperfect speech should have been in the more general theory of discourse that he struggled to formulate. Characteristically, he never completed it.

Instead, he asserted like Berkeley that "processes of thought might be carried on independent and apart from spoken or written language." He was haunted by the possibility that "if language had been denied or withheld from man . . . thought, as thought, would have been a process more simple, more easy, and more perfect than the present, and would both have included and evolved other and better means for its own manifestations, than any that exist now" (*TT,* p. 311). Here he went much further than Reid and Blair in ascribing not just emotional but intellectual potential to nonverbal language. Reservations about the adequacy of language were typical of linguistic theories like Coleridge's that make words represent neither ideas nor things but relations. Though prudishness made him reject as an interpolation the Porter's smutty wordplay in *Macbeth,* he warmly defended Shakespeare's propriety in composing punning swansongs for dying characters like Mercutio and John of Gaunt. He found in "vindictive anger striving to ease itself by contempt—the most frequent origin of Puns, next to that of scornful Triumph exulting and insulting."[45] His alter ego, Hamlet, likewise expires with terminal wisecracks about "this fell sergeant Death." It is therefore tempting to apply Coleridge's psychological insight to his own habitual punning. His puns represent more than Romantic irony dramatizing verbal artifice in order to triumph over it. Puns also help discharge the anger that he normally turned inward upon himself in the form of copious guilt. Sometimes his puns express the rage of a mind confronting life's seemingly ineluctable limits. Though he claimed to have no "horror of death, simply as death," he confessed "that it was *dying* he dreaded" (*TT,* p. 62). In the beginning was the Verb, of course, but we also have to reckon with it at the end. Such philosophic nicety seems both admirable and ludicrous. Seldom a drag, his wordplay was often a drug. Among the ailments he joked about obsessively was the constipation his opium habit caused; newly discovered verses include quite a few bawdy poems about shit.[46] But as a genuine verbal stimulant puns proved a safer and more creative addiction than opium.

As the *Aids to Reflection* (1825) guardedly put it, "There sometimes occurs an apparent *Play* on words, which not only to the Moralizer, but even to the philosophical Etymologist, appears more than a mere Play" (p. 42). In developing what has been aptly styled "etymologic," Coleridge bequeathed to the nineteenth century a stylistic and heuristic technique that safely sanitized the shallow skepticism of that radical culture hero Horne Tooke, the Tom Paine of philology. Etymologic became a major weapon in the arsenal of the Victorian sage, who was more often than not essentially conservative. Relatively lucid and undogmatic, the *Aids* did more than any other work to disseminate Coleridge's ideas about language in America. In 1829 James Marsh reorganized the curriculum at the University of Vermont along Coleridgean lines and began to churn out devoted disciples. At the semicentennial in 1854 alumni in Burlington were exhorted to chant, "I believe in Coleridge! I believe in Professor Marsh!" as the climactic articles of their school's intellectual creed.[47] When Marsh's campaign for Christian unity bogged down in the aridities of Kantian terminology, he waited for help from Coleridge's promised "Elements of Discourse." That help never materialized, of course, and Marsh's Christian hopes for Boston Transcendentalism faded. Like his master's, his concept of Reason was ambiguous in its relation to faith but not elastic enough to accommodate Emerson's leaps and bounds. The Vermont Transcendentalists were a conservative vanguard. But they took up Coleridge with such a vengeance that the first collected edition of his works appeared in the United States. Marsh's edition of the *Aids* had a catalytic effect on religious thinkers like Connecticut's Horace Bushnell, who also hoped that a truer philosophy of language could deepen people's reading of Scripture and update New England's Calvinist theology. Like Emerson, many Harvard divinity students promptly acquired copies. It became the hornbook of budding Transcendentalists.

3/

Parsing the Language of Nature

> The main difficulty . . . is for the examiner to . . . arrive at the simple philosophy of the subject. So accumulated and perplexing, too, is the body of mere learning, under the name of philology, grammar, and their kindred arts, that there is constant danger of being mazed in the wilderness of words, and losing the essential principle, in the multiplicity of conflicting authorities, of incidental facts and associations.
>
> — William S. Cardell, *Elements of English Grammar* (1826)

Murray's Grammar and the Mania for Etymological Parsing

Webster's *Philosophical and Practical Grammar of the English Language* (1807) enshrined his belief in the eternal truth of the *Diversions of Purley*. But his grammar never acquired the ascendancy over its rivals that his speller and dictionary did. Throughout the first half of the nineteenth century Lindley Murray's *English Grammar* (1795) remained the most popular introduction to the subject, appearing in numerous abridgments and adaptations. The National Union Catalogue lists well over two hundred American editions of this standard text between 1800 and 1850, and that listing is scarcely exhaustive.[1] Among the four grammars that Thoreau owned was an edition published in Hallowell, Maine, in 1823. Printshops in many American hamlets spawned similar versions for use in local schools.

How was a pupil who desired to understand the structure of his language encouraged to do so? "ENGLISH GRAMMAR is the art of speaking and writing the English language with propriety," Murray began. "It is divided into four parts, viz. ORTHOGRAPHY, ETYMOLOGY, SYNTAX, AND PROSODY." But the student marching through this schema would soon discern that greatest among the four grammatical cardinal virtues was *etymology*. Forty percent of the text was devoted to what Murray called etymology, for that category included the parts of speech and their inflections. Orthography was elementary stuff; two dozen pages sufficed to enumerate the letters of the alphabet and a few simple spelling rules. The appendage on prosody required little more space, for Murray's treatment of pronunciation and versification made these seem matters of faintly irrelevant refinement. The backbone of grammar was clearly etymology. Not only were nearly a hundred pages devoted to it, but the ensuing section on syntax took the parts of speech as its organizing principle and seemed merely a commentary on etymology.

Murray was hardly peculiar in this respect. His categories represented the received grammatical wisdom of the day and were echoed throughout the first half of the nineteenth century by almost all other grammarians. That era's understanding of *etymology* differed from ours, for the term then embraced what a modern linguist would call *morphology*: how the words of a language at a given point in time are declined, conjugated, and modified to yield other acceptable verbal forms. But the term also included our modern meaning. The result was conceptual confusion. Struggling to clarify it, in 1825 another grammarian suggested distinguishing grammatical etymology from "what I will venture to call *comparative etymology*"—that is, the historical study of the derivation of one language from others.[2] But this tentative wording shows how idiosyncratic such a distinction was; in fact, it never gained currency in the period. In antebellum America *etymology* was a multipurpose concept, cloudily conflating kinds of inquiry that we take to be sharply distinct. Far from being sidelined to scholarly obscurity, it was impressed upon the beginner as the quintessence of the whole grammatical enterprise. Once having grasped that *men* is a plural of *man* and that *sits* is another form of the verb *sit,* a tot became by definition a little etymologist.

Murray's treatment of the parts of speech thus culminated naturally in a chapter "Of derivation," where the rules of morphology lead to "a sketch of the steps, by which the English language has risen to its present state of refinement."[3] Indeed, to define substantives, adjectives, verbs, conjunctions, interjections, and so forth was very likely to engage in etymological analysis, insofar as the eighteenth-century grammatical tradition persistently sought the origin of some parts of speech in others. Did language begin with the interjection, as Rousseau postulated? with the impersonal verb, as Adam Smith suggested? or was Tooke right in his bias for the noun? A nineteenth-century teacher prepared students to parse sentences amid muffled echoes of inveterate debate over the primal word.

Indeed, in the middle of the nineteenth century etymology displaced orthography as the crucial linguistic skill. Spelling bees celebrated an age of romantic innocence, when the American Adam could walk naked in the garden and name the animals in happy unself-consciousness. Grammatical etymology, however, demanded that the names themselves be named. In *An Introductory Lecture on the Metaphysics and Philosophy of Language* (Philadelphia, 1819) Peter Chazotte explained that our first parents needed grammatical ligaments only after the Fall. Speaking the language of nature became an art, and the technique practiced by its apprentices was parsing. Before midcentury composition was seldom taught. "Although we studied English grammar for seven years and received a silver medal for proficiency, we never wrote a sentence of English at school, and never did anything that had to do with writing or conversation," one student recalled.[4] Instead, children were relentlessly urged to analyze sentences in their texts. But this analysis only partly resembled the process of diagramming sentences that survives in some modern classrooms—alas, not all—for early nineteenth-century schools lacked blackboards.

They also lacked our concept of the structure of a sentence. Whereas modern grammar takes the sentence as the basic unit of language and works backward from that to the role of individual words, for American grammarians before 1850 the word remained the primary unit of speech. Their approach to language was Lockean and atomistic—they were determined to build up complex wholes in a step-by-step fashion from the simplest elements. They lacked the Kantian perspective that might have stressed synthesizing a priori structures. Thus their grammars regularly began with orthography, for at heart they aspired to make grammar quite literally *grammar*—the study of *letters* in combination. Partly because of this atomistic outlook, syntax received less attention than etymology, where attention focused on classifying the parts of speech.

Diagramming sentences displays their architecture in a way that Gertrude Stein found exhilarating. "At school the really completely exciting thing was diagramming sentences and that has been to me ever since the one thing that has been completely exciting and completely completing," she recalled. "I like the feeling the everlasting feeling of sentences as they diagram themselves."[5] In parsing, however, the blueprint of the verbal structure is scanted. You focus on the role of the individual building block, the word. A class parsing a sentence would march through it identifying each word in order at the teacher's command and reciting from Murray by rote the grammatical terms and rules involved. Dudley Leavitt explained:

> *Etymological parsing* consists in telling what part of speech any word is, and in what form . . . it is with respect to the variations pertaining to that part of speech, but has nothing to do with the rules of syntax.
>
> *Syntactical parsing* is the parsing of words not only according to the principles of etymology, but also agreeably to the rules of syntax.
>
> *Analytical parsing* is the parsing of words either etymologically or syntactically and giving the reasons *why* they are parsed as they are.
>
> When a word is to be parsed, the first thing to be considered is what part of speech it is.[6]

Leavitt's definitions manifest the mania for analysis that underlay parsing. In its conviction that to give verbal processes high-sounding names must be to understand them, nineteenth-century grammar joined hands with twentieth-century grammatology. But for all his effort at logical rigor, the intellectual poverty of the parsing process is also apparent. That he feels compelled to create his own novel category of *analytical parsing* only reveals how much parsing depended on rote for which the student was not expected to supply reasons.

Moreover, Leavitt's distinctions cannot be sustained. To refute his claim that etymological parsing "has nothing to do with the rules of syntax," we need only ask how one should parse the word *rules* in that sentence, in accord with his dictum that "the first thing to be considered is what part of speech it is." Is *rules* the plural of the noun or the third-person present indicative of the verb? Etymological analysis alone can give no answer, of course; the word can be classified correctly only by understanding its syntactic function in the sentence as a noun designated by the article *the* and governed by the preposition *with*.

Leavitt, however, sought to extricate himself from such dilemmas by resorting to Murray's semantic definition of the parts of speech, with predictably ludicrous consequences: "The following examples may be useful to explain the subject to learners. — 'A *tune* is a noun because it is the name of something of which we have an idea or notion.' 'Tune the instrument.' Here *tune* is a verb because it signifies to *do* something" (p. 21). Explaining to learners why songs are things but singing is an activity required far greater philosophical talents than Dudley Leavitt's. Since his *Complete Directions for Parsing the English Language* do not even equip students to parse his own directions, teachers and students alike were understandably frustrated by the ambiguities engendered in Murray's grammar. Indeed, the entire parsing process encouraged students to view language as a quicksand of multiple meanings shifting beneath unwary feet. If spelling drill suggested the magical potency of language, parsing represented an attempt to tame its unruly powers by insisting on unequivocal meaning. The sorcerer's apprentices who peopled the nation's classrooms often got the genie back in the bottle. But by no means always, for their key concept of *etymology* (etymologically "true word") remained itself deeply equivocal.

Troubled by the difficulty of isolating etymology from syntax, Allen Fuller devoted his *Grammatical Exercises* (Plymouth, Mass.: Danforth, 1822) to blending them together since "these two divisions are so systematically connected that one cannot be fully explained without the other; for as the parts of speech are known by the office that they perform in the sentence, and some words may be used for several parts of speech, it follows that without knowing something of the relation and connection of words, one cannot understand their division into classes" (p. 81). In *Rudimental Lessons in Etymology and Syntax in Which These Two Parts of Grammar Are Exhibited in Parallel Columns* (Providence, R.I.: Cranston, 1826) Manasseh Robbins tried to heal the breach with another novel method of organization he hoped would make parsing less "disgusting and fatiguing" (p. 3).

Such books attest to the uneasiness often felt by grammarians working in the tradition of Murray as well as to their reluctance to abandon that tradition. Of perhaps five million grammars printed in America before 1850, a million are estimated to have been editions of Murray — with another half million to a million representing adaptations of Murray. But though this text was the standard against which others were measured, it did not dominate its market like Webster's speller. Forty percent of Americans may have owed their grammatical training to Murray, but a host of domestic competitors appeared in the first half of the nineteenth century. The 1820s were the boom decade, witnessing more than eighty new grammars written by Americans, but the swelling army of native grammarians recruited largely through midcentury, with the 1830s and 1840s each adding more than sixty contenders. Like James Brown, the author of *An American Grammar* (1820), these stalwarts patriotically opposed Murray and royalty but were obviously in favor of royalties.

The Lurking Transcendentalism of William Cardell's "Philosophic Parsing"

One of the leading spirits in this grammatical revolution was William S. Cardell of New York, who in 1820 founded the American Academy of Belles Lettres in avowed imitation of the French Academy. His attempts to enlist the support of Thomas Jefferson and James Madison failed, for they feared that any linguistic authority would try to fix and so stultify the language. But men like John Marshall, John Trumbull, and John Adams warmly suppported it. Alas, the congressional endowment that Adams hoped for never materialized, and the academy collapsed in the wake of hostile criticism from the *North American Review,* so founding the National Endowment for the Humanities had to await more enlightened political leadership.

Nothing daunted, Cardell adopted a more forthrightly reformist stance than his efforts to secure bipartisan support for the academy had allowed. In his *Essay on Language, as Connected with the Faculties of the Mind and as Applied to Things in Nature and Art* (New York: Wiley, 1825) he conceded that most Americans felt that any attempt to go beyond Murray was chancy. He aimed to put the study of language on a more scientific basis by attending "to etymology; to the comparison of various languages, in the literal, transitive, idiomatic, and figurative meanings of words; and to the best systems of logic and mental philosophy, compared with the consciousness of what is passing in the mind" (pp. v–vi). Education should show how language is shaped by our civil and moral history, by the physical and social condition of man. "Instead of treating words as the theme of contempt, and explaining them according to the metaphysics of the twelfth-century," grammar would again become the gateway to all knowledge if enriched with the insights of modern philosophy. What passed for analysis of language "is alike opposed to fact, to science, and to common sense: for under no other name but that of grammar, could such gross inconsistencies be admitted in schools of the present day and pass for instruction."

This unfortunate situation Cardell sought to rectify with an "Introductory Dissertation" sketching the history and philosophy of language. He vouched for its effectiveness in stimulating young minds and fostering philosophic reflection in the classroom. In that gentler age New York schoolboys were evidently moved to shun dangling participles by flights of periodic eloquence:

> When we consider the faculty of speech as the distinguishing gift of the Creator to our race: as inwoven with all the wants, enjoyments, and improvements of man: as the index to the progress of society from barbarism to refinement, and of its downward course through luxury, imbecility, and crime to the depths of national degradation; contemplating the structure of speech as blended with the whole internal organization of society; with instruction, laws, religious sentiments, moral conduct, and habits of thought; when we consider it as the means of the Christian's present consolation and future hope, and still extend our views to the faculty of speech as the medium of social bliss for superior intelligences in an eternal world: what benighted man, rejecting the bounty of his Maker, shall come forward and say that the study of language is dull, or low, or unprofitable? (p. 2)

Their emphasis on the importance of self-culture meant that like many academics today Unitarians seemed at times to equate Heaven with Harvard. But the celestial seminars of William Ellery Channing's eschatology pale beside Cardell's more democratic vision of a transcendental grammar school in the sky.

Cardell also composed two grammars designed to adapt his theories of language to the classroom. *Elements of English Grammar Deduced from Science and Practice, Adapted to the Capacity of Learners* (1826) dignified the subject by developing the connection between language and thought adumbrated in the *Essay*. Although Bacon, Locke, Tooke, and Stewart were his principal philosophical authorities, the influence of Humboldt, Coleridge, and Schlegel also peeps out. But ultimately he revered the structure of language as the embodied democratic wisdom of the average man. Language is where "the plain common sense of mankind has reposited its enduring treasures; and where the investigator . . . must repair for his choicest means of induction."[7] Or, as he phrased this core conviction even more boldly in his *Philosophic Grammar of the English Language, in connection with the laws of matter and of thought* (Philadelphia: U. Hunt, 1827), which amplified and slightly altered his *Elements,* "the nations of unlettered men so adapted their language to philosophic truth, that all physical and intellectual research can find no essential rule to reject or change" (p. 91).

Philosophic truth consisted for Cardell in the proposition that "all language, and the reasoning connected with it, rest primarily on the evidence of the senses. If, from slight inspection, it should appear to any, that such reasoning leads to the degrading, comfortless doctrine of materialism, into which some theorists have fallen, nothing is farther from such a tendency" (*Elements,* p. xxxii). Grammar, as he grandly conceived it, needed to explain not just the structure of language but the structure of the world. He did this by classifying all things into material, mental, imaginary, or spiritual substances, then categorizing them by attendant circumstances, affections of the mind, complex ideas, and relative or absolute names. The difficulty in establishing such distinctions did not trouble him unduly. "No skill can draw a complete separating line between them," he admitted, but these philosophical categories intermingled in nature, so it was unnecessary "to aim at infallibility in the application of principles, the unerring use of which would require nothing less than the perfection of knowledge" (*Essay,* p. 59).

He wished to supplement conventional grammatical analysis with a technique that he termed "philosophic parsing." In practice this amounted to requiring pupils to give a pious empirical account of the italicized words in set passages:

> You may show a *child* a *house* and teach him the *fact* that such an *edifice* could not have made itself; in *proof* of which *opinion,* you may show him *masons* and *carpenters* at their *work.* Then direct his *attention* to the heavenly *orbs;* the *earth;* and the numerous *animals* and *vegetables,* and *minerals* which God has formed for the *use* of *man,* and say to the little *boy* or *girl,* how much superior is the *world* we inhabit, to that *house!* Can the *universe,* then, have organized its own *structure.* How ought our

souls to glow with *gratitude* and *admiration* for the *Author* of such *wisdom* and *goodness.—Paraphrase from Fenelon.*

Child, absolute name of persons.

All names of persons are mixed or complex ideas, including the union of body and mind.

House, sensible object.

Fact, attendant circumstance of matter.

It alludes to some operation on material substances.

Animals, class of sensible objects, including the relative idea of life.

Vegetables, sensible objects; but the name always relates to the manner of growth.

Minerals, sensible objects but always relative, as being found in mines.

God, highest mental object.

As mind is superior to matter, and the Creator is the highest mental existence, so the idea is the most *sublime* which the mind can conceive.

Universe, most complex of all ideas, including all objects, qualities, and relations, as a collective whole.

Structure, attendant circumstance of matter.

Souls, mental object. (*Essay,* pp. 197–99)

Could philosophic parsing win mental objects like souls for literature, Christ, and John Locke? That was the question for Enoch Pond. In his adaptation of Murray's *English Grammar* (1826; Ward, Conn.: 1828) that conservative minister expressed a nervous skepticism rooted in his commitment to Calvinist orthodoxy in Connecticut. Did Cardell's reliance on Tooke's doctrine of conjunctions as covert imperatives really breed a more philosophical view of language than Murray's?

> The writer has no difficulty with those who have means and leisure, and are disposed to amuse themselves with investigating the roots of English words; but they, who urge the results of such investigations to overturn the established principles of our language, allowing but two or three parts of speech; making no distinction between active, neuter and passive verbs; admitting only three modes and tenses; with other innovations equally unfounded and ridiculous; and who would bring all this into common schools, under the imposing title of scientific and philosophical grammar—such persons, he honestly thinks, might be better employed. It is obviously a much more useful exercise, to take the principles of our language, as taught by the best masters . . . and make them plain to the capacities of learners, than to raise new theories, however specious, and however captivating to the lovers of novelty. (pp. 5–6)

Etymological speculation à la Tooke might be all very well for affluent members of the leisure class, Pond implied, but introducing it into common schools might breed grammatical Jacobinism among the lower orders. Nonetheless, the lower orders proceeded to elect Andrew Jackson, a president who dismayed good New England Federalists by his penchant for articulating the *vox populi* in solecisms. Pond removed to a professorship at the theological seminary in Bangor, Maine. A quarter-century later, when Horace Bushnell's newfangled philosophy of language set all the Congregational lily pads rocking, from that northern fastness the voice of his frogship was once again heard, croaking imprecations against the Hartford minister's doctrines in the accents of contemporary Know-Nothingism.

Cardell's ruling philosophical ideas did have curious consequences for his conception of grammar proper. Harmonizing grammar with science, he found that Newtonian physics invalidated the traditional grammatical classification of passive verbs:

> Every verb denotes *action;* because, *First;* there is no other office which it can perform, or by which it *could* acquire meaning or use; and,
>
> *Second;* Because the sublime truth that every thing *acts,* at every moment, is a prime law of nature, the experience of human life from the cradle to the grave, the predominating habit of thought, and the ruling principle of construction, in every form of speech. (*Elements,* pp. xxii–xxiii)

Though supported with an ingenious argument, Cardell's evangelistic zeal on this point might just as well be viewed as the expression of a patriotic populism that aligns him with Jefferson and Jackson. For Cardell the verb embodied the same expansive energy that characterized America's dynamic provincialism. His democratic ideals biased him against grammatical class distinctions. At heart he held these truths to be self-evident: that all verbs were created equal and endowed by their Creator with a certain inalienable right to action.

Despite his scientific reasoning here, Cardell was right to contrast his thought to materialism. He wanted to broaden the concept of action well beyond Newtonian physics:

> It will not be supposed that the animal frame, barely as an organized mass of matter, can act. There must be some unseen active principle within it: and by what law the incorporeal spirit exists in the body, or directs its locomotion, in all the surprisingly varying modes, is entirely incomprehensible to human skill. According to the habit of thought and expression, the vital power is the *cause* of animal motions; but within the province of science, properly so called, neither this cause, nor any other, is understood, except as inferred from its effects. The principle is the same through the whole range of created things, as far as they are known; and there is no clear line of demarcation between beings possessed of *animal vitality,* and those imbued, as all are, with other *living* or inherently *active qualities.* Men of science, in character as such, do not appear to recognize, under any name, a distinctive sort of things which can not spontaneously act. (*Philosophical Grammar,* p. 27)

Tocqueville was shrewdly to observe that in its tendency to obliterate all distinctions pantheism should appeal strongly to democratic Americans. In that direction Cardell's imagination inexorably moved, undoubtedly to Pond's distrust. His grammar mapped a universe instinct in every detail with vital, divine power. Thus for philosophic reasons he wanted to erase all distinctions between the copula, transitive, and intransitive verbs.

The capstone of his system was an elaborate etymological exegesis of the "*Word of Words, the Verb* TO BE" (*Elements,* p. 135). It proceeded along Tookean lines, but Tooke was filtered through Herder and Coleridge to sift out the skeptical materialism. Taking wing from the Hebrew *aur,* light, Cardell explained the irregular parts of *to be* thus:

> *a, are, art,* these are the same word. . . .
>
> "They are," means first, they *air,* or *are themselves;* they *supply themselves* with air; they *vivify, inspirit* and *preserve themselves* by means of *air;* and applied to the lower ranks of creatures, they continue themselves in *air,* . . . do something as nearly analogous to the same *action* as their various natures and circumstances will admit. (*Elements,* p. 136)

These forms he connected with "*Aurora:* the *air,* the *light,* the *morning dawn,* deified in the pagan mythology." *Aur* inferentially signified God and "figuratively signified instruction, the *light* of the mind, intellectual talent. In English, the noun *art* is a participial formation from the verb, as *cleft* is from *cleave.* A person's *art* is that with which he is *lighted,* instructed, or *skilled*" (*Essay,* pp. 143–45). Cardell's etymological equations between light, life, air, dawn, divine inspiration, and art were so unenlightened as to be thoroughly delightful.

"No man can state a falsehood in saying *I am;* for no one can utter it, if it is not true," he averred. Thus this compound of noun and verb fittingly designates the self-sustaining source of all truth. "*I am,* as a noun, could never be thus used, but by the *Ever living God;* and . . . it can be taken only as a *nominative* word, or as the *actor,*" Cardell argued. Since the unchanging God is "above all influence of inferior *actors,* he can not in strictness be contemplated as the object of any *action*" (*Elements,* pp. 135–38). After analyzing the individual Hebrew characters composing I AM as "hieroglyphic symbols" of breathing, duration, and power, Cardell concludes that "this expression . . . presents an idea of the incomprehensible Sovereign, who *was,* and *is,* and *is to be,* in a manner which it would be presumptuous in the writer of this essay to attempt farther to explain" (*Essay,* pp. 156–58). Nonetheless, despite this modest disclaimer, Cardell does seem to regard himself as sketching a Coleridgean solution to Tooke's conundrum about whether noun or verb had priority by locating the origin of all language in a hybrid form designating the Deity. In Cardell's books this nominalized copula becomes both a model for physical science and the divinely tuned motor geared to the transmission of human speech.

If Cardell's treatment of the verb *to be* was his philosophical motor, the transcendental etymologies on which it ran were certainly gas. Virtually without exception they were vaporous. Yet when ignited by the imagination they form an explosive mixture. Before dismissing Cardell's philological innocence with a condescending smile, ask yourself how many readers today would know that his derivations were erroneous unless thoughtfully informed of that fact. Most twentieth-century teachers of English know fewer languages than he did and could hardly contradict his claims without help. Our era abounds in theories of language more advanced than Cardell's, but our literary culture is not so familiar with them, and our linguistic experts have done less to spread them abroad. If in some respects we have advanced beyond Cardell's age, in other respects we lag behind. However erroneous, Cardell's theories of language at least made him a fairly effective writer. Modern academics deconstructing his prose might not construct it as well. Many grammatical and critical theories now in vogue will no doubt strike future ages as hugely amusing. Cardell's grammar must be judged as an aesthetic construct, with a modicum of respect for the past and a modicum of humility about ourselves.

Approached in these terms, Cardell reveals himself as a contemporary of Emerson's, sharing many aims with the Transcendentalists. His assault on Murray's tripartite classification of verbs as active, passive, and intransitive has both scientific and political dimensions, to be sure. But its ultimate basis is religious and moral. *In principio erat Verbum:* in the beginning was the Verb. In denying Murray's grammatical trinity Cardell resembles a Boston Unitarian articulating a simpler and more rational theology. But rationalism alone proves unsatisfying and fails to convey his sense of the world. Hence his occasional resort to the cryptic and elliptical, his habit of unveiling etymological secrets in a manner calculated slightly to shock. His right hand wants to reinject the divine into the universe of discourse from which his left hand has banished it. An enormous moral earnestness underlies his insistence that all verbs are active. Passive and intransitive verbs threaten the faculty of choice, and he relies on self-cultivation and moral choice to endow his world with a meaning jeopardized by the departure of special grace.

But neither Channingesque moral intensity nor aesthetic self-cultivation is enough—he wants an ecstatic sense of being alive based on some more direct contact with godhead. Thus he insists that as the Creator constantly sustains creation and creatures, so a man must deliberately sustain his carefully cultivated self: "In order to be, as this verb asserts, *he must,* by continual alternations, *inhale* and *respire the air; inflate* his *lungs,* and by their instrumentality, *impart oxygen* to chyle and blood: he must *eat* and *drink, sleep* and *wake, feel sensations . . .* and *exert himself* in various ways: he must *repeat* the *pulsations* of his heart . . . and *maintain* all his complex vital *organs* in their proper tone of action" (*Philosophic Grammar,* pp. 86–87).

This seems like self-consciousness with a vengeance, and the Transcendentalists were nothing if not self-conscious. One thinks of Emerson, who with uncanny poise modulates between endless reflections on the moral law and moments of exhilarated awareness when "the currents of the Universal Being circulate through me" (*CW,* 1:10). But Emerson sharply distinguishes such numinous self-apprehension from "all mean egotism." Cardell also sees ideal existence as inviting a radical self-awareness that is only partly conscious:

> So far as verbal affirmations *have* any *concern* with the action of *living,* it is not of the least importance whether its complex movements are regulated by consciousness and will, or by . . . the corporeal frame. . . .
>
> It is far more absurd to deny the high *action* of *living,* because, from habit, *it is,* in part, unconsciously *performed,* than to *re-assert* the exploded *belief* that the *earth has* no *motion,* because its rapid progress is not felt. (*Philosophic Grammar,* p. 87)

Both writers aim to make readers aware of what Cardell calls "the high action of living." Before we laugh too heartily at his transcendental grammar, we might wonder whether our transformational grammars transform many students or heighten their sense of life.

Sherman's Attack on Cardell: Grammar Enters Politics — and Vice Versa

To believe John Sherman, many New Yorkers took Cardell's grammar very seriously: "It has made a powerful impression in the city of New York; has received the approbation of a large number of its scientific citizens and teachers; has actually forced its way into many of its schools, the High school not excepted; and is applauded, in the most unqualified terms, in some of the public journals."[8] Encouraged by the favor shown grammatical innovation but burning to launch his own novel textbook, *The Philosophy of Language Illustrated: An Entirely New System of Grammar; Wholly Divested of Scholastic Rubbish, of Traditionary Falsehood, and Absurdity, and Reduced to the Principles of Fact and Common Sense* (1826), Sherman unfurled and affixed thereto a preface designed to steal the wind from Cardell's sales, while taking advantage of every favorable puff for himself. Rather like Cardell, he flew the flag of "a Republican in grammar," excoriating Murray as "too aristocratick for me. . . . Here we own not the *quidities* of the *few*, but the MAJESTY of the MULTITUDE" (p. 170). But though his spread-eagle linguistics might seem to link him with Cardell, he was actually a far harsher critic than Pond had been.

The harshness was partly temperamental. Educated for the ministry at Yale, this grandson of Roger Sherman professed the orthodox faith and was ordained to pastor in northeastern Connecticut. There he came under the influence of Harvard's more liberal theology. When denominational battle lines began to be drawn, he was one of the first casualties— a fate he seems to have courted by dancing on the parapets and thumbing his nose at the enemy. These were now his orthodox brethren from Yale. He published *One God in One Person Only: and Jesus Christ a Being Distinct from God, Dependent upon Him for His Existence, and His Various Powers* (Worcester: Thomas, 1805). Though he framed his argument with unctuous appeals for catholic charity and theological tolerance, it was actually a rather contentious document—perhaps the first polemical statement of Boston Unitarianism. Expelled by outraged Calvinists from his Connecticut parish, he accepted a call from Trenton, New York, where in 1806 his tiny congregation of fourteen became the first Unitarian church in the state. It gradually grew, but so did his family. He sought to provide for them by establishing an academy, over which he presided. He also built a gazebo to accommodate those who wished to share his Unitarian raptures over the local scenery. Eventually he added a hotel.

To publicize it he wrote *A Description of Trenton Falls, Oneida County, N.Y.* (1827; New York: Colyer, 1844), an odd twenty-page tract. Near the hotel, at the deep, romantic chasm of Kauy-a-hoo-ra, the Reverend Sherman had decreed a stately pleasure dome, where the West Canada branch of the Mohawk ran, with cascades measureless to man, down toward New York City. "Here a flight of stairs leads up to a house of refreshment, styled the RURAL RETREAT, 20 feet above the summit of the high falls, and in a direct line with them—a house 30 by 16, with a well furnished bar, and also a room for gentlemen and ladies . . . from the front platform and windows of which, is a full view of the inverted scenery of the falls" (p. 9). This commodious hut commanded a more exciting prospect than Walden Pond. From its vantage a budding Transcendentalist could contemplate "the magnificence, the beauty, the grandeur and sublimity of the scene" in silent awe if he chose (p. 4).

Sherman felt that nature was best worshiped collectively, however, for "the large party enjoy with more zest their association, as they can sit together, make philosophical observations, and communicate their mutual impressions" (pp. 16-17). There would be plenty to talk about. For example, "in the bosom of the excavation a Fairy makes her appearance at a certain hour of sunshine, and dances through the mist, modestly retiring as the visitor changes his position, and blushing all colours when she finds him gazing at her irised beauties" (p. 7). There was a display of fossil specimens collected in the conviction that "an irreligious geologist 'is mad.'" Estimating the rate of erosion as one inch per year, Sherman calculated that the three-hundred-yard gorge had required "between 5 and 6000 years to produce this effect: which corresponds with sufficient exactness to the Mosaic account of the period in which the solid surface of the earth emerged from its preexistent state" (p. 13-14). But all his ingenious arithmetic did not quite preclude the possibility that in the gorge one might be observing "the operations of incalculable ages" (p. 4). Verily, in Sherman's hostelry the customer could always be right. It was the ambition of mine host (apparently realized) to preside over an early version of Chautauqua, an environment both intellectual and profitable, "where the God of nature himself preaches the most eloquent and impressive lectures to every visiter" (pp. 14-15). Here "philosopher and divine may make their sage remarks and draw their grave conclusions; the weary rest from their labors, the hungry and dry recruit their exhausted spirits, the sociable of all grades and nations converse freely and unknown together, the facetious display the corruscations [*sic*] of their wit, and the cheerful enjoy the innocent glee of hilarity" (pp. 9-10). If the weather failed or nature proved uncommunicative, there were always puns and the well-furnished bar. They provoked very few instances "of the least deviation from gentility or politeness. We record this fact with pleasure, as characteristic of the dignified refinement of the age" (p. 16).

In the 1820s an increasingly numerous and mobile American bourgeoisie betook themselves to watering places in such a spirit. Sherman hoped that the midstate location of his resort near Utica, enhanced by his ingenuity, would make it a small nondenominational Disneyland that could cut into the trade of Niagara Falls. But speaking the language of nature relied increasingly on grammar and science. As Emerson was to suggest in *Nature,* both these were comprehended in the early nineteenth-century conception of *art*, which denotes the blending of human will with "essences unchanged by man" and essentially unchangeable (*CW,* 1:8). With cheerful confidence, therefore, Sherman set about articulating the syntax of nature scientifically. Even wordless communion with nature involved engineering ingenuity. His pamphlet proudly emphasizes the "pathway... blasted at considerable expense" to permit ascent through the gorge (p. 5). There "the deep volleying thunder of the grand cataract" produces "a paralizing impression of Omnipotence" sufficient to humble the infidel "son of pride," in a way that "it is the prerogative of nature alone to do" (pp. 9–10). Nonetheless, a son of pride emancipated from Calvinism might recover imperiled self-respect when he realized that the answering volley of many a "fortunate blast" displacing "five tons" of rock echoed through Kauy-a-hoo-ra annually in efforts to improve Sherman's walkway, by which several separate cataracts, like the fossils that he found with "circular perforations in the parities of the cell, . . . become one connected system" (pp. 6, 21).

The result was perceptively versified by the anonymous author of a travel sketch describing vacation areas newly opened up by the Erie Canal. His essay concluded with stanzas on Trenton Falls, which he thought "alone worth traveling two hundred miles to see":

> Ye hills! who have for ages stood
> Sublimely in your solitude
>   List'ning to the wild waters roar,
> As thund'ring down from steep to steep,
> Along your wave-worn sides they sweep,
>   Dashing their foam from shore to shore!

> Wild birds that loved the deep recess,
> Fell beasts that rov'd the wilderness,
>   And savage men have hover'd round;
> But startled at the bellowing waves,
> Your frowning cliffs and echoing caves,
>   Affrighted fled the enchanted ground.

> How chang'd the scene! your lofty trees
> Which bent but to the mountain breeze,
>   Have sunk beneath the woodman's blade;
> Now sun-light through your forest pours,
> Paths wind along your sides and shores,
>   And footsteps all your haunts invade.

> Now boor, and beau, and lady fair,
> In gay costume, each day repair
>   Where your proud rocks exposed stand;
> While echo from his old retreats,
> With babbling tongue strange words repeats,
>   From babblers on your stony strand.

And see! your river's rocky floor,
With names and dates all scribbled o'er,
      Vile blurs on nature's heraldry;
O! bid your torrent in its race,
These mean memorials soon efface,
      And keep your own proud album free.

Languid its tides, and quell'd its powers,
But soon Autumnus, with his showers
      Shall all its wasted strength restore;
Then will these venturers down the steep,
With terror pale, their distance keep,
      Nor dare to touch thy trembling shore.

But spare, oh! river in thy rage,
One name upon thy stony page,
      'Tis hers—the fairest of the fair;
And when she comes these scenes to scan,
Then tell her, echo, if you can,
      His humble name who wrote it there.[9]

The Bryantesque side of this writer finds his gorge rising as the waters fall, permitting an annoyingly easy familiarity with the river not only to fashionable visitors but to local "boors." Their jarring discordancy with nature is registered by grotesque attempts to superimpose their language on hers. Hence the "strange words . . . from babblers," scribbled names and dates in the timeless streambed, "mean memorials" that endeavor to reduce her authorship to the level of their own tourist albums. Any visitor to our national parks today knows whereof he speaks. But in a final twist the writer reveals that he is one of them. His sweetheart's name is chalked on a rock too, and he would have used spray paint if it had been invented. Ironically "humble," this self-consciously cultivated gentleman merges anonymously with the masses at boorish play, as if to do otherwise would be undemocratic. He too would cheerfully swap the sublime for the beautiful, except that he doubts that in the long run it is possible, for the true aristocracy of nature's proud heraldry will probably reassert itself to erase the unyielding page upon which he has scribbled. "Forgive me, nature!" Sherman likewise cried at one point, sure that he had undertaken "too much for art to imitate, or eloquence to represent" (p. 11). But he was not unduly worried. Born of a booming era, both his art and his science were quite at home in this peculiarly American synthesis of the sublime and the beautiful, "for what is NATURE but the *systematic course of divine operation?*" (p. 15).

To defray the cost of further systematizing it, in 1825 Sherman gladly accepted a loan of $5,000 from his good friend Philip Hone, mayor of New York at the time and a power in Whig politics for decades to come. It was altogether fitting that Hone was the first guest to enjoy the improvements that he financed at Kauy-a-hoo-ra, which undoubtedly boosted the first season's modest receipts of $187.55. These visionary businessmen would have agreed with Emerson that there is a "property" in the landscape "which no man has but he whose eye can integrate all the parts, that is, the poet." (Hone was a major patron of the Hudson River painters.) But they would surely have rejected the Emersonian corollary that to that property once integrated "their warranty-deeds give them no title" (*CW*, 1:9). In the *Description of Trenton Falls* the author is frankly styled the "proprietor" of the Rural Retreat and its environs.

Moreover, having bankrolled Sherman in systematizing the language of nature, Hone then financed his analogous effort to systematize the nature of language. Dedicated to Hone, Sherman's *New System of Grammar* gratefully acknowledges that worthy's patronage for the grand goal of divesting the English language of "scholastic rubbish" much as he had blasted obstructing rubble from his American ravine. In the mine of language encrusted falsehood was enveloped in an atmosphere so volatile that "I really tremble at the idea of approaching it with the lamp of TRUTH, as much as I should do to inspect a magazine of gunpowder with a fire-brand" (p. 85). Interestingly, one of Sherman's key grammatical innovations is separating all "POSSESSIVES" from nouns, pronouns, and adjectives and exalting them into an independent ninth part of speech. "The sole office of this class is to denote that one person or thing has possession in or over another," and the dignity of that function is best not diluted by extraneous considerations (p. 32).

Murray, who was essentially prescriptive, had defined grammar as an art, though acknowledging the grammarian's factual obligation as an observer and recorder of common usage. Sherman was scarcely less prescriptive, but nonetheless he was sure that "this science is based *wholly upon facts*; as entirely so as the science of Chemistry" (p. 26). Although democratic leanings flawed Cardell's grammar, Sherman had even less respect for the radical Horne Tooke, whose cavalier attitude toward the parts of speech authorized grammarians "to put all the words of the Dictionary into a bag, shake them well together, then turn them out promiscuously and say, 'here you have the *science* and *philosophy* of English Grammar.'" Sherman saw that Tooke's etymological approach involved an extraordinary naïveté about syntax. Maybe Tooke excelled at tracing things back etymologically to primary particles like atoms. "But do these atomic materials *set the universe in order? . . .* Atheism says they do; and so says the grammatical atheism of Horne Tooke." In the *Diversions* "relations, bearings, applications, dependencies, connexions, office, use are all out of the question. The congregation of simple ideas, no matter how fortuitious, constitutes the system of grammar, the *philosophy* of speech" (pp. 31–32).

Indeed, Sherman wished to scrap Murray's basic four-part schema. "As Grammar is not a Spelling-book, but a study of a higher and different order, orthography is here detached from it, together with etymology and prosody," he explained. After naming and classifying words properly the true grammarian should focus on "their syntactical relations in discourse." At times his categorical exclusiveness seemed merely a pedagogical convenience. But elsewhere he violently denied any grammatical relevance to etymology. Just as no carpenter manufactures his tools, so no grammarian needs to be an etymologist: "Etymology and Grammar are, therefore, as perfectly distinct and unrelated, as any two branches of knowledge whatever. Etymology has for its department the derivation of words. A display of their *import* is the business of the Lexicographer. To the Grammarian it is left to class them, to show their relations and connections in speech, and to illustrate the philosophy of their application" (p. 17). His sense that this idea is novel, an "*important truth*, never yet divulged," helps account for his stridor on this theme (p. iii). So also does the gout, which exacerbated a temper not sweet to begin with. Etymology was clearly the main sort of "scholastic rubbish" and "traditionary falsehood" of which he hoped to rid the study of language, while arrogating to grammar the exposition of linguistic *philosophy*.

This was the core of his opposition to Cardell. "The principal embarrassment, which has prevented Mr. C. from forming a correct system of Grammar, is his researches in Etymology," he averred. "No learned Etymologist ever has formed or can form a system of Grammar, which corresponds to the language of modern times." Other Cardellian sins, like reducing the parts of speech to six and ultimately to three, instead of the nine that Sherman advocated, were venial by comparison, though by itself this fundamental error was "so obvious, that it carries a death-warrant upon its forehead" (pp. 214–15).

If, as Sherman says, "the Verb is Mr. C's HOBBY," then etymology was his hobbyhorse. Sherman aimed to blast him out of the saddle:

Here then, is DEATH, EVERLASTING ANNIHILATION to the IMPERATIVE MOOD, and to Mr. C's. *future tense* of this mood. There *is* no such mood:

There *never has been* such a mood: And there *never will be* such a mood among any nation, kindred, tongue, or people on the globe. All the examples in illustration of an Imperative mood, of whatever language, are the result of profound stupidity, the best proof ever afforded, that wise men may be deranged QUOAD HOC, though perfectly sane in all other respects. (pp. 217-19)

He was determined to interpret all imperative utterances as truncated declaratives (*Go* = *I charge you to go*). Like Cardell, he was reluctant to concede the importance of pure linguistic form, but whereas Cardell often tried to interpret form semantically, Sherman wanted to define it intentionally. What interested him was "the *authoritative attitude* . . . expressed in a declarative form," though he felt compelled to reject "the new doctrine of Dewar and his followers, that 'all language is imperative'" (p. 219). Had he seriously developed this line of thought by distinguishing the various purposes for which formally "declarative" utterances are used, he might—in about a century—have emerged with John Austin's useful doctrines concerning illocutionary and perlocutionary forces.

Instead, he deployed it in general terms chiefly to attack Cardell's referential theories:

> What has deluded Mr. Cardell, and led some of the learned Gentlemen of New York to sanction his Grammar, is, that, at first view, it would seem to be really *grounded on fact,* because he makes language to be the exact picture of the objects in nature, and applies the philosophy of the latter as an illustration of the principles of the former. But this is sophistical, inasmuch as it assumes for *general* or *universal,* what is *partial* or *limited.*
>
> . . . .
>
> The MIND, although dependent for her primary ideas upon the objects in nature, has peculiar powers, which she is capable of exercising according to her volitions. She can abstract or compound, restrict or extend her *notions* of things at pleasure. . . . Her paintings are often the pictures of fancy. . . . She, sometimes indeed, draws from nature with great exactness; but her pictures are more frequently her own invention, according to the impressions she designs to make upon the minds of others.
>
> The case is plain, that *Language is the fabrication of the mind, and of the Mind alone. . . . The Intentions of the mind, as exhibited in words, constitute, therefore, the broad fact upon which the philosophy of language is grounded:* And . . . Etymology cannot furnish the fashion of her dress, nor can the Philosophy of Nature delineate the features of her form. (pp. 230-31)

Though Emerson would have deplored Sherman's manner, he might grudgingly have approved the thrust of this argument, for the correspondence theory of *Nature* tries to synthesize Cardell's nature-centered philosophy of language with Sherman's mentalist approach. In rejecting

Cardell's Philosophy of Being and Action as "wholly foreign from the subject of Grammar," Sherman opened up new ground that was both linguistically and transcendentally promising in stressing the shaping power of the creative imagination (p. 232). He could deny that the verb *to be* is transitive because his own bombastic rhetoric gave language explosive energy: "This example pronounces the sentence of DEATH upon Mr. Cardell's principle, and it lies at the foot of TRUTH, pale and breathless as a corpse" (p. 235). To his credit Sherman did suspect that functional definitions of the parts of speech would clarify sentences more than Newtonian physics. Instead of looking at verbs as a manifestation of physical energy, he just rechristened them *assertors* and asserted that they had sentence-making power. To his discredit, however, in the heat of combat with Cardell he forgot that earlier he had defined grammar as "a science based *wholly upon facts*—as entirely so as the science of Chemistry" (p. 26). With Emersonian scorn for foolish consistency, he now argued that Cardell's philosophical and scientific etymology "has no more relation to Grammar than a Lexicon or Laboratory" (p. 229).

Moreover, he ignored an important critique of scientific thinking implicit in Cardell's linguistic philosophy, for Cardell's *Philosophic Grammar* was to argue that grammar was not simply dependent on science for its laws but gave laws to science:

> It will not always seem a paradox that the deep secrets of nature are chiefly to be sought in words; for the inquirer in this department of knowledge, will find that after devoting years to the subject, and trying to understand the best authors on natural science, he can have no definite and extensive views of his divisions between *substances, properties,* and *actions,* but in coming back upon language, to see how the terms which, according to general experience, denote them, assume their relations with regard to each other. (p. 37)

Cardell had the wit to see that the categories of early nineteenth-century science were sometimes simply naive reifications of grammatical categories, which language shared with science. Those categories were neither the creation nor the discovery of scientists but the long-matured wisdom of the human race as democratically embodied in the structure of speech. If the animistic tendencies of the primitive mind are writ large in the history of language, then, Cardell felt, that evidence merits respect from physicists as well as philosophers. Wondering "whether the word *grammar* applies in strictness, to the essential principles of language, or the system of rules to explain them," he trusted that the rules of grammar (which were also the rules of science) corresponded effectively with reality. "If the explanatory system is just, the two things are virtually the same," he decided—but even if it were not, he doubted the capacity of men to think effectively outside the categories of speech (*Essay,* p. 39). He had formulated an early version of the Sapir-Whorf hypothesis (indeed, in the 1930s Whorf's interest in language was sparked by reading outmoded grammarians like Cardell to support eccentric religious beliefs). Of course, whereas Whorf saw different grammars as all imposing different worldviews that were absolute and reciprocally untranslatable, Cardell saw all speech as sharing the same universal grammar. For him the central issue was not translation but grammar's correspondence to the structure of the external world. Though much more elaborate, detailed, and sophisticated, Whorf's doctrine remains a bit simpleminded. Now that modern linguistics is once again flirting with universal grammar, Cardell's speculations may seem more au courant.

Sherman was also a believer in universal grammar, and a singularly naive and contentious one. Though his treatment of universal grammar is ludicrous enough, he grasped a major shortcoming that Cardell inherited from the Tookean tradition of etymological speculation, its indifference to syntax. "As to Mr. C's. Rules of Construction, they, of course, are shaped to his general theory, and give a very meager and a very false account of the philoshphy [*sic*] of the English language," he grumbled. Only a quarter of his own book deals with syntax, but he was rightly eager to emphasize its importance (p. 249).

The most far-reaching and characteristic rule that he proposed to revolutionize parsing was his fourth: "An ellipsis of words, both in speaking and writing, occurs almost incessantly. These words, in parsing, must all be supplied, exactly and fully, as the sense demands." The sense demanded a lot, as this sample sentence demonstrated:

> "Agesilaus, King of Sparta, being asked, What things he thought proper for BOYS to learn? answered; Those things which they ought to practise, when they come to be men."
>
> If, by supplying the ellipsis, we illustrate the sense of this passage, it will read thus.
>
> Agesilaus, who was King of Sparta, being asked, which asking or enquiry was, that he would tell, What are the things, which things he thought it proper for boys, that they should learn? answered; which answer was. It is proper for boys, that they should learn those things, which things they ought [or are obligated] that they should practise, when they come to the age or period, that they shall be men.
>
> This expresses the ideas in full, without any subaudition.

As the faintly transformational flavor of this process suggests, Sherman was groping for a way of clarifying sentence embedding. In his hands, however, it became a tacit rationale for his own prolixity. We see a truly laconic utterance being transformed into a specimen of Victorian windiness, with no gain in logic or clarity. Believing as firmly as any Spartan that "the object of grammar is to make *boys* men," Sherman insisted that a boy called to parse a sentence should be required "to supply all the elliptical words, and to give the sense or import of each term in the sentence, before he enters on the grammatical resolution of it. This seems a most extravagant demand; but it is absolutely indispensable" (p. 300). It was indispensable not only because the challenge turned boys into men; it also offered a handy-dandy escape from any syntactically problematic sentence, which could be altered to suit the parser by the addition of enough "understood" words to delete any difficulties. Sherman's theological hermeneutics had proceeded similarly, for in interpreting the many undeniably Trinitarian passages of Scripture he either denounced them as textual corruptions and so tried to blast them out of the way or expanded them by interpolating "understood" words and phrases until the entire passage sustained a Unitarian position. The same hermeneutic tactic that revealed the meaning of Scripture also parsed the syntax of nature at Kauy-a-hoo-ra, by a judicious mixture of demolition and construction.

By Sherman's testimony children instructed under his system grew mightily sophisticated. He illustrated this with a sample dialogue between himself and his nine-year-old scholar James:

Ques. James! Do you ever think *to parse* what you see and hear, when you go through the streets of Utica of New York?

Ans. I *do* Sir. Since I have studied the Philosophy of Language, I am thinking upon *every thing*, which I see and hear. I stopt, the other day, in Utica at a *Grocer's sign*, and considered how it ought to be parsed. It read thus:

Rum	Raisins	Rice
Wine	Tobacco	Indigo
Gin	Coffee	Almonds
Brandy	Sugar	Cod Fish

It puzzled me for as much as ten minutes. Here is nothing but a group of names. At length the question came to mind, *What is the object* in hanging out such a sign? I felt mortified, and bit my thumb, and said to myself, "James, you are an *ignoramus* to be ten minutes in parsing a sign. There is an ellipsis in language, of which this is a very evident example. The sign reads thus: "Rum, Wine, &c. *is for sale here*." (pp. 319–20)

Despite James's concluding solecism such trenchant analysis convinced Sherman that his pupil was becoming a philosopher in language. Overjoyed, his teacher rewarded him with three cents and wished that it could be three dollars. But the manly lad replied, "I feel more thankful for this lesson, my dear Sir, than if you had given me ten thousand pounds."

Learning how liquor is sold convinced James that grammar was a veritable gold mine. His teacher heartily concurred: "True, James: For there is such a thing as a rich *rascal* and a rich *ignoramus;* but *the only truly rich man,* is one, who has that intellectual mahogany furniture in his upper story . . . which silver and gold can never purchase" (p. 321).

After enumerating a mere eighteen rules of syntax, however, Sherman abandoned his scientific model of grammar on realizing that few rules applied universally. Most were matters of taste and depended on circumstances. For example, "there *are* cases, in which the beauty, the force, and even the elegance of the sentence, requires a violation of the primary rule, that we should not close a period with a Relative or Preposition." Concluding lamely that rules "are therefore superfluous, especially to the student of Grammar, having no other influence than to fetter his genius and encumber his memory," he found himself reposing on the accommodating bosom of grammatical art rather than science. He immediately recoiled from this refuge: "To the literary student it is left to advance to elegance and eloquence; neither of which has any more relation to Grammar, than Chemistry or Oryctology."

"The departments of the mind are not on the march but on the wing," he marveled. Mediating between science and art, philosophy became his final model for understanding language in this new era.

> He, who has this knowledge, need spend no time on the uncertain and fanciful rules, concerning correctness of expression and the right collocation of words. His philosophy will be to him like the web to the spider, a perfect system in all its radiations, the vibration of each chord of which being felt at the center, he knows, exactly, the direct course to his object. As in Arithmetick, he, who understands the principles of the science, has always before him a Rule for any and every case that may arise; so he, who understands the philosophy of language, will be at no loss for correctness of expression and a right collocation of terms. A just knowledge of this philosophy would spare all, that has been writ in our Grammars on this subject, and would lead the mind to the proper expression of its ideas or intentions, just as naturally as water runs down hill. (pp. 303-4)

Of course, water running downhill naturally at Kauy-a-hoo-ra turned a profitable philosophical gristmill. In his devotion to the queen of the sciences Sherman was no impractical visionary but remained an adroit businessman like his patron Philip Hone. The linguistic utility of philosophic analysis he located precisely in its labor-saving potential. Thus a single sample sentence, "of *eleven words only,* knocks all Latin, Greek, and English Grammars in the head. It is a bursting bomb, which causes an explosion of the whole magazine" (p. 319). Then as now, the study of methodology promised to spare literary intellectuals a lot of hard work.

Academician, minister, capitalist—structuralist, deconstructionist, neo-Marxist—all like to turn an easy dollar by engaging in philosophical *speculation.*

Unequivocal Eminence Achieved!!! The Language of Nature Mechanized!!!

Sherman's attack on Cardell was seconded on another front by James Brown, a pugnacious New Englander who had migrated to the City of Brotherly Love via New York. When peace was concluded with Great Britain in 1815, Brown had immediately enlisted for his country's service in the wars of the grammarians by publishing *A Treatise on the Nature and Reasons of the English Grammar, Illustrated by a Machine Constructed for That Purpose* (Boston: Clapp, 1815). From the beginning Brown was less interested than most grammarians in etymology and more interested in syntax. His conception of this was idiosyncratic, however. "Upon examination you will learn, that a natural law attends the formation of things, by which their component parts are governed; and language, being the representative of things, has the same natural law attending *its* formation and governing its component parts," he argued. "The power of coherence in words, therefore . . . is no other, than the power of coherence in things, for which those words stand." How Adam communicated with God is a mystery, but Scripture assures us that he named what he saw. Brown stressed that directly inspired nomenclature was restricted to christening the creatures as organic wholes. Adam may have named the elephant at first sight, but the word for the trunk had to wait for the analytic baggage of language to catch up.

Magnetized by the mysterious natural force that makes parts cohere as wholes—a force that at this stage he viewed as also unifying language—Brown's grammatical exegesis revolved obsessively about that theme. As "the mould in which they are supposed to have been cast," things are the prototype for words. "The prototype for the noun is a union or cohesion of so many simple parts as are implied by the name given to that union of parts, one of which simple parts must be the prototype for the verb." Illustrating how verbs endow things with existence, at the center of his machine was "a spring which we shall call the verbal primordium or the last mentioned important part. This being the origin of life and action, is seen to communicate that life and action to the brass wheels and globes, which may be seen on pages 4 and 6" (pp. 16-19). Alas, when we turn back eagerly to pages 4 and 6 to glance at this marvelous machine, brass wheels and globes are nowhere to be found. Indeed, this bewildering tract advances its argument by referring to earlier pages for supporting evidence that never appears there or anywhere else. Perhaps Brown's printer cheated him. Explaining that "nouns when taken in their most extensive signification, do not admit articles before them, as will be seen by p. 1," he offers us another tantalizing glimpse of this trailblazing design: "On the same page the balls which are entered partly into the machine, are designed or taken for the whole human race. The word man directly above, whose power or extensive properties are represented by the brass running directly from the word, shows that the word is not limited, but extends to each and every individual" (p. 23). Unfortunately, the rare Columbia copy of Brown's tract begins at page 3, so unless a perfect copy of this odd volume turns up, we must remain forever tantalized by his vision. From the hints scattered throughout the text it is hard to know whether he thought he had created simply a diagram illustrating his philosophy of language (it could stand clarification), a piece of pedagogical equipment, a design for a primitive word processor, or an operating model of a verbally powered perpetual motion machine.

So bizarre was Brown's New England debut that it is startling when he surfaces five years later in the Hudson River valley as the relatively lucid author of *An American Grammar, Developing the Principles of Our Language* (Troy, N.Y.: Adancourt, 1820). From the onset Brown displayed a revolutionary zeal and a determination to throw off the grammatical shackles of British tyranny. His grammar commenced with a radical declaration of linguistic equality: "Language is a genus of definers, commonly called words, by which we point out ideas. Under this genus there are several species of definers, which will be classed according to their separate characters." At a stroke the cumbersome class structure of British grammar was swept aside. As in the French Revolution the three estates were merged into one with the common title of *citizen*, so in *An American Grammar* the various parts of speech were merged into one with the common title of *definer*. Though they were gradually redifferentiated as "primary definers," "secondary definers," "helping definers," "pro definers," "vital definers," and so forth—indeed, Brown wound up enumerating thirty-three varieties of definers, including "superfluous definers"—in his new republic of words the underlying fraternal bond remained clear (pp. 1–3).

But clarity did not always mark Brown's exposition. Witness the exercise that "best illustrated" the three distinct positions active, passive, and neuter:

> The right *hand* strikes the right *ear* by the left *ear*.—The right *hand* takes the active position; the right *ear* the *passive* position, and the left *ear* the

neutral position. The left *hand* did hit the left *ear* near the right *ear.*—Here the left hand takes the *active* position, the ear the *passive* position; and the right ear, which before took the passive position, now takes the *neuter.* Perhaps it will be thought, that the right hand in the last examples should be in the neuter position, in as much as the action is not yet done; but the rule for determining the positions of words is the particular state under which the writer speaks of the person, place or thing. Hence if there be *doubt* respecting the actual performance of the action, the things take the same position which they would take provided no doubt existed; as, if the right hand do hit the left *ear.* Things require these three positions, which the genius of the language demands to be subdivided into six; viz. *direct*, active, and *oblique* active; *direct* passive and *oblique* passive; *direct* neuter and *oblique* neuter. (pp. 20-21)

Naturally enough, the oblique positions required very oblique words called "*oblective* definers. This will be understood from examples" (p. 52).

Brown now attached such importance to syntax that he was immediately compelled to redefine it: "Instead therefore of laying it down that any part of grammar is an agreement between words, I shall say that *this* part of grammar consists in the agreement between the *properties* of words. And instead of calling this part of grammar *syntax*, I shall call it what it really is, namely, CORRESPONDENCY." Its basis was religious, for "when we view the mind drawing into itself, through organic avenues, the various objects with which the body is surrounded, and forming by an act of decomposition, correct notions of their character and nature, and when we see the vocal organs attached to the body, making the air into sounds for the communication of those notions, we behold the three Gods when they said, let us make man" (pp. 70-71).

Brown thus differed from most grammarians in basing his idea of grammar on syntax rather than etymology. But his notion of syntax remained unique. "It is the business of language to communicate man's ideas, but it is the business of grammar to shape and smooth language . . . to produce the most agreeable emotions in the mind." Restricted thus to a secondary aesthetic function, grammar has only a limited right "to exercise authority in the construction of language," for wherever "her interference is detrimental to perspicuity and brevity of sentences, . . . no longer are the directions of this dame to be regarded by the writer or speaker" (pp. 71-72). Instead of linking grammar with logic or perspicuity, he suggests that it is mainly a matter of prettifying language rhetorically, as if human communication, like the language of nature, could roll on its majestic course more comfortably sans syntax. Unlike Sherman and Cardell, Brown allowed grammar to deal mainly with linguistic forms, for "the mental sonorous palate is better pleased when . . . words appear in some forms than in others" (p. 72). But like them he suspected that such artificial entities could not be truly important. Hence his conviction that grammar deals merely with the surface of language. Hence also his ambiguous doctrine of correspondency, expounded in highly charged corporeal metaphors that link language and the physical world as Cardell did. Brown's own first *Treatise* (1815) assumed just such a link, of course. He still could not repudiate it wholeheartedly despite the main thrust of his argument.

Understandably, Brown's novel terminology proved too much for many to swallow, as he himself admitted. Therefore he temporarily shelved it. Resuming the older grammatical vocabulary, he published a dozen new editions throughout the 1820s. Some were purported abridgments that seem to be longer than the original text; some were apparently reworked and retitled as the *American System of English Grammar*. Laboring industriously to expand and improve his textbook, he also worked hard to market it by cadging testimonials. An early edition secured an impressive endorsement from His Excellency DeWitt Clinton, a power in New York political and intellectual life until his death in 1828. Brown reprinted this testimonial in subsequent grammars even when they differed sharply from the book that Clinton endorsed.

Clinton had praised Brown as "a man of great personal modesty," but as recommendations and editions of his grammar multiplied, that modesty seems to have eroded somewhat. Disturbed by the fact that "even the *constitution* of the *United States* cannot be understood by two impartial statesmen in the *same* way," Brown diagnosed the problem as "a want of *skill* in the language which is used." The adoption of his grammar might "calm the storms which ambition directs by riding upon the clouds of the *constitution*," he felt. "It is in these clouds, that ambition lurks—yes, it is from these, that the thunder of eloquence will burst—it is from these, that the lightning of genius will play, first to the consternation, then to the *destruction* of our political EDEN."[10] For some reason neither President John Quincy Adams nor Congress accepted his tactful offer to moderate their conflicts. But for Brown, as for Hamlet, the readiness was all.

Like many a professor of English turned political activist, Brown sprang to the defense of the Constitution in the conviction that "a REPUBLIC must advance; or it must retrograde" (p. x). Moreover, since "this Republic came into being by political revolution . . . it must attain its destined rank and sway by *literary innovation*." Predictably, he was soon opposed by entrenched conservatives who found more clouds in his grammar than in the Constitution. Thus the first chapter of Brown's

Appeal summarizes his controversy with the Right Reverend Bishop John Croes, who was disturbed when three schools in New Brunswick, New Jersey, adopted some edition of Brown's *Grammar*. From Brown's rehearsal of their newspaper debate in 1823-24 that haughty prelate was understandably hampered by the difficulty of pinpointing his opponent's doctrines and terminology, since these fluctuated from one edition to the next. In their debate Brown acquitted himself—to his own satisfaction, at least—by assuring readers that the novel terminology that aggravated the bishop did not come from the school edition but from a research version privately printed for a few lovers of grammatical truth in all her naked majesty. He comforted himself with the thought that "whenever innovation has travailed in improvement some human heart has engendered foul detraction" (p. 20). In the 1830s Brown became embroiled in similar pamphlet wars with Martin Roche of Philadelphia and the Reverend Dr. Robert Breckinridge of Baltimore, whose all-too-human hearts were likewise foully provoked by the *American Grammar*.

From the Pisgah perspective of his more advanced views Brown glanced back at Cardell with mingled contempt and jealousy: "We confess that we pay very little respect to Mr. Cardell's *matter* and *thought* Grammar." Their divergence was partly philosophical, for Brown could no longer accept Cardell's equation of semantic with syntactic criteria. But deeper undercurrents accounted for his animosity toward Cardell, for Brown's *American Grammar* "was, by Mr. *Cardell*, made the object and subject of *ridicule*." Before their relation dissolved into a professional feud, young Brown had seen Cardell as a potential ally, and not without reason, for both began from similar premises from which Brown only gradually distanced himself. But by 1828 he was convinced that etymology had "buried the erudition of a Took [*sic*] beneath a huge pile of Anglosaxon verbiage," and he taunts Cardell for relying on Tooke's authority in asserting that the article "a and one are the same in meaning" (pp. 179, 399).

Brown thought that his textbooks should immortalize him together with DeWitt Clinton. Before its glorious completion Clinton's Erie Canal had to overcome as many prejudiced tongues as "the particles of earth, thrown out in the excavation." Brown's work was also a noble shortcut, opening up new vistas. The *American Grammar* "smooths the rugged road to knowledge, over which the *Grammatical* vehicle has for ages rumbled," he explained. "It is a system obviously differing from all others: it is a species of INNOVATION which must meet, and withstand the usual opposition." What Brown hoped to open up was not the interior of the American continent but the interior of the American sentence. His attention to syntax finally flowered in a better understanding of its independence from semantics than many compatriots possessed:

> A hypothetical tree, comprising as many parts as our language has words, each part yielding fruit, and the whole tree producing just as many kinds of fruit as the British grammarians have made parts of speech, may aid in giving a correct, and clear view of the erroneous course pursued by these distinguished scholars in forming their system of English Grammar. Now, what construction, mechanism, is to the frame-work of this tree, grammar is to the frame-work of a language, or a sentence. And as the construction, the anatomy of the tree, is not the fruit which its component parts yield, so the grammar of a language, is not the ideas which its words express. As grammar bears the same relation to language, which mechanism does to the tree, the proper course in forming a system of grammar, or construction, is to divide the words of a sentence, not according to their dictionary signification, but according to their constructive principles. (*An Appeal:* 1836, pp. xix–xx, xxv)

This is well said, for a major weakness of the tradition transmitted by Lindley Murray had been its effort to construct sentences from individually isolated words, the parts of speech. Strikingly absent from Murray and his fellow parsers are such syntactic concepts as the phrase and the clause. Within the structure of a sentence these play roles like those of individual words. Brown correctly saw that by focusing more attention on these intermediary syntactic units he could clarify not only syntax but thought. He had blundered on the principles of sentence diagramming and grasped, in a fitful way, that for students of a living language such a process is even more helpful in deciphering sentences than in forming them.

But our praise must be heavily qualified, for Brown's metaphors reveal how confused his conception of syntactic structure remained. Though he compares language to a tree in the foregoing passage, he talks variously about the "construction," "frame-work," "mechanism," or "anatomy" of the tree. This is surely a very odd arboreal species, at which even Joyce Kilmer might have boggled. Organicism was perhaps the dominant concept of the Romantic era. Ever since Humboldt, plant metaphors had been used brilliantly to define language as an organic growth. Yet Brown flounders about comparing syntax to almost every kind of coherence *except the organic principle* that his own botanic metaphor invites. His failure to do so is all the stranger in view of his intermittent awareness that the various kinds of structure differ substantially. As he insists elsewhere with admirable precision:

> 1. If the construction belongs to a *house*, we call it, (the construction) architecture.
> 2. If the construction belongs to a *machine*, we call it mechanism.

3. If the construction belongs to *trees*, or *plants*, we call it organization.

4. If the construction belongs to an animal body, we call it anatomy.

5. If the construction belongs to a work, or a sentence, or to a language, we call it *syntax*.

We speak of the architecture of a house . . . a bridge . . . &c., as fine, or otherwise. But we never speak of the *mechanism* of a house. Nor do we ever speak of the *anatomy* of a watch, or the syntax of a clock: we say the *mechanism* of a *watch*, the *mechanism* of a clock. Nor do we say the *organization* of a *word*, the *organization* of a *sentence*, the *organization* of a *language*. We say the *syntax* of a *word*, the *syntax* of a *sentence*, the *syntax* of a *language*.[11]

What accounts for the grotesqueness of Brown's arboreal conception of syntax? This same deformation, apparently half-conscious, pervades his entire treatment of the subject. His technical terms for syntactic units—*cormos*, *monoramus*, and the like—are all artificial constructions though etymologically botanic, "founded upon the *trunk*, and *branch* relation existing between the collective portions of a sentence" (*Appeal*: 1836, p. 42). As his syntactic system blossomed, Brown relied increasingly on artwork. Indeed, by this stage he could proudly declare, "Nothing is to be *memorized*: every thing is illustrated through the medium of diagrams, or plates" (*Exegesis*: 1840, p. iv). Most of these are drawings of trees. In their shade, presumably, the grammatical tyro may cool his overheated memory (see figs. 6, 7). But the visual effect is singular in the extreme, for all these trees illustrating clauses and phrases are leafless. Often floating disembodied on the pages, their denuded branches are sometimes connected to trunks by mortise and tenon joints. Visually the student of Brownian syntax wanders in a surreal landscape—in a mechanical forest. In Brown's grammatical lumberyard, the language of nature must constantly be reassembled like a jigsaw puzzle, by fitting tab A into slot B.

Unlike Sherman at Kauy-a-hoo-ra, Brown never heard the language of nature. He could only see it—and even then nature had to be pulped so that the words could be displayed visually on her page. If Brown looked at a forest, he saw furniture in the making. Despite his flirtation with organic metaphor, Brown's mechanical trees suggest that his governing conception of language remained what it had been in his first treatise: the machine. Whenever Brown touches upon this theme, his imagination fires: "In construction, a sentence is a mere *table*, a mere *chair*; it is two, or more words so *packed*, that they form a complete bridge over which one mind can cross to another. But in *import* a sentence is an engine for transmitting *thought*; and, the better one understands its beautiful *mechanism*, the more *distinctly*, *easily*, and *forcibly*

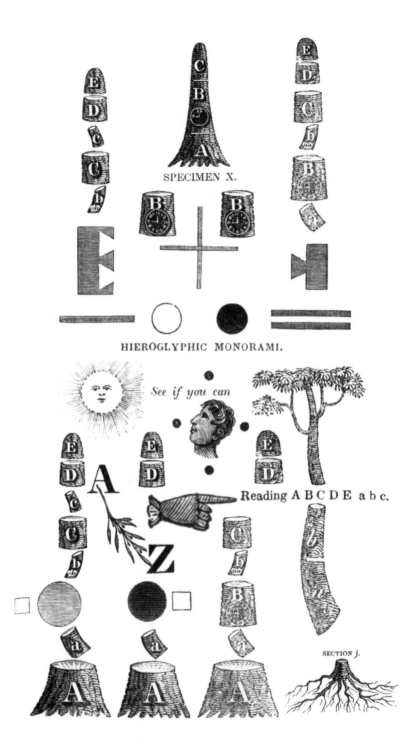

SPECIMEN X.

HIEROGLYPHIC MONORAMI.

See if you can

Reading A B C D E a b c.

SECTION j.

Fig. 6. Montage of cuts from James Brown, *The American System of English Syntax* (Philadelphia: Blackmarr, 1837). Courtesy, Nietz Textbook Collection, University of Pittsburgh Library System.

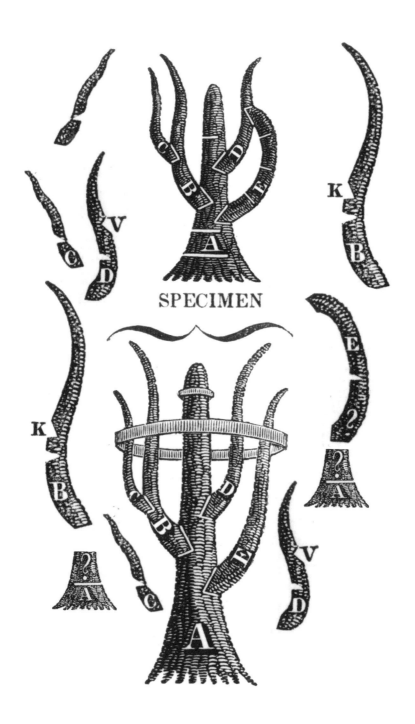

SPECIMEN

Fig. 7. Montage of cuts from James Brown, *The American System of English Syntax* (Philadelphia: Blackmarr, 1837). Courtesy, Nietz Textbook Collection, University of Pittsburgh Library System.

he can transfer this mental fluid to others; and the more *clearly*, and *readily*, can he *see* it as *they* pass it to *him*."[12] Though he had evidently drunk deep of this mental fluid, it did not quite free his conception of language from a simple-minded corporeal basis. While one foot tested the dangerously abstract waters of structuralism, from the beginning of his career to the end the other foot remained safely planted on a corpuscular concept of thought.

Thus his effort to explain syntax structurally spawns paradoxes. "Now, *actors*, *actions*, and *objects* may hold a conspicuous place in a system of *metaphysics*; but how they can become parts of a system of grammar, is not so very clear," he avers. Why should prior grammarians

> after making *actors*, *actions*, *being*, and *objects*, the principal parts of their system, . . . proceed upon the ground that *language* itself is an *abstract nothing*, and a sentence the mere child of the imagination? Language, considered in its true character, seems to be as tangible as a clock; and a *sentence* as much a piece of mechanism as a watch. A sentence is a frame-work of words. A word is a sort of house, a kind of temple, constructed of sound, ink, paint, metal, or other matter, and is occupied by the *meaning*, the *signification* itself. Thus a *sentence* is a little *village*, a cluster of buildings, various in their shape, size, and occupants. Thus, too, while a chapter is a whole ward of a verbal city, and a sentence one block of houses in this ward, a whole book is the entire city, peopled by those significant citizens that are engaged exclusively in the commerce of ideas. . . . Hence, he who attempts to make a book to unfold the syntax, the mechanism of any language, should confine himself to *constructive* principles. To say what a word in any sentence *means*, is to leave the *frame-work*, the *architecture* of the house for its occupants. Bear this in mind: the grammarian is not to teach the nature of the *liquid*, but to illustrate the *construction* of the *vessel*! (*Exegesis*: 1840, pp. 30–31)

What begins as an argument for detaching language from too close a dependence on the physical world turns effortless flip-flops to avoid its own Platonic implications. Cardell had stressed the grammatical importance of actors, actions, and objects, but his matter-and-thought grammar insisted that these were not simply metaphysical but physical concepts. Moreover, Brown's own structural analogies suggest that the cohesive "principles" must be distinguished from their material embodiments, that grammar needs metaphysical concepts even more than physical ones. But when push comes to shove, he simply cannot conceive of such principles except by reifying them naively. He cannot distinguish between an architect's blueprints and a builder's two-by-fours, between the geometry of clockwork and a clock, between a map of Philadelphia and Philadelphia. All are equally "tangible," and so is language, for the distinction between rules of syntax and words arranged according to those rules also vanishes.

But perhaps the supreme irony is that his theory of syntax gave Brown a weapon to demolish the much-mistrusted Tooke and his etymology. Had Sherman gotten his hands on such a nifty dueling pistol, he would have pulled the trigger with sadistic glee to defend the linguistic honor of the mind. Brown not only fails to administer the coup de grace but seems to have forgotten that he ever challenged Tooke and his second Cardell to a duel. Upon no intellectual compulsion he now bemusedly endows syntax with the same naively materialistic basis that he rejects for etymology.

At the root of the problem is Brown's resolutely unequivocal vision. With the best of intentions, he cannot think symbolically. His metaphors remain didactic and mechanical. His correspondency theory of syntax resembles Transcendental thought, but at bottom he has trouble imagining that there are really *two* realms that need to coincide. "Language is fossil poetry," Emerson was boldly proclaiming, while for the more literal Brown "a word is . . . a kind of temple only." What more could one want? Foreign to him is the faint melancholy that tinges Cardell's grave inquiries and lies behind Sherman's tight Unitarian smile. He gazes for a moment at his "verbal city" peopled by significant citizens hawking their ideas—then, like W. C. Fields, he concludes that he'd rather be in Philadelphia. Whitman would look at the same verbal city, make it the theme of great poetry, and so transform his Mannahatta into a more genuine abode of brotherly love than Philadelphia, where ideal and real, fused by his soaring Emersonian parataxis, dissolve the boundary between present and future tenses. Brown's prose proceeds mechanically, with logical connectives linking every other sentence to the past: Fit tab A into slot B. . . .

But boys like Meccano sets. One midcentury visitor to the United States noted that given half a chance American schoolboys would cheerfully doodle steamboats and locomotives on their slates. In addressing them mechanically Brown glamorized grammar by couching it in terms that many wanted to understand. During the American Renaissance the machine became a totem of tribal power, secondary but far more accessible than iconoclastic Protestantism's invisible Divinity. As such it could unite elder and neophytes in classroom puberty rituals even more effectively than Noah Webster's Christian exhortations. Grammar became not only a science but the sacred formula that might unlock the energy of the universe and enable youths to speak its secret language as initiated adults.

The aridity of etymological parsing Brown replaced with *construing*. This would canalize the language of nature, so to speak, let it flow usefully in people's minds.

> To him who is well skilled in CONSTRUING, a sentence ceases to be *dead matter*; it ceases to be a lifeless mass of inseparable particles! The whole period rises into life, and seems a *moving* battalion, breaking into *files* of different grades, and each *inferior* file *marching* to its own superior, under the directions and command of the sense itself! No, the man skilled in CONSTRUING, does not survey a sentence like another—he looks upon the period, and it falls into distinct and separate *groups*! These groups *winged* with the *sense* of the writer, leave their places upon the paper, and fly into their respective mechanical positions in the machine which they constitute! . . . It is not the solution of *single words*! It is the solution of *whole sentences*. CONSTRUING is founded on the *constructive* policy of the *collective* parts of a period. . . . This exercise, by *forcing* the pupil to trace out the connexion from following the filiments [*sic*] by which it is produced, fits the mind to discern the energy of the writer, through the power of his language. Made familiar with this process, the pupil sees the language rise into a species of muscular action. (*Appeal*: 1828, pp. 101-3)

Flush with the excitement of his discovery, Brown momentarily transcends the habitual grotesqueness of his prose. Here he conveys the energizing novelty that a better conception of syntax could bring to the ancient scholastic rituals for prose analysis. As Ian Michael says, the Enlightenment approach to English grammar "was doomed to be trivial: a necessary descriptive procedure in the elementary study of a foreign tongue" but "irrelevant, sterile and dull when applied to a vernacular."[13] But with his notion of construing, Brown tried to revitalize American grammatical pedagogy by fusing it with rhetorical and logical analysis in a way that would recapture the lost unity of the medieval trivium, with its fruitful interplay between potentially allied approaches to language and literature. Conceived as part of the trivium, the grammatical study of English is scarcely trivial. Moreover, it might help redeem from sterility modes of rhetorical and critical analysis that in our time threaten to lose touch with the classroom, with the linguistic matrix of literature, and with the socioeconomic reasons why American society generously if perhaps misguidedly funds literary study.

Brown's English Syntax Institution and the Peripatetic Tradition, 1836-1856

To reproach Brown simply for failing to unify discourse about language and literature when twentieth-century intellectuals have also failed to do so would be unfair. But the effort to understand why

Brown in particular failed can yield useful lessons. The inadequacy of Brown and his fellows should not necessarily be attributed to low pay. In Victorian America English teachers gradually achieved parity with classical grammarians in pay and respect. Indeed, Brown's intellectual evangelizing failed partly because it was too profitable. Experiences with other grammarians made him wary of plagiarism. He always worried lest his idiosyncratic syntactic approach be compromised by conventional terms flawed by ambiguity. Thus his later texts abandon mere grammar to study what the title of one proclaims as *English Syntithology . . . developing the constructive principles of the English language by appropriate polymorphy terms, used in this science only, each form of the same word having but one meaning* (Philadelphia: Grubb, 1847). Three motives led him to couch the principles of his new science in "appropriate polymorphy terms": a philosopher's zeal for intellectual purity, a businessman's concern to advertise and trademark his goods, and an autodidact's delight in exotic nomenclature for its own sake that equated it naively with understanding.

Brown's effort to elevate grammar to full scientific dignity took the form of a textbook accompanied by an instrument he denominated the syntascope. In the prefatory "OBSERVATIONS TO JOHN, THE PUPIL," that worthy was cautioned to avoid fidgeting, not "to play with his knife, and watch-chain, to wring and pull his fingers, or child-like, to amuse himself with the pointer of the SYNTASCOPE." John's initial nervousness was amply justified, for by the third chapter he found himself staring at material like the following:

> The Epoagical Analysis of the Epecons in the GNOMOD which constitutes the FIRST SECTION OF THE SYNTASCOPE
>
> I presume, John, that the introduction of this new word, Epecon, produces no very agreeable emotion in your mind. But technical words are the tongue with which I teach you, and, if you deprive me of these, you of course close my mouth at once. Technicals are, in teaching, what teeth are in eating—both are necessary in a thorough mastication. I must masticate with my technical teeth; and you must swallow, and digest.
>
> The first section of the SYNTASCOPE contains one Gnomod, or Sentence, and this is divided into three monos. These monos are called epecons. The word, epecon, is derived from the Greek, epos, a word, and eikon, an image, a picture, a likeness. . . . These epecons are the mirror in which, if you will look, you can see the image of the epoagical character of the words of any verbal mono which can be found in our language. But you must become well acquainted with the epoagical character of each epecon before you can see any thing in it. I shall, therefore, endeavour to make you acquainted with the epoage of these epecons at once. I shall begin with that which is called an AGNOMECLAD. The first clade in this

epecon, is marked A; and, from the size, and form to its tenon, you can see
that it belongs to the corme, F. Hence this part, A, is e-po-a-giz-ed thus—
A, a clade of the uni corme relation, belonging to F.[14]

This may be unequivocal. But it is also hard to decode, at least without
consulting one's syntascope. That was probably the point, for pupils
were apparently to steer by the diagrams and the well-twiddled dial of
their mechanical marvel.

John's reactions to his teacher are not on record, for Brown never
imagines his saying anything. Indeed, Brownian pedagogical theory is
explicitly grounded on the notion that the pupil should open his mouth
as little as possible, especially when error seems likely to emerge. From
some hints "for teachers of Private Classes" we may glean Brown's own
classroom practice:

> Allow no time to lapse between the pupil's error and your correction.
>
> By close attention to the posture of the pupil's lips, you may ascertain
> even before he speaks, whether he is right or wrong. If he is wrong, inform
> him before he expresses his error. . . .
>
> Do not use more than two words in telling the pupil that he is wrong.
>
> *Say,*—wrong, *sir*—or *wrong.*[15]

Johnny was evidently to be taught syntithology in much the same fashion that Rover is housebroken. Called on the grammatical carpet for an
answer, he would be promptly swatted if threatening to stain it with piddling mistakes, lest the lapses become habitual. Some linguistic puppies
undoubtedly responded to Brown's fond discipline by developing a
dogged Pavlovian affection for the sound of their master's voice. But
many students in nineteenth-century classrooms were just as quick as
their modern counterparts to sniff out needless pomposity in critical jargon. "What, is the word NEPOECLID, to be rejected because the word,
conjunction, is already in use?" their teacher might cry. "Let both names
have a place."[16] But like twentieth-century undergraduates, some students mightily resented the self-gratulatory proliferation of hermetic terminology.

In his fear of multiple meanings and his ludicrous overvaluation of
definition as a method of learning, Brown remained a thorough grammarian at heart, however unorthodox. He was elated that his new terminology reduced the number of technical definitions necessary from
ninety-three to forty-four. This efficiency he sought to turn to profit by
circulars advertising "ENGLISH SYNTAX TAUGHT IN SEVEN DAYS WITHOUT
MEMORIZING." Aware that in making this claim he might seem like a
"sciolist and . . . charlatan," he promised "to impart a better knowledge
of the constructive principles of the English language, in seven days, six

hours a day" than would be possible by any other method in fifty years. His record of success would sooner or later sever him "from the detestable empiric, and the loathsome mountebank." His grammatical sensitivity training catered frankly to those burned in encounters with Murray yet still questing for syntactic salvation. "Particular attention is paid to punctuation." Though no money-back guarantee was offered, "all who are not satisfied with the knowledge which they acquire in one week, are permitted to continue as long as they wish" (*Appeal:* 1836, p. vi).

Commencing operations at 86 Arch Street in Philadelphia, he had broadened his vision three years later:

> The author, believing the work to be as important to his country as it is novel in the annals of science, has deemed it his duty to attempt to found an INSTITUTION,
>
> *First,* To qualify those who wish to become lecturers on his system, to do so with credit to themselves, and advantage to the public.
>
> *Secondly,* To render that aid which those teachers who wish to use the system in their schools, may need to enable them to do justice to their pupils,—and,
>
> *Thirdly,* To teach adults, and children of both sexes, the constructive principles of the English Language in a few days without the slavish process of memorizing opponent definitions, absurd rules, and irrelevant notes.
>
> All who wish to become teachers of the system, or venders of the works, are invited to call on the principal of the Institution, No. 70, Chestnut Street, where he will be happy to do all in his power to enable them to pursue a lucrative, and an honorable business.[17]

The higher learning so throve at 70 Chestnut Street that next year Brown removed to a new location six blocks westward. At 90 South Eighth Street the Institute kept serving its established clientele while adding a new track, ENGLISH SYNTAX ACQUIRED WITHOUT A TEACHER, for those capable of self-instruction, that is, almost everyone, for "any one who can acquire even a partial knowledge of English grammar upon the old plan with the aid of a teacher, can acquire a complete knowledge of it from his system without any such aid" (*Exegesis:* 1840, p. iv).

This ambitious claim may have represented overexpansion, for it would seem to undercut the Institute's graduate program. Perhaps for that reason next year's Philadelphia city directory mentions no James Brown, teacher, at that address but lists a James Brown doing business at 234 Chestnut Street as the proprietor of a "Nat. saloon." The directory of 1844 shows a James Brown residing at 282 Chestnut Street who gives no occupation. This may not be the same man, for the third edition of Brown's *Appeal* (1845) shows the Institute still very much on his mind;

he devoted ten pages to defending one of its graduate lecturers, whose espousal of Brownian doctrines in Baltimore a few years earlier had triggered Rev. Dr. Breckinridge's attack. Any interlude as a self-styled gentleman of leisure was short-lived, for the 1850 directory has James Brown—now advanced to the dignity of "author"—dwelling at 52 Wistar Street. Three years later James Brown, author, had removed to 15 South 10th Street. A circular from 1856, shortly before Brown finally vanishes from view, shows him still doing business there, offering private classes ("Five Dollars for a course of twelve Lessons") and vending his books—but with no more rash talk about cutting teacher out of the educational action.

This late advertisement ends on a plaintive note: "N.B. To remove the only objection which has ever been made to the new system, the author has recently restored the old technical terms to their accustomed places" (*Book Second*: 1856, p. 2). The change may have been overdue, for another text published that year directs clientele to 118 Arch Street, third story. After four decades of struggling to free his fellow Americans from Murray's grammatical tyranny, Brown "found them as loath to leave their prison house of error as was the old inmate of the Bastile, his cell of darkness."

There cracked a noble heart, we may think—and surely an offbeat one. Our temptation is to imagine Brown as oscillating between the roles of crank reformer and con man, a grammatical lightning-rod salesman, with a well-meant sideline in syntactic snake oil. One inevitably thinks of the King and the Duke in *Huck Finn*, whose schemes include setting up as traveling teachers of "yellocution" and who must invariably decamp one step ahead of their enraged dupes. But this would be to waste either pity or contempt on Brown when both should focus elsewhere in American education. Though the English Syntax Institute shuttled from one location to another, they were all within a twenty-block radius. For two decades it at least paid the rent, and probably more than that. Only by comparison with Murray can Brown be deemed an unsuccessful grammarian. The two hundred American editions of Murray's grammar made it the best-selling text. But with sixty editions of various grammatical books to his credit, Brown was no contemptible figure himself. His texts are adorned with page after page of testimonials that could not have been faked in such numbers by anyone doing business in the same city for two decades. The president and vice provost of the University of Pennsylvania were among those enthusiastically endorsing his approach, as was the principal of its affiliated academy. His franchising system apparently worked; some of his trainees made a living as schoolmasters. The Pennsylvania legislature voted a resolution in favor of his system and allocated $1,000 for the purchase of Brown's textbooks. He commanded a good chunk of the school market, especially in the Middle Atlantic States, with consequences for the intellectual life of that region that remain to be explored. Believing that "this great branch of learning . . . has ever been open to as various and worthless a set of quacks and plagiaries as have ever figured in any other," the arch-conservative Goold Brown might well sniff contemptuously about James Brown's "fantastical works."[18] But they were so many that he frankly declined to list them all in his comprehensive bibliography, and the two Browns both sold briskly. We are so accustomed to thinking of all nineteenth-century grammarians as dry, prescriptive arbiters of correctness like Goold Brown that we have forgotten that from his wintry perspective the field teemed with "numerous . . . visionaries" like his namesake (p. 35).

In "A Circular to Teachers" the aging pedagogue touted what he now called his "Rational System of English Grammar." This swan song reveals a mind-set pervading even more American classrooms than his textbooks succeeded in penetrating:

> As the well taught astronomer sees perfect harmony, and clear method throughout this wonderful machinery of lights, so the skilful sectionizer of a sentence, apprehends the exact import of this verbal structure, with a certainty, and a strength which nothing but a capacity to divide a sentence into sections, and ascertain their true *sense* relation can give to the mind. As the reader proceeds, the entire thought of the writer becomes almost *visible* to him; and he breaks it into sections which he classes as *trunks* and *branches* of the same mental assemblage, with as much ease and accuracy as a well taught botanist would classify the component parts of a tree. . . . CONSTRUING . . . enable[s] him to map off, and connect the different ideas of the writer with as much ease, and correctness as a practised engineer can sketch a *canal*, *dock*, or *harbor* upon paper. . . . SCANNING . . . is not only calculated to enable pupils to investigate the mind of another through the medium of his writings, but to enable them to promote the growth of their own minds to almost any extent. . . . Perhaps, while a *dissected* map of the United States represents a *sectionized* sentence as clearly as any other thing which can be found, the act of putting its component parts together, represents the process of *Scanning*, and *Construing* with as much precision, and *perspicuity* as any other operation which is common among us. The entire map is the entire sentence—and the division of it into the different States, the division of a sentence into different sections.[19]

In urging the merits of syntactic analysis Brown is troubled by no Wordsworthian worries that we may murder to dissect. The student is to march through the sentence breaking off branches from trees, confident in his ability to reconstruct them. But the model for the constructive process is largely mechanical. Every "mental assemblage" will be faithfully reassembled by making the nation's classrooms into a kind of assembly line. Despite respect for the "well taught botanist," the "practised engineer" is Brown's real hero. By assimilating his scientific methods grammar can help open the nation up for commerce and share in the conquest of a continent. Indeed, if students learn to "investigate" others' minds properly, they may "promote the growth of their minds to almost any extent." But the preferred goal of such growth is rather clearly predetermined: after the conquest of the continent, the conquest of space! Brown's marked desire to spatialize language is only the most obvious aspect of his determination to publicize all activity of mind. There is no recognition that language might be helpful for shaping private thoughts of an antisocial character, that some authors like Thoreau might not wish to be read in quite the way this passage prescribes—might even seek to frustrate it. Brownian grammar is dedicated to the exploration of the outer world, not the exposition of an inner world. Today such desires to make "the entire thought of the writer . . . almost visible" to students will lead them not to books but to television, and to the *Tonight Show* at that.

But it is all too easy simply to dismiss Brown in such terms, for his culturally loaded metaphors do convey the excitement in analyzing a sentence that Gertrude Stein was later to feel. Such relentless analysis does empower students by giving them conscious control over their language. Virtually all university classes today contain mostly students who have never been taught traditional grammatical analysis of the form (if not the style) that Brown espoused; they have never diagrammed sentences. Their lack of any common, working terminology for understanding their own language is a serious handicap in what still remains a print culture. Their inability to understand much instruction about how to improve their writing should keep us from laughing too heartily at Brown's agnomeclads. His zany grammar beats with the authentic pulse of his culture: "As in the *dissected* map, a State may be located far from the particular States which actually bound it, so in the sectionized sentence, a *sub-section* may be placed far from its own *super-section*." Students are to connect displaced clauses to the main body of the American sentence just as the entire nation realized its manifest destiny by annexing Texas and claiming Oregon. Though territorial expansion is now out of fashion, even in the later twentieth century we have tried to correct such dangling modifiers as Hawaii and Alaska.

The degree to which Brown puts grammar at the service of American commerce will doubtless exasperate many academics. But one reason for the ineffectiveness of modern university English departments is their tendency to serve as employer of last resort for intellectuals out of touch with the mainstream of their culture. Too much time is spent evolving elaborate literary theories rationalizing, deploring, or denying their own insignificance, while too little time goes to help students articulate significant thought in writing. Nearly automatic hostility to business culture results in pedagogy every bit as ridiculous as Brown's unexamined support of it. Literary academics need to realize that as sentences are not just agglomerations of individual words, so societies are not composed of isolated "interpretive communities." Whether we ground grammar boldly like Brown in the interplay of the Trinity or settle for an interplay between branches of the trivium, full communication between persons should be the aim. That will entail better communication between scholarly disciplines. The modern literary scene recalls those twelfth-century debates between grammar and dialectic, which ended with clerkly intolerance trivializing the entire trivium.[20] In his eminently muddled way Brown was seeking to construe America as a whole. Perhaps that remains a better approach for her grammarians than muddled attempts to deconstruct it. Like Brown I pontificate, I know. But then to *pontificate* (from Latin *pons*) may yet be a way to build bridges.

4 /

Antebellum America Goes Gaga over Grammar

> One of the greatest evils attending our modern system (or rather, no sys-
> tem) of instruction is the frequent changing of elementary books. It is
> truly disheartening to the pupil . . . if he be unfortunately subject to that
> caprice and love of change which frequently attend the members of our
> profession. . . . Even the verbal discrepancies of half a dozen grammars
> must be annoying.
>   — Poe's teacher William Burke, *Rudiments of Latin Grammar*
>   (Richmond: Shepherd, 1832)

The Heirs of Cardell, Legal and Illegal

Sherman was convinced that he had destroyed his health in the effort to
elucidate language. Kauy-a-hoo-ra offered solace, so "here the writer . . .
retired at midnight for contemplation, to familiarize himself with mortality" (*Description*, p. 18). When familiarity ripened into a lasting fellowship in 1828, Sherman could at least rest satisfied in knowing that
his adversary Cardell accompanied him to the grave that same year.
After a mildly derisive notice in William Cullen Bryant's *U.S. Review
and Literary Gazette*, Sherman's *Philosophy of Language* was never
reprinted. But Cardell's grammars were ballyhooed by New York's Democratic press. The *New York Literary Gazette* serialized prepublication
excerpts, confidently predicting "the overthrow of the old system."[1]
After Cardell's death his books enjoyed a definite afterlife in the age of
Jackson. Reprinted occasionally, his works were plagiarized just as
often. The influential Boston educator William B. Fowle ranked him
among "the only distinguished writers upon our language and upon
grammar."[2] E. Smith's *Philosophical Grammar of the English Language,
in Connection with the Laws of Matter and Thought . . . to Which Is
Added a Hieroglyphical Key* (York, Pa.: Glossbrenner, 1833) was confessedly extracted from Cardell's work of that title—so largely, in fact,
that Cardell's estate should have been concerned. Joshua Jones was
another disciple of Cardell who tried to dignify grammar by approaching it philosophically:

> We shall now treat of the application of words to simple ideas, and, to
> thoughts prepared for utterance. In the prosecution of which, we shall

unfold the propensities of that part of speech which . . . is denominated the VERB.

Our range of thought is extensive. All objects presented to the mind, as well as the distinguishing properties, relations, and actions of those objects (which we call attributes) constitute objects of thought.[3]

Characteristic was his ponderous insistence that verbs could not be understood without understanding all thought and knowledge, which the first section of his textbook purported to set forth. His intellectual ambition was often ludicrous. "We shall now consider the COMMUNICA-TIVE RELATIONS subsisting between objects of thought, when prepared for utterance," he began his discussion of syntax. "Or, in other words, we shall treat of what is called 'the government and agreement of words in a sentence'" (p. 105). No twentieth-century teacher of "language arts" could have exhibited a more touching faith in the power of pompous nomenclature to elevate the subject of grammar and purge the lingering terrors inspired by its terminology. For Jones "all the phrases of a sentence, together with its verb, represent the attributes of the subject under an abstract conception of those attributes." By emphasizing logical relations it was the job of abstract syntax to distill communicative thoughts like "I see a bird resting upon a shrub, extracting nourishment from the flowers" from the buzzing perceptual confusion in which language is always originated by "a *flower-nourishment-extracting shrub-resting bird-seeing* person" (pp. 156–57). As his nominalizing tendency suggests, Jones departed slightly from Cardell's veneration for the verb and questioned whether existence is the effect of action, but he remained convinced that "I AM, is the AUTHOR, and existence is the universal attribute of nature" (pp. 34–35).

On the Middle Border B. F. Ells's reverence for English mingled oddly with a tinkerer's desire to improve it. Exceeding all others in sublimity, splendor, and richness, this "last formed language in the world, . . . without doubt, will continue to be the last, till time shall have been lost in the vortex of Eternity." It will soon be the language of the world. But English "is far from the acme of perfection, notwithstanding its future growing prospects. Much remains to be done to make it what it ought to be." For marketing and export purposes he discarded "Mr. James Brown's new-fangled doctrines . . . that *English nouns and pronouns have no case.*" Further streamlining eliminated passive verbs and the potential mood. Naturally enough, in achieving linguistic perfection "the names of the *Imperfect* and *Perfect Tenses* are made to change places." Ells also had fundamental objections to integrated approaches like Brown's. "The greatest defect in the popular system, is the blending of the primary principles with the philosophical notes," he felt (pp. vii-viii). Thus his *Dialogue Grammar* (South Hanover, Ind.: Hanover College Press, 1834) begins by treating mechanical rules, then shifts to a dialogue on "The Philosophy of Grammar."

When Ells's teacher inquires, "What books have you found to be so interesting, as to cause the hours to fly so swiftly," his pupil saucily explains, "I have been entertained with 'Horn Took's Diversions of Purley,' 'Webster's, Murray's, Brown's, Cardell's, Hull's and Kirkham's Grammars.' In which I have found many curious things, which, peradventure, may lead me to become more inquisitive than becomes a pupil" (pp. 97-98). To his credit, Ells realized the perplexity of the tradition and sought to clarify it by discussing such intriguing issues as whether language was confined to men, as Cardell thought, or shared with animals, as Webster argued. But his freedom of inquiry was limited by his belief that Hebrew was the primitive language given to Adam in the Garden, and "its principal words . . . are always significant of the characters of the persons to whom they were given." Spreading from Paradise through every region of the world, Hebrew begat all the modern languages of Europe through the intermediary Celtic tongue "first introduced . . . by the descendants of Magog and Gomer, the sons of Japheth." The most extensively spoken language in the world, the Chinese, "is an immediate offspring of the Hebrew." An unbecomingly inquisitive pupil might ask why this nearer relative of the Adamic language, spoken by "more than one third of the human family," is destined to be displaced by English (pp. 101-10). Ells seems not to anticipate that question from young heretics in South Hanover, Indiana. His explanation of why "adjectives, philosophically speaking, cannot be compared" represents the normal level of argument: "We will begin with the adjective *good*. . . . It is a term, that *implies no evil*. Therefore, when I say, that John is *good*, the adjective *good* denotes, that he has no evil about him; consequently, no one can be *better* than he" (pp. 178-79).

Sans benefit of comparative philology, youth in South Hanover could easily hear no evil, see no evil, and speak no evil; but they had the devil of a time understanding what Cardell meant by *etymology*:

> B. I think that Mr. Cardell advances a strange idea, when he says,—speaking of grammar, 'Its design is to teach the right understanding and use of words.'
>
> A. It is the province of dictionaries to teach the 'right understanding of words' by giving their meanings; but grammar may be said to teach their right use in speaking and writing.
>
> B. Perhaps Mr. C. intended to convey the idea, that dictionary is a minor

part of grammar; for he says, that, 'Etymology teaches the *meaning* of words,' and what more can a dictionary do? and yet, (strange to tell!) Mr. C. has left this part of his grammar unillustrated. (pp. 112-13)

In discussing grammatical etymology in his *Elements* Cardell indeed gave no specific example of its relation to "the origin and history of words" with which a lengthy footnote connected it. Therefore, he had anticipated that "without the proper connection and accompanying proof," his concepts were "probably liable to be misunderstood" (pp. 43, 38). But historical etymology is so extensively illustrated in his prefatory Synopsis that it takes some obtuseness to miss his point. That Ells had such trouble fathoming the double meaning of *etymology* suggests that Eggleston did not exaggerate much in caricaturing grammatical savants of the Hoosier frontier. What a sensitive but naive student might have imagined while puzzling over Cardell in such a milieu is almost beyond conjecture. But the experience could certainly open up a brave new world where nothing of him remained but suffered a sea-change into something rich and strange.

Twenty years after Cardell's death another disciple acknowledged his influence. He drew on Cardell's notion of the breathy copula but felt largely alone in his peculiar views. Colored also by Tooke and Court de Gébelin, N. Vernon's version of the origin of language has a distinctly French flavor that suggests how small-town intellectuals in midcentury America could resemble parochial Enlightenment savants:

> The letter *h*, was doubtless one of the first, if not the first, which became a distinct part of speech.... Let us suppose two individuals destitute of verbal language, to be examining a third, apparently lifeless. One feels assured that life has not become extinct; and intimates . . . by a forcible breathing, that such is the fact.
>
> His companion, after a more thorough exam . . . gives his assent in like manner. This aspiration has now acquired a meaning. Articulate it, and it becomes *ah*, *ha* or *he*, a word denoting breath, to breathe, and by an extended application, *life* and *to live*. By a farther application it becomes a noun, denoting the being who breathes, lives, and performs the functions of life.[4]

Vernon went Condillac one better by showing the language of action sparking speech. As two panting brutes point to the body of their dazed fellow and struggle with the primal articulation, "He am!" the locomotive of language begins chuffing down the tracks.

Like de Brosses and Court de Gébelin, Vernon made much of the similarity between words for *father*. He wished to interpret the entire alphabet on the basis of semantic phonetics, with the letter *S,* for example, uniformly signifying to *shoot, dart*, or *throw out* in such words as "*see*, to shoot, or dart the eye; *say*, to throw out words; *sane*, to shoot or dart the wits" (p. 6). Vernon defended Court de Gébelin from Webster's fundamentalist strictures about God's direct gift of artificial speech, preferring a deistic explanation. How did God speak with primeval man? "The answer is obvious. In the same language in which his communications are ever made. This language is written upon every page of *Nature's volume*. It is alike understood by all." Terrifying the guilty nations of the earth with cataclysms or declaring his power and goodness in roaring cataract and murmuring rill, "such is the *language* of NATURE. The *language* of NATURE'S GOD" (pp. 24-25). Vernon colored this naturalistic vision with just enough Christianity to comport with his position as professor of science at a female seminary in Maryland.

That a professor of science should write a Cardellian grammar is less surprising when we consider the marked affiliations between nineteenth-century disciplines now regarded as methodologically distinct. The historical origins of language attracted investigators with interests in natural history.[5] Indeed, one of Cardell's most famous pupils never became a grammarian at all yet remained in some ways a faithful disciple: his half-brother Reuben Hyde Walworth. In 1804 Cardell, then a Williams College dropout, tutored his younger half-brother in Latin and mathematics for the brief spell of fourteen weeks. That was the only brush with classical education that Reuben Hyde Walworth ever had, but it helped imbue him with the etymological method.

While Cardell went on to teach French and English in New York City and struggled vainly to get his American Academy of Belles-Lettres funded, his younger brother took to the law and Democratic politics. DeWitt Clinton named Walworth chancellor of the state of New York the same year that Cardell died discouraged by American indifference to literary education. Perhaps he was in the wrong field. Throughout the early decades of the Republic a taste for letters often led to the practice of law. In his *Law Miscellanies* (1814) Hugh Henry Brackenridge explained that the lawyer must "understand the precise meanings of words; this is not to be collected from dictionaries; so well at least, as from the roots of the words, which are found in these Languages from which our own is derived."[6] While statutes and precedents remained scanty, etymological sophistication readily converted into legal expertise.

The renown Cardell just missed as a grammarian his brother achieved for shaping American equity jurisprudence. Whereas Cardell's books were concerned with simplifying and reforming grammatical rules scientifically, Walworth's *Rules and Orders* (1829) began a twenty-year campaign to simplify court procedures in the spirit of Benthamite reform. Partly because of his careful attention to standards of evidence, legal precedents proved more rewarding than linguistic precedents. By the time the office of chancellor was abolished in 1846, his opinions were cited in British courts. He earned honorary degrees from Harvard, Yale, and Princeton and the accolade of Justice Story as "the greatest equity jurist living." Retiring from the bench, he declined a cabinet post under Buchanan to prosecute the chief interest of his latter years, genealogy. The main result was his authoritative *Hyde Genealogy* (1864), two massive volumes totaling nearly fifteen hundred pages, a model of painstaking historical research. To it we owe virtually all our biographical knowledge of Cardell. Whereas the elder brother traced the genealogy of words with disappointing results, the younger brother devoted himself to the genealogy of the law so profitably that he was at last able to investigate his own genealogy and save his half-brother from oblivion.

A genetic approach to English study was widespread. In Whitesboro, New York, Jonathan Badgley, for example, organized his entire grammar etymologically "to observe how one part of speech seems to arise and grow out of another." Badgley instructed his students to begin their grammatical studies by imagining what they would do if devoid of speech: "Our first step would, undoubtedly, be the assignation of names to the different objects around us. This we may observe among children in their first efforts toward speech. Hence arises that class of words which we call nouns. A noun is a name. It is the foundation of grammar; as all the other parts of speech arise from it and necessarily depend upon it."[7] Next arose the verb, so complex, intricate and abstruse that Badgley found himself taxed to explain the origin of this part of speech in which "the subtle and profound metaphysics of language appear" (p. 33). He turned gratefully to the process whereby "nouns become adjectives," not allowing the flow of his grand grammatical narrative to be roiled by the fact that "on the other hand, adjectives often become nouns" (p. 63). Adverbs and pronouns came next. Then, after "men had invented words for limiting the signification of nouns . . . and had contrived substitutes for nouns to render language less tedious . . . still language must have remained very imperfect and unintelligible, if they had not devised some means of showing the relations which different things bear to each other" (p. 72). As soon as prepositions had been patented, men needed to find some means to connect their thoughts. "This is the office of conjunctions" (p. 77). Linguistic technology had created a ready market for them, and they duly made their appearance, much as the locomotive followed hard upon the steamboat.

In Badgley's imagination the primitive brutes whom the Enlightenment delighted to envision "inventing" language became equated with his own generation of Romantic American tinkerers churning out mechanical inventions sparked by the need to conquer a continent. The genetic organization of his grammar represents in extreme form a common underlying assumption: the child should begin the study of his own language as if forced to reinvent it. "To enable children to comprehend the *abstract idea* that all the words in a language consist but of *nine kinds*, it will be found useful to explain how *savage tribes . . . having no language*, would first invent one, beginning with interjections and nouns, and proceeding from one part of speech to another as their introduction might successively be called for by necessity or luxury," was the opinion of David Blair, whom Goold Brown quotes in his massive *Grammar of Grammars* (1851).[8] Brown strove to refute this idea for ignoring the authority of Genesis. That Brown's grammatical encyclopedia, an eleven-hundred-page compilation gleaned from four hundred grammarians, itself went through about twenty printings in the nineteenth century suggests the seriousness that invested such ideas.

Like Blair's, Badgley's pedagogy was a direct legacy from Tooke. He referred ambitious students to the *Diversions of Purley* but feared the book might baffle those already baffled by the parts of speech. For the tender minds of "mere English" students he devised lively dialogues in which Schoolmaster Peter Puzzle and Simeon Rust, a Candidate for a District School, struggle to explain the mysteries of parsing to a motley crew including Farmer Bellmouth's entire family and such familiar student types as John Faithful, William Strut, and Charles Burly. Though adult instruction en famille is no longer common, Rust survives today as the hapless university teaching assistant assigned to night school classes, while Professor Peter Puzzle continues to perplex Faithful, Strut, and Burly in his English courses (unless the football tutor shrewdly steers Burly into Speech 101).

Indeed, the grip of grammar upon the midcentury American imagination transcended the schoolroom setting. Like spelling, it evolved its own evening rituals for the working portion of the community. The burgeoning lyceum movement was hospitable, so citizens of Galena, Illinois, heard D'Arcy A. French deliver two lectures that were subsequently published as *English grammar simplified: in which it is clearly proved that in the grammars most commonly used in our schools, the principles, in the most important constructions, are grossly erroneous and defective* (Galena: Thomas, 1846). How much French improved Galena's grammar is hard to say. But the town's most illustrious citizen was to command a stark, driving prose as impressively when he wrote his memoirs as when he commanded the Union armies in the field. Though no American president performed more poorly in office, perhaps no president has written a better book. Clear, laconic, stripped to their syntactic bone and muscle, U. S. Grant's classic battlefield dispatches might still be models for any bureaucrat gestating a memo. Struggling to finish his memoirs on his deathbed, the old general defined his core identity grammatically. "I think I am a verb instead of a personal pronoun," he jotted down in a note as throat cancer robbed him of speech. "A verb is anything that signifies to be; to do; or to suffer. I signify all three."[9]

Elsewhere in Illinois a self-educated lawyer with a penchant for puns addressing a Springfield audience in 1859 on "Discoveries and Inventions" could quite naturally spend most of the evening discussing the supreme invention of human speech. Like most subsequent technology, Adam and Eve's fig-leaf aprons required speech, he argued, whether Divine gift or invention, for shared knowledge is the engine of human progress. Lincoln's surviving notes for that lecture are not profound, to be sure, but they show that Grant's commander in chief honed his eloquence in the same tradition as Badgley.

"A new pronoun has been invented, to supply the deficiency in the language . . . when employing a generic noun of the singular number," a midwestern disciple of James Brown proudly announced. "For instance, *parent* may be either masculine or feminine. We can not, therefore, say *he* or *she* loves, because it may be either."[10] Troubled by this deficiency, William Hall of Columbus, Ohio, ransacked Anglo-Saxon roots in vain for a suitable word. He finally pitched on

> the Latin word *nonnemo,* which signifies *a person of either sex.* This word in its present form, would not do. But by taking fragments of it, we can make something that would approximate convenience. Thus
>
> 1. Nom. *Ne;* as, The person I referred to, when *ne* was beheaded, never murmured nor groaned.
>
> 2. Poss. *nis;* as, The person who will embrace this doctrine shall receive the pardon of all *nis* transgressions.
>
> 3. Obj. *nim;* as, I refer to *nim* who was drowned on last Sabbath.

Though he wisely doubted that it would soon be adopted, he was confident that ultimately "men of erudition will see the necessity of such a word" (pp. 209-12n). It seems not to have entered his mind that women of erudition would see the necessity even more keenly or that he might ever figure as a footnote in the annals of herstory. Nor did he imagine that in systematically replacing men and women with persons (from the Latin *persona, per sonum,* through sound, as in *dramatis personae*) we risk peopling the world with theatrical performers wearing masks as megaphones in order to make a loud noise in public. But it would be unjust to reproach Hall for not anticipating issues ignored by many in the modern movement for degendered language. Scientific accuracy was evidently the driving ideal behind this linguistic tinkerer's invention, which had no discernible link to nineteenth-century feminism. He was not just another literary pedant grotesquely peddling nis politics.

In Providence a clarion call like French's was sounded by William S. Balch when he mounted the podium for an evening lecture series sponsored by a Baptist youth group. These so edified them that they voted to publish his *Lectures on Language, as Particularly Connected with English Grammar* (Providence, R.I.: Cranston, 1838). That decision was probably swayed by the fact that he was their pastor. Current grammars satisfied none, he proclaimed. "The seventy-three attempts to improve and simplify Murray have only acted intransitively, and accomplished very little if any good, save the employment given to printers, paper makers, and booksellers" (p. 177). Why? Learners focused on the mere forms of words without ever looking at what the word meant. Away with memorizing "arbitrary, false, and contradictory rules, which the brightest geniuses could never understand!" (p. 151). Instead, youth should be taught to seek out the etymology of words, which would focus them on the things signified. "This is the business of philosophy, under whatever name it may be taught; for grammar, rhetoric, logic, and the science of the mind are intimately blended, and should always be taught in connection" (p. 219).

If all this sounds familiar, that is because Balch was a fervent disciple of William S. Cardell. That bright star in the firmament of American literature reduced these principles to a system taught triumphantly by Daniel H. Barnes, formerly of New-York High School, "one of the most distinguished teachers who ever officiated in that high and responsible capacity in our country." Precipitously summoned "by the aid of their transcendant intellects, to unseen realities in the world of spirits," these two gentlemen were soon "embosomed in the light and love of the Great Parent Intellect" (pp. vi–vii). Both mantles fell to the young prophet. Perhaps because system was not his forte, half a dozen editions of his own *Inductive Grammar* (Windsor, Vt.: Ide, 1829) failed to alter the status quo. Pulpit and podium were his natural habitat. As grandly conceived by Cardell, grammar had to describe not just language but the structure of all thought and knowledge. American optimism led Balch to treat that as already accomplished by his old high school teacher's refinement of philosophic parsing.

Like Cardell, Balch rejected the distinction between transitive and intransitive verbs as meaningless. To call *lie* a neuter verb was to enforce "in these days of light and improvement, the groveling doctrine of neutrality, the relic of the peripatetic philosophy" (p. 128). He proposed to replace traditional grammatical categories with a system based on modes of action. B his hostility to the peripatetic tradition was not inveterate, for his analysis of verbal forms soon modulates into a paean to "the all-sufficient and ever-present agency of the Almighty Father, the UNCAUSED CAUSE of all things and beings; who spoke into existence the universe" (p. 146). Trotting out the Cardellian etymologies, he equates *to be* with verbs of action. Having emanated from the Divine *Word*, all *worth* may yet return to it. Yet though all worth wills return to God, we cannot say that all worth will return to God, for "of the future we can know nothing definitely." Only God knows the future, so no human words can express it. However uncertain the future tense, it seems more substantial than the present, for all knowledge of the present derives from the past. Is the timeless infinitive infinite or nonexistent? Balch stresses that "the Hebrew, which is strictly a philosophic language, admits no present; only a past and future." Subjected to this linguistic legerdemain, the past too begins to vanish, for "it has ceased to be. Its works are ended." We are left with a Baptist minister's violently teleological sense of time where "the present is a mere line—nothing as it were—which is constantly passing unchecked from the past to the future" (p. 201). Thoreau spoke like a grammarian, albeit one less enamored of Hebrew verbs, when he aimed "to stand on the meeting of two eternities, . . . to toe that line" (*Walden,* p. 17).

To palliate Balch's philosophic innocence it may be urged that, unlike some twentieth-century existentialists, he was more or less aware when his discussion of Being became a discussion of grammatical categories. His linguistic concerns made him a lively stylist with a knack for humorous exemplification. His imagination oscillated vibrantly between the palmier realms of abstract spirituality and a naive neo-Lockean cosmos where concrete objects bombard the hapless cerebellum into consciousness, where "words . . . are the expression of ideas, and ideas are the impression of things" (p. 136). When the materialistic fit was on him, he asserted that his own analytic "principles exist in fact and must be observed," and his language constantly strains to reify facts and treat them as things. Though his most ardent affection seemed reserved for the incorporeal verb, the subject of six of the ten lectures that he devoted to individual parts of speech, he was clear "that action, as such, can never exist distinct from the thing that acts." His *Inductive Grammar* found it "highly probable that most verbs originally had objects expressed," so that *Tom walks* really means *Tom walks a walk* (p. 66). Relational particles he derived in a Tookean vein. *There*, *where*, and *here* represent contractions of the noun *area*, meaning respectively *the area*, *wha-icht area*, and *hic area*. "*While* is another spelling for *wheel*. 'To while away our time' is to *pass*, spend, or *wheel* it away" (*Lectures*, p. 246).

Beautiful Dreamers: Philosophical Grammarians and Their Homespun Hermeneutics

Throughout the American Renaissance language was conceptualized, often illogically, by people wheeling away their time playing with words. They were not so much thinkers as tinkerers with ideas. The intellectual historian's temptation to analyze concepts, categorize them, and trace their affiliations is constantly frustrated by the fact that each tinkerer could reformulate these ideas and blend them idiosyncratically for his own purposes. The popular view of language was not shaped by philosophers who produced theories with any clarity; it was shaped by schoolteachers. What resulted was no clear-cut debate between two or three well-defined intellectual positions as some scholars have suggested. The topic of language was canvassed with unusual intensity by American grammarians, but their discussion generated more heat than light. Resemblances between them dissolve upon closer inspection as often as not. Seen all together, American grammars form a phantasmagoria of uneasily shifting viewpoints on language, shading into each other unconsciously, so hazy, contradictory, and perplexed as virtually to defy summary.

But we can say that the stereotype of our nineteenth-century grammarians encouraged by H. L. Mencken is partial and inaccurate. Scorning the collective silliness of America's literary gogues, Mencken did not grossly underestimate them, but he did fail to emphasize that in the nineteenth century many were silly in unpedantic ways. Apostles of dry, rulebound correctness predominated, to be sure, but they were constantly challenged by a minority whose stock in trade was translunary imagination. The juicy, speculative quality of much antebellum grammatical pedagogy has been sadly neglected in accounts of the era's intellectual life. To understand the classics of the American Renaissance we must shelve our notion of the schoolmarm Miss Throttlebottom, with her pursed lips, and expand our sense of how American authors *and* readers were in fact taught to approach language.

Like Cardell, Sherman, Brown, and Balch, many were troubled by what they saw as the philosophical poverty of grammar. In his *Analytical Outlines of the English Language . . . in the Form of Familiar Dialogues*

Intended to Accompany Grammatical Studies (Richmond: Shepherd, 1825), John Lewis entered the lists bent on deploying Baconian induction in "a philosophical examination of Language" (p. vii). To keep students from parsing sentences unaware of their meaning he penned twenty-six dialogues in which a father supervises his son's study of grammar. Tooke showed that all words reduce either to nouns or verbs, Papa explains, and failed likewise to reduce the verb only because of lingering "metaphysical errors" since dissipated by Dugald Stewart and other able philosophers. Under Papa's indulgent tutelage the scales fall from George's eyes. Dazzled, he cries, "I now see clearly the conclusion to which you would lead me, that all words in language are *nouns or names,* and that the sentific suggestion arises in the mind from the use of the *signs* of things, in the same manner that thoughts arise from the presence of the objects themselves to the senses" (p. 143). Though the *North American Review* thought Lewis too fervent a worshiper of Tooke, it found his approach useful for the intelligent teacher of grammar. Lewis's doughty adherence to Scottish commonsense philosophy seemed a bulwark against what the *Review* saw as an unparalleled vogue for philosophico-grammatical "charlatanry" (23:114).

Two Hoosier schoolmasters saw a need for their *Western Grammar of the English Language* (1843; Terre-Haute, Ind.: T. Dowling, 1845). Its conventional approach was belied by a title coyly suggesting that effete eastern grammarians would no longer be allowed to perplex any plain-speaking plainsman who might grumble that we'uns talks different out here. As Shakespeare's Caliban curses Prospero "for learning me your language," so many a Kokomo Caliban tuned with a hickory stick cussed his teachers for larnin' him theirs. More ambitious was Noble Butler's *Practical Grammar* (Louisville: Morton & Griswold, 1846). Hailed by Cincinnati newspapers as an addition to "our Western literature," the book also bore testimonials from eastern luminaries. "I am especially pleased with the *philosophical accuracy* which pervades the work," wrote Harvard's Professor Convers Francis. "When grammar goes below the surface and recognizes the great principles and laws of language, it is apt to become obscure," but without philosophy "it is apt to become superficial" (n.p.).

"I have served in the private ranks," wrote Ezekiel Hildreth of his thirty-five years as a teacher. "And though serving in this humble station, I have not been a mere incurious drudge, performing my daily task without observation, and without inspection into the nature and reasons for the various evolutions, maneuvres and discipline, practised in the field of literary campaigns." With beguiling modesty this veteran decided to raise a monument to his educational victories in the West Virginia Panhandle—a little book called *Logopolis, or City of Words; Containing a Development of the Science, Grammar, Syntax, Logic, and Rhetoric of the English Language* (Pittsburgh: Jaynes, 1843, p. iii). Hildreth possessed a mildly ironic self-awareness that set him apart from some heroes vaunting their feats on the grammatical battlefield. Despite his eccentricities, which were manifold, this odd drillmaster probably trained troops who gave a fairly good account of themselves in later life.

Power fascinated Hildreth. His book aimed to show that "language is a transcript not only of nature material in her visible and tangible properties . . . but also of her powers and energies" (p. vi). For him as for Webster the locus of power was the verb. Syntax germinates from exploding vocabulary because "single words, whether simple or compounded, are necessarily abbreviated and imperfect sentences." Verbs are the most explosive words. Hildreth's chapter "Philosophy of the Verb" is a rhapsody about *power*. He traces the word to the Greek verb *poein* = make, which is also the root of the word *poet*. Of course, he was wrong. *Poetry* has less to do with *power*, alas, than antebellum etymologists (or modern deconstructionists) might suppose. But at times he does create an awkward but powerful poetry of ideas. Like Coleridge and Cardell he derives the copula from the divine I AM and asserts that its active nature supports everything else. Since it operates reciprocally, power applies "to all created beings, both as communicants, and as recipients of it." To communicate is to share divine power. "The term passive does not apply with much propriety, either to the action of the verb, or to the act of utterance; . . . it applies wholly to the condition of the subject or nominative of the verb." There are no passive verbs, only passive people. Evidently the study of grammar can overcome their inertia, enabling them to tap the divine energy of the universe. No academic Marxist was ever more intoxicated with the notion that literary criticism might empower people—including, of course, the professor himself.

"O logic! if thy votaries would but follow thee into thy sequestered abode, thou wouldst feed them with thy rich and pure historical milk, whereby they would grow up to literary manhood." Determining the proper application of words in sentences would create a bountiful "economy of language." The mind craves its proper food, and syllogistic logic cannot provide it. He strove to articulate a grander conception of logical reasoning. After he derived the term *evidence* correctly from a Latin root meaning to see or discern clearly, etymological evidence then enabled him to discern clearly that "the noun *proof* is derived . . . from the Greek compound verb *probaino,* signifying to go before one. . . .

Proof represents the object, as *coming* before the mind and shewing itself; while *evidence* represents the object, as *standing* before the mind, and shewing itself."

Investing the mind with all the dignity of the Appalachian bar, he sought a model for philosophy in legal process:

> Argument comes to us from the Latin noun *argumentum,* compounded of *argutum* and *mentis;* but the Latins took their verb *arquo,* from the Hebrew verb *arg,* signifying to weave, to entwine . . . therefore the noun means a web, texture or fabric. But in the word *judgment,* we find that which gives beauty, order, simplicity, strength, and unity to the whole structure; for our noun *idea,* which is the same in Greek—the Greek verb *eido* or *eideo,* and the Latin verb *judico,* are all from one and the same origin or root, namely, from the Hebrew verb *idaa,* signifying to see with the organic eye, or with the mind's eye; that is, to know, understand, &c. So that our word *judgment, (judicium mentis,)* the Latin *judicium,* the Greek and English *idea,* literally mean a form or image, which the mind beholds, like that presented through the natural eye.
>
> Thus we have proof or evidence, argument, and judgment, the three grand pillars on which rests the broad and extensive platform of judicial economy. . . . Charges or predications set forth in questions, sentences, propositions or declarations, are all tried, and found to be *true* or *false,* by one and the same process of mind; whether they are brought before it seated on the tribunal of public justice, or sitting in the private *chair* of its own chancellor dignity. A *declaration* is first made, in which some demand, claim, or charge is set forth as TRUE . . . ; the *truth* of which is *attested* or *denied* by the several *proofs* or *evidences* standing by as witnesses; and "by the mouth of *two* or *three* witnesses every thing is established." Therefore, upon the *argument* or texture of these *proofs,* the declaration or charge will stand or fall as this contains, *yea* or *nay,* on which judgment is rendered and stamped accordingly. (pp. 154-55)

Seeing alternately with the organic eye or with the mind's eye made Hildreth's philosophy engagingly cockeyed. So did the bogus etymologies underpinning his new legal logic. Arguments and judgments are no more weavings or verdicts of the mind than the Latin *flumen* = river means a flow of mind; the Latin root *-men* is just a common suffix objectifying verbal force in nouns, quite distinct from *mens.* Hildreth was lavish in laying out the dishes at his intellectual banquet because he believed that the mind would naturally select its proper food. His legal logic was but an appetizer "before I proceed to explain the peculiar mode, called *reasoning.*" No mere logic could satisfy him; he wanted a full-blown holistic epistemology. Deriving *reason* correctly from the Latin *reor,* to think, Hildreth questioned logicians who restricted it to ratiocination. To foster an ampler view Hildreth traced the genealogy of *reason* further back to the Hebrew noun *roue* signifying "the Spirit of God, the human mind, wind, air, breath, &c." as well as to "the Greek verb *reo,* signifying the flowing motion of a stream or liquid, and also that of the breath in talking or making articulate sounds in speech" (p. 165). It follows that "reason and rhetoric have a common origin." In point of fact, the Latin *reor* and the Greek *rheo* are as unconnected with each other as both are with the Hebrew *roue;* but Hildreth was convinced that he had demonstrated their underlying unity. After all, as he explained in another bogus etymology, "the verb *demonstrate* . . . literally and definitely means, to strew, spread, or scatter the mountain . . . so that the organic or mental eye can discern objects that were concealed behind it," and he had certainly moved mountains to link literature with philosophy (p. 168). Achieving a unified theory of language was a challenge as great as unifying the country. But where the route from ignorance to knowledge "has been circuitous, laborious, and slow, that pioneer, who can open the road and level the way, that lies directly between them, will certainly be the easiest to follow, and the cheapest in the end" (p. vii). Since reason refers "to the flowing energies of the mind, while rhetoric has as direct reference to flowing words," a grammarian who connected them was simply canalizing the language of nature (p. 166).

Hildreth was not content to incorporate rhetoric in reasoning, for in his hierarchy of mental faculties reason did not reign supreme. To be sure, reason was superior to demonstration, just as demonstration itself presupposed contemplation and meditation:

> *Contemplation* is derived from three Latin words, viz. *con* or *cum,* signifying with, or in company; *tempus,* signifying time; and the verb *pleo,* signifying to fill up, to finish, end, &c. Therefore, to *contemplate* an object, is to fill up or pass away time with it, in our inspection of what belongs to it.
>
> *Meditation* comes from two Latin words, viz. *medius,* signifying in the midst, or among, &c. and the verb *ito,* signifying to frequent, or to go often to, &c. Therefore to *meditate* is to go often to and be conversant with things, in order to know them.

With these garbled derivations Hildreth subordinated the contemplative faculties to the heart-stirring activity of moving mountains in the same way that engineering enterprises begin with preliminary surveys. (The genuine etymologies would have been more to his purpose.) But philosophical balance was speedily restored by subsuming the engineer's approach within that of the sage, who in turn yields the ultimate intellectual honors to another figure: "Reasoning includes demonstration— demonstration includes contemplation and meditation; but *theorizing* includes the whole four. For, to theorize means, to see as God sees; that is, to know and understand, &c." (pp. 167–68). Few more pregnant *et ceteras* have ever been penned.

On the topmost rung of Hildreth's *scala perfectionis* stands the sublime theorist, God's right-hand man. Insofar as his lineaments are discernible, they bear a curious resemblance to those of a philosophical grammarian like Hildreth himself. Wheeling might think his a humble station, but few if any of its townsfolk could know the lofty satisfaction of laying down the laws for everyone else's intellectual activity. To echo the elder brother in Milton's *Comus*, "How charming is divine philosophy!" Hildreth's intoxication with his fancied methodological dictatorship is palpable and endearing. He reminds one of Fielding's archetypal Abraham Adams, an estimable soul rendered ridiculous by his characteristic delusion that grammarians have the most important occupation in the world.

Of course, Hildreth's enthusiasm for theory is widely shared in literary academia today, where the search for the magic formula that will make English teachers into philosopher kings and priests of culture goes on unabated. So far it has only made some more grotesque than ever in the public eye. But within the cozy groves at least it promises to elevate some grammarians over others, while gratefully diverting everybody's attention from the humiliating business of mending comma splices. English teachers must constantly compensate for their deep-seated sense of inferiority grounded in the fact that professing one's mother tongue does not strike the world at large as a notably difficult enterprise. With a complicated hermeneutics, they try to maintain the ancient pedagogical rituals demanding that youths master a secret language as part of their initiation into adulthood. (*Hermeneutics* itself is a satisfyingly occult term.) Unfortunately, their literary theories may yield no more divine insight than Hildreth's. They share Hildreth's belief that to *theorize* is to see as God sees. Alas, the etymology is mistaken. Theory derives not from the Greek *theos* = god, but from the Greek *thēa* = spectacle. The words are from two distinct Indo-European roots. Etymologically speaking, theorists do not see as God sees. They just make a spectacle of themselves with intellectual theatrics.

Thoreau and the Educational Establishment

"Grammar, taught according to the usual system, is productive of little practical good," Samuel Shattuck reported to the Concord town meeting in 1830 on behalf of the school committee (in Lyman, p. 143). Dissatisfaction with grammatical theories and the public grammar school was not new. In 1822 four of the town's leading citizens had joined to establish the Concord Academy as an alternative. Thoreau's family scrimped to send him to this private school in 1828. The eleven-year-old boy may not have entirely relished the change. "I was fitted, or rather made unfit, for college, at Concord Academy & elsewhere, mainly by myself, with the countenance of Phineas Allen, Preceptor," Thoreau wryly wrote twenty years later. Allen was a Harvard graduate whom some regarded as a perfect encyclopedia with a command of five languages besides English. But one of Thoreau's classmates at the Concord Academy who later rose to be attorney general of the United States called his schooling there "as bad, as could reasonably be desired," while another successful alumnus harbored memories of "the poorest teacher and worst school I ever knew anything about personally."[11] Twenty years after leaving Concord, Allen came back for a Sunday school convention. "I found I could not take two steps with him," Thoreau commented dryly in his journal, noting that his old teacher "wished much to see the town again, but nothing living and fair in it" (21 Oct. 1855). Aside from a demolished tavern, Allen's recollections of Concord revolved around a caged fool who lived near his boardinghouse and the scamps and sots among his students. Neither teacher nor pupil recalled their time together with much sentiment.

In the records of the academy there survives a schoolboy poem written by "T." The handwriting is so unlike Thoreau's that it is excluded from the canon, but he was the only pupil whose last name began with that letter. Whether or not "The Contrast, Written in an hour of gloom and despondency" is his, its plangent clichés suggest the *cri du coeur* of an American preppie toiling away at conjugations, who regrets the more relaxed atmosphere of public school, marked equally by less snobbery and less homework:

> My days of youth were crowned with joys—
> Then, friends carressed [sic]—for fortune smiled.
> Now blighted hopes my peace destroys,
> And sorrow claims me as her child.
> How different now my humble lot
> From that which marked life's early dawn:—
> By those I loved remembered not,
> And doomed to bear the proud world's scorn.
> To reap hard labour's scanty fruits,
> O'er leisure hours I've no controul:—
> For toils must sacrifice pursuits
> The most congenial to my soul.[12]

Whoever wrote this melancholy effusion, which ends lugubriously by anticipating that "Soon will . . . life's . . . current ceace [*sic*] to move," had not toiled so unremittingly over English grammar and spelling as to avoid all errors.

Indeed, instruction in English does not bulk large in Allen's curriculum, though spelling, reading, grammar, composition, and declamation were all taught at some level during Thoreau's first year at the academy. No particular grammar was specified, but Blair's *Rhetoric* was a required text. Allen did demand themes, and one of the twelve-year-old Thoreau's entitled "The Seasons" happily survives. There are half a dozen spelling errors in this holograph, uncorrected by Allen, and only three of its twenty simple sentences achieve grammatical complexity. This juvenile effort would seem even more prophetic in its interests were short themes on this topic not a staple of American schooling.[13] For advertising purposes, however, more time was spent cataloging instruction offered in Greek, Latin, French, and Italian, while Allen's encyclopedic abilities were also exercised expounding standard textbooks in mathematics, history, geography, natural philosophy, chemistry, logic, and "the theory of the moral sentiments." If he was a pedant, he appears a thorough one. When Thoreau squeaked into Harvard on probation in Greek, Latin, and mathematics, the fault was probably not Allen's; for Thoreau's schoolmate and Harvard roommate Charles Stearns Wheeler passed the entrance exams with flying colors. Allen's students generally ranked in the upper third of their classes at Harvard, as Thoreau himself was to do. How many students enter Harvard today as well prepared is an interesting question.

Certainly Allen did not stifle Thoreau's burgeoning interest in languages. In addition to the required classical authors who constituted the core of the curriculum, at Harvard Thoreau zealously pursued courses in German, Italian, French, and Spanish, though only one modern language was required. He chose to take only one course in natural history, though others were offered—a fact especially relevant for those who consider him primarily a naturalist by inclination. One contemporary found him distinguished in college for "local pride and Concord self-conceit."[14] Did he preen himself on his Concord Academy training in languages? He even dipped into Anglo-Saxon on his own, partly because of Professor Channing's encouragement, partly because of Longfellow's lectures on the subject, but mainly because "Saxonism" was coming into vogue.

Thoreau's dull college themes show that he had familiarized himself with the *Diversions of Purley*. His essay on the potentially deceptive titles of books describes a naive student eager to read this celebrated treatise but

puzzled that "so learned a philologist as Mr. Tooke should have condescended to dabble in light literature, or have sacrificed a moment
in . . . diversions of any kind" (*Essays*, p. 91). With all the lofty sophistication of a Harvard senior about to graduate, Thoreau was probably recalling his own first encounter as a sophomore with that deceptive book. The
same inquisitive spirit that led him to read Court de Gébelin's *Monde
primitif* also drove him to explore Anglo-Saxon further before graduating.
As August's Commencement loomed, his college notebooks are full of
extracts from Bosworth's *Elements of Anglo-Saxon Grammar* (1823),
including carefully transcribed versions of the Moeso-Gothic and Runic
alphabets for comparison. He ransacked Conybeare's *Illustrations of
Anglo-Saxon Poetry* (1826) and noted, "In Bosworth the Saxon form of
the letters appears to have been more closely adhered to."[15] But in copying
out Caedmon's Hymn from Conybeare he decided, "I shall *not use the
Saxon* letters." For other extracts from Bosworth he did use Anglo-Saxon
characters, sometimes accompanying them with translations from Sharon
Turner's *History of the Anglo-Saxons* (1807) or other sources.

This was strictly amateur philology. There is no reason to think that
Thoreau ever became as proficient in Old English as Noah Webster or
Thomas Jefferson, and their knowledge was tatty enough. But the fact
that he was still copying specimens of prose and poetry in 1838, well
after his graduation, suggests that it was a little more than a summer's
fancy. He even tried his hand at versifying a selection from Bede as "The
Speech of the Saxon Ealdormann." Yet by the time that Longfellow's
appreciative and influential essay "Anglo-Saxon Literature" appeared in
the *North American Review* for July 1838, Thoreau's own enthusiasm
was waning. "After all that has been said in praise of the Saxon race,"
he commented in his journal, "we must allow that our blue-eyed and
fair-haired ancestors were originally an ungodly and reckless crew" (15
Jan. 1838). Of course, a French strain made his own ancestry equivocal,
like that of Chaucer. Though in *A Week* he was to praise Chaucer's vigorous Saxon English, there he also disparaged "the meagre pastures of
Saxon and ante-Chaucerian poetry," finding little sympathy between it
and the present (p. 370).

As a college junior he again tackled his favorite theme by reviewing
William Howitt's *Book of the Seasons* (1831), probably for his literary
fraternity. With modest dash this essay ticks off the first eight months in
a series of paragraphs that begin by deriving their names etymologically,
whereas Howitt had buried this information in the middle of each chapter. Thus we are quickly told that "April is so called from the Latin . . .
Aperire, to open" (*Essays*, p. 30). Either he found less food for thought

in the numerical derivations of the last four months, or he did not care to explain why the Latin September = Seventh month is our ninth. After Channing's tutelage his spelling errors now average one a page instead of one a paragraph, and his sentence structure has improved greatly since "The Seasons." Two charming mock-heroic paragraphs depart from Howitt's English scenes to portray American boys opening hunting season on birds with a borrowed blunderbuss. In describing the gang's *scatteration* when their ancient piece is about to be fired Thoreau exploits the New England vernacular with a sophisticated awareness of how etymological incongruity can generate laughter. But it would have taken an unusually prescient fraternity brother to have wagered on the author's future greatness. Channing saw nothing special; he graded Thoreau as an average student. English was not one of Thoreau's strongest subjects at Harvard.

During his junior year Thoreau took a term off from Harvard to make money teaching school in nearby Canton. His initial interview with the town's Unitarian minister became a lively discussion lasting until midnight. He was promptly hired, for the Reverend Orestes Brownson was a power on the school committee. During the six weeks Thoreau lived in Brownson's home he may not have distinguished himself as a teacher, but performing in concert with this Transcendental one-man band more than made up for any unpopularity in the classroom. The two studied German together, held wide-ranging discussions, and generally reciprocated each other's high regard. Writing Brownson two years later Thoreau recalled those days as the dawn of "an era in my life—the morning of a new *Lebenstag*." The self-conscious display of this letter, mixing Transcendental ethics and German, reveals a high-minded young intellectual who desired to be "responsible only to that Reason of which he is a particle, for his thoughts and his actions."[16] Alas, after graduation in 1837 he had become responsible to the Concord public school committee, which hired him to preside over his own first alma mater. Though the job carried a good salary in the midst of a depression, he soon threw it up. The supervisor insisted that he discipline pupils more vigorously, so he caned several particles of Reason at random to parody the committee's unreasonableness, then resigned to pursue better methods of making youth smart.

In addition to demonstrating his ability to kindle "metaphysical catsticks" on the hearth of the heart, his letter to Brownson of 30 December 1837 was thus a feeler for another teaching job where he could profess "freedom proportionate to the dignity of his nature." Despite Brownson's goodwill none offered. Brownson himself was reformulating his attitudes toward authority seasonally in the pages of the *Boston Quarterly Review*. In 1844 he converted to Catholicism, swayed partly by the belief that despite apparent linguistic diversity all the languages in the world "are only modifications of one and the same original tongue"—the gift of the one true God.[17] On the philological rock of linguistic devolution Brownson buttressed his despair at the sins of the Democratic Party.

During his first year after graduating from Harvard Thoreau looked industriously but unsuccessfully for a teaching job. Intermittent pencil-making and pencil-pushing did not yield him a satisfactory living, so in June 1838 he founded his own school. When the master of the Concord Academy opportunely resigned at summer's end, Thoreau took over its premises and name. Thus he came to preside over his second alma mater. After a slow start in the fall term, he found himself with enough pupils in winter to summon his more popular brother John to join him for the spring term of 1839. Henry would continue to preside over "the classical department" while "the English branches" would be taught by John. "N.B. Writing will be particularly attended to" John's ad in the *Yeoman's Gazette* for 9 February 1839 assured parents (in Harding, *Days,* p. 76). For the next two years the brothers kept the Concord Academy together until John's ill health forced them to abandon their prospering enterprise. The academy dismissed its twenty-five pupils on April Fool's Day 1841.

Thoreau applied without success for a position at the newly founded Perkins Institute. Instructing the blind in Boston may have seemed more glamorous than teaching them in Concord. Then later that month he happily became Emerson's literary handyman. He tutored Margaret Fuller's brother for admission to Harvard in 1842 and served as tutor to the Staten Island family of Emerson's brother in 1843. Brownson's disciple Isaac Hecker, who boarded briefly with the Thoreaus in 1844, was so struck by his penetrating aperçus on language that he contemplated engaging him as a classical tutor, then tried to inveigle him into a walking tour of Europe. But Thoreau suspected that all Hecker's linguistic roads led (like Brownson's) to Rome and declined the pilgrimage. By the time that he moved to Walden on Independence Day 1845, he felt that he had abandoned schoolmastering for good.

Verbal Fever Rages on the Ohio—and Elsewhere

For good or for ill, schoolmastering had nonetheless marked Thoreau as it marked Whitman and Melville. Teaching was his main occupation from 1837 to 1841, and those were years of extraordinary educational ferment, both locally and nationwide. As secretary of the Massachusetts Board of Education Horace Mann launched his energetic campaign to improve schooling across the state the same year that Thoreau took over Concord's public school. While the beginning teacher walked off the job after two weeks, renouncing his salary of $500, at a salary only twice that Mann commenced his twelve-year campaign to enlighten the state's school committees. They were ready to be enlightened if approached rightly. Mann's reports had a galvanizing effect across the country because discontent with education was widespread. No topic was more controversial than grammar. The four annual surveys that Mann conducted between 1837 and 1841 to discover what texts were being used in Massachusetts schools paint a picture of grammatical turmoil. During those four years the number of towns using Murray's grammar fell by half. Roswell Smith's pretentious Pestalozzian grammar was the most popular across the state. In three hundred towns two dozen different grammars competed for school boards' adoption with varying success. Yet grammars popular in other states did not penetrate the Massachusetts market. Kirkham, who dominated the New York market, was a very minor factor in the Bay State—and no towns used Cardell or Goold Brown. Pond held sway in the Worcester area, where he was a favorite son.

Amid the lively confusion noted by Mann, one minor trend stands out. Though only two towns in the state reported teaching composition independently, increasing use of Parker's *Progressive Exercises in English Composition* showed that subject encroaching on formal grammar. Only thirteen towns used Parker's grammar in 1837, but twenty had adopted it by 1840 to fill the vacuum left by Murray's decline. It was Parker's line of relatively progressive texts that the Thoreau brothers chose for the Concord Academy when they promised special attention to composition. "The first difficulty which perplexes the beginner, is *what to* say about his subject," Parker advised. "Before taking up his pen to *write*, it will be well to *think* for some time on the subject . . . and when difficulties of that kind occur, determining the true import of a word by its etymology or derivation."[18]

Nationally the same confusion of textbooks was replicated on a far grander scale. By 1838 Kirkham dominated Murray in the New York market two to one; but Brown, Smith, and Greenleaf had significant minor shares. Other grammarians had their followings in the 1840s; among the more popular were Comly, Bullions, and Wells. Effective innovation did not come until Samuel Greene's *Treatise of the Structure of the English Language* (1847) introduced a sentence-based approach that soon displaced parsing. Greene's success owed much to the air of crisis. Teachers and public were aroused; disgust with old methods was approaching meltdown. "It would seem impossible for a scholar to parse a stanza of Childe Harold correctly, and yet fail to see the force of the metaphors, etc.," proclaimed the Boston School Report of 1845, "yet this is done sometimes" (in Lyman, p. 140). The analytic-synthetic method with diagramming came to predominate in the 1850s and 1860s, while the rhetorical approach to grammar waxed powerful in the 1870s and 1880s. But in the 1840s the grammar of the American language was up for grabs. An old linguistic paradigm was dying, no clear successor had emerged, and theory jostled theory in splendid cacophony.

Among grammar's chief advantages was "the discipline which it affords to the mind," felt Smith B. Goodenow. In distinguishing shades of meaning the *judgment* was exercised; classifying words trained *abstraction* and *generalization*; and retaining it all in the mind flexed the sinews of *memory*. His faculty psychology had little room for invention or creativity. He worried that most young people, lacking a thorough liberal education, were thereby denied "efficient mental culture." Since colleges honed minds on foreign languages and higher mathematics, he frankly conceived of English grammar as a popular substitute for calculus and foreign languages. The higher walks of literature he reserved for college, but if Americans diligently analyzed their mother tongue in school, the eminently practical mental discipline of grammar would fit them for their "high duties as citizens of this great republic."

Obstreperous citizens were evidently not desired, at least in great numbers. To emphasize this point, his *New England Grammar* opens with a "map of etymology city" laid out neatly in a grid (see fig. 8). Thoroughfares like substantive street and verb street, adjective street and particle street, intersect lesser byways like pronoun row, unsubjective row, and connective row. There are no alleys. Etymology city is surrounded by "guards," and one suspects that they patrol it carefully at night. Goodenow's grammatical Levittown is actually rather innovative in conception and terminology. He not only quotes James Brown with gusto but pilfers most of Brown's testimonials from luminaries proclaiming the bankruptcy of Murray's system, while specific praise of Brown is edited out. Cardell, Fowle, Balch, and Balch's Baptist youth group are also happily cited. But Goodenow carefully eschews Brown's flaunting claims to radical novelty. "Few ideas do we produce, which have not the sanction of high authorities," he proclaims, genuflecting to grammarians of prior ages, especially the eighteenth century. His conservative pose was partly disingenuous but partly accurate, reflecting the outlook of a Congregational pastor who would later publish a discourse titled *Everlasting Punishment Attended with Everlasting Decay*. Aspiring to be "one harmonious system" like a New England town, Etymology City was deaf to more complex harmonies heard in Concord, Massachusetts.[19]

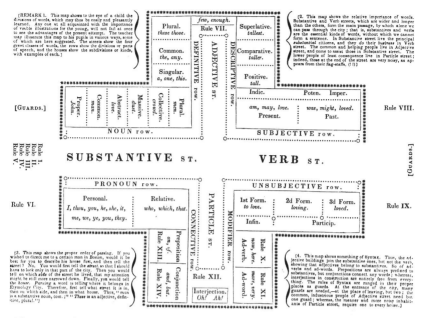

Fig. 8. Smith B. Goodenow, "map of etymology city," *New England Grammar* (1839; Boston: Lewis & Sampson, 1843), reproduced from the original textbook held in the Historical Textbooks Collection, Monroe C. Gutman Library Special Collections, Harvard Graduate School of Education.

"The present age is distinguished, above all others, for its different theories of English grammar, no less than for its wonder-working and labor-saving machines," wrote John Goldsbury. "These different theories do not differ more from all their predecessors, than they differ from each other; at the same time, each theory claims to be the only true one, to the exclusion of all others." He surveyed the field as a defender of Murray, but one who conceded that Murray required improvement. Those disaffected with Murray's system were ridiculing it, so he returned the compliment by scoffing at their grammatical zeal:

> They would like to have some high-pressure steam power,—some railroad system,—by means of which they can pass over in a day what now require the labor of years to accomplish. So infected is the public mind with this mania, and so ready are some to take advantage of it, that it would not be strange, ere long, to hear of the discovery of some mesmerizing process, by which a person can, at once, and without any effort on his part, obtain a thorough knowledge of English grammar. Should such a discovery ever be made, it may fitly be called, "the labor-saving grammar," or "the railroad grammar."[20]

Three of the four chief engineers on the grammatical railroad whom he genteelly sought to derail were Smith Goodenow, James Brown and William Balch. After four pages straight-facedly illustrating Brown's terminology, he concludes that its technical terms alone are more baffling than Murray's entire system. Balch's explanation of universal grammar according to the Cardellian principles of truth, common sense, and independent thought he mocks as grandiose, dryly concluding that "this author, by attempting too much, has defeated his own object, and therefore accomplished but little" (p. 18). Goodenow's claims to traditional authority are deflated by gravely wondering what authorities sanctioned beginning with elocution and prosody, while his rationale for classifying adverbs, prepositions, conjunctions, and interjections together as particles draws this Johnsonian rejoinder: "As well might we infer that 'it is not possible for any human skill' to distinguish between *black* and *white*; these colors are so much alike,—so 'very similar in their nature, often running into each other, so that they cannot be told apart;' and that it is better, not to attempt to distinguish between them, but to give them some common name, like *gray,* for instance, so as to prevent all mistakes, with regard to their *name*s, their *colors,* or their *uses*" (p. 60).

For the popular grammar of Oliver Peirce, Goldsbury had more respect. "This work contains many good things," he admitted. "Yet it so abounds with egotism, sarcasm, raillery and bombast, that one can scarcely have patience to read it." Peirce's bombastic controversial style was much like Sherman's. Goldsbury quotes Peirce's fulminations against Murray and others at length, then declines to give further specimens, primly concluding that it is improper "to put into the hands of children any text-book which deals in jibes and jeers" (pp. 31-33). Though he soberly strains to give a neutral summary of Peirce's ideas, his own style, as if magnetized by his opponent's, veers inexorably into sarcasm: "From these specimens, no one can doubt, that this is 'the automathic system' or self-explaining grammar, as it so fully explains itself!" (p. 44). Goldsbury's book is earnestly committed to the belief that grammarians must conduct their affairs with professional dignity. "We have aimed to be respectful in language, and to use fair and honorable arguments," he piously concludes. But with the best will in the world he could not make that aim good. He seems to have sensed that a profession that attempted to stand on its nonexistent intellectual dignity would only render itself more ridiculous in the long run. The perplexed grammatical tradition that midcentury America inherited often drove its abler practitioners into the embrace of irony—in some ways its natural culmination.

All this merry pluralism could paralyze both pedagogues and popu-
lace. Reporting on the condition of common schools in 1848, the Ohio
secretary of state found some districts refusing to offer grammar and
barely half the state's instructors competent to teach it. Undermanned
districts objected to licensing teachers in grammar because then "they
would be required to understand" it. Whereas 3,200 students cheerfully
pursued spelling in Seneca County, only 420 studied grammar. Pennsylvania did not require grammar until 1854. As the superintendent of Indiana County reported in that year, "A rough knowledge of spelling,
reading, writing, and ciphering is deemed all sufficient, whilst a knowledge of grammar . . . is most heartily repudiated."[21] Rural America
clung to the speller as a paradigm of language; grammar was advanced
stuff for high schools. And farmers could scarcely be blamed for concluding that this occult science had little to teach them.

But while some were paralyzed by this linguistic confusion, others
were liberated. Educational energies were mobilized to meet the needs
revealed by inadequate grammatical instruction. Like Murray's and
Kirkham's, the grammars most in vogue throughout the American
Renaissance were generally dull, prescriptive, and somewhat inaccurate. But a substantial minority of grammarians revolted against the
dominant mode. Like most surveyed here, they advocated a more
"philosophical" approach. They felt that grammar could have the
glamor it enjoyed when medieval men coined that derivative word
because they saw grammar as the source of occult power. By constant
agitation the philosophical grammarians went some distance toward
glamorizing it intellectually. Their persistent confusion of formal,
structural, syntactic, and semantic criteria made them even more inaccurate than the tradition they contested; but they were also far more
stimulating.

The Enlightenment tradition that America had inherited sundered
grammar from both logic and rhetoric and thus trivialized it as a way of
studying the vernacular. Eighteenth-century British grammars "are surprisingly, distressingly self-contained. In them grammar had become
such an impacted discipline that it could scarcely be modified from outside," notes Ian Michael. "There are few references to Locke's *Essay*,
and no sign that it influenced the treatment of the parts of speech or the
categorical framework generally. In the 18th century the idea of universal grammar had lost the connection with logic which made it linguistically important and was used by the grammarians merely to assure their
pupils that in studying one language they were being prepared to learn
them all."[22]

By contrast, even the nineteenth-century American grammars derived from Murray seem more embedded in cultural history. Though he proudly borrowed his practical rules from Murray, Samuel Kirkham cribbed from Tooke and Webster to add a "System of Philosophical Grammar, in Notes" to his best-seller, in a grudging concession to "a kind of *philosophical mania*" that he thought had arisen of late.[23] Frequently cited by Murray's adapters, Locke is a lively presence for the philosophical grammarians, as is Stewart. But perhaps the most seminal philosopher of language was John Horne Tooke. In midcentury America most literati agreed that the *Diversions of Purley* were more than diverting. Its paradoxical materialism lent itself surprisingly well to Transcendentalism, as Emerson's borrowings in *Nature* suggest. Tooke taught Webster as he had taught Coleridge, and etymological speculation inspired by the *Diversions* broke ground for Transcendentalism across America in hamlets where Coleridge never penetrated. The question of linguistic origins that Tooke had skeptically raised was answered by American grammarians with interpretations of Genesis or conjectures about primal man. The dominant rhetorics were those of Campbell, Blair, and Whately. All three sadly neglected the notion of invention. To compensate for its deemphasis Tookean etymological speculation seems to have taken over some of its functions. The idea of universal grammar was alive and kicking in the American Renaissance, though more often in historical than in logical terms. Before a sound comparative philology was imported from Europe, the tree of language exfoliated in wild and wonderful forms. The linguistic theories of the American Renaissance are maddeningly hard to label, precisely because each small-town savant could easily brew his own private blend, often with a grand disregard for consistency. Side by side with the legacy of Condillac, organic concepts—half transplanted, half native—arose to explain the language of nature.

American elementary schools teemed with talented educators who spoke the language of nature fluently. Or so thought Rufus Blanchard when he set about marketing a teaching aid. "The Grammatical Tree is respectfully offered to the youth of America as an Assistant in obtaining a knowledge of the Elementary Rudiments of English Grammar," he began. "The design has been to excite a literary curiosity in the mind of the uninitiated pupil, to please as well as to instruct the grammatical tyro, and to open a field to the genius of the teacher by combining the beauties of nature with the scientific classification of English words." What Blanchard was trying to sell teachers of genius was a fold-out chart for display in the classroom—*The Grammatical Tree* (New York: Colton, ca. 1853). His brief prospectus says nothing explicit about linguistic organicism, but his visual aid seems designed to stamp that doctrine indelibly upon the minds of tots and teachers incapable of absorbing it through artificial language. Instead of James Brown's denuded, deracinated, dismembered mechanical trees, he offers a handsome specimen in full bloom: "A limb is devoted to each part of speech, and the medallions on each limb are colored with a view to assist the eye in tracing out the classes and properties belonging to the part of speech assigned to it. . . . The limbs containing the Adverb and Participle are made to branch from the limb containing the Verb, because one comes from the Verb and the other qualifies it" (see fig. 9).

To be sure, the chart conveys the beauties of nature perhaps less forcefully than the beauties of chromolithography. But the pastel palate is a pleasing one, as the public school principal Josiah Reeve commented in an accompanying testimonial: "In my judgment the work cannot fail to attract the attention of pupils, not only by its intrinsic value, but by its tasteful and beautiful appearance" (n.p.). If James Brown's illustrations portrayed sentences in the style of a demented horticultural Chirico, Blanchard's chart sought to imbue New York schoolchildren with the painterly vision of a grammatical Chagall. After plucking the fruit of knowledge so temptingly displayed, urban urchins could sneak innocently back into Eden and shinny up the Tree of Life. By rendering the language of nature in glowing technicolor, the Grammatical Tree not only excited literary curiosity but fostered botanic science and art appreciation as well. It was clearly a bargain at the price.

Studying and teaching in Concord and Cambridge, Thoreau laid the foundations for a dynamic view of language that finally flowered in extraordinary prose. To be sure, his were unusual educational advantages in the America of his day. But it would be a mistake to suppose that such a vision could flourish only near the eastern seaboard. Living in what was then western Virginia's Wheeling in 1842, Ezekiel Hildreth dwelt in a cultural environment more limited than Concord. Pittsburgh, the nearest thing to a local metropolis, was even more provincial than the Hub of the Universe. Still it hummed with kinds of activity unknown to Anglophilic Boston. Visiting that year, Charles Dickens was dryly amused by its American boosterism: "Pittsburgh is like Birmingham in England, at least its townspeople say so," he observed. "It certainly has a great quantity of smoke hanging over it, and is famous for its iron works." A few years earlier the French visitor Michel Chevalier had concluded, "Nowhere in the world is everybody so regularly and continually busy."[24]

Forty miles away in the more bucolic environs of Wheeling, Hildreth was also busy, expounding his Philosophy of the Verb. A few years earlier the establishment of the town's first iron mill had "suddenly

Fig. 9. Rufus Blanchard, *The Grammatical Tree* (New York: Colton, ca. 1853). Courtesy, American Antiquarian Society.

awakened the people of Wheeling as from a Rip Van Winkle slumber, and many were the wild schemes for the aggrandizement of the city that were imagined."[25] The town's first iron tycoon was bankrupt by 1840, a victim of variable tariff policy. His immediate successors did little better. But despite the failure of the first local blast furnace, visions of Wheeling dealing in steel kept tantalizing the Panhandle's citizenry, among them Ezekiel. Hildreth had married a daughter of the Zane family, who pioneered the area. While tutoring his young son for college, he took the boy for nature walks and lectured him on the geology of the region. This schoolmaster wondered what might be the relation between his business and Wheeling's, between Wheeling's future business and Pittsburgh's. In a sense *Logopolis* was an effort to answer those questions.

"Be it life or death, we crave only reality," Thoreau was to write — then promptly set about mining for it (*Walden*, p. 98). After a life devoted to words, Hildreth harbored a similar craving. He knew what reality was. "The word is compounded of two Latin words, viz: *res* or *re*, a universal term applied to any being, fact or truth, like our word *thing*; and *sal, salis,* or *als, alis,* signifying salt; and *realis* literally means the essence of salt or the savour of salt, which if it has lost, what is it good for?" he explained. "Therefore *reality* signifies the essence or savour of a thing" (p. 169). But what was the essence of the metropolis looming upriver under clouds of smoke? Wherewith was Pittsburgh salted? Motion, said Chevalier, or commotion. Therefore the essence of *Logopolis* is likewise motion, as manifested in its Websterian doctrine of energetic primal verbs underpinning all reality. Like Noah Webster but more sunnily, Hildreth was convinced that constant motion or actual change "is the origin and foundation of all verbs whatever. But this motion . . . is contrasted under two grand general heads, diametrically opposite in their natures. One is direct, unchanging, forward motion; and the other is constantly changing, or circular motion." From this dichotomy he wrung our two contrasted adjectives *right* and *wrong*, deemed the perfect participles of *rig* and *wring* respectively. "*Right* then has reference to motion or actions begun in a fit and proper direction, and . . . *right* in that direction. But *wrong* has reference to motion or action, constantly changing its direction" (p. 189). Our country was on the go and needed a corresponding philosophy of language. The motion of its wheels — like the motion of the planets — might be wrong, but the American locomotive was clearly on the right track.

Hildreth was not the last intellectual to admire technological progress but deplore technological instability. He caustically dismissed instructors who offer "mere *information* of what has taken place among men and things, rather than a development of the cause or causes that produced it." By philosophic grammar he would show that "truths in principle or elements of science, include all operative powers, together with . . . their own degrees of energy . . . as they exist in their social relations and intercommunion with each other." Embodying the social relations of scientific truths in Logopolis, he envisioned a booming verbal borough with "a wonderful . . . economy of language" (p. 155).

Dynamic urban language required exactly the same fuel that powered Pittsburgh:

> In proof of this, let us inquire . . . what is meant by the term *verb*? The Latin word *verbum*, from which our term verb is derived, comes from ferveo, fervere, fervi, or ferbui, and the noun would be *ferbum;* but we know, that the consonants *f* and *v* are interchangeable. . . . The word is very happily chosen as a term of classification of those words arranged under this head, since they all signify power operative and operating. And the term itself implies the fervor of heat or caloric, or even of any power in its active movement. (p. 49)

The verb is the source of all language, and the source of the verb is heat. By deriving the word *verb* erroneously from the Latin root meaning to *seethe* or *boil* Hildreth linked the crucible of language imaginatively to the smelters of Wheeling and Pittsburgh. They refined metal ore; he refined mental ore. Indeed, his imagination seethed, and so did the nation's. Aglow with economic and literary zeal, this grammarian had the wit to suggest that the vernal fever of the American Renaissance was more truly conceived of as *verbal fever.*

During the 1850s similar thoughts occurred to a young man in Concord watching the spring snow melt off in a railroad cut. In literary, philological, and intellectual sophistication the gap between Thoreau and Hildreth was great. But they had much in common. For Hildreth, too, was a Harvard crank, who had migrated to greener albeit sootier pastures on the Ohio. One of his nephews was a classmate of Thoreau's at Harvard, while another Harvard nephew, the historian Richard Hildreth, had preceded Phineas Allen as preceptor of the Concord Academy.[26] Thoreau and Ezekiel Hildreth were kindred spirits in many respects—and in some ways Hildreth was the bolder. The Concord author wrote a very subtle book; but the educational ferment that shaped him extended across the country, and there was an audience in Wheeling that could appreciate some of *Walden's* implications more shrewdly than most citizens in Concord or Wheeling today.

5 /

Copyrighting Etymological Ecstasy

The study of language and my vocation, have also led me to make many inquiries, and in one of those moments of rapture, when the mind seems to detach itself from earthly things, and become, as it were, a part of that which language calls *sublime*, I thought that a *single idea*, proved more forcibly the existence of a first cause, of an Omnipotent Creator, than the view of the stars, the sun, and the earth I trod upon.

> — Peter S. Chazotte, *An Introductory Lecture on the Metaphysics and Philosophy of Languages. Being the First No. of a Philosophical and Practical Grammar of the English and French Languages* (Philadelphia: Author, 1819)

Pop Philology—The Vogue of American Etymological Manuals

Conflating grammatical with historical etymology focused attention on the origins of words. In his *Abstract of the First Principles of English Grammar* (Philadelphia: Bioren, 1810) Joseph Hutchins, D.D., tried to clarify that science with an etymology of etymology—an "Index Pointing Out the Etymologies of the Principal Grammatical Terms" (p. 197). Sure that youth would flock to a warbling instructor, F. McReady composed his *Art of English Grammar in Verse*. This pedagogical Pied Piper rhapsodized about the history of English:

> Ere we of derivation end the theme
> It may be curious to our youth
> Scholastic, here to know the true descent
> Original our English language came:
> Thro' all the tribes, and nations whence,
> Came strength, and copiousness, and all
> Refinement, elegance, and pleasing grace.
>   When first the sons of Anglia oppress'd,
> By Picts and Scots, their Borean neighbors wild,
> Invok'd the sun of hope, to beam one cheering ray,
> From old, consistent fam'd Germania . . .[1]

As the century wore on, confusion between grammatical and historical etymology dwindled. Used alone, the word increasingly denoted the latter as an independent discipline. Forward-looking educators began using it to beef up elementary English instruction.

Hence there arose a new class of textbooks offering etymological sensitivity training to a broad audience. Novel spellers paved their way. Samuel Gummere published *The Progressive Spelling-Book in Two Parts . . . Including Extensive Tables of Words Deduced from their Greek and Latin Roots* (Philadelphia: Kimber & Sharpless, 1836). William B. Fowle's *Common School Speller* (Claremont, N.H.: Claremont Mfg. Co., 1842) also served two masters by dividing words syllabically to encourage both proper pronunciation and etymological insight. The first aim still had priority, he explained, but fortunately "the cases are not numerous in which these great objects clash with each other" (p. 6).

By midcentury Almon Ticknor disagreed. "The great fault of the many spelling-books now extant, appears to be the crowding into them too much of that which appertains to the higher departments of learning, and to the scientific principles of language generally," he complained in his *Columbian Spelling-Book* (Pottsville, Pa.: Bannan, 1849). Their authors wrote as if the tyro speller knew "the roots and idioms of the ancient classics. But are they not sadly in error? . . . By presenting these formidable barriers to their advancement, are they not thwarting and discouraging the mind of the young learner?" (pp. 3-4).

Not if Tocqueville's diagnosis of the Jacksonian passion for etymology was accurate. "Men living in democratic countries know but little of the language that was spoken at Athens or at Rome," he observed. But despite their lack of erudition, "vanity will induce them to search for roots from the dead languages. . . . The most ignorant, it sometimes happens, will use them most. The eminently democratic desire to get above their own sphere will often lead them to dignify a vulgar profession by a Greek or Latin name. The lower the calling is and the more remote from learning, the more pompous and erudite is its appellation."[2] So undertakers would blossom into morticians—so teachers became educators.

Webster's *American Spelling Book* had a section on derivation that purported to instill "some knowledge of the formation of the language." But his attention was focused elsewhere. By 1836 he grudgingly acknowledged a new market. He met the competition with an advanced supplement to his speller. In it, he promised,

> the explanations of the prefixes, and affixes will be useful to all classes of pupils, whose understandings are sufficiently enlarged to comprehend them. The derivations of English words from the Latin and Greek languages may not be so generally wanted; but they may be of some use even to mere English scholars; and they must be very useful to such as are intended for an education in our higher seminaries. There are books in the market containing similar explanations; but I have seen none which are free from material errors.

> In the section containing the derivations from the Latin language the radix or primary word is translated; but most of the derivations left without being rendered into English as exercises for the pupils.[3]

He did not want to alienate the vast audience for his spellers by suggesting that his bread-and-butter text was deficient, so his overture toward this new market was restrained. Explaining that the new meanings created by prefixes and suffixes were not always self-evident, he hastened to add that "a book of this kind cannot be a substitute for a good dictionary, which every pupil should consult." His lack of enthusiasm for *The Teacher*'s approach scuttled the book. It reached a fourth edition but never took off.

One of Webster's competitors sold very widely indeed. The previous year Salem Town had published *An Analysis of the Derivative Words in the English Language, or A Key to Their Precise Analytic Definitions* (1835; Cooperstown, N.Y.: Phinney, 1847). This Town wrongly believed to be "the first attempt to present the *component parts* of English derivative words, in their distinctive character . . . in anything like SYSTEM." He scorned Webster's pedagogy. Parroting unmeaning words left the student with a vocabulary he could not use intelligently in later life. Town painted a bleak picture of the embarrassment that ensued. A man suddenly responsible for the precise ideas his words convey "is often compelled to make frequent appeals to his dictionary in relation to some of the most common words in the language. Who does not know this from his own experience, when just stepping into public life?" For twelve years Town racked his brains for a solution. He passed through many states, "conversed with many scientific men, and, in May, 1835, at the General Assembly in Pittsburgh, availed himself of the opinions of many others, some of whom, at least, were men of undoubted qualifications." After canvassing Presbyterian experts, he had the remedy. Since his book tried to supplement rather than replace other texts, his title page recommended it for schools of all grades, where it would "confer some of the important benefits which the classical student now receives almost exclusively, on our common English scholars" (pp. 3–9).

Patriotism made Town burn to "unlock the whole amount of derivative words in the Language." Like many, he feared that Jacksonian democracy's extension of the franchise threatened republican self-government unless the electorate could be liberally educated for new responsibilities formerly discharged by an elite, thus:

in un.	Discover, f. To lay open to view, to reveal or find out.
anti	
aristo theo	Demo,cracy, gr. *Demos,* the people, and *Cratos,* power; hence, a government by the people. (p. 131)

To forestall aristocratic or antidemocratic tendencies as well as mob rule, he empowered people by drilling students in the meanings of prefixes and suffixes, then applying these to root-words identified as coming variously from French, Saxon, Norman, Greek, German, Dutch, Irish, Italian, Spanish, Welsh, Danish, and Gothic (if unspecified, a Latin origin was to be assumed). They could thus build their vocabularies on knowledge they already possessed, for though "few children could tell what *agglutinative,* means . . . who of them does not know what is meant by *glue?*" (p. 4).

With the teacher's help a pupil would analyze words derived from the same root much "as the classical student is exercised in Greek and Latin. . . . He can easily trace each shade of difference, from the plain, literal signification, to the most beautiful figurative applications" (p. 9). Learning to spell and define words in this manner would inculcate "the *radical* principles, in the formation of ALL derivative words." English would lose its mystery. "Proper mental discipline, continued in this manner" (by which he apparently meant consulting a dictionary's etymologies) would "unavoidably ensure clearness of thought, and perspicuity of expression for life" (p. 71). Clarity in composition was the supreme and self-evident goal; he never worried that he might create rather than unlock a secret language.

He correctly forecast the popularity of his book, which saw three editions within a year of publication. Town's *Analysis* went to town, claiming a thirty-third edition in 1846 and leaving seventeen actual editions recorded in the National Union Catalogue. Webster's *The Teacher* straggled in its dust. In 1838 Town came out with his own piggyback *Spelling, and Defining, Book; Being an Introduction to Town's Analysis.* It proved even more popular. Although its claimed one hundredth edition in 1843 may be wishful thinking, Town's spellers gave Webster's some of their stiffest competition and boosted sales of the *Analysis.* Town was active in summer institutes for retraining teachers, while his political bent got him elected to the New York legislature. He glad-handed at educational conventions as unflaggingly as he buttonholed Presbyterians in Pittsburgh. Just before the Civil War fifty thousand copies of his Speller and Definer were printed annually, and half a million of his popular readers were sold each year. In 1864 his obituary proudly claimed that over a million copies of his books were printed yearly, and they were recommended by more than a thousand authorities.

William Smeaton was also distressed by the inability of those without Greek or Latin "to scan out the meaning of what issues from the pulpit or the press, even when it has been written designedly for their benefit." The potted classical education that he advocated made less claim to novelty than Town's; he cited Scottish textbooks as models. But the Scots had apparently ignored German. Smeaton's manual classified roots in three tables—Greek, Latin, and miscellaneous (including Saxon)—then traced their relations to both English and French.

> Take the word 'occurrence.' The teacher may ask such questions as the following. Of what parts is 'occurrence' composed? *(oc, curr ence)*. Whence are these derived? *(ob curro ens entis)*. What does 'ob' signify? Can you give any other examples of 'oc' having the same signification? (Such as *oc*casion, *oc*cult, *oc*cupy). What other forms does 'ob' take? *(of, op, os)*. Can you give an example of each? (Such as *of*fer, *op*pose, *os*tensible). What does 'ens entis' signify? . . . What does curro signify? Can you give other derivations from '*curro*' (such as current, currency, curricle, coureur, recur, incursion. . . . Such derivations as 'corsair' and 'vancourier' should be omitted till the pupil is familiar with the preceding). What then is the literal meaning of 'occurrence?' Can you mention any other root of a similar meaning with 'curro?' (such as *loopen*, to run). Give examples of it; (such as e*lope*, e*lope*ment, inter*loper*). Can you give any other root still? (if the pupil has learned so far as *dremo*, to run). And examples from it; (such as *drome*dary, hippo*drome*, palin*drome*, dia*drome*).[4]

This was vocabulary building with a vengeance! Almost as an afterthought, Smeaton added that "besides the literal meaning of these examples, the pupil should be called on to give their common acceptation." It did occur to him that all this might be more than some pupils wanted, so he dropped the French examples from his abridged version, *An Etymological Manual of the English Language; Comprising the Principal Latin, Greek and Saxon Roots* (1843). But it sold no better than its parent. Smeaton had to wait thirty years before once again entering the educational lists with *A New System of English Etymology* (1876).

Far more popular was James Napoleon McElligott's *Manual, Analytical and Synthetical, of Orthography and Definition* (New York, 1845). It enjoyed a second edition in the year of its issue, two more the following year, and several more before the Civil War. McElligott anticipated that calamity by conducting a barely civil war of his own with Salem Town. Like Town, McElligott had immediately followed up his initial success with a simpler speller, *The Young Analyzer* (New York, 1846). Town charged to the defense of his market share with charges of plagiarism. McElligott responded with *The "Analysis" Analyzed: or, Ten Points of Difference between McElligott's Analytical Manual and Town's Analysis* (New York, 1847). After Town and

McElligott had exhaustively analyzed each other's analyses, the latter was elected president of the New York Teachers Association in 1849. Reputation apparently unimpaired, McElligott became editor of the *Teacher's Advocate*. He turned his rhetorical energies from debate with Town to the larger problem that had inspired Town's *Analysis*: the plight of the would-be orator without classical training. McElligott drew fruitfully upon his experience as principal of the School of Mechanics and Tradesmen in New York. His *American Debater* (New York, 1855) became his most successful textbook. Whereas sales of the correspondential *Manual* tapered off with the Civil War, demand for the *American Debater* scarcely abated. His antagonist Town died shortly before the end of the war, and McElligott did not long survive it. But both belligerents went to their graves happily degreed as Doctors of Laws.

"As the standard of education in our country has advanced," enthused James Lynd, "increased attention has been paid to the study of the etymology of language." Several manuals had recently been published, he noted, but somehow none satisfied this professor of belles-lettres in Delaware College. He issued his own *Class-Book of Etymology, Designed to Promote Precision in the Use . . . of the English Language* (1847; Philadelphia: Biddle, 1848). His introduction sketched the origin and growth of language with copious etymological examples. Lynd doubted that language was the direct gift of God, but he found no difficulty believing that all languages spoken descend from one common parent. "What this original language was, or the order in which others are derived for it, we are unable to ascertain" (p. 9). Still his *Class-Book* aimed to help people make intelligent guesses. Part One expounded the prefixes and suffixes while Part Two dealt with classical roots and a few French words. Lynd especially prided himself that "the THIRD PART, containing a copious list of words of Gothic origin, is a new feature in school text-books on Etymology" (p. 3).

Those not ready for such challenges were catered to separately with a *First Book of Etymology, Designed . . . for Beginners* (1847; Philadelphia: Biddle, 1848). Like Town's and McElligott's feeder primers, this was an abridged version intended to serve as a bridge to the larger text and to Oswald's *Etymological Dictionary*, which Lynd edited for Biddle. Because its format was seductively abbreviated, timid beginners might be cajoled into mastering just a few inviting polysyllables like "abbreviate—*brev-is*, short" (p. 49). Despite his fruitful labors in the etymological vineyard, he never acceded to the dignity of an LL.D. like McElligott, but James Lynd, A.M., had the more solid satisfaction of outselling that be-laureled rival. By the Civil War one hundred thousand copies of his two textbooks were in circulation. "The value of such aids to an accurate knowledge of the English language can hardly be overestimated," wrote one supporter. "If our public speakers, and newspaper and other editors, would master their contents, we should have fewer offenses against philological propriety."⁵ Biddle recruited Joseph Thomas to produce a further simplified version of the *First Book* by revising it so that "where the *etymological* or *literal* differs from the *proper* or *usually accepted* meaning of the English derivative, such difference is explained. The great value of this feature will be fully appreciated by every competent instructor" (1854 ed., p. 2). Doubtless every incompetent instructor appreciated it even more.

McElligott eventually countered Thomas's simplified version of Lynd's *First Book* by sanctioning Charles W. Sanders's *Analysis of English Words* (New York: Ivison and Phinney, 1859), a further simplification of his own simplified texts. Sanders felt that neither teachers nor pupils had to know any language but English to enjoy the benefits of etymological analysis. He deplored "the strangely forbidding aspect which the process is made to assume in most of the books prepared expressly to teach it." Gothic roots he dismissed as conjectural and irrelevant. Touting his book's simplicity, Sanders made a virtue of necessity by palliating the linguistic ignorance of many teachers using it. Desire to offer a potted classical education dwindled markedly in his manual. He merely aimed to provide scientific help in dealing with Greco-Roman derivatives, "the most difficult words in the language." Essentially, he was peddling etymological simplification to simpletons. As "a decided *improvement*, to Sanders American Educational Series," the book kept McElligott in contention with Lynd by going through seven editions in the 1860s (pp. iii–iv).

Native Roots—Walt Whitman and America's Anglo-Saxon Zealots

Though Sanders happily ignored the Teutonic heritage, Lynd hardly stressed Gothic etymology enough to satisfy some. Germanic roots were generally treated like poor relations of their more esteemed classical kin. With *Elements of English Grammar* (London, 1842) the Dorsetshire poet and clergyman William Barnes began a dogged campaign "to keep up the purity of the Saxon English language" while explaining etymology.⁶ Barnes's efforts culminated in his *Outline of English Speech-craft* (1878), but well before that a parallel movement was active across the Atlantic. Thoreau registered its early stirrings at Harvard. Thomas Jefferson and

Noah Webster had linked the Anglo-Saxon language with free political institutions. This theme was developed with mildly racist relish by the versatile Vermonter George Perkins Marsh, politico, environmentalist, Transcendental sympathizer, and pioneering Scandinavian scholar. His tract *The Goths in New England* (1843) portrayed virtuous Teutonic pilgrims boarding the *Mayflower* for religious freedom, then battling "Roman" redcoats at Bunker Hill. Emerson not only made much of Saxon virtues in *English Traits* (1856) but found "abundant points of resemblance between the Germans of the Hercynian forest and our *Hoosiers*, *Suckers*, and *Badgers* of the American woods" (*W*, 5:48).

By 1850 there was a burgeoning educational market for texts in the field. A Saxonist zealot like the principal of Philadelphia's Central High School made three and a half years of Anglo-Saxon *compulsory* there between 1850 and 1854, even before regular courses in the subject penetrated college curricula. Among the lesser monuments of this movement are several textbooks published by a group calling itself A Literary Association. The preface to one features an imaginary dialogue dated Saturday afternoon, 14 January 1853, when "a practical teacher" calls upon a member of A Literary Association:

> Teacher: I have seen your Hand-Book of Anglo-Saxon Orthography and am much pleased with it. You have another Hand-Book?
>
> Member: Two, sir. . . . In these books the child is led over the whole domain of the English language. He follows its *historical growth* from the half-formed words, pa and ma, to the awful names of God and eternal things.
>
> Teacher: The growth of language! Sir, has language a growth?
>
> Member: An instructive and beautiful one. It is the body of thought, and, like our own bodies, grows into an organic whole. Every word is a member, and increases with the increase of every part. . . .
>
> Teacher: Allow me, Sir, to return to the Hand-Books? What do you propose to do in your first one?
>
> Member: To teach the Anglo-Saxon root-words. We begin with the *childhood* of the language. It becomes the young mind. What do we want with derivative words till we have learned their roots?[7]

By excluding foreign frippery to focus on essentials, this *Hand-Book of Anglo-Saxon Root-Words* aimed to meet the needs of children about eight years of age.

Echoing the common misconception encouraged by Bopp, the book solemnly explains that English has for "its native home . . . the far-famed India" (p. x). Anglo-Saxon is its basic stock, with Gothic, Celtic, French, Italian, and Greek merely engraftings. To Anglo-Saxon we owe not only our grammar but our words for home, heart, and early life, our sensible and practical vocabulary. It is thus preeminently suitable for instructing the young, for whom "speech breaks up the silence of the heart" so that "we think and feel aloud" (p. 14). Neither Latin nor Norman French should clutter the tyro's mind, for the former is too abstract while "the French portion of our language is associated with wrong and oppression." By tapping the wellsprings of pure Anglo-Saxon for domestic intercourse American teachers would perform not only their patriotic duty but an act of filial piety: "Our old mother-tongue has endured two captivities: one under the Norman French, the other under the Latin and Greek. From the former, it was delivered under the reign of a king; from the latter, it is about to return under a president."[8] Far from seeing this method of English study as Anglophil-iac, A Literary Association boldly titles it "The American System of Education" and presents it as the natural republican outgrowth of the freedom-loving British stock.

One thousand words of Anglo-Saxon origin are grouped topically because the child learns more from models than from words. First studied is HOME, "the dearest spot on earth. The heart turns to it, wherever we may be." Nineteenth-century domestic piety is relentlessly inculcated, in a way that might have startled the roving Anglo-Saxons who coined the words while migrating across Europe to England:

> HOME, a cover; the place where one lives. *Teacher.*—Is *home* a dear place? *Child.*—Home is a dear place.
> STEAD, a stand; room or place. *Teacher.*—Shall I answer in your *stead*. *Child.* You may answer in my stead.
> HOMESTEAD, the place of home; one's abode. *Teacher.*—Do you like the old *homestead*? *Child.*—I do like the old homestead.
>
> (*Hand-Book of Anglo-Saxon Root-Words*, p. 36)

The sentimental morality is buttressed with quotations from poems like Samuel Woodworth's "The Old Oaken Bucket." But in finding Anglo-Saxon names for dwellings ranging from wigwams to palaces a discriminating taste is also cultivated. "Are cottages pretty?" invites an affirmative answer, but a certain consternation underlies the question, "Do poor people live in cots?"—that is, in "something cut off for a cover; a very small, rude house." Asked, "Have the Irish *huts*?" the child is left in little doubt that a hut is "a small cover; a small poor place to live in"—even if situated beside Walden Pond (p. 41). *Outhouses*, however, "are a very useful kind of buildings. They belong to every fine home in the country" (p. 40). Barns, sheds, cribs, and stalls are carefully described in accordance with the dictum that "no word should be allowed to find its way into the mind without a knowledge of its use" (p. 28). Except possibly for the admonition that "neat outhouses adorn a place," one important function of the generic term is discreetly ignored. Sentimental nostalgia tinges the question, "Is the *outhouse* old?" (pp. 40–41). Oddly enough, the *Hand-Book*'s domestic piety focuses less on the hearth than on the old oaken outhouse that stood near the well.

Of course, buildings alone do not make a home. "Furniture is also needed." But that term is French in origin. So the pupil is marched through a catalog of "household-stuff," where the solid Saxon *stand* doughtily does duty for the Latinate *table*. *Crock, pan,* and *dish* are enumerated, but this household contains no *pot*. Whether aesthetic or philological scruple excluded it is hard to say because the word does appear late in Old English but may be borrowed from Celtic or late Latin forms. Or it may simply have been discarded in accordance with the Thoreauvian definition of stuff as "that which fills; household articles. Shall we keep useless *stuff*?" (pp. 43–44).

Ultimately, "the house, food, clothing and furniture, are all little or nothing compared with man" (p. 4). Chattels should always suggest a family, so the *Hand-Book* warmly proceeds to the "many dear names in the household—names of love" (p. 45). Its exposition of kindred terminology is often dubious or downright wrong. A *wife* is probably not "one who weaves" nor a *father* "one who feeds," and a *son* is certainly not "a light." But a *bairn* is indeed one "born" ("is the *bairn* good?"). Good bairns who conned this book were expected to decompose nineteenth-century America into elemental processes. Learning that *milk* is "what is got by stroking" while "what is made by striking" is *butter* left the pupil with a provocative half-truth. Despite appearances, battered cream does not produce butter, at least etymologically speaking, but the Indo-European root for *to milk* does also mean *to rub*. Such meditation bridged the increasing gap between urban students and the agrarian realities their parents had known. Revealingly, the *Hand-Book*'s discussion of food is preceded by a section on hired help, perhaps even more fundamental to this home. "Servants form a very useful class of men and women," the pupil is assured (p. 46). Anglo-Saxon terms for fifteen different servants are enumerated, ranging from cook, house-maid, washer-woman, and hireling to teamster, ploughman, footman, and steward. (By contrast, ten terms suffice to itemize Anglo-Saxon food). Though the loyalty of a henchman is praised, one senses that some pupils might be more familiar with the services of a butler. But since that functionary derives his title from late Latin, the temperance of this modern Saxon household is not violated by any uncorking of bottles.

After household members the *Hand-Book* inventories bodily parts, the soul, business, human tools and works, the works of the Creator, place, time, and finally God. The same panoramic progression is repeated in cataloging adjectives and verbs for elemental qualities and actions. The movement of the book is insistently from Home to Higher Things. Each of the three sections concludes with a grand Christian view of the universe grounded presumably in the concrete details of language. Thus the 156th Lesson, "Events of God," happily follows Tooke in explaining that Heaven means "lifted up" (i.e., heaved), then supplements this with other vital cosmological definitions, all presented as etymologically self-evident: "EARTH, dust . . . SUN, the shiner . . . MOON, what directs . . . STAR, what steers . . . WORLD, round . . . MAN, strong . . . GOSPEL, good-speaking . . . PEACE, pressed down" (p. 140).

Except for the derivation of *Gospel*, this is a riot of pious misinformation. *Dust*, for example, has no linguistic connection with *earth* but is cognate with *fume*, *dew*, and *cloud*. The *stars* do not steer but *stand*; the *moon* does not direct but *measures*. *Man* is a primitive term unconnected with the Indo-European root *magh-* denoting power; likewise, the Indo-European roots for *sun* and *shine* are independent. Obviously the Anglo-Saxons did not anticipate Columbus in surmising the *world* was *round*. One might have imagined that much even if ignorant of the word's genuine derivation from the anthropocentric concept *wer-ald*, age of man, but fancies about the world as *whirled* apparently prevailed here. *Peace* does not require the religious suppression of evil but originates from a human (albeit Latinate) *pact*. "Is Christ our *daysman*?" the pupil is asked ("Daysman, the strength of day; one who unites parties, as sinful man and offended God"). Such relentlessly elemental catechism gave students the heady sense of discovering all the eternal verities whereas in point of fact their mentors were free-associating in a linguistic daze. "I have never seen boys more interested in any intellectual pursuit," claimed one teacher using the *Hand-Book* for a class of intermediate readers. "The enthusiasm actually became contagious, boys begging to be admitted into the class, in addition to their other studies." Since among other exotica they learned that "the slaves who waited at the shrine of the mother of the earth, were drowned in the secret lake," A Literary Association's handbooks may well have given Ned Buntline's a run for the money (*Derivatives*, pref., n.p., and p. 92).

The ambition to lift the youthful mind to higher things bred a distinctive version of Humboldtian doctrine. The *Hand-Book* was committed to the belief that God "taught man at first, some words and their combinations, and so fitted the body and world to the soul, and the soul to them, as to make the after-growth of words a part of our life." But the determination to ground language in spirit as did Humboldt was balanced by considerable attention to the physical basis of speech. Indeed, the third part of the *Hand-Book* recategorized all its words under bodily parts or physical stimuli to emphasize the sensory roots of words in Lockean terms. Thus it was prudent to insist that "the body and the world could not produce a single word . . . without the soul and God. Words are . . . thoughts, and require mind in their production." Since speech springs from the soul, "the organ of speech and the body can only be regarded as the verbal instrument from which it awakens sound" (*Derivatives*, p. 268). Words and the body were both objectified in instrumental terms. "The word, *organ*, is the same as an instrument, or a tool. The hand is an organ: so is the eye." Likewise words are "the weapons or tools of the mind" (pp. 27–28). The resulting view of language manages to be both consciously organic and thoroughly mechanical: the biological impulse toward speech is identified with the mechanical procedure of writing. Encouraged to regard his talk, his tongue, and his pen as all tools in an intellectual kit, the student was on his way to becoming a linguistic technician. Like Thoreau, he might also become conscious "of a part of me, which, as it were, is not a part of me" (*Walden*, p. 135).

The *Hand-Book of Anglo-Saxon Derivatives* (1853) enumerated sixty-seven native English terminations, prefixes and suffixes to expand the basic vocabulary of one thousand terms in the *Hand-Book of Root-Words* until it embraced "some five thousand of the choicest Anglo-Saxon words, and their meanings" (p. v). So fortified against undue foreign influence, the student was then ready for a manual of Gothic, Celtic, French, and Classic elements—the *Hand-Book of the Engrafted Words of the English Language*. A Literary Association was not for Saxon purists like Barnes. Its members recognized the contribution of other languages to modern English and had no real desire to remodel it, since its composite nature especially suited it to "the Great American Nation, *Unum e Pluribus*" (p. iv). They just wished to anatomize the English language in a manner that would highlight its Saxon bone and muscle and give those priority in etymological study. The books fostered not simple ancestral piety but enlightened shock at the poverty and brutality of Anglo-Saxon culture, as one surviving student essay reprinted for publicity purposes makes clear. Naively racist hero-worship was not the aim of texts that gravely described how "the early Saxons were without outhouses" (*Derivatives*, p. 82). Before the Civil War WASP piety lacked the strong biological basis that Darwinism would later lend it. These Saxonists were less promoters of invidious racial distinctions than cheerful boosters—and not uncritical ones—of a national character that they believed quite capable of assimilating foreign elements without imperiling its cultural identity.

One may question whether the *Hand-Book* "unfolds in a natural manner the Anglo-Saxon part of our language." It is not so easy to refute A Literary Association's claim that its textbook "makes our boys *thinkers*" (*Derivatives*, pref.). That was the explicit aim of *First Thoughts; or, Beginning to Think* (1853), another of its textbooks. Also published were *A Hand-book of English Orthography* (1853), *Outlines of English Grammar. On the Basis of the Anglo-Saxon* (1853), *The Sentential Reader* (1853), and *The Verbal Reader* (1853). After prospering with other publishers as the American System of Education, these eight textbooks were acquired by D. Appleton and Company in 1854. They were reprinted at least until 1857. Their influence was probably strongest in the New York area, where A Literary Association was based. The Reverend James Scott, D.D., a moving spirit in the group, shares with John Liddell Chapman the copyright for early volumes. He was pastor of the First Reformed Dutch Church in Newark, New Jersey. His chief contribution to Gotham's literary life appeared posthumously as *The Guardian Angel: A Poem in Three Books* (1859). But A Literary Association's influence extended beyond the Middle Atlantic states. Under the banner of the American Party, Know-Nothing political power reached its zenith in 1854. The books may have appealed to nativist sentiment at large more than the outright study of foreign languages. Two of the four editions of the *Hand-Book of Anglo-Saxon Orthography* were issued by a Massachusetts firm. Newspaper publicity claiming that the series was attracting favorable attention in England is unreliable. But during 1853 Scott's campaign to have the Brooklyn Board of Education adopt the texts attracted very favorable attention from an American newspaperman who harbored inchoate ambitions as a poet. Whether or not the Brooklyn school board adopted the books, Walt Whitman certainly did.

Borrowing directly from the *Hand-Book of Engrafted Words,* he was also influenced by the *Hand-Book of Anglo-Saxon Root-Words.* The only surviving manuscript page of the first edition of *Leaves of Grass* bears on its verso a list of ninety-one words copied from the former. Each word is followed with the abbreviation g, f, l, or c, carefully specifying its origin as either Gothic, French, Latin, or Celtic. This was evidently a worksheet for "Song of the Broad-Axe," which first appeared in the 1856 edition of *Leaves of Grass*, employing several words on the list. But the first edition of 1855 had already embodied A Literary Association's doctrine in poetic form. Its textbooks emphasize that the child learns nouns from the names of familiar things, then converts these primary words into adjectives and verbs and applies them to the world at large: "The child picks up whole words as he picks up whole flowers. He picks them up in connection with things. He goes forth and *names* whatever he sees and feels" (*Root-Words*, p. vi). The series stresses this notion of the learning process with the key phrase "child goes forth." Thus from words for home "the child goes forth to the wide world" (*Engrafted Words*, p. 114).

Whitman's "There Was a Child Went Forth," with its incantatory description of a boy exploring Eden, might seem a poetic primitive's evocation of his Long Island childhood. But it is actually a rhapsody about A Literary Association's linguistic epistemology:

> There was a child went forth every day,
> And the first object he looked upon and received with wonder or pity or
>   love or dread, that object he became,
> And that object became part of him for the day or a certain part of the
>   day . . . or for many years or stretching cycles of years.
>   (*LG*, Variorum ed., 3:149-52)

The poem catalogs the homely household details that the child encounters, from objects to rural flowers and animals to parents and other people to a panorama that finally embraces the distant city and sky. The child incorporates his world imaginatively by acquiring a vocabulary for it from "the mother with mild words. . . . / The father, strong . . . mean, angered, unjust, / The blow, the quick loud word . . . / The family usages, the language, the company, the furniture." In the first edition the conclusion strongly emphasized that what is described is learning language: "These became part of that child who went forth every day, and who now goes and will always go forth every day, / And these become of him or her that peruses them now." Later dropped, Whitman's original last line stressed that the reader too enters the child's imagination through homely domestic words that embody it with peculiar poetic force. A Literary Association's approach suggested a magical power in its primitive English words: "I speak, for instance, the word, *rose*, and it is a sign to you of what I mean. You *see* and *smell* that sweet flower" (*Root-Words*, p. 1). By the end of the poem Whitman's child-author is like a graduate of the American System of Education, who at the end of the course "finds the 'kindred points of heaven and home' united in his language" (*Engrafted Words*, p. 114). Indeed, Whitman's essay on language "America's Mightiest Inheritance" (1856) applauds philologists and reformers who advocate improved textbooks for elementary schooling like those of A Literary Association. The Saxonist theorizing of the American Renaissance was one inspiration for his novel poetic.

The Scholar's Companion (1836) Becomes the Businessman's Friend

The most popular manual of the period was American only by adoption and naturalization: Richard W. Green's *The Scholar's Companion; or, A Guide to the Orthography, Pronunciation, and Derivation of the English Language . . . Arranged on the Basis of the 15th London ed. of Butter's Etymological Expositor* (Philadelphia: H. Perkins, 1836). Henry Butter was an English Swedenborgian whose taste for occult correspondences led him to publish an *Etymological Spelling Book and Expositor; Containing above 3500 Words Deduced from Their Greek and Latin Roots* (London, 1830). It long dominated the British market, claiming its 353d edition in 1874. Green's adaptation for the American market was almost as successful. Within a year of publication *The Scholar's Companion* had run through seven editions. It became the standard text in its field, probably outselling all its rivals put together. But the competition from Salem Town and his cohorts was keen enough so that eventually the publishers entrusted it to Rufus W. Bailey for revision. Understandably enough, he declined to alter it radically. As he explained in the preface to his revision of 1854, with more than a hundred editions totaling half a million copies it did not need any endorsement. Extensive overhaul "would render the new edition unfit to be used with those already in extensive use in the schools." Bailey's concern with compatibility suggests that the audience for textbooks far exceeded the number of copies in circulation, since many were apparently reused yearly by school boards who did not want to see their investment rendered obsolete. With sales steadily increasing, very minor revisions were "all the Publishers deem necessary to meet the wishes of its numerous patrons" (n.p.).

Eschewing the newfangled taste for Gothic roots, the *Scholar's Companion* fed pupils choice Greco-Roman esculents, in the conviction that language "is not only the instrument but the nutriment of thought." It gestured toward the Teutonic heritage in chapter 3, "Equivocal Words," by explaining that because of the various sources of English, two words of entirely different origin and meaning were often spelled and pronounced alike. The multiple meanings of *bark* were correctly traced to its various ancestors: Anglo-Saxon *beorcan*, a dog's bark; French *barque*, a boat; and Danish *bark*, rind of a tree. But such tidbits only spiced the book's main rationale: to offset the average student's lack of classical learning. To that end 120 pages were given over to a dictionary of Latin words and their derivatives, while another 30 pages surveyed Greek derivatives. The virtues of a classical education were extolled, while exercises allowed those confined to English to learn the root meanings of its words. Bailey was wise not to let the quest for greater philological sophistication detract from this basically snobbish formula for success. With his modest revisions the book continued to triumph over superior competition.

Walden appeared in the same year as this revised best-seller—and *Walden* also sought an audience of poor scholars. Whereas Bailey catered to them, Thoreau challenged them. But *Walden* cannot be fully understood except as the chief literary monument of the etymological fervor that permeated the American Renaissance. The sudden popularity of elementary manuals is only the most obvious sign of how midcentury America sought salvation in etymology. Educators catered to this need with other books too. Students who survived basic training could proceed to advanced critical work in an anthology like *The Etymological Reader* (Philadelphia: Butler, 1872), in which Epes Sargent and Amasa May supplied two hundred brief passages of prose and verse glossed in the conviction that "our noblest authors . . . employ words with a view to their etymological meaning." Ferreting it out would provide "a new zest to the reading lesson" (pp. 5-6). Webster tried to use *The Teacher* to sell his dictionary. Likewise, Lynd's manual was calculated to kite sales of John Oswald's *Etymological Dictionary of the English Language,* another staple on his publisher's list. Originally published in Edinburgh in 1833, it was gussied up for the American market by J. M. Keagy in 1836, "especially adapted to the purpose of teaching English composition in schools and academies." Lynd and Joseph Thomas, M.D., further expanded it, and Thoreau acquired a copy of this work. By the Civil War ten editions were satisfying public curiosity for information about English suffixes like this:

> ACIOUS, (Latin-ax) . . . signifies *much; very* or *greatly; accustomed to* or *greatly addicted to; strongly:* as, au *dacious,* daring *much, very* daring; vera cious, *accustomed* to telling the truth, truthful; menda *cious,* lying *much,* greatly addicted to lying; tena *cious,* holding strongly or *firmly,* holding fast to. . . . This termination in Latin may be considered as an intensive form of the present active participle. Thus *audax* seems to be equivalent to *audens multum,* "daring greatly;" *tenax,* to *tenens firmiter* &c. &c. (s.v.)

A Thoreau pencil checked this passage in his copy of the 1844 edition. His journal entry for 2 September 1851 records the results of his browsing:

> Old Cato says well, "*Patremfamilias vendacem, non emacem, esse opportet.*" These Latin terminations express better than any English that I know the greediness, as it were, and tenacity of purpose with which the husbandman and householder is required to be a seller and not a buyer,—with mastiff-like tenacity,—these *lipped* words, which, like the lips of moose and browsing creatures, gather in the herbage and twigs with a certain greed. This termination *cious* adds force to a word, like the lips of browsing creatures, which greedily collect what the jaw holds; as in the word "tenacious" the first half represents the kind of jaw which holds, the last the lips which collect. It can only be pronounced by a certain opening and protruding of the lips; so "avaricious." These words express the sense of their simple roots with the addition, as it were, of a certain lip greediness. Hence "capacious" and "capacity," "emacity." When these expressive words are used, the hearer gets something to chew upon. . . . The audacious man not only dares, but he greedily collects more danger to dare. The avaricious man not only desires and satisfies his desire, but he collects ever new browse in anticipation of his ever-springing desires. What is *luscious* is especially enjoyed by the lips. The mastiff-mouthed are tenacious. To be a seller with mastiff-mouthed tenacity of purpose, with moose-lipped greediness,—ability to browse! (W, 8:442–43)

How eagerly Thoreau accepted Oswald's offhand invitation, expressed in ampersands, to speculate further about Latin and English words in *-ax*, *-acious*! An uneasy fascination with eating suffuses the passage. Despite his overt rejection of the greedy morality of buying and selling, Thoreau seems to empathize with it strikingly. And well he should, for he was greedily browsing on what American publishers were selling, in the hope that they would buy his own work-in-progress. Resembling the moose he describes, Thoreau meandered through lexicons, munching etymologies like some great verbivorous animal. Seldom has an author's lip-smacking relish for words been more vividly if ambiguously rendered.

Though midcentury Americans happily appropriated this standard etymological dictionary from Britain, they were not dependent upon it. More than a decade before Oswald, the American William Grimshaw had produced what he claimed (wrongly) was the first etymological dictionary of English. It was first published in Philadelphia in 1821, and two later editions expanded its modest stock of words from six to seven thousand. Conceived before the educational heyday of etymology, it was designed not as a school text but as a reference work for professional men and literati. To spur buyers, Grimshaw raised the grim specter of solecism:

> There is little likelihood (though there is some,) of mistaking the true significance of our *vernacular* dialect,—the Anglo-Saxon. But this cannot be said of the modern portion of our language. Not having been required in youth, it has been neglected; and we are hurried from a society who speak the other, into a maturer and more refined, whose discussion is in a great measure unintelligible to us. We know not which is the literal, which the figurative import of a word; how far the former may be extended,— within what bounds the latter should be confined. We have derived our knowledge from those who were either not competent, or not willing to instruct; who have misled us through ignorance, or deceived us through design. We resemble a vessel without a pilot, which is subject to the variable direction of her crew, and in tracing the windings of the channel, is wrecked upon its banks.[9]

For eighty-four cents merchants might purchase the linguistic equivalent of marine insurance, since "the best verbal pilot is etymology."

With his vision of a vast pedagogical conspiracy deceiving innocent pupils by design, Grimshaw appealed to free-floating grammatical paranoia in the populace at large. Were many professional men haunted by the sinister possibility that their lack of a classical education could be embarrassingly exposed? By uprooting people from stable small towns like Concord, increasing mobility and urbanization made it possible for many to pose as what they were not—or at least to dream of doing so. The supreme literary poseur was Poe, who ransacked thesauruses to eke out the classical background expected of a Virginia gentleman. Similar forces helped account for the American vogue of phrenology, which offered deracinated countrymen crowding cities a way of safely typing anonymous strangers by the bumps on their heads. Grimshaw's dictionary promised to smooth out the revealing etymological bumps in one's vocabulary by showing how English words were derived from Greek, Latin, and French. Though he claimed that Anglo-Saxon roots were less likely to cause mistakes, his argument really implied that they were unlikely to cause embarrassing mistakes, since fewer people were capable of detecting them.

Grimshaw actually omitted Anglo-Saxon etymology not because he felt it irrelevant but because he felt himself inadequate. With touching humility, he avowed the supreme authority of Horne Tooke. Had Tooke's plan embraced derivatives from the learned languages, "no occasion had offered for so inferior a philologist, as the author of the present work, to undertake this task" (p. viii). Genuflecting toward his revered predecessor, his *Etymological Dictionary* presented itself on a smaller scale as a classical *Diversions of Philadelphia*. Confessing his philological inferiority complex like this was not calculated to hurt sales but rather to attract an adult audience who shared it.

Other American lexicographers catered to the need for linguistic security. Daniel J. Browne compiled *The Etymological Encyclopedia of Technical Terms and Phrases Used in the Arts and Sciences and of Many Words in Common Use, with Popular Quotations From Foreign Languages and their Translators* (Boston: Hyde, 1832). Whereas Grimshaw aimed at professional men and merchants, Browne supplied the etymological needs of farmers and artisans. The five thousand terms in his encyclopedia include a goodly medley of foreign phrases. His derivations of English words occasionally ranged beyond Indo-European roots: "Abbot, s. [Syr. *abba,* father]. The chief of a convent or fellowship of canons" (s.v.). But most of his derivations were from Greek and Latin, as befitted his emphasis on our scientific and technical vocabulary. This civil engineer later traveled widely, then edited the paper the *American Agriculturalist* while writing treatises on trees and poultry. His literary career culminated with *The American Muck Book* (1851), which led to an appointment in the Patent Office. That terminated unhappily eight years later amid charges of scandal, but obviously the author knew what to expect when he set out to clean up the mess in Washington.

Treasuries of Words—From Roget to John Williams of Lancaster, Ohio

So vigorous was American demand for such books that English works often sold better here than at home. George Frederick Graham's *English Synonyms Classified and Explained* (London, 1846) saw its second British edition in 1853. But by then the American version of the text, which Henry Reed, LL.D., had edited (i.e., pirated) with lightning speed in the same year as the London original, had gone through seven editions and was to go through nearly twenty more. Of all the major Victorian writers Carlyle was the most addicted to etymological speculation as a stylistic mannerism. It is perhaps no accident that his prose found zealous admirers in America before his British reputation was firmly established.

Thus when Peter Mark Roget published his *Thesaurus of English Words and Phrases* (London, 1852), three publishers brought out different American editions within the next two years. The most popular was augmented by Barnas Sears, who had succeeded Horace Mann as secretary of the Massachusetts Board of Education. When Thoreau included a Roget in the catalog of his library, it was probably that edition.[10]

Roget's *Thesaurus* is a book that is widely used and widely abused. It has gone through so many editions and revisions that most people are unfamiliar with the aims Roget set forth in his original preface. Cofounder of the Society for the Diffusion of Useful Knowledge and for many years secretary to the Royal Society, Roget was a polymath with a subsidiary interest in language. This British physician wrote numerous books on physical science, authored one of the Bridgewater treatises on natural religion, invented a new kind of slide rule, and wiled away his leisure hours composing and publishing chess problems. He had in mind a grander goal than a memory-jogger to help harried authors find synonyms. Since language is the medium of thought as well as communication, reviewing a catalog of analogous words would suggest "other trains of thought, which, presenting the subject under new and varied aspects, will vastly expand the sphere of our mental vision. Some striking similitude or appropriate image, some excursive flight or brilliant conception, may flash on the mind."[11] The *Thesaurus* was actually to be used as a dictionary of intellectual analogies and antithetically correlated concepts. The heart of the book is its taxonomy of ideas, for which science was his professed model: "The sectional divisions I have formed, correspond to Natural Families in Botany and Zoology, and the filiation of words presents a network analogous to the natural filiation of plants and animals" (p. xxviii).

He was emulating those rationalist philosophers who wished to map the totality of concepts available to the human mind. His original thesaurus enumerated exactly one thousand categories, as if both mind and universe were governed by Pythagorean harmonies. He linked his work to Enlightenment speculation about a universal language. Except for the *Amera Cosha*, translated by Henry Colebrooke as *Vocabulary of the Sanskrit Language* (1808), the only predecessors he acknowledged were Bishop Wilkins's *Essay towards a Real Character and a Philosophical Language* (1668) and the anonymous French *Pasigraphie* (1797). His preface invoked that tradition to aim his thesaurus at "metaphysicians" investigating the philosophy of language by analyzing the ideas underlying our words:

> Such analyses alone can determine the principles on which a strictly *Philosophical Language* might be constructed. The probable result of the construction of such a language would be its eventual adoption by every civilized nation; thus realizing that splendid aspiration of philanthropists,—the establishment of a Universal Language. However utopian such a project may appear to the present generation . . . its accomplishment is surely not beset with greater difficulties than have impeded the progress to many other beneficial objects, which . . . yet were successfully achieved by the continued and persevering exertions of the human intellect. . . . Some new and bolder effort of genius towards the solution of this great problem may be crowned with success. . . . Nothing, indeed, would conduce more directly to bring about a golden age of union and harmony among the several nations and races of mankind. (pp. xxviii–xxix)

Was this universal language to be invented or recovered? As the first installment of this project, his taxonomy of words professed "no concern with their etymologies, or with the history of their transformations" (p. xxiii). Yet Roget approached science as Natural *History*. His preface features etymological analysis in Trench's vein and looks forward to an English dictionary on historical principles. Indeed, he anticipates a historical version of his thesaurus. Such works in other languages would then yield "a *Polyglot Lexicon* constructed on this system" (p. xxviii). As the ultimate fruition of his taxonomy Roget envisioned a multilingual dictionary of ideas with historical evidence, which resembled the Philosophical Dictionary that Gérando had dreamed of half a century earlier.

Unfortunately (from Roget's point of view), the allure of a universal language was dissipated by trends in Victorian philosophy and philology. Indo-European studies largely renounced their claim to privileged investigation of ideas. With the decline of etymological metaphysics such lexicons seemed unlikely to yield conceptual insight proportionate to the effort involved. A more copious index was added by Roget's son, so that those who consult the book for synonyms can now locate words without paying any attention to its underlying intellectual structure: the six main categories embracing the knowable under the headings of Abstract Relations, Space, Matter, Intellect, Volition, and Affections.

Roget ignored one predecessor, David Booth. Whereas Roget's taxonomy began with Abstract Relations as befitted a closet rationalist of French extraction, Booth was staunchly English with an empirical scheme for organizing the roots of language:

> Pleasure and pain, apparently the result of the impressions of outward objects, must lead him more generally to attend to the organs of his body, by which those impressions are received; and, therefore, we shall not be accused of an unnatural arrangement, if we begin our definitions with an account of the human race.
>
> The word MAN . . . is common to all the Gothic dialects.[12]

Beginning with kinship terms, Booth's anthropologically oriented synonymy never surveyed the whole English vocabulary though he labored on it for thirty years. In 1806 he published the first half of his project as an independent volume. Its yeasty etymological ferment gained it a second edition, but ultimately the British public preferred Booth's *Art of Brewing*. That saw several editions superintended by the Society for the Diffusion of Useful Knowledge.

What Booth could not complete John Williams of Lancaster, Ohio, could. The intellectual luminary of that town had migrated to Ohio with his family in 1814, conning textbooks as a boy while camped beside a Conestoga wagon. Almost entirely self-educated, he taught himself Greek, Latin, French, German, and Spanish as well as higher mathematics from the library of a kindly Ohio doctor. He read law and acquired a medical degree in Cincinnati. But, head echoing with Homer and the orations of Cicero, he settled instead on teaching. After twenty years serving in backwoods Ohio academies, in 1851 he was named county superintendent of schools. Lancaster's historian revered him as a pure, honest Christian, an honor to the human race, with a mighty intellect comparable to Sir Isaac Newton's. But he held that post only five years, for "his usefulness was somewhat circumscribed from insufficient executive ability . . . and somewhat of awkwardness in manners and dress."[13] Freed from administrative duties, this unkempt polymath completed an ambitious, innovative synonymy that he styled *The Readable Dictionary* (1860). By including etymologies and definitions, the village Newton came closer than Roget or perhaps anyone previously to realizing Gérando's dream:

> The topical classification of words brings together the different terms derived from the same root. Now, the definition of a Latin or Greek root will frequently shed such light upon a number of English terms derived from this root, as to render it unnecessary to define the derivatives separately. . . . Another advantage of studying words in connection with their roots, is, that the connection often gives a force and beauty to the meaning of the derivatives, which would be entirely lost in any definition which disregarded this connection!
>
> Nearly all the Latin and Greek roots from which important English words have been derived will be found in the present work, the most of them occurring more than once. The study of this volume may therefore serve, in some degree, as a substitute for the study of the Greek and Latin languages.
>
> . . . .
>
> A common dictionary may be compared to a cabinet of minerals, in which the specimens are arranged according to their shape, size, or color, and not according their chemical nature. The object of the present undertaking is to sort the specimens, and to arrange them according to their natural affinities, assigning to the earths, the metallic ores, and the precious stones distinct compartments, and appropriating a separate shelf to each species.[14]

Williams's taxonomy was independent of both Booth's and Roget's. Beginning neither with abstractions nor with man, his categories inventory the physical universe, though he may have taken a hint from Booth in organizing it sensationally. But Genesis reverberates equally in the choice of his opening category—Light. From it the world unfolds in Lockean majesty: "Color, Heat, Sound, Sapors, Odors, Mechanical Properties of Matter, Mechanical Action Overcoming Cohesion, Mechanical Action Affecting Solid Bodies Otherwise than by Separating their Parts, Mechanical Properties of Liquids, of Water, Air, Gravitation, Form, Number, Magnitude, Quantity, Measure, Anatomy, Physiology, Disease, Civil Government, Warfare, Property, Commerce, Astronomy, Chemistry, Animals, Mankind, Spiritual Beings, Magic and Witchcraft, Mythology, Morals, Religion, Schools of Philosophy, the Mind, Will, Mental States, Language, Literary Schools . . . Agents, Make, Skill, Build, Take, Hold, Cover, Hide, Clothing, Beauty, Purity and Impurity." In 360 pages the American Adam was given a Cook's Etymological Tour of the universe revealed by the divine Fiat, before being brought back shamefacedly to recognize that he might still be naked in the garden.

"To BE is not susceptible of definition," Williams felt. Therefore, to explain that "*Being* is the state implied by the verb *to be*" was not to explain much. He did aver that the verb "is applied either to the accidents of things, or to the substances of things." Without Greek or Latin roots to rely on, he remained clear that "A *Being* is, 1. Any object that is. 2. An object that possesses an intellectual or spiritual nature. God, angels, and men are *beings*" (p. 297). There the matter rested. Etymology whirled Williams wider than Uranus flies, then let him down into the world again like Walt Whitman "to feel the puzzle of puzzles / And that we call Being" (*LG*, 56). Both Whitman and Williams found an American audience for their ecstatic cataloging of essences. Philologically the *Readable Dictionary* was outdated, but that hardly mattered to the public who bought up four editions. And with good reason. Williams was one of the more sensible etymological metaphysicians. His definitions were often rewarding, and his topical format was illuminating. A very readable dictionary it was, and it remains a readable dictionary today. There is nothing in print exactly like it.

Picking Flowers from Florilegia—Thoreau and the Etymological Entertainers

"True words are those, as Trench says,—transport, rapture, ravishment, ecstasy," Thoreau confided to his journal for 15 January 1853. He was referring to Archbishop Richard Chenevix Trench's *On the Study of Words* (1851; New York: Redfield, 1852). This etymological florilegium was even more popular here than in England, with two American publishers claiming some thirty editions by the Civil War. "Take three or four of these words," Trench had written. "'Transport,' that which *carries* us, as 'rapture,' or 'ravishment,' that which *snatches* us, out of and above ourselves; and 'ecstasy' is very nearly the same, only drawn from the Greek" (p. 19). Thoreau was certainly ravished by such concretely rooted abstractions. "These are the words I want," he exclaimed. "This is the effect of music. I am rapt away by it, out of myself. These are truly poetical words. I am inspired, elevated, expanded." And with a rapturous pun he profanely concludes, "I am on the mount."

The etymological ecstasy that prompted sermons on the mount from both Trench and Thoreau reflects Emersonian influence in each case, since Trench's *Study of Words* cites and develops the notion of language as "fossil poetry" set forth in "The Poet." But Thoreau cultivated it with a single-minded ardor that Emerson was incapable of, copying thirty of Trench's derivations into a notebook. He was particularly intrigued by Trench's claim that *rivals* are those who dwell on the opposite banks of the same stream. Four years earlier he had begun his first published book by explaining the etymology of "the Musketaquid, or Grass-ground River," to which English settlers in 1835 gave "the other but kindred name of CONCORD from the first plantation on its banks, which appears to have been commenced in a spirit of peace and harmony. It will be Grass-ground River as long as grass grows and water runs here; it will be Concord River only while men lead peaceable lives on its banks" (*A Week*, p. 5). Since Trench's derivation threatened his sense of riverside harmony, he immediately consulted his copy of Nathan Bailey's *Universal Etymological English Dictionary* (1721), where he found it corroborated. Finally, by playing around with words like *privilege* and *brawl* he harmonized his newfound knowledge with his earlier intuitions:

> Trench says that "'rivals,' in the primary sense of the word, are those who dwell . . . on opposite banks," but as he says . . . since the use of water-rights is a fruitful source of contention between such neighbors, the word has acquired this secondary sense. My friends are my *rivals* on the Concord, in the primary sense of the word. There is no strife between us respecting the use of the stream. The Concord offers many privileges, but none to quarrel about. It is a peaceful, not a brawling, stream. It has not made *rivals* out of neighbors *that lived on its banks*, but friends. My friends are my *rivals*; we dwell on opposite banks of the stream, but the stream is the Concord, which flows without a ripple or a murmur, without a rapid or a brawl, and offers no petty privileges to quarrel about. (16 Jan. 1853)

But all this speculation about riverside neighborliness suggests that Trench's derivation touched a nerve. "Here I have been on what the world would call friendly terms with one fourteen years," Thoreau had journalized, "and yet our hate is stronger than our love. Why are we related—yet thus unsatisfactorily. We are almost a sore to one another" (10 Oct. 1851). Thoreau's relations with Emerson cooled as the younger man struggled to find his own voice: "Ah, I yearn toward thee, my friend, but I have not confidence in thee. I am not thou; thou art not I. We trust each other today, but we distrust tomorrow," he agonized. "I know not how it is that our distrust, our hate, is stronger than our love." The Journal's tortuous meditations on friendship show that Thoreau felt one particular friend to be a rival in every sense of that word. The spelling book of Joseph Emerson Worcester taught proper Bostonians that *friend* was derived from the Anglo-Saxon root *freon*, to free, to love. But teaching proper Bostonians how to love freely was a rather more difficult task. Five years later, when *Walden* had given him a modest reputation, Thoreau finally mellowed into plausibility: "Here are all the friends I ever had or shall have, and as friendly as ever. Why, I never had any quarrel with a friend but it was just as sweet as unanimity could be" (1 Nov. 1858).

"Trench says a wild man is a *willed* man. Well, then, a man of will who does what he wills or wishes, a man of hope and of the future tense, for not only the obstinate is willed, but far more the constant and persevering. The obstinate man, properly speaking, is one who will not. The perseverance of the saints is positive willedness, not a mere passive willingness. The fates are wild, for they *will*; and the Almighty is wild above all, as fate is" (27 Jan. 1853). Since by following in Tooke's wake Trench had confused two distinct Indo-European roots, this was both wild and willful on Thoreau's part. Nonetheless, such speculations helped shape the paean to wildness best expressed in "Walking" and "Wild Apples."

In extending Trench's philology by distinguishing *obstinate* and *persevering* "properly speaking," Thoreau drew upon synonymies like Taylor's *English Synonyms Discriminated* (1813). The best-known was George Crabb's *English Synonymes Explained* (1816; New York: Harper, 1839). After deriving *obstinate* from the Latin *obstinans*, "standing in the way of another," Crabb tried to discriminate it from such related terms as *stubborn*, *headstrong*, and *heady*. In this case etymology was little help. Obstinacy is "a habit of the mind," he decided, "while the *stubborn* and *headstrong* are species of the *obstinate*; the former lies altogether in a perversion of the will; the latter in the perversion of the judgment" (p. 209). This attempt to regulate usage philosophically was in his own terms certainly obstinate and possibly headstrong as well. Likewise, in contrasting *continue*, *persevere*, and *persist*, he insisted that "*persevere* or *persist* marks a direct temper of the mind; the former is always used in a good sense. . . . Examples are to be found in English authors of *persevere* in a bad sense, and *persist* in a good sense, but modern writers have uniformly observed the distinction" (p. 264). In fact, nineteenth-century writers were scarcely uniform on this point. Crabb persevered or persisted in efforts to make them so by drawing crabbed distinctions that often clarified usage but sometimes distorted it. A public avid for correctness jumped into the search for verbal essences. America kept the book in print until after World War II, and Crabb's name became a synonym for discriminating synonyms.

Trench sparked the wordplay in one of Thoreau's most beautiful paragraphs:

> Ah, the pickerel of Walden! when I see them lying on the ice, or in the well which the fisherman cuts in the ice, making a little hole to admit the water, I am always surprised by their rare beauty, as if they were fabulous fishes, they are so foreign to the streets, even to the woods, foreign as Arabia to our Concord life. They possess a quite dazzling and transcendent beauty which separates them by a wide interval from the cadaverous cod and haddock whose fame is trumpeted in our streets. They are not green like the pines, nor gray like the stones, nor blue like the sky; but they have, to my eyes, if possible, yet rarer colors, like flowers and precious stones, as if they were the pearls, the animalized *nuclei* or crystals of the Walden water. They, of course, are Walden all over and all through; are themselves small Waldens in the animal kingdom, Waldenses. It is surprising that they are caught here,—that in this deep and capacious spring, far beneath the rattling teams and chaises and tinkling sleighs that travel the Walden road, this great gold and emerald fish swims. . . . Easily, with a few convulsive quirks, they give up their watery ghosts, like a mortal translated before his time to the thin air of heaven. (*Walden*, pp. 284-85)

What energizes this passage is the striking comparison of the pickerel to Walden itself and then to Waldenses—those medieval martyrs who were too pure for a corrupt world to appreciate. Startling but utterly right, pathetic yet witty enough to check sentimentality, this pun crystallizes the main theme—the imaginative leap that lets us find beauty in the quotidian.

Yet surprisingly the pun is absent from Thoreau's earliest draft. The pickerel are first described when his journal is pondering Trench's book, and many details are carried over into *Walden* from that entry. But he excluded these among other sentences: "They are something tropical. . . . They are true topazes, inasmuch as you can only conjecture what place they came from" (25 Jan. 1853). This conceit derives directly from Trench's discussion of the etymological meaning of various gems, where he exclaims, "What curious legends belong to the explanation of . . . the 'topaz,' so called, as some said, because men were only able to conjecture (τωπαζειν) the place whence it was brought" (p. 105).

As Thoreau revised, the fish became a true trope rather than simply tropical, so *tropical*, with its jarring connotations of South Seas sensuality, was dropped. The topaz-like pickerel grew in his mind through a process of etymological conjecture. Tinkering around, Thoreau first expanded the notion of "fabulous fish" thus: "fresh water dolphins eldest sons of Walden, for whose behalf this whole world is but a dauphin edition to study."[15] The French crown prince has been styled the Dauphin ever since the Lords of Viennois, whose coat of arms bore three dolphins, ceded the province Dauphiné to the crown in 1349. Famous editions of the classics were prepared for Louis XIV's grandson by Jesuit scholars, *in usum serenissimi Delphini*, and Thoreau himself owned several Delphins.

He finally canceled this conceit as too bookish and heavy-handed, but not before it suggested the trope that replaced the topaz comparison in his final version; for the Dauphiné was home to the Waldenses, whose status had been a matter of topical interest since Charles Albert of Sardinia issued an Edict of Emancipation in 1848. "The Waldenses, or Wallenses, it was declared by . . . the Church of Rome, were justly so called, as dwelling 'in valle densa,' in the thick valley of darkness and ignorance," Trench would note in later editions, but the origins of the sect remained a puzzle to him: "Were the Waldenses so called from one Waldus, to whom these 'Poor Men of Lyons,' as they were at first called, owed their origin?"[16] They were indeed, but Thoreau could not be sure of that and did not want to be, lest their derivation from Peter Waldo stress his own derivation from Ralph Waldo.

"The boundaries of the actual are no more fixed and rigid than the elasticity of our imaginations," Thoreau believed (31 May 1853). By fishing so assiduously for etymological comparisons his prose makes the pickerel suggest less any unequivocal truth than our power to organize and transform the world imaginatively with language. "It is remarkable that many men will go with eagerness in the winter to Walden Pond to fish for pickerel and yet not seem to care for the landscape," he wrote. "Now I go a-fishing . . . every day, but omit the fish" (26 Jan. 1853). One trophy from Trench that he mounted handsomely in *Walden* was the notion that "the *shore* is *shorn*" because changes in water level kill off trees (p. 181). Another was proudly displayed in the journal: "What are our fields but *felds* or *felled* woods" (27 Jan. 1853). Despite Thoreau's ingenuity in stuffing these catches, both specimens remained faintly fishy, though lifelike. Trench dropped the Tookean felled field from later editions along with willed wildness, but both bogus derivations shaped Thoreau's cosmology.

Trench was not the only etymological essayist to edify Americans. Two years earlier the Philadelphian Henry Wharton Griffith had published *A Lift for the Lazy* (New York: Putnam, 1849). This native florilegium showcased a gentlemanly collection of specimen derivations. Griffith was struck by the origin that Dr. Johnson attributed to *saunter*: "According to Mme. Piozzi, he said that the verb . . . came originally, from *Sainte Terre*, the Holy Land" (p. 37). This oft-quoted aperçu (alas, mistaken) became the organizing donnée of Thoreau's magnificent essay "Walking."

> I have met with but one or two persons in the course of my life who understood the art of Walking, that is, of taking walks,—who had a genius, so to speak, for *sauntering*: which word is beautifully derived "from idle people who roved about the country in the Middle Ages, and asked charity, under pretense of going a la Sainte Terre," to the Holy Land, till the children exclaimed, "There goes a *Sainte-Terrer*," a Saunterer, a Holy Lander. . . . Some, however, would derive the word from *sans terre*, without land or home, which, therefore, in the good sense, will mean, having no particular home, but equally at home everywhere. . . . But I prefer the first, which indeed, is the most probable derivation. For every walk is a sort of crusade preached by some Peter the Hermit in us, to go forth and reconquer the Holy Land from the hands of the Infidels. (W, 5:205-6)

Essayists in the eighteenth-century manner loved to style themselves *Ramblers* or *Idlers*, while chucking the resolute Johnsonian antitheses that tempered the casual stance. Thoreau developed the Saunterer's pose into a metaphor for life and art. Ambling from one etymology to another in this opening paragraph, he saunters throughout the essay hands-in-pockets like a Yankee boulevardier, then returns home to the governing pilgrim analogy at the end. Quite aware of its dandiacal tendencies, Thoreau's prose relies on verbal roots to temper his claim to be living what another essay styled "Life without Principle."

With polite vagueness Griffith also called attention to the derivation of *manure* from *manoeuvre*—"literally, to work with the hand, to cultivate, or till—in its present use, to cultivate by the addition of other substances of a fertilizing nature" (p. 69). In *Walden* Thoreau sported with this etymology in describing his decision to plant no more beans but only "such seeds, if the seed is not lost, as sincerity, truth, simplicity, faith, innocence, and the like, and see if they will not grow in this soil, even with less toil and manurance" (p. 164). But earlier he emphasized that his beans got "no manure." Raising a crop paradoxically with less than no manurance forces the reader to recover the radical meaning of the word. Preferring austere self-discipline to unnecessary effort, Thoreau invites us with this pun to realize the degrading nature of excessive physical labor, by which "this soil has . . . been exhausted" together with those who till it.

As a young farmhand in Pennsylvania Dutch country Samuel K. Hoshour learned more about manuring fields than he wished to know. He studied for the Lutheran ministry, then became a Campbellite and sauntered to the freshly plowed territory of Indiana. The Disciples of Christ were tight-fisted, so he schoolmastered from 1835 to 1846. At the Cambridge Seminary he taught all comers, from men and women who were grounded in the humanities by studying Latin, Greek, French, and German, to "the toilers in rudimentary English."[17] To enliven their toil, he resorted to more innovative methods than the trusty hickory. He told stories about "*Grammar City*—a city of a hundred thousand inhabitants (words), residing that time in ten streets—the parts of speech). The class entered the city on *Article* street, where none but little folks . . . lived."[18] Cambridge City was poverty-stricken beside Grammar City, where many big folks maintained several residences. The teacher strove mightily to explain the value of a dollar to the community: "Mr. Hoshour's pupils were made aware that Count Schliecken first made that coin in a valley of Bohemia; and that the German word for valley is Thal—that the Count's coins were in demand because they contained but little alloy—that they were called *Thaler* (pronounced *tahler*) or val-leyers. This the Danes converted into a Dhaler, and the English into Dollar!" The town marveled but declined to raise his salary, so Hoshour left teaching for preaching and farming. Alas, that proved just as unprofitable.

He had earned a reputation as a fine professor who knew how to dispel classroom doldrums with sudden conundrums like "Why is a certain kind of grain named 'buck-wheat?'" (Ans.: "The buck-wheat grain and the beech nut are alike in shape; but *buche* is the German for beech, and the Danes use *ack* for *ch*, and hence buck in this connection means *beech*"). To enliven his classes he also composed and published a short epistolary novel, *Letters to Esq. Pedant, in the East* (1844), recounting the picaresque adventures of Lorenzo Altisonant and his dog Indagator.

> The publisher intends these Letters, among other things, as a stepping stone from the everyday, and current English, to the Latin. Their language is mostly *latino* and *graeco* English. Any one that has ever studied the Latin tongue, knows what trouble he had in retaining the meaning of Latin words, while trying to construe a sentence. . . . Here the perplexity in construing a sentence is absent, and the definition only to be attended to—and when the learner gets into the Latin, the definitions of many

words of that language will already be familiar, and hence less division of mind in deciphering a Latin sentence. Should the student of the Letters never study Latin or Greek, still, he will feel himself at home whenever, in reading authors, he meets an unusual word.[19]

Lorenzo's fans certainly met many unusual words as the hero migrates westward in pursuit of his fortune. Bunking with farmers and tavern-keepers, listening to parsons and stump orators, jailed and bailed, encountering snakes, quack doctors, fortune-tellers and Millerite camp meetings, Lorenzo relates his garish journey in an imperturbably learned prose. The cynarctomachy in which the faithful Indagator "terminated his subastral vitality" is a fair specimen of Hoshour's narrative: "In the circumgyrations of the combatants, Indagator rendered Bruin excaudate; but Bruin being ungiculated seized Ind. at his neb and capillaceious and dermal integument in the lateral part, and almost exenterated him, aye, indeed suggilated him. By an extra conatus he effectuated his eluctation from Bruin; but his claudication from the arena of concertation, prompted the most puissant ululations" (p. 23).

Hoshour's hifalutin style is clearly mock-heroic, though there may be little exaggeration when his stump speaker inveighs against whiggism in this way. To imagine like one recent study that Hoshour was seriously trying to revive Elizabethan inkhornism and aureate diction is to carry scholarly humorlessness well beyond the call of academic duty. The preface is clear that the book is "a pleasant means of obtaining the meaning of the greater part of the unusual words of the English language, on the principle of 'association of ideas.'" By meeting the far-fetched words of Webster's speller in a narrative where context helped define them, the student might learn more than from spellers and dictionaries. Whether or not this educational theory was true, the results were amusing enough for four editions.

Hoshour was a well-intentioned educator, whose own *Autobiography* was written as straightforwardly as one might expect of a Campbellite. But this mild-mannnered minister was also the etymological counterpart of the era's vernacular humorists. Whereas they exaggerated the native, colloquial element in English for comic effect, by exaggerating its classical element Hoshour blended educational uplift with satire of hifalutin prose. To be sure, the Hoosier sense of irony was so uncertain that "it may be urged . . . that it is not desireable that youths should know the meaning of the words employed in these letters, as it might dispose them to become pedantic and turgid in their style." Earnestly explaining the point of the joke, the publisher warned that the style of the letters was not to be imitated "unless when old schoolmates who had studied them should accidentally meet, and would wish to enjoy the reminiscences of the past; then it might be allowable to spice the social chat a little with some of Altisonant's phrases." As the title page proclaimed, the book was "published for the benefit of youth: by a lover of the studious"—and fully copyrighted. Though prosperity eluded this lover of the studious, it is nice to note that like Lorenzo's adventures, his *Autobiography* has a happy ending. After more hardscrabble farming he ended his days as a professor of languages at Butler University, grubbing for roots in more congenial fields.

Three Ramblers among Words—Whitman, Thoreau, and William Swinton

In 1854 *Putnam's Magazine* carried two "Rambles over the Realms of Verbs and Substantives," just as it had serialized Thoreau's rambles over the province of Quebec the year before. The author was William Swinton, an émigré Scot educated in Canada, then briefly at Amherst. During 1855–58 he taught in New York. He quickly began reviewing for the *Times*, authoring perhaps the most perceptive early notice of *Leaves of Grass* (if one excludes Whitman's own anonymous reviews, self-promotion that Swinton exposed and criticized). Meeting in late 1855, Swinton and Whitman had been drawn together by love of the theater. When the celebrated Mademoiselle Rachel began performing in French on the New York stage, Swinton reviewed all performances. Whitman saw *Athalie* as Swinton's guest, relying on him for interpretation. Swinton fascinated Whitman no less for his fluent French than for his energy and sophistication. In later years the poet recalled that "my friend who used to translate Hugo for me—he would sit at the other side of the table and talk across—was very lively, very animated—almost danced some of his verses out."[20]

Among his many projects Swinton was working on a translation of Rousseau's *Social Contract*, using Whitman as a sounding board. Since the poet had sent a copy of his first book to Emerson with gratifying results, Swinton did too. His accompanying letter of 21 August 1856 offered to do research for Emerson in the Astor Library and mentioned that the poet was "to bring us a new sheaf of 'Leaves' in a day or so."[21] When Whitman exasperated Emerson later that month by emblazoning his tribute on the spine of the second edition of *Leaves of Grass*, Swinton was eager to consolidate his own standing with the Concord sage. The Transcendental busybody Bronson Alcott was in New York as an advance guard for a visit from Emerson. He met the poet on 4 October and was fascinated. Alcott also got Thoreau a job surveying in New Jersey. Soon Thoreau was visiting in New York. Alcott's *Journal* for

7 November records, "Henry Thoreau comes from Eagleswood and sees Swinton the Scotchman at my rooms."[22] Besides common interests like etymology, their discussion probably covered Emerson's annoyance at Whitman's pilfered testimonial. Next week Swinton's review rebuked the poet for taking this liberty. But it was also sympathetically insightful, and Whitman did not mind being at the center of controversy if that might sell books. He and Swinton remained on warm terms, as Alcott's *Journal* for 20 November reveals: "Swinton comes and we cross to Brooklyn and dine with Whitman. I am well paid for this visit, and bring home spoils for great uses."

Thoreau also felt himself well repaid for visiting Whitman with Alcott on 10 November. Alcott memorably describes the two authors encountering "like two beasts, each wondering what the other would do, whether to snap or run," each secretly thinking of the other, "Well, you're almost as great as I am!" To their credit, each managed to look beyond the more off-putting elements of the other's pose—Thoreau's fastidious superciliousness, Whitman's blustering physical pretentiousness—and sense that the other might be devoted to sniffing out what Alcott called "all Nature" with "a sagacity potent, penetrating, and peerless as his own." Despite Whitman's claims to appreciate genius in everyone, Thoreau would prove the more perceptive in his frank admiration. The copy of *Leaves of Grass* that he flaunted about Concord shows a desire to *épater les bourgeois*, to be sure. But a surprising generosity of spirit is manifest in the Yankee's verdict—"He is a great fellow" (*Correspondence*, p. 445).

Thoreau asked Whitman whether he were familiar with the great books of the Orient. "No: tell me about them," Whitman answered. His frank curiosity was not quite candid. Whitman liked to act as if a Bowery b'hoy could rewrite the Bhagavad-Gita from scratch. His own review had touted the American bard of *Leaves of Grass* as "talking like a man unaware that there was ever hitherto such a production as a book."[23] In fact, he was keenly conscious of his intellectual lacunae. Newspaper culture filled gaps; so did public libraries. But neither offered anything like the training in languages that Emerson and Thoreau got at Harvard. Whitman felt the lack. His relationship with Swinton became an informal tutorial in philology. Swinton gave Whitman his copy of Maximilian Schele de Vere's *Outlines of Comparative Philology* (New York: Putnam, 1853), which the poet kept until his death. Material from it was transcribed into the voluminous notebooks on language that Whitman was keeping shortly after meeting Swinton. His homemade scrapbook called "Words" gives the flavor of his earnest attempts at philological self-cultivation:

? of Swinton
What are the Turanian Languages?
Arian—(Greek)
Turanian, (Turk)
Semitic, (Hebrew)
("Arian Brahman")
What the Arian?

The Arians are the higher classes, late-comers, conquerors of India —as the Normans under William the Conqueror, in England—they were the Brahmanic Caste	The Arian seem to be those that have flowed out, or have an allied character with the Hindustan, the Sanskrit, the "Dekhan",—the land of the Ganges *(DBN, 3:721-22)*

Such entries suggest the baffled notes of an eager sophomore auditing a graduate seminar in linguistics.

This sophomore was conscientious, however. His scribbled self-admonitions show a determination "to get in the habit of tracing words to their root-meanings / as for instance in the phrase 'Rev. Mr. Conway' trace 'Reverend' / 'Mr.' / -how inapplicable and superfluous so many words are!" *(DBN*, 3:725). He had been doing so even before encountering Swinton. Early experience as a country schoolteacher on Long Island whetted his curiosity about words. His scrapbooks contain a few clippings on language from the 1840s and show him seeking out authorities for personal advice when possible. In the so-called 1847 Notebook he reminds himself to "ask Mr. Dwight about the highest numeral term known" (in Bernbrock, p. 7). Benjamin W. Dwight, principal of a Brooklyn high school, later published *Modern Philology: Its Discoveries, History, and Influence* (New York, 1859), a well-informed survey of continental scholarship, so Swinton was not the first philologist whose acquaintance Whitman cultivated. But just as Emerson catalyzed Whitman's Transcendentalism, so Swinton brought the poet's philological imagination, already simmering over A Literary Association's textbooks, to a boil. Within six months of meeting him Whitman had published "America's Mightiest Inheritance" in the phrenological periodical *Life Illustrated*. In this essay he extolled the English language as "by far the noblest now spoken—probably ever spoken—upon this earth" because of its highly synthetic and derivative origins.[24] To aid linguistic amalgamation he added a list of foreign words, chiefly French, and urged his audience to incorporate these in their speech. For naive readers, definitions and notes on pronunciation were included. Perhaps the poet should have done the same for *Leaves of Grass* (1860), when he paradoxically proclaimed, "I say for ornaments nothing outre can be allowed," and then addressed the nation in "Apostrophe" with such imports as these—"O mater! O fils! / O brood continental! / O flowers of the prairies!" (*LG*, p. 600).

The notebooks of 1856-58 show him knee-deep in etymology: "Every principal word ?name in our language is a condensed octavo The word *Jehovah* weaves the meaning of the past, present and future tenses—*personalizes* Time, as it was, is and ever shall be The word name 'Buddha'- intelligence? the word *Homer* i.e. compiler Editor."[25] Whether his response to Thoreau's query had represented real or feigned ignorance, Whitman was now doing his amateurish mite to eclaircise the myths Asiastic, consulting his friend whenever perplexed to eclaircise the facts philological: "question for Swinton / to tell me of Etruria."[26] Like other authors, he was struck by the fact that April was "from the Latin verb Aperio—I open (April was anciently 2d. month of year)." His etymological study persuaded him that "in These States, there must be new Names for all the Months of the year—They must be characteristic of America—The South, North, East, and West must be represented in them—What is the name . . . January to us?—Or March to us?. . . March commemorates Mars—the bloody god of war, for the sake of War!" (*DBN*, 3:693, 700-701). Unlike the French Revolution, *Leaves of Grass* promulged no new names for the months but sporadically continued the Quaker tradition of identifying them by number.

So intoxicating was home-brewed philology that Whitman quickly decided that a new dictionary was needed. "*A Perfect English Dictionary has yet to be Written,*" he proclaimed in "America's Mightiest Inheritance" (p. 59). He emphasized the same need in the letter appended to the second edition of *Leaves of Grass*. After surveying the deficiencies of eleven lexicographers from Samuel Johnson through Webster and Worcester, he hoped that "some coming American worthy the sublime work" would take up the task. Actually he had himself in mind. In the 1850s the success of Bartlett's *Dictionary of Americanisms* (1849) bred a slew of wannabe lexicographers, and he was one of them. The masses of material that Whitman collected fill several notebooks. Some eventually leaked into print as the essay "Slang in America" (1885) and the posthumously edited *American Primer*. His qualifications for systematic lexicography were nil, of course, as he finally realized. His own collecting efforts tapered off after the first volume of *New English Dictionary* was published in 1884.

Actually, the chief monument to Whitman's linguistic zeal appeared twenty-five years earlier. Brilliant but mercurial, Swinton came to New York aglow with projects. He taught school and toyed with the idea of becoming a Presbyterian minister, then pursued a more controversial but exciting career as a war correspondent. After nearly being shot when U. S. Grant caught him hiding in a closet to obtain a scoop, he became a professor of English. He neglected his duties notoriously, then finally resigned from the University of California when his and Henry George's joint plan for populist control of the Board of Regents fell through. As a free-lance author of many profitable textbooks he was businesslike enough to read the galleys as lectures to California students, pausing at the lectern to correct proof, but later he often sold the copyrights for a song because imprudence left him short of ready cash. His two etymological essays for *Putnam's Magazine* were foretastes of a projected book. The metropolis proved so diverting that at first he did little to finish it. After five years he published *Rambles among Words* (New York: Scribner's, 1859). The book was confessedly indebted to Trench. Indeed, the *Atlantic Monthly*'s reviewer thought it rather too much indebted. But it was quite successful. Two American publishers brought out later editions, the latter twice reprinted, and a London edition appeared in 1864. Though not so popular as Trench's book, *Rambles among Words* outsold Griffith's *A Lift for the Lazy* to become the most widely circulated etymological florilegium that midcentury America produced.

It is a stridently American book—but schizophrenically so, for the émigré Scotsman had acquired a native collaborator. Needing help to expand his manuscript to book length, he enlisted the expertise of a fellow journalist who had already written a successful temperance potboiler, allegedly by lubricating his inspiration over three days with gin cocktails. Putting this ghostwriter's name on the title page would not have enhanced sales; indeed, it might have harmed them. As C. Carroll Hollis pointed out in 1958, Walt Whitman is in fact the unacknowledged coauthor of the era's best-selling American etymological anthology.

Swinton undoubtedly contributed the bulk of the etymologies, insofar as they are original. Many are taken from the *Dictionary* of Charles Richardson, a staunch disciple of Tooke, for which the *Atlantic Monthly*'s reviewer chided Swinton. The spurious derivations of *wild*, *saunter*, and *craven* (the word "basely confesses that he has craved . . . his life at an enemy's hand," p. 104), echo Trench or Richardson, while *plagiarism* is cheerfully traced to the Latin word "*Plagium* . . . among the Romans the name given to man-stealing" (p. 84). Meditating upon that correct etymology may have refined the morals of the book's readers more than those of its compilers. They were convinced that the idea of *seriousness* was derived from the Latin *sine risu*, without a smile. "Words are born of a passionate yearning. And it is through the senses that the mind goes out to Nature," the book argues, parading Fichte,

Humboldt, Schlegel, Coleridge, and Emerson as witnesses. But an important authority remained Tooke, who by deriving *think* from *thing* had proved that sensory thought was a primary law of language. Tooke is also the apparent source for the bogus derivation of *morn*, "a sweet poem coming to us from an old Gothic verb *Mergan*, to dissipate . . . just the time when darkness is . . . *dispersed*" (p. 58).

Besides this stock etymological aubade the book offers many tidbits for a budding Transcendentalist. Citing scientific diction to prove that sight is the most spiritual sense, the book links etymology with visionary power: "SEER, again, is simply one who sees—a see-er—whose eye has been unsealed to the 'open secret' of the universe, in Fichte's grand thought—a secret hidden from the wise and prudent (in their own imaginings), and yet 'revealed'—*revelo*—*unveiled* to those exercising the faith and humility of babes" (pp. 29-30). Obviously the Victorian sage will reveal his wisdom by deciphering such open secrets as the origin of the word *seer* itself. The epigraph to the second chapter comes from Lorenz Oken: "Speech is the perfect expression of the Senses. Words are but the representations of the disintegrated body of Man" (p. 20). We hear also of Oken's insight "that the whole animal kingdom is simply man disintegrated" (p. 149). As Emerson's disciple, Whitman did not need to import body mysticism from Germany, but Oken's aperçus resemble the doctrine of human body language expressed in "A Song of the Rolling Earth" (1856) more than does anything in *Nature*. Given Whitman's devotion to the body and nudism, he may especially have relished learning from Swinton the etymological truth that "a ROBE is cousin-german to *rob*" (p. 43).

Rambles explains the origins of such words as *exaggerate, parlor, pecuniary,* and *extravagant,* among those that Thoreau sported with in *Walden*. Though Whitman's prophetic style rarely puns like Thoreau's, the poem "City of Ships" (1865) employs *extravagant* with an awareness of its literal meaning *wandering beyond*. Hailing New York as the "City of the World," ringed with myriad ships for global commerce, his apostrophe builds to a climax:

> City of the sea: city of hurried and glittering tides:
> City whose gleeful tides continually rush or recede, whirling in and out
>   with eddies of foam,
> City of wharves and stores—city of tall facades of marble and iron!
> Proud and passionate city—mettlesome, mad, extravagant city!
>
>   (*LG*, p. 294)

Indeed, this poem owes its very title to an etymological aperçu. Trench had erroneously explained that London, "according to the most probable etymology, is a name formed out of two Celtic words, and means, 'city of ships'" (1852 ed., pp. 223-24). Trench found this name especially appropriate for the great commercial capital of the world, but in Whitman's exultant paean maritime Manhattan challenges for that title.

But the most fertile hint that Whitman took from *Rambles* was an etymology that Swinton found dubious. For the derivation of *calamity* the book cites Francis Bacon's speculation that "the word *calamitas*, was first derived from *calamus, when the corn coulde not get out of the stalke*" (pp. 68-69). The poems that became "Calamus" in the 1860 edition derive from a masculine attachment ending in renunciation that Whitman experienced in 1856-57. But the dozen poems first composed took as their governing symbol the live oak tree, its leaves and moss. Then in the spring of 1859 he composed the bulk of what is now "Scented Herbage of My Breast," the second poem in the sequence. The first draft of these anguished lines focuses on the calamus plant as the symbol of his thwarted longing:

> O slender leaves! O blossoms of my blood: I permit you to tell, in your own way, of the heart that is under you, where your roots are!
> O aching and throbbing! O these hungering desires!
> Surely one day they will be pacified—all will be accomplished
> O I know not what you mean—you are not happiness—you are often too bitter!
> Yet you are beautiful to me, you faint-tinged roots! you make me think of death,
> Death is beautiful from you—what is so beautiful as death and love?[27]

As Whitman confronted his ambiguous sexuality, the phallic stalks of calamus condemned to grow in swamps blended in his imagination with leaves of grain sprouting from the breast of the mummified Osiris, which he had seen illustrated in a book on Egyptian antiquities. "Give me your tone therefore O Death and manly Love that I may accord with it," his first draft begged (p. 74). The tortuous symbolism of this poem reflects the plight of a man whose phallus had provided a disastrous surprise, committing him to a love that seemed incapable of bearing fruit except in death. The calamus so engrossed his imagination as a symbol that he then decided to marshal his poems of manly attachment under that flag, writing the opening lines of "Scented Herbage" and "In Paths Untrodden," the first poem of the group, to carry out that programmatic intent. Whitman's choice of this rush as the central symbol for his sexual identity was probably influenced by its etymological associations with calamity. But in his final version of the poem it became a beloved disaster. "Emblematic and capricious blades I leave you, now you serve me not, / I will say what I have to say by itself," he wrote. "I will raise it with immortal reverberations through the States, / I will give an example to lovers to take permanent shape and will through the States" (*LG*, pp. 114-15). By embracing his misfortune boldly he sought to dispel its calamitousness.

Was he also etymologist enough to know that *capricious* behavior involves goatlike lustiness? Undoubtedly, for quoting Shakespeare's reference to "the most capricious poet, honest Ovid," *Rambles* had explained the occult pun lurking in *capricious* that made the epithet "luminous" (p. 173). Citing Carlyle as an authority, *Rambles* also stressed that etymologically *health* was a state of *wholeness,* linked to such cognates as *heal* and *hale* (p. 69). That belief is writ large throughout the body of Whitman's poetry, which is ultimately both wholesome and healing. Few poets come from families exhibiting more varieties of sickness. Like the aging poet, his father became a chronic invalid. One brother was an epileptic idiot, another died young of tuberculosis and alcoholism, while a third had to be committed for outbreaks of ungovernable violence probably stemming from syphilis. Living with all this disease turned his sister Hannah into a neurotic hypochondriac. But Walt made a heroic effort to absorb health imaginatively by grasping things whole.

Fortunately, unlike Tooke, Swinton knew enough not to connect health with the Anglo-Saxon *helan*, to cover, to conceal. For Whitman complete secrecy would have led not to healing over and recovery but to Hell. Both poetically and morally his instinct to promulge was sound. Seldom yielding to the seduction of camp, the valetudinarian sage of *Democratic Vistas* retained the belief that he first enunciated in the *Preface*: "Sanity and ensemble characterize the great master. . . . He sees health for himself in being one of the mass" (*LG*, pp. 719-20). Hence his insouciant claim to be a kosmos. His beatific visions of fusion with the All, when "health puts you in rapport with the Universe" (*LG*, p. 342), were often compensatory, to be sure. But whether cosmic or merely cosmetic, they were also therapeutic.

In discussing French loan-words, *Rambles* listed many used in Whitman's appendix to "America's Mightiest Inheritance." It justified such borrowing by citing Chaucer's example. "But it cannot be that Chaucer did anything more than crystallize into literature verbal forms already in solution among the floating word-capital of the day," it added. "For never otherwise could he have been the popular poet he was" (p. 274). Was Chaucer a linguistic innovator of genius or a typical speaker of

Middle English? The book seems unsure, and a like ambivalence about Chaucer's French diction is reflected in articles on the poet that Whitman clipped and annotated. The question was not academic, for Chaucer was a model for Whitman in his linguistic role as a national bard.[28] *Rambles* finally solves the riddle of how to be both popular and a pathbreaker by suggesting that the national poet works in harmony with needs and tendencies in the language that the people may not fully recognize. Thus English rejected many of Chaucer's French importations. "In Chaucer I find such Gallicisms as these—'gaillard' (gay), 'debonair' (good-natured), . . . 'rondeur' (roundness—the 'Earth's rondeur'), with scores of such like, some of which will no doubt again make their appearance in our language, many of them expressing thoughts or things not so well expressed by any we have" (p. 276). When Whitman apostrophized the earth in "Passage to India" as "Thou rondure of the world at last accomplished . . . / O vast Rondure, swimming in space" (*LG*, p. 414), he was a philological poet self-consciously resuming Chaucer's effort to enrich the language. His ungainly imports were an ostentatious wedding gift to his people—"For you these from me, O Democracy, to serve you ma femme" (*LG*, p. 272). The husky groom cut an awkward figure in his rented finery. But somehow it was the thought that mattered.

"A petrified and mechanical national mind will certainly appear in a petrified and mechanical language. . . . The renovation of language is provided for, as the renovation of races is provided for, by a subtle chemistry. The sublime democracy of speech!" (p. 11). *Rambles* rambles from Swinton's specific philological facts to perfervid Emersonian meditations on the development of language, where Whitman's accents are unmistakable:

> To Modern times and to America, too, the thought of Naming presents itself. Once, we know, every name was significant. There have been seasons, in the elder ages, of flood-tides in the creative faculties, when Nature disclosed her secret thought and gave it to man to name her—when to mountain and stream, field and flood were added names that are poems. Why should not we, too, come into this Orphic secret? . . . Imperative is the demand for a fresh, free appropriate nomenclature for American Geography, Inventions, Contributions, Personalities. Already the new needs make the old perfections meagre and inadequate. To you, Poets and Builders, sublime invitations! To quarry and to build in the new architecture of humanity. (pp. 228-29)

A new era brings exciting challenges. A more adequate treatment of English synonyms is needed, for Crabb's work is outdated, the book argues. "Of much profounder philosophic significance is the Thesaurus of Mr. Roget, who has given us a metaphysical classification of Thoughts and Things with their corresponding Verbal Symbols" (pp. 230-31). (Indeed, Whitman's grand conceptual inventories and loosely parallel epithets sometimes read as if quarried from the pages of Roget.) For this lexicographical task "the constant law of *Desynonymizing*, as Coleridge expressively terms it, comes into play" (p. 234).

But for hundreds of years English scholars and literati have tried to curb neology. "What starvation has this insane purism effected!" (p. 289). Though Shakespeare, Milton, Wordsworth, and Dickens some-how throve in this repressive climate, desynonymizing must render English no longer synonymous with American. In this evolutionary pro-cess the continuity of the "Japhetic" tongues will be maintained because "they alone have reached the altitude of free intellectual individuality and organism. To them belongs the splendid plasticity of Sanskrit, Greek, German, English! . . . Sounds and structures—words and forms—that were heard along the Ganges, five thousand years ago . . . are now scaling the Rocky Mountains of the Western world!" (pp. 269-70). The rising tide of Indo-European bears Whitman where "new cre-ations surge and swell the ampler currents of our time! New thoughts, new things, all unnamed!" His intoxication at riding the crest of this linguistic wave into a land of literary opportunity is palpable. "Where is the theory of literary expression that stands for the new politics and sociology? What puts itself abreast the vast divine tendencies of Sci-ence? that absorbs the superb suggestions of the Grand Opera? I can see but one limitation to the theory of Words—the theory of Things. . . . Freely, then, may the American literat . . . build" (p. 289). His slight reservation does him credit, but he seems not too worried that the splendid progress of the plastic American language might ever be checked by plastic American culture. Indeed, with their fondness for throw-away theories of literary expression couched suitably in throwaway dic-tion, modern literats often seem little more sophisticated than Whitman, and much less exciting.

With advancing years Whitman himself became a rather sterile lit-erat. As the Golden Age of American culture yielded to the Gilded Age, he yielded to the tempting role of pundit that his book had created. Instead of exploring the gaps between his vision of America and the social facts, he relied on empty assertion to mask the discrepancy. "O earth that hast no voice, confide to me a voice," he implores in "The Return of the Heroes" (1867). But the voice that "the lavish brown par-turient earth" confided to him for such postwar propaganda was increasingly Latinate (*LG*, p. 358). "Spirit that formed this scene," he wrote in Colorado's Platte Canyon in 1879,

These formless wild arrays, for reasons of their own,
I know thee, savage spirit—we have communed together,
Mine too such wild arrays, for reasons of their own;
Was't charged against my chants they had forgotten art?
To fuse within themselves its rules precise and delicatesse?
The lyrist's measured beat, the wrought-out temple's grace—column and
    polished arch forgot?
But thou that revelest here—spirit that form'd this scene,
They have remember'd thee. (*LG*, p. 486)

But these lines themselves, with their archaisms, artful inversions, and tediously abstract diction, smack more of the study than of wild nature. The infatuation with French that produced insouciant gaucheries was balanced at first by Whitman's determined use of the concrete, colloquial Anglo-Saxon vocabulary endorsed by A Literary Association. But with age and a measure of renown, there emerged a sinister preference for abstract words of Romance-Latin origin—not necessarily new imports— which are twice as frequent in the postwar poetry. The empty orotundity of Whitman's later bardic manner is owing in large measure to this proliferation of vague, genteelly literary diction.

Whitman's veneration for the human voice helped save his great poetry from the sterile theorizing of the literat. The oratorical sublime fascinated him. He dreamed of becoming an orator himself, filling notebooks with hints culled from authorities on elocution. From his peculiar sensitivity to the timbre of singers' and speakers' voices he evolved a mystique that he called vocalism. It led him on some strange tangents; for example, he was convinced that in softening the consonantal endings of English words Negro speech was paving the way for an American grand opera as singable as the Italian. But it also led him to *Leaves of Grass*. Upon his return from New Orleans in 1848 he did not strike his brother as more abstracted than usual, but George recalled that "it was about those years he had an idea he could lecture. He wrote what mother called 'barrels' of lectures. We did not know what he was writing." He seems never to have completed a draft of a single speech, although he filled his notebooks with hints on public speaking and toyed with titles for a collection of his lectures:

"Lectures" or "Lessons"
The idea of strong live addresses directly to the people, adm. 10¢, North and South, East, and West - at Washington,—at the different State Capitols—Jefferson (Mo.)—Richmond (Va.)—Albany—Washington +c promulging the grand ideas of American ensemble liberty, concentrativeness, individuality, spirituality +c +c
Keep steadily understood, with respect to the effects and fascinations of *Elocution* (so broad, spacious, and vital) that although the Lectures may

be printed and sold at the end of every performance, nothing can make up for that *irresistible attraction and robust living* treat of the vocalization of the lecture, by me,—which must defy all competition with the printed word and read repetition of the Lectures.

Though he doodled drafts of posters for these unwritten lectures, they were never delivered. Perhaps they could not have been, for he may well have lacked all *"the amazing and splendid athletic magnetism of . . . vocalization"* that he wished to bill himself as possessing.[29]

He never wandered the continent as prophet-priest of Democracy, enchanting audiences for a dime. But he did evolve a novel literary form to express his ideas. Many peculiar stylistic virtues of *Leaves of Grass* are efforts to achieve with print alone the audience rapport that a charismatic speaker attains viva voce. In the first edition the rhapsodic prose of the Preface, with marks of ellipsis pointing rhetorical cadences, blends almost imperceptibly into the free verse of the poems. The striking penchant for direct address to the reader is only the most notable platform mannerism incorporated in his new poetic.

As vocalism molded his literary style, so it is reflected in the linguistic doctrines preached in *Rambles among Words*. The Humboldtian theory that he picked up from Swinton reinforced his devotion to the oral sublime. The book invokes linguistic organicism to insist that the legatees of speech inherit its creators' imaginative struggle:

> Language is indeed alive! Primordial creation and manifestation of the mind, Language throbs with the pulses of our life. This is the wondrous babe, begotten of the blended love of spirit and of matter—physical, mystical, the Sphinx! Through Speech man realizes and incarnates himself; and Oken has an oracular utterance that 'without speech there is no world.'
>
> It is one of the current wranglings, How language originated: as though Language were not an innate energy and aspiration! Language is not a cunning conventionalism arbitrarily agreed upon: it is an internal necessity. Language is not a fiction, but a truth. Language is begotten of a lustful longing to express, through the plastic vocal energy, man's secret sense of his unity with nature. (pp. 265-66)

Whitman's vision of the linguistic process was ongoing and open-ended, emphasizing neology as much as etymology. By sublimating his oratorical aspirations this essentially solitary man managed to express not only his oneness with nature but his secret sense of unity with an audience. As its punning title suggests, his great book fuses literary and organic conceptions of language. Putting out new roots of its own, *Leaves of Grass* claimed freedom of speech to create a world. For one golden decade before its precarious linguistic synthesis disintegrated, the result was some astonishing poetry.

6 /

Thoreau and the Life of Words

Do they not know I can laugh?
— Thoreau (16 April 1854)

Sporting with Etymological Metaphysics on a Sandbank

"When occasionally I have ventured out of that magic circle of Silence which seems to be an Eternity enclosing Absolute Truth—I find clouds arise—& myself lose the vision," the Transcendental busybody Elizabeth Palmer Peabody lamented to her aunt. "We have lost the key to language, that great instrument by means of which the finite mind is to compensate itself for its being fixed to a point in space & compelled to the limitations of the succession which we call time. We use words that are no longer symbols but counters—Our logomachy does not coincide with the eternal logos." Peabody was convinced that the émigré Hungarian sage Charles Kraitsir, then schoolmastering in Boston, could remedy this sad state of affairs. "I intend to put myself under his tuition . . . & in the course of *a year or two*, I think I may possibly get weaponed to contend with the great Silence adequately and win from her the Expression of what God has been graciously pleased to say *to me* individually."[1] Peabody and Kraitsir assaulted the great Silence jointly by promoting a series of lectures by the Hungarian. Elizabeth attended raptly, took careful notes, submitted them to Kraitsir for review and expansion, and self-abnegatingly published the resulting fifty-page tract in his name as *The Significance of the Alphabet* (Boston, 1846).

With visionary propensities that made her collide with a tree she "saw" but did not "realize" and once led her to sit absentmindedly on a litter of kittens in Hawthorne's armchair, Peabody seems a dingbat in quest of the *Ding-an-sich*. But Kraitsir's eccentric theories intrigued wiser Bostonians, including Emerson. Kraitsir's pamphlet figured in Thoreau's modest library, which listed more works under the rubric philology than any other specific heading. In the early 1850s Thoreau also transcribed parts of Kraitsir's *Glossology: Being a Treatise on the Nature of Language and on the Language of Nature* (New York: Putnam, 1852) from Emerson's copy. Preferring a more familiar and explanatory treatment like that in the etymological florilegia, reviewers complained that the latter work was too learned, so compressed as to be painful to read. But Kraitsir demurred. "Only minds unaccustomed to masticate the food, offered to them in the infinite realm of creation, will find the style obscure," he explained (p. iii). The reader "must spin out our hints with elastic, yet steady mind. Perpetual chewing on our part would furnish him pleasant pulpy baby-pap, without strengthening the digestive power of his brain" (p. 165). Zealous in pursuing recondite etymological parallels, Kraitsir loved to exploit them stylistically, forcing his audience to make the necessary connections: "The reader must use his brain as a spirited, spreading, sprouting, sprightly steel-spring; not as a lazy, letting-alone, leaden, lumbersome, lymphatic gland" (p. 209).

In Thoreau Kraitsir's elliptical contortions found a skilled interpreter. *Walden* records his conviction that "books must be read as deliberately and reservedly as they were written," and it is governed from the beginning by a stylistic rationale like Kraitsir's (p. 101). Thoreau's oblique wordplay only heightens what he took to be the inescapable ambiguity of language, its need for conscious interpretation. Too much explicitness would deny readers the delight of discovery and the mental training that accompanies it. "In this part of the world it is considered a ground for complaint if a man's writings admit of more than one interpretation. While England endeavors to cure the potato-rot, will not any endeavor to cure the brain-rot, which prevails so much more widely and fatally?" (*Walden*, p. 315). Thus he denounces "the ridiculous demand which England and America make, that you shall speak so that they can understand you," as stunting intellectual growth (*Walden*, p. 324).

"Pupils frequently ask the philological teacher, if he does not draw upon his imagination for his facts. Certainly he *ought* to do so," declared Kraitsir. "He cannot remember personally, and he must *imagine*, the circumstances of humanity, when it was in such vigorous and healthy condition, as to receive impressions, and give them forth again in so much order, as all primitive languages exhibit" (*Significance*, p. 57). In Kraitsir Thoreau found a scholar who sanctioned his bent for etymological speculation without undue worry about Grimm's laws. Thus in *Walden* he can assert that "the works of the great poets have never yet been read by mankind, for only great poets can read them," and we find him urging the study of ancient literature with Kraitsir's emphasis on the imaginative recreation of the text: "The heroic books . . . will always be in a language dead to degenerate times; and we must laboriously seek the meaning of each word . . . conjecturing a larger sense than common use permits out of what wisdom and valor and generosity we have" (p. 100).

The Hungarian believed that his major contribution to philology was the discovery of "the best and universal language . . . the essential, uncorrupted basis of all human tongues" (*Glossology*, p. 193). All languages resemble each other in employing three kinds of sounds representing three different speech organs to denote three basic categories of nature: cause, living and moving effect, dead or dormant effect. An examination of languages reveals "that the causal, or what appears causal, is not expressed without gutturals; what is living and moving not without labials and linguals; what is dead or dormant not without dentals" (*Significance*, pp. 3-4). This schema lies at the heart of Kraitsir's thought. Since most ideas combine two or more natural categories, the roots of words often blend these elementary sounds. Kraitsir illustrates this doctrine as follows:

> To determine a root, we must consider three things: the quality of the object, the idea of it, and the organ, by which it is expressed. A root may be a letter of one class, or composed of letters of two classes, or of letters of all three classes. An object or action which expresses the several dimensions of length, breadth and highth, or depth, will need one of each class; . . . thus *crp, glb, grp, blk, glm, krp, klp,* are roots of *corpus, globe, grope, crop, block, bulk, bulge, grab, group, conglomerate,* and words of similar meanings. These roots are essentially the same. So an object or action, which expresses free outward motion, or that in thought, which is naturally symbolized by free outward motion, will need labials and the liquids, thus: *lb, lv , lf, fr, fl, pl, pr,* are roots (or different forms of a root,) which vegetate into the words *labia, live, lip, liber, love, laub, life, free, flow, blow, bear, fare, plane, flat, pluvia, flamma, fire.* If the object or thing moves from within its own being, which implies deep, internal, essential action, we have a guttural and the liquid, thus *gl, ql, cl, gr, cr,* which are roots of *glide, globe, glare, glance, vogel, eagle, volucris, creo, gradior, cylinder, columna, columba, aquila, circle,* &c. (pp. 29-30)

Except for his triadic conception of cause-and-effect relationships, Kraitsir's semantic phonetics was not entirely novel. Many of his claims about the inherent meanings of sounds simply show him quarrying without acknowledgment from De Brosses and Court de Gébelin. Thoreau knew enough about those French theorists to view Kraitsir's argument in perspective. He was undoubtedly aware of alternative theories about the inherent meaning of sounds. But though he did not suppose that the Hungarian had discovered the ultimate truth about language, he found his theories provocative. They suggested many details in one of *Walden*'s core passages, where he describes the thawing sandbank exposed by the railroad cut in "Spring."

> You find thus in the very sands an anticipation of the vegetable leaf. No wonder that the earth expresses itself outwardly in leaves, it so labors with

the idea inwardly. The atoms have already learned this law, and are pregnant by it. The overhanging leaf sees here its prototype. *Internally,* whether in the globe or animal body, it is a moist thick *lobe,* a word especially applicable to the liver and lungs and the *leaves* of fat, (λειβω, *labor, lapsus,* to flow or slip downward, a lapsing: λοβος, *globus,* lobe, globe; also lap, flap, and many other words,) *externally* a dry thin *leaf,* even as the *f* and *v* are a pressed and dried *b.* The radicals of lobe are *lb,* the soft mass of the *b* (single lobed, or B, double lobed,) with a liquid *l* behind it pressing it forward. In globe, *glb,* the guttural *g* adds to the meaning the capacity of the throat. The feathers and wings of birds are still drier and thinner leaves. Thus, also, you pass from the lumpish grub in the earth to the airy and fluttering butterfly. The very globe continually transcends and translates itself, and becomes winged in its orbit. (*Walden,* pp. 306-7)

But this passage is by no means a testament of simpleminded faith in Kraitsir like Elizabeth Peabody's. Instead, it demonstrates Thoreau's ability to apply glossological techniques independently while borrowing from other sources to develop this line of speculation playfully. In *The Music of Nature; or, An Attempt to Prove That What Is Passionate and Pleasing in the Art of Singing, Speaking, and Performing upon Musical Instruments Is Derived from the Sounds of the Animated World* (1832; Boston: Wilkins, 1837), the Englishman William Gardner likewise developed an elaborate semantic phonology that equated the forms of alphabetic characters with the sounds of the letters and the shapes of the vocal organs involved. Thus "the two semi-circles in the letter B represent the lips as closely pressed together in the act of forcing that explosive sound; and the consonant P, having but one nerve, would intimate a slighter effect of the same kind. These delineations were probably the first attempts at representing sounds by written characters . . . analogous to the recording of musical sounds by notes" (p. 42). Despite its eminent implausibility, the book went through four American editions before the Civil War. Thoreau merrily borrowed a strain from the music of nature to eke out Kraitsir's rather different speculations about the language of nature, without necessarily proclaiming discipleship to either guru. Like Goethe, who in his *Italian Journey* described inventing such a flippant theory of language as a running joke to pass the time, Thoreau is no more than half-serious.

Like Goethe in his *Metamorphosis of Plants* (1790), Kraitsir's etymologies often equate flowing material with vegetation and body parts. Both men encouraged Thoreau to see that "this sandy overflow is something such a foliaceous mass as the vitals of the animal body" (*Walden,* p. 306). In a remarkable passage Thoreau weaves Kraitsir's philological comparisons between feet and fluid, lips and leaves, arms and branches, into a triumphantly independent statement:

What is man but a mass of thawing clay? The ball of the human finger is but a drop congealed. The fingers and toes flow to their extent from the thawing mass of the body. Who knows what the human body would expand and flow out to under a more genial heaven? Is not the hand a spreading *palm* leaf with its lobes and veins? The ear may be regarded, fancifully, as a lichen, *umbilicaria,* on the side of the head, with its lobe or drop. The lip (*labium,* from *labor* (?)) laps or lapses from the sides of the cavernous mouth. The nose is a manifest congealed drop or stalactite. The chin is a still larger drop, the confluent dripping of the face. . . . Each rounded lobe of the vegetable leaf, too, is a thick and now loitering drop, larger or smaller; the lobes are the fingers of the leaf; and as many lobes as it has, in so many directions it tends to flow, and more heat or other genial influences would have caused it to flow yet farther.

Thus it seemed that this one hillside illustrated the principle of all the operations of Nature. The Maker of this earth but patented a leaf. What Champollion will decipher this hieroglyphic for us, that we may turn over a new leaf at last? (pp. 307-8)

It has been argued that Thoreau's own prose in the sandbank passage reflects the same deliberate employment of gutturals, labials, and dentals.[2] There is little evidence that Thoreau believed in Kraitsir's anagogic phonetic triad to the point that he structured his own sentences devoutly upon it. But there is a further sense in which Kraitsirian glossology is a Rosetta stone that helps decipher Thoreau's vision of the sandbank, if not of the universe.

His metaphor above describes nature as a hieroglyphic, a form of language that, though secret, can be read by patient study. The relationship between nature and language fascinated Kraitsir. As a disciple of German Romantic scholarship, he early committed himself to the central belief that "language is a living organism." He quotes Humboldt's famous definition of language, amplifies it, and proceeds to offer his own definition: "Language . . . cannot but be the aim and end of the whole complex of human energies, the only adequate memento of . . . a people and . . . each man, while they and he yet live; and still more so after they had made their exeunt from the theatre of their activity" (*Glossology*, pp. 22-24). For Kraitsir language functions as the *telos* of the *Weltgeist,* the dynamic of human progress, and the mode of man's immortality. As the chief end of man, it replaces the glorification of God enjoined in the Westminster Catechism. Or rather, for Kraitsir the word *is* God: "The spirit is spread-ing, sprout-ing, going, gas-like, a ghost (Germ. geist, self-acting, gush-ing.) God's highest manifestation, as far as it can be felt by us, is in our spirit, especially in our mental faculties" (ibid., p. 159). Hence the highest form of mental culture, the study of language, is the best worship. Semantic analysis is the new revelation: "Get, got = go + to = cau-se + end . . . symbol of first, of beginning, tending to an aim, and attaining it. Hence God and good. The latter not an epithet of sickly sentimentality, but of reasonable conscious aim-viewing, of apt- or fitness" (ibid., p. 197).

Believing like Kraitsir that "*articulate* may go together with *organic*" (ibid., p. 69), Thoreau sees the natural world as pregnant with its fundamental and universal language. The heaps of cast-off innards and appendages on the sandbank might appall a sickly sentimentalist with their excrementitiousness; but they are simply the discarded forms, the outmoded grammar, as it were, of an essentially linguistic *Weltgeist* pressing forward in its search for greater articulacy. This theme of spirit working itself out through the metamorphoses of matter lies at the heart of *Walden*. It is memorably dramatized in the penultimate paragraph when the strong and beautiful bug gnaws its way out of the apple-tree table. Viewing language as the *Weltgeist*, Thoreau, too, hesitates to bar its progress. While his style does yeoman service clearing away petrified impedimenta, he resists the seductions of form. All articulations must be discarded: "In view of the future or possible, we should live quite laxly and undefined in front, our outlines dim and misty on that side; as our shadows reveal an insensible perspiration toward the sun. The volatile truth of our words should continually betray the inadequacy of the residual statement" (*Walden*, pp. 324–25).

Another passage in *Walden*'s "Spring" betrays the impact of glossology when Thoreau describes the thawing pond: "Walden is melting apace. . . . A great field of ice has cracked off from the main body. I hear a song-sparrow singing from the bushes on the shore,—*olit, olit, olit,—chip, chip, chip, che, char—che, wiss, wiss, wiss*. He too is helping to crack it. How handsome the great sweeping curves in the edge of the ice, answering somewhat to those of the shore, but more regular!" (p. 235).

The amateur of Thoreauvian wordplay needs no glossology to see that he is punning on two senses of *crack* (shatter, talk) and that in crying *chip* repeatedly the sparrow is imagined to be chipping the ice. But Kraitsir's speculations cast more light:

> Why is a *curve* called *curve*? The *c* being produced in the curvature of the organs of speech (in the guttur), is the symbol of the *angle*, of the *break of a line*. The *r*, as a symbol of repetition, and of movement, inherent in *breaking*, denotes repetition of the angle designated by *c*, not only as to its geometrical qualities, but also as to our organs of hearing. Thence it comes that *curvus, circus, crux*, on the one hand, and *crepo, increpo, to cry*, are symbolized by the same combination. The difference between *crepo* and *frango*, is very delicate; for *crepo* is a kind of augmentative of *frango*, whose correlative, as to sound, is *fragor*, and so on. (*Significance*, p. 38)

A major preoccupation of Thoreau's was understanding the phenomena of nature by means of their organic interconnections. He amassed mountains of data in efforts to construct a calendar of correspondences that would predict the spring thaw. "I hear the bluebirds in the air," he journalized, "the blue curls of their warblings,—harbingers of serene and warm weather, little azure rills of melody trickling here and there from out the air, their short warble trilled in the air reminding of so many corkscrews assaulting and thawing the torpid mass of winter, assisting the ice and snow to melt and the streams to flow" (17 Mar. 1853). Behind the lyricism here is the conviction that since both water and birds are said to *trill* (a word containing both liquid consonants and the shorter word *rill*) ice melts because of some sympathetic vibration throughout nature. "The very grain of the air seems to have undergone a change and is ready to split into the form of the bluebird's warble," he imagined. "The air over these fields is a foundry full of moulds for casting bluebirds' warbles. Any sound uttered now would take that form, not of the harsh vibrating, rending scream of the jay, but a softer, flowing, curling warble, like a purling stream or the lobes of flowing sand and clay" (18 Feb. 1857). The notes of this bird's spring song suggest an occult Pythagorean harmony pervading nature. "His soft warble melts in the ear, as the snow is melting in the valleys around. The bluebird comes and with his warble drills the ice and sets free the rivers and ponds and frozen ground. As the sand flows down the slopes a little way, assuming the forms of foliage where the frost comes out of the ground, so this little rill of melody flows a short way down the concave of the sky" (2 Mar. 1859).

In speculating about the hidden harmonies of springtime Thoreau must have welcomed Kraitsir's ideas as a clue. For glossology suggests that there is an occult link between the *break*-up of ice and bird-*cries*, that fragmentation and sound are organically related like *frango* and *fragor* or *rigor* and *rigo*. Thoreau's sparrow flourishes his guttural song like an ice pick, for he seems to participate in a system of correspondences where the notes *c* and *r* are repeated blows, echoed by the curves of the shore and the "answering curves" of the ice.

Walden's Dirty Language and Walter Whiter's Geocentric Etymology

Stimulating though Kraitsir undoubtedly was, for his fundamental conception of the sandbank Thoreau was indebted to another philologist. On the shelves of Emerson's library, where Thoreau often browsed, stood a copy of Walter Whiter's *Etymologicon Magnum, or Universal*

Etymological Dictionary on a New Plan (Cambridge, Eng.: Cambridge University Press, 1800). Believing that sounds had intrinsic meaning, this Fellow of Clare College found a profound resemblance between the English word *earth*, the Hebrew *aretz*, and the Arabic *erd*. Further, "we may well imagine, that the name of an object so important as the *Earth*, could supply the origin to a great race of words expressing the various operations which are attached to it; and in all these instances likewise, should we expect to find the same coincidence. We shall instantly perceive, how by this idea the supposed similarity of languages is extended" (pp. xxi-xxii). Since Whiter ignored vowels and viewed all cognate consonants as indiscriminately interchangeable, he was indeed able to demonstrate the similarity of all languages—especially when he discovered that under certain conditions even consonants that were not cognate could pass into each other.

Occasionally he could wonder whether "the reader perchance, in the spirit of captious objection, should be disposed to observe, that I have assumed to myself an ample sphere for the exercise of my Theory or my Invention; and that with such a latitude of change, transformations of every kind may readily be effected" (p. xvi). But such doubts were soon dispelled by the magic radical RTH (convertible when necessary to any other consonants) and the infinitely fertile concept of the earth. This bulks with peculiar importance in Whiter's theory. While sounds correspond to objects and have inherent, imperishable meanings, the earth looms in Whiter's imagination as the overwhelming object first confronted by primeval man: "It is impossible, I imagine, to deny or to doubt this fact" (pp. xxiv-xxv). Implied though never quite stated is his solution to the riddle of the origin of language: by sympathetic vibration, so to speak, the earth generated it.

In the eighteenth century Poisinet de Sivry had derived all language from fire, and Rousseau from water, while Herder's climatic theories stressed the shaping influence of the air on human speech. But it remained for this stalwart Englishman to ground language solidly on the first of the Four Elements, terra firma. True to his promise, he did not relinquish this theme. Incorporating and expanding his first work, two volumes duly appeared with the title *Etymologicon Universale . . . in which it is shown . . . that languages contain the same fundamental idea; and that they are derived from the Earth and the operations, accidents, and properties belonging to it* (Cambridge, Eng.: Cambridge University Press, 1811). Twelve hundred pages of exegesis expound the "*one great Universal* object,—ever present—ever visible and perpetually pressing upon the attention of man" (1:82). Whiter insists that his etymologies are no dead language. Not only did the earth "seize on the mind of man, in suggesting the *first* or *prevailing* ideas communicated by Language" (1:77), but it has preserved the language that it formed. Thus he concludes that "THE ORIGINAL ELEMENTS OF LANGUAGE, which were once vocal in the inventions and emotions of primeval Man . . . continue to be instinct with the energies of Mind; and to record in mystic, though in faithful characters, the secret History of the Ancient World" (2:1263).

This marvelous fact leads Whiter to make explicit a religious analogy underlying his conception of language: the doctrine of transmigration. He believes that "the Element, by which a race of words is generated and preserved, may be compared to that *primitive* and *unperishing particle*, in which, according to the doctrine of the visionary Philosophers, consists the Essence of the Soul. . . . The material vesture, with which the divine particle is enveloped, and through which it communicates with the world around it, is ever passing into an infinite variety of shapes and appearances; but the Soul itself still continues to preserve inviolate its peculiar force and characteristic energy." Thus the capstone to Whiter's geocentric theory of language is a muddy metaphysic somewhat like Berkeley's in the *Siris*. Once we understand how words are derived from the earth, "it will surely be acknowledged, that the doctrine of these visionary Philosophers affords a strong and striking resemblance to the principles of the theory, which in the present volume I have laboured with such solicitude to unfold and establish. The *Elements* of *Language* and of *Life* are employed in the same work, and their operations are directed to the same purpose" (2:1255–57).

With death approaching, Whiter crowned his labors in 1825 with a third volume of the *Etymologicon Universale*. It amplified and reformulated his theory that human language sprang from the dirt. But he was increasingly preoccupied with earth in fluid forms. Hence the third volume chronicles not the transmogrification of the elementary character RTH but devotes more than five hundred pages to "the two forms BS &c. and MC &c." (p. 4). These two are really one, for the latter is essentially a form of BS.

Four hundred pages chronicle the adventures of the radical BC, the progenitor of such key terms as Bog, Pash, Peat, Puddle, Pit, and Bottom, "those words which relate to the BASE or *Low* Spot, to the PUDGE spot or matter" (p. 7). Throughout this volume particular stress is laid on the derivation of anatomical terminology. Thus "there are various terms, belonging to our Element BC, &c. which relate to the *Mouth, Lips, Cheeks*, &c.," apparently "from the idea of PUDG*ing*, or *Swelling out*" (p. 206). Likewise we find in the "words *Pulpa, Puls, Pulmentum*,

Pulmo, the *Rising* up—Swelling out substances, as of *Mud*-matter." Not only the pulpy lungs but the legs are derived from mud, since the Latin *Pedes*, feet, are apparently connected with the French "PATrouiller, To tread in . . . a Muddy place" (p. 31). Comparable derivations account for most of our organs.

In explaining how we should trace "to the Plastic nature of PUDGE, or *v*-ISC*ous* Matter . . . PHIZ, (Eng.) VIS*age* (Eng.) with its parallels" and also "WISE, WIT, WITTY . . . with their parallels," Whiter comes close to depicting the fluid birth of anatomy that Thoreau saw in the thawing sandbank. Indeed, what Whiter envisions here is nothing less than the genesis of mind from matter:

> I might state my hypothesis by observing, that these terms expressing *Form, Appearance, Sight, Knowledge*, are derived from the Pliant, *Plastic* nature of OOZY, *v*-ISCous matter, which is readily or easily moved, *Stirred* about, together, &c. which quickly or readily gives way so as to receive, or admit of *Form*, and hence it relates to that *Quick, Pliant*, or *Ready* Faculty of the Mind, able to *Form* images to deVISE, Invent &c. or to the Quick Powers of the *Imagination*, as we express it. In the same manner we see, that the term *Imagination* belongs to Image, which I shall show to be derived from the Plastic *Matter* of *Mud*. That the Greek words relating to sight are connected with the notion of OOZE Matter, under some process, is evident from . . . ID*os*, Ἴδος sudor. (pp. 391–92)

Increasingly the idea of washy dirt becomes the primal clue linking myriads of seemingly unrelated words. What the book thus offers is a vision of language erupting from the primeval slime.

Fittingly enough, Whiter concludes his *Etymologicon* by passing from the radical BS/BC to MC, MD, etc., which "receive their force, as I imagine, from such terms as Mud, Muck, &c" (p. 4). His final 140 pages are an extended meditation on "the MATTER of MUD." An English writer is lucky to have a term "such as MUD, which is so common in every species of style, so comprehensive, and so intelligible to all . . . an advantage, which no other Language is able to supply." Colored by the consciousness of his own approaching demise, his etymologies have initially a rather somber cast. Upon analysis, mud yields three leading ideas. First, we have words "which relate more particularly to the Ground, Dirt, Filth, &c.," such as *Mushroom*, and hence "to What is Foul, Vile, Bad, &c." As we might expect, this section shows off his polyglot vocabulary for various forms of excrement. Second, we get "those terms, which relate to a MASHED, or MUD like state, as of Destruction, Dissolution, Decay, Disorder . . . in the *Frame*, or the *Mind* of Man, and other animals, as MUT, (Heb.) Death, MAC*ies*, (Lat.) Consumption." The gloomy atmosphere inspired by such meditations is finally dispelled, however, by contemplating a third quality of mud "in a state of Consistency, as *Being in*, or as *Collected* into a MASS, Lump, Heap, &c. or as *Rising, Swelling*, or *Bulging up, out*." In this guise mud becomes more benign. The *Etymologicon* concludes with this bachelor's enthusiastic account of the "Generative Powers, &c... which are derived, as I conceive, from the MATTER of MUD, under the idea of The MATTER, or Substance, The *Formative*, or *Formed* Matter, or *Substance*, the *Creative, Creating*, or the *Created* Substance, the *Creature*,—The MAKing, or MADE MATTER" (pp. 401–4). Scholastic tradition held that this MATTER is obviously our MOTHER, and the reader accustomed to Whiter's linguistic legerdemain will experience no surprise in learning that mud is also to be connected etymologically with springtime, for "the term MAY, *Maius*, quasi MAJ, MAJus is the *Producing* Month" (p. 528).

Whiter's muddy linguistics surely parallels *Walden*'s vision in the railroad cut. What Thoreau confronts in the flowing sand is not just the birth pangs of vegetable and animal life. As his wordplay with *globe-lapse-labor* suggests, he is also wittily recapitulating the Fall of Man. Because life is mortal, it is inextricably mingled with excrement in what strikes the eye as a charnel house of destruction:

> This phenomenon is more exhilarating to me than the luxuriance and fertility of vineyards. True, it is somewhat excrementitious in its character, and there is no end to the heaps of liver, lights and bowels, as if the globe were turned wrong side outward; but this suggests at least that nature has some bowels, and there again is mother of humanity. This is the frost coming out of the ground; this is Spring. . . . I know of nothing more purgative of winter fumes and indigestions. It convinces me that Earth is still in her swaddling clothes, and stretches forth baby fingers on every side. Fresh curls spring from the baldest brow. There is nothing inorganic. These foliaceous heaps lie along the bank like the slag of a furnace, showing that nature is "in full blast" within. The earth is not a mere fragment of dead history, stratum upon stratum like the leaves of a book, to be studied by geologists and antiquaries chiefly, but living poetry like the leaves of a tree, which precede flowers and fruit—not a fossil earth, but a living earth; compared with whose great central life all animal and vegetable life is merely parasitic. Its throes will heave our exuviae from their graves. (pp. 308–9)

The birth pangs that Thoreau witnesses are also throes of death. This world needs toilet training, for earth attests to her status as both ageless and newborn by rioting in senile and infantile incontinence. Like Ezekiel Hildreth, Thoreau can equate fertility with industrial productivity. But lacking Hildreth's confidence in "our factory system," which is criticized elsewhere in *Walden* (p. 26), what Thoreau contemplates here is not so much the glowing creativity of nature's blast furnace (which remains hidden) as the prodigal waste left by her creative process: the slag heaps, the sewage, the offal of the abattoir.

Like Whiter, both Court de Gébelin and Emerson encouraged Thoreau to see linguistic creativity as fecal. In his *Dictionnaire étymologique de la langue latine* the Frenchman boldly connected the Latin *creo* = create, *screo* = spit, *crepo* = make a sudden farting noise, *scoria* = slag, and *excrementum* = excrement. He treated all these as conceptually related cognates derived from the same primitive onomatopoetic root "CRA, CRE, CRI, CRO, COR, &c" (pp. 467ff.) Since the actual Indo-European roots *ker-^{2}*= make a sound and *ker-^{3}*= grow are apparently distinct, and neither is connected with the Indo-European *sker-^{4}*= to cut off, the source of *excrementum*, *scoria*, and probably *screo*, these equations created some radical discrepancies. But to be told that many of these resemblances were groundless would probably not trouble Thoreau much, for he could take satisfaction in a genuine linguistic analogy not exploited by Court de Gébelin: the fact that the Latin *excrementum* and *scribere* both derive from the same Indo-European root *sker-^{4}*. Etymologically, writing is indeed a form of excreting.

A similar thought had occurred to Emerson, for in *Nature*'s section "Language" he quoted Elizabeth Peabody's manuscript translation of the French Swedenborgian Guillaume Oegger: "'Material objects,' said a French philosopher, 'are necessarily kinds of *scoriae* of the substantial thoughts of the Creator, which must always preserve an exact relation to their first origin'" (CW, 1:22–23). Rightly noting that "this doctrine is . . . abstruse though the images of . . . 'scoriae' . . . may stimulate the fancy," Emerson proceeds to "summon the aid of subtler and more vital expositors to make it plain." Emersonian correspondence theory was quite capable of imagining the universe as both the Divine Author's handwriting and God's excrement. "What is there of the divine in . . . a privy?" he journalized in 1834. "Much. All" (*JMN*, 4:307). Emerson's grandfatherly manner tempts modern readers to overlook how daring his doctrine of nature as a language really was. We tend simply to murmur, "Oh, yes," when we should exclaim, "Holy shit!"

Despite its gruesomeness, Thoreau is able to view the sandbank with high spirits because what he sees in the sands is a world travailing to give birth to speech. Life and language are not only coordinates; all life seems to aspire to linguistic *expression*. His own style denies the mimic Fall of Man by making it issue not in work but in verbal play. With Whiter's aid, Thoreau inverts Emerson's dictum that language is fossil poetry by treating earth as poetry and fossils as baby talk. Court de Gébelin had expressed a similar view in his *Dictionnaire étymologique de la langue Latine*, for the Latin word *ferre* means both *to bear* and *to say*. After he derived the noun *ver* = spring correctly from it, the noun *verbum* = word was also plausibly (though incorrectly) traced to the same source, much as Ezekiel Hildreth would do later. The two words, together with such French cognates as *verdure* and *parole*, were treated as the descendants of the same primitive root BAR (pp. 160-61). Like *Logopolis*, therefore, both the *Monde primitif* and the *Etymologicon* purport to furnish ample evidence that in the formation of words "Earth is still in her swaddling clothes, and stretches forth baby fingers on every side." Thus for Thoreau language and the other social institutions that earth generates remain "plastic like clay in the hands of the potter." This means that as "the very globe continually transcends and translates itself in its orbit," such social excrescences as the railroad traversing one corner of the pond may be eliminated by purer forms of communication. Insofar as the Fitchburg line carries little traffic now while Walden reflects an occasional airplane, this prophecy has proved true enough. Thoreau might have been less chipper had he foreseen the cars on the highway that has replaced the Middlesex Pike a stone's throw from his hut. But like other social institutions, that too is transient—hence his positive glee at the bracing spectacle of universal mortality.

To say that "there is nothing inorganic" may seem to insist that everything except the earth is mortal. But not quite. For by translating itself into language the globe transcends itself into a timeless sphere. Dead languages there may be, but as *Walden*'s chapter "Reading" emphasizes, with heroic effort they can still be read. If language is an organism, it is a curiously abstract, nonbiological organism that seems in some ways deathless—in principle, at least. Hence Court de Gébelin, Kraitsir, and Whiter all worship it as incarnating the eternal element of their cosmologies. Whether such faith would be rewarded was, of course, a question glinting with irony that some etymological metaphysicians had to confront. In *Philosophic Etymology* (1816) James Gilchrist fretted over it:

> Etymologicon Magnum . . . I have twenty times attempted to read and twenty times laid down with deep regret: but whatever I may think of the work as often mystical, I have great respect for the author. . . . Had he first of all studied himself into the true nature of alphabetic signs . . . he could not have lost himself in such a wilderness. . . . This notice which I have been led unintentionally to take of the labours of Mr. Whiter diffuses a tender melancholy over my mind for in turning from them I have often said to myself with an involuntary sigh, what a poor fallible thing is the

human understanding! Perhaps after all this anxious thinking and toilsome enquiry I shall only make a book to lie on the same shelf, or be thrown to the same heap, with Etymologicon Magnum.[3]

Alas, Gilchrist's melancholy forebodings were amply justified. Later in the century nagging doubts about his own book *Phrasis* (1864) drove the American philologue Jacob Wilson into a similar ironic stance.

Whiter's career neatly concatenates several themes running through the tradition of etymological metaphysics. His first publication was *A Specimen of a Commentary on Shakespeare . . . on a new principle of criticism, derived from Mr. Locke's doctrine of the association of ideas* (1794). In this pioneering work he focused on the poet's wordplay, for he had rightly noticed that "certain terms containing an equivocal meaning, or sounds suggesting such a meaning, will often serve to introduce other words and expressions of a similar nature."[4] He thus furnished ammunition for Coleridge to mount his defense of Shakespearean wordplay a few years later. Moving on to the labor of his *Etymologicon*, Whiter refreshed himself annually by throwing a birthday picnic for Shakespeare garnished with commemorative verses in English and Latin. Publishing some of these tributes to the immortal bard at the age of sixty, he also emerged from his labyrinth that year to issue his *Dissertation on the Disorder of Death, or That State Called Suspended Animation* (1819). In that tract he mingles medical lore with Shakespearean passages treating death as sleep to argue that attempts to resuscitate the dead should always be performed. The novelist George Borrow relished his company for his knowledge of twenty languages, including Romany. A character in *Lavengro* (1851) describes him thus: "He has got queer notions in his head—wrote a book to prove that all words came originally from the earth—who knows? Words have roots, and roots live in the earth; but, upon the whole, I should not call him altogether a sound man."[5] With that estimate of this aggressively eccentric clergyman, who boxed, doted on cold baths, and lived as a quasi-hermit, we may agree.

In his preoccupation with punning, etymology, bodily decay, and literary immortality, Thoreau rather resembled him.

Thoreau's Hydraulic Psychology of Humor

"A written word is the choicest of relics," Thoreau argues in *Walden*. "It may be translated into every language, and not only be read but actually breathed from all human lips . . . carved out of the breath of life itself" (p. 102). When he marvels at how "the symbol of an ancient man's thought becomes a modern man's speech," he expresses an attitude toward language that informs all his writing. Like the Tookean tradition, linguistic organicism deriving from Humboldt tempted him to conceive of words biologically. He eked out this basic stance idiosyncratically with hints culled from the exuberant speculation of the American Renaissance. Though not wholly consistent, the resulting mix of ideas has imaginative coherence. For want of a better term, we might call Thoreau's mystique of language verbal vitalism.

Underlying Thoreau's pronouncements about speech is the notion that words are either alive or virtually so. "We cannot write well or truly but what we write with gusto. The body the senses must conspire with the spirit— Expression is the act of the whole man . . . that our speech may be vascular" (2 Sept. 1851). Speech comes from the human body and seems to have a body of its own that shares the circulation of its parent. When "the poet sings how the blood flows in his veins . . . he performs his functions. . . . His song is a vital function like breathing, and an integral result like weight" (*Week*, p. 91). The organs of the body must supply the verbal organism too. "The intellect is powerless to express thought without the aid of the heart and liver and of every member." Physical life pumps through language, so that it is vain "to sit down to write when you have not stood up to live. Methinks that the moment my legs begin to move, my thoughts begin to flow—as if I had given vent to the stream at the lower end & consequently new fountains flowed into it at the upper." Linking verbal fluency with the circulation of bodily fluids, Thoreau works out this hydraulic conception of diction with meticulous detail: "You need to increase the draught below—as the owners of meadows on C. River say of the Billerica Dam. Only while we are in action is the circulation perfect. The writing which consists with habitual sitting is mechanical wooden dull to read" (19 Aug. 1851). A vascular utterance requires the author to establish proper drainage for his physique, so unfortunately "a perfectly healthy sentence . . . is extremely rare" (*Week*, p. 103).

Nonetheless, "a few sentences spring like sward in its native pasture, where its roots were never disturbed" (*Week*, p. 100). Thoreau's praise of early literature in *A Week* is built on this organic premise. Early sentences are "verdurous and blooming as evergreen and flowers because they are rooted in fact and experience, but our false and florid sentences have only the tints of flowers without their sap or roots" (*Week*, p. 104). The man of science studied nature as a dead language, Thoreau thought, and the result was reflected in scientific writing. "What a keepsake a manual of botany! In which is uttered breathed, man's love of flowers. It is dry as a *hortus siccus*.— Flowers are pressed into the botanist's service" (30 Jan. 1852). As his wordplay with *pressed* here demonstrates,

Thoreau wanted no such funereal album. Happily, "there are many words which are genuine and indigenous and have their root in our natures, not made by scholars" (1 Jan. 1858). Nevertheless, "some men have a peculiar taste for bad words . . . like 'tribal' and 'ornamentation,' which drag a dead tail after them. They will pick you out of a thousand the stillborn words, the falsettos, the wing-clipped and lame words" (26 Jan. 1858). Belief in the rooted vitality of the verbal organism underlies his contempt for "a writer who . . . uses torpid words, wooden or lifeless words, such words as 'humanitary,' which have a paralysis in their tails" (14 July 1852). Thoreau's waspish rejection of such crippled diction reflects a desire for speech lively enough to sting. "My work is writing, and . . . no subject is too trivial for me, tried by ordinary standards; for, ye fools, the theme is nothing, the life is everything" (18 Oct. 1856).

"All that interests the reader is the depth and intensity of the life excited," Thoreau continues. To excite life in the reader requires the writer to render his own life. His sentences "must have the essence or oil of himself, tried out of the fat of his experience and joy," for "however mean and limited, it must be a genuine and contented life that he speaks out of" (23 Dec. 1856). Ergo, writing on set themes is vain. "We must wait till they have kindled a flame in our minds. There must be the copulating & generating force of love behind every effort destined to be successful. The cold resolve gives birth to—begets, nothing" (30 Jan. 1852). Our titillated era makes it hard to imagine that Thoreau's chastity was not a cold resolve. It was his artistic and amatory response to "the theme that seeks me, not I it. The poet's relation to this theme is the relation of lovers. It is no more to be courted. Obey—report." As this passage extolling verbal copulation suggests, Thoreau shared Emerson's desire for "spermatic, prophesying, man-making words" (*JMN*, 8:148). He often imagined language as seeds germinating in an audience. "Facts collected by a poet are set down at last as winged seeds of truth, samarae, tinged with his expectation. Oh, may my words be verdurous and sempiternal as the hills! Facts fall from the poetic observer as ripe seeds" (19 June 1852).

But nobody realizes just how deeply he believed in language as sublimated libido. As *Walden*'s chapter "Higher Laws" reveals, he was sufficiently influenced by Hindu tradition to flirt with the notion that seminal retention enhances creativity. "The generative energy, which, when we are loose, dissipates and makes us unclean, when we are continent invigorates and inspires us. Chastity is the flowering of man" (pp. 219–20). Thus he regrets that "there is to be attributed to sensuality the loss to language of how many pregnant symbols" (6:207). Because of his hydraulic physiology and psychology Thoreau took his responsibility for disseminating ideas far more literally than we might suppose:

> The mind may perchance be persuaded to act—to energize—by the action and energy of the body. Any kind of liquid will fetch the pump.
>
> We all have our states of fullness & of emptiness—but we overflow at different points. One overflows through the sensual outlets—another through his heart another through his head—& another perchance only through the higher part of his head, or his poetic faculty. . . . We can perchance thus direct our nutriment to those organs we specially use. (7 Sept. 1851)

If he ever applied his crude theory of biofeedback, most morsels must have been religiously routed over the high road of the mind, while gastrointestinal traffic was diverted from the dangerous junction of the crotch. "Genius is the abundance of life or health," he opined, but it needs to be properly husbanded, so that "if we have not dissipated the vital, the divine, fluids, there is . . . a circulation of vitality beyond our bodies" (11 July 1852).

It was awkward reconciling this ascetic strain with his vascular theory of verbal expression emanating from the whole man: "Often I feel that my head stands out too dry, when it should be immersed. A writer, a man writing, is the scribe of all nature; he is the corn and the grass and the atmosphere writing." If recording "whatever things I perceive with my entire man . . . will be poetry," the entire man definitely included what he had elsewhere dismissed as "the superfluous juices of the body" (14 Dec. 1840). Thus he ends this meditation on vascular writing rather ambiguously: "It is always essential that we love to do what we are doing, do it with a heart. The maturity of the mind, however, may perchance consist with a certain dryness." Another lengthy meditation on writing concludes rather surprisingly that "we seek too soon to ally the perceptions of the mind to the experience of the hand—to prove our gossamer truths practical—to show their connection with our everyday life. . . . Ah give me pure mind—pure thought!" (25 Dec. 1851). So he complained on the Christian festival celebrating the Word's loving incarnation of itself.

Yet when he experienced pure mind in its scientific incarnation he was often repelled. "It turns the man of science to stone. I feel that I am dissipated by so many observations." Brushing his hand against a rock while studying lichens, he found himself smoothing back his skin as if "prepared to study lichens there. I look upon man but as a fungus. I have almost a slight, dry headache as the result of all this observing. How to observe is how to behave. O for a little Lethe! To crown all, lichens which are so thin, are described in the *dry* state, as they are most commonly, not most truly seen. Truly, they are *dryly* described" (23 Mar. 1853). More than the Wordsworthian fear of murdering to dissect underlies this passage. What troubles Thoreau most is how scientific observation kills the observer. Nineteenth-century science was moving away from the creative perceiver whom Berkeley had insisted on. Its highest ideal became the elimination of all subjectivity—its characteristic vice, collecting masses of dead data. Inadvertently becoming the object of his own observation, Thoreau finds himself amalgamated to the rock and the lichen—painfully so. Thus objectified, man risks becoming a fungus himself. With determined punning on *dry* Thoreau seeks to extricate himself from the toils of a dead scientific language involving a hypertrophy of intellect. Etymologically, one antidote to excessive dryness was *humor* (from Latin *umor* = moisture).

Elizabethans, Indians, and Animated Nature-Writing

As a poetic naturalist Thoreau believed that "the truest description, and that by which another living man can most readily recognize a flower, is the unmeasured and eloquent one which the sight of it inspires. No scientific description will supply the want of this, though you should count and measure and analyze every atom that seems to compose it. Surely poetry and eloquence are a more universal language than that Latin which is confessedly dead" (13 Oct. 1860). His hostility here is directed against Linnaean botanic terminology because of the fixed, uniform, and unequivocal meaning at which it aims. That aim, rather than its being couched in Latin, makes it a dead language. As he complains elsewhere, "the most important part of an animal is its *anima*, its vital spirit, on which is based its character. . . . Yet most scientific books which treat of animals leave this out altogether, and what they describe are as it were phenomena of dead matter" (18 Feb. 1860). Their *dead* nomenclature kills like formaldehyde, so "as soon as I begin to be aware of the life of any creature, I at once forget its name. . . . The best and most harmless names are those which are an imitation of the voice or note of an animal, or the most poetic ones." From his belief that "if you have undertaken to write the biography of an animal, you will have to present to us the living creature," it follows that stylistically "a history of animated nature must itself be animated." Like modern field biology and ecological studies— lineal descendants in many ways—the tradition within which Thoreau worked did not take physics as the model for all science. Reserving a role for the scientist as participant, natural history sanctioned observations that cannot readily be replicated in a lab, falsified, or verified.

Therefore Thoreau made a cult of the older naturalists. He found their vital language more suited than scientific terms to the description of nature. On 16 December 1859 he traveled to Cambridge, "where I read in Gerard's Herbal. His admirable though quaint descriptions, are, to my mind, greatly superior to the modern more scientific ones. He describes not according to rule but to his natural delight in the plants." Quoting Edward Topsell's description of antelope which "are bred in India and Syria, near the river Euphrates . . . and delight much to drink of the cold water thereof" from the *History of Four-Footed Beasts* (1607), Thoreau adds, "The beasts which most modern naturalists describe do not *delight* in anything, and their water is neither hot nor cold" (16 Feb. 1860). Gerard and Topsell shared the natural impulses that they found in flora and fauna. Thus their descriptions were vibrantly phrased, and their own prose throbbed with nature's vitality. Whereas "modern botanical descriptions approach ever nearer to the dryness of an algebraic formula, as if $x + y$ were = to a love letter," Gerard wrote with "the keen joy and discrimination of the child who has just seen a flower for the first time and comes running in with it to its friends. How much better to describe your object in fresh English words rather than in these conventional Latinisms" (16 Dec. 1859).

In Thoreau's imagination delightful fresh flowers demand delighted fresh words. Gerard could supply organically fresh diction because he "has not only heard of and seen and raised a plant, but felt and smelled and tasted it, applying all his senses to it" (13 Oct. 1860). Moreover, his fluid Elizabethan syntax projects a truly organic view of nature:

> You are not distracted from the thing to system or arrangement. In the true natural order the order or system is not insisted on. Each is first, and each last. That which presents itself to us this moment occupies the whole of the present and rests on the very topmost point of the sphere, under the zenith. The species and individuals of all the natural kingdoms ask our attention and admiration in a round robin. We make straight lines . . . where Nature has made curves to which belongs their own sphere-music. It is indispensable for us to square her circles, and we offer our rewards to him who will do it. (13 Oct. 1860)

The Linnaean system of classification thus resembles the artificial systems of grammar that prompted Thoreau to exclaim, "When I read some of the rules for speaking and writing the English language correctly,—as that a sentence must never end with a particle,—and perceive how implicitly even the learned obey it, I think—Any fool can make a rule / And every fool will mind it" (3 Feb. 1860). What he preferred was the "wild and dusky knowledge" of natural language for which "the

Spaniards have a good term . . . *Gramatica parda*, tawny grammar," a kind of mother-wit derived from the leopard (W, 5:289).

Thoreau's preference for the older naturalists was rooted in the following convictions:

> As in the expression of moral truths we admire any closeness to the physical fact which in all language is the symbol of the spiritual, so, finally, when natural objects are described, it is an advantage if words derived originally from nature, it is true, but which have been turned (*tropes*) from their primary signification to a moral sense, are used, *i.e.*, if the object is personified. The one who loves and understands a thing best will incline to use the personal pronouns in speaking of it. To him there is no *neuter* gender. Many of the words of the old naturalists were in this sense doubly tropes. (15 Feb. 1860)

In *Walden* Thoreau complained that modern *philosophers* were not really lovers of wisdom. He surely could have made a similar complaint about modern philologists. We are not so naive as to assume that literary scholars should write as though they loved language, but Thoreau would have argued the point. He would also have speculated about why there is no corresponding term for a naturalist—like, say, a *philophysicist*. For he assumed that the naturalist was—or should be—fundamentally a *lover of nature*. Even Linnaeus called himself a Botanophile. As lovers of nature, Gerard and Topsell were able to describe flora and fauna appropriately in language animated by the same creative power as their subjects.

But the passage suggests that Thoreau would push this rationale even further and extend it to describing natural *objects*. As a history of animated nature should be animated, so should a history of inanimate nature. Even for the *philophysicist* there is no neuter gender. By moralizing and personifying nature, in words that were doubly tropes, the older naturalists attested to the belief that Thoreau proclaimed at the sandbank as a philogeologist: "There is nothing inorganic." Though in his wilder flights Emerson was capable of almost anything, he tended not to go quite so far. Man and the moral law were the poles of his thought, and the thrust of *Nature* was to subordinate the world to both. But Thoreau wrote in the Wordsworthian conviction that "Nature is reported not by him who goes forth consciously as an observer, but in the fullness of life. To such a one she rushes to make her report. To the full heart she is all but a figure of speech" (2 July 1852). To speak her language the poetic observer had to approach her as a lover, for "Love is the burden of all Nature's odes. The song of the birds is an epithalamium, a hymeneal. The marriage of the flowers spots the meadows and fringes the hedges with pearls and diamonds. In the deep water, in the high air, in woods and pastures, and the bowels of the earth, this is the employment and condition of all things" (2 Mar. 1840). The naturalist's employment was to merge with her for a loving moment so that his figures of speech would echo the pulsating rhythm pervading every nook and cranny, both organic and inorganic.

Deploring modern manuals, where "I rarely read a sentence . . . which reminds me of flowers or living plants" (22 Sept. 1860), Thoreau was likewise drawn to John Evelyn's *Sylva: or A Discourse of Forest-Trees* (1662). He notes that the author's "love of his subject teaches him to use many expressive words, some imported from the Latin, which I wonder how we can do without. . . . Many of his words show a poetic genius" (9 June 1852). This expressive style was possible because

> Evelyn and others wrote when the language was in a tender, nascent state and could be moulded to express the shades of meaning; when sesquipedalian words, long since cut and apparently dried and drawn to mill,—not yet to the dictionary lumber-yard—put forth a fringe of green sprouts here and there along in the angles of their rugged bark, their very bulk insuring some sap remaining; some florid suckers they sustain at least. Which words, split into shingles and laths, will supply poets for ages to come. (23 Mar. 1853)

Evelyn's sesquipedalian diction seemed vivid to Thoreau because, though Latinate, it was freshly derived, unlike words with dead tails. Though Evelyn did not coin most of these words, they were so newly transplanted that the soil still clung to their roots. Like his homely Saxon diction, this language sprang from the earth. Such words seemed ideally suited to describe trees because they embodied stylistically the force animating plants, language, and ultimately the earth itself. Thoreau's own sentence reflects the same vital power when he takes the cut and dried phrase *cut and dried* and literalizes it with a deliberately florid conceit comparing expressions to timber. His prose playfully demonstrates that two centuries after Evelyn's exuberant linguistic springtime the tree of the English language has enough sap remaining to put out a few suckers yet. Of course, Thoreau's prose especially aims to put out suckers who rely on their dictionaries as if words were authoritatively embalmed there rather than using them etymologically as sources of inspiration for living language.

For all his learning, Thoreau did not approach language as an antiquary but as a highly innovative author. His description of New England's stately elm trees overshadowing "the manikins beneath" in their villages shows how many intellectual surprises he could spring just by playing around with one pair of etymologies:

I find that into my idea of the village has entered more of the elm than the human being. They are worth many a political borough. They constitute a borough. The poor human representative of his party sent out from beneath their shade will not suggest a tithe of the dignity, the true nobleness and comprehensiveness of view, the sturdiness and independence, and the serene beneficence that they do. . . . A fragment of their bark is worth the backs of all the politicians in the union. They are free-soilers in their own broad sense. They send their roots north and south and east and west into many a conservative's Kansas and Carolina, who does not expect such underground railroad,—they improve the subsoil he has never disturbed,—and many times their length, if the support of their principles requires it. . . . See what scars they bear, what limbs they lost before we were born! Yet they never adjourn; they steadily vote for their principles, and send their roots further and wider from the *same centre*. They die at their posts, and they leave a tough butt for the choppers to exercise themselves about, and a stump which serves for their monument. They attend no caucus, they make no compromise, they use no policy. Their one principle is growth. They combine a true radicalism with a true conservatism. Their radicalism is not cutting away of roots, but an infinite multiplication and extension of them under all surrounding institutions. They take a firmer hold on the earth that they may rise higher into the heavens. Their conservative heart-wood, in which sap no longer flows, does not impoverish their growth, but is a firm column to support it. . . . Their conservatism is a dead but solid heart-wood, which is the pivot and firm column of support to all this growth, appropriating nothing to itself, but forever by its support assisting to extend the area of their radicalism. Half a century after they are dead at the core, they are preserved by radical reforms. They do not, like men, from radicals turn conservative. Their conservative part dies out first; their radical and growing part survives. (24 Jan. 1856)

From the root meanings of *radical* and *conservative* this passage extends itself in sinewy tentacles. Like the elms, its one principle is growth, both radically exploratory and conservatively ringed. Subsidiary wordplay branches off from the same center: borough/burrow, free-soilers, comprehensiveness, underground railroads, support, limbs, reforms. The passage contains some of the sharpest political satire ever penned by an American, with one audacious conceit following another until our conventional notions of radicalism and conservatism are inverted. But the final effect is one of serene beneficence like the elms, of a self-delighting verbal energy that dwarfs its satiric targets without needing to communicate with them, so massive is its irony.

Stylistically, Thoreau buttressed his conservative radicalism on previous eras. Quotations from Renaissance explorers and early New England historians stud his works.[6] He relished their expressions just as he preferred the early naturalists:

> What a strong and hearty but reckless, hit-or-miss style had some of the early writers of New England, like Josselyn and William Wood . . . as if they spoke with a relish, smacking their lips like a coach-whip, caring more to speak heartily than scientifically true. They are not to be caught napping by the wonders of Nature in a new country, and perhaps are often more ready to appreciate them than she is to exhibit them. They give you one piece of nature, at any rate, and that is themselves. (Cotton Mather, too, has a rich phrase.) They use a strong, coarse, homely speech which cannot always be found in the dictionary, nor sometimes be heard in polite society, but which brings you very near to the thing itself described. The strong new soil speaks through them. . . . Certainly that generation stood nearer to nature, nearer to the facts, than this, and hence their books have more life in them. (9 Jan. 1855)

Not denying their kinship with nature for a bogus objectivity, their speech resonates sympathetically with the objects they describe. Their awareness of physical facts vivifies their language. Thoreau quotes with admiration a lengthy passage in which Mather describes cattle buried in a blizzard, "interred (shall I say) or innived, in the snow" (3 Feb. 1856). Such apt and quirkily original phrase-making proved to Thoreau that "the forcible writer stands bodily behind his words with his experience. He does not make books out of books, but he has been *there* in person" (3 Feb. 1852). Earlier writers benefit as observers from not having their experience filtered through literature. Indeed, the best thing about their works is the difficulty of consulting them, which may help preserve the modern writer's tenuous and imperiled originality. "Nature, at least, takes no pains to introduce him to the works of his predecessors, but only presents him with her own *Opera Omnia*."

Thoreau was also deeply interested in the American Indian languages. What he could glean of Penobscot from his Maine guide Joe Polis fascinated him. Our botanic term *arbor vitae* seemed barren by comparison. "It is not a *tree* of *life*. But there are twenty words for the tree and its different parts which the Indian gave, which are not in our botanies, which imply a more practical and vital science," he noted (5 Mar. 1858). Our Linnaean term is a petrified classification because we have lost touch with the facts behind its root meaning. If we enjoyed a vital relation to it like the Indian, the tree of language would burst out with a score of lively terms that smack more of their origin. The vitality of Indian expression was among the "primitive" traits that led Thoreau to fill notebook after notebook copying information about Indians that would total nearly a million words. Likewise, during his last years he was planning a work to show the superiority of Pliny and other pre-scientific naturalists in portraying nature.

Making Prose Spring from the Earth

Both these major projects showcase his ideas about vital, natural expression. But though he lived long enough to produce a considerable oeuvre, both projects remained inchoate. He was neither an Elizabethan nor an Indian but an audacious nineteenth-century intellectual who wrote jocular letters in Latin to his schoolteaching sisters. How did he propose to get a suitable style for the works about animate nature that he actually did write?

> Where is the literature which gives expression to Nature? He would be a poet who could impress the winds and streams into his service, to speak for him; who nailed words to their primitive senses, as farmers drive down stakes in the spring, which the frost has heaved; who derived his words as often as he used them—transplanted them to his page with earth adhering to their roots; whose words were so true and fresh and natural that they would appear to expand like the buds at the approach of spring, though they lay half smothered between two musty leaves in a library—aye, to bloom and bear fruit there . . . for the faithful reader, in sympathy with surrounding Nature.
>
> I do not know any poetry to quote which adequately expresses this yearning for the Wild. Approached from this side, the best poetry is tame. I do not know where to find in any literature, ancient or modern, any account which contents me of that Nature with which even I am acquainted. . . . I demand something which no Augustan nor Elizabethan age, which no *culture*, in short, can give. Mythology comes nearer to it than anything. (W, 5:232)

The *wild* was the *willed*, Thoreau thought, so despite Romantic sputterings against the intellect, a mythological style demanded patient effort. "Write often, write upon a thousand themes rather than long at a time, not trying to turn too many feeble somersets in the air,—and so come down upon your head at last," he urged. "Antaeus-like, be not long absent from the ground. Those sentences are good and well discharged which are like so many little resiliencies from the spring floor of our life, a distinct fruit and kernel itself, springing from terra firma." He wanted a prose so alive to the earthy meanings in which words were rooted that its leaps and bounds could make a reader sense the physical analogies from which the spring sprang. Little resiliencies might help us feel the physical tensions in the farmer's activity when he "drives down stakes in the spring, which the frost has heaved."

So he continues his acrobatic manifesto:

> Let there be as many distinct plants as the soil and the light can sustain. Take as many bounds in a day as possible. Sentences uttered with your back to the wall. Those are the admirable bounds when the performer has

lately touched the springboard. A good bound into the air . . . is a good and wholesome experience, but what shall we say to a man's leaping off precipices in the attempt to fly? He comes down like lead. In the meanwhile you have got your feet planted upon the rock, with the rock also at your back, and . . . can say,

> "Come one, come all! this rock shall fly
> From its firm base as soon as I."

Such, uttered or not, is the strength of your sentence. Sentences in which there is no strain. (*W*, 9:107-8)

With so little strain that it is scarcely noticeable except to those willing to jog along as they read, the "distinct fruit and kernel, springing from terra firma" becomes "as many distinct plants as the soil . . . can sustain." Only six sentences later does it become clear that Thoreau is also talking here about *planting your feet distinctly when you run or walk* (Roman farmers planted seeds by stamping them into the soil with the footsole = *planta*, hence the etymological connection). The grandiloquent quotation from Scott that Thoreau fancifully imagines as the writer's tacit motto is better left unuttered, of course, for once the intellectual strength of such sentences is made manifest it may seem *strain*.

Given Thoreau's professed desire not to turn too many feeble somersaults in his writing, one wonders what the verbal gymnast who pulled off this full-twisting Tsukahara effortlessly in the privacy of his journal would consider a strained display of strength. The contrast with Carlyle is instructive. Wordplay of various sorts, especially involving overt etymological redefinition of terms, is a pronounced Carlylean mannerism. Thoreau relished Carlyle's humorous style. During his stay at Walden he busied himself writing the essay "Thomas Carlyle and His Works," in which he claims that "humor is not so distinct a quality for the purposes of criticism . . . as . . . it is commonly regarded, but allied to every, even the divinest faculty." Terming it essential to sanity, he argues that transcendentalism in particular needs "the leaven of humor to render it light and digestible." But despite his admiration, Thoreau insists that Carlyle's is not the purest and finest form of humor. That is "more quiet the more profound it is." Carlyle's overflowing verbal exuberance is too copious and boisterous, whereas Thoreau wants "a man's diamond edition of his thought . . . so clipped and condensed down to the very essence of it, that time will have little to do. We know not but we shall immigrate soon, and would fain take with us . . . all kinds of *dry* portable soups, in small tin cannisters, which contain whole herds of English beeves boiled down." This punning statement rationalizes the drier, more condensed, and less obvious wordplay that he preferred to Carlyle's straining after effect. Carlyle's self-dramatizing jocularity meant that on rereading there is "no *double entendre* . . . for the alert reader" (*Essays*, pp. 235-41). In the oxymoronic concept of *dry humor* Thoreau found a way to balance the cerebral and physical currents that make man "the hydrostatic paradox—the counterpoise of the system" (18 Feb. 1841). Though unlike blood, "humors will not feed a man. . . . They circulate" about the heart (18 Mar. 1842). Hydraulic psychology let Thoreau imagine that by venting the system even humorous speech helped drain and regulate it, so serving the cause of vascular expression.

To be succinct required painstaking revision. "Thinkers & writers are in foolish haste to come before the world with crude works," Thoreau felt. Alas, scholars too often ignore his warning. The spate of half-baked studies supposedly honoring Thoreau would have exasperated him, for he well understood the academic milieu from which it flows. "Young men are persuaded by their friends or by their own restless ambition, to write a course of lectures in a summer against the ensuing winter," he noted, "and what it took the lecturer a summer to write, it will take his audience but an hour to forget" (16 Nov. 1851). The winnowing process by which good writing slowly matures demands that the writer do his own forgetting. "Often I can give the truest and most interesting account of any adventure I have had after years have elapsed, for then I am not confused, only the most significant facts surviving in my memory" (28 Mar. 1857).

Granted, such pronouncements jibe oddly with Thoreau's aesthetic of sensory immediacy, with his notion of the writer as the man on the scene. Elsewhere he advised: "Write while the heat is in you. When the farmer burns a hole in his yoke—he carries the hot iron quickly from the fire to the wood—for every moment it is less effectual to penetrate (pierce) it. . . . The writer who postpones the recording of his thoughts—uses an iron which has cooled to burn a hole with. He cannot inflame the minds of his audience" (10 Feb. 1852). But even as he wrote this heated injunction, he began to revise it by fiddling with the diction. Which was the better word, *penetrate* or *pierce*? The latter seemed more piercing, but he was not yet sure, so he inserted it parenthetically, leaving the final choice to cooler reflection since "to the poet considered as an artist, his words must be as the relation of his oldest and finest memory—and wisdom derived from the remotest experience" (*PJ*, 2:89).

"Obey the spur of the moment. These accumulated it is that make the impulse & the impetus of the life of genius.— These are the spongioles or rootlets by which its trunk is fed. If you neglect the moments—if you cut off your fibrous roots—what but a languishing life is to be expected. Let the spurs of countless moments goad us incessantly into life." So spoke this young Romantic as he worked himself up to cry, "I feel the spur of the moment thrust deep into my side." But what it seemed to goad him into was not life but a whimsical elaboration of his conceit: "The present is an inexorable rider. The moment always spurs either with a sharp or a blunt spur. Are my sides calloused?" Had he used this passage for a finished essay, some of these freewheeling, jazzy improvisations might have been cut:

> Whatever wit has been produced on the spur of the moment will bear to be reconsidered and reformed with phlegm. The arrow had best not be loosely shot. The most transient and passing remark must be reconsidered by the writer, made sure and warranted, as if the earth had rested on its axle to back it, and all the natural forces lay behind it. The writer must direct his sentences as carefully and leisurely as the marksman his rifle, who shoots sitting and with a rest, with patent sights and conical balls beside. He must not merely seem to speak the truth. He must really speak it. If you foresee that a part of your essay will topple down after the lapse of time, throw it down now yourself. (26 Jan. 1852)

Revising his prose thus appealed to the cold-blooded killer in Thoreau who enjoyed hunting but ultimately found it "nobler game to shoot one's self" (*Walden*, p. 320). But the hunt for stylistic weaknesses was not lethal, for its victims could be resuscitated. "In correcting my manuscripts, which I do with sufficient phlegm, I find that I invariably turn out much that is good along with the bad, which it is then impossible for me to distinguish—so much for keeping bad company; but after the lapse of time, having purified the main body and thus created a distinct standard for comparison, I can review the rejected sentences and easily detect those which deserve to be readmitted" (1 Mar. 1854). Annihilating some words, reprieving others in a riot of creative power, Thoreau undertook literary revision with the wanton relish of the Demiurge in the railroad cut. "The writer must to some extent inspire himself," he found. "Most of his sentences may at first lie dead in his essay, but when all are arranged, some life and color will be reflected on them from the mature and successful lines; they will appear to pulsate with fresh life, and he will be enabled to eke out their slumbering sense, and make them worthy of their neighborhood. . . . Each clear thought that he attains to draws in its train many divided thoughts and perceptions" (3 Feb. 1859). Transcendentalism's omnivorous vagueness complicated his life as a writer. To tell the truth, he confidently proclaimed, "I lie," slyly adding, "and relie on the earth" (16 Nov. 1850). But the earth was a more solid subject than Life. When it offered no fertile suggestions, he had to rely on words. This passage reveals a writer who often discovered his subject not so much by embracing experience as by allowing words to rub against each other.

Sometimes this process involved definition. The time-hallowed appeal to a dictionary tempted him less than efforts to generate his own definitions by speculative discrimination like Crabb's. "The combined voice of the race makes nicer distinctions than any individual. There are the words diversion and amusement," he noted, developing a hint from Trench. "It takes more to amuse than to divert. We must be surrendered to our amusements, but only turned aside to our diversions. We have no will in the former—but oversee the latter. We are oftenest diverted in the street—but amused in our chambers. We are diverted from our engagements—but amused when we are listless." When otherwise listless, he could amuse himself with words. "We may be diverted from an amusement—and amused by a diversion," he decided. Indeed, "it often happens that a diversion becomes our amusement—and our amusement our employment" (27 Feb. 1841). So it does, and Thoreau's employment became writing.

Beside Emerson's comprehensive experience of the world, the New England earth that Thoreau chose to till as an author seemed meager when all was said and done. He knew how unyielding it could be. He needed a strategy to cope with it:

> It is of no use to plow deeper than the soil is, unless you mean to follow up that mode of cultivation persistently, manuring highly and carting on muck at each plowing,—making a soil, in short. Yet many a man likes to tackle mighty themes, like immortality, but in his discourse he turns up nothing but yellow sand, under which what little fertile and available surface soil he may have is quite buried and lost. He should teach frugality rather,—how to postpone the fatal hour,—should plant a crop of beans. He might have raised enough of these to make a deacon of him, though never a preacher. Many a man runs his plow so deep in heavy or stony soil that it sticks fast in the furrow. It is a great art in the writer to improve from day to day just that soil and fertility which he has, to harvest that crop which his life yields, whatever it may be, not be straining as if to reach apples or oranges when he yields only ground-nuts. He should be digging, not soaring. Just as earnest as your life is, so deep is your soil. If strong and deep, you will sow wheat and raise bread of life in it. (9 Nov. 1858)

Whereas Emerson's travels and wide reading manured his soil, Thoreau was determined to raise a native crop. Yet even that required a strategy for improving just what soil and fertility he had by daily labor. Although he gave his beans no manure, *Walden* describes how he hoed them vigorously on John Evelyn's theory that there is "no compost or laetation whatsoever comparable to this continual motion, repastination, and turning of the mould with the spade" (p. 162). To improve his experience meant to dig deeper into himself when expressing it. Words were the primary tools for self-cultivation. "I do not think much of that chemistry that can extract corn and potatoes out of a barren," he journalized, "but rather of that chemistry that can extract thoughts and sentiments out of the life of a man on any soil" (23 Jan. 1858). Spading over his journal might help him live more intensely. But not necessarily. The year he published *Walden* he found himself so busy writing that he failed to notice a change in the seasons. "This is the life most lead in respect to Nature," he lamented. "How different from my habitual one! It is hasty, coarse, and trivial, as if you were a spindle in a factory" (8 Dec. 1854). But normally the process of revising seemed anything but sterile. "The Scripture rule, 'Unto him that hath shall be given,' is true of composition," he decided. "The more you have thought and written on a given theme, the more you can still write. Thought breeds thought. It grows under your hands" (13 Feb. 1860). With Thoreau as supreme arbiter, word jostled word into life or expired on the page. He found that "time never passes so quickly and unaccountably as when I am engaged in composition. Clocks seem to have been put forward" (26 Jan. 1858). When he was in this frame of mind, the seasons scarcely mattered. He came to live most intensely by writing.

Getting the Point of Thoreau's Puns

"If thou art a writer, write as if the time were short, for it is indeed short at the longest." So he wrote—then, overcome by *Weltschmerz*, exclaimed, "In thy journal let there be never a jest! To the earnest there is nothing ludicrous" (24 Jan. 1852). The mood was not isolated, but neither was it lasting. "By spells seriousness will be forced to cut capers, and drink a deep and refreshing draught of silliness," he found. "I exult in stark inanity, leering on nature and the soul. We think the gods reveal themselves only to sedate and musing gentlemen, but not so, the buffoon in the midst of his antics, catches unobserved glimpses, which he treasures for the lonely hour. When I have been playing tom fool I have been driven to exchange the old for a more liberal and catholic philosophy" (24 Jan. 1841). Some puns in the journal are bad enough to defy any effort to justify them philosophically. Reflecting that a public official has a hard time returning to private life, he remarks, "His ex-honorableness-ship stands seriously in his way, whether he is a lawyer or a shopkeeper. He can't get ex-honorated" (3 Jan. 1856). Had he gone on to work up this pleasantly whimsical passage treating public service as guilt ex officio, this contorted joke might well have been cut. Other puns are less strained. "Even bleak and barren November wears these *gems* on her breast in sign of the coming year," he wrote of an autumn azalea, aware that the Latin *gemma* = bud (25 Oct. 1858). The family cat Min was robbed of a mouse by a rooster who strutted over, tossed it up and swallowed it alive, then crowed to celebrate the feat. "It might be set down among the *gesta* (if not *digesta*) *Gallorum*," he observed (4 Dec. 1856). The Latin word *Gallorum* can mean either *Gauls'* or *roosters'*, so this learned mock-heroic joke is neat enough. But one is loath to imagine Thoreau treasuring it as a divine epiphany for a lonely hour. The net effect is still one of Carlylean strain. The best are deadpan puns that almost escape notice. "Walked to see an old-schoolmate who is going to help make the Welland canal navigable for ships round Niagara," one entry notes. "Well and good I must confess" (17 Mar. 1843). "I have a cousin . . . who regularly eats his bowl of bread and milk just before going to bed, however late. He is a very stirring man" (18 Mar. 1861). No more is said—and no more needs to be said—to demolish that methodical milksop.

Thoreau mistrusted his facility with puns. While revising the manuscript of *Walden* he listed stylistic self-indulgences to watch out for:

> My faults are—
> Paradoxes,—saying just the opposite,—a style which may be imitated.
> Ingenious.
> Playing with words,—getting the laugh,—not always simple, strong, and broad. . . .
> Not always earnest. (*Journal*, 7:7-8)

The charge was accurate, the verdict harsh. The writer who proclaimed homeliness "next to beauty, and a very high art" because it was "almost as great a merit in a book as in a house, if the reader would abide there," overestimated the ease of imitating such insouciant etymological paradoxes (*Week*, p. 108). While he pondered the importance of being earnest, his epigrammatic elegance rivaled Oscar Wilde's. "We check & repress the divinity that stirs within us," he grumbled, "to fall down & worship the divinity that is dead without us" (16 Nov. 1851). A few months after *Walden*'s publication he was exasperated to find himself with a reputation as a humorist that did not quite please him. "What a grovelling appetite for profitless jest and amusement our countrymen have," he exploded. "Curators of lyceums write to me:—DEAR SIR,—I hear that you have a lecture of some humor. Will you do us the favor to read it before the Bungtown Institute?" (20 Dec. 1854). The proverbial village of Bungtown was celebrated in comic almanacs, and Bungtown's thirst for amusement was about to beget a whole new school of native

American humorists. Scores of Phunny Phellows like Artemus Ward, Josh Billings, Bill Arp, and Petroleum V. Nasby sated the country's craving for comic lectures between 1855 and 1895, with febrile wordplay their distinguishing trait. In *Doesticks What He Says* (1855) Mortimer Thompson explained that his sketches were "dressed up in a lingual garb . . . quaint, eccentric, fantastic, or extravagant," and "it is undoubtedly this trick of phrase, this affectation of a newfound style, which has caused their widespread notoriety." The Phunny Phellows read tepidly enough now. Their platform drollery evaporated in print, and they compensated for its loss by overindulging in cacography. Mass-produced, their japes stale on the page without the serious vision that informs Thoreau's puns. In newspapers where they cavorted, he found "a singular disposition to wit and humor, but rarely the slightest real success" (*Week*, pp. 185–86). But Bungtown was right to treat Thoreau as its kinsman. His writing was not always simple, strong, and broad, for the man himself was remarkably complex, nimble, and sharp.

"When I criticize my own writing, I go by the scent," he claimed. "By it I detect earthiness" (8 May 1852). Puns are appropriately pungent. Far from being merely clever, his wordplay often provides the earthiness that anchors an otherwise ethereal passage:

> For years my appetite was so strong that I fed—I browsed—on the pine forest's edge seen against the winter horizon. How cheap my diet still! Dry sand that has fallen in railroad cuts and slid on the snow beneath is condiment to my walk. I ranged about like a gray moose, looking at the spiring tops of the trees, and fed my imagination on them,—far-away, ideal trees, not disturbed by the axe of the woodcutter, nearer and nearer fringes and eyelashes of my eye. Where was the sap, the fruit, the value of the forest for me, but in that line where it was relieved against the sky? That was my wood-lot; that was my lot in the woods. The silvery needles of the pine straining the light. (3 Dec. 1856)

What an aesthete this Yankee was! His strong appetite was actually the finicky taste of a sensory epicure. He has affinities with the American luminists and other painters. Here he ranges the woods less like a moose than like James McNeill Whistler, composing monochromatic landscapes by squinting experimentally. With Japanese delicacy the pines are brushed in as a line against the sky. As their tops blur into ideal trees and into his eyelashes, we may well wonder "where was the sap . . . of the forest." The passage risks overrefinement as it risks sentimentality: "Woodman, woodman, spare that tree. . . ." What pulls it back from both is the penultimate sentence. Its marvelous pun makes it clear that binocular vision keeps this observer from being imprisoned by his carefully cultivated perspectives. The joke is not only ingenious but broader than anything else in the passage. The aesthete who strains his light through pine needles is the same homely soul who enjoys a cheap diet. Yes, this man saw a lot in the woods.

"In criticising your writing, trust your fine instinct," he urged himself. "There are many things which we come very near questioning, but do not question" (31 Mar. 1854). Despite second thoughts, his finest instinct was often to pun, and he learned to trust it:

> There is always some accident in the best things, whether thoughts or expressions or deeds. The memorable thought, the happy expression, the admirable deed are only partly ours. The thought came to us because we were in a fit mood; also we were unconscious and did not know that we had said or done a good thing. We must walk consciously only part way toward our goal, and then leap in the dark to our success. What we do best or most perfectly is what we have most thoroughly learned by the longest practice, and at length it falls from us without our notice, as a leaf from a tree. It is the *last* time we shall do it,—our unconscious leavings. (11 Mar. 1859)

When a leaf finally left it felt right. The word uttered unconsciously at last might last. Since all perception of truth is the detection of an analogy, we should "improve the opportunity to draw analogies.... Improve the suggestion of each object however humble—however slight & transient the provocation—what else is there to be improved?" (4 Sept. 1851). The mind's vagaries had to be trusted. Etymological brainstorming led to invention. "I would say to the orator and poet Flow freely & *lavishly* as a brook that is full—without stint—perchance I have stumbled upon the origin of the word lavish" (12 Feb. 1851). With witty wordplay he could "probe the universe in a myriad points," using his pen as a sharp tool.

His habitually pointed style was not just a calculated mannerism. Much of the time it was a half-conscious experimental impulse, testing the word and the world in the conviction that "you must try a thousand themes before you find the right one—as nature makes a thousand acorns to get one oak" (4 Sept. 1851). He wanted "sentences which suggest far more than they say, which have an atmosphere about them— sentences which do not merely report an old, but make a new impression—sentences which suggest as many things and are as durable as a Roman Aqueduct." Fluent writers like De Quincey, he complained, "lack moderation and sententiousness—they do not affect us by an ineffectual earnestness and a reserve of meaning—like a stutterer—they say all they mean. Their sentences are not concentrated and nutty" (22 Aug.

1851). Though not always earnest, Thoreau's puns were certainly nutty. With their aid he achieved the kind of style that he admired, "style . . . kinked and knotted up into something hard and significant, which you could swallow like a diamond, without digesting." It was perhaps a little kinky for this surveyor to complain that during a week spent perambulating Concord's bounds "with the *select* men of this and the surrounding towns" he dealt only with "emphatically *trivial* things" (20 Sept. 1851). But etymological puns were a way of puncturing the pomposity of the local politicians who hired him.

"My mother says that she has been to the charitable society," he recorded. "One old jester of the town used to call it 'the chattable society'" (11 Mar. 1859). The old jester's impulse was healthy, for "the analogies of words are never whimsical and meaningless, but stand for real likenesses— Only the ethics of mankind, and not of any particular man, give point and vigor to our speech" (*PJ*, 1:92). We must learn to trust language as "the record of men's second thoughts, a more faithful utterance than they can momentarily give." The moralist must venture into it boldly, for "the state of complete manhood is virtue—and virtue and bravery are one— This truth has long been in the languages. All the relations of the subject are hinted at in the derivation and analogies of the Latin words *vir* and *virtus*, and the Greek αγαθος and αριστος" (*PJ*, 1:92). Coaxed and teased, words teach us that "the soldier is the degenerate hero, as the priest is the degenerate saint. . . . The one's virtue is bravery, the other's bravery virtue" (*W*, 7:101-02n) "Fortitude is that alchemy which turns all things to good Fortune," he noted after reading Plutarch. "The man of fortitude, whom the Latins called *fortis*, is no other than that lucky person whom *fors* favors" (*PJ*, 1:98). Yet etymology also allowed him to escape any disagreeable conclusion it suggested, like the notion that heroism is a matter of chance. "A true happiness never happens, but rather is proof against all haps," he later decided. "I would not be a happy, that is, a lucky man, but rather a necessitated and doomed one" (*PJ*, 1:221).

By exploring analogies between the sounds of words, however coincidental, the perceptive listener may suddenly overhear the universal harmony. Then, struck by the beauty of the world, his body vibrates like a tuning fork. A man blowing a horn one still evening seemed "like the plaint of nature in these times. . . . It is as if the earth spoke." Clarified and dehumanized by distance,

> it is a strangely healthy sound for these disjointed times.— It is a rare soundness when cow-bells and horns are heard from over the fields— And now I see the beauty and full meaning of that word sound. Nature always

possesses a certain sonorousness, as in the hum of insects—the booming of ice—the crowing of cocks in the morning, and the barking of dogs in the night—which indicates her sound state. God's voice is but a clear bell sound. I drink in a wonderful health—a cordial in sound. The effect of the slightest tinkling in the horizon measures my own soundness. I thank God for sound it always mounts, and makes me mount. (3 Mar. 1841)

The slightest tinkling in words could likewise stimulate health and send Thoreau soaring skyward in etymological ecstasy.

Not that he took leave of his senses at any jingle. Asked how the name Quebec was derived, an Indian guide explained, "Well, when the English ships came up the river, they could not go any farther, it was so narrow there; they must go back,—go-back,—that's Quebec" (*Maine Woods*, p. 142). "I mention this," subjoins Thoreau, "to show the value of his authority in other cases." But by definition no whisper from nature could be truly *absurd*.

For these reasons Thoreau's mistrust of punning did not curb his indulgence in it. Most of the foregoing specimens come from his journal. Many more might be added; but in its fourteen volumes they remain random raisins in a very bulky plumcake. When he revised passages of his journal for publication, some wordplay was eliminated, to be sure. But for every pun that revision excised, two were added. Thus the texture of his wordplay in some of his published works—notably *Walden*—is even denser.

"Attended the auction of Deacon Brown's effects a little while to-day,—a great proportion of old traps, rubbish, or trumpery, which began to accumulate in his father's day, and now, after lying half a century in his garret and other dust-holes, is not burned, but surviving neighbors collect and view it, and buy it, and carefully transport it to their garrets and dust-holes, to lie there till their estates are settled, when it will start again. Among his effects was a dried tapeworm and various articles too numerous and worthless to mention. A pair of old snow shoes is almost regularly sold on these occasions, though none of this generation has seen them worn here" (27 Jan. 1854). So runs a journal entry during his final, hectic revisions of the manuscripts that became *Walden*. The passage was incorporated into the book, where it appeared six months later in the following form:

> Not long since I was present at the auction of a deacon's effects, for his life had not been ineffectual:-
>
> "The evil that men do lives after them."
>
> As usual, a great proportion was trumpery which had begun to accumulate in his father's day. Among the rest was a dried tapeworm. And now,

after lying half a century in his garret and other dust holes, these things were not burned; instead of a *bonfire*, or purifying destruction of them, there was an *auction*, or increasing of them. The neighbors eagerly collected to view them, bought them all, and carefully transported them to their garrets and dust holes, to lie there till their estates are settled, when they will start again. When a man dies, he kicks the dust. (pp. 67-68)

Though the entry was hardly expanded, several details were added and others dropped. Virtually all the additions involve wordplay. Revising the passage, Thoreau pitched upon the ironic possibilities in the word *effects*. He mocks the Deacon's Christianity as *ineffectual* in not discouraging the laying up treasures upon earth. Similar verbal whimsy inspired the bogus definition of an *auction* as the multiplication of goods whereas the Latin root really refers to the increasing of prices. Allusions to Shakespeare and Homer resonate oddly as the original meaning of key terms is slightly warped by the context; at the same time modern slang is jangled by scrambling the phrases "kick the bucket" and "bite the dust."[7] Indeed, the reference to Homeric heroes whose heels drummed the dust in their death throes literalizes that idea until we may be tempted to equate the *settling* of an estate with the *settling* of dust in garrets. It becomes only natural that *trumpery lie* there, since the function of trumpery (from French *tromper*) is to *deceive*. Thoreau knew that etymologically a *bonfire* was a *baneful* fire. But by the time that he inserted this detail in the passage, his mind had become so sensitized to the radical meanings of its words that he probably toyed with the notion that such purifying destruction as Hector's pyre might also be called a *bone* fire and was in any event surely a *good* fire.

If Thoreau amused himself with such speculations while composing the passage, our aim in reading *Walden* need not be to reproduce them all. One may certainly conclude that such writing tries too hard to prove his thesis in "Reading" that "it is not all books that are as dull as their readers" (p. 107). "To read true books in a true spirit," he there argues, "is a noble exercise, and one that will task the reader more than any exercise which the customs of the day esteem. It requires a training such as the athletes underwent, the steady intention of almost the whole life to this object" (p. 101). The metaphor is extremely suggestive. To catch all Thoreau's wordplay would indeed require prolonged philological training. A lifetime spent practicing to read *Walden* in this sense would almost surely be misspent—a grotesque series of philological Texas drills culminating in a sorry Super Bowl of the mind. His language insists on a physical element in intellectual discipline: both are *exercises*. A professional athlete reading *Walden* might not understand that "the steady *intention* of the whole life to that object" involves stretching the mind and bending it steadily like a bow so that the intent reader can live with intensity. Still, those accustomed to stretch their tendons can appreciate aspects of Thoreau's style that conventional academic analysis scarcely touches. A scholar like me can clarify his intent and the etymologies underpinning it. But my reading will be just as impoverished if I forget that this book was written neither for professional athletes *nor* professional scholars but for "poor students" (p. 4). Better to miss some of the wit with which Thoreau tried to lure us into becoming better readers than to miss the main goal of that activity. When he says that we must apply our whole life to reading, he means not our lifetime but our *whole* life—a life that is integrated, healthy, and wholesome. On this subject academics may have less to teach others than they might wish. Fortunately, for a halfway sensitive reader the glorious rhetoric of *Walden* not only exposes cultural complacency but punctures the hot-air balloons in which literary intellectuals love to ride while they loftily survey that terrain.

Etymologically, puns are *pointed* words. They are thus well suited to puncture conventionalism. In most writing "a very little information or wit is mixed up with a great deal of conventionalism in the style of expressing it," Thoreau felt. "Some life is not simply expressed, but a long-winded speech is made, with an occasional attempt to put a little life into it" (25 Nov. 1857). His wordplay stems from a determination to put a lot of life into his prose. His puns are the snap, pop, and crackle of words that quietly explode as they suck vitality from the earth. Fusing popular humor with the snappish insights of the Victorian sage, his learned wisecracks can still be appreciated by anyone with the wit to recognize them. Even if they only elicit a groan, at least it attests that the audience is still alive.

7/

The Ironic Drift in Antebellum Language Philosophy

I am acquainted with only one person, my esteemed friend, Mr. John Wesley Huff of Philadelphia, whom I would hopefully ask for a critical opinion of my work. This is surely a singular condition for an old man in a thronged city, where he ought to have 'troops of friends,' of congenial study. I often feel like one o'clock sounds at midnight, solitary yet tuneful. And thus what a sorry target is a metaphysician to shoot taunts and gibes at; nevertheless, I have fearlessly bared my breast to thee, my reader.

—John Gaskell, *Sense and Sound as They Reciprocally Form Any Sign of Mind* (Philadelphia: Collins, 1854)

Alexander Bryan Johnson: Utica's Philosophical Emperor of Empiricism

In post-Kantian idealism the highway of language study led straight to irony. America's empirical back roads meandered that way too. In Alexander Bryan Johnson, who emigrated to America at fourteen, British empiricism threw up on these shores a fascinating philosopher of language. He was the sole thinker in philosophical history to anticipate views of language expounded in the twentieth century by Russell, Wittgenstein, and the British school. The books embodying his trenchant insights were ignored. He felt his lack of influence keenly, and it partly explains his near-total neglect by histories of philosophy. But why have intellectual historians not paid more attention to this intriguing figure? This frustrated philosophical reformer was also an original economic thinker, an enterprising banker (sometimes too enterprising), a Jacksonian Democrat who authored political satires, married John Quincy Adams's niece, and corresponded cordially with both her illustrious relatives. His ten books and forty-odd articles campaign loftily against everything from slavery and taxes to tight-lacing. Eddying in the crosscurrents of the American Renaissance, he suggests how philosophical achievement, however austere, inevitably mirrors its era.

Bryan Johnson preceded his son to America from Britain by four years. He kept a store in Old Fort Schuyler, New York. When it was proposed to rename the village, Bryan suggested Kent, but a wit on the committee "ridiculed it with an indelicate euphemism."[1] Old Fort Schuyler became Utica, another bustling upstate hamlet aspiring with charming naïveté to neoclassical dignity—and not always achieving it. The young lad noted that "obscene conversation among men at their social feasts . . . was the ordinary source of mirth and good fellowship." Though Americans struck him as primmer than British, Johnson concluded that "the strict practical chastity which I believe marked the period . . . sought a compensation in the license of speech" (*PB*, pp. 34-35). With Johnson helping out in the store, the family prospered. By 1807, when he attained his majority, they had amassed a modest fortune of $50,000. They sold the store to live as gentlefolk of leisure. In a custom-built chaise attended by his liveried slave Frank, he set off for the fashionable Sans Souci Hotel in Ballston Spa to find a wife. All he found was the truth of the local saying that "people went to the Sans Souci and returned *sans six sous*" (*PB*, p. 46). He returned to Utica determined to multiply his family's capital. Organizing a factory to make window glass, he proved a better promoter and lobbyist than administrator. His own windows were broken in a labor dispute, and the directors replaced him as secretary.

Bank stocks proved more tempting. A prudent and thoughtful speculator, he was soon reading Adam Smith and Lauderdale. In 1813 he published *An Inquiry into the Nature and Value of Capital: And into the Operations of Government Loans, Banking Institutions and Private Credit,* with an appendix on "the Causes which Regulate the Rate of Interest and the Price of Stock." It was the most significant of more than a dozen economic works he authored over the next half-century. This cautious investor was a surprisingly radical economic thinker, an early New Dealer and Keynesian who argued that government borrowing simply increased the national capital by the amount of the new securities. Whereas the public debt was expansive and beneficial, taxing was deflationary and undesirable. Tax only to support a minimalist government and service the debt, which no citizen perceived as lessening his own wealth. In a specie-short economy the national debt was like a gold strike. As a private banker, Johnson bitterly opposed hard-money laws requiring banks to redeem notes in specie. To the Second Bank of the United States he objected strongly, staunchly supporting President Jackson's effort to clip its wings. He himself organized innovative state bond schemes to construct canals and keep credit flowing in New York. When Martin Van Buren pushed for Federal subtreasuries, Johnson bolted the Democrats to support the Whigs, authoring *The Philosophical Emperor: A Political Experiment* (1841), a satiric allegory on Jacksonian and post-Jacksonian monetary policy.

Before Jackson ushered in the era of free banking from 1836 to 1863, Johnson's capacity for innovative schemes had flowered in the Utica Insurance Company. He was serving unremuneratively as a state-appointed director of the newly chartered Bank of Utica. Like other existing banks, it disliked competition, so legislative bank charters were hard to come by. In 1816 Johnson therefore drew up an insurance company charter that "was so cunningly worded that while it seemed to convey only permission to insure property, it granted, as was manifest to the reader aware of its intent, the privilege of banking also."[2] Such verbal cunning amounted to punning. Johnson maneuvered his bill nervously through the state legislature. Then the Utica Insurance Company quickly sold out its stock issue and began circulating banknotes. Opposition rallied, however. The legislature amended an old restraining law, and the state attorney general Martin Van Buren brought suit. In 1818 the Utica Insurance Company suspended banking operations and soon after liquidated its pro forma insurance program. Though at first priding himself on his ability to exploit verbal ambiguity, Johnson came to repent his duplicity profoundly. "I never performed an act that I have so much regretted," his autobiography confesses. "I was deceived in its character by the absence of proper ethical knowledge in my education and associations" (*PB*, p. 96). Was he thinking of his autodidactic upbringing in a Utica given to "license of speech"?

His financial prowess had already helped him form better associations in Utica. In 1814 he met the sixteen-year-old Abigail Adams there. This impecunious granddaughter of our second president regarded Johnson's fondness for money as no vice but a virtue not honored by Adamses. Their ten-week courtship was scarely an erotic whirlwind. Johnson says that "the marriage on the side of bride and groom was purely intellectual." Nor did he ever repent it as a hasty investment decision. They were a happy couple, and his connections with the Adamses brought him great satisfaction. The Quincy patriarch wrote the new husband with a special message for "my lovely hussy Abby," jocularly advising him to soothe her fancied annoyance at "such a vulgar word" by explaining that "hussy . . . means housewife, and I hope she will know how a pot should be boiled and a spit turned" (*PB*, pp. 81, 89). The lovely hussy eventually produced nine children. Johnson wanted to help them avoid the deficiencies of his own Utica self-education. He remembered lonely struggles with Murray's grammar: "I was twenty years old, and perhaps more, before I could apply the rules of syntax to my own compositions and properly understood the etymology of words, so as to consult a dictionary understandingly."[3]

The alphabetical organization of dictionaries kept them from teaching conceptually related words. To use English well, we need nouns, adjectives, verbs, and adverbs in sets. When these parts of speech differ in form, the inquirer is at a loss. "Why should we not find under the word *vanish* . . . that its adjective is *evanescent*?" With Webster's organization, "if irony were suited to so grave an evil, a lexicographer might say to students . . . what a celebrated cookery book says of cooking a hare—first, 'catch it.'" For example, Johnson said he thought that English contained an adjective he could not find corresponding to the noun *stepmother*. He wanted to correlate etymologically and conceptually linked words. For philosophical reasons, his ideal dictionary should provide not only synonyms but antonyms because "man is so constituted that he can recognize no quality till he can recognize also its privative." The Scriptural doctrine of God's omnipresence may be misleading, for "were his omnipresence as apparent to all our sense as light is to our eyes . . . his unintermitted presence would prevent us from recognizing his presence" (*Method*, pp. 6-13).

During 1830-34 Johnson campaigned for a new dictionary by lecturing and publishing two pamphlets. He explained how he had begun to compile it:

> I procured two blank folio books. Each is the size of a volume of newspapers. On the outer edge of every second page, the book binder pasted a column, cut from an English dictionary.
>
> Having a whole dictionary thus formed of single columns, with a blank margin of almost two folio pages to every column, I took another dictionary, and with a scissors cut out for instance, the word, *abacus,* with its definition. This word purports to be a counting table. I pasted it in my dictionary against the verb *to count*. But abacus is also "the uppermost member of a column." I therefore cut another *abacus* with its definition, from a supplemental dictionary and pasted it into mine, against the word *column*.
>
> After a little familiarity with the labour, and with the assistance of my children to whom it was a pleasant and instructive amusement, I could generally cut out two hundred words of an evening, and place them appropriately in my dictionary. (*Method*, pp. 11-12)

Alas, such pleasant evenings bred no brilliant brood like the Adams clan. John Quincy Adams wrote superciliously to explain that the adjectival form of *stepmother* was *novercal*. More enthusiastic was the Philadelphia philologue Peter Du Ponceau, who before emigrating had been Court de Gébelin's secretary in France. Urging completion of the dictionary, Du Ponceau pointed out its resemblance to the *Monde primitif*: "The only difference is that he classes the words in families with respect to their Etymologies whereas you would do it in respect to the Sense."

Because his offspring were uninterested in carrying the project through, Johnson cast about for someone else to shoulder the work while prudently copyrighting his plan for a "Collated Dictionary" (*LV*, pp. 101-3). But ambivalence about sharing his copyright kept him from finding a collaborator. The Collated Dictionary languished. Two decades later, when Roget's *Thesaurus* appeared, Johnson wrote the Englishman to find out whether his own pamphlets had helped shape that opus. The answer was an indignant no. Rationalist in its premises and unalphabetized at first, Roget's work does differ from Johnson's plan. But the fireside education of his American household very nearly earned Johnson a measure of the renown he craved.

Not unwisely, he had pinned his main hopes for fame on philosophy. He published *The Philosophy of Human Knowledge, or A Treatise on Language* (New York: Carvill, 1828), which then appeared in a revised and enlarged edition as *A Treatise on Language: or The Relation Which Words Bear to Things* (New York: Harper, 1836). Two decades later, he reworked his ideas into *The Meaning of Words: Analyzed into Words and Unverbal Things* (New York: Appleton, 1854; 2d ed. 1862). He also published *The Physiology of the Senses: or How and What We See, Hear, Taste, Feel and Smell* (New York: Derby & Jackson, 1856), as well as the privately printed *Deep Sea Soundings and Explorations of the Bottom; or The Ultimate Analysis of Human Knowledge* (Boston, 1861). Except for *Rees' Cyclopedia*, his philosophical reading hardly extended beyond the British empiricists, but he developed their nominalism in a way that was systematic, idiosyncratic, and amazingly prescient, if sometimes naive. When he suggested that his own work constituted that "new logic and critic which Locke began to suspect at the close of his Essay on Human Understanding" (*Meaning*, p. 255), he surely had some reason to think so.

"What is denominated the Philosophy of Mind, consists of but little more than a contentious verbal criticism," Johnson argued. "Every natural existence we deem a mere representative of some word. Language usurps thus, to an astonishing extent, the dignity which truly belongs to creation. I know we usually say words are the signs of things. Practically, we make things the signs of words."[4] Insistently repeated until it became almost a mantra, his great theme was the need "to subordinate language to nature,—to make nature the expositor of words, instead of making words the expositors of nature." This promises "a great revolution in every branch of learning" (*Tr.*, p. 40).

Like his empirical forefathers, Johnson believed that we apprehend the external universe as a mass of sights, sounds, tastes, feels, and smells that impinge on us in bundles of various kinds: "A sight and a feel that are invariably associated, we call fire. . . . Another group, consisting of a certain sight, feel, and taste, we call bread. Another group, consisting wholly of sights, we call a rainbow" (*Tr.*, p. 48). Following Berkeley, he holds that our sources of sensory information are entirely independent of each other, so that sights can tell us nothing about sounds or tangible substance. Even more radically, he argues for independence among sensory experiences of the same class.[5] He denies Locke's claim that a rainbow can be described to someone who has seen only the particular colors that compose it, denies Hume's suggestion that a blue spectrum with a missing band can be filled in by the imagination. "So rigid is nature on this subject that the most intimate acquaintance with two sights will not enable me to know the appearance which they will present when blended. The same law regulates all our senses: after drinking two liquors, endeavor to combine their flavor, and when you think the mental combination is complete, mingle the liquors, and the moment you taste them you will be conscious of a new taste" (*Tr.*, p. 154).

A man who never drank a glass of alcohol in his life (but who pretended to do so for sociability and who opposed prohibition), Johnson violates his own principles with this example. Whatever experiments he conducted with sarsaparilla and lemonade should not have allowed this radical empiricist to predict that familiarity with gin and vermouth unmixed gives no sense of a martini. But the insight was plausible. It left him inhabiting an atomistic universe without clear relational principles, where no sensible experience supplies reliable information about any other.[6] His vagueness about how cognition then takes place was a serious philosophical weakness, but he developed no detailed explanation beyond assuming a certain "organic" congruence between mind and world. His main interest lay elsewhere.

It followed that language was both systematically and unsystematically ambiguous:

> Nearly every word has a signification which refers to our senses, and another which refers to words. The verbal signification is usually termed a definition. It is regulated by principles wholly different from those which govern the sensible signification. The sensible signification is the phenomena to which the word refers, and therefore nothing but our senses can reveal to us this signification; but the verbal signification of a word may be known to any person who possesses hearing, and even to those who are void of hearing, if they have acquired the art of reading. The blind may discourse eloquently about fires and illuminations; and the deaf mutes in our asylums may write pertinently about melody; but it is only the verbal signification of these words of which either have any knowledge. (*Tr.*, p. 150)

This key distinction, Johnson rightly thought, was ignored by prior philosophers. Not only do words often confuse the data of our discrete senses; all verbal signification is constantly being mistaken for sensible signification, with results as awkward for science as for metaphysics.

Thus Hume's skeptical insistence that "no visible connection exists between any cause and its effect" is simply a bogus metaphysical conundrum rooted in illegitimate language, for "to talk . . . of seeing a cause and its effect connected, as we see the connection of two links, is to talk of seeing at the same time either a present sight and a past, or a present and a future" (*Tr.*, p. 285). Such speculation is as absurd as to ask, "How would memory look if we could see it?" (*Tr.*, p. 253). Likewise, "theories are beneficial to science; but when we say that water ascends in a vacuum by means of the pressure of the atmosphere, we should discriminate the theoretical pressure from the feel to which the word pressure is ordinarily applied. Pressure like every other word, possesses no invariable signification, nor any inherent signification . . . When it refers to the effort of my hand against this table, it names a feel; and when applied to the ascent of water in a vacuum, it names the ascent. If we suppose it names also some insensible operation of the air on the water, this is merely our theory, which signifies nothing; or rather it signifies all to which we refer in proof of the pressure" (*Tr.*, p. 227). Like metaphysics, scientific theories have mainly verbal significance. Their key concepts must not be reified or confused with the sensible data of experience. Thus when popular writers on science marveled at the translucency of glass, they simply confused the motion of light with the motion of physical bodies: "Wonder is produced only . . . when we suppose the passage of the light through crystal to be the same as the passage of my hand through crystal" (*Tr.*, p. 120, and cf. p. 89). As a quondam glass manufacturer whose windows were shattered when a disgruntled worker heaved bricks, Johnson was clear that philosophical distinction was in order here.

Despite affinities, Johnson was thus much more sophisticated than naive philosophical materialists like Tooke and Cardell. He appreciated the importance of theoretical abstraction in generating knowledge. His concept of "verbal signification" was never strictly defined, for his style was shaped by the podium and sought to appeal aphoristically to a popular audience impatient with nice definitions. He had obviously thought a fair amount about analytic propositions and with self-conscious audacity was willing to go so far as to ground logic itself ultimately in experience. Words denoting emotions he categorized separately from those purporting to describe the external world, resolving the problem of other minds by showing that the "similarity" of our internal experiences differs logically from the "similarity" of other people's feelings insofar as the latter concept presupposes reference to observable behavior. Though he has been accused of conflating meaning with reference, certain inconsistencies in his terminology suggest that he was at least fitfully aware of the issues involved. Had he faced them more squarely, he might have been an even greater philosopher. But either he was not interested in them or he knew his limits. "To investigate the sights, sounds, feels, tastes, and smells, which separately, and in various associations, constitute the external universe, is not my present object; nor shall I discuss whether sights, sounds, tastes, feels, and smells, are words which appropriately designate external existences. I adopt the phraseology as a means of investigating the nature of language" (*Tr.*, p. 55).

He never articulated a thoroughgoing ontology or a semantic system because he cared less about the relation between words and their denotata than about the peculiar semantic abuses that occur when words shift between multiple meanings. But within his limits, as Rynin argues, he was astonishingly original. He was the first philosopher to analyze the logic of language in detail as the starting point for resolving a host of philosophical problems. Long before Russell, Wittgenstein, and logical positivism, he argued for the verifiability of statements as a criterion of meaning, sharply and systematically distinguishing between the untrue and the insignificant in a way that showed many philosophical conundrums to be neither false nor mysterious but simply senseless and therefore incapable of being answered. Long before Pierce, Mach, and P. W. Bridgman, he developed the implications of this view for science by arguing that metaphysical objectivity is irrelevant to the scientific value of secondary qualities like appearance and substance, that theories are practical instruments for ordering sense data efficiently, and that without operational consequences or experimental tests theories lack sensible significance. Long before modern behaviorism he saw the fundamental duality of psychological language as authorizing the scientific study of the human mind. Failure to clarify the structure of the universe or to classify all the ways in which words function productively may perhaps be forgiven so doughty a pioneer.

Were intellectual and stylistic distinction the criteria for expanding the canon of American literature, Johnson would merit space in anthologies far more than many now included. If we exclude Emerson as belletristic, he is the most notable American philosopher between Jonathan Edwards and Charles Sanders Peirce. His *Treatise* provides an indispensable counterweight to Emerson's *Nature.* In the twenty-first century his philosophical legacy is arguably more relevant than Edwards's or even Emerson's.

Ironing Out Utica's Antinomies with Irony

Academics impatient with a white male Protestant canon can take comfort in the fact that Johnson was of Jewish origins. Temperamentally aloof, this autodidactic émigré considered himself an outsider. When not striving to remedy his lonely lot, he consoled himself by viewing it as the basis of his prosperity and originality. Diffidence and arrogance both contributed to his own neglect—which was not total. There were a few favorable reviews of the *Treatise,* and at least one educator plundered it to compose a philosophical grammar for school use.[7] But neglected Johnson was. In nineteenth-century America nothing did more to marginalize his opinions on language than their theological implications. For he launched a devastating attack on natural theology. To Paley's argument that "nothing can be God which is ordered by a wisdom and a will superior to its own," he responded, "Why? For one reason only; the word God excludes from its signification these consequences" (*Tr.,* 189). Likewise, the notion of "Creation" simply implied the Creator verbally. "Why must bricks have a creator?" Johnson queried. "Try to produce a brick, and you will discover. . . . But when you ask me why the sun must have a creator, I cannot tell you to produce a sun, and thus discover the necessity." Since we can postulate a series of prior creators for the sun ad infinitum, "we are compelled eventually to abandon the process, and admit that we are arrived where the process is no longer applicable. This alone ought to teach us that the whole process is insignificant where it refers to no sensible archetype" (*Tr.,* pp. 202–3). Johnson knew that he was treading on thin ice here, that "this doctrine is so novel, that I may be accused of saying that the sun had no creator." But explaining that such an assertion was no more significant than its converse did not allay anxiety.

Johnson was no unbeliever but an ecumenical Christian gentleman who disliked dogmatism. He embraced his wife's Presbyterianism to marry but bridled when the Utica Session rebuked him for advocating mail transport on the Sabbath. He finished his days in the Episcopal Communion of his youth, claiming that he would never hire a man who did not attend church. "I never knew but one atheist," he explained in the *Treatise,* "and his unbelief was fortified by the doctrines of natural theology. When you attempted his conversion, by alleging the necessity of a creator for the sun, moon, etc.," the atheist cheerfully took refuge from God in an infinite regress of creators. "Had this atheist known that language is impertinent to the whole discussion, he would have seen that verbal incompatibilities afford no cause to disbelieve the being and attributes of Deity" (*Tr.,* p. 208).

For Johnson as for Franklin, much of the case for religion rested on moral utilitarianism, but he was no covert deist winding up his own clockwork god. "Fully impressed with the paramount authority of the Holy Scriptures," he felt that "no heresy is so pernicious as the persuasion that God can be discovered by reason" (*Tr.,* pp. 208–9). In his apologia *Religion in Its Relation to the Present Life* (New York: Harpers, 1841) he defended the Bible as an encyclopedia of concrete truths that were not generalities "whose meaning, like a riddle's, is anything and everything to which ingenuity can affix it" (p. 167). Revelation was essential in Johnson's view, but he gave it a characteristic twist:

> When the Lord answered from the flaming bush the inquiry of Moses, by saying "I am that I am," the answer was wonderfully expressive of the nature of language, which can in no instance accomplish more than it effected in that. We may say to life, What are thou? and to death, What art thou? and we may address a like inquiry to the sun, the earth, the sea, the revolution of the seasons, the alternations of day and night, the fluctuation of the tides, the attraction of magnetism, and the gravitation of stones; but language can furnish them with no better answer than, I am that I am. Would we learn more in relation to them, we must seek it from our senses. (*Tr.,* p. 244)

Like Wittgenstein in the *Tractatus,* who felt that language may *show* what it cannot *say,* Johnson argued that "we can no more exemplify with words that there is a limit to their applicability, than a painter can demonstrate with colours, that there are phenomena which colours cannot delineate" (*Tr.,* p. 246). Yet here Scriptural poetry paradoxically reveals the limits of Scriptural language. That is Revelation with a capital R. "If you cannot catch my meaning by a few hints," as Johnson observed, "you will not by a tedious detail" (*Tr.,* p. 95).

Alas, like the Pharisees most missed his hints. Even the acute John Quincy Adams confessed himself nervous about the apparent mindlessness of his nephew's sensationalism. Warm notices by Timothy Flint and Horace Bushnell found the *Treatise* theologically barren. In later editions Johnson modified his radical empiricism slightly to accommodate such objections but with no great success.

"If you examine the various theories of philosophers," he shrewdly observed, "you will generally be able to divine the science with whose phenomena the philosopher is familiar. If the formation of rocks is to be accounted for by a chemist, they are caused by a chemical precipitation among the waters of a flood, by crystallizations, and by chemical combinations. If a physician becomes geologist, the interior of the earth suffers convulsions; volcanoes vomit up rocks, and the ocean fractures them into smaller stones" (*Tr.*, p. 256). Johnson's *Treatise on Language* is likewise swayed by the discipline with which he was most familiar—economics. That helps explain why he backed off from his most uncompromising linguistic empiricism. He was an amateur philosopher, with no classical education and no foreign languages to speak of; but he was a professional banker and financial theorist in the country that first adopted paper money on a wide scale. During 1825-75 no issue except slavery dominated American politics more than the debate about coined versus paper money. Economists have often sensed analogies between money and language. Turgot and Adam Smith, for example, both wrote discourses on etymology, and the latter's heavily noun-centered view of language has intriguing parallels with his capitalist ideology. In nineteenth-century America the relation was reciprocal. Thus writers called for an aesthetic gold standard, with Emerson complaining that our linguistic degeneracy meant that "old words are perverted to stand for things which are not; a paper currency is employed when there is no bullion in the vaults" (*CW,* 1:30).

The argument of Johnson's *Treatise* seems oddly at odds with the main thrust of his economic thought. As a politician Johnson zealously defended soft-money policies, arguing that the symbolic and practical value of paper currency was unimpaired by sundering its connection with specie. As a linguistic thinker, however, he marshaled his eloquence and ingenuity to warn against debasing words by disregarding the hard physical evidence on which they all depended for significance "as a pronoun refers for signification to the substantive whose place it supplies" (*Tr.*, p. 118). "An object of capital must be an object of desire," wrote the expansive economist, "and the business of life is to secure objects of desire" (*PB*, p. 67). But the student of words warned that we must retrench our desires sharply because many could never be embodied in objects. By devising novel financial instruments the banker labored cheerfully to keep *credit* flowing. But the philosopher did less than he might have to defend language as a novel theoretical instrument, and by undermining the *credit* in words he caused a mild panic in theological circles.

This antinomy suggests that Utica's upstate Stoic felt more tensions than at first appear. His linguistic philosophy tried to resolve them by showing how "conflicting general propositions often harmonize when we know the particulars to which they refer" (*Tr.*, p. 130). But his empiricism left him trusting even less than Kant in any ultimate authority of logic. "Why cannot the same thing both be and not be?" he asks, then answers unflinchingly that "our assent to such propositions is founded on our sensible experience." Though a spot can be both white and hard, it cannot be both white and black, for reasons that finally go beyond definition: "Try if you can effect such a coincidence, and you will discover why. The impossibility is what you will experience. It possesses no other meaning" (*Tr.*, pp. 194-95).

Therefore, if Johnson encountered an experience that seemed absolutely contradictory, like Schlegel he was in no position to banish it by appealing to Transcendental logic. Contradiction might be the logic of psychology, a psychologic where A = not-A was unimpeachably authenticated by experience. The publication of the revised edition of the *Treatise* in 1836 forcibly demonstrated that, for it was attended by the death on July 4th of Abigail Adams Johnson. Holding her husband's hand, she died after three days of agony, the last punctuated by audible evidence of national rejoicing. A = not-A?

Johnson met this calamity with anything but the Roman fortitude his *Treatise* suggests. "To never have married is probably better than any connubial state," he wrote one friend, "to never have had children is probably better than to possess them, and never to have possessed life is probably better than all other states" (*PB*, p. 233). Insisting that her death by ovarian cancer had been inevitable, his doctors invited him to attend the last stages of her autopsy and witness the proof. For such sensible significations he had no appetite. He filed their autopsy report away unread and clung instead to the belief that her death was an avoidable consequence of tight corsets, the target of a Johnsonian diatribe in *Mothers Magazine*.

So profound was his gloom that the family consulted Professor Tully of the Yale Medical School. Noting recurrent episodes in Johnson's life, Tully concluded that the depression was constitutional and would probably become worse because Abigail's death had been only the trigger. Feverish activity in combating the bank crises beginning in 1837, remarriage in 1838, and a vigorous intellect eventually pulled Johnson out of his depression, though he conceded that Tully's prediction might well have come true (*PB*, p. 234). Like his insistence on the intellectual necessity of antonyms, the episode highlights a marked polarizing tendency running through Johnson's thought. "We may suppose that life has an individuality, but we recognize it not, even in our own bodies," he had speculated earlier. "Could we, however, become conscious of what 'not life' is we should immediately attain to knowledge of life"

(*Method*, p. 9). Whether he ever attained the elusive knowledge of life is unclear. His reluctance to view his wife's body suggests that the requisite consciousness of "not life" came hard indeed. But the philosophy of his final years, especially the peculiar *Deep Sea Soundings and Explorations of the Bottom,* increasingly stressed the polar character of concepts and the dialectical nature of consciousness. "The contrast principle, the 'figure-ground' relationship of Gestalt psychology lies at the very basis of awareness and thought," as Rynin puts it. "The essential dependence of life upon death, light upon darkness, pleasure upon pain, sound upon silence, feast upon famine, all show the necessity for every positive of its corresponding negative."[8] Such ideas may surprise those familiar only with Johnson's earlier books, which might make him seem a nominalistic empiricist and nothing more.

"To deem ourselves shut up in the universe with no capacity to know or even speak any thing of it but what our senses reveal, seems a narrower range than we are accustomed to attribute to our knowledge," Johnson admits with a touch of melancholy. "Still, such is our situation. Language cannot enable us to pass the barrier of our senses" (*Tr.,* p. 250). If the sensory universe struck him occasionally as a prison, it still seemed far roomier than language, for "language is a collection of general terms, but creation is a congregation of individual existences." The multifariousness of the sensory world Johnson generally regards not with melancholy but with a sober joy: "Individuality is no anomaly of nature. It is nature's regular production, and boundless richness" (*Tr.,* pp. 79–80). He marvels that with "but thirty-eight thousand words" we can express infinite shades of sensation and feeling as well as we do. In this fact lies "the necessity that every word should possess a multitude of meanings" (*Tr.,* p. 113). Had Johnson paid more attention to syntax than to vocabulary, he might have seen grammar as the finite body of rules that enables our finite vocabulary to generate an infinite number of sentences. Instead, his focus on isolated words (typical of the era) led him to conclude that in a world where "no two existences are as identical in nature as in name" the identity implied by language is "the expedient by which a finite language comprehends an infinitely diverse creation" (*Tr.,* pp. 87–88). For Johnson as for the German Romantics, then, since language requires multiple meanings, punning is virtually its central structural principle; but he is diametrically opposed to them in insisting (much like Stewart) that truth can be found only by resisting the seductions of equivocation.

Though closer to Cardell in deemphasizing mind, on etymology Johnson sided with Sherman. It furnished no unitary meaning to polyvalent words: "Etymology has pursued [metaphysics] through all the torturous wanderings of words, up to their pristine signification. Discovering hence, that *spirit* signified originally *breath,* she concludes that the word has still no other import[,] . . . overlooking the most important characteristic of language, that every word possesses as many meanings as it possesses applications to different phenomena" (*Tr.,* p. 35). In Johnson's case this commonsense position reflected extraphilosophical concerns. Since arriving in America the youth had rankled at constitutional provisos debarring foreign-born citizens from the land's highest offices. During the War of 1812 he was vexed to find himself called an Englishman so he published a pamphlet on expatriation warmly asserting the natural right of men to change their national identity. Johnson's parents had abandoned their Jewish faith, but his closest relatives were Jewish. Throughout his life Johnson corresponded affectionately with a cousin who expostulated "cousin Zalick" (= Selig) to return to the faith of Abraham. But though he toyed with the notion that "the intellect of the Jews differs somewhat from that of other people" (*PB,* p. 295), this Episcopal vestryman treated his rabbinical ancestry as a dark secret.

Living out Crèvecoeur's dream of the American as a new man, Johnson had poignant personal reasons to deny that roots determined the meaning of names. Indeed, restricting the meaning of terms to a speaker's sensible experience made it hard to explain how statements about the future or past are to be understood. Characteristically, he interprets such statements as disguised references to the speaker's *present* attitudes. Though philosophically problematic, this strategy suited his stance as an American determined neither to be bound by his past nor limited to a specific future, one who believed with Thoreau that "God himself culminates in the present moment" (*Walden,* p. 97). Likewise, denying etymological meaning meant that his nominalism enforced no clear standard of propriety for words. Usage was for him the supreme arbiter. Words meant chiefly what *individuals* chose to designate by them. Confusions he resolved by clarifying the particular reference of words in a given instance but seldom by suggesting alternative terminology. His concern was the misinterpretation of words, not the misuse. In this sense his approach to language was populist to the core, probably more so than this Hunker Democrat intended. Despite his concern for educating his family decorously, despite his labor on the Collated Dictionary, his philosophy allowed individuals to appropriate words for their own purposes because words had no inner life of their own. The linguistic confusion that he struggled against was simply human social confusion, not a Tookean linguistic organism transcending man and threatening to throttle him in its coils. Nature rather than Webster was his ultimate authority, a dictionary that everyone must consult for himself like Natty Bumppo. The *Treatise* thus licensed more radical stylistic innovations than Johnson ever practiced or contemplated.

For Johnson there was no better example of language's tendency to foist nonexistent verbal unity on a pluralistic social and physical world than the concept of identity itself. Ultimately *identity* possessed no more stable identity than words or people:

> The word identity itself is merely a general term, expressive of a multitude of varying existences and relations. A man who is blind from his birth, knows roundness from feel. Should he attain sight and see a ball, he will not recognize it as the round object of his former amusement. When, however, he shall have learnt roundness by the sight, he may inquire how the visible ball and the tangible are identical. Their identity is different from the identity of his person now, and his person a few moments previously. The identity of John when an infant, and the same John when a decrepid old man, differs from both the other identities. The identity which exists between an acorn and the oak from which it originated, differs from all the other identities. To seek in each of these cases for something that is common to them all, and as similar in all as the similarity of the word identity, is to seek in nature for what is only a contrivance of language. (*Tr.*, pp. 86–87)

In so arguing, Johnson's *Treatise* of 1828 posed a challenge to the Transcendentalists. When Emerson's *Nature* (1836) argued that "man is conscious of a universal soul within or behind his individual life" (*CW*, 1:18), he challenged the nominalist position taken by Johnson that "no two men possess the perfect identity which the sameness of their manhood implies; nor possesses any one man, at all times, and under all circumstances, the complete identity with which language invests his individuality" (*Tr.*, pp. 80–81). "The American Scholar" unfolds from "a doctrine ever new and sublime; that there is One Man" (*CW*, 1:53). To exalt the Transcendentalist, the Johnsonian position had to be roundly dismissed: "The sensual man conforms thoughts to things; the poet conforms things to his thoughts" (*CW*, 1:31). Of course, from the viewpoint of a sensual man like Johnson, the rhapsodies in *Nature* about "this Unity, that . . . easily seen . . . lies under the undermost garment of Nature, and betrays its source in Universal Spirit" (*CW*, 1:27–28) showed Emerson titillated embarrassingly by a linguistic dance of the veils. Johnson's own philosophical *Explorations of the Bottom* made him less eager to peep beneath Nature's nethermost garment.

Johnson's skepticism about identity had one curious result for his moral philosophy. Personality was not fixed but malleable and improvable.

Though resisting direct intellectual dictatorship, our feelings can be cultivated through our actions and words. In the absence of an active and independent concept of mind he came to regard these as levers for manipulating the emotions. In an American tradition that runs from Benjamin Franklin through Norman Vincent Peale, he is one of the more sophisticated advocates of positive thinking: "Mark out for yourself, then, such a character as you desire to possess, and by speaking consonantly thereto you will attain the desired character as certainly as you will a coat after going to your tailor and ordering it." His own marriage had taught him that "the feeling that causes a man to kiss his wife he can excite in himself at any time by kissing her."[9]

During Utica's horrifying cholera epidemic of 1832 Johnson became convinced that the symptoms of terror and cholera were so similar that one might produce the other (the philosopher's insistence on rigorous sensory distinctions had its limits). He therefore forbade his family to discuss the plague. When they violated that edict and his own peace of mind, "I immediately said I was not well; and I rushed into the open air and began to walk, whistle, sing and dance to divert my thoughts as the best way of allaying my fear" (PB, p. 196). Shortly thereafter, he removed his startled family to the country, where they all survived unscathed, a blessing he ascribed to positive thinking.

Sincerity is thus a poor guide for ethical action. For a man "to insist that he will not speak as duty requires, by reason of his not possessing the congenial feelings, is as unreasonable as for a sailor to insist that he will not hoist his anchor by reason of his not first being underway" (LV, p. 39). Johnson traced one friend's spiritual depression to the "erroneous opinion that religion must be preceded by an intellectual faith in the scriptures," whereas faith was actually best created by participating in liturgical worship (PB, pp. 194-95). He developed this theme in his essay "The Effects of Language on the Speaker and Hearer," which appeared in An Encyclopedia of Instruction: or Apologues and Breviats on Men and Manners (1857). It also figured largely in his Religion in Its Relation to the Present Life (1841)—so largely, in fact, that when Harpers wished to reprint that volume as part of its popular Family Library, on the advice of a clergyman the firm stipulated that certain sections that "inculcated hypocrisy" be excised. But avid for influence though he was, Johnson somehow could not find in himself hypocrisy enough to consent to the expurgation.

That this arch-empiricist thus wound up espousing (somewhat like his master Berkeley) an almost magical view of language is but one paradox among many. His advocacy of moral role-playing envisioned a world where deception was difficult because we "are masquerading before others who have masqueraded themselves, and they know every turn of the game as well as you" (*PB*, p. 273). But despite stressing our self-creating fictions, he scorned fiction as a literary genre. This teetotaling antiprohibitionist was an opponent of slavery feted by Utica's blacks, but he could not embrace abolition because of his dedication to states' rights. As an investor he speculated; as a man he abhorred gambling. "Refrain from all attempts to excite laughter," he advised his sons. Anyone voluntarily assuming the lowly job of a paid jester "must be a fool indeed." But his condemnation is itself wittily couched, for he knew that discreet humor could aid our gravest aspirations. So he distinguished "brilliant conversation" from mere jesting. Its desirable aim was "to recreate rather than instruct,—to be playful rather than serious, and sprightly rather than profound." Even sheer frivolity was thus a legitimate objective, so "he ought to be satisfied . . . who can amuse without diminishing the esteem in which he is held by his companions, though he should fail of exciting their admiration" (*Encyclopedia*, p. 268).

Ambiguity about humor pervades the philosophical magnum opus in which he tried vainly to excite the world's admiration. By the second edition of the *Treatise* (1836) Johnson knew how readily he was misunderstood. He was not shrewd enough to eliminate perhaps the chief cause of that—the lack of symbols like quotation marks or italics for distinguishing between the words considered in themselves and their denotata. But he labored mightily to make himself clear, devising an elaborate scheme for the *Treatise*. Twenty-nine topically organized lectures were subdivided into four groups and then into numbered paragraphs with subheadings. Yet he kept returning so insistently to his main theme, the need to interpret words by things, that the linear argument is often unclear. The *Treatise* blunders like a moth around this light. The result reads rather like a collection of brilliant aphorisms in the vein of Schlegel's *Athenaeum Fragments* or Wittgenstein's *Tractatus*. At the end of his long life Johnson sturdily professed to believe that "in artistic construction" his works were unsurpassed for conciseness and clarity (*PB*, p. 353). Thus "when my language or positions shall, in a casual perusal, seem absurd, (and such cases may be frequent)," he pleaded in the second edition for more thoughtful interpretation (*Tr.*, p. 28). Yet his plea attests to awareness of the gap between himself and his audience. "In detail then we must proceed," he cautioned. "Patience, then, must be *your* characteristic and *my* motto" (*Tr.*, p. 125). Alas, when Americans need patience, they want it immediately. Instead of the oracular confidence with which Emerson prophesies in *Nature*, Johnson's *Treatise* is suffused with an ironic awareness of its own impotence. Believing that language cannot define its own limits, he had to warn his readers that "if you desire to know what the universe truly is, you must dismiss my names . . . and contemplate the universe externally with your senses" (*Tr.*, p. 161).

This impasse Johnson sought to transcend by hemming his Enlightenment toga with a homespun Romantic irony. Whereas Greek philosophers had been notable for eloquence, modern philosophical writing usually combined "slovenly composition with sterility of ornament." It was monumentally boring. "I will endeavour to believe that Philosophy is not necessarily so frowning and sluggish a divinity as her ministers usually represent," he assured his timorous audience. "Her limbs are masculine I admit, and her discourse is grave"—an invitation to envision a deity like the androgynous goddess gracing the frontispiece of Webster's *Speller*—"but her language may be tasteful, and her decorations gay" (*Tr.*, p. 41). True to his promise, Johnson spiced his *Treatise* with ironic observations:

> When men first attempted to spell, they resolved every word into such letters as would best express the sound of the word. The sound was the standard, and the letters approximated to it as well as they could. In our days, however, the process is reversed. The letters are the standard, (in our country at least,) of the sound of the word; and very awkwardly sounding words the superficially learned (who adopt this unnatural standard) occasionally make. Thus to subordinate oral words to the letters into which orthography resolves words, is a species of retribution on words for the authority that words have usurped over natural existences. (*Tr.*, p. 116)

In one breath the superficially learned are mocked for ignorant pretension, in the next they are enlisted as allies in the Johnsonian program for subverting the usurped authority of words, and the audience reading the lectures is left wondering how much his written words can be trusted if they conform to an "unnatural standard." Such a conceit may seem too ponderous and convoluted to be alluring. But the moment we insist on the gaiety promised, Johnson assures us with the grave mien of an economist that "every thing estimable must be costly." Now a winsome philosophical style seems a contradiction in terms, for "if knowledge were attainable without effort, it might possess, like air and water, a theoretical homage; but it would command no practical reverence" (*Tr.*, p. 186). Tedium becomes for the nonce the criterion of philosophical value.

Elsewhere the stylistic economist clearly mocks his own premises:

> We might reasonably imagine that a man who devotes his life to literature (a devotion in itself perverse,) would select subjects in which the playfulness of fancy, or the vivacity of wit, would relieve the irksomeness of composition;

at least, that he would avoid the labyrinths of metaphysics, and the straits of logick: toils which seldom can supply even the consolation that a French authoress extracted from an assimilation of herself with a lamp; that she consumes to enlighten others. Yet in literature also the rugged walks are voluntarily thronged equally with the most agreeable. This thought is gloomy, but it happily suggests the subject of our lecture. (*Tr.*, p. 145)

Johnson's lectures often begin with such ironic self-deprecation. Thus he devises an allegory that "bears but slightly on our subject" to explain that his "not very alluring motive" for continuing the lectures is shame at abandoning them. And the *Treatise* as a whole is framed by two ironic digressions. After promising us philosophical gaiety and a pleasing style, Johnson ends his introductory lecture with a wry fantasy about being at the mercy of a demon who deludes men into magnifying their vices. Suddenly the demon appears in a vision. "His language was harmonious,— his actions were profoundly respectful. Delight hung upon his lips, and conviction attended his communication. An unusual complacency expanded my breast. I extended my arms in the attitude of oratory, and prepared to welcome him with all the figures of rhetorick; when suddenly, approaching the fiend, his eyes were averted, and his face was distorted in ridicule. He dissolved into air, and, as he vanished, I discovered his name, Vanity, stamped upon his back" (*Tr.*, pp. 44-45). With this flowery flight Johnson undermines his own professed aim of investing philosophy with ironic beauties of style. Here we are not far from Schlegel's sense of the Irony of Irony. It is not surprising that the *Treatise* concludes with allusions to the philosopher in *Rasselas* who believed that his calculations controlled the winds and rains and that a mistake on his part would either deluge the earth or devastate it with tempests. Though Johnson presents him as a symbol of "our errour" in seeking to influence nature through words, the trope spirals into an ironic exordium on philosophers that questions their ability to influence mankind. As well he might. During his final years, labor on his intellectual *summa* kept him from auditing accounts vigilantly. In a sad irony, the philosophical banker's own bank collapsed in the wake of embezzlement.

Whether Romantic or not, Johnson's ironic stance stemmed naturally from his American experiences and his view of language. As philosophy dwindled into conceptual clarification, his naive bearer-theory of meaning left him pointing to a world he could hardly describe. Time and again words led him to the threshold of reality, but once the philosopher's foot was on the sill he had to revert to something like Condillac's gestural language of nature. Johnson's relentless iteration of his central point seems only partly a pedagogical strategy. On a deeper level it functions like a mantra, dissolving the meaning of words in an effort to let him come to his senses. His conviction that "nature is no party to our philology" left him with a fragmented world in which he lived comfortably enough (*Tr.*, p. 62). His metallic, aphoristic style mirrors its tensions at the same time that his philosophy wages war against ambiguity. "*Copper* has the English derivative *coppery,*" he noted, and "*iron* has the adjective, *irony*" (*Method*, p. 6). The dictionary of his dreams would have informed him that the adjective *irony* has absolutely no etymological connection with the noun that is its English homonym. That is only another of the ironies of language that Johnson understood quite well.

Rational Theology and Its Discontents

Many American ministers shared Johnson's Lockean view of language at the same time that they recoiled from his metaphysical skepticism. Unlike Britain, where theologians could slumber undisturbed in the bosom of an established church, America's religious freedom fostered sectarian competition. Colleges were often supported by denominations to train their ministry. Since the capture of the Hollis Chair of Divinity in 1805, Harvard had spawned Unitarian ministers. Disgruntled Congregationalists founded Andover Theological Seminary in response and continued to rule the roost at Yale while Presbyterians held sway at Princeton. As the Protestant sects struggled to interpret Scripture self-justifyingly, biblical hermeneutics flirted increasingly with philosophy of language.

"The art of interpretation derives its origin from the *intrinsic ambiguity of language,*" explained Harvard's leading theological light Andrews Norton in his *Statement of Reasons for Not Believing the Doctrines of Trinitarians* (1819).[10] Sometimes styled the Unitarian pope, he elucidated Scripture with a Lockean view of language rather like Johnson's but less complicated. The *summa* that he produced for his denomination revolved around Sections VII and VIII, "On the Principles of the Interpretation of Language" and "On a Fundamental Error Concerning Language." Like all popular writings, the Scriptures are couched in an emotive language "very different from that of philosophical accuracy." In the Oriental poetry of the Bible "different senses in which such language may be understood often present themselves" (p. 142). Hence the need for hermeneutics. "The object of interpretation is to enable us to solve the difficulties presented by the intrinsic ambiguity of language. It first teaches us to perceive the different meanings which any sentence may be used to express . . . and it then teaches us . . . to distinguish, among *possible* meanings, the *actual* meaning of the sentence" (pp. 147-48). Norton approached figurative language with a wary Enlightenment mentality. Symbols had to be shucked to get at their kernel of meaning. For Norton the biblical authors were clumsy primitives groping for logical statements neither their culture nor language let them make well. With the help of Germanic Higher Criticism, scholars like Norton could now disentangle their ambiguities and pick out the "essential" meaning capable of being expressed in precise, straightforward prose unequivocal to all with common sense.

The Trinitarian passages of the Bible were certainly equivocal. But the principles of linguistic interpretation codified by Norton required the reader to select the one meaning most agreeable to historical context and common sense. Norton abhorred logical contradiction. "There is nothing clear in language, no proposition of any sort can be affirmed to be true, if we cannot affirm this to be true,—that it is impossible that the same being should be finite and infinite" (p. 58). Repugnant to common sense, "the doctrine has turned the Scriptures . . . into a book of riddles, and, what is worse, of riddles admitting no solution" (p. 61). Like Johnson, Norton regretted this result, but unlike Johnson he remained confident in language's metaphysical utility. There are undoubtedly truths above reason that men could not now grasp, but such truths lie entirely beyond language's power to express. Nor does biblical language try to express them:

> Words are only human instruments for the expression of human ideas; and it is impossible that they should express anything else. The meaning of words is that aggregate of ideas which men have associated with certain sounds or letters. They have no other meaning than what is given them by men; and this meaning must always be such as the human understanding is capable of conceiving; for we can associate with sounds or letters no idea or aggregate of ideas which we have not. Ideas, therefore, with which the human understanding is conversant, are all that can be expressed by words. (pp. 162-63)

Abstractions like "infinity" and "identity" cannot be pictured to the imagination, but Norton differed from Johnson in supposing that the understanding still has a tolerably clear grasp of them sans sensory reference. For expressing such ideas language is quite adequate. But though we have clear concepts of *identity* and *infinity,* we can have no clear notion of the identity of the finite and the infinite. In claiming such a union, the Doctrine of the Trinity struck Norton as intelligible enough—but absurd. "This is not an incomprehensible mystery; it is plain nonsense" (p. 170). At the root of the problem was the double meaning of the word *Logos,* which by signifying either *reason* or *word* identified the Son ambiguously with the Father as the uttered discourse of God. Norton brusquely dismissed Trinitarian doctrine as "the confusion of ideas produced by this confusion of the meanings of the word 'Logos!'" (pp. 371-72).

Boston Unitarians of the first generation thus shared with Johnson a Lockean view of language radically opposed to verbal ambiguity. But they struggled to ground their religion metaphysically, whereas his theological skepticism pointed him toward ethics as an objective domain where religion should be empirically based. For the Rhode Island businessman Rowland Gibson Hazard, however, neither an empirical nor a metaphysical basis would ever suffice religion. In *Language: Its Connexion with the Present Condition and Future Prospects of Man* (1836) he divided language into three overlapping realms—factual, abstract, and poetical. All supplement each other, but the imagination, "by analogies to what was before known, and by refinements of the language which already exists, has a greater celerity than reason, which follows with assured and cautious steps, and has to adapt a language of terms to every new discovery."[11] Poetic language was the cutting edge of all intellectual advance, including science. Because of our "ethereal nature" religion especially demanded "never-ending expansion" (p. 66), for "a religion which is contained in precise finite terms is inadequate to the boundless cravings of the soul."

Hazard's Romantic theory of imaginative "ideal" language offered trenchant analysis of the spiritual malaise affecting many Unitarians when "their advancement in thought . . . outstripped their improvement of its signs" (p. 90). "The great mission of our age is to unite the infinite and the finite," proclaimed Orestes Brownson—a difficult task given his conviction that "every positive form, however satisfactory it may be for the present, contains a germ of opposition to future progress."[12] Like the reformer, the Transcendental Artist "sees this vision of perfection in his mind, and attempts to embody it," claimed the punning Transcendentalist George Ripley. "But the result is never equal to his conception, he still imagines more glorious forms of beauty, than any which he has produced, his soul communes with an ideal perfectness, that no human hand can ever call into being" (*TR,* p. 140). While Norton clung to the Gospel miracles as historical warrant for Christ's divinity, Emerson wanted his miracles now, began to worship the moral sense, and bypassed the Trinity to genuflect before a quasi-Schlegelian Absolute vaguely conceived of as a bipolar unity.

"There is somewhat in all life untranslatable into language," ran the manifesto he composed for the *Dial*. "He who keeps his eye on that will write better than others, and think less of his writing, and of all writing. Every thought has a certain imprisoning as well as uplifting quality" (*TR*, p. 250). Gradually, grudgingly, Unitarians followed the Transcendental lead toward pantheism, praying as if "to whom it may concern," while orthodox Calvinists clucked in dismay and muttered, "I told you so."

Andover Theological Seminary's Moses Stuart soaked up German Higher Criticism to duel with Norton on behalf of Congregationalism. His scholarship unsettled as much as it corroborated, however, for Andover graduates fanning out into the backwoods with their heads full of Hebrew points sometimes disdained the "secondary meanings" of proof-texts their congregations had been wont to depend on. As Unitarianism splintered, religious journals proliferated. During 1820–50 a steady trickle of articles in the *Christian Examiner,* the *Scriptural Interpreter, Biblical Repository, Biblioteca Sacra,* and the *Princeton Review* worried the topic of language. With their revivalist tradition and their shrinking flock, Congregational ministers were especially sensitive to what Leonard Bacon censured in the *Biblical Repository* for 1839 as "Some Causes of the Corruption of Christian Eloquence." Already Unitarianism had captured Boston's elite by politely declining to trouble them about damnation. Now in Connecticut, where Calvinism seemed increasingly out of style, Episcopalianism was making inroads among the genteel, who demanded a more tasteful religion than theological argument could provide. In a series of articles for that journal, Edwards Park distinguished between "The Theology of the Intellect and That of the Feelings." His essays "The Proper Mode of Exhibiting Theological Truth" and "Connection between Theological Study and Pulpit Eloquence" show a sensitive logician speculating whether an approach to language based on Lockean logic-chopping was the best way to interpret or communicate religious truths. Perhaps words were not Norton's Lockean counters arbitrarily agreed upon by men, Frederic A. Adams suggested in "The Collocation of Words in the Greek and Latin Languages Examined in Relation to the Laws of Thought" (*Biblioteca Sacra,* 1848). If they were indelibly stamped by the divinely organic structure of the human mind, then pulpit eloquence, like "The Lyrical Poetry of the Bible" itself (*Biblical Repository,* 1847), must be couched in the language of nature—not that of theological abstraction. If a true God of reason needed Christ to express himself as the Living Word, then ministers needed to find living words for the pulpit that could incarnate their God oratorically.

From Paradigm to Paradox: Horace Bushnell Shakes Up American Protestantism

In 1849 the trickle of linguistic articles became a spate, for a Connecticut minister trained at Yale to defend the Congregational faith published a book titled *God in Christ: Three Discourses Delivered at New Haven, Cambridge, and Andover, with a Preliminary Dissertation on Language.* It climaxed an extraordinary period for Horace Bushnell. In 1845 a physical breakdown had left him expecting speedy death from consumption. But in 1848 he experienced a regenerative vision that convinced him he had glimpsed the gospel light. On the strength of his growing reputation as an Orthodox liberal, he was invited to speak at Yale, Andover, and Harvard. Indeed, Harvard was considering him as a leading candidate for the Hollis Chair. After discoursing on the Atonement for the Divinity School, he was chosen Phi Beta Kappa speaker for Harvard's Commencement that year. In the opinion of the Unitarian minister Cyrus Bartol, a Transcendental fellow traveler, "probably no oration at Cambridge had ever resounded more sweetly afar than his, in 1848, on 'Work and Play.'"[13] Emerson himself acknowledged the triumph, exclaiming, "We have not had since ten years a pamphlet which I have saved to bind! and here at last is Bushnell's."[14] The enthusiasm that inspired Emerson to bracket Bushnell first with Thoreau, then fancifully with Greeley and Mann as one of "The Three Horatii" (*JMN,* 11:275), was prompted by an oration that domesticated Schiller's *Spieltrieb* by treating science, morality, and religion as essentially sportive propensities. Bushnell argued that man is "a creature of play, essentially a poet in that which constitutes his higher life."[15]

Like many, Bartol was especially struck by Bushnell's peculiar blend of wit and gravity. Bushnell once left Bartol with an Orthodox clergyman who pleasantly tried to convert him. When Bushnell came back, he asked his colleague, "What have you been doing with my friend Bartol?" "I have not been doing anything but laying out the Presbyterian creed to him," was the reply. "You mean that you have been putting a shroud on it, I suppose, for that's what they do when they lay things out," rejoined Bushnell, with "that laugh which always began in the gray eyes, and only left its last audible ripple . . . in his mouth" (in Cheney, p. 187). Deluged with invitations from liberals to expound orthodox views, Bushnell hoped that the novel approach of *God in Christ* might heal the breach between Unitarianism and Orthodoxy. Alas, after their ostentatious courtship Harvard's

Unitarians left him dangling with no offer, while back home the book sparked such outrage that the Hartford Central Association of Ministers tried him for heresy. Let off with a censure, he published *Christ in Theology* (1851) to clarify his views. Nonetheless, he was isolated in his denomination. Fellow Congregational ministers refused to exchange pulpits with him. By the time the furor died down, its reverberations had been felt in every New England parsonage. Nearly two dozen reviews, some of astonishing length, appeared in various publications. Bushnell's notoriety ensured that issues debated within the manse were known to the community, if mainly through indignant sermons.

He had obviously touched a nerve, but how? The key to Bushnell's thinking about the Trinity and most other religious subjects lay in his Dissertation on Language. Unlike those devout souls who hoped that philology might pinpoint the paradisal language, he thought that irrecoverable after Babel. Anyway, he insisted, Genesis showed God teaching Adam no one particular language but simply endowing him with the capacity to create languages. Assuming a direct Divine origin exalted language more than Bushnell wished. Nor, despite his study under Josiah Willard Gibbs at Yale, did Bushnell see onomatopoetic imitation as dictating the shape of primal languages. Though some Germans, "in general coincidence with the scheme of Schlegel," had elaborated a "most subtle and beautiful theory" to that effect, ultimately "all theories about the representative nature of names, taken as sounds, would seem to be idle, in the last degree."[16] After Babel Bushnell imagined small groups developing their own noun-languages independently by naming physical objects in the world around them on a largely arbitrary basis. He resolved Tooke's dilemma about the priority of nouns or verbs by arguing that "verbs are originally mere names of acts, or phenomena of action, not distinguished from what are called nouns, or names of things, until use settles them into place in propositions or forms of affirmation" (*GC*, pp. 27–28). Originally *sun* and *shine* named the same phenomenon, and their function was differentiated only with the subsequent formation of grammar. Drawing on Gibbs's theories, Bushnell suggested that all grammatical structure evolves from our effort to locate things in space.

Since grammatical structure derived—like the names of things—from physical objects, the emergence of grammar provoked less speculation from him than it should have. For Bushnell the key issue was instead the emergence of names for nonphysical phenomena—our emotions and intellectual concepts. As one of Johnson's few perceptive readers, he recognized that words might mislead by confusing data from different senses. "This subject was labored some years ago by one of our countrymen, Mr. Johnson, in a 'Treatise on Language, or The Relations of Words to Things,'" Bushnell observed. "The latter part of his title, however, is all that is justified; for to language in its more comprehensive sense, as a vehicle of spirit, thought, sentiment, he appears to have scarcely directed his inquiries." The inaccuracies cataloged by Johnson Bushnell joyfully acknowledged, but for him the crucial question was explaining how words let us communicate as well as they do. The primal noun language distorted somewhat insofar as names are general categories for specific things, but at least men could keep tabs on common nouns by pointing to the objects categorized. When concrete nouns became metaphors for formless concepts and emotions, how could men know what they were talking about? To check on the meaning of abstract words they could not point to their ideas. To claim with Tooke that the moral term *right* simply reduces to the notion of a *straight line* was not enough. There is nothing inherently linear about mental states like goodness, nothing inherently curvy about sin, so one has to explain "why a crooked line, which is the more graceful in itself, should not have been the natural instinct, and so the symbol of the right, as it now is of the wrong." For abstract terms ever to have arisen etymologically, individuals must somehow have agreed about the analogies involved. Beyond saying vaguely that there was something "organic" about the mind, Johnson like most other thinkers seemed too incurious about how verbal language ever managed to say anything about the realms of intellect, emotion, and spirituality. When the mind sought to serve itself with object-words, "on the one hand, is form; on the other is the formless. The first represents, and is somehow fellow to, the other; how, we cannot discover" (GC, pp. 43–44).

Herder, for one, invited him to imagine language as evolving organically from a unitary primitive consciousness that left mind and matter undifferentiated, rather than as a mechanical invention requiring a social contract. But despite his reading of Humboldt and his sympathy with organicism, all Bushnell could imagine was a Transcendental answer where

> the outer world is seen to be a vast menstruum of thought or intelligence. There is a logos in the forms of things, by which they are prepared to serve as types or images of what is inmost in our souls; and then there is a logos also of construction in the relations of space, the position, qualities, connections, and predicates of things, by which they are framed into grammar. In one word, the outer world, which envelops our being, is itself language,

the power of all language. . . . And if the outer world is the vast dictionary and grammar of thought we speak of, then it is also itself an organ throughout of Intelligence. (*GC*, p. 43)

Like many leading philologists, Humboldt seemed on the right track in supposing that speech "must really be considered as inherent in man: language could not have been invented without its type pre-existing in man" (*GC*, p. 19). Many modern psycholinguists would agree. But unlike modern linguistics, Bushnell insisted with Plato and Berkeley that the principle of analogy structuring intellectual language must exist not only in the mind but also in the world, that the physical universe was indeed a language in which the mind of God expressed itself to men. In the Trinity, the logos was "the Word, or Word of Life, that peculiar power in the Divine nature by which God is able to represent Himself outwardly in the forms of things" (*GC*, p. 187). But theology could supply no blueprint for the internal relations of the three Persons, whose function was expressive in any event, "the wording forth of God" (*GC*, p. 175). Linguistic ambiguity forbade any such precision, for abstract terms were simply analogies. They could suggest meaning but never designate it as words designate physical objects. "Since all words"—except for purely self-referential systems like logic and mathematics—"are inexact representations of thought, mere types or analogies . . . it follows that language will be ever trying to mend its own deficiencies, by multiplying its forms of representation." Denying that rigorous definition could ever purge metaphysical diction of its potentially misleading physical roots, Bushnell argued that the truest language drops all pretense of philosophic objectivity to dramatize its own struggles: "Thus, as form battles form, and one form neutralizes another, all the insufficiencies of words are filled out, the contrarieties liquidated, and the mind settles into a full and just apprehension of the pure spiritual truth. Accordingly we never come so near to a truly well rounded view of any truth as when it is offered paradoxically" (*GC*, p. 55).

"Poets, then, are the true metaphysicians," Bushnell concluded (*GC*, p. 73). He stood Norton and Stuart on their heads by arguing that Scripture was not clumsy logic but that their theology was clumsy literary criticism. When Norton dismissed the Trinity as a hyperbolic fancy, he did not really understand "the nature, capacities, and incapacities of language, as a vehicle of truth" (*GC*, p. 40). Symbols were both feebler and more powerful than he supposed. And they were inescapable. By worshiping God in one Person, Unitarians still symbolized the Absolute, but with much graver risk of anthropomorphism (*GC*, pp. 138-39). The

multiple metaphors of Father, Son, and Spirit guarded against anthropomorphic debasement on the one hand and against pantheistic dispersion
on the other, while their paradoxicality made them self-canceling vehicles
of a dynamic revelation that was always fresh. Bushnell sympathized with
the Unitarians' protest against the frozen logic of orthodoxy, but they
simply exacerbated the theological disease by renouncing the great Christian myths like depravity, grace, and regeneration. Without such concrete
but flexible biblical symbols "the tone or tonic energy of the gospel is
lost" (GC, p. 99). Proof-text theology wandered in logical mazes built
from single figures of speech, much as if trying "to compress the whole
tragic force of Lear into some one sentence of Edgar's gibberish."[17]

For this approach to theology Bushnell claimed to owe more to Coleridge's work than to any other writing except Scripture. He came from a
raw country family where cultivated conversation was unknown, and he
matriculated late at Yale "when the vernacular type of language is cast."
Expressing himself there was painfully awkward. "I had no language,
and if I chanced to have an idea, nothing came to give it expression. The
problem was, in fact, from that point onward, how to get a language,
and where." By stressing the primacy of figurative speech, Marsh's edition of Coleridge's Aids gave the young man confidence in his right to
construct abstract terminology for himself from his own concrete vocabulary and experiences. Writing became "to a considerable extent, the
making of a language, and not a going to the dictionaries." The result
was an exhilarating sense of verbal freedom and power. "Finding the air
full of wings about me, buoyant all and free, I have let them come under
and lift. The second, third, and thirtieth senses of words—all but the
physical first sense—belong to the empyrean, and are given, as we see in
the prophets, to be inspired by." But, he characteristically added, "of
course, they must be genuinely used—in their nature, and not contrary
to it" (Cheney, pp. 208-9). Menacing thought even as they give birth to
it, physical objects safeguard the meanings of terms but threaten constantly to distort intellectual discourse. Thus Young's line "Zeal and
humility, her wings to heaven" would almost certainly jar on a sensitive
reader because etymologically humility means groundling "even when a
classical education has not revealed it to his view." Etymology "controls
the speech of the ignorant not the less certainly, because it is itself
unknown to them. On the contrary, its sway is even the more absolute,
that it governs by a latent presence" (GC, p. 51).

Bushnell's effusive gratitude to Coleridge may camouflage other
latent presences by which he was governed in framing his theology. With
its analogical logos, his doctrine of language obviously resembles that

articulated thirteen years earlier by Emerson in *Nature* (1836). But though Emerson welcomed Bushnell as an ally, nowhere does *God in Christ* mention Emerson's influence. Elsewhere Bushnell trenchantly criticized him. Coleridge was a safer source, for in Connecticut Transcendentalism meant pantheism. A man wishing to reconcile Unitarianism with Orthodoxy had good reason to maintain discreet silence about any influence from that quarter. In one important respect Bushnell disagreed with *Nature*, for in that early work Emerson had suggested with the Swedenborgian Sampson Reed that *particular* natural facts were signs of *particular* spiritual facts. In later essays such as "The Poet" Emerson specifically rejected the one-to-one Swedenborgian concept of correspondence, talking instead as if any symbol might mean everything and all meanings had myriad symbols.[18] Bushnell more steadily held that though the forms of things rule out some analogical uses as illegitimate, any natural object can yield multiple though not infinite analogies.

As a quondam farmhand Bushnell had a knack for things that the unhandy Emerson notably lacked. "He had it in him to be an artist, architect, road-builder, and city-builder, as well as scholar," observed Cyrus Bartol. "I have never known faculties so manifold in better order" (Cheney, p. 186) It was characteristic that Bushnell called his conception of the Trinity instrumental rather than modal, for he grasped words as a craftsman handles tools. It was also characteristic that Bushnell's correspondence theory welcomed science even more warmly than Emerson's. Despite the inevitable distortions of metaphorical language, he envisioned "one hope for mental and religious truth . . . which I confess I see but dimly, and can but faintly express or indicate. It is, that physical science, leading the way, setting outward things in their true proportions . . . revealing their genesis and final causes and laws, and weaving all into the unity of a real universe, will so perfect our knowledge and conceptions of them, that we can use them, in the second department of language, with more exactness." Scientists might clarify the "laws of nature" by providing "an internal grammar, which is certain, as it is evolved, to pass into language, and be an internal grammar in that, systematizing and steadying its uses" (*GC*, p. 78). If physical science ever unified its theories successfully, then perhaps a *summa theologica* would be possible. In the meantime, Bushnell's instrumentalism allowed him better than Emerson to appreciate the analogic value of scientific concepts limited to specific disciplines, without worrying whether chemists and physicists explained the same physical properties differently. Emerson, by contrast, though he read widely and profitably in popular science, was too eager to believe that a unified field theory was at hand. As an imaginative naturalist, Thoreau had to move toward Bushnell's appreciation of correspondences that were neither fixed nor infinitely suggestive because their scientific usefulness demanded limiting their scope as hypotheses.

In this respect as in others, Bushnell's language theory may owe more to Johnson than he cared to admit. Working from different premises as a Lockean empiricist and a Coleridgean etymologist, as Crosby emphasizes, banker and preacher still agreed on important points. Stressing the limitations of language, both saw words as irredeemably ambiguous. Both minimized the value of logic. Ecumenically minded, both tried to show how contradictory statements could each point to truth; and from trying to harmonize opposing viewpoints both at first pleased partisans of neither. Their respect for science was tempered by a clear understanding of its instrumentalism. Both distrusted natural theology as pseudo-science, sapping religion rather than nurturing its emotional roots. Both defended religious experience experientially by treating it as the self-sufficient domain of the heart, impervious to logic and requiring scant metaphysical sanction. Doubting the power of theological argument to convert unbelievers, they saw religious language as communicating only feelings already shared, reawakening faith rather than conveying it. Though each man labored to organize his insights and to some extent professed the value of system, systematic definition was alien to the deepest convictions of both. Their philosophical masterworks seem assemblages of powerfully suggestive fragments rather than fully convincing wholes. Like *A Treatise on Language*, Bushnell's *God in Christ* seems haunted by a truth that it can point to but not incarnate because words "are only hints, or images, held up before the mind of another, to put *him* on generating or reproducing the same thought" (*GC*, p. 46).

"Fragments," Schlegel had claimed, "are the proper form of universal philosophy" (*KA*, 2:209). If much in Bushnell seems reminiscent of Schlegel, that is no accident. Extolling Romantic literary techniques was novel only within the "stern, iron-limbed . . . New England theology" that Bushnell was trying to bend into a new theology of limber irony (*GC*, p. 96). Even there Bushnell's endorsement of mixed metaphors just echoed Dugald Stewart's recommendation of thirty years earlier (see chapter 2 after note 14). His rationale for holy paradox had been seminally formulated by Schlegel at the end of the eighteenth century: "All highest truths of every kind are thoroughly trivialized; hence there's nothing more necessary than to express them always anew and, where possible, ever more paradoxically, so that we don't forget that they still exist and that they can never be completely articulated" ("On Incomprehensibility," *KA*, 2:366). If a Scottish commonsense philosopher and a German Romantic sage could reach similar stylistic conclusions, one need not assume Bushnell's direct indebtedness to the latter. Paradoxicality could have swum into his ken on many currents of Romantic thought.

Nor need we suppose that *God in Christ* (1849) sparked Thoreau's meditations:

> It is related that Giorgio Barbarelli Titian's friend, defending painting against the charge of being an incomplete art, because it could exhibit but one side of a picture—laid a wager with some sculptor that he could represent the back face & both profiles of a man, without the spectator being obliged to walk round it as a statue. He painted "a warrior, who, having his back turned towards the spectator, stood looking at himself in a fountain, in whose limpid waters his full front figure was reflected. At the left of the warrior was suspended his suit of polished steel armor. . . . At the right was painted a looking-glass, which reflected that side"; and thus he won the wager.
>
> So I would fain represent some truths as roundly and solidly as a statue—or as completely & in all their relations as Barbarelli his warrior. So that you may see round them. (25 Apr. 1852)

Thoreau figured out for himself that representing some truths required multiple perspectives. He and Bushnell agreed that to see round depictions of truth you need to see through them.

At one point Bushnell quotes in translation from Schlegel's *Philosophy of Language*. There are Kantian overtones in his philosophy of language, and Schlegel's book could well have given him a sense of the approach taken by German idealism.[19] Whatever Bushnell's access to Schlegel's thought, Anglo-American philosophy of language was converging independently on a native concept of Romantic irony. "Full of jokes and bright sayings . . . and fond of writing droll doggerel," Bushnell left many observers trying to define his peculiar sense of humor (Cheney, p. 19). "Playfulness I should call one of Dr. Bushnell's marked traits," wrote Cyrus Bartol, but "seldom, if ever, exploding aloud" (Cheney, p. 186). "His ordinary conversation was not humorous in the strict sense of the word," observed W. L. Sage, "but flashes of wit, bright, illuminative, and unexpected, darted from sentence to sentence" (Cheney, p. 255). "Witty . . . biting in his sarcasm against pomp and falseness," this preacher's darker ironies made him seem to Charles L. Brace "the most independent and muscular sermonizer in the American pulpit" (Cheney, p. 80). Yet his health was in constant peril, forcing him to resign his ministry early. An autopsy disclosed only one functioning lung. Coughing up quips and blood from "this restless play of being," he seemed to his daughter to exemplify Carlyle's dictum that "the very excess of life in him . . . brought on disease" (Cheney, p. 265).

After Andrews Norton dismissed the Trinity as a bad pun, this man undertook like Charles Lamb to defend it as such. Only a Logos at loggerheads with itself, Bushnell felt, could break the emotional logjam of New England theology. *God in Christ* opened an era for liberal Protestantism in the United States. Eddying, like his other books, in dizzying cultural crosscurrents, his philosophy of language reflects a "tragic optimism" that placed him among midcentury America's most eloquent spokesmen for "the party of Irony."[20]

8 /

Go Slow—Man Thinking

> When the mind is braced by labor and invention, the page of whatever book we read becomes luminous with manifold allusion. Every sentence is doubly significant.
>
> — Emerson, "The American Scholar"

Emerson Whips Words Until the Silence *Reverberates*

Throughout the reign of literary modernism Emerson suffered a partial eclipse. The voice that liberated nineteenth-century America rang on twentieth-century ears like an ossified fuddy-duddy's. Emerson seemed a purveyor of high-sounding thoughts so incoherent as scarcely to merit the name of philosophy. New Critical methods honed on poetry and fiction hardly illuminated his peculiar achievement as a writer. Even today I find no author in the standard survey anthologies more difficult to teach. "How do you get a handle on this guy?" one baffled student earnestly asked when our survey reached "The American Scholar." What should I have said while young Ira's pen hovered eagerly over his notebook? It had been my own question thirty years earlier. The same question vexed the elder Henry James when he exclaimed in exasperated admiration, "Oh you man without a handle!"[1] And it remains a fair, even a penetrating question.

"First, put down the pen," a good reply might have begun. "Listen to my voice." And then, with what eloquence I could muster, I might have tried to explain that Emerson's unique rhetorical style was designed precisely to make it difficult to label him. He aimed to be not a thinker but Man Thinking. At his best, he brilliantly realized that ambition. Transfixed on the page with a hi-liter and treated as "ideas," even his best maxims assume a frozen grandeur. What Emerson intended as living thoughts become simply thoughts to live by when set down in a notebook. His finest passages may congeal unless the reader attends not only to the words but to the spaces between them. With the publication in recent decades of an accurate edition of his remarkable journals, it has become easier to grasp how far the oracular manner of the essays was a deliberately contrived pose, a literary creation. At home in his study the

Orphic Bard became foxy grandpa. Rightly read, Emerson's public prose floats and shimmers unlike any other nineteenth-century oratory. Misgauge his podium manner, and the essays can collapse into empty, florid grandiloquence.

Almost everything that makes Emerson's writing memorable emerges from his preoccupation with language. Here as elsewhere his thinking is fissured with contradictions. "Language is the great study of man," he early decided, "and the degree of its perfection is I suppose an unerring index of the degree of civilization" (*JMN*, 2:55–56). But how could man perfect it when "each word is like a work of nature, determined a thousand years ago, & not alterable. We confer & dispute, & settle the meaning so or so, but it remains what it was in spite of us. The word beats all the speakers & definers of it, & stands to their children what it stood to their fathers" (*JMN*, 11:232).

The Diversions of Purley, which he plundered to furbish *Nature*'s famous section on "Language," encouraged precisely this fear. Insofar as Tooke allowed for linguistic change, it seemed a process beyond man's control. "How much language thinks for us," Emerson marveled, a trifle apprehensively (*JMN*, 11:267). Often, indeed, this seemed beneficial: "A man may find his words mean more than he thought when he uttered them & be glad to employ them again in a new sense" (*JMN*, 5:409). But the supposed organic autonomy of language also posed a threat to man's independence. "We die of words. We are hanged, drawn & quartered by dictionaries" (*JMN*, 7:240). Fidelity to self meant treason to language, and its punishment was severe. In such moods he felt that "only words that are new fit exactly the thing" (*JMN*, 5:246). But how to come by them when the authorities he transcribed informed him that "no fact is more certain . . . than that words neither have been nor are now *invented;* but that they always have been compounded from existing words in the dialect—or borrowed from some collateral source" (*JMN*, 12:48). Too starchy to be a vulgar neologizer like Poe or Whitman, he was gored painfully on the horns of this literary dilemma. How could he be the Poet as Language-maker and primal Namer? Fitting new words he could neither coin nor compound freely, but "those that are old like old scoriae that have been long exposed to the air & sunshine, have lost the sharpness of their mould & fit loosely" (*JMN*, 5:246). At such moments perhaps all words seemed turds.

"It seems as though this present age of words should naturally be followed by an age of silence when men should speak only through facts & so regain their health" (*JMN*, 8:240). Recoiling in disgust from the disease of language, he flirted with the Transcendental mystique of silence.

"There are two in every man, a sane and an insane. The sane thinks; the insane speaks. Our thought is . . . great . . . our speech petty" (*JMN*, 8:188). Language might be superfluous. "It seemed to men that words came nearer to the thing; described the fact; were the fact. They learn later that they only suggest it. It is an operose circuitous way of putting us in mind of the thing,—of flagellating our attention" (*JMN*, 8:286). He wanted instead to whip words. Like the Swedenborgian Sampson Reed, at times he was confident that "the day will come when speech will be adequate, commensurate with thought" (*JMN*, 8:188). Elsewhere language seemed too petty a goal for human development: "But with all progress this happens, that speech becomes less, finally ceases in a nobler silence" (*JMN*, 8:286-87). This was a theme he could wax eloquent upon: "It is better to hear than to speak. As long as I hear truth, I am . . . not conscious of any limits to my nature . . . . But if I speak, then I define, confine, & am less. Silence is a menstruum that dissolves personality & gives us leave to be great & universal" (*JMN*, 5:391).

This encomium was, of course, paradoxically eloquent. The value of silence depended on speech; only language made it possible to hear truth. Indeed, truth is fundamentally linguistic, not a property of nature. Only sentences can be true or false. There are no true trees, only real ones, nor are there any true words by themselves. Moreover, in dissolving personality the menstruum of Silence might menace the self more than words ever did. "Speech is the sign of artificiality, difference, ignorance, and the more perfect the understanding, the less need of words," Emerson might protest after scanning the Chinese pictographs in Marshman's translation of Confucius (*JMN*, 7:106). "The great Idea baffles wit," the Orphic Bard proclaimed haltingly, "Language falters under it" (*W*, 9:298). But all this Romantic courtship of the ineffable only led the frustrated suitor back to the fact of speech:

> The end and the means, the gamester and the game,—life is made up of the intermixture and reaction of these two amicable powers, whose marriage appears beforehand monstrous, as each denies and tends to abolish the other. We must reconcile the contradictions as we can, but their discord and their concord introduce wild absurdities into our thinking and speech. No sentence will hold the whole truth, and the only way in which we can be just, is by giving ourselves the lie; Speech is better than silence; silence is better than speech. (*CW*, 3:143-44)

Unitarians whose ancestors had expelled the Quakers were now looking to India for a fresh appreciation of religious silence. There is something funny about these earnest efforts to woo the Void, chanting *om* with a Boston twang. But the *dialectic* of speech and silence led Emerson down more fruitful paths. A language of things might be awkward for philosophers, as Swift had mockingly shown in *Gulliver's Travels*. But another alternative to words suggested itself. Come the millennium, Emerson dreamed, "the only speech will at last be action, as Confucius describes the Speech of God" (*JMN*, 7:106). No reader of Genesis or Coleridge should need the Confucian example to imagine this happy state. For two millennia classical rhetoric had classified *action* as a form of oratorical discourse. Across America tykes were sawing the air declaiming patriotic speeches from school readers. Noah Webster suggested that language originated with verbs of action, and the relation of verbs to nouns bred interminable wrangling among America's philosophical grammarians. However the idea first popped into his head, Emerson developed it gleefully. "Words & deeds are quite indifferent modes of the divine energy," he declared in his journal. "Cease talking with such bellowing emphasis against words. They also are actions" (*JMN*, 8:252).

He was addressing himself of course. When he had bellowed emphatically against words, that was largely because of Tooke's influence. Etymologically he had remained oddly and needlessly materialist. "Language is made up of images or poetic tropes which now in their familiar secondary use have quite ceased to remind us of their poetic origins, as *howl* from *owl*, *ravenous* from *raven*," he wrote in 1841 (*JMN*, 8:160). Despite the nominalizing bias of his philosophy, Tooke had never decided whether noun or verb came first, and Coleridge had long since opted for the latter as the better source of derivations for an idealist. Yet here is Emerson doggedly deriving a verb and an adjective from nouns, when a minute's reflection clearly suggests a reverse process. It is preposterous to imagine primitive man needing an owl to denominate howls—unless one is fantasizing about the isolated brute beloved of French savants, who somehow became our ancestor sans exposure to a baby's crying. And even if such an isolato could exist, it is absurd to imagine him pointing to a raven to express hunger rather than to his own mouth or belly. Surely the sensible inference is that both nouns derive from verbal roots: owls are howlers and ravenous ravens raven. (In point of fact the last connection is bogus, but that is another story.) Partly because Emerson had trouble imagining verbal origins, his etymologic failed to grow and exfoliate like Coleridge's. Max Müller dedicated his studies of Indo-European roots to Emerson for harping on the concrete origins of words, but Emerson twangled the etymological lyre so monotonously that its harmonies blend into those of the sitar.

Though in this area he never shook off Tooke's nominalizing bias, the oscillating dialectic between speech and silence helped prod Emerson into action. It oriented him not to the Void but to the Verb. Vibrating between the poles of speech and silence made silence reverberate. If words were "poetic tropes," what were *tropes* themselves? *Turns*. The etymological essence of metaphoric troping is "change," which the poet controls. Viewed from this angle, words became not Tooke's gigantic bullies but charging bulls, whose power the writer could gracefully turn aside with a flourish of his cape. Writing became diversion—or better yet diverting—when words were used as *versatile* tools. "Every word we speak is millionfaced or convertible to an indefinite number of applications," Emerson reflected. "If it were not so we could read no book. Your remark would only fit your case not mine" (*JMN*, 8:157). Seeing words as multipurpose tools for thinking linked language fruitfully to its past. As "the first & simplest vehicle of mind," language "is of all things next to the mind, & the vigorous Saxon that uses it well is of the same block as the vigorous Saxon that formed it & works after the same manner" (*JMN*, 3:319). By approaching language as linguistic *activity*, not a bag of fixed forms, an author might extend it while remaining true to its essence, just as he could reclaim it. "The vocabulary of two omniscient men would embrace words & images now excluded from polite conversation" (*JMN*, 5:398). When Whitman took such advice, Emerson blenched but did not recant. Even the intellectual smokers loftily cultivated by the Transcendentalists embraced the same activity, for their beloved art of *conversation* was—in more than one sense—a series of turns.

Here was a notion that could be turned to account—to many accounts. Some rhetoricians ranked puns among reputable tropes, and Emerson was not immune to their appeal. In his journal he set down five conundrums that caught his fancy: "Why is one playing blindman's bluff, like sympathy? 'Tis a *Fellow feeling for a fellow Creature*. What reason to think the Carthaginians had domestic animals? Virgil says 'Dido et dux,' 'et pig e-bit Elisa.'" (*JMN*, 11:301; cf. 9:91). Schoolboy guffaws gleaned from George Bancroft would not serve his turn, but the Dog Latin does suggest a more genteel method of troping. Distinguishing "Elegant turns, either on the word, or on the thought" from "Points of Wit, and Quirks of Epigram," Dryden's *Discourse on Satire* had claimed that Ovid, Juvenal, and Virgil all used them. Throughout eighteenth-century criticism such fine turns on the thought alone could mean playing with synonyms, one scholar observes. "But normally the turn requires repetition of a word or root."[2] When Emerson evolved a prose style for his Orphic hero that gave gentle twists to the meaning of words, not quite puns in themselves but akin to satiric wit, he was not diverging all that far from neoclassic taste.

"A mistake of the main end to which they labor is incident to literary men, who, dealing with the organ of language,—the subtlest, strongest, and longest-lived of man's creations, and only fitly used as the weapon of thought and of justice,—learn to enjoy the pride of playing with this splendid engine, but rob it of its almightiness by failing to work with it" (*CW,* 1:110). So Emerson declaimed in *Literary Ethics, An Oration Delivered Before the Literary Societies of Dartmouth College* in 1838. This seems an unblushingly earnest credo, garden-variety commencement rhetoric. But notice the slight shocks in the diction. Language is variously an *organ, long-lived,* a *weapon,* and a *splendid engine.* These synonyms equivocally straddle the great divide between mechanical and organic conceptions of language. If we imagine literary men abusing this organ by playing with it, are they profaning a church organ dedicated to *almightiness?* profaning their tongues? or profaning another bodily organ in a weird form of linguistic self-abuse? In the early 1840s, as Joel Porte notes, Emerson regularly equated sexual and literary expression, calling for "a spermatic book" and "initiative, spermatic, prophesying, man-making words."[3] One may learn to enjoy playing, but what kind of *pride* must one normally "learn to enjoy"? (One of the word's older meanings is *sexual heat.*) Did Emerson's audience of students think that *they* had learned to enjoy play at Dartmouth? If the "splendid engine" of language is a "weapon," is this tool more useful or dangerous? Is language safe to keep around the house? If this weapon belongs to "thought and justice," can it be robbed? or only stolen? (Here the verb jerks us back to the animated, organic language of the early epithets.) If only thought and justice can fitly use language, does that mean that the speaker actually wants burglars to observe pious silence? Whom need truth and justice fear anyway? Are some literary men perhaps covertly eyeing the goods of conventional "thought and justice"? Does this help explain the very odd fact that literary men are initially said to "labor," albeit to a mistaken end, whereas by the end of the sentence we are told that they are "failing to work?" (A turn of 180 degrees.) Is the passage finally a *strong* statement of literary responsibility? or *subtle* to the point of bewilderment? tactfully reassuring or bizarrely unsettling? Is its author humble or proud? If the latter, should he be? Is he working with language or playing with it?

Three tempting but facile explanations must be quickly dismissed: first, Emerson was confused; second, Emerson just couldn't write any better; or third, Emerson was a hypocrite, trying to be all things to all people. As a philosopher Emerson often exhibits considerable fuzziness, but he was perfectly aware of the distinction between mechanical and organic language theories. As a rhetorician he just chose to blur it in this sentence, which fairly represents the middling prose of the early essays. As to its merits, one is free to call it bad prose. A student who handed me writing like this would receive a tart comment, I confess. But if we judge Emerson's writing harshly, we must admit that it is not helplessly bad here but deliberately so. The journal entries quoted above offer overwhelming evidence of his ability to write pungently when he chose. This sentence's orotund dance of the veils corresponds closely to aesthetic observations he worked out there and then published. "The only way we can be just, is by giving ourselves the lie" (CW, 3:143–44). If a student whose essay I had criticized brought me a journal as shrewd as Emerson's to justify his stylistic idiosyncrasies, I might become more interested in learning to read his essays on their own terms, however inappropriate those might be for normal exposition. As for hypocrisy, in prophetic prose like this Emerson was indeed trying to be all things to all people. But he was perfectly candid about this aim, not only journalizing about his desire to be "great & universal" but openly essaying the task of becoming Man Thinking. By 1838 the Emersonian program was public, the oracular pose understood. Few Dartmouth students judging this performance worried unduly about its sincerity, one suspects. They were there, after all, for the show—to have the sage they'd invited do his turn, turn them on, *convert* them. In his word games they were players, in his literary "labor" *collaborators*.

So deceptive is Emerson's podium style that most readers will require a second look to realize that he was *not* telling Dartmouth students to take language seriously rather than trifle with it. The conventional opposition between play and work is precisely what he wants to turn around, to undermine, to *subvert*. Thus his sentence describes "playing with this splendid engine" as something that literary men "labor . . . to . . . learn." And it assumes that *only* by "playing" with language will literary men ever be able to "work with it." Rather than urging a serious approach to language, the sentence suggests that sobriety would rob words of their almightiness as surely as frivolity. Indeed, the sentence embodies its own dictum stylistically. It accomplishes serious, potentially long-lived work by replacing a conventional intellectual antithesis with something that looks like a bipolar unity, where work and play grow out of each other like two sides of the same coin. But it contrives to dissolve dualism only momentarily—and then only by fooling around with words. Stare fixedly enough, and the verbal sleight of hand risks exposure. Could there be a bipolar unity that is not a contradiction in terms? But like a good magician Emerson has many ways of keeping his audience from staring fixedly. Only painfully dull skeptics go to magic shows hell-bent on spotting the wires. A wise reader will not emulate them.

"It is a happy talent to know how to play," Emerson confessed wistfully. "Some men must always work if they would be respectable; for the moment they trifle, they are silly. Others show most talent when they trifle" (*JMN*, 5:32). For all his aversion to respectability he was a disciplined worker. His voluminous output was not produced without great effort. Literary triflers like Ellery Channing Jr. inspired from him both envy and reproach. Passages like this show that the fusion of work and play that he preached to Dartmouth undergraduates did not come naturally to this scion of Puritanism. A New Englander had to work to achieve it. And work at playing he did, romping awkwardly with his children, transcribing conundrums in his journal, sheepishly accepting his own ineptitude at games but not letting that deter him from joining in. Or at least from watching. "We go to the gymnasium and the swimming school to see the power and beauty of the body: there is the like pleasure . . . from witnessing intellectual feats of all kinds, as feats of memory, of mathematical combination, great power of abstraction," he decided. "Foremost among these activities are the summersaults, spells, and resurrections wrought by the imagination" (*CW*, 4:10). Spectator sport paid handsome literary dividends. Games became a key metaphor for imagining his own writing. "Some play at chess, some at cards, some at the Stock Exchange," he journalized in 1840. "I prefer to play at cause and effect" (*JMN*, 6:228). Elsewhere the writer's life itself seemed sport when contrasted to the drudgery of the respectable. "My life is a May game, I will live as I like," he exulted in 1839. "I defy your strait laced, weary social ways & modes. . . . I will play my game out" (*JMN*, 7:208). This imagery of play blended naturally into imagery of motion, with which all the Transcendentalists were obsessed. "The wild fertility of nature is felt," he wrote, "by comparing our rigid names with our fluid consciousness" (*W*, 2:131). But rigid names might yield to courageous authors, he meditated, for "Heroes do not fix but flow, bend forward ever & invent a resource for every moment" (*JMN*, 7:539). Dedicated to "the constant evolution of truth, not the petrification of opinion," the Transcendental organ the *Dial* laid claim to "a station on which the light may fall; which is open to the rising sun; and from which it may correctly report the progress of the hour and the day."[4]

Exploding the Correspondence Theory of *Nature* (1836)

But how does all this square with the famous theory of language that Emerson set forth in *Nature* (1836), the manifesto of the Transcendental movement? In chapter 4 he argued, "Words are signs of natural facts. . . . Particular natural facts are symbols of particular spiritual facts. . . . Nature is the symbol of spirit." Raiding Tooke for examples, he explained that "children and savages use only nouns or names of things, which they convert into verbs, and apply to analogous mental acts." Built into the structure of the universe, "there is nothing lucky or capricious in these analogies, but . . . they are constant, and pervade nature," so that "the same symbols are found to make the original elements of all languages." Waging war against linguistic corruption, wise men seeking the universal language of nature "pierce this rotten diction and fasten words again to visible things," but they do so only by connecting "thought with its proper symbol" (*CW*, 1:17–20). Drawing heavily on the Swedenborgian writers Sampson Reed and Guillaume Oegger, as Philip Gura has shown in detail, *Nature* seems to assume that the links between words, things, and spirit are one-to-one, fixed, and unique, absorbed by the mind more than created.

As man thinking linguistically Emerson struggled to emancipate himself from his early formulation. The Swedenborgian correspondences that initially seemed liberating threatened to render the mind as passive as the Lockean tabula rasa they challenged. "It is not so in your experience . . . but is so in another world," Samson Reed once told him. "Other world," responded Emerson, "there is no other world; here or nowhere is the whole fact. All the universe over there is but one thing; the old double, creator-creature, mind-matter, right-wrong."[5] Swedenborgianism leaned too heavily on a separate spiritual world, whereas Emerson groped toward a monistic dualism in one world that might express itself in double meanings. Like any contemplative religious genius Reed seemed "jealous of the artist as of one who is already marketing, or at last making grammar of Beauty & Soul" (*TN*, 3:54). By the time Emerson published "The Poet" (1844) he had decided that, unlike a mystic, one must not nail "a symbol to one sense, which was a true sense for a moment, but soon becomes old and false. For all symbols are fluxional; all language is vehicular and transitive, and is good as ferries and horses are, for conveyance." For this reason he christened the Poet not just the Namer but the "Language-maker," for as the etymology of the word *poet* itself suggests, "the poets *made* all the words" (*CW*, 3:20, 13, emphasis added).

Emerson's mature philosophy of language is thus much more active, creative, and dynamic than the static conception first adumbrated in *Nature*. Yet the early essay mesmerizes scholars and cows students, banefully fixing the terms in which Emerson's prose of process is often misread. Why? As the locus classicus for Emerson's symbolic doctrine, *Nature* served the modernist literary sensibility well enough—or at least better than anything else of his. *Nature* fostered a conception of Emerson as a mystic seer of timeless essences, which was congenial to modernism's effort to elevate works of art to a timeless realm remote from history. It allowed New Critics accustomed to hunting Christ-figures through fiction and bringing them to bay with a pack of symbols to fancy that they should do the same thing with Emerson's prose (while catering to the common undergraduate tendency to over-read almost anything symbolically). By linking that prose to poetry it camouflaged New Criticism's lack of adequate tools for analyzing expository writing.

And *Nature* lent itself to the interests not only of New Critics but of Americanists, especially those with a commitment to American Studies. Scholars eager for disciplinary independence wanted to believe that American culture was an autonomous growth that could be fruitfully studied apart from English literature and European intellectual history. Though the great American intellectual historian Perry Miller had labored mightily to make the Puritans interesting, colonial American studies remains a rather parched field, with little appeal to undergraduates. Naturally colonialists were eager to hitch their leaky little brigantine to the svelte clipper manned by the major American Romantics, naturally Romanticists were happy to make their seven dwarfs and a princess seem *echt* American figures. This could be done by producing a version of Puritanism in which the baleful old ogre Jonathan Edwards turned out to be Ralph Waldo Emerson in disguise. Miller happily obliged.[6] At a stroke the terrors and icy beauties of Calvinism were decorously muted for undergraduates while by marinating that old-time religion in typology and Edwardsean aesthetics Miller made it palatable to literati leery of church. In Miller's typological enterprise *Nature* was crucial. Never mind that precious few Transcendentalists showed the slightest interest in Puritan theology. Never mind that whenever one tracks their reading as this study does, their ideas derive from European Romanticism or the Enlightenment more often than one might suppose, from their contemporaries less than one might wish, and from their American predecessors scarcely at all. Americanists score Brownie points and shorten bibliographies by focusing attention on native roots—thus avoiding the awkward question of whether matters deemed peculiarly "American" differ significantly from European parallels.

As Philip Gura has wisely observed, "earlier in Emerson's career the notion of symbolic literature was not Emerson's main concern. He was less interested in man's ability to comprehend 'symbolic' experience than he was in reaffirming his belief that there did, indeed, exist a realm of spirit approachable in moments of illumination."[7] We might go even further and say that as a writer of prose Emerson was rarely symbolic. The language doctrine of *Nature* had several useful consequences, to be sure. In dignifying all natural objects it emboldened Emerson to use concrete imagery freely. The intellectual confidence it bred let him develop his oracular tone. In his Orphic poetry it sometimes gave birth to genuine symbols. And it was demonstrably important to other American Romantics. But oddly, it may have intrigued others more than it did Emerson himself. Except for those objects that *Nature* explicitly proclaims to be symbols ("an enraged man is a lion," *CW*, 1:18), his nouns do not vibrate symbolically. Even these two nouns do not function quite like symbols, for without his equation we would not make the connection. The celebrated one-lane bridge between man and spirit has been rather a *pons asinorum,* focusing attention on linguistic fixities when the action in Emerson's prose lies elsewhere.

The book ends, after all, with this poetic promise:

> Nature is not fixed but fluid. Spirit alters, moulds, makes it. The immobility or bruteness of nature, is the absence of spirit; to pure spirit, it is fluid, it is volatile, it is obedient. Every spirit builds itself a house; and beyond its house, a world; and beyond its world, a heaven. Know then, that the world exists for you. For you is the phenomenon perfect. What we are, that only can we see. All that Adam had, all that Caesar could, you have and can do. Adam called his house, heaven and earth; Caesar called his house, Rome; you perhaps call yours, a cobler's trade; a hundred acres of ploughed land; or a scholar's garret. Yet line for line and point for point, your dominion is as great as theirs, though without fine names. Build, therefore, your own world. As fast as you conform your life to the pure idea in your mind, that will unfold its great proportions. A correspondent revolution in things will attend the influx of the spirit. So fast will disagreeable appearances, swine, spiders, snakes, pests, madhouses, prisons, enemies, vanish; they are temporary and shall be no more seen. The sordor and filths of nature, the sun shall dry up, and the wind exhale. . . . The kingdom of man over nature, which cometh not with observation,—a dominion such as now is beyond his dream of God,—he shall enter without more wonder than the blind man feels who is gradually restored to perfect sight. (*CW*, 1:44-45)

The eerie effect of such writing is hard to analyze, but the task should not be shirked. Its first Unitarian reviewer, Francis Bowen, was no fool, and that philosopher's reactions remain a useful point of departure. "We find beautiful writing and sound philosophy in this little work," he conceded, but "injured by occasional vagueness of expression, and by a vein of mysticism that pervades the writer's whole course of thought. . . . No one can read it without tasking his faculties to the utmost, and relapsing into fits of severe meditation. But the effort of perusal is often painful, the thoughts excited are frequently bewildering, and the results to which they lead us, uncertain and obscure. The reader feels as in a disturbed dream, in which shows of surpassing beauty are around him, and he is conversant with disembodied spirits, yet he is all the time harassed by an uneasy sort of consciousness, that the whole combination of phenomena is fantastic and unreal." As a general description, this is finely perceptive. Moreover, Bowen pinpointed the main cause of this effect: "As the object and method of philosophizing are thus altered, it is obvious that language also must be modified, and made to subserve other purposes than those for which it was originally designed." How, specifically, is this effect achieved in these Orphic sentences, which even the Transcendental *Western Messenger* found "especially dark to our misty vision"?[8]

Notice first the equivocations by which Emerson turns the meaning of words: nature is "fluid," yet solid too, for Spirit "moulds" it. Insofar as Spirit "alters" and "makes" it, nature seems both to precede and emanate from Spirit. When the word *fluid* is repeated, its meaning is turned once again, for now it describes not a quality of nature but a relation to Spirit. *Bruteness* is a word unknown to Webster then or now, and the *OED* cites Emerson as the first to use it thus designating the irrationality of the material universe. As this mild innovation is imposed, we feel the shaping force of Spirit, that is, of the author's linguistic imagination. And Emerson has it both ways, for with this term the brute (= irrational, insentient) materiality of brute facts (isolated ones) is tamed by assimilation to the organic world of brute creatures. He is not content with a rational but inanimate physical universe obeying scientific law, for the last sentence of *Nature*, playing around with Luke 17:20, firmly rejects Baconian "observation." Instead, the word *obedient* immediately turns bruteness back toward biology by making nature seem a dumb brute harking to her master's voice.

Another repetition then turns "pure spirit" into an ethereal carpenter with ambiguous Pauline credentials: "He who hath built the house hath more honour than the house. For every house is builded by some man; but he that built all things is God" (Heb. 3:3-4). So hypnotic repetitions of the word *beyond* try to dissolve the metaphor of house-builder even as it arises. Does "heaven" lie *beyond* this world as this world extends *beyond* a house? Not necessarily so, for Oegger's *Le Vrai Messie,* which sparked Emerson's imagination through Elizabeth Peabody's translation, concluded from the necessity of physical emblems that "our future life cannot be so metaphysical as is sometimes imagined.... The future life is evidently Berkeley's world."[9] Playing around with Berkeleian immaterialism, the Orphic Poet reverses fields as easily as he reverses the word order of his sentences. "The world exists for you. For you ..." Who, me? That we can see only what we are would point to a dispiriting solipsism. But another Orphic inversion, and presto! almost everyone may be pleased. "What we are, that only can we see." The conventionally pious are condescendingly assured of the legitimacy of belief in a future world necessarily invisible to mortal eyes or glimpsed in the Pauline glass darkly. At the same time, the sentence tempts the Transcendental elect to imagine that "what we are" is as plastic as Emerson's language. With purified perception and morals they may realize that they are already *in* heaven.

This entire arabesque is underpinned by fundamental equivocations on the terms *we* and *you.* "Every spirit builds itself *a* world," but nonetheless "*the* world" seems to exist expansively "for you" *all.* Yet in the next sentence *phenomenon* is singular, so *you* shrinks once again in that direction. This double reference carries through *we.* Christians may safely apply it to the whole human race, but a sensitive soul avid for Transcendental chic may feel the Orphic hand descend on his shoulder as so often in "Song of Myself." It's you and me, baby, "only ... we see." Many readers, including Transcendentalists, have probably managed to oscillate between both strands of meaning. What ecstatic vibrations one may feel caressing the multiple meanings of "his dream of God"!

Vibration of that kind powers Emerson's prose. There is generally an escape hatch for those who may not fancy their eternity in the company of Bronson Alcott. But it *is* powerful prose, make no mistake, with an impressive ability to hold multiple meanings in suspension. Readers who bail out early cheat themselves of a unique experience, far more challenging and rewarding than they suppose. Consider the sentence beginning "As fast...." What on earth does it mean? Does *great* have the same meaning here that it did two sentences above? What does *fast* mean? But all pivots on the ambiguous pronouns. What are the antecedents of *that* and *its*? Your life will unfold its great proportions? The pure idea will unfold its great proportions? Your life will unfold the pure idea's great proportions? The mind will unfold the pure idea's great proportions? Its own proportions? And so on. Though not endless, there are scads more permutations and combinations.

Most that first occur simply blur *life, idea,* and *mind* together in some way. In a sense this is Emerson's main philosophical effort. But left at that level the ambiguity is trivial. Nouns alone cannot generate the meaning that makes this sentence suddenly luminous. Consider finally this clumsy paraphrase: "As rapidly *and* closely as you square the concrete experiences of your life with the pure conceptions in your mind, that temporal *activity* of conforming experience to idea will make your mind's already large proportions morally and spiritually great." Aha! So indeed it may. The maneuver is rather like the wonderful equivocation on *that* by which Keats resolves the dialectic of Truth and Beauty at the end of "Ode on a Grecian Urn." But Keats is at last content to balance real and ideal whereas Emerson nervously presses on toward fusion.

This interpretation asks us to violate a grammatical rule that holds it poor form to make implied verbal activity in one clause the subject of the next: for example, "George goes to bed early, which is good." *A habit* which is good, teacher wearily scribbles. But for all his Tookean nominalizing, Emerson really does not want to turn verbs into nouns. Earlier he imagines language growing when children and savages convert nouns to verbs. Far from endorsing a static view of words nailed to things by Platonic essences, *Nature* drives toward the idea of growth. It even embodies it structurally. The main theme of the essay is man's need to gain power over nature. It reaches one surprising climax near the end of "Idealism," and his last sentence promises a "kingdom of man over nature" undreamed of by science.

In our passage the preoccupation with power over things surfaces in words like "dominion." After previous concrete references to a hundred acres, Rome, and the whole earth, we assume "dominion" means *domain* here. But this yields an absurdity. While our nascent labor movement was agitating for the distribution of free public land to hardpressed mechanics, Emerson does not believe that every American owns at least a hundred acres or ought to, nor does he want every village cobbler a Napoleon trying to conquer the world. Note the beautiful turn inviting you to realize that "your dominion is as great as theirs" only if you understand that *dominion* here means *inherent power, potential control.* The meaning of this noun is diverted so as to recapture its inherent verbal force. *Dominion* is the *action* of *dominating, dominions* merely its temporary concretion. The mastery that Emerson wants us to exercise over things is powered mainly by the energy of verbs.

Verbs dominate the rhetoric of the book's ending. They do not out-number nouns, nor are they all transitive. But because of the many odd disjunctions between nouns, even Emerson's copula seems actively to connect.[10] Like "fixed" and "fluid," many adjectives retain verbal force. Thus "volatile" seems to mean *flying* rather than *equipped with wings,* while "perfect" trembles on the verge of *perfected.* At the other pole from these Latinisms gutsy basic English verbs carry enormous weight: *moulds, makes, builds, see, have, do, call.* Notice especially the claim that all that Adam and Caesar had or could, "you have and can do." When building a house it's easy to imagine how we can have what we do. But how can we do what we have? By tempting us to ask precisely that awkward question the contorted word order of this sentence invites us to realize that possessions are only activity temporarily congealed; the potential energy of things craves issue again in the heat of action. *Have* and *can* should lead to *do,* just as naturally as the reverse process.

Two imperatives underpin the passage: "Know then" and "Build, therefore." Tempered only slightly by the connectives (for logic too has its very modest place in Emerson's thought, though Aristotle's binary either/or often yields to the semiotic both/and of C. S. Peirce), their imperious power permeates the Orphic Poet's entire message almost as commandingly as the words dominate the sentences that they govern grammatically. Indeed, if one had to conjecture what "pure idea" lurks in the Orphic Poet's mind, one might guess from his tone that he is driven to speech by nothing less than a dream of pure *power.*

Unlike many academics, I have few pure ideas, so I see this but dimly. But through the haze I do see that Emerson's mind, too, is more impure than commonly supposed. It is important to remember that the serene Waldo is *not* the Orphic Poet. Still, power did fascinate Emerson. Its ter-minology, as Poirier remarks, is everywhere in his writing. So it is hardly surprising that some Transcendentalists, like many earnest, well-meaning souls in academia today, drew from him the lesson that intellectuals—those with pure ideas, at least—were peculiarly qualified to assume the reins of power and restructure society. These efforts were sometimes val-iant and useful, like Theodore Parker's devotion to reform. Like Bronson Alcott's devotion to education, they sometimes verged on the absurd, especially when that sage peddler of ideas devoted himself loftily to teach-ing his family rather than feeding them. And some efforts were painfully sad, like George Ripley's futile Utopianism.

Emerson, of course, shied away from Brook Farm and other reform causes like abolition. Some Transcendentalists accused him of betraying his own message, and they have their modern academic defenders. Oft told, this story needs little elaboration here. But a careful reading of the Orphic Poet's language shows that Emerson was true to himself and misinterpreted by those demanding a reformist messiah. Reading this passage, transparent eyeballs were teased by the claim that "a correspondent revolution in things will attend the influx of the spirit." Orestes Brownson surely drew from Transcendentalism the lesson that a social revolution was at hand; but when the Democratic Party failed to carry it out promptly, he converted in despair to political reaction and conservative Catholicism. If those of his ilk looked closely, however, they might note that the undoubted political implications of the term *revolution* are immediately *reversed* by the next sentence. "Mad-houses, prisons, enemies" are indeed said to vanish as the Transcendental Spirit bloweth where it listeth, but they vanish in conjunction with "swine, spiders, snakes." It should have given the barmiest reformer pause to imagine a new political dispensation that would remove *all* these "pests." Indeed, as the pigs fly away, we may wonder just where they are winging it if the universe, like language, is built on eternal analogies grounding spiritual meaning in things. How now will the Orphic Poet orph? What is the future of poetry?

As we have observed, Emerson was shortly to abandon the language theory of chapter 4. Even in *Nature* his commitment to it was less than wholehearted. It may be temporary philosophical scaffolding left untidily in place after finishing construction. It may even be a joke of sorts. But the Orphic Poet's conclusion can be reconciled to it, more or less, thus. Come the Transcendental millennium, what will vanish first is "disagreeable appearances." And that is all. The pigs will remain, for unlike Thoreau and other Transcendental vegetarians, Emerson relished his bacon. "Let the stoics say what they please, we do not eat for the good of living," he insisted, "but because the meat is savory and the appetite is keen" (*CW*, 3:108). The madhouses will remain too. Like Hawthorne, Emerson is perfectly aware that with the swarms of disgruntled intellectuals that any age spawns, madhouses will be needed for those lapsing into the starker forms of insanity. (From a neighbor's grounds in Concord the screams of a madwoman wafted regularly through Emerson's windows.) In fact, the whole panoply of natural pests and social ills will remain. But they will *appear* different to us. Pigs will no more be *swine,* for we will have learned to accept their piggishness as natural, not morally reprehensible. Either we will learn to enjoy the sight of professors oinking their merry way to the trough, or we may invent some new emblem to describe the greedy grunting around their federal pork barrels.

Here Emerson's theory of moral correspondences begins to disintegrate, for he was less willing to give up values than the concrete analogies that he claimed cemented them. Still, as the snake slithers away the Orphic Poet bids a smiling farewell to Christianity's unhealthy fascination with evil. So much for Jonathan Edwards and typology—we can call it Uncle Wiggly now! Like prisons, capital punishment may remain—but if so, we will learn to view executions as benign. And our enemies? The Christian may suppose that they will vanish when we finally learn to love them all in the Spirit. But the true Transcendentalist sees deeper. Yes, our enemies will vanish when we finally realize that those who criticize us most justly are our best friends—while those who tax us unfairly, like all poor critics, are nature's indispensable though faintly contemptible clowns.

Is all this radically naive? The answer, as so often with Emerson, is both yes and no. But surely the Orphic Poet is no social revolutionary. He wants things left as they are. How is the new Transcendental philosophy to be practiced? Look again. You are to "conform your life to the pure idea in your mind." Rather strikingly, the author who would soon proclaim that "whoso would be a man, must be a non-conformist" here employs the vocabulary of social convention to characterize his ideal disciple. One might think this sarcastic inversion—cleave fast to the ideal only, and kiss off social conformity. But it is not sarcasm, for when Emerson gained a disciple whose thought ran in such channels, he advised Thoreau to pay his poll tax and not kick against society's pricks quite so much. A running theme in Emerson's journal, one reflected in his comfortable bourgeois lifestyle, is the folly of wasting precious energy in pointless social defiance. Lo and behold, *conforming* your life more closely to the "pure idea," according to Emerson, turns out to mean bringing your pure ideas into closer contact with conventional social living. Only a reciprocal process can refine ideas, and overrefinement needs the coarsening grit of society. Thus after the crushing loss of his first wife, Ellen, Emerson abandoned mourning resolved to "conform himself to circumstances . . . and carry forward the brilliant game" (*JMN*, 2:375–76).

How should the literary scholar in his garret "unfold" his pure idea? Neither by running to the barricades nor to the woods, nor even to abstruse French theorists, Emerson suggests. The best way for scholars to *unfold* pure ideas is simply to *explicate* them well. That process may involve crumpling many a page in disgust, then retrieving it for another painful start.

The Playthings in the Playhouse of the Children

Myriad relevant meanings lurk in the Orphic Poet's conclusion—if we help make them, build our houses, as it were. That explains why the Poet's house seems so "fantastic and unreal," as Bowen noted, so ethereal in contrast to the solid white clapboard housing Emerson on Concord's main street. Notice that almost no concrete details apply to houses in the passage. These houses seem genuine *buildings* only in that they are fundamentally verbs. Emerson bequeathes us a lot—a lot surveyed "line for line and point for point." But this abstract geometry may not be Euclidean—we suspect that for the Orphic Poet parallel lines meet at infinity. Emerson's blueprint specifies no materials. What shall we build with—clapboard, brick, logs, or deerskin? Shall there be gingerbread spandrels or aluminum siding? He left many choices open to careful readers. That's why he's fascinated them so.

"Here comes one among the wellbeloved stonecutters and plans with decision and science," wrote Whitman, one eye on Emerson, one on himself, "and sees the solid and beautiful forms of the future where there are now no solid forms" (*LG*, 712). Emerson was the abstract planner among stonecutters, but the solid and beautiful future Whitman saw was his own. He could see it clearly because Emerson left "no solid forms" to block his vision. "If you have built castles in the air, your work need not be lost; that is where they should be," concluded Thoreau (*Walden*, p. 324). "Now put the foundations under them." The first sentence might have been addressed to Emerson, but with the second Thoreau's eye was on his own excavation project beside Walden. He could not have dug on Emerson's woodlot had Emerson himself built there. In Salem the house acquired seven scowling gables as if to rebuke what seemed Emerson's serene optimism, but there is an element of charade to all the Puritan gloom. Snakes and swine fly away at the end, and all the characters but one emerge safe into the sunlight for a final bow and a photograph. Poe likewise filled his fiction with gloomy houses and hung them with drapes to shut out the sun. While Emerson's Poet "turns the world to glass" (*CW*, 3:12), Edgar Poe uses it as a dark mirror. But in all the red-velvet defiance of nature, the note of charade persists. In Melville's "I and My Chimney" the narrator Dacres is plagued by a wife whose Emersonian mission in life is eternally remodeling houses. With comic fervor he cuddles up to the phallic chimney rooting him to the earth (his very name is an arsy-versy anagram for *sacred*) because no such detail is specified in Emerson's airy, see-through architecture of the Spirit.

During a violent thunderstorm in Amherst, livid with lightning,

> The Birds put up the Bars to Nests—
> The Cattle fled to Barns—
> There came one drop of Giant Rain—
> And then as if the Hands—
> That held the Dams had parted hold—
> The Waters Wrecked the Sky—
> But overlooked my Father's House—
> Just quartering a Tree. (#824)

The house of Emily Dickinson's Father had many mansions, and she dwelt in several. She rather collected fathers, among them Emerson. Could she have shuttled so nimbly among them all without him? This poem is quite *astonishing,* in the literal sense of that word, which she well knew. Here its flickering symbols invite us to entertain all the following notions simultaneously: (1) God, like that thundering male lecher Zeus, may be rather a bastard; (2) Daddy may be rather a bastard, too, though what he chiefly lusts after is self-righteousness; (3) But I am God's little girl and Daddy's daughter, baptized in water and the Spirit, so what does that make me? (4) God's in his heaven, I *wuv* my Daddy, and all's right with the world! These female, feline lines show a "livid Claw" of their own emerging from the lacy mitt. Had Emerson's spacious, empty, ethereal house been occupied as Edward Dickinson's was, would Emily have been able to juggle these ideas quite so insouciantly?

So the greatest gift Emerson left his children was razing his house even as it rose. His building permit also licensed demolition. He left them space. Space like Silence. Like the spaces between words. To fill such space concrete words set in concrete need not apply. Instead of nailing words to things, he really craved words that would dissolve things by dissolving themselves like a flash of lightning. He had wanted that from boyhood. "I remember when a child in the pew on Sundays amusing myself with saying over common words as 'black,' 'white,' 'board,' etc. & I began to doubt which was the right name for the thing, when I saw that neither had any natural relation, but all were arbitrary," he recalled. "It was a child's first lesson in idealism" (*JMN*, 8:30). Before the sorcerer's hope of manipulating things through words magically linked to their essences, there was simply a child bored silly with sermons, hoping that words, things, and boredom would all vanish if words were repeated enough. Repeated four times at the end of *Nature,* the word *house* is not an incantatory expression of power over a natural symbol but an effort to suggest that there are no natural symbols. The process of symbolizing may interest the Orphic Poet but chiefly as a means of destroying fixed symbols. Unlike real houses, this one will never become a home, not even for the imagination. The Orphic Poet already knows what Emerson made explicit in "The Poet" a decade later—that "fluxional" linguistic symbols are "good, as ferries and horses are, for conveyance, not as . . . houses are, for homestead" (*CW*, 3:20).

Building houses and worlds that promise so little permanence, so little hominess, might strike one as frustrating. In his great poem "Directive," Robert Frost, another of Emerson's children, caught the poignance of standing where "there is a house that is no more a house." When both Christianity and Emersonian Transcendentalism were regarded as "playthings in the playhouse of the children," he asked his readers to "weep for what little things could make them glad."[11] Most of Emerson's children who shouldered the burden of constantly reimagining the world from scratch felt this way at times, Mark Twain as much as any. In chapter 9 of *Huckleberry Finn* Huck and Jim are encamped in the cave on Jackson's Island watching a thunderstorm more violent than Emily Dickinson's:

> It was one of these regular summer storms. It would get so dark that it looked all blue-black outside, and lovely; and the rain would thrash along by so thick that the trees off a little ways looked dim and spider-webby; and here would come a blast of wind that would bend the trees down and turn up the pale underside of the leaves; and then a perfect ripper of a gust would follow along and set the branches to tossing their arms as if they was just wild; and next, when it was just about the bluest and blackest— fst! it was as bright as glory and you'd have a little glimpse of tree-tops a-plunging about, away off yonder in the storm, hundreds of yards further than you could see before; dark as sin again in a second, and now you'd hear the thunder let go with an awful crash and then go rumbling, grumbling, tumbling down the sky towards the under side of the world, like rolling empty barrels down stairs, where it's long stairs and they bounce a good deal, you know.

We are watching a world rent apart and reimagined by lightning flashes of language. The spontaneous poetry of Huck's slang here discovers meanings in American nature that neither we nor perhaps even Twain suspected. The terrifying beauty that Huck and Jim are gazing into seems like Schlegel's Abounding Fullness, the free play of dynamic energy denying all stasis. It is fitfully glimpsed because neither language nor perception can sustain the vision long. "Jim, this is nice," says Huck. "I wouldn't want to be nowhere else but here."[12] But these smug words scarcely do justice to what his language has just seen and rendered for us. This storm is not nice but awesome, not beautiful but sublime. Claiming no desire to be elsewhere, Huck ignores the seductive appeal of the storm to Romantics like Schlegel, who would see in the branches "tossing their arms as if they was just wild" a corybantic invitation to merge with nature's energy in self-destructive ecstasy. Schlegel's Romanticism aspires to fuse the safety of being in the cave with the bliss of becoming in the storm. So does Twain's, for one's memory of the book can be dominated by this and by the Emersonian moments on the raft when, lulled into silence gazing at the stars, Huck and Jim become transparent eyeballs through whom the universal currents of the river seem to circulate. The episodic plot of the novel is overpowered by the dissolving flow of the Mississippi. The book poignantly suggests that Huck's longing for secure stasis is foredoomed. Like a child of Emerson, he must learn that the cave and Jackson's Island are only halfway houses, "fluxional," that neither offers any imaginative "homestead." Breaking into houses throughout the book and then leaving, he is never housebroken. At the end Huck is suspended between Being and Becoming, a boy who declines to be fixed by society, an adolescent who can never become a man. Like his ideal of freedom for Jim, his deepest intimations about nature resist formulation, for the language he commands is still tainted by social absurdities. He can only escape being housed by lighting out for the wordless terra incognita of the Territories. Trapped within the limits of Huck's language, the reader escapes from the first-person narrative only by the spiraling staircase of Romantic irony.

For all his children Emerson was Houdini. His rope tricks with words taught them their trade as escape artists. However variously they were tempted to build their houses, they shared his fundamental fascination with words that would first dissolve things, set them free. Writing to Margaret Fuller in 1841, Emerson was candid about this:

> I know but one solution to my nature & relations, which I find in the remembering the joy with which in my boyhood I caught the first hint of the Berkleian philosophy, and which I certainly never lost sight of afterwards. There is a foolish man who goes up & down the country giving lectures on electricity;—this one secret he has, to draw a spark out of every object, from desk, & lamp, & wooden log, & the farmer's blue frock, & by this he gets his living: for paupers & negroes will pay to see this celestial emanation from their own basket & their own body. Well, I was not an electrician, but an Idealist. I could see that there was a cause behind every stump & clod, & by the help of some fine words could make every old wagon & woodpile & stone wall oscillate a little & threaten to dance: nay, give me fair field,—& the Selectmen of Concord & the Reverend Doctor Poundmedown himself began to look unstable & vaporous. . . . Now there is this difference between the Electrician,—Mr. Quimby—is his name?—(I never saw him)—and the Idealist, namely, that the spark is to that philosopher a toy, but the dance is to the Idealist terror & beauty, life & light. It is & it ought to be; & yet sometimes there will be a sinful

empiric who loves exhibition too much. This Insight is so precious to society that where the least glimmer of it appears all men should befriend & protect it for its own sake. (*Letters*, 2:384-85)

The conception of language lying behind this letter has little to do with names linked to things by physical analogy. Emerson never saw Quimby, is foggy about his proper name, and doesn't care much. But he cares greatly about language. Note his implication that he could not have created this picture in words if they did not first demolish. A blank page can terrify some writers, looming like Moby-Dick. But Moby-Dick terrified Melville more than he did Emerson. Emerson knows as much as Melville about idealist terror and beauty, but at bottom he wants blank paper to start on. He needs words to "give me fair field" by exploding and distancing things, so the Reverend Doctor Poundmedown is blown away by an absurd name. His words are pencils with erasers, and he uses the eraser end first. Only when his field of vision is clear of obstacles can he create—which is why, as Poirier observes, he was in some ways the first writer to relish the literary opportunities of being American. With a fair field full of nothing, he can build what he wants. His words conjure up a vivid comic scene that he never saw, with Phineas Parkhurst Quimby electrifying the gaping yokels. The verbal power to make everything "oscillate a little and threaten to dance" seems humorous here, partly because it is so far-fetched and fanciful. Commanding capering wagons and woodpiles, this sorcerer's apprentice is funny, a figure from Disney. Such verbal power often makes reading the essays feel like watching intellectual cartoons. They are philosophical phantasmagorias where words, ideas, and images swirl around fancifully.

What Quimby regards as a "toy" Emerson treats seriously. The spark is turned into the Idealist's notion of language, electrical energy leaping across a gap between two poles. Without the gap, the space, the Silence, the spark could not exist. By its flickering light the mind sees, catching at least a glimmer of "Insight" as subject and object fuse in expression. Or if not electric current, he speculated, nonetheless "our strength is transitional, alternating; or, shall I say, a thread of two strands. The seashore, sea seen from shore, shore seen from sea; the taste of two metals in contact . . . the experience of poetic creativeness, which is not found in staying at home nor yet in traveling, but in transitions from one to the other, which must therefore be adroitly managed to present as much transitional surface as possible" (*CW*, 4:31-32). Here the underlying electrolytic metaphor is a reworking in scientific terms of a polar theory from theology. "The Germans believe in the necessary Trinity of God,—the Infinite; the finite; and the passage from

Inf. into Fin.: or, the Creation," he had noted as early as 1835. "It is typified in the act of thinking. Whilst we contemplate we are infinite; the thought we express is partial and finite; the expression is the third part and is equivalent to the act of Creation" (*JMN*, 5:30). But serious though all these analogies indeed are, their very multiplicity shows that none can be taken by itself with entire seriousness. While Emerson plays intently and fruitfully with all these ideas, electricity remains for him as for Quimby a toy, albeit a toy tool. His own analogies "threaten to dance" away from him.

These analogies highlight the nature of speech as active, temporal, transitive, bipolar, and creative. They represent serious thinking. Behind them all one senses the influence of German idealism. Indeed, if there is a ghostly presence behind Emerson's attitude toward language, Jonathan Edwards seems a less likely candidate than Wilhelm von Humboldt. With his doctrine that all understanding is simultaneously a misunderstanding and his basic commitment to the ineffable, Humboldt's oft-quoted formulation comes as close as any to capturing the essence of Emerson's linguistic thinking: Speech "is the ever-repeated *mental labor* of making *articulate* sound capable of expressing thought."[13] Whereas the correspondence theory of *Nature* has the etymological stamp of Cardell, the essay moves inexorably toward the mentalism crudely stressed by Sherman, recapitulating for Transcendentalism their New York debate. Though Humboldt's linguistic formulations really drew their impetus from Condillac, Diderot, and Gérando, as Hans Aarsleff has shown, their chic philosophical garb was tailored from the same German idealistic vocabulary that Friedrich Schlegel used to drape the theory of Romantic irony. And it should now be apparent that many aspects of Emerson's writing reflect that sensibility. *Nature,* for example, involves at least two fictitious characters, Emerson-qua-Sage and the intrusive Orphic Poet. The book's argument about language shows signs of imploding, and the entire work is couched in a powerful self-canceling rhetoric involving turns upon words. Other essays are even more disorganized than *Nature* and read like intellectual fantasias. Indeed, one critic has shrewdly argued that Emerson's essays resemble playpens. As the author toddles off for his nap, ideas and images are left scattered about like toy tools after an hour of intellectual fun and games.[14] In "The Poet" Emerson argues that the best aesthetic forms derive from nature, so his essays tend to imitate what he praised as her "frolic architecture" (*W,* 9:43).

Approached from this angle, Emerson's doctrine of the symbol changes oddly. Cut off by the collapse of his correspondence theory from any pretensions to unique meaning, natural objects remained "symbols, because nature is a symbol, in the whole, and in every part." But now authors had "to explore the double meaning, or, shall I say, the quadruple, or the centuple, or much more manifold meaning, of every sensuous fact." Unlike Bushnell, Emerson applied no brake to creative analogy. Recoiling from fixity to stress "the accidency and fugacity of the symbol," he undermined its claim to serious meaning (*CW*, 3:3-4, 12). Anything could symbolize everything and vice versa, so he began to feel that nothing symbolized much. "There is no word in our language that cannot become typical to us of nature by giving it emphasis," he decided. "The world is a Dancer, it is a Rosary, it is a Torrent" (*JMN*, 8:23). Playing with words, he is like a child with a kaleidoscope. "The use of symbols has a certain power of emancipation and exhilaration for all men. We seem to be touched by a wand, which makes us dance and run about happily, like children." But since only "the metamorphosis excites in the beholder an emotion of joy," men must keep twisting their symbolic kaleidoscopes. Symbols "must be held lightly" (*CW*, 3:17, 20).

When trivialized in this way, Emerson's emblems act much like pleasant visual puns. Though they carry no grave meaning, they free us for a moment from single vision. Indeed, Emerson's most famous symbol (a synechdoche, actually) rests on a pun: "I become a transparent eye-ball. I am nothing. I see all" (*CW*, 1:10). Christopher Cranch's famous cartoon-sketch (fig. 10) of Emerson parading about as a gigantic eyeball with top hat and walking stick might seem hostile. But as a minor Transcendentalist Cranch admired Emerson. If the eyeball's spindly legs represent humorous awareness of *Nature*'s stilted rhetoric here, Emerson too might well have laughed over this and the other sketches depicting him as a pumped-up pumpkin, etc. (see fig. 11). Not purely caricatures, Cranch's cartoons faithfully render the deliberate comedy of Emerson's style. As his skeptical sense of flux grew, the writing remained crisp, but the things of the world seem more and more like juggled toys, meeting only in chance collisions. When he claims in "Circles" that "Moons are no more bounds to spiritual power than bat-balls," that visual analogy carries little more weight than a homonymic pun (*CW*, 2:180). When the stream of such epigrammatic wisecracks becomes oppressive, Emerson the emblematic spritzer sounds oddly like one of the Phunny Phellows.

But such were the toys in the children's playhouse, where "every word has a double, treble, or centuple use and meaning" (*W*, 6:304). Weep for what little things could make them glad.

"Standing on the bare ground, — my head bathed by the blithe air, & uplifted into infinite space, — all mean egotism vanishes. I become a transparent Eyeball."

Nature, p. 13.

Fig. 10. Christopher Pearse Cranch, "becoming a transparent eyeball . . ." fMS Am 1506, by permission of the Houghton Library, Harvard University.

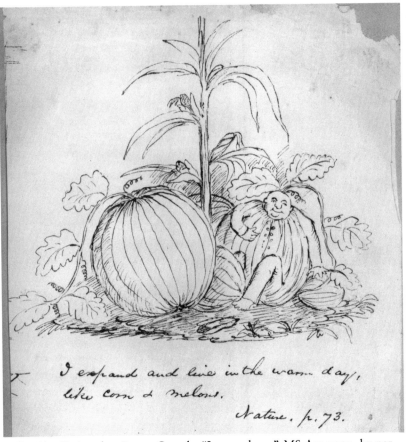

I expand and live in the warm days,
like corn & melons.

Nature. p. 73.

Fig. 11. Christopher Pearse Cranch, "I expand . . ." MS Am 1505, by permission of the Houghton Library, Harvard University.

The Inarticulacy of Old Man Eloquent

If too much ink has been spilled over fixed symbols in Emerson's prose, too little attention has been paid to his writing as an outgrowth of oratory. This neglect reflects the organization of contemporary English studies, where rhetoric is condescendingly relegated to freshman courses, with public speaking encamped beyond the pale in a competing department of speech and communication. Its scholars publish in journals not scanned by the honchos of lit crit. Despite his age's desire to see him as purveying unsettling "philosophy," Emerson himself more than once expressed surprised regret that no college had boldly offered him a professorship of rhetoric. The essays were often delivered first as lectures, and his theory of language, like Whitman's, was shaped by an underlying conception of himself as an orator.

Speech is the basic form of language for Emerson, not writing. Definitions of language as energy flickering momentarily between two poles point that way. So does his stress on language as action, for a long rhetorical tradition insists that the orator employs his body as a form of speech, with a vocabulary of gesture that Emerson exploited rarely but tellingly on the platform. The Emersonian mystique of silence also emerges from his practice as an orator, for a skillful public speaker learns to make silence resonate as a form of eloquence. The various techniques that he developed to slow readers down, to exploit the "white spaces" between words, to whip words till they reverberated on the page, are literary substitutes for the practiced speaker's emphatic pause and raised eyebrow. Oliver Wendell Holmes recalled Emerson's conversation as studded with pregnant hiatuses, while James Russell Lowell, describing his "deliberate utterance" on the podium, noted how pausing let him produce perfect phrases with a "glance of humor."[15] All the self-canceling Romantic ironies that Emerson deploys on the page aim at recapturing for writing the evanescent fluidity of uttered discourse. The orator's fleeting words do dissolve themselves in air, and his inspiration expires with every breath.

"Propose no methods, prepare no words, select no traditions," Emerson advised himself in his journal, "but fix your eyes on the audience, and the fit word will utter itself as when the eye seeks the person in the remote corner of the house the voice accommodates itself to the area to be filled" (*JMN*, 5:223). This conception of speech-making tended toward dialogue, with the orator's pauses letting the audience participate by thinking or even clapping. "An audience is not a simple addition of the individuals that compose it. Their sympathy gives them a certain social organism, which fills each member, in his own degree, and most of all the orator," Emerson explained, "as a jar in a battery is charged with the whole electricity of the battery." According to his neglected essay "Eloquence," the electrical currents flowed both ways. "No one can survey the face of an excited assembly, without being apprised of a new opportunity for painting in fire human thought, and being agitated to agitate" (*W*, 7:64–65). The heady joys of verbal intercourse are felt perhaps most sensually by a charismatic speaker. Ravishing an audience, Emerson enjoyed an almost orgasmic release when language suddenly cohered to "the ejaculative, eruptive experience inside." At times the physical energy of language seemed positively erotic, and stage fright became foreplay: "Hence the necessity of speech and song, hence these throbs and heartbeatings in the orator, at the door of the assembly, to the end, namely, that thought may be ejaculated as Logos, or Word" (*CW*, 3:23).

It is easy to chuckle snidely at all this. Emerson's ejaculative conception of "spermatic" speech reached its height as sexual relations with Lidian cooled. But the rhetorical transactions between Emerson and his audiences were real, and it is also easy to ignore that. If his rhetoric strives to incarnate the Logos, etymologically *orations* are prayers. And prayers may be essentially performative utterances in Austin's sense. "Such a doctrine," one critic writes of Emerson's equation between words and actions, "is perfectly appropriate to the self-conscious predicament of an alienated artistic or intellectual class: only speak, and the words go forth as deeds without any further exertion."[16] There is a grain of truth here, but it must be taken with several grains of salt. Emerson did not "only speak" once, he spoke energetically again and again, stumping the land for his novel ideas. Then, with great exertion, he wrote book after book, struggling to devise a novel style that would carry his message not just to the intelligentsia but to the public at large. And any reading of the historical record shows that he succeeded grandly in that aim. What "further exertion" should he have made? It's not easy to imagine. Literary academics who criticize Emerson for not being an intellectual *engagé* because of his reluctance to address political questions directly are themselves an alienated intelligentsia no more directly or effectively involved in public affairs than he was; indeed, few of them can match his modest record of service as alternate delegate to the Republican convention of 1856 and later as vice-president of the Women's Suffrage Society.

Moreover, to his eternal credit, Emerson *did* invent a new conception of the American Scholar that put intellectuals of his era in sympathetic vibration with the age, if not in the seats of power. His words ring down prophetically to our alienated intelligentsia. "I look upon the discontent of the literary class, as a mere announcement of the fact, that they find themselves not in the state of mind of their fathers, and regret the coming state as untried," that great essay confides. But "this time, like all times, is a very good one, if we but know what to do with it" (*CW*, 1:67). There is no better illustration of his dictum that "the aim of the author is not to tell truth—that he cannot do, but to suggest it" (*JMN*, 5:51). In "The American Scholar" he did all he could to suggest a saving truth to modern literary intellectuals. But many have little idea what to do with it, and some have not the foggiest idea what it is.

Late in life the truth became foggy for Emerson too. After 1865 his mental deterioration became obvious to his family. They lovingly strove to conceal it from outsiders, but it was well known to old friends—indeed to many in the public at large. Not well understood, however.

They simply saw his loss of memory as "senility." In fact, minor strokes rendered Emerson for the last fifteen years of his life an increasingly helpless victim of aphasia. As Roman Jakobson has explained, two very different forms of this common brain dysfunction correspond to two distinct abilities in users of language. Some aphasics suffer from "contiguity disorder," which affects our ability to combine words syntactically into sentences. As the ability to articulate spatial relations deteriorates, grammatical governance vanishes together with the capacity to express those contiguous part-whole relationships that rhetoric calls metonymies. With the sense of context impaired, linguistic units cannot be subordinated in sentences. Victims blurt out heaps of words linked mainly by similarities.

But that was precisely what Emerson could not do, for he suffered instead from "similarity disorder." In such aphasia the ability to form sentences and to describe contiguous relations remains intact. But words in sentences depend for meaning not just on grammatical context but on a person's total vocabulary and its semantic relation to the world. Victims of similarity disorder cannot select appropriate synonyms for naming objects. The myriad of synonyms baffles when one cannot grasp metaphoric relations between them. And though sentence syntax remains intact, extended discourse suffers, for the "logical" relations between sentences are governed not by grammar but by *analogical* resemblances between their topics. Such metaphoric relations between ideas elude the victim of similarity disorder. To compensate for his crippled metaphoric power, his speech may rely increasingly on the perception of spatial contiguity and the figure of metonymy. To avoid disorientation, linguistic context becomes overwhelmingly important; he can carry on a conversation more easily than he can start one.

This ailment created more than its share of poignant ironies for Emerson before the grand old man of American letters died in 1882. He could read but not consecutively. "He read anything which he picked up from the table," Oliver Wendell Holmes observed, "but he read the same things over, and whispered the words like a child. . . . He enjoyed pictures in books and showed them with delight to guests."[17] But pictures create their own problems for the aphasic. Gesturing at a portrait of Carlyle, Emerson could only say, "That is that man—my man."[18] The great Namer or Language-maker could no longer make language yield his friend's proper name. For such aphasics, as Jakobson explains, "the picture of an object will cause suppression of its name: a verbal sign is supplanted by a pictorial sign."[19] What troubled Emerson here was the apparent redundancy of language—the difficulty of selecting the correct verbal sign from among thousands when all verbal signs seemed superfluous. How must it feel for an aphasic, A. B. Paulson shrewdly asks, "to inhabit such a universe, one marked by a plethora of signification?"[20]

One can only reply that Emerson must have felt much as he had for decades, only more so. What he experienced before Carlyle's picture he had long felt about all emblems—that the connections between words and things, things and things, were so manifold and trivial as scarcely to be worth denominating. Now that the effort involved was greater, he could not and did not. Instead, in his aphasia he often turned to action to supplement failing speech. Some of his gestures attained an uncanny purity of expression beyond anything in the language of nature dreamed of by Condillac. One morning Mrs. Emerson and his doctor led him into the garden to see her roses. Struck by one unusually fine specimen, the doctor repeated a line from George Herbert's "Vertue," which Emerson had recited to him at length many years before. Emerson gazed at the rose in admiration, then as if on impulse gently lifted his hat and said with a low bow, "I take off my hat to it" (Holmes, *Emerson*, p. 345). That was the heroic act of a very great orator, who, as words failed him, still contrived with diminished vocabulary to match the eloquence of his prime.

In his aphasia nouns slipped away from Emerson as verbs did not. "There was something striking in the kind of forgetfulness by which he suffered," Dr. Holmes observed. "He remembered the realities and uses of things when he could not recall their names. He would describe what he wanted or thought of; when he could not recall 'chair' he could speak of that which supports the human frame, and 'the implement that cultivates the soil' must do for plough" (*Emerson*, p. 343). Wanting an umbrella but unable to recall the word, he said, "I can't tell its name, but I can tell its history. Strangers take it away."[21] Old age thus exposed a preference long apparent in his style but never before revealed with such stark clarity: his bias for the verb. "The world being thus put under the mind for Verb and Noun," he had long ago written, "the Poet is he who can articulate it" (*CW*, 3:12). Now when his mind could only decline physically, linguistically he could still conjugate.

The umbrella anecdote also reveals the old man's effort to locate things not through name or function but in space. Ultimately, he imagines the missing umbrella's history positionally. One hot day he invited a companion into the shade by saying, "Isn't there too much heaven on you there?" Unable to name the sun properly, he resorted to metonymy and gesture to place it as part of a larger whole. When his secretary

Cabot met him on the street in Boston one day and asked where he was going, Emerson replied, "To dine with an old and very dear friend. I know where she lives, but I hope she won't ask me her name . . . the mother of the wife of the young man—the tall man—who speaks so well" (Cabot, 2:651). He could navigate through familiar space, but he could explain his goal only by awkwardly linking people in a series of essentially positional relations. Struggling to make his grasp of contiguity do the work of his crippled power to name metaphorically, he was dealt a cruel blow in 1872 when his Concord house burned. Now as a tenant at the Old Manse he could no longer rely on a network of familiar spatial relations to express his needs verbally and gesturally. To his family the move seemed crucial in hastening his disorientation.

And there is an even more poignant irony in the disaster. Three dozen years earlier he had confidently built a house for the imagination that the final paragraph of *Nature* unbuilt as it arose. Its dissolving walls of glass seemed—and were—a triumph of the spirit. But when his real house burned to the ground, he found himself forced to live in the children's playhouse as a full-time tenant. When he finally lost all sense of a concrete place anchoring him to the earth, tenanting a world where all symbols dissolved as they arose proved a far harder task than he had imagined in "The Poet."

A daunting task, one might think. And these cruel ironies might well have crushed a lesser man. But bowing humorously before the rose he could no longer name to praise, time and again in his declining years Emerson turned his humiliating handicap into an occasion for small triumphs of the spirit. Before entering the ministry a sense of humor had marked him, prompting verbal high jinks like a rebus letter to his older brother. But during maturity he had muffled his humor in irony. Dignity and reticence often made him reluctant to laugh aloud. "Humour," perhaps, "was unlaughed fun" (*JMN*, 8:392). Now as he shuffled in comic incompetence through his daily routines, he smiled and laughed more openly. He was laughing, of course, at himself. He sensed as shrewdly as we must the Irony of Ironies overwhelming his life. It was not that aphasia had stricken an eloquent man dumb, for he could still talk. Rather, aphasia heightened the peculiarities of his great prose until he became a living parody of his own thought. Words are a form of action, he had claimed, and here he was pantomiming his needs. His vision of flux had always sought to dissolve names, symbols, and nominalization; now they had fled him completely. All larger coherence was gone with them, so he was penned syntactically within the individual sentence that had always been the core of his epigrammatic style—those same sentences from which "with very little system & . . . the most fragmentary result," as he had confessed to Carlyle, he struggled to compose his "paragraphs incompressible each sentence an infinitely repellent particle."²² Glimpsed through the gaps between words, the void had always energized his prose. "There must be the Abyss, Nox, and Chaos out of which all come," he had held, "and they must never be far off. Cut off the connexion between any of our works and this dread origin and the work is shallow and unsatisfying" (*JMN*, 9:325). Now as sentences absolutely refused to join, the Abyss loomed before his eyes. He tottered unsteadily on its brink.

From this perspective we must judge those occasions late in life when the family trundled him out for public readings. His few late works were ghost-edited to impose some coherence, but on the platform he stood alone. An old man who had lost his place in his house, he often lost his place in his pages, shuffling them arbitrarily at the podium or reading the same page twice. His daughter agonized. Scheduled to lecture on education to a Concord audience in 1878, he faithfully rehearsed his reading beforehand but kept forgetting what the subject was. The situation amused him keenly. "A funny occasion it will be—a lecturer who has no idea what he is lecturing about," he joked, "and an audience who don't know what he *can* mean" (Rusk, *Life*, p. 498).

What especially tickled him, we may surmise, was an awareness that things had never been very different. Hearing him lecture in 1868, James Russell Lowell found him "more disjointed even than common," as though he had shuffled his paragraphs in despair of ordering them. But in this "chaos full of shooting-stars, a jumble of creative forces," Lowell insisted that he saw no "falling-off in anything that ever was essential to the charm of Mr. Emerson's peculiar style of thought or phrase." Disconnected? "So were the stars that seemed larger to our eyes, still keen with that excitement, as we walked homeward with prouder stride over the creaking snow. And were *they* not knit together by a higher logic than our mere sense could master?"

Emerson shared with his public a perspective from which the sage's incoherences were subsumed in a higher order. That perspective was Romantic irony. "We do not go to hear what Emerson says," Lowell observed, "so much as to hear Emerson" (Konvitz, pp. 45–47). Beyond the inadequacies of words they felt they glimpsed in the old man himself an active embodiment of his message. And so perhaps they did. When he read across the gaps left by missing pages in his manuscript with a pause and a daffy smile, Emerson was hovering over the Abyss with great grace of spirit. At heart he had always been a devotee of Schlegel's Irony of Ironies. Now there was nothing left to do but embrace that as it enfolded him. Christian fundamentalists and the legions of political correctness may cluck in dismay that this was bogus transcendence. They may quarrel—they doubtless will—over whether to recommend him to the tender mercies of the Unitarian ministry or the bracing labor of social reform. But the rest of us may still feel—together with his original audiences—that even in his dotage the great great-granddaddy of American Romantic irony was somehow wiser than both lots. He comprehended them all, but they scarcely comprehend him. Purity and sweetness made his a rare soul; poise and balance made it a big one.

Man Thinking about American Scholars

But it would be a shame to fade out on the doddering Emerson smiling seraphically at the lectern, a sad, absurd reduction of his own mental powers. So let us take leave of him at the top of his game in "The American Scholar." After that glorious summons to "creative reading as well as creative writing" the entire American tradition of progressive education can seem like a long, dull, and often silly footnote. My text is a paragraph from the middle of the essay, where Emerson defines the duties of the intellectual as Man Thinking. It comes after a paragraph on the intellectual's proper method of working that would exclude many academic studies now churned out in pursuit of proper methodology and tenure. Emerson there argues that the scholar determined to remain true to himself will find that hotly debated questions of the day are probably "not worth the poorest thought which the scholar has lost in listening to the controversy." But he will eventually feel impelled to publish his thoughts, Emerson declares, and to his surprise he will find a broad *public* audience: "The orator distrusts at first the fitness of his frank confessions,—his want of knowledge of the persons he addresses,—until he finds that he is the complement of his hearers . . . most acceptable, most public, and universally true."

This paragraph develops the theme of scholarly nervousness about speaking the truth:

> In self-trust, all the virtues are comprehended. Free should the scholar be,—free and brave. Free even to the definition of freedom, "without any hindrance that does not arise out of his own constitution." Brave; for fear is a thing which a scholar by his very function puts behind him. Fear always springs from ignorance. It is a shame to him if his tranquillity, amid dangerous times, arise from the presumption that like children and women, his is a protected class; or if he seek a temporary peace by the diversion of his thoughts from politics or vexed questions, hiding his head like an ostrich in the flowering bushes, peeping into microscopes, and turning rhymes, as a boy whistles to keep his courage up. So is the danger

a danger still; so is the fear worse. Manlike let him turn and face it. Let him look into its eye and search its nature, inspect its origin,—see the whelping of this lion,—which lies no great way back; he will then find in himself a perfect comprehension of its nature and extent; he will have made his hands meet on the other side, and can henceforth defy it, and pass on superior. The world is his who can see through its pretension. What deafness, what stone-blind custom, what overgrown error you behold, is there only by sufferance,—by your sufferance. See it to be a lie, and you have already dealt it its mortal blow. (*CW*, 1:63–64)

No doubt the paragraph can be interpreted in different ways. But the previous paragraph charges me to make sense of it in a personal way and publish that. And surely one must *make* sense of it, for the more one looks at it the more puzzling questions arise.

To begin with, why is the scholar—after being advised in the previous paragraph to ignore popular controversy—now told that "the diversion of his thoughts from politics or vexed questions" is shameful? Does self-trust really comprehend all the virtues? Then why are there so many confident nincompoops and bullies? Does *all* fear spring from ignorance? Is it really true that all scholars put fear behind them upon first donning their Ph.D. robes? This question especially perplexes me since both my own motives in becoming a professor and thirty years' observation of *homo academicus* tempt me to endorse the folk wisdom that most scholars choose academic careers because they are frightened of life. (There is reason to think this question troubled Emerson and his Harvard audience.) Then there are the echoes. Though the scholar is warned not to be turning rhymes as a boy does, several words are rung repeatedly like chiming bells: "Free . . . free . . . free . . . freedom," "comprehended . . . comprehension," "fear . . . Fear . . . fear," "turning . . . turn." And most startlingly of all: "lion . . . lies . . . a lie."

Gradually some answers emerge for me. To begin with, scholarly self-trust does not *contain* all the virtues unless we equate self-trust with Aristotelian *megalopsychia* and buy the doctrine of the *Nicomachean Ethics*. Emerson may have one eye on Aristotle here, but surely he also knew that the claim runs counter to moral common sense. It is precisely because many scholars view self-assurance as the quintessential virtue that academic arrogance flourishes in so many forms. Among them we may instance the literary professoriat's current "pretension" that expertise in culture especially qualifies it to advise on national affairs that secretaries and carpenters presumably knew less about when they voted in administrations not to academia's taste. Would Emerson really relish an academy packed with Aristotle's strutting "great souls"? Perhaps he also wants us to entertain the possibility that with trust in his own peculiar mission a scholar may simply come to *understand* all the virtues, including many he may lack and some rarely seen in academia. Thus the word *comprehend* is turned in that direction by being repeated later in the passage.

The second sentence begins by positing an ideal freedom that scholars should have but may not. Heroic liberality? a free cosmopolitanism like Emerson's own? freedom from all institutions? Whatever it is, this ideal freedom is quickly restricted by reminding American scholars that they dwell in a land where a national anthem links freedom and bravery, so as Americans they are limited by our particular society and its political "constitution." Even as "the definition of freedom" seems to expand it, paradoxically the ideal freedom is limited still further by reminding us of those linguistic constraints that Emerson was so aware of.

Whether Emerson would have endorsed our current institutional concept of academic freedom is an interesting speculation. Whereas modern American scholars insist on their right to employment regardless of the offensiveness of their opinions, Emerson felt that his heterodoxy obliged him to resign his pulpit even though his congregation wished him to stay. Would a writer so alive to various meanings of this word want us to realize that when "academic freedom" is extended to tenure university personnel such as librarians, the word is being *turned* from its original purpose of safeguarding "free inquiry" and converted into its virtual opposite—that is, job *security* in lieu of high wages?

After racking my brains to understand why the scholar is now rebuked for avoiding political controversy when the previous paragraph urged him to remain aloof from it, I am still unclear. But Emerson's straddling both sides of this issue suggests a larger perspective than those now clashing in campus wars over political correctness. He sees the issue's complexity and is reluctant to oversimplify it. Does a resolution lie in his stipulation that the scholar should not seek a "temporary peace" by avoiding politics? If a biologist peeped into microscopes throughout a revolution because he was totally absorbed in his research and well funded, one doubts that Emerson would shoo him from his lab into the streets in the name of higher responsibilities. But if he huddled in fear over his slides while rocks were thrown through the lab windows, then, Emerson suggests, he is deluding himself with the notion of dwelling in an ivory tower. In other words, scholarship need not court political involvement to be valuable, and it always enters the fray at some risk; but it may become politically involved, especially in circumstances where politics hamper its prosecution. That may sound like simple common sense, like nothing so grand as "philosophy." But it is a form of Emersonian common sense all too rare in literary academia today.

Emerson's treatment of intellectual fear, on the other hand, is not commonsensical but brilliantly original. At first the linkage of fear and ignorance as attitudes that the scholar "by his very function puts behind him" seems to proclaim grandly that intellectuals are above such groveling concerns. Who, we may ask, is kidding whom? But the next sentence reminds us that timidity is a shameful scholarly stereotype, so obviously all scholars are not above fear. As this dawns on us, we may begin to realize that we are ignorant of the author's meaning. Indeed, the realization of our own ignorance may be a little frightening. We are being invited to penetrate our own fear and ignorance to realize that scholars are not immune to these attitudes by virtue of any "function" understood as an *office* or *class*. Rather, scholars who are neither bold nor omniscient learn to overcome fear and ignorance daily by their "function," their activity, their *functioning*. Evidently the scholarly vocation does not exempt people from craven ignorance but condemns them to it as their native element through which they must always move toward the truth. The scholar puts fear "behind him" only in the sense of moving through it—hence the startling turn on "turn" when he is told, "Manlike . . . turn and face it." The scholar must admit his fear if he is ever to overcome it. Among the myriad unacknowledged fears that plague academic intellectuals, like the fear of seeming old-fashioned, we may instance the fear of being exposed as no smarter than anyone else—students, colleagues, other professionals, just plain folk. Being put to shame by amateurs, by "children and women," as it were, threatens the financial underpinning of their "protected class." Academic jargon—a language of fixed, rigidly stipulated meanings, a priestly language difficult of access—is the most common defense against this fear.

When the scholar turns to face fear, what does he see? "It" gradually—only gradually—assumes the form of a lion. This is a masterstroke. A year earlier Emerson had claimed that the lion was a permanent type of wrath, yet here the lion is made to stand for the antithesis of all its traditional symbolic associations. It is an emblem of fear, not bravery (another sign that the correspondence theory of *Nature* was lightly held). It seems, in fact, our old friend the Cowardly Lion straight from Oz. What does this bizarre reversal suggest? Evidently fear and bravery are not distinct. We confront another of Emerson's bipolar unities, which asks us to imagine that fear is essential to bravery. Without fear, courage is mere foolhardiness. Bravery is fear overcome. We can grasp that notion without too much strain, for Homer embedded it in the Western heroic tradition. But to suggest that courage also inheres in fear is more novel. How can this be? And then we realize that the timorous scholar "hiding his head like an ostrich" actually runs more risks through fear than he would through courage. His fear is a form of *recklessness.*

Gazing into the eye of the beast, the scholar must learn to "see the whelping of this lion,—which lies no great way back." Notice the eerie way in which the lion begins to dissolve even as it takes shape. Physical eyesight may take in a couching beast, but only a transparent eyeball can simultaneously imagine its birth. In locating the whelping of the lion "no great way back," a temporal event is being displaced confusingly onto space (a trait that blossomed in Emerson's aphasia). The pun on "lies" invites us to realize this. Once the scholar grasps the limits of the visual emblem, "he will then find in himself a perfect comprehension of its nature and extent." He comes to *understand* the illusory lion perfectly by realizing that he entirely *contains* it. If he struck out at the lion, in either terror or bravery, his hands would not "meet on the other side." Only when he tries to *apprehend* his own *apprehension* will it vanish so that he can "pass on superior." He is the Cowardly Lion, and he must learn to see through his own "pretension."

Chief, perhaps, among his pretensions is the idea that his scholarly language (i.e., academic jargon) consists of words whose meaning can be safely fixed, whether by Emersonian correspondence theory or by the current literary mania for stipulative philosophical definition. The pangs of fear that the scholar suffers are by his own "sufferance." He allows them—just as he allows "deafness" to flourish in the world with erroneous custom when he takes refuge in the comforting jargon of the schools. That fixed jargon, like the "lion," is a "lie." See that, and the American scholar reclaims his freedom with a pun by speaking the essentially fluid language of public discourse. Ordinary language has philosophical drawbacks, to be sure, but philosophical jargon has far more.

Emerson's oratorical sublime drives like this paragraph toward the necessity of making choices and taking action. "The American Scholar" emerges from the skeptical play of a powerful intelligence capable of turning the whole world momentarily to glass. But if he often dwelt in a glass playhouse, Emerson was willing to throw stones, and as the shades of evening fell he toddled back to Main Street. Some deconstructionists may suppose that, like theirs, his mind revolved eternally in a jocose and sterile skepticism. Others may believe that he sounded a clarion to action that he was hypocritically unwilling to embark on. But the Romantic irony that colors Emerson's rhetoric mediates deftly between these two extremes. He wanted action, expected it, demanded it—and got it. "The American Scholar" is steeped in moral urgency that will not be divorced from social action. But it is also steeped in awareness of how manifold and complex our alternatives for social action are. His style invites us to weigh all the alternative consequences of action as it invites us to weigh all the alternative meanings of words. Like single vision, single-issue politics was anathema to him. His Romantic rhetoric does not aim at sheer self-expression; rather it presupposes a democratic society of individuals who must make moral choices. Unlike academics who prate of the "death of the author," Emerson knows that the individual is always free to make those choices. Choice is *not* preempted by society, as his disciple Thoreau was impressively to demonstrate. But Emerson also knows that in this democratic society, where single issues are filtered through a two-party system, the political expression of moral choice in a sound vote requires the ability to map and balance whole constellations of competing ideals. At its best, then, Emerson's rhetoric is eminently *engagé,* for it exercises the discriminative powers of all people bent on voting responsibly in American democracy.

"How do you get a handle on this guy?" my student Ira asked. It's hard, I admit. One can sympathize with the critic who argues that "we cannot simply render or present an Emerson of process. . . . We must show him . . . engaged in his dynamic constructions of meaning through our own active and dynamic constructions, in our making of it happen."[23] But even this claim may be dangerous if it reinforces an assumption that valid criticism must be philosophical and analytical. Hence the current obsession with "theory," with finding the right "method" for criticism. Emerson's own unsystematic essays on figures ranging from Shakespeare to Thoreau can be quite perceptive in *describing* the effects of literary style sans analysis. Impressionistic criticism has been in the academic doghouse for most of the twentieth century. Yet it is a perfectly legitimate mode. Most of the great critics of history practiced it at some point, and in their hands it yielded unique and permanently valuable insights. Criticism will remain a marginal activity in our culture so long as academics refuse on principle to employ all the resources of language to describe literature, so long as they refuse to see criticism itself *as* literary activity. Surely that thesis is implicit in the argument of "The American Scholar." Also implicit there is a wise skepticism that American scholars will ever find a "method" for creating either literature or criticism worth reading.

"I see the selfsame energy & action in a boy at football, that I admire in the intellectual play of Burke or Pindar" (*JMN,* 14:132). The sentence is provocative and enlightening even when detached from its roots in Emerson's aesthetic. So let me finally give an answer to my student's question in a manner that Emerson, I think, would approve. View it as an intrusion by an Orphic Poet if you wish.

"How do you get a handle on this guy, Ira? You don't. Look at this paragraph in 'The American Scholar.' Just imagine the situation. Fifty years of political independence and our culture is still being stomped. The American team is down 20-zip at the half, our boys have yet to get on the board. Man-to-man the Brits outweigh them by thirty pounds. They're a cocksure bunch of authors, all right. And why not? This is their game, their field, their language. Now it's the beginning of the second half. There's a new American quarterback. Ralph Waldo Emerson, the program says. This skinny guy don't look like much of a threat as he stands in the end zone, hands on hips, waiting. They've picked a reserve quarterback for kickoff return? Good grief, this is a whole new philosophy!

"The kick is up and it's a beauty, pinwheeling lazily in the sun. Emerson takes it deep in the end zone—hesitates a moment. Will he drop to one knee and start at the twenty? No, he was just reading the field, taking it all in, *comprehending* it. Now he's off! At the fifteen-yard line three Brits converge on him. But he picks up a block from a dictionary definition, pivots twice on the word *freedom*. All three Brits go sprawling! Now the word *fear* comes at him from two sides, but he zigzags, puts it behind him. He cuts to his left in the direction of *politics*, then cuts right again—yowsah, he juked that word out of its jockstrap! Ahead looms a literary *lion*—old Sam Johnson rearing up to trap him with his dictionary? Emerson straightarms the British *lion,* sends him spinning like a top. Whooee! That word *lion* hasn't a clue what it means now! Look into its eye, and you see the English language itself was only whelped a few centuries ago. Waldo's not gonna let it stop him now, no way!

"Now at midfield a lane opens up down the left sideline of language, and he's gone. The *world* or the *word* is his who can see through its pretension. All over the field English words are colliding as Swivel-hips Waldo glides past. He's America's original Galloping Ghost—he's here, he's there, he's everywhere, Ira, even where you least expect him. And right now he's here in this classroom telling you not to worry about the big mazumbas of literature like himself, because you own the language just as much as they do. You can do it too, dude, and anything else is a *lie*. Just remember that for the midterm.

"Knees pumping, he drives for the goal of the essay, the touchdown that will finally put America on the cultural scoreboard—creative reading and writing. Look at that sucker go! He's at the twenty, the ten . . . But wait! From the sidelines a scrawny figure scrambles onto the field. Look, it's D. H. Lawrence from the British bench! Despite himself he can't bear to see the momentum swing just because of a Man Thinking in print.

"'Oh, Waldo,' he snarls, 'your disintegrating white psyche will never make it. You lack blood-consciousness. Gotcha.' He launches himself at Emerson's ankles.

"Quick as a wink Waldo leaps into the air with a half-twist, hurdles the flying tackle, and comes down with his back to the goal line. Facing the prostrate Lawrence, he moonwalks backward into the end zone, ejaculating the last spermatic words of his oration all over the surly Brit. He spikes the ball gracefully over his shoulder. And only then do we realize that Emerson's features glimpsed through the mask are grinning in blackface. . . ."

That's what I should have told Ira. Now why did words fail me?

9 /
Wordplay, Romantic Irony, and the Forms of Antebellum Fiction

> You asserted that . . . Richter's novels are not novels but a colorful hodge-podge of sickly wit. . . .
> I admit the colorful hodgepodge of sickly wit; but I shall defend it and emphatically maintain that such grotesques . . . are the only romantic productions of our unromantic age.
>
> — Friedrich Schlegel, "Letter about the Novel," trans. Behler and Strug

Irving's Bawdy Double Entendres

The uniqueness of nineteenth-century American fiction has perhaps most often been ascribed to authors' taking the imaginative romance as their model rather than the novel form favored by the masters of British and European social realism. Less noticed, however, has been the extent to which America's great romancers spun stories rather different in tone from those of British figures like the Brontës, for example—comic romances or grotesque fictions that even when dark are ironically colored by American authors' preoccupation with wordplay, so that sheer stylistic virtuosity may suggest vistas broader than those commanded by the characters.

When together with friends Washington Irving undertook *Salmagundi* (1807-8) to elevate the *ton* of the town, wordplay figured prominently in their program. "The Philadelphians do absolutely 'live and move and have a being' entirely upon puns," wrote Irving to a friend while visiting there in 1807. "I absolutely shudder with horror—think what miseries I suffer—Me to whom a pun is an abomination" (6:363). With such mock-squeamishness about wordplay *Salmagundi* described a New Yorker contracting "a violent fit of the *pun* mania" in Philadelphia:

> Accosted by a good-looking young gentleman from New-Jersey, who had caught the infection—he took me by the button and informed me of a contest that had lately taken place between a tailor and a shoemaker about I forget what;—SNIP was pronounced a fellow of great *capability*, a man of gentlemanly *habits*, who would doubtless *suit* every body. The shoemaker *bristled* up at this, and *waxed* exceeding wroth—swore the tailor was but

a *half-souled* fellow, and that it was easy to *shew* he was never *cut-out* for a gentleman. The *choler* of the tailor was up in an instant, he swore by his thimble that he would never *pocket* such an insult, but would *baste* any man who dared to repeat it. (6:185–86)

Philadelphians, *Salmagundi* concludes, are "an honest, worthy, square, good-looking, regular uniform ... kind of people, who always go to work methodically, never put the cart before the horse, talk like a book, walk mathematically ... think syllogistically, and pun theoretically, according to the genuine rules of Cicero and Dean Swift." Like their rectangular, grid-patterned city, their mechanical raillery reflects a communal sensibility resolutely rooted in Enlightenment geometry, "whereas the people of New-York—God help them—tossed about over hills and dales, through lanes and alleys, and crooked streets ... are the most irregular, crazy headed, quicksilver, eccentric, whim-whamsical set of mortals that ever were jumbled together in this uneven, villanous revolving globe, and are the very antipodeans to the philadelphians." To rational Enlightenment satirists like Joseph Dennie and Ben Franklin, gifted merely with "hum drum regularity," *Salmagundi* opposes a vision of New York as a dynamic metropolis, growing organically, pulsating with life, unmaking and remaking itself daily. By pretending that Philadelphians excel New Yorkers in punning, Irving backhandedly dismisses their comic rhetoric as a bewigged and static eighteenth-century hangover while prophetically staking out the opening territory of Romantic irony for Manhattan punsters.

With its bawdy breeches humor his jocular *History of New York* perfected the Knickerbocker manner. Along with gargantuan eating and drinking, flatulence and defecation loom large. Mocking the quest for origins conducted by writers such as Jacob Bryant, bogus etymologies abound in this historical burlesque. Does Manna-hata mean Island of Manna? Or did squaws wear men's hats, so the name *Manhattan* = man-hat-on? Contradictory punning explanations suggest that the original meaning of words is no more readily recovered than a land flowing with milk and honey. Irving differed from Transcendentalists like Emerson and Thoreau for whom etymology was a clew into the Minotaur's lair of the past. The early stirrings of Romantic philology failed to stir his imagination when he encountered the works of Sir William Jones and Tooke; his habitual response was suave but shallow amusement at linguistic pedantry. Hieroglyphic fragments fallen from the moon show that "the universal language there is high dutch," joshed *Salmagundi*, "thereby proving it to be the most ancient and original tongue" (6:313).

Recoiling from the "pure unadulterated LOGOCRACY or government of words" exemplified in America's windy politics (6:142-43), Irving longs nostalgically not for primitive languages but for the speechless Eden of infancy (Latin *infans* = not speaking). His comic history of Dutch Manhattan becomes a parable of the corruption of infantile pleasure by language. Led by Oloffe the Dreamer, the Dutch craftily acquired the island from the Indians because "the Indians were much given to long talks and the Dutch to long silence" (7:63). They enjoyed their golden age under their first governor, Wouter Van Twiller, whose forebears "had comported themselves with such singular wisdom and propriety, that they were never either heard or talked of" (7:92). Only parson and council clerk could read, so Van Twiller signed his name with a cross. In Wouter the Doubter's prelinguistic paradise, the Dutch sucked their pipes in peace, gourmandized mightily, defecated accordingly, and propagated lustily.

With the demise of the drowsy Wouter this idyllic lubberland vanishes. He was succeeded by Wilhelmus Kieft, whose name, "according to the most authetic etymologists, was a corruption of Kyver; that is to say a *wrangler* or a *scolder.*" Irving's burlesque veers into satire in mocking Thomas Jefferson as William the Testy. Having made "gallant inroads . . . into the dead languages" (7:130-31) and "dabbled in Egyptian hieroglyphics and the mystic symbols of the obelisks," this Aeolist par excellence put his faith in "the art of fighting by proclamation and defending a country by trumpeters and windmills" (7:159-63). Corrupted by his blustering verbosity, the Dutch develop a "passion for endless harrangues . . . a cruel and distressing disease . . . continually breaking out in alarming and obnoxious flatulencies, whereby the said body politic is grievously affected, as with a wind cholic."[1] Political squabbling that replaces defense policy with rhetoric undoes Kieft's vainglorious but valiant successor Peter Stuyvesant, so a sensual paradise founded by dumb dreamers and doubters is lost by the talkativeness of the testy and headstrong.

Lost forever? Dreamer and doubter that he was, Irving seems unsure. His burlesque fable reflects his alienation from the course of American history. From Knickerbocker's arsy-versy perspective all our official heroes seems villains. Wistfully Irving dreams of recapturing the primal joy of Creation, of liberating the sensual instincts harnessed in the service of a sober and industrious civilization. In the early years of the nineteenth century tall tales of American abundance often sprang up among marginal groups who felt themselves at the mercy of the dominant mercantile classes. But his family's stake in hardware kept him from repudiating mercantilism wholeheartedly. Despite his nostalgia for New Amsterdam's golden age of childish giants, he is skeptical about recapturing the past.

The comic mannerisms that Irving pioneered in the *History* show him a romantic ironist at heart long before 1825 found him transcribing the theories of A. W. Schlegel. In his demented narrative of "*how the town of New Amsterdam arose out of mud*," Diedrich Knickerbocker's intrusive denunciations of windiness become suspiciously long-winded (7:102). The philosophical historian merges with the authorities whom he assaults. "It has ever been the task of one race of philosophers to demolish the works of their predecessors, and elevate more splendid fantasies in their stead, which in their turn are demolished and replaced by the air castles of a succeeding generation" (7:30). Composing and decomposing his book simultaneously, Knickerbocker asserts proudly that "my work shall, in a manner, echo the nature of the subject . . . this being an improvement in history, which I claim the merit of having invented" (7:35). He bids his reader farewell by flaunting the planned obsolescence of his magnum opus: "That many will hereafter spring up and surpass me in excellence, I have very little doubt and still less care" (7:293). The new world Knickerbocker wants us to discover hardly resembles the land reached, according to "vulgar opinion, . . . on the 12th of October, 1492, by Christovallo Colon . . . clumsily nicknamed Columbus." But we may share his own vulgar opinion that "this country should have been called Colonia, after his name" (7:35). Dilettante though Irving was, few have written history with eyes more jealously fixed on posteriority. Republican rhetoric struck him as the flatulence of the mob while rounding up Federalist voters in New York's Negro ward nauseated him with the "sweet smelling savour" of an election day crowd (23:232). But if the body odors of the body politic were disgusting, explosive scatological puns might help dispel such democratic vapors.

Romantic irony also informs the charming tales by which he is best remembered. Today they strike us as innocuous, fit for treatment by Disney. On their first publication, however, they were often denounced for risqué humor. The author was seeking "to smuggle impurity" into the home through "equivocal" remarks "that no woman could bear to read . . . aloud," complained *Blackwood's*.[2] The complaint was in measure justified, for Irving was determined to distinguish his work from the scads of legendary and romantic tales the press spewed out. He needed a novel approach to capitalize on his idiosyncrasies, he decided, depending on style rather than plot. He elaborated on his subtleties in a letter to his editor: "I fancy much of what I value myself upon in writing, escapes the observation of the great mass of my readers, who are intent more upon the story than the way in which it is told. . . . It is the play of thought, and sentiment and language . . . the familiar and faithful exhibition of scenes in common life; and the half concealed vein of humour that is often playing through the whole—these are among what I aim at" (24:90).

Irving's two fictional masterpieces are serio-comic ghost stories in which an ambiguous Gothic plot sparks a train of double meanings. Beginning with a bogus etymology for Tarry Town, allegedly named by country housewives from their husbands' propensity to linger at the tavern there, "The Legend of Sleepy Hollow" ends with an ironic fillip at the credibility of the tale itself. The play of thought, sentiment, and language that flickers around "Rip Van Winkle" likewise lets us wonder whether Irving's "half concealed vein of humor" includes sexual innuendo about the curious fondness for Rip shown by the village housewives and their children. While the supernatural is foregrounded, the story invites another interpretation closer to the common life Irving claimed to exhibit: an unhappily married man with an eye for the women deserts his family and lights out for parts unknown like Ichabod Crane. Chastened by lonely old age, he returns twenty years later seeking to pick up the threads of family life, with a tall tale to justify his absence. Sentimentalist though Irving was, his vision spans the depressingly mundane scenes enacted daily in modern Bureaus of Missing Persons. Like the eerily "melancholy party of pleasure" in the glen, the language of the story is two-faced. Read on one level it yields smiling romance or pathos, read on another drab reality or a dirty joke.

Like *A History of New York,* which he completed to solace his grief at the death of his fiancée, this comic masterpiece was composed while Irving labored under a depression so profound as to worry his family. In June 1818 his despondency stemmed from his brothers' bankruptcy and the collapse of the family fortunes. Rip took shape in a mind split like Hudson's melancholy party of pleasure, materializing to rescue his creator from the slough of despond. The short story genre that Irving pioneered came from a divided consciousness. In the volumes that followed, the most successful tales are generally serio-comic ghost stories with a bawdy strain underlying ironic Gothic machinery, like "The Adventure of the Bold Dragoon," "The Adventure of My Aunt," and "Dolph Heyliger." Just as Irving was attracted to punning, so he gravitated toward narratives that turn on double meanings, often risqué ones, to the increasing discomfiture of reviewers. "If Mr. Geoffrey Crayon is not a thought more careful," complained the *U.S. Literary Gazette* in 1824, "the more recondite meaning of his double entendres will become a little too apparent" (in Hedges, p. 198n).

The fictional form that Irving bequeathed to his country was thus in essence an expanded pun. The play of thought and language on which he prided his tales was the shimmer of Romantic irony. By comparison with later figures in the American Renaissance, Irving's ironic manner too often seems the lazy refuge of an author unwilling to face cultural contradictions squarely. Too often the ideals subtended by his Romantic irony remain sentimental or vague. But his best stories are miniature masterpieces that blaze the way for the achievements of Hawthorne and Melville. "The Stout Gentleman" is a notable example. Throughout the tale the narrator fantasizes in obsessive detail about a mysterious guest at an inn who is never seen. Rushing to the window the next morning, he just glimpses the rear of a person mounting a coach. "The skirts of a brown coat parted behind, and gave me a full view of the broad disk of a pair of drab breeches. The door closed—'all right' was the word—the coach whirled off—and that was all I ever saw of the stout gentleman!" (9:52-56). The story burlesques Gothic conventions, of course, but it transcends parody to dramatize larger issues that would become central to American Romanticism: the bias inherent in physical observation, the linguistic basis of understanding. At the end the narrator's multiple meanings collide cheekily with the inscrutable universe of Hawthorne and Melville, and Irving offers us a startling comic vision of the world as Scarlet Arse, as Moby Buttock.

Leatherstocking and the Languages of Nature

Had Irving christened a character Nate Bumppo, we might safely guffaw at the dirty joke. But Cooper took scant pleasure in verbal ambiguity, and his fiction seldom encourages us to enjoy it. "There is a half hidden looseness, an indelicacy of allusion," in "The Stout Gentleman," he complained, "which should have no place in a book destined, if not designed, as an ornament to the sopha, and as a modest companion at the parlor window."[3] "The common faults of American language are an ambition to effect, a want of simplicity, and a turgid abuse of terms," wrote Cooper in *The American Democrat* (1838), recoiling like Irving from popular rant. "To these may be added ambiguity of expression. Many perversions of significations also exist, and a formality of speech, which, while it renders conversation ungraceful, and destroys its playfulness, seriously weakens the power of the language, by applying to ordinary ideas, words that are suited only to themes of gravity and dignity."[4]

Like Tocqueville, Cooper regarded the American melting pot as a giant smelter for puns, since "a democratic people double the meaning of a word" in refusing to respect its class-determined import.[5] Whereas rhetorical exaggeration inspired Irving to develop a punning mock-heroic style that could playfully parody it, Cooper rejected such verbal cleverness as unworthy a gentleman. In an era of populist turbulence "ambiguity of expression" was extending the term *gentleman* further than he wished. It also jeopardized epic aspirations. The romantic sublimity at which his style aims is seldom enhanced by his clumsy levity. Thus Natty Bumppo indulges his humor chiefly by "the silent laugh for which he was so remarkable" (*Pioneers,* p. 154).

Of eighteen authorial notes in *The Prairie* the majority deal with etymologies like the derivation of the title-word itself. Yet for Cooper as for Irving and A. B. Johnson, etymology offered no linguistic stability, no guarantee of correctness. The Leatherstocking Tales are permeated with the conviction that verbal expression is radically ambiguous. The mute grandeur of Cooper's wilderness is always menaced by a babel of languages, by diverse dialects and idiolects competing for center stage. Each undermines the others' claims to represent the world truly. Like other noise, speech often seems dangerous by threatening to betray wanderers to marauding Indians. His landscapes are properly read only by those who realize with Natty that no "title of convention" offered by human language can faithfully render the visual language of nature. If silence is golden in the wilderness, the most golden tongues belong to the Indians. By their laconic standard "the palefaces are prattling women: they have two words for each thing" (*Last,* p. 91). By contrast, "Hugh!" suffices Cooper's Indians for myriad purposes, while they distrust the "forked tongues" of whites.

Even in portraying formal Indian oratory, where "not a word was uttered, that did not convey the meaning of the speaker, in the simplest and most energetic form," Cooper insists on their economical vocabulary and the superior force of physical signs, "those significant gestures with which an Indian always illustrates his eloquence" (pp. 241–42, 106). In Cooper's Ossianic renderings of Indian speech according to the theories of Reid, Blair, and Herder, the most frequent metaphors equate sense organs with the faculties they serve or parts of the body with mental traits. Cooper's Indians describe their hearing as "my ears" or speech as "the tongue" on an average of ten times a novel. Like the early ethnologists whom he followed, by insisting on the physicality of Indian languages Cooper tempted readers to imagine a primitive consciousness that had somehow avoided the Cartesian split between mind and body, word and world. Heckewelder had noted no instance in Delaware where the verb *I am* appeared by itself, apart from the idea of the act to be done. So perhaps (as Cardell had conjectured) that tongue held the answer to Tooke's nagging dualistic riddle—a fluid, transactional concept of personal identity, "a primary, integrated state of being" prior to "the self-other and verb-noun differentiations so prominent in other languages."[6]

"Society is always a loser by mistaking names for things," Cooper roundly declared in *The American Democrat* (p. 118). Time and again the Leatherstocking novels invite us to bypass names and read things directly as natural signs. When an Indian orator speaks, every eye is riveted on his face, for auditors interpret not just his words but his features. Decoding traces of emotion on a face is much like the challenge of deciphering tracks, another elaborate semiotic system in the Leatherstocking novels. For all Pathfinder's adeptness at tracking, Hawk-eye cannot match his Indian comrade Uncas in reading the language of nature this way. He even suggests that familiarity with languages tainted by writing may blunt the ability to discriminate visual signs. Fugitives may try to falsify their trails, but such efforts rarely succeed. It is as if the wilderness speaks a language that cannot lie. Following a trail triumphantly to his quarry, Natty whispers, "There they are, by all the truth of signs!" (*Last,* p. 205). His vocabulary includes no higher oath.

"What's your name?" Hetty Hutter asks Natty in *The Deerslayer*. It takes him two pages to answer, for young though he is, he already has five names to his credit: Bumppo, Straight-tongue, Pigeon, Lap-ear, and Deerslayer. "My names have come nat'rally," he explains, "and I suppose the one I bear now, will be of no great lasting" (pp. 67–69). In later life he will acquire as many more, almost all earned by some talent or attribute. Of such names he styles himself "an admirator... although the Christian fashions fall far below savage customs in this particular. The biggest coward I ever knew was called Lyon; and his wife, Patience, would scold you out of hearing" (*Last,* p. 57). To Hetty's observation that "Bumppo isn't as pretty as Hutter, is it?" he replies, "Why that's as people fancy. Bumppo has no lofty sound, I admit, and yet men have bumped through the world with it." The rare pun points to no occult etymological connection but rather to his amusement (like A. W. Schlegel's) at language's sheer arbitrariness. "I put no great dependence, therefore, on names" (*Deerslayer,* p. 423).

In the Leatherstocking novels opposed semiotic systems are contesting for the American continent. Natty's deeper allegiance remains to the nomenclature of action, the wordless language of signs, and the transparent icons of nature. He is reluctant "to disturb natur' with a name." He prefers the titles bestowed by Indians or hunters, who "are likely to call the place by something reasonable and resembling" (pp. 45–46). Yet at some level the virginal Natty wishes his beloved Glimmerglass would not have to bear any name, not an Indian one or even his own. All naming violates the purity of his sweetheart nature, just as the lost innocence of the heroine Judith remains too vulnerable to exposure by a word to make her a fit wife for this bachelor of nature. Like naming and sex, naming and appropriation go hand in hand. When the pioneer Ishmael Bush encounters the aging Natty wandering the prairie to escape the pressure of settlers, he is prompt to inquire, "What may you name the district, hereaway?" Pointing upward significantly, the old trapper replies, "By what name . . . would you call the spot, where you see yonder cloud?" (*Prairie*, p. 17). But the answer only baffles the Bush family, who suspect him of joking. Like the civilization they represent, they simply cannot conceive of nature unsegmented by verbal language.

Neither, one must add, can Natty, or perhaps any except feral mutes. Hence a certain ambivalence tinges his attitude toward names. Like his creator, who invested enormous energy in suing scurrilous editors successfully for libel, Natty sometimes *does* care what he is called, itemizing his sobriquets for Hetty with modest pride. Throughout *The Prairie* Cooper makes a great show of referring to him anonymously as "the trapper, whom in future we shall choose to designate by his pursuit" (p. 22). Yet Natty sets no traps in the book. Moreover, one of its great emotional climaxes occurs when he encounters the grandson of his old friend Heyward wandering the plains. Middleton informs him that his own middle name is Uncas, while three other family members have names derived from Natty's. "Do you mean the actual name itself; spelt with the very same letters; beginning with an N, and ending with an L?" inquires the excited Natty, whose illiteracy is evidently not quite total. The news that his Christian name, coyly withheld from the reader, is perpetuated in that family reduces him to joyful tears: "Do ye hear that. . . . A name! it is wonderful! very wonderful!" (pp. 113–15).

And the great set piece of his death scene is likewise dominated by his mysteriously unspecified name. As if in response to a divine roll call, he rises suddenly to his feet, pronounces the single word "Here!" and expires. He dies uncertain whether he will meet Indian friends of different religion in the hereafter. Yet Christian faith does not keep him from thinking that if "the same meaning is hid under different words, we shall yet stand together . . . before the face of your Wahcondah who will then be no other than my God" (pp. 382–86). Unsettling linguistic diversity in this word is counterbalanced by faith that in the next "the Master of Life has an ear for every language" (p. 282). With such vague trust in universals, Natty dies cherishing his Christian name enough to request a gravestone to perpetuate it. His saga closes on a note of muted linguistic optimism unlike the ironic fate in *The Pioneers* of his comrade Chingachgook, the last of the Mohicans, whose name was misspelled on the very gravestone erected by white friends to commemorate it.

Similar ambivalence about words pervades Natty's saga from the beginning. Captured by hostile Indians, Deerslayer is released to carry a message to the Hutter family, promising to return to his captors. Judith Hutter asks him "why they have sent you on parole, to make us some offer," only to receive a backwoods lecture on diction:

> "Furlough, Judith; furlough is the word; and it carries the same meaning with a captive at large, as it does with a soldier who has leave to quit his colors. In both cases the word is past to come back, and now I remember to have heard that's the ra'al signification; 'furlough' meaning a 'word' passed for the doing of any thing of the like. Parole I rather think is Dutch, and has something to do with the tattoos of the garrisons. But this makes no great difference, since the varture of a pledge lies in the idee, and not in the word." (pp. 391–92)

Natty garbles the etymologies, attributing to the Dutch-derived *furlough* the original meaning that actually belongs to the French *parole,* which he confuses with the drum roll mustering for payroll. As the narrator elsewhere observes, "the reader will have remarked that Deerslayer had not very critically studied his dictionary" (p. 212). Yet at the same time—and surely this is Cooper's point—Natty has a more exalted conception of language than any Tookean etymologist, for he is scrupulously governed in his actions not by dead roots but by the intended meaning of his word. The plot revolves around his refusal to rescind his oath or tell any lies whatsoever. Indeed, the Straight-tongue seems to regard all uttered words as compacts sworn before God, inviolable since "the woods are but the ears of the Almighty, the air is his breath, and the light of the sun is little more than a glance of his eye" (p. 405).

"Book! What have such as I . . . to do with books!" the illiterate Natty exclaims in a famous outburst. "I never read but in one, and the words that are written there are too simple and too plain to need much schooling" (*Last,* p. 117). Whereas the Bible may be true, the Book of Nature that Natty prizes is truth itself. Its natural signs seem not merely to point to God but to embody him. At moments like these, reading Cooper's language of nature seems to require neither imagination nor interpretation—just open eyes.

But that is only half the story, of course, for Natty has a great deal to do with books. He is the literary hero of five. Cooper's authorial intrusions insist that interpreting them requires literary imagination, "it is unnecessary to warn the practised reader" (*Prairie*, pp. 13-14). Author and character are both torn between signs and words, but whereas Natty's primary allegiance remains to the former, Cooper the novelist must deal in the latter. So how did Cooper proceed as a writer to render a consciousness to which writing was alien?

On one memorable occasion Natty finds himself arguing with his friends Chingachgook and Uncas over the proper route for their party to take. At first, the argument goes against the scout "because, from the lingering pride of colour, he rather affected the cold and inartificial manner, which characterizes all classes of Anglo-Americans, when unexcited." Then suddenly, before the eyes of the outsider Duncan Heyward,

> he arose [to his feet,] and shaking off his apathy, [he . . . assumed the manner of an Indian, and] adopted all the arts of native eloquence. Elevating an arm, he pointed out the track of the sun, repeating the gesture for every day [that was] necessary [to accomplish their object]. Then he delineated a long and painful path, amid rocks and water courses. The age and weakness of the slumbering [and unconscious] Munro were indicated by signs too palpable to be mistaken. . . . Then came [the representation of] the light and graceful movements of a canoe, set in forcible contrast to the tottering steps of one enfeebled and tired. He concluded by pointing to the scalp of the Oneida, and apparently urging the necessity of their departing speedily, and in a manner that should leave no trail. (*Last*, p. 199, my brackets)

Gesture carries the day. Chingachgook and Uncas convert to a water route, and even Heyward can follow the argument despite his ignorance of Delaware. Note how the striking contrast between Natty the verbalist and Natty the pantomimist is reproduced in the prose of the passage itself. Here representing the civilized viewpoint of the observer Duncan Heyward, it is a fairly typical specimen of Cooper's ponderous narrative style justly criticized by Poe and Twain. As the bracketed redundancies suggest, it is prolix in the extreme, and a moment's thought suffices to condense other phrases that cannot be omitted outright. "Signs too palpable to be mistaken" boil down to "unmistakable signs," while the concluding clause craves to be expressed in half as many words—"urged a speedy departure without leaving any trail." The diction is marked by genteel inflations like "necessity" for "need," "enfeebled" for "feeble," and "delineated" for "sketched." Yet in this passage all these vices almost become stylistic virtues, enforcing on us the key contrast between Natty's "light and graceful movements" and the awkwardness of Heyward/Cooper's conventional civilized discourse. One could scarcely ask for a more graphic illustration of Magua's claim that the palefaces have two words for each thing.

To call this deliberate irony is perhaps too much, for concise narration was frankly not one of Cooper's gifts. But if he could not readily write otherwise, at least he knew his limitations as a storyteller. "Much less time was consumed in the occurrence of these events," he remarks in *The Pioneers,* "than in their narration" (p. 272). Alas, too true! Cooper lets us hear the creakiness of his medium to suggest through cracks in his narrative technique why the silent languages of nature need no novelists. His narrator oscillates between omniscience and uncertainty, between locutions like "Truth obliges us to say" and "it seemed that. . . ." Some events "the reader will readily imagine," but elsewhere narrative assurance yields to the melancholy possibility that "we have spilled much ink in vain" (*Prairie,* pp. 207, 321). A tense scene of impending torture is interrupted by "a sudden and unlooked for announcement, that . . . put a momentary check to the whole proceedings." Whereupon the screen goes blank, the lights come on, and Cooper's audience is encouraged to file out for popcorn: "As this interruption has a close connection with the denouement of our story, it shall be given in a succeeding chapter" (*Deerslayer,* p. 507). Verbal narrative itself seems now a cramped distortion of reality—"Our limits will not permit a detail"—now simply superfluous—"It is needless to say" (*Prairie,* pp. 365, 230). The net effect of such constantly shifting locutions is to unsettle the authority of the narration, to make the reader aware of its artificiality.

Romantic irony does not loom so large in Cooper's fictions as in Irving's. Yet one further stylistic tic suggests how pervasive were Cooper's linguistic misgivings—his fondness for periphrases like "the man they call Gamut," "her who has been called Cora," and "the colour called sorrel" (*Last,* pp. 323, 21–22). Identifying things thus questions the adequacy of names. Cooper wants readers to realize that terms for colors are not colors themselves. But though he must render them in black and white, he surely wants his readers to *see* colors, to *see* characters, to *see* landscapes. Time and again his slow-moving narratives grind to a halt so that the author can engage in explicit portraiture or scene-painting.

Oft-noted, Cooper's pictorial aims are not unique; other writers like Irving and Bryant shared a taste for the picturesque that links them with Catlin, Mount, and the Hudson River painters. But in the Leatherstocking tales Cooper's penchant for grandiose landscapes becomes uniquely expressive. As in Cole's paintings, the unbroken expanses of wild forest or deserted prairie dwarf the figures who move through them. Except for

Natty, most characters seem insensible to the visual grandeur enveloping them. With wordy definitions, they are bent on segmenting it into private property. Natty himself is an ironic champion of the iconic. He shuns written language yet paves the way for the civilization that will displace him and the illiterate native peoples by imposing a grid of print upon nature. And the adventures of this self-annihilating hero are appropriately described in a style that repeatedly pauses as if to dissolve its own narrative medium, its historic momentum. Nostalgic but not notably sentimental, Cooper's literary picture-painting seeks to remind his audience of what may have been lost when readers of visual signs became readers of novels. Drawing much of their energy from Cooper's ambivalence about public language in America, the Leatherstocking tales deploy Romantic irony to help us reimagine the language of nature.

The Gothic Grotesquerie of Poe's Grinning Skull

During Poe's year at the University of Virginia his guardian John Allan fumed that he seemed to be paying too much attention to Joe Miller's jestbook. That was probably familiar to Poe, for a sense of humor marked him from youth. His earliest juvenilia imitated the tragicomic brio of Byron's *Don Juan,* with its coruscating Romantic ironies. Over the next twenty-five years Poe spun ever more complicated arabesques to elaborate this sardonic pose. For saving laughter he often turned to puns. So did his family. Conundrums brightened their fireside when fuel was scarce. His faithful housekeeper Aunt Maria cherished them, jotting down naive specimens for future reference: "What was Eves bridal dress? A bear skin."[7] Poe himself could condescend to that level. "Why does a lady in tight corsets never need comfort?" he queried. "Because she's already so laced.—*solaced.*"[8] But his efforts to intellectualize the form could smother the humor. "Why is the fifteenth letter of the alphabet, when mutilated, like a Parisian cockney?" he asked, then explained with lofty sophistication, "Because it is a bad O.—*badaud.*"

Aborted by Allan, Poe's classical education was patchy, leaving him fluent only in Latin and French. His Greek and Italian were sketchy while his efforts to fake a knowledge of German are so inept as to suggest that he could scarcely read it. In 1844–45 he still regarded Horne Tooke as a notable grammatical sage. Drawing on a handful of favorite compendia to simulate scholarly authority, as an editor he cultivated the pose of a gentlemanly savant qualified to review everything from belles lettres to grammars and dictionaries. Superficial though Poe's cosmopolitanism was, it came as a tonic to American criticsm. Using the adjective *linguistic* ten years before the earliest citation in the *OED*, this rather limited linguist was a bold neologizer who may have pioneered as many as a thousand words.

In 1839, while promising to crack any cipher readers submitted, he also offered to solve riddles. His essay "Enigmatical and Conundrumical" contrasted riddles and puns:

> Modern taste, . . . at least modern newspaper taste, affects rather the conundrum than the enigma proper. The former has more spice in its composition, and its brevity gives it force. A good enigma, we have said, is a good thing, but a good conundrum *may be* a better. Consequently, we see our brethren of the press trying their hands at *cons* in all directions, and as soon as they perpetrate a decent one (after a severe effort) they set up a cackle forthwith, and the bantling goes the round of the papers in a kind of *ovation*. This inordinate estimation of conundrums arises from the chance haphazard manner in which they are conceived, making their conception a difficult thing. With a little . . . *method* . . . they may be manufactured by the yard—yes, and of good quality too. (Brigham, pp. 13–14)

As proof, he churned out twenty-five for *Alexander's Weekly Messenger.* Then, recycling a third (which suggests they were not so speedily manufactured as he claimed), he published two more series of conundrums in the *Saturday Museum* in 1843.

More learned macaronic puns stud the *Marginalia,* three hundred aphorisms published in magazines during 1844–49, chaotic years as Poe spiraled toward breakdown. Appearing a month before Poe's death in 1849, the last installment of the *Marginalia* concludes appropriately with three paragraphs analyzing the humor of Thomas Hood, who enjoyed enormous popularity. Poe now judged that largely undeserved:

> In fact, he was a literary merchant, whose main stock in trade was *littleness*; for during the larger portion of his life, he seemed to breathe only for the purpose of perpetrating puns—things of so despicable a platitude that the man who is capable of habitually committing them, is seldom found capable of anything else. Whatever merit *may* be discovered in a pun, arises altogether from *unexpectedness*. This is the pun's element and is two-fold. First, we demand that the *combination* of the pun be unexpected; and, secondly, we require the most entire unexpectedness in the pun *per se*. A rare pun, rarely appearing, is, to a certain extent, a pleasurable effect; but to no mind, however debased in taste, is a continuous effort at punning otherwise than unendurable. (*Essays*, p. 1471)

Noting that habitual despondency meant that Hood had to force himself to write, Poe concludes that his puns "leave upon us a painful impression; for too evidently they are the hypochondriac's struggles at mirth— the grinnings of the death's head." This penetrating analysis of Hood's wordplay is surprisingly harsh, for earlier references to Hood and to punning are more generous. Beneath the hood one inevitably sees Poe's own grinning skull.

The vogue for puns tempted Fanny Fern to sexual double entendres and spurred her estranged brother N. P. Willis, Poe's friend and editorial benefactor, to fluffy prose and witty *vers de société* while absorbing the deaths of his mother, wife, child, and youngest sister.[9] But it stirred deeper echoes in Poe's troubled psyche. His last name offered good sport for a gamesome age. "Why ought the author of the 'Grotesque and Arabesque' to be a good writer of verses?" queried Poe himself, then crowed, "Because he's a poet to a *t*. Add *t* to Poe makes it Poet" (Brigham, p. 16). His inamorata Sarah Power Whitman shored up her temporary belief that she and Poe were soul mates by deriving family names on both sides from a supposed common ancestor the Chevalier le Poer. "Another cousin or twin star," she enthused in verse, "We drop the W, he the R" (*EAP*, p. 361). But no aristocratic background had been ascribed to the Irish-American Poes by the New York reviewers who in 1809 ridiculed Edgar's actor-father David for mispronouncing foreign words. Advising him to limit his roles to footmen, they lampooned him in French doggerel verses "Sur un POE de Chambre" (*EAP*, p. 7). Throughout the War of the Literati unfriendly critics gleefully pooh-poohed Poe's poetry as poo-poo. "Poh! Poh!" clucked the *Boston Evening Transcript,* while Poe's opponent T. D. English wrote that others had "converted the paper on which his sketches were written to its legitimate use—like to like" (*EAP*, pp. 268, 309). Poe was himself a walking pun, where one intent was at odds with another. Orphaned at three, he never mourned his mother properly, so his entire life became a protracted ritual of mourning in which remembering and forgetting were equally painful. Byronic rebelliousness went hand in hand with a child-like dependence on motherly women like his aunt, while the childishness was camouflaged by marrying an even more childlike wife in his thir-teen-year-old cousin. Stylistically Poe denounced ambiguity. But when this devotee of double entendres turned to fiction, he produced stories in which characters are frequently doubled. Dupin resembles his antagonist the Minister D——, that dupe of duplicity, while "William Wilson" is the classic American treatment of the doppelganger annihilating his own namesake.

Like his last name, Poe's middle name offered enigmas when his foster father disinherited him. No matter how much he craved love or money from the man he once called Pa, now he would get neither. Shortly thereafter Poe dropped the full middle name he had proudly flaunted, signing later letters and works simply with the middle initial A.

But the name he was not legally entitled to bear haunted his imagination as Kenneth Silverman suggests, lurking anagrammatically in a slew of characters christened with abundant double *a*'s and double *l*'s, from Annabel Lee to (perhaps most revealingly) Allamistakeo. Buried in the coffin of his hopes, the lost Allan name seems always about to rear up and confront him. Abandoned as an infant by his natural father, then disinherited by his foster father, Poe had reason to wonder what either of his surnames meant. Partly for this reason, skepticism often tinges the etymological speculations that he culled from authors like Jacob Bryant and H. N. Coleridge for the *Pinakidia* and *Marginalia*. Like Irving, he cultivated the bogus etymology with gusto. "The derivation of the word *cab* is not quite certain," he began one essay.

> According to Dr. Lumberskull, of Gutt-stuffin University, the word comes from the lately discovered antediluvian Arabic. In that language, *caba* means *go-ahead*—hence a cab, a thing for going ahead. But with due deference to the doctor's erudition, we are inclined to think that the word comes from the Greek. In the Island of Naxos, the word *kabos* means *tub*. Now it is believed by some, and we are of that number, that the tub of . . . Diogenes, was not one of your vulgar washingtubs, but a circular box, on wheels, drawn, probably, by a donkey—possibly by a Newfoundland dog. This being the fact, the weight of evidence inclines to the Greek; for the word *kabos* is in Schrevilius, and has not been lost, as we have shown, in the modern dialect. . . . The word cab, however, sounds like English, inasmuch as it expresses the nature of the thing itself, for it has a squat, angular sound—cab! (*Works,* 3:1091-92).

Behind this phlight of phunny phellow phancy lurks an orfan's suspicion that names, like people, all too readily become detached from their origins. Thus given two plausible derivations of the term *weeping willow,* Poe is certain that most philologists would pick the wrong one because they look for more exact correspondence between names and things than exists. "Here then is a subtle source of error which Lord Bacon has neglected," he concludes. "It is an Idol of the Wit" (*Marg.* #47).

Despite his reputation as a grand panjandrum for unity of effect, Poe's aesthetic theory honors his contradictory impulses. In his struggle to apprehend "supernal Loveliness" the poet must juggle the things of this world in "multiform combinations" (*Essays,* pp. 76-77). For Poe the imagination and fancy are allies. By harmonious combinations the imagination strives to suggest a supernal beauty it cannot create or even embody. Juggling combinations until they blur destructively, fancy may try to reveal truth through discords that result in grotesquerie like "The Raven" or arch humor like his poem "Fairy-Land." There is a certain archness in *Eureka,* the long prose poem in which Poe envisioned a finite materialistic universe. Driven by gravitational attraction and electrical repulsion, pulsating like a giant heart, it is quasi-identical with the mind of God. Yearning for unity, its atoms are ceaselessly flung out, then reabsorbed in new combinations, so that the logical principle A = A fails to apply. In the Schlegels such a vision begat the doctrine of Romantic irony, and Poe is very much a Schlegelian.[10]

With the connivance of anthologists, most read Poe solely as the author of tales of terror, as an explorer of abnormal psychology in extremis. But the majority of his sixty-odd stories are clearly humorous. Some are parodies like "A Tale of Jerusalem," a send-up of Horace Smith's novel of that title, where Smith's name was vulgarly anagrammatized in Poe's central character Abel-Shittim. Some tales are whimsies involving grotesque literalization of a key phrase like "Loss of Breath" or "Never Bet the Devil Your Head," which satirizes Transcendentalism's reverence for the physical roots of words. A celebrated instance is "Berenice," where like the modern musical comedy *The Little Shop of Horrors* Poe sports with the idea of a demented dentist. "The history of all Magazines," he explained to his publisher, "shows plainly that those which have attained celebrity were indebted for it to articles *similar in nature — to Berenice*. . . . You ask me in what does this nature consist? In the ludicrous heightened into the grotesque: the fearful coloured into the horrible: the witty exaggerated into the burlesque: the singular wrought out into the strange and mystical" (*Letters,* 1:58).

"You are nearly, but not altogether right in relation to the satire of some of my *Tales*," Poe confessed to a patron who praised him for yoking heterogeneous attitudes with a "*serio tragi comic*" style. "Most of them were intended for half banter, half satire—although I might not have fully acknowledged this to be their aim even to myself" (*Letters,* 1:84). With this tortured concept of intentions beyond his awareness, Poe confessed that his humor was not always under control. Self-parody was his own imp of the perverse. His most strenuous tales of impending dissolution threaten to dissolve their own Gothic machinery at the touch of a stray word or wordplay. His critical prescriptions for total authorial control are just a reaction against the essential waywardness of his verbal fancy.

Thus his Gothic chef d'oeuvre "The Fall of the House of Usher" derives much of its uncanniness from black humor. As the commonsense narrator explains, the title is a pun denoting "both the family and the family mansion." Usher himself is "alternately vivacious and sullen," his normal gloom relieved on occasion by wildly gay improvisations in poetry and music. The narrator nervously intones passages from the

Mad Trist of Sir Lancelot Canning—a bogus romance that parodies Poe's own tale. After hysterical laughter the doomed Usher is borne to the floor by his returning sister. The horrified narrator flees as the house falls. We are left with many ambiguities in the explained Gothic mode, so literalists may cling to scientific and psychological explanations: Madeline revives from an epileptic fit, Usher succumbs to the ill effects of swamp gas or auto-suggestion, and the distraught narrator fails to bethink him that the electrical storm might naturally have triggered a cataclysmic explosion in the copper-lined vault used for storing gunpowder. Yet perhaps—just *perhaps*—the punning title links house and family more intimately than Ben Franklin or Freud would imagine. Usher's speculations about "the sentience of all vegetable things" which "trespassed, under certain conditions, upon the kingdom of inorganization" are buttressed by the narrative footnote to scientific authorities who "have thought thus." Perhaps the isolated Usher family and their crumbling stone house covered with fungi have evolved together in the peculiar "atmosphere which . . . reeked up from the decayed trees, and the gray wall and the silent tarn."[11] Now they constitute one huge, quasi-biological organism, a perverse ecosystem that must expire in toto with the demise of any vital part. Perhaps language is a similar organism. Which is ultimately more unsettling—the linguistic arbitrariness of A. W. Schlegel that issues in Poe's normally jokey, fortuitous puns, or the linguistic determinism of Tooke suggesting that all our words are bound to their roots as inextricably as the two senses of *house*? If the tree of language is a family tree that decays instead of growing, a dead or decadent language, what deformed participles dangle from its branches?

Perched on the bust of Pallas over the door, Poe's notorious raven suggests similar thoughts. The spectacle of a rational dog or parrot "would be in an extreme degree offensive and painful," the popular philosopher Dugald Stewart had claimed. "But why should one look with 'horror' at an animal differing in shape very widely from ourselves, but possessing similar powers of reason and speech?"[12] Poe dramatizes this philosophical conundrum with his usual ambiguity. As his account in "The Philosophy of Composition" explains, after deciding to compose a poem of about one hundred lines, for artistic piquancy he pitched upon the gimmick of a refrain that would produce "continuously novel effects, by the variation of the application," a refrain uttered by "a *non-reasoning* creature capable of speech."[13] This refrain amounts to a running play on words in a poem that deliberately verges on the ludicrous. The bereaved lover first accosts the raven jocularly. Even after its first two replies the bird is "still beguiling my sad fancy into smiling," as he tries to guess what "this ominous bird of yore . . . / Meant in croaking 'Nevermore.'" But gradually startled from his original nonchalance by the melancholy repetition of the word, Poe explains, the lover "wildly propounds queries of a far different character . . . because he experiences a phrenzied pleasure in so modeling his question as to receive from the *expected* 'Nevermore' the most delicious because the most intolerable of sorrow." From the pleasure of solving an enigma the lover passes, then, to the pleasure of framing inverse conundrums, and this sentimental orgy concludes with the first pun in his own right, ostentatiously italicized: "And the Raven, never flitting, still is sitting, *still* is sitting / On the pallid bust of Pallas just above my chamber door."

The lover is lacerated by the memory of Lenore, painful to recall, still more painful to forget. But he is also tyrannized by language, hard to interpret, harder to ignore. Often dismissed as pointless technical virtuosity, the alliteration actually renders the sense of a mind at the mercy of words, buffeted by verbal associations, some significant, some fortuitous. The syncopated rhymes and rhythms *are* vulgar, but they are out of place only if one assumes that the poem seeks to express unmitigated gloom. Close one eye, however, and what one views resembles Emmeline Grangerford's comic mourning scene in *Huck Finn*. "The Philosophy of Composition" to the contrary, Poe's real subject is not seductively plangent melancholy but the grotesqueness of manic-depressive disorder, here dramatized as if highs and lows were occurring at once. *Mournful and Never-ending Remembrance,* the emblematic label that Poe's essay finally proposes for the raven, is oddly blended with scornful and ever-rending amusement at literary clichés. As apt replies accumulate, they become more ominous and more ludicrous at once, for repetition only emphasizes the bird's scant vocabulary, the utter meaninglessness of the word the lover as a man of letters tries with increasing "success" to "interpret." How much of the poem's popularity with the unlettered rests, like "The Philosophy of Composition," on its burlesque of literary criticism?

From Aristophanes on, talking birds have lent themselves to many shades of humor, from the merry to the menacing, blurring the boundaries of our humanity in an eerie way that is the hallmark of the grotesque. Poe's raven is unique in seeming by turns an innocent orphan of the storm, Heckle the cartoon crow croaking for Jeckle, a frightening bird of ill omen, a cuckoo without a clock, a demonic denizen of another world, and a stuffed symbol in search of a critical scarecrow to perch on. Flirting and fluttering gaily between these alternatives makes the poem a memorably unsettling specimen of the grotesque, immune to its rash of parodies because it deftly anticipates them all.

Apropos of "The House of Usher," one contemporary critic claimed that its theme was "the revulsion of feeling consequent upon discovering that for a long period of time we have been mistaking sounds of agony, for those of mirth or indifference."[14] This perceptive comment applies rather well to "The Raven" too. But then its converse also fits both works: they leave us with a feeling of revulsion at having mistaken mirth or indifference for agony. Peculiar tours de force, many of Poe's best works yoke inflated sensationalism with deflationary humor as closely as a pun binds two meanings together. However harrowing, they generally make us wonder whether we are being gulled by a bad joke.

Such individual works fuse tendencies evident throughout his oeuvre as tales parody other tales.[15] In "How to Write a Blackwood Article" the intrepid lady reporter Psyche Zenobia thrusts her head through an aperture in a tower clock to view Edinburgh, then is caught thus. The descending minute hand gradually decapitates her while she dauntlessly details her sensations. Her burlesque encounter with "the ponderous and terrific *Scythe of Time* (for I had now discovered the literal import of that classical phrase)" is echoed at several points in the phraseology of "The Pit and the Pendulum," that harrowing and apparently straightforward account of impending vivisection by a giant blade (*Works*, 2:353–54). But the more Poe one reads the less straightforwardness is apparent. Like converging comets, his sparkling burlesques and livid horror stories seem to attract each other gravitationally, narrowly miss, then pinwheel round each other eternally twinned. With its deadpan claim of a transatlantic flight in 1844, "The Balloon Hoax" drew crowds that bought out an extra edition for the *New York Sun*. Later Poe burlesqued it in "Mellonta Tauta," a mock balloon voyage supposedly undertaken by the lady correspondent Pundita on 1 April 2848, a millenium after its publication. But both the hyperrealistic hoax and the satiric allegory had their origins in "Hans Pfaall" (1835). With a burlesque frame enclosing an enthusiastic account of the possibility of space travel, this balloon trip to the moon veers erratically between spoof and science fiction. Uncertain how to proceed because of his contradictory impulses, Poe later refined the theme in two opposite styles, each still bearing the seeds of the other. "King Pest" burlesques "The Masque of the Red Death." Other comic inversions of obsessive Poe themes include "The Premature Burial" and "Spectacles," which spoofs his preoccupation with incest and double identity by having a nearsighted young man fall in love with his own great-great-grandmother. Indeed, the first two paragraphs of Poe's horrific masterpiece "Ligeia" were simply recycled to begin his prophetic satire of media manipulation in American politics, "The Man Who Was Used Up: A Tale of the Late Bugaboo and Kickapoo Campaign," thereby setting what may be a record for extended narrative double entendres.

The trailblazing tales of ratiocination were followed by "Thou Art the Man," which has been called the first comic detective story. With "a tone of unsuitable levity," the narrator leads us through a complicated and deceptive plot, unmasking an unlikely murderer at the end by having the body of his victim rear up to accuse him (*Works,* 3:1042). Ventriloquism and a spring explain the hoax. When coffins are prised open in Poe's tales, what pops out may be either a corpse or a jack-in-the-box. "Thou Art the Man" foregrounds an element of playfulness common to all Poe's pioneering detective stories, as well as to most by his successors. Dupin's narrator-friend marvels at the taste for *bizarrerie* and "wild whims" that leads the detective to conclude that investigating the brutal murders in the Rue Morgue "will afford us amusement." As the Watsonesque sidekick observes, "I thought this an odd term, so applied, but said nothing." The opening defines the analytic temperament as one "fond of enigmas, of conundrums, of hieroglyphics; exhibiting in his solutions of each a degree of *acumen* which appears to the ordinary apprehension praeternatural." In his debut story this prototypical literary detective demonstrates his acumen by following a train of unspoken thoughts to their conclusion and apparently reading his friend's mind. He deciphers facial expressions as the language of physiognomy and tracks the mind through punning interactions with the environment. "Here your countenance brightened up, and, perceiving your lips move, I could not doubt that you murmured the word 'stereotomy,' a term very affectedly applied to this species of pavement," Dupin explains. "I knew that you could not say to yourself 'stereotomy' without being brought to think of atomies, and thus of the theories of Epicurus" (*Works,* 2:528–46). The detective genre popularized by Poe neutralizes the brutality of murder by encouraging the reader to approach it as a puzzle to be solved through speculation akin to etymological wordplay.

By contrast, *The Narrative of Arthur Gordon Pym* (1838) seethes with more brutality and violence than its etymological wordplay can tame. So hoaxical is the framework of authorial disclaimers, so poorly plotted the implausible narrative, and so melodramatic the violence of this polar voyage that one suspects much running parody upon boys' pulp adventure stories, bedizened haphazardly with symbolic implications.[16] Even so, the impact is powerful. Toward the end the reader is thoughtfully provided with sketches of the dark labyrinth within which Pym finds himself (the looping recesses of which strongly resemble human entrails, the favorite diet of the native black Tsalalians) and of the mysterious petroglyphs on its walls. Footnotes point out that the petroglyphs represent the Ethiopian verbal root "To be shady," the Arabic verbal root "To be white," and the Egyptian word meaning "the region of the south" (pp. 207-8). Indeed they do, for Poe culled the words from Gesenius's *Lexicon* and other authorities. Perhaps he intended to identify the Tsalalians as demonic Hamitic offspring of a lost tribe of Israel, whose depraved language mires spiritual meaning in physical fact.[17] But this flirtation with etymology functions mainly as a teaser, hinting at more meaning than the story probably could deliver if completed. Psychoanalytic criticism sees the nine-month voyage as a regression to primitive society and infantile behavior. The strange speech of the Tsalalians sounds like aggressive baby talk. Burying the visiting whites beneath a mountain of dirt, theirs seems a society deficient in toilet training. By the same token, their petroglyphs may be crap, serving mainly to mark the way in which etymological analysis of written language must grind to a halt, unable to capture in black-and-white print the essence of prelinguistic behavior. "Silence is the voice of God," wrote the young Poe, lamenting that "Ours is a world of words" (*Works*, 1:104). But his "Sonnet—Silence" and his prose parable "Silence—A Fable" portray the hush of inhuman nature as the ultimate horror. Corresponding perhaps in white to the black petroglyph of a man with outstretched arms, the gigantic white figure whom Pym confronts at the end is awesomely ambiguous, not least as to gender. To read this riddle language seems of no avail; the only solution is dissolution. One suspects that Poe's Ethiopian root hinting at a connection between Tsalal and the wisdom of Solomon is *shady* in several respects.

Achieving a press circulation of some three hundred thousand copies, "The Gold-Bug" was Poe's most popular story and remains one of the best-known in the world. Its cryptographer hero the impoverished southern aristocrat Legrand bears obvious analogies to Poe, not the least in being "subject to perverse moods of alternate enthusiasm and melancholy," according to the rather obtuse narrator (*Works*, 3:806-44). He interprets the parchment with a death's head at one corner and a drawing of a young goat at the other as carrying "a kind of punning or hieroglyphical signature" for Captain Kidd. This lets him establish and then decode "the text for my context," since the pun on Kidd is possible only in English. With etymological insight he links Kidd's reference to Bishop's Hostel with an ancient Negro's memories of a place called Bessop's Castle—and wins a chest of gold to revive his family fortunes. "The bug, which gives title to the story, is used only in the way of mystification," one contemporary critic noted, "having throughout a seeming and no real connection with the subject."[18] As Legrand himself emphasizes afterward, the "accidents and coincidences" that led him to the treasure were so extraordinary that chance aided him as much as deduction. But though in one sense a false lead, the insect does precipitate Legrand's discovery. "Jupiter's silly words, about the bug being of solid gold, had a remarkable effect on my fancy," he explains. He is "bitten" by the gold-bug in entertaining two senses in which the insect can be called gold, while resolving its resemblance to a skull into sheer coincidence. Using language with due awareness of both its logic and its arbitrariness, its grammar and its referents, he maps it scientifically onto the Carolina terrain and solves Kidd's conundrum. Oscillating between melancholy and mania, between sullen skull and sportive kid, Legrand's imagination fuses both perspectives in final triumph by reading the bug warily as a visual and verbal pun.

Links between visual, verbal, and musical languages were stressed by Cotesworth P. Bronson, a leading figure in the elocutionary movement who lectured widely and was usually addressed as "Professor." His *Abstract of Elocution and Music* (1842) was expanded into *Elocution; or, Mental and Vocal Philosophy* (Louisville: Morton & Griswold, 1845). This standard text saw many editions. To inculcate good speech habits he mingled musical analogies, plates illustrating gestures, and literary texts. Puns figured frequently in his text as specimens of pedagogical and oratorical wit. Zeal for untrammeled expression made him advocate a practice he called *Laughing Scientifically*:

> The following suggestions are given for the formation of *laughing glee clubs*; in the hope that this remarkably *healthful* and *anti-melancholy* exercise, may aid in accomplishing its very beneficial effect in *old* and *young*, *male* and *female*. Let a number of persons, say six, or eight, form a circle, sitting, or standing, erectly, with the shoulders thrown back, and the leader commence, by giving one laugh, in the use of the syllable *huh*: then, let the one at his right hand repeat it, which is to be reiterated by each one till it comes round; then, without any loss of time, let the leader *repeat* the word, adding another, (huh, huh,) . . . till there follows a complete round of shouts, and roars of laughter. (p. 77)

If scientific laughter did not avert melancholy, the professor stood ready to vent that by other avenues. His textbook waged war on inhibition by classifying all the passions and encouraging their full expression vocally and physiognomically. "In the *vowel* sounds of our language, are involved all the elements of music," he felt, making "Elocution and Music . . . inseparable in their nature" (p. 34). Bronson met Poe in the summer of 1847, despondent about his wife's death and his poverty, and urged him to write something for recitation.

The result was "Ulalume," shaped, as were "The Bells" and "Annabel Lee" subsequently, to show off an elocutionist's vocal gamut. "*U*, when long, at the beginning of a word, or syllable, is preceded by the consonant sound of *y*: i.e., it has this *consonant* and its own *vowel* sound," Bronson advised pupils. "Never pronounce duty, *dooty* . . . Sound all the syllables full, for a time, regardless of sense" (p. 28). The unique fantasia that Poe created shows him an apt pupil indeed, chewing each syllable lingeringly while eschewing sense. Of scientific laughing there is none, but of methodical musical mourning there is so much that it may well stir laughter. In the last stanza Psyche and the speaker break into a formal duet that virtually drowns out the painful meaning. Reviewing it, N. P. Willis recognized as much by calling it "a curiosity . . . and a delicious one . . . in its philologic flavor."[19] Poe's assault on referential language mirrors the speaker's effort to escape the memory of his lost love. Both fail, but by the narrowest of margins. Much as he wishes to, the speaker cannot forget Ulalume; much as he tries, Poe cannot quite write nonsense.

Also mingling anguish and amusement, Poe's quintessential tale may be "The Cask of Amontillado" so often tapped by anthologists. "A wrong is unredressed when retribution overtakes its redresser," says Montresor. "It is equally unredressed when the avenger fails to make himself felt as such to him who has done the wrong" (*Works*, 3:1256–63). Revenge as he defines it is a species of irony, for it requires a secret meaning concealed from most but disclosed to the victim. From this central irony flow the myriad ironies of the tale. Montresor's anticipatory smile at his victim is misunderstood as goodwill. By ordering his servants to remain at home he ensures their disappearance, by discouraging Fortunato he lures him on. "I shall not die of a cough," says the victim. "True—true," replies Montresor. The name of that wealthy unfortunate means either *lucky* or *fated*. He marches drunkenly to his doom in a jester's costume. Quizzing Montresor in sign language to learn if he "is of the masons," he is answered with the visual pun of the trowel. When nearly immured, Fortunato suddenly speaks in a changed voice, "a sad voice" that forlornly insists, "Ha! ha! ha!—he! he!—a very good joke indeed—an excellent jest." Montresor persistently repeats Fortunato's words, loading them with double meanings, and the climax comes in an orgy of repetition:

'... Let us begone'
'Yes' I said, 'let us be gone.'
'*For the love of God, Montresor.*'
'Yes,' I said, 'for the love of God!'

We are left with the dark irony of an honor-bound aristocrat punningly invoking religious faith as a reason to murder a parvenu freethinker of the Masons. He hints at the possibility of a guilty conscience, but that may be only a jibe at the reader's assumptions. "My heart grew sick—on account of the dampness of the catacombs." That the tale may be told as a death-bed confession to a priest, yet lacks clear signs of repentance, only deepens the ironies. "*In pace requiescat!*" concludes Montresor. We are left to wonder whether he relishes the peace of absolution or relishes a piece of absolute revenge, for his final words may twist a solemn prayer for the soul's repose into a gleeful wish that a body go undiscovered.

What did Poe think composing such savage revenge fantasies as this and "Hop-Frog" in his last years while smarting from the Wars of the Literati? The avenging jester Hop-Frog clearly escapes unscathed and unrepentant, thumbing his nose at all Poe's previous tales stressing that murder will out. But in the case of Montresor we really cannot say. In that respect Poe victimizes his reader much as Montresor victimizes Fortunato, avenging his injuries openly but leaving the insult undefined. Even if we let Montresor include us among those "who know so well the nature of my soul," that may not make us privy to his creator's. "In the construction of *plot*, for example, in fictitious literature, we should aim at so arranging the incidents, that we shall not be able to determine, of any one of them, whether it depends from any one other or upholds it," Poe would shortly argue in *Eureka* (1848). "In this sense, of course, *perfection* of *plot* is really, or practically, unattainable—but only because it is a finite intelligence that constructs. The plots of God are perfect. The universe is a plot of God's."[20] But like *Eureka*, "The Cask of Amontillado" may be only a striking plot of Poe's. Is the last sentence of the story piety? or blasphemy? or some barely conceivable fusion of the two, welded together in a pun? Through mordant Romantic irony Poe revenges himself after death upon readers who could not know him when alive.

The Spell of a Scarlet Letter

"He is to a considerable degree ironical—this is part of his charm—part, even, one may say, of his brightness; but he is neither bitter nor cynical—he is rarely even what I should call tragical." Unlike Melville, who lauded his friend's intuitive power of blackness, Henry James claimed that

Hawthorne's fancy found "license to amuse itself" by picking Puritan morality for its "playground." We tend to see Hawthorne through Melville's eyes, so James's urbane demurrer comes as a tonic. "There have been observers more humorous, more hilarious," James allows, "though on the whole Hawthorne's observation has a smile in it oftener than may at first appear; but there has rarely been an observer more serene, less agitated . . . and less disposed to call things deeply into question."[21]

"Your picture gallery of auxiliary verbs is an admirable fantasy," wrote Hawthorne to his fiancée. Sophia Peabody studied Hebrew for recreation, but on this occasion her artistic demon made her draw auxiliary verbs.[22] Her grammatical caricatures vastly amused Hawthorne. "You are certainly the first mortal to whom it was given to behold a verb; though, it seems as if they ought to be visible, being creatures whose office it is (if I remember my Grammar aright) 'to be, to do, and to suffer.' Therein is comprehended all that we mortals are capable of." But he toyed with this fancy only to reject it strenuously. "No; for according to this definition, verbs do not feel, and cannot enjoy—they only exist, and act, and are miserable. My Dove and I are no verbs—or if so, we are passive verbs, and therefore happy ones."[23] Here the author whom Melville heard pealing forth No! in thunder thunderously proclaims his desire to be a passive verb. He challenges grammar, not the universe, staging a mock rebellion against Lindley Murray rather than Jehovah.

Verbal high jinks like Sophia's had intrigued him from his schoolboy days under the lexicographer Joseph Emerson Worcester. "Of all Lexicographers, you seem to me best to combine a sense of the *sacredness* of language with a recognition of the changes which time and human vicissitude inevitably work upon it," he later assured his old tutor (18:376). By comparison he faulted his school in Maine for "not being dear enough . . . and not near enough" (15:112). At Bowdoin he proved a tolerable Latinist but an indifferent student. Budding politicos honed their skills in florid eloquence, but Hawthorne refused to declaim, paying fines for nonparticipation. Instead he took the lead in organizing the Pot-8-o Club, a secret society whose members roasted spuds and each other's compositions. After graduation he returned to Salem and set about making himself an author.

To relieve the solitude of his garret, over the next decade he read his way through some seven hundred volumes from the Athenaeum. Among them were John Wilkins's *Essay Toward a Real Character and Philosophical Language* (1668), Joseph Ames's *Typographical Antiquities* (1749), and James Rush's *Philosophy of the Human Voice* (1833). Domestically, the Hawthornes cultivated a semiprivate punning language that led Nathaniel to use etymological aliases like Theodore, Diodate, and de L'Aubepine. His notebooks show him playing around with ideas for stories, often by playing around with words or letters. Perhaps reflecting his reading of Tooke, one abortive project was "to personify If—But—And—Though—&c" (8:242). For future use he jotted down the name "Miss Polly Syllable—a schoolmistress" (8:236). In a more serious etymological vein he thought "Pearl—the English of Margaret— a pretty name for a girl in a story" (8:242). He was inspired to toy with graphic fantasies by perusing such a volume as Edmund Fry's *Pantographia* (1799), which featured handsome plates illustrating all the known alphabets in the world, including *lettres fleuries* in the shape of men, animals, and flowers, as well as ornamental English A's from the eighth to the sixteenth centuries. "Letters in the shape of figures of men &c." he mused. "At a distance the words composed by the letters were alone distinguishable. Close at hand, the figures alone were seen, and not distinguished as letters. Thus things may have a positive, a relative, and a composite meaning, when seen at the proper distance &."[24] Here was a vision of people dissolving into letters and vice versa, moralized via multiple meanings.

Elsewhere he sports with fancies to no very clear purpose. A man trying to kindle a fire with fireflies "would be symbolical of something" (*LN,* p. 80). A meditation about the main gas pipe of a city "might be made emblematical of something" (*LN,* p. 56). Verbal fancifulness could spark the genesis of fictional characters. "To make literal pictures of figurative expressions," Hawthorne mused, "for instance, he burst into tears—a man suddenly turned into a shower of briny drops. An explosion of laughter—a man blowing up, and his fragments flying about on all sides. He cast his eyes on the ground—a man standing eyeless, with his eyes on the ground, staring up at him in wonderment" (8:254).

But just before this entry the writer who entertained such whimsies had jotted down an idea about "the life of a woman, who, by the old colony law, was condemned always to wear the letter A, sewed on her garment, in token of her having committed adultery." That too could be made emblematical of something, of many things—of anything? Hester Prynne was created by an author who used wordplay to discover the meanings of his stories. By his own admission his sketches were written only half in earnest to display "the art of extracting the mirth which lies hidden like latent caloric in almost everything."[25] Writing in Concord, he felt free "to utter the extremest nonsense, or the profoundest wisdom, or that etherial product of the mind which partakes of both, and may become one or the other" (10:24).

Among the books from the Salem Athenaeum that Hawthorne perused during his apprenticeship was Charles Davy's *Conjectural Observations on the Origin and Progress of Alphabetical Writings* (London, 1772). Davy mistrusted the ambiguity of Egyptian hieroglyphics, for symbolic characters could only breed vague interpretations and religious absurdities. Such pictographs encouraged the Israelites to worship idols after leaving Egypt. Together with the Ten Commandments, alphabetic writing was first revealed to the Hebrews in the wilderness by Divine Providence, according to Davy, "to put a stop to the progress of the contagion" (p. 54). The clarity of a phonetic alphabet squeezed out all undesirable ambiguity. "Alpha was pronounced with a considerable aperture of the mouth," Davy explained. "Now nothing could more exactly represent the opening of the lips in profile for the purpose than the character of this letter reclined, in which the cross has delineated or pointed out the situation of the teeth; though this letter was afterwards erected for the sake of taking up less room" (pp. 84-85). With such mnemonic aids Jehovah encouraged proper penmanship and pronunciation, offering the Decalogue as an unambiguous ethical primer.

Hawthorne took a more complex view of the Ten Commandments, including the Seventh. And he could hardly agree with Davy that a phonetic alphabet eliminated ambiguity and idolatry. His college instructor in philosophy Thomas Upham stressed a hermeneutic approach to language like Dugald Stewart's. "When we look upon the page of an author we say it has meaning or that it is full of thought," argued Upham in the first important American philosophical textbook, "whereas in truth, in consequence of a long continued and obstinate association, of which we are hardly sensible ourselves, we transport the meaning or thought out of ourselves and spread it upon the page. The thought or meaning is in ourselves, but is placed by us, through the means of a casual but very strong association, in the written marks, which are before us."[26] Writing offers no escape from ambiguity unless it makes a reader confront ambiguities within himself. College philosophy had taught Hawthorne that Davy's view of the alphabet still verges on verbal idolatry. With remarkable ingenuity, his greatest novel rings changes on potential meanings of the first letter of the alphabet. The word *adultery* never appears in the book, and alternatives proliferate: A = Angel? the Almighty? Authority? Adam? Able? Art? Arthur? Amor? the Absurd?

"Mother dear, what does this scarlet letter mean?—and why dost thou wear it on thy bosom?—and why does the minister keep his hand over his heart?" So asks seven-year-old Pearl, whose "inevitable tendency to hover about the enigma of the scarlet letter seemed an innate quality of her being." In her isolation Hester craves sympathy, but she can neither repent her passion nor frankly avow her sexuality to her daughter. "Silly Pearl," she replies, "what questions are these? There are many things in this world that a child must not ask about. What know I of the minister's heart? And as for the scarlet letter, I wear it for the sake of its gold thread!" Dismissing the question of meaning, her answer suggests that the letter exists only as a physical ornament, pointing to nothing beyond itself. For the first time in seven years she is "false to the symbol on her bosom," for one of her motives in wearing it is surely to accentuate a bosom of which she is proud (1:179-81). Pearl's questions are not silly. Though Hawthorne flirts with Hester's notion that signs may be forms without referents, he here treats as a serious lapse her refusal to read the symbol, to supply a serious meaning of her own and "spread it upon the page," in Upham's words. Interpreting the alphabet is far more difficult than philologists like Davy imagined. But that people read the letter A in many different ways does not make it so indeterminate as to be meaningless. Initially contradictory, its multiple meanings finally come to seem complementary.

The Puritan community may seem excessive in its reverence for authority, its reliance on the letter of the law. But in Pearl we confront the alternative. Resembling both her mother and father, the girl is "the living hieroglyphic" of the secret Hester and Dimmesdale seek to hide (1:207). She is "the scarlet letter in another form; the scarlet letter endowed with life." This resemblance her mother carefully enhances by clothing her in a peculiar crimson velvet tunic, abundantly embroidered, lavishing "many hours of morbid ingenuity, to create an analogy between the object of her affection, and the emblem of her guilt and torture. But, in truth, Pearl was the one, as well as the other." The analogy Hester fancies herself to be creating is in fact an identity, and not always a healthy one. In temperament the girl "seemed the unpremeditated offshoot of a passionate moment." Ostracized by other children and teased, she screams horrifically and pursues her persecutors like "an infant pestilence,—the scarlet fever, or some such half-fledged angel of judgment" (1:102-3). Whether or not Pearl is an awesome pestilential scourge, at times she is surely an awful pest. Amid all her charming freaks Hawthorne never lets us lose sight of an unruliness that suggests a delinquent in the making. Dancing on gravestones, covering her mother's dress with prickly burrs, spattering the Governor from a cattle-trough, she prompts Chillingworth to ask Dimmesdale, "Is the imp altogether evil. Hath she affections? Hath she any discoverable principle of being?" "None, save the freedom of a broken law," answers the minister quietly. "Whether capable of good, I know not" (1:134).

Pearl is indeed capable of good, but she needs the law to develop it. Her untrammeled self-expressiveness could use some of the restraining authority that weighs so heavily on Puritan discourse. In the simplest human terms, this child needs the fatherly discipline that her parents' passionate, undisciplined act has denied her. Her nature "lacked reference and adaptation to the world into which she was born" (1:91). Despite her fantasy of being plucked from a rose bush, that world is a social world, as Hawthorne well knows. Like her behavior, her language sometimes lacks social or semantic reference. Promising to identify Chillingworth to her father, "Pearl mumbled something into his ear, that sounded indeed like human language, but was only...gibberish" (1:156). Pearl is no happy passive verb but a hyperactive one. She needs parsing. Tinged faintly with diabolism, her nonsensical childish utterance must accommodate itself to social and grammatical rules. When her "errand as a messenger of anguish was all fulfilled," that is what finally allows her to join the world as a woman (1:256).

While much in the novel suggests the relativism of human values, not all of Hawthorne's linguistic reading did. James Rush's musical analysis of speech posited "two essentially different modes of expressing the various states of mind." Passions, shared by men and brutes, are deeply lodged "in the voice and in other muscular functions" and can be universally understood. But attitudes rooted in human intelligence and social relations lack such natural signs. "Thus there are natural expressions both in the vocal organs and in other parts of the body, for pain . . . but none of any definite character for hope."[27] When Dimmesdale's Election Sermon prophesies a glorious future for New England, what impresses folk is "a certain deep, sad undertone of pathos." The plaintive, wavelike semitones of his voice convey a meaning to distant auditors "entirely apart from its indistinguishable words. These, perhaps, if more distinctly heard, might have been only a grosser medium, and have clogged the spiritual sense" (1:147-49). Arguing that whereas the nonverbal language of nature can well express grief or pain, "fortitude . . . remorse . . . or generosity . . . must be shown in action, or, described in words," Rush's theory sharply distinguishes Dimmesdale's Election Sermon from his final confession on the scaffold (p. 343).

In his wry prefatory sketch "The Custom-House," Hawthorne pretends first to have encountered the scarlet letter as "a riddle which . . . I saw little hope of solving" (1:31). In one sense the book is indeed a riddle. We too readily forget that among other things, A = Amusement. In the chapter "The New England Holiday" Hawthorne remarks that the Puritans in the story, though somber, were by no means humorless but rather "the offspring of sires who had known how to be merry in their day" (1:165). The American descendants of the original settlers, by contrast, "wore the blackest shade of Puritanism, and so darkened the national visage with it, that . . . [we] have yet to learn again the forgotten art of gayety" (1:165). Her high spirits make Pearl the book's preeminent virtuosa in that art. Perhaps her preternatural vivacity was itself a disease, Hawthorne shrewdly adds, "but the reflex of the wild energy with which Hester had fought against her sorrows, before Pearl's birth" (1:184). As the conscious and unconscious creation of Hester's ideals, Pearl embodies the humor of heartbreak that figures notably in her mother—the love of fancy and fantasy demonstrated in Hester's embroidery, the playfulness that makes her often feel "a sportive impulse . . . in the midst of her deepest suffering" (1:98). If *The Scarlet Letter* is an entertaining riddle, Hester makes it so.

But in what sense does A = Answer? If the scarlet letter is a riddle, it is one that Hawthorne professes "little hope of solving." When its office is done, he is eager to erase it from his brain, where meditation has fixed it in "very undesirable distinctness." A riddle requires a solution, whereas no one interpretation promises to "solve" the novel to his satisfaction. Therefore we may do better to think of the book as a vastly expanded etymological pun, where various meanings of *A* can simultaneously be true. Since the riddle cannot be solved, different meanings are resolved, like desynonymized derivatives, into one shadowy original *logos,* in a manner reminiscent of Coleridge and Bushnell.[28] "Distinctness" hardly helps us understand the scarlet letter because it fosters exclusive interpretations of the form "either A or B"—either society or the individual, either men or women, either justice or mercy. Instead Hawthorne invites us to envision the scarlet letter as "both A_1 and A_2"—both change and continuity, both nature and culture, both gloom and gaiety. Like an Emersonian bipolar unity, such a word must be indistinct, so in contrast to Davy's enlightened alphabet A = Ambiguity. Within the novel distinct interpretations breed conflict, whereas the ambiguity of the scarlet letter is a sign of tolerance: A = Accommodation. In its glowing shadow Dimmesdale learns to show mercy to himself and dies penitent; with the dowry left her by old Roger Chillingworth a humanized Pearl marries happily; and in a spirit of reconciliation Hester and the Puritans are transformed, accepting their mutual dependency, each embracing on faith what neither can understand in the other.

For all its Christian coloring, this reconciling vision of accommodation is also a blueprint for a liberal, pluralistic society.[29] Indeed, Hawthorne's political convictions as a northern Democrat who supported Franklin Pierce are clearer than his religious views. Appearing in the 1850s as America slid down the slope to the Civil War, the novel's plea for accommodation embraced northerners and southerners. Slavery was among the mysterious flaws that Hawthorne, unlike John Brown, was willing to tolerate in the name of higher unity. Gazing from the window of his fiction like an observer in one novel, he found himself "getting pretty well acquainted with that little portion of the backside of the universe which it presented to my view" (3:148). With no burning desire for closer encounters, he was still curious about it. As its satiric preface "The Custom-House" demonstrates, the author of *The Scarlet Letter* was not politically naive. But partisanship made it hard for a writer to get an ampler view of the universal backside. He needed distance. Hence all the Romantic ironies of the preface, where Hawthorne as historical narrator evades paternity for the scarlet letter much as Dimmesdale evades paternity for Pearl. Hence the deliberate thinness of historical texture in the story, where most key elements of Puritan theology go unmentioned while the community's patriarchs are so busy ruling that they never appear at work or among their families. Hence, in short, Hawthorne's theory of the romance.

His books tried to create "a mood in which all imaginative people . . . love to indulge. In this frame of mind, they sometime find their profoundest truths side by side with the idlest jest, and utter one or the other, apparently without distinguishing which is the most valuable, or assigning any considerable value to either." This form of fantasy, half-serious, half-mirthful, takes one "into a certain airy region, lifting up—as it is so pleasant to feel them lifted— . . . heavy earthy feet from the actual soil of life." The world is "set afloat, as it were, for a moment" (4:16). What he describes is of course Romantic irony.

Hawthorne's irony in *The Scarlet Letter* involves tender mockery, not the sardonic, self-annihilating laughter vented at memorable moments by characters like Dimmesdale, Young Goodman Brown, Robin Molyneux, and Ethan Brand. In a letter to his friend Horatio Bridge he wondered whether the Custom-House preface was sunny enough to balance the book. As for the main narrative, he wrote, "it is— (I hope Mrs. Bridge is not present)—positively a h-ll-fired story, into which I found it almost impossible to throw any cheering light" (16:312). Thank goodness, A = Almost!

Fortunately, Hawthorne wrote fiction with one eye on readers like Mrs. Bridge. In the epistemological debates spawned by British empiricism there figured a celebrated experiment that he had doubtless encountered. The surgeon William Cheselden reported to Locke the result of a cataract operation that gave sudden sight to a boy blind from birth. "Now scarlet he thought the most beautiful of all colors," runs the report as anthologized by Hawthorne's college philosophy professor, "whereas the first time he saw black it gave him great uneasiness, yet after a little time he was reconciled to it."[30] This naif's instinctive attraction to scarlet as "most gay" suggests an innate value in that hue more perdurable than the dark. Hawthorne knew that even the blind need light to see blackness. Annihilating its own nihilism in a spirit of Romantic irony, the scarlet letter dances through the book like a pun, casting its spell, shadowing meanings, illumining the shadows it casts.

The Whale's Tale and Other Literary Flukes

Melville's schooling commenced auspiciously enough at the private New York Male High School, which was led by a devotee of Cardellian philosophical parsing. But whatever first principles of grammar he imbibed did not extend to spelling the name of that science aright. "This is the third letter that I ever wrote so you must not think it will be very good," the nine-year-old schoolboy explained to his grandmother. "I now study Geography, Gramar, Arithmetic, Writing, Speaking, Spelling and read in the Scientific class book."[31] Advanced to the dignity of monitor, he surprised his father by emerging as the best speaker in the elementary division. But with the decline of the family's fortunes twelve-year-old Herman was forced to withdraw from the Albany Academy to clerk in a bank, and later attendance for a couple of terms left him almost completely ignorant of Latin. Shouldering responsibility for his own district school at the age of eighteen made Herman "intimately . . . acquainted with . . . those evils which . . . exist in Common-Schools," he explained to an affectionate uncle. One was physical danger, for there is an anecdote that he was once booted out of his schoolroom by two oversized students. He "established a system in my mode of instruction"—apparently by sizing up the "charactars" of the biggest "schollars" disposed to challenge it and then thrashing them. This afforded the fledgling pedagogue "a few intervals which I improve by occasional writting & reading."[32] Indeed, despite his membership in the Philologus Debating Society, his spelling still needed improvement. In a tempestuous newspaper controversy with its former president Charles Van Loon he could pun briskly enough about that worthy's being in the van of brainless loons, but his own letters to the fray were signed alternately "Philologian" and "Philologean." Evidently the society cultivated scant philological nicety in its members. A merchant voyage to Liverpool was followed by another brief spell of schoolmastering, but after a term that petered out like his first. Unable to find work elsewhere, by the end of 1840 he had signed on with the whaler *Acushnet*. "The transition is a keen one, I assure you, from a schoolmaster to a sailor," Ishmael explains in *Moby-Dick*, especially "if just previous to putting your hand into the tar-pot you have been lording it as a country schoolmaster, making the tallest boys stand in awe of you" (6:6). For a depressed young man whose haphazard encounters with formal education had not been notably successful, shipping out seemed better than suicide. "A whale-ship was my Yale College and my Harvard," cries Ishmael, mocking his own prior avatar as the pale Usher who supplies the opening etymological extracts: "He loved to dust his old grammars; it somehow mildly reminded him of his mortality" (6:112, xv).

After four years of seafaring, Melville returned to New York to begin mining his adventures for *Typee* (1846) and the early novels that followed that best-seller. With his new riches he acquired not only a wife but a thirty-seven-volume set of translated Greco-Roman classics that he had never read in the original—and three copies of Webster's *Dictionary* to boot. He also acquired new friends among the literati of New York City known as Young America. They enlisted his services for the comic weekly *Yankee Doodle*, to which he contributed "Authentic Anecdotes of 'Old Zack,'" seven facetious installments about the hero of the Mexican War. One typical joke described the general's anger when an enemy shell disturbed his dinner by flipping a pie-pan onto his head. "I 'spect you go now, Massa, lick the Mexicans," chortles his comic slave Sambo. "You armed *cap a pie*—cause ain't you got the hot pie for a cap, ha ha!" (9:224). Self-education evidently drove Sambo to consult Webster's just as much as did Melville. This elephantine jest reveals an author wading into the journalistic punning of the era while honoring Young America's hopes for a native literature founded on Rabelaisean humor.

Typee (1846) contained just two puns and *Omoo* (1847) only three.[33] But as Melville veered into the orbit of Young America, his wordplay increased sharply. There are six puns in *Redburn* (1849), sixteen in *White-Jacket* (1850), and twenty-nine in *Mardi* (1849). An exuberant linguistic skepticism colors his wordplay. "What's the use of bein' *snivelized*?" asks a cynical sailor in *Redburn* (4:100). "Dogma . . . should be thrown to the dogs," *Mardi* proclaims, and that satiric allegory strives to realize that aim (3:290). Without the classical training to trace roots, Melville was predisposed to the Johnsonian etymological skepticism underpinning the claim that "words are but algebraic signs, conveying no meaning except what you please" (3:269). Babbalanja, the book's philosophical jester, ponders "the essence of things; the mystery that lieth beyond; the elements of the tear which much laughter provoketh; that which is beneath the seeming" (3:352). When King Media merrily remarks, "No pastime is lost time," wordplay melds jest and earnest. "My lord, that maxim may be good as it stands," solemnly puns Babbalanja, "but had you made six words of it instead of six syllables, you had uttered a better and a deeper" (3:212).

Into the making of *Moby-Dick* (1851) Melville poured both his own past times, his hypos, and Ishmael's pastimes, his puns. The metaphysical chaos that the book seeks to anatomize is insistently rendered in oxymorons. Thrown from his "madly merry" craft into the vast expanse of ocean, with no "gloomy-jolly" tambourine to play, Pip has his unsettling vision of "the joyous, heartless, ever-juvenile eternities." What he sees is akin to Schlegel's Abounding Fullness. Gauged by mortal Reason this self-contradictory vision seems "absurd and frantic" yet "celestial." Ineffable, it leaves man feeling "uncompromised, indifferent as his God" (6:411–14). Pip's detached madness is but one manifestation of the Romantic irony in which the book abounds. Another is the allusive, elusive, intrusive Ishmael, sometimes a character in the past time of the story, sometimes a survivor embroidering it as a present pastime, and sometimes so self-annihilating a narrator as to seem just Herman Melville himself, undermining the credibility of his main fiction with a flaunting medley of other genres. These range from etymological florilegium, dictionary, essay, sermon, encyclopedia, whaling handbook, and travel narrative through short story, satire, blank-verse drama, prose poem, and epic romance.

Among the subgenres Melville cultivates in this olla-podrida are the pun and the dirty joke. There are at least fifty-eight puns in *Moby-Dick*, more than in all his earlier books combined. "Like so many ant-hills of powder, they all stand before me," puns Ahab grimly after facing down his crew, "and I their match. Oh, hard: that to fire others, the match itself must needs be wasting!" (6:168). The book's explosive humor is sometimes scatological. Ambergris results from dyspepsia in the whale, explains Ishmael. "How to cure such a dyspepsia it were hard to say," he adds, "unless by administering three or four boat loads of Brandreth's pills, and then running out of harm's way, as laborers do in blasting rock" (6:408–9). Sometimes scatology shades into sexual humor, as in the description of the bull whale's harem or the sentimentality experienced by sailors squeezing out sperm in what looks like a circle jerk. The dissection of the bull-whale's penis, "the grandissimus, as the mariners call it," sets up the bawdiest pun in the book.³⁴ Flayed and stretched, the jet pelt is converted into a "cassock" for the sailor who presides religiously over the process of mincing blubber for boiling into thin slices called "bible leaves." Arrayed in phallic canonicals of "decent black; occupying a conspicuous pulpit; intent on bible leaves," Melville concludes, "what a candidate for an archbishoprick, what a lad for a Pope were this mincer" (6:420).

With his "almost impious good-humor" the *Pequod*'s second mate Stubb is the book's purest incarnation of the comic spirit (6:119). A sick old whale defecates in fear, making the water behind him bubble malodorously. "Who's got some paregoric?" cries Stubb. "Lord, think of having half an acre of stomach-ache!" (6:352). With old Fleece the cook he stages an impromptu minstrel show, ordering that worthy to preach his mock sermon to sharks. The sunny calms that inspire Starbuck with dogged faith and prompt Ahab to ponder his own agnosticism make the second mate treat the sea as his native element: "I am Stubb, and Stubb has his history; but here Stubb takes oaths that he has always been jolly" (6:492). In Stubb's philosophy "a laugh's the wisest, easiest answer to all that's queer," so he sedulously takes the humorous view of life.³⁵ "I know not all that may be coming, but be what it will, I'll go to it laughing," he early promises, "such a waggish leering as lurks in all your horribles!" (6:171). He braves the typhoon with a comic song. The corpusants test this desperado philosophy, startling him into a prayer for mercy. But when Starbuck upbraids him with inconsistency, he wiggles out as nimbly as Falstaff. "I said the corpusants have mercy on us all; and I hope they will," he justifies himself. "But do they only have mercy on long faces?—have they no bowels for a laugh?" (6:504-6). When Moby-Dick sinks the *Pequod*, Stubb welcomes death with wordplay. "My God, stand by me now!" cries the pious Starbuck. "Stand not by me, but stand under me, whoever you are that will now help Stubb," chimes in the second mate. "Stubb, too, sticks here. I grin at thee, thou grinning whale!" Tearing off shoes and jacket, the ship's clown is determined to "die in his drawers," a resolutely comic figure (6:570-71).

"What soulless thing is this that laughs before a wreck?" asks Ahab, appalled by Stubb's relentless jesting. "Man, man! did I not know thee brave as fearless fire (and as mechanical) I could swear thou wert a poltroon" (6:553). Reciprocal incomprehension sunders captain and second mate. "I guess he's got what some folks ashore call a conscience," says Stubb of Ahab. "It's a kind of Tic-Dolly-row they say—worse nor a toothache. Well, well; I don't know what it is, but the Lord keep me from catching it." Both seem monomaniacs with a psychological tic that renders each quasi-mechanical. "Think not, is my eleventh commandment," proclaims Stubb, "and sleep when you can, is my twelfth" (6:128). The question of meaning that he habitually laughs off is Ahab's intellectual obsession. It leaves the captain no humor except the mirthless, sardonic kind displayed in his catechisms of the carpenter as a *deus in machina.* "Faith, sir . . ." begins the carpenter, only to draw the captain's quibble, "Faith? What's that?" Ahab exults in making the carpenter parse his own sentence to reveal faith as no noun but an expletive, "only a sort of exclamation-like—that's all, sir" (6:528). For making legs, coffins, and life-buoys indifferently, Ahab calls the carpenter "as unprincipled as the gods, and as much of a jack-of-all-trades." "But I do not mean anything, sir," replies the carpenter. "I do as I do" (6:527–28). That is a godlike disclaimer of responsibility that Ahab cannot abide.

"The Sperm Whale has no tongue," asserts Ishmael, and the beast's great genius is "declared in his pyramidical silence." Though Sir William Jones read in thirty languages, he could not decipher the elements of physiognomy, so "how may the unlettered Ishmael hope to read the awful Chaldee of the Sperm Whale's brow? I but put that brow before you. Read it if you can" (6:347). That challenge Ahab accepts. He is convinced that he can read Moby-Dick, much as Noah Webster was convinced that he could trace the original Adamic tongue in the Chaldee. Webster argued that through grammatical development some thirty or forty primitive verbs denoting motion generated "most of the nouns, adjectives, and other parts of speech belonging to each family."[36] Stripping away the grammatical accretions that constituted nouns as separate "things," the Websterian etymologist verged upon the magic moment when words derived their meaning referentially by pointing to the divine flux of matter and energy that gave language its initial impetus.

"All visible objects, man, are but as pasteboard masks," claims Ahab. "But in each event—in the living act, the undoubted deed—there, some unknown but still reasoning thing puts forth the moldings of its features from behind the unreasoning mask." In his determination to reach "the little lower layer" by striking through the mask of objects to grasp the living act of a governing consciousness, Ahab resembles a Websterian etymologist or Emerson in "Nature" at his most restrictively correspondential. He hunts for a source outside language to fix meaning within language, as if otherwise it might leak away. "Let it leak!" he rants to Starbuck anent oil seepage. "I'm all aleak myself. Aye! leaks in leaks! not only full of leaky casks but those leaky casks are in a leaky ship . . . Yet I don't stop to plug my leak" (6:474). The obsessive repetitions that characterize his rhetoric throughout the book suggest a mind wringing words for some essential meaning.[37] "I am madness maddened," he cries, "in the midst of the personified impersonal, a personality stands here" (6:168, 507). When his intensive doubling dwindles into punning, there is a note of subdued rage at the slipperiness of language. "Here's a man from Man," he tells the Manxman, "a man born in once independent Man, and now unmanned of Man" 6:521). Unmanned by the whale, Ahab tries to put himself back together by confronting the contradictory meanings of words.

In the seminal chapter "The Doubloon" Ahab and the crew read the symbolic coin nailed to the mainmast. Like Ahab, all the interpreters in the hermeneutic parade explain it with marked egocentricity, and all ground the meaning of the coin in some external reality that it must denote. Like their captain, they are thus all etymologists. But the response that Stubb notes in Pip bespeaks a different kind of etymologist:

> "I look, you look, he looks; we look, ye look, they look."
> "Upon my soul, he's been studying Murray's Grammar! Improving his mind, poor fellow! But what's that he says now—hist!"
> "I look, you look, he looks; we look, ye look, they look."
> "Why he's getting it by heart—hist! again."
> "I look, you look, he looks; we look, ye look, they look." (6:434)

Murray is Pip's linguistic authority, not Webster. He practices grammatical rather than historical etymology. Instead of deriving meanings of words from something outside language, Pip emphasizes how meanings derive from the structure of language itself. He looks and parses others' looks in a way that lets one separate the meaning of *the whale* from the meaning of *whaling*. He offers no interpretation of the coin—just an interpretation of interpreters. By conjugating the varieties of relativism he links them in a coherent statement.

Highly formal though it is, it retains a referential dimension. The first person locates Pip among those who look. Without the crew's attempt to spy out meanings, however partial, his conjugation would be a more trivial exercise of little value. Pip's analysis of the subjective limits of interpretation is inspired, but it is also deranged. The formal insights of his detached grammatical overview in three persons are purchased only by the loss of his own personal identity after immersion in the sea. To believe that there may be no meaning beyond language is to be "too crazy-witty for my sanity," in Stubb's words.

As Mark Bauerlein argues, the characters in *Moby-Dick* seem doomed to oscillate between the interpretive poles of etymology and grammar, meaning and form, genesis and structure. Human beings feel compelled to "delineate chaos" even when they suspect that their sketch owes as much to the contours of their linguistic medium as to the structure of the universe (6:12). And regardless of the distortions involved, they do so personally with some faith that their language does correspond to a world beyond itself. "Here's the ship's navel, this doubloon here, and they are all on fire to unscrew it," says Pip truly. "But unscrew your navel, and what's the consequence?" The consequence, according to folk wisdom, is that your ass falls off. But like Ahab, the crew of the *Pequod* will risk that part of their anatomy in the quest for more fundamental truth.

Articulating these insights is Ishmael's task. "Call me Ishmael," he begins with a nod to the provisional, arbitrary, and possibly delusive nature of naming. He makes no overt interpretation of the doubloon. Like Pip he is fascinated by how different readers read nature differently. To explain how Ahab unifies the diverse crew behind his monomaniacal quest "would be to dive deeper than Ishmael can go" (6:187). But he shares Ahab's lust for meaning, for he himself feels that "some certain significance lurks in all things, else all things are little worth, and the round world itself but an empty cipher, except to sell by the cartload, as they do hills about Boston, to fill up some morass in the Milky Way" (6:430).

Yet even as he expresses this belief irony tempers it. Then he indulges in a "free and easy sort of genial, desperado philosophy" that is not the captain's but essentially that of Stubb. Ishmael likes Stubb better than anyone except Queequeg. "I lack the low, enjoying power," says Ahab truly (6:167). Neither Stubb nor punning Ishmael could say the same.

"That mortal man who hath more of joy than sorrow in him, that mortal man cannot be true—not true, or undeveloped," argues Ishmael. "The truest of all men was the Man of Sorrows, and the truest of all books is Solomon's, and Ecclesiastes is the fine hammered steel of woe." But if Stubb is wanting in his obsessive joking, so too is Ahab, for "there is a wisdom that is woe; but there is a woe that is madness." Monomania stunts Stubb and maims Ahab. By contrast, Ishmael continues, "there is a Catskill eagle in some souls that can alike dive down into the blackest gorges, and soar out of them again and become invisible in the sunny spaces. And even if he for ever flies within the gorge, that gorge is in the mountains; so that even in his lowest swoop the mountain eagle is still higher than other birds upon the plain, even though they soar" (6:424–25). That eagle is Ishmael's imaginative faith swooping between Stubb's and Ahab's perspectives, from frivolity to deadly earnest.[38]

Moby-Dick may have a similar imagination, for Melville stresses that the peculiar placement of the whale's eyes denies him binocular vision. Ishmael doubts the whale's synthesizing powers. With glimpses of two diametrically opposed pictures, "all between must be profound darkness and nothingness to him" (6:330–31). If so, the whale resembles Ahab more than Ishmael, for Ahab's polarized view of a black-and-white universe cannot tolerate grayness or ambiguity. That limitation Ishmael strives to transcend. To establish his humanity Ahab confronts nature with negations, for negatives are not found in nature. But the tactic risks nihilism. By contrast, a striking feature of Ishmael's grammar is his relish for double negatives. As Gayle Smith observes, in *Moby-Dick* at least sixty-five words with negative prefixes or an accompanying *no* or *not* are themselves negated, and sixty-two of these formulas are Ishmael's.

This stylistic tic has large implications. Citing American usage, Webster had defended double negatives from British authorities who condemned them as illogical. The more double negatives Ishmael uses, the less they seem to cancel each other out to yield the straightforward positive stipulated by many schoolroom grammarians. "Savage though he was, and hideously marred about the face," says Ishmael upon first beholding Queequeg, "his countenance yet had a something it it which was by no means disagreeable" (6:49). In calling something *not disagreeable* Ishmael rebuts simple negation without implying that Queequeg's face was simply agreeable. His litotes suggests that between the linguistic poles *agreeable/disagreeable* he envisions a spectrum of meanings accessible to thoughtful readers. Double negatives of this sort produce "a pleasing and delicate variety of expression," claimed the grammarian Peter Bullions, and Melville evidently took to heart this counsel from his old headmaster at the Albany Academy.[39] Ishmael's first tentative impressions of Ahab also culminate in an evasive but suggestive litotes: "I . . . felt a strange awe of him; but that sort of awe, which I cannot at all describe, was not exactly awe; I do not know what it was. But I felt it; and it did not disincline me towards him" (6:80). Here Bushnellian paradox colors this rhetorical figure, for by it Ishmael begins to describe what he says he "cannot at all describe." He uses it fifteen times in chapters 41 and 42 describing Moby-Dick.

Whereas Ahab apostrophizes the calm sea's "unnamable imminglings," Ishmael imagines storm-tossed billows as "a nameless yeast" (6:497, 12). The word *nameless* is a favorite of his, and Ishmael regularly employs it as the first step toward naming what Ahab might dismiss as unnamable. Compounding words audaciously, pluralizing abstract nouns, turning participles into modifiers, making nouns into verbs and vice versa, Ishmael's rhetoric warps grammatical categories to find new ways of naming. Whereas failures of correspondence embitter Ahab, Ishmael learns to take the slippage of words for granted. Baroque rodomontades of diction are offset with nautical slang. Punning is one of the techniques he improvises to highlight the imperfect fit between the bipolar structures of language and the seamlessness of a chaotic world. Ahab's quarrel with God is subsumed in Ishmael's quarrel with words. And that remains a lover's quarrel despite all the sensitivity to the oceanic ineffable displayed in "The Mast-head" and "The Gilder." In a world where Moby-Dick's whiteness seems "the visible absence of color" Ishmael's many-shaded voice always offers the audible presence of a rainbow (6:195). Negating negation itself, he alone survives, floating above meaninglessness on the coffin-lifebuoy of Romantic irony.

Skeptical about the pursuit of Truth, Ishmael does not despair of suggesting truths in language. Nor did Melville, who after the publication of *Moby-Dick* kept embodying limited truths in powerful short stories. His longer narratives, however, aspired to tell all, in ways that made it increasingly hard for him to say anything.[40] Among the verbal incongruities that Ishmael trawls from the depths, correspondences glimmer; *requin,* the French word for shark, comes from the Latin *requiem,* a footnote to chapter 32 informs us. But in Melville's later fiction wordplay loses its ebullience. Punning is pandemic in *The Confidence-Man,* published on April Fools' Day 1857. Asked whether he will relieve an unfortunate man, one stingy soul snorts, "Let the unfortunate man relieve himself" (10:48). The puns are mainly mirthless equivocations by which philosophical con-men gull victims or dupes gull themselves. "But is analogy argument? You are a punster," one recalcitrant victim vainly objects. "Yes, you pun with ideas as another man may with words" (10:124). One con-man observes that "the least lovable men in history seem to have had for humor not only a disrelish, but a hatred; and this in some cases, along with an extraordinary dry taste for practical punning" (10:164). Judged by this criterion *The Confidence-Man* teems with enough practical punning to make it a peculiarly humorless and unlovable book.

When late in life Melville patched up a truce with fiction to write *Billy Budd,* a story of natural innocence refracted through ineluctable duplicity, puns remained suspect. Billy's impressment into the British navy plunges him into a world of double meanings. "Good-bye to you too, old *Rights of Man!*" he calls out nostalgically to his old ship while being ferried to *H M S Bellipotent.* The farewell draws a stern rebuke from the lieutenant, along with a suppressed smile, for he suspects "a covert sally on the new recruit's part." But the pun is unintended and suspicion unwarranted, for Billy was "by no means of a satirical turn. . . . To deal in double meanings and insinuations of any sort was quite foreign to his nature."[41] By contrast, his enemy the master-at-arms Claggart is a master ironist, whose stock-in-trade is innuendo.

Willy-nilly the narrator's epithets may share such "sinister dexterity" with words (itself an etymological pun), for in British gay argot an *angel* is a faggot, an *Adam* is a first partner, and a *bud* is a young latent homosexual.[42] When Claggart falsely accuses Billy before Captain Vere, the handsome sailor's speech impediment prevents his replying. "Speak: Defend yourself!" the captain commands—then seeing Billy's tongue-tied paroxysms urges him sympathetically to take his time. But with an effect exactly opposite to what Vere intends, his fatherly words only worsen Billy's paralysis. "The next instant, quick as the flame from a discharged cannon at night, his right arm shot out" (*BB,* pp. 98-99).

Billy's action in killing Claggart is a form of rhetoric, the body language of nature. "The discovering passions instantly as they arise, being essential to our well being, and often necessary to self-preservation, the author of our nature, attentive to our wants, hath provided a passage to the heart, which can never be obstructed while our external senses remain entire," proclaimed Gilbert Austin's *Chironomia; or, A Treatise on Rhetorical Delivery* (London: Cadell, 1806). Melville's brother acquired a copy of this treatise that Herman probably dipped into, for as a youth he also was enamored of oratorical distinction.[43] The aging author may have recalled the rhetorician's common thesis that while words suffice for intellectual communication, gesture taps a deeper truth. "The external signs of passion are a strong indication, that man, by his very constitution, is framed to be open and sincere," argued Austin. "The total suppression of the voluntary signs during any vivid passion, begets the utmost uneasiness, which cannot be endured for any considerable time" (pp. 472-74).

Yet even the gestural language of nature enmeshes Billy in a web of double meanings, for Vere, whose own words inadvertently prompted his gesture, must now consider its inadvertent significance under the code of military discipline. When Billy hangs, his apparent suppression of gesture transcends the language of nature but still produces no agreement about its meaning. After the grotesquely distorted account of his act in the naval gazette, the inside narrative trails off with the sailors' legends about the Handsome Sailor, culminating in the ballad composed by one of his shipmates gifted "with an artless *poetic* temperament." But moving though "Billy in the Darbies" is as a dramatic monologue, it too falsifies his "unconscious simplicity" by making him speak in puns. "O, 'tis me, not the sentence they'll suspend," his fellow foretopman implausibly imagines him saying, "Aye, aye, all is up; and I must up too."[44] The poetic temperament is a punster's temperament, Melville implies, not an etymologist's and still less an innocent's. Etymologically speaking, *poetry* is *fabrication*. If art shares with theology and history a fallen language, it may be impossible to get to the root of Billy Budd except by faith. *Moby-Dick* begins with a bogus Hebrew etymology, causing editors no little confusion, but it is perhaps no accident that the Hebrew characters Melville supplied form the word not for *whale* but for *grace*.[45]

10 /

Savoring the Wiles of Words

When the thinking mind comes into direct contact with the object, thing
or idea it has 'felt after' and found,—the words which it then weaves into
the visible garment of its mingled emotion and conception are words sur-
charged and flooded with life,—words which are living things, endowed
with the power, not only to communicate ideas, but to convey, as by spiritual conduction, the shock and thrill which attended their conception.

> —"The Use and Misuse of Words," *North American Review*
> 79 (1854): 141-42

A Word that breathes distinctly
Has not the power to die
Cohesive as the Spirit
It may expire if He—
"Made Flesh and dwelt among us"
Could condescension be
Like this consent of Language
This loved Philology   (*Poems*, #1651)

Dickinson's Love Affair with Dictionaries

"The Doctor's pun was happy," wrote Emily Dickinson late in life to a
correspondent sharing a witticism with her. "How lovely are the wiles of
Words!" (2:612). An Amherst upbringing sensitized her to their wiliness.
With its two colleges the town was intellectual, a newspaper quipped, but
"also spiritual with a score of liquor-holes."[1] It had been home to the lexicographer Noah Webster. His son-in-law the grammarian William
Chauncy Fowler also lived there, and Webster's granddaughter was one of
Emily's girlhood chums. Fowler's disciple Francis A. March taught briefly
at Amherst and later corresponded with Emily. Her friend Maria Whitney
taught French and German at Smith while Maria's brother William
Dwight Whitney pioneered linguistics at Yale. Yet another philologue in
the family orbit was Emily's confidant and cousin John Graves, whose
commencement address in 1855 dealt with "Philological Philosophy."

Daily life in the Dickinson household normally began with her
father's reading the family a chapter from Scripture. Once when her par-

ents left her at home with her brother Austin, the younger Dickinsons celebrated their freedom by installing the big Webster's on the kitchen table while they wrote letters to friends. In Emily's youth the family's lexicons sparked sociability. "I am glad you took the Latin lexicon," she wrote to her brother at boarding school, "because I have had good luck in borrowing one" (1:4). One young man with whom she read German plays recalled her sitting "close beside me so as to look out words from the same Dictionary."[2] During her gradual withdrawal from the world, books became substitute sociability, exhilarating but not entirely satisfying. She was overdramatizing her isolation when she wrote T. W. Higginson in 1862 that "for several years, my Lexicon—was my only companion" (2:404). But a poem of ca. 1863 does suggest the compensatory intensity of her relationship to dictionaries: "Easing my famine / At my Lexicon— / Logarithm—had I—for Drink— / 'Twas a dry wine" (#728).

A *logarithm* acquired a touch of effervescence, however, when Emily misconstrued its Greek root meaning *the ratio of a number* as signifying instead *the rhythm of words*. Though she long spelled a few words like *wo* and *extasy* by Webster's eccentric canons, her attitude toward authority was scarcely slavish. "Orthography always baffled me, and to 'N's' I had an especial aversion, as they always seemed unfinished M's," she confessed in one letter. "I can best express my contrition in the words of the Prayer of a Clergyman I heard when a child—'Oh thou who sittest upon the Apex of the Cherubim, look down upon this, thine unworthy Terrapin!'" "God—spell the word! I—can't," she pouts in one poem (#296). Her onomatopoetic ornithology would have charmed Thoreau. "I used to spell the one [bird] by that name *'Fee Bee'* when a Child, and have seen no need to improve!" she proclaimed defiantly. "Should I spell all the things as they sounded to me, and say all the facts as I saw them, it would send consternation among more than the 'Fee Bees!'" (3:774).

One striking poetic legacy of her love affair with dictionaries is her fondness for verse definitions. Over one hundred of her poems—about 7 percent of her output—are efforts to grasp and state the essence of some word. "'Hope' is the thing with feathers— / That perches in the soul," she writes as if trying to explain the concept to a child, "And sings the tune without the words— / And never stops—at all" (#254). Like Webster's, her attempts at precision may involve subdefinitions: "'Morning'— means 'Milking'—to the Farmer— / Dawn—to the Teneriffe," she begins one poem, then reels off eight further illustrations (#300). A definition of *Nature* is elaborately schematic, with three quatrains structured on the progression, "'Nature' is what we see ... Nature is what we hear ... Nature is what we know" (#668). Some definitions are quizzical: "'Heaven'—is what I cannot reach! / The Apple on the Tree— / Provided it do hopeless—hang— / That—'Heaven' is to Me!" (#239). Others are spiritually probing, pushing beyond lexicography to inventory the soul. "Remorse—is Memory—awake— / Her parties all astir— / A Presence of Departed Acts— / At window—and at Door," begins one poem that concludes, "Remorse is cureless—the Disease / Not even God—can heal— / For 'tis His Institution—and / The Adequate of Hell" (#744).

Some poems echo the descriptive synonymies, for a copy of Crabb's *English Synonymes* (Boston: Ewer, 1819) reposed on the family bookshelves.

> Escape is such a thankful Word
> I often in the Night
> Consider it unto myself
> No spectacle in sight
>
> Escape—it is the basket
> In which the Heart is caught
> When down some awful Battlement
> The rest of Life is dropt—
>
> 'Tis not to sight the Savior—
> It is to be the saved—
> And that is why I lay my Head
> Upon this trusty word— (#1347)

These lines boldly explore the terrain between waking and dreaming. Is the poet tossing in insomnia because of some unnamable angst, courting sleep by counting words like sheep? Or is she struggling to stay awake because she dreads being yielded to Piranesian nightmares shadowed by the second stanza? The poem portrays a consciousness riven between painful reality and more painful dreams. In this tormented state the word *escape* becomes her lifeline, inscribed on the blackboard of the mind in implicit contrast to *elude* and *evade*. "The idea of being disengaged from that which is not agreeable is comprehended in all three terms," Crabb wrote, "but *escape* designates no means by which this is effected; *elude* and *evade* define the means, namely, the efforts which are used by one's self: we are simply disengaged when we *escape*; but we disengage ourselves when we *elude* and *evade*; we *escape* from danger; we *elude* the search: our *escapes* are often providential, and often narrow; our success in *eluding* depends on our skill." Overwhelmed, the poet pillows her head on a word that connotes rescue by superior force. Waking in bed to find himself paralyzed, Dr. Johnson tested his sanity by mentally composing some Latin verses. For Emily Dickinson the power of definition seems the saving residue of intellectual control.

At Amherst Academy and Mount Holyoke Emily studied Latin for at least four years, German for a few months, and probably a little Greek and French too. By the standards of the day, her scientific training was thorough. Its technical terms stirred her imagination and stamped her poetic vocabulary. Along with hard science her popular botany textbook offered a sentimental guide to "the Symbolical Language of Flowers."[3]

To her encounter with the classics she owed at least a nodding acquaintance with Simonides and Horace. Later allusions to set pieces by each suggest how powerfully such masters inculcated the virtue of concision. Simonides' famous epitaph on the Spartan dead at Thermopylae—"Stranger, go tell the Lacedemonians / That we lie here obeying our country's laws"—prompts a response from Dickinson only slightly less laconic:

> "Go tell it"—What a Message—
> To whom—is specified—
> Not murmur—not endearment—
> But simply—we—obeyed—
> Obeyed—a Lure—A Longing?
> Oh Nature—none of this—
> To Law—said sweet Thermopylae
> I give my dying Kiss— (#1554)

Recoil mingles with respect as this American Romantic grapples with a central strand in our classical heritage: the disciplined subordination of the self to a communal ethos. For a poet whose major themes included both the renunciation of fulfilled passion and the sovereignty of the self, classical culture was a provocative stimulus. She doubtless knew that sweet Antigone bestowed her dying kiss elsewhere than Thermopylae. Her poem is a dialogue between love and the law, with *nomos* and *physis* embracing surreptitiously in the last two lines. Her training in Latin composition at the academy, where Ramshorn's *Latin Synonymes* was a text, reinforced the link between Stoic control and the classics. "It don't sound so terrible—quite—as it did— / I run it over—'Dead',— Brain, 'Dead.' / Put it in Latin—left of my school— / Seems it don't shriek so— under rule" (#426).

Schoolgirl efforts to construe the classics truly opened her mind:

> A precious—mouldering pleasure—'tis—
> To meet an Antique Book—
> In just the Dress his Century wore—
> A privilege—I think—

His venerable Hand to take—
And warming in our own—
A passage back—or two—to make—
To Times when he—was young—

His quaint opinions—to inspect—
His thought to ascertain
On Themes concern our mutual mind—
The Literature of Man—

What Interested Scholars—most—
When Competitions ran—
When Plato—was a Certainty—
And Sophocles—a Man—

When Sappho—was a living Girl—
And Beatrice wore
The Gown that Dante—deified—
Facts Centuries before

He traverses—familiar—
As One should come to Town—
And tell you all your Dreams—were true
He lived—where Dreams were born—

His presence is Enchantment—
You beg him not to go—
Old Volumes shake their Vellum Heads
And tantalize—just so— (#371)

What raises this above stock tributes to a classical education is Dickinson's awareness that construing Greek texts is more an imaginative than a grammatical challenge. It provides at best but a "mouldering pleasure." To clasp a Greek author's hand requires warming it in one's own. While she gives Beatrice's name the proper Italian pronunciation, she seems less sanguine than Thoreau about communing with the past as a heroic reader. What the classics confirm is not truth but dreams. Old volumes recede from our interrogation, shaking their heads mournfully at attempts to invoke their authority. Dickinson had studied the classics enough to know that our word *tantalize* is rooted in a Greek myth about ineluctable frustration. They tantalize just as she now tantalizes with her last words "just so." She knew that if one goes to antiquity looking for quick answers, the result can be grandly unsatisfying.

"It has been an April of meaning to me," wrote Dickinson to her suitor Judge Otis Lord after the demise of the Reverend Charles Wadsworth. "I have been in your Bosom. My Philadelphia has passed from

Earth, and . . . Ralph Waldo Emerson . . . Which Earth are we in?" (3:727). Her schooling taught her that etymologically an April of meaning was an *opening* of meaning, and the unfolding of meanings was what made that particular month memorable. "If the foolish, call them 'Flowers' / Need the wiser *tell*? / If the Savants 'classify' them / It is just as well. / Those who read the 'Revelations' / Must not criticise / Those who read the same Edition— / With beclouded Eyes," another poem begins (#168). Here the conceit is inspired by Webster's mistaken notion that the primary sense of *glory,* from Latin *gloria,* "seems to be to open, to expand, to enlarge," and the Latin *floreo,* "to blossom, to flower . . . is probably of the same family."[4]

"How many times these low feet staggered" seems to end by mocking the negligence of an "Indolent Housewife—in Daisies—lain!" (#187). But Dickinson's epithet is informed with the knowledge that etymologically *indolent* means *feeling no pain,* so behind the mockery lurks a shrewd sympathy for this long-suffering victim of her chores. "If night stands first—*then* noon / To gird us for the sun, / What gaze!" she exclaimed, "When from a thousand skies / On our *developed* eyes / Noons blaze!" (#63). Here the imagery shows her aware that the radical meaning of *developed* is *unveiled.* The knowledge that the Latin *pallium* means *cloak* underlies her claim that "the Shivering Fancy turns / To a Fictitious Country / To palliate a Cold" (#562). "These are the Nights that Beetles Love" describes an intrusive insect as "a Bomb upon the Ceiling," for moths of the family *bombycidae,* like our word *bomb,* derive their name from a Greco-Roman root designating a booming, buzzing noise (#1128). "Who built this little Alban House / And shut the windows down so close / My spirit cannot see?" she inquires, taking over Horace's domicile as a trope for her body. "Who'll let me out some gala day / With implements to fly away, / Passing pomposity?" (#128). Here she imagines her liberated spirit "passing pomposity" in two senses: first, excelling magnificence in its habiliments; second, flying over her own funeral procession, which the Latin *pompa* denotes. The impish sprite who toys with buzzing her own cortege elsewhere dryly hails an undertaker as "the Man / Of the Appalling Trade" (#389).

Luxury attracted Dickinson more than pomposity. "Wild Nights— Wild Nights! / Were I with thee / Wild Nights should be / Our luxury!" (#249). But in this love lyric the word is loaded with the knowledge that its root denotes rank fertility, so that in medieval Latin *luxuria* names lechery, the seventh deadly sin. A spinster whose imagination overflowed in such diction had reason to be wary of exposing her thoughts to insensitive readers.

> Publication—is the Auction
> Of the Mind of Man—
> Poverty—be justifying
> For so foul a thing
>
> Possibly—but We—would rather
> From Our Garret go
> White—Unto the White Creator—
> Than invest—Our Snow— (#709)

Of the dozen poems published during her life some were tampered with by editors impatient with her idiosyncratic punctuation and such eccentric syntax as "be justifying." Like T. W. Higginson, they sought to clothe her perverse verse in more orthodox stylistic garb for the marketplace. Discomfited, in these lines she regally defends the imaginative autonomy of her garret by declining to "invest our snow." She avows higher standards than the marketplace with diction that claims a larger meaning than commercial publishers might acknowledge. The lofty refusal to let finances govern language becomes a mischievous, delicate striptease, however, when the radical meaning of *invest* is considered. Her style is often flirtatious, on the principle that "the thought beneath so slight a film— / Is more distinctly seen— / As laces just reveal the surge— / Or Mists—the Apennine" (#210). "To their apartment deep / No ribaldry may creep," she chastely begins one gnomic quatrain, then belies that claim with a surprising double entendre, "Untumbled their abode / By any man but God" (#1701).

After Judge Lord's death, Dickinson continued to think of him fondly. "On my way to my sleep, last night, I paused at the Portrait," she wrote his executor.

> Had I not loved it, I had feared it, the Face had such ascension.

> Go thy great way!
> The Stars thou meetst
> Are even as Thyself—
> For what are stars but Asterisks
> To point a human Life? (3:860, #1638)

But she was not so overwhelmed by grief as to forget her Greek. The conceit of the stars as heavenly punctuation marks for the ellipsis of decease, referring the reader to matter below, is grounded in the derivation of *asterisk* from a Greek word meaning *little star*.

A dawning vocation let a self-sustaining spirit relish her intellectual isolation:

> Once more, my now bewildered Dove
> Bestirs her puzzled wings

> Once more her mistress, on the deep
> Her troubled question flings—
>
> Thrice to the floating casement
> The Patriarch's bird returned,
> Courage! My brave Columba!
> There may yet be *Land*! (#48)

Bobbing like Noah on an inundation, this female speaker shares her ark with no crew of contented couples. Unlike the Patriarch she is on intimate terms with her Dove, a female creative principle like the Holy Spirit but here linked to her own poetic imagination. Courage was a higher value than bravery, according to Crabb, denoting a principled intellectual persistence in valor rather than an instinctive physical reaction to momentary danger. The persistence asked of the Dove is underscored when she apostrophizes it by its Latin name *Columba,* for the term makes the bird seem almost a transvestite Columbus. Columbus returned from his new world as a condition of discovering it. But the Patriarch's bird did not. The poet's Dove is loath to leave her, and for all her bravado we may wonder whether she really craves landfall if that means the loss of her pet. That it may be immortalized as the constellation Columba, Noah's Dove, seems only partial compensation.

Though overt etymological wordplay like this occurs in relatively few of her 1,775 poems, it surely fulfills her prescription for poetry in that it "distills amazing sense / From ordinary meanings" (#448). It is the prime example of a more generalized etymological sensitivity that energizes her verse. "We used to think, Joseph, when I was an unsifted girl and you so scholarly that words were cheap and weak," she wrote her friend Lyman. "Now I don't know of anything so mighty. There are to which I lift my hat when I see them sitting princelike among their peers on the page. Sometimes I write one, and look at his outlines till he glows as no sapphire" (*Life,* 2:675). Soirées with her lexicon made her acutely aware of the different registers of English vocabulary.

> Many a phrase has the English language—
> I have heard but one—
> Low as the laughter of the Cricket,
> Loud as the Thunder's tongue—
>
> Murmuring, like old Caspian Choirs,
> When the Tide's a'lull—
> Saying itself in new inflection—
> Like a Whippowil—

Breaking in bright Orthography
On my simple sleep—
Thundering it's Prospective—
Till I stir and weep—

Not for Sorrow, done me—
But the push of Joy—
Say it again, Saxon!
Hush—Only to me! (#276)

The unspoken phrase is of course the homely Anglo-Saxon "I love you."
The power of this declaration is doubled by suppression—and trebled by
contrast to more ornate diction. Each of the first three stanzas has at
least five polysyllables, and the third hinges on two erudite abstract
words of classical origin. With the final stanza monosyllables come to
the fore in the awkward but powerful phrase "the push of Joy," almost
as if language itself were a lover, before the poem subsides in a colloquial
whisper. Here Dickinson happily reflects Webster's mistaken conviction
that "*joy . . . and the like affections, are from the sense of rousing, exciting, lively action*" (Preface, p. xxxvii). The linguistic images of the first
three stanzas suggest a subtle progression from phonetics through grammar to literacy. The evolution of language is also hinted at in the simile
comparing the English phrase first to old Caspian choirs murmuring in
the putative homeland of Indo-European and then to a whippowil's new
inflection, Webster's spelling setting off the American from the English
whipoorwill.[5]

Though Dickinson was apparently unaware that the Caspian Sea has
no tides, she was keenly alert to the perpetual ebb and flow of English
between its various sources. "Presentiment—is that long Shadow—on
the Lawn— / Indicative that Suns go down," she begins one poem, tentatively defining a Latinate abstraction with another polysyllabic Latin
derivative, then shifts the emphasis to Saxon vernacular, "The Notice to
the startled Grass / That Darkness—is about to pass—" (#764). "I dwell
in Possibility— / A fairer House than Prose," she proclaims—and also a
more obviously Latinate one (#657).

Elsewhere that movement reverses direction: "The Carriage held but
just Ourselves— / And Immortality" (#712). In this her most famous
poem three stanzas end in punchy monosyllables, while the other three,
including the last, trail off with Latinate abstract nouns in -y: *Immortality,
Civility, Eternity.* As the years went by, this tendency hardened into a mannerism. Of the four hundred poems written during 1863–65, for example,
nearly 10 percent end with an abstract Latinate polysyllable in -y.[6] Since
the primary accent in such words does not fall on the last syllable, her

closing rhymes are often feminine. Their note of tentative, wavering irresolution is compounded by her fondness for slant rhyme. Many of her lyrics also end with contradictions, questions, qualifications, or suspended judgments. The net effect contrasts sharply with the ringing "masculine" closure of most nineteenth-century poems.

Like Whitman's, her diction grew more abstract with advancing years. Foreign loan-words bedizen its stark Anglo-Saxon base, not always with happy results: "A nearness to Tremendousness— / An Agony procures— / Affliction ranges Boundlessness— / Vicinity to Laws / Contentment's quiet Suburb— / Affliction cannot stay / In Acres—its Location / Is Illocality" (#962). In such writing the stamp of experience yields to the stump, and her Orphic pose, like the later Whitman's, degenerates into obnoxious one-upmanship.

What redeems her Latinate diction is that unlike the autodidactic Whitman she was aware of its tendency to pomposity. She often exploited that with irony. "To be a Flower, is profound / Responsibility," one amusing poem concludes with that deliberate inflation characteristic of the mock-heroic style (#1058). In a later poem the various registers of her vocabulary are finely tuned for ironic effect:

> That short—potential stir
> That each can make but once—
> That Bustle so illustrious
> 'Tis almost Consequence—
>
> Is the eclat of Death—
> Oh, thou unknown Renown
> That not a Beggar would accept
> Had he the power to spurn— (#1307)

The poem unpacks its meaning through pointed phrases: *potential stir, illustrious bustle, almost consequence, death's eclat, unknown renown*. All are faintly contradictory, all hint at a tempestuous teapot. The portentous fuss triggered by death is *potential* in several senses: potent, evanescent, and only hypothetical insofar as it is not really the dead person who makes it. This contradictoriness is accented by the slight clash between the Latinate abstraction and the two Saxon monosyllables that bracket it. The following phrases also couple terse Anglo-Saxon words for homely realities with polysyllabic Latin or Romance derivatives suggesting social pretentiousness. The poem's energy sparks from the delicate collisions that Dickinson engineers between conflicting elements of her vocabulary.

This technique is scarcely novel. Chaucer had similar fun with aureate diction. Like other seventeenth-century writers whom she loved,

Shakespeare called forth a gorgeous counterpointed rhetoric from the multiple heritage of the English word-stock. But her etymological sensitivity helped her tap the energy trapped between different strata of the language more effectively than any other nineteenth-century American poet—more effectively, indeed, than all but a handful of those who have written English verse. Like Dryden and Pope, she sets Saxon against slightly inflated classical diction most brilliantly as a form of wit. Obsessed with diminutiveness and differences in scale, hers seems an essentially mock-heroic art. "She knows herself an incense small— / Yet *small*—she sighs—if *All*—is *All*- / *How larger*—be?" (#284). Aware that the word *small* includes *all*, she either treats the trivial grandiosely or tries to domesticate the infinite.

A Punning Humorist Grows Up in Amherst

"Dennis was happy yesterday, and it made him graceful—I saw him waltzing with the Cow," wrote Dickinson to her nephew anent the family's Irish handyman. "You told me he hadn't tasted Liquor since his Wife's decease—then she must have been living at six o'clock last Evening" (2:641). Toward one fat, pious neighbor, she was less charitable. "Mrs. S. gets bigger, and rolls down the lane to church like a reverend marble," she observed (2:470). Despite cattiness, the joke was too good to abandon, so in another gossipy letter to her favorite cousins it was elaborated: "There is that which is called an 'awakening' in the church, and I know of no choicer ecstasy than to see [her] roll out in crape every morning, I suppose to intimidate antichrist; at least it would have that effect on me" (2:505-6).

As a girl she possessed a wicked wit. At Amherst Academy she wrote a comic column for a manuscript magazine organized by her friends. As one recalled it,

> Emily's contributions were often in the style of a funny little sermon, long since vanished, which went the rounds of the newspapers for two years and was recited from lyceum platforms and declaimed in village schools, from this text: "He played on a harp of a thousand strings, sperrets of just men made perfec'," the art of which consisted in bringing most incongruous things together, such as . . . samphire and camphire (camphor) . . . ending always with the same refrain, "He played on a harp of a thousand strings, sperrets of just men made perfec'." . . . One bit was stolen by a roguish editor for the College paper, where her touch was instantly recognized; and there were two paragraphs in *The Springfield Republican*.[7]

Writing from college, she favored an uncle with a mock-tirade invoking stock comic characters like B. P. Shillaber's Mrs. Partington and Douglas

Jerrold's Mrs. Caudle. That reflects her youthful immersion in the mainstream of Victorian humor. "Has the Mexican war terminated yet & how? Are we beat?" she inquired of her brother during her stay at Mount Holyoke. "Do you know of any nation about to besiege South Hadley? If so, do inform me of it, for I would be glad of a chance to escape, if we are to be stormed. I suppose Miss Lyon would furnish us all with daggers & order us to fight for our lives" (1:49).

Eluding doctrinaire religion and feminism by returning home to Amherst, she threw herself into the thick of village amusements. She enjoyed a reputation as a cut-up. Combining a burlesque sermon with mock-epic, her earliest surviving manuscript poem is a comic valentine. She cultivated this genre assiduously. Forbidden by Mount Holyoke authorities, it allowed her to skewer clichés, parody religious, political, and academic bombast, and generally exercise a talent for whimsical nonsense:

> Oh "veni, vidi, vici!"
>   Oh caput cap-a-pie!
> And oh "memento mori"
>   When I am far from thee!
>
> Hurrah for Peter Parley!
>   Hurrah for Daniel Boone!
> Three cheers, sir, for the gentleman
>   Who first observed the moon!
>
> Peter, put up the sunshine;
>   Pattie, arrange the stars;
> Tell Luna, tea is waiting,
>   And call your brother Mars!
>
> Put down the apple, Adam,
>   And come away with me,
> So shalt thou have a *pippin*
>   From off my father's tree!
>
> I climb the "Hill of Science,"
>   I "view the landscape o'er;"
> Such transcendental prospect
>   I ne'er beheld before!
>
> Unto the Legislature
>   My country bids me go;
> I'll take my india rubbers,
>   In case the wind should blow! (#3)

This valentine so amused its recipient and others who copied it that it wound up in the *Springfield Daily Republican* in 1852 (the first of Dickinson's poems known to have been published). The first two stanzas above mock textbooks, the third discombobulates the nursery rhyme "Polly, put the kettle up," while the fifth travesties Watts's hymn "There is a land of pure delight" by adapting it to an academic nirvana. Like most hymn lyrics her poetry took shape as parody—that is, *par-odia,* to suit an existing tune.[8] With its punning distaste for political rhetoric (*india rubbers* = overshoes/erasers) in the very year that her father was elected to Congress, this *jeu d'esprit* suggests how humor helped her maintain a safe distance from people and events with deep claims on her allegiance. The punning theology of the fourth stanza above (*pippin* = an apple/a beauty) lets her present herself coyly as a seductive Eve. The effusive Romanticism of sentimental valentines is mocked in a way that honors the intelligence of the reader, yet the irony creates such intimacy with whoever fathoms it that one wonders whether the missive is devoid of conventional sentiment.

Surely the Valentine letter to George Gould that popped up in the Amherst literary magazine he edited may cloak real feeling under a pose of mocking extravagance:

> Magnum bonum, "harum scarum," zounds et sounds, et war alarum, man reformam, life perfectum, mundum changum, all things flarum?
>
> Sir, I desire an interview; meet me at sunrise, or sunset, or the new moon—the place is immaterial. In gold, or in purple, or sackcloth—I look not upon the *raiment.* With sword, or with pen, or with plough—the weapons are less than the *wielder.* In coach, or in wagon, or walking, the *equipage* far from the *man.* With soul, or spirit, or body, they are all alike to me. With host or alone, in sunshine or storm, in heaven or earth, *some* how or *no* how—I propose, sir, to see you.
>
> And not to *see* merely, but a chat, sir, or a tete-a-tete, a confab, a mingling of opposite minds is what I propose to have. I feel sir that we shall agree. We will be David and Jonathan, or Damon and Pythias, or what is better than either, the United States of America. We will talk over what we have learned in our geographies, and listened to from the pulpit, the Press and the Sabbath School.
>
> This is strong language sir, but none the less true. So hurrah for North Carolina, since we are on this point. (1:92–93)

Promising that at their tryst on Valentine morning "we'll pull society up to the roots, and plant it in a different place . . . build Alms-houses, and transcendental State prisons, and scaffolds," this letter does indeed (as the undergraduate editors warmly noted) quicken the imagination and make the blood "frolic through the veins" (*Life,* 2:419). But what stirs the blood most is the idea that for all the mockery of ritual vows of eternal friendship, the strong language is true. Dickinson sounds eager to see Gould, and not just to discuss the last paragraphs of Emerson's *Nature*. The two shared a taste for Romantic irony that had led Gould to lecture on Jean Paul Richter. One would give much to read the other letters that she wrote him, of which he kept "quite a treasured batch" until late in life (*Life*, 2:751).

Some friends fell away. Girlhood chums moved or subsided into a conventionality beyond her reach. She developed a passionate affection for her sister-in-law, but in time that too disappointed. And of course many of her poems from the early 1860s on as well as the famous "Master" letters suggest painful attachment to a shadowy man, perhaps a minister like Gould or the Reverend Charles Wadsworth, always cherished but perforce renounced.[9]

But as darker shades enveloped her, she never renounced her humor. Rereading the Bible, she was surprised by it. "I had known it as an arid book," she confessed to a friend, "but looking I saw how infinitely wise & merry it is" (*Life*, 2:695). With the inspiration of humor she was able to coin her Tenth Beatitude: "Blessed are they that play, for theirs is the kingdom of heaven" (*Letters*, 3:691). Her workaholic father's illness she ascribed to its neglect. "I think his physical life don't want to live any longer," she wrote her Norcross cousins. "You know he never played, and the straightest engine has its leaning hour" (2:486). Her own preferred amusement was authorship. "You asked me if I wrote now?" she replied to T. W. Higginson. "I have no other Playmate" (2:588). Correspondence became a game for her and poetry her favorite form of play. Such poetic poses as child and drunkard are frankly comic. Even her cherished role as Queen of Calvary can verge on the ludicrous in its hyperbole. With niece and nephew she played the roles of fairy godmother and co-conspirator to the hilt. With Amherst she engaged in a monumental game of hide-and-seek.

She played hide-and-seek with her readers too, challenging them to ferret out a joke:

> Alone and in a Circumstance
> Reluctant to be told
> A spider on my reticence
> Assiduously crawled
>
> And so much more at Home than I
> Immediately grew
> I felt myself a visitor
> And hurriedly withdrew

Revisiting my late abode
With articles of claim
I found it quietly assumed
As a Gymnasium

Where Tax asleep and Title off
The inmates of the Air
Perpetual presumption took
As each were special Heir—
If any strike me on the street
I can return the Blow—
If any take my property
According to the Law
The Statute is my Learned friend
But what redress can be
For an offense nor here nor there
So not in Equity—
The Larceny of time and mind
The marrow of the Day
By spider, or forbid it Lord
That I should specify. (#1167)

Dickinson's editor suspects here a complaint about time wasted reading George Sand's *Mauprat,* while others detect a dark indictment of God and nature befitting her tragic muse.[10] These are remarkably solemn interpretations of a comic episode that apparently took place in the Dickinsons' outhouse. It features the poet as a demure Little Miss Muffet, who is frightened from the privy by a spider's crawling upon her. Just what part of her anatomy was involved we may surmise from the spider's *assi*duousness (from Latin *assidere* = sit down beside). By the time she nerved herself to return with a broom, she found the outhouse a gymnasium (from Greek *gymnos* = naked) festooned with cobwebs for gymnastic apparatus, spiders illegally squatting where the Dickinsons nakedly squatted. Doubtless the outhouse was reclaimed, but the spiders could not be swept from her mind. With mock-legal solemnity the lawyer's daughter is left pondering the difficulty of a suit to recover psychological damages from spiders in a case involving neither battery nor theft. Whatever the last two lines hint at (an absent lover seems as likely a preoccupation as George Sand or divine injustice), it is surely subordinate to the humor of tone and circumstance.

Sometimes her poetic games seem a form of solitaire.

The Angle of a Landscape—
That every time I wake—
Between my Curtain and the Wall
Upon an ample Crack—

Like a Venetian—waiting—
Accosts my open eye—
Is just a Bough of Apples—
Held slanting, in the Sky—

The Pattern of a Chimney—
The Forehead of a Hill—
Sometimes—a Vane's Forefinger—
But that's—Occasional—

The Seasons—shift—my picture—
Upon my Emerald Bough,
I wake—to find no—Emeralds—
Then—Diamonds—which the Snow

From Polar Caskets—fetched me—
The Chimney—and the Hill
And just the Steeple's finger—
These—never stir at all— (#375)

This prospect may seem suffocating in its minimalism, the view of a reluctant prisoner. After lines 12-13 promise seasonal variety, it can come as a mild shock, an anticlimax, when three of four elements composing this narrow landscape recur unchanged. But that anticlimax is part of the joke on midcentury Americans who reveled in the Hudson River painters' sense of boundless space. They preferred panoramas like those from Mount Tom in nearby Holyoke or the famous Ox-Bow of the Connecticut River in Northampton, grand vistas unified by hints at divine design. Dickinson, however, peeps out from an "ample Crack."

How ample? To answer that question one must parse the phrase "like a Venetian," which her odd punctuation leaves obscurely dangling. Evidently the vertical gap between her curtain and window makes her think of the horizontal gaps in a Venetian blind. But no sooner does that idea occur than by syntactic ambiguity the landscape itself is fancifully transmuted into an opulent Venetian gentleman after Titian, waiting to accost her eye when it opens. Like the jeweled liveries on the bough or the intimations of human form in the landscape's details, this bizarre simile suggests how hyperactive was the poet's imagination. Like Emerson, she is alert to discover patterns in her world, but what she cannot discover she will happily invent. Anyone who can invent a Venetian visitor on the spur of the moment, with no other resources than a window blind and the vagaries of language, would appear amply provided with imaginary playmates. If one wonders from what fantasies such a visionary awakes, one begins to see why the chimney, hill, and steeple—the known, unchanging elements of her view—might strike her as welcome evidence of security rather than confinement. Thoreau said he had traveled widely in Concord. Dickinson too dramatized humorously the deceptive amplitude of the fixed prospect framed by her window.

Was a mind of such self-reliant agility oppressed by God? Did it need God? Dickinson's feud with the fading orthodoxy of her day was a lover's quarrel. No major American poet makes more use of the Bible. Her poems on religious topics span a spectrum of attitudes ranging from hostility to devotion. The lady who found the Bible a wise and merry book, who was overwhelmed by fine sermons but burlesqued silly ones, shunned church throughout her adult life. Without presuming to encapsulate her beliefs, we may simply note at this point that she drew no clear line between piety and humor.

> I've known a Heaven, like a Tent
> To wrap it's shining Yards—
> Pluck up it's stakes, and disappear—
> Without the sound of Boards
> Or rip of Nail—Or Carpenter—
> But just the miles of Stare—
> That signalize a show's Retreat—
> In North America—
>
> No trace—no Figment of the Thing
> That dazzled, Yesterday,
> No ring—no Marvel—
> Men and Feats—
> Dissolved as utterly—
> As Bird's far Navigation
> Discloses just a Hue—
> A plash of Oars, a Gaiety—
> Then swallowed up, of View. (#243)

What dazzled yesterday but now cannot be found is more than sunshine, surely, for a cloudy day follows a sunny one without startling us. And the sideling glance at historical perspective "in North America" distinguishes this loss from some merely personal tragedy. This disappearing Heaven is the edifice of faith erected by a carpenter all too familiar with joined boards and the rip of nails. Yet the passion that erected the edifice is scarcely felt at its collapse. The circus strikes its tent and slouches off sans parade, bystanders staring stupidly at its departure. As the red-and-gold wagons fade into the distance a glint comes back, like the glint of an oriole's wings before it's swallowed from view. What we last glimpse is "a Gaiety," reminding us of the promise the shining canvas once enfolded.

And then the show is gone. Nostalgic but no dirge, the poem recalls Oliver Wendell Holmes's "The Deacon's Masterpiece." That comic allegory of the demise of Calvinism appeared in the *Atlantic Monthly* in 1858. Like the collapse of the one-hoss shay Dickinson's poem is light-hearted. Heaven vanishes with a parting twinkle of gaiety. Though the circus is utterly dissolved, its sudden disappearance almost seems a final stunt, leaving a lingering awe at this climactic feat. A last hurrah? Circuses circled through town all her life. "There was a circus, too, and I watched it away at half past three that morning. They said 'hoy, hoy' to their horses," she wrote one year, but a year later "we are to have another 'Circus,' and again the Procession from Algiers will pass the Chamber-Window" (2:507, 524).

"Dear friend. *'May'* I, or is it still April?" Dickinson began one letter (3:915). Like Holmes and the culture at large, she doted on puns.[11] "I give you a Pear that was given me" ran one note to her sister-in-law. "Would that it were a Pair, but Nature is penurious" (3:848). The childlike frivolity of these examples tinges many of her poetic puns. Nature lyrics often tap this goofy vein that scarcely rises to the level of wit: "The Orchis binds her feather on / For her old lover—Don the Sun!" (#64). "Bring me the sunset in a cup," she cries, "Reckon the morning's flagon's up / And say how many Dew" (#128). The equivocation *dew* = *do* = *suffice* is imperfect, for the mass noun makes no grammatical sense after *many,* but the very silliness of the wordplay chimes with the mood of drunken exuberance. "We—Bee and I—live by the quaffing," proclaims the little tippler in another mock drinking lyric that ends with both sprawled out dead drunk in a comic tableau: "Noon—our last Cup— / 'Found dead'—'of Nectar'— / By a humming Coroner— / In a By-Thyme!" (#230). The stretch from "moment of leisure" to "secluded thyme-bed" is hardly worth the effort unless one agrees with Lamb that the worst puns are the best. Like the bird who "squandered such a Note," we should not expect small change back when paying for ecstasy (#1600). "I tend my flowers for thee— / Bright absentee! / My Fuchsia's Coral Seams / Rip—while the Sower— dreams," cries an addled gardener-seamstress (#339). "The happy—happy Leaves— / That just abroad His Window / Have Summer's leave to play" may still suggest frolicsome double meanings after the advent of sterner weather: "The Winds went out their martial ways / The Leaves obtained excuse— / November hung his Granite Hat / Upon a nail of Plush" (#498, 1140). If autumn cannot be put off, a pun may at least divert attention from it to physics until we hardly realize what is at hand: "The pungent atom in the Air / Admits of no debate— / All that is named of Summer Days / Relinquished our Estate" (#1191).

Smarmy enough to be printed during her lifetime, these familiar quatrains read a little less obnoxiously if one understands that the speaker is not Dickinson but a bird:

> Some keep the Sabbath going to Church—
> I keep it, staying at Home—
> With a Bobolink for a Chorister—
> And an Orchard, for a Dome—
>
> Some keep the Sabbath in Surplice—
> I just wear my Wings—
> And instead of tolling the Bell, for Church,
> Our little Sexton—sings.
>
> God preaches, a noted Clergyman—
> And the sermon is never long,
> So instead of getting to Heaven, at last
> I'm going, all along. (#324)

They read better yet if one fancies that some keep the Sabbath in surplus, while God's status as a "noted" clergyman suggests that the sermon is birdsong.[12]

As Dickinson turns her wordplay to religious subjects, it acquires more weight, almost a metaphysical density at times. From Matthew 27:57-60 we learn that Christ's body was borne to Joseph of Arimathea's tomb at that rich man's personal expense. Dickinson gives Scripture an oblique verbal twist in drawing her own moral from the Resurrection: "'Twas Christ's own personal Expanse / That bore him from the Tomb" (#1543).

Elsewhere she devotes eight probing stanzas to surveying the many modes of human misery. "I measure every Grief I meet / With narrow, probing Eyes— / I wonder if It weighs like Mine— / Or has an Easier size." A striking conclusion explains the result of her effort to distinguish and appreciate the styles of grief: "And though I may not guess the kind— / Correctly—yet to me / A piercing Comfort it affords / In passing Calvary— / To note the fashions—of the Cross— / And how they're mostly worn— / Still fascinated to presume / That Some—are like My Own" (#561). Like patterns from *Godey's Lady's Book*, the patterns of grief pass before her. However modish they were in revival-prone Amherst, however alien to her own tastes, however "worn" in the sense of *démodé*, through "the fashions of the Cross" she glimpses the Passions of the Cross and is comforted by that pattern in human suffering.

Christ was more easily glimpsed than God, who could play hide-and-seek with Dickinson as she did with Amherst. Poem #576 echoes Sir Thomas Browne's regret that unlike Moses we have not even spied God's hindquarters. She remains ever alert:

I know that He exists.
Somewhere—in Silence—
He has hid his rare life
From our gross eyes.

'Tis an instant's play.
'Tis a fond Ambush—
Just to make Bliss
Earn her own surprise!
But—should the play
Prove piercing earnest—
Should the glee—glaze—
In Death's—stiff—stare—

Would not the fun
Look too expensive!
Would not the jest—
Have crawled too far! (#338)

Even if God's rare life is so rarefied as to prove nonexistent, making the game a foolish ambush rather than a loving one, she could face that cosmic joke with her own jokes. But she doubted the Cosmic Joker would go quite so far. "God cannot discontinue/annul himself," she mused. "This appalling trust is at times all that remains" (3:913). Buoyed by it, she consigned herself to an elaborately rehearsed finale with enough hope of divine mercy to end with an insouciant pun: "I made my soul familiar—with her extremity— / That at the last, it should not be a novel Agony— / But she, and Death, acquainted— / Meet tranquilly, as friends— / Salute, and pass, without a Hint— / And there, the Matter ends" (#412).

And if no mercy, no matter. "The truth I do not dare to know / I muffle with a jest" (#1715).

Hell held few terrors for Dickinson, whose eclecticism blandly waived doctrines she found distasteful in her Calvinist heritage, even at the risk of trivializing it.

A Tooth upon Our Peace
The Peace cannot deface—
Then Wherefore be the Tooth?
To vitalize the Grace—

The Heaven hath a Hell—
Itself to signalize—
And every sign before the Place
Is Gilt with Sacrifice— (#459)

Hell is Heaven's signboard, where guilt is gilded with grace. Remorse (from Latin *remordere* = bite again) is all we need of hell. Here she seems convinced that its nip is temporary. Her own triumphant sacrifices let her toy with the efficacy of a greater one.

The Paradoxical Power of Webster's Primal Words

Analogous to puns are Dickinson's experiments with homonymic or identical rimes. So-called *rime riche* is characteristic of French poetics. It flourished in Chaucer and the early English Renaissance but fell into disfavor when James I formally proscribed it. This royal ban Dickinson quirkily ignores, just as her off-rhymes flout the authority of English poetic tradition. The outcome is such rimes as *new/knew, Our's/Hours, too/to, be/Bee, I/eye, side/beside, found/profound, prefer/infer, go/ago, way/away.* "How lonesome the wind must feel Nights— / When People have put out the Lights / And everything that has an Inn / Closes the shutter and goes In" exemplifies one kind of naive wordplay that results (#1418).

But the technique also lends itself to more sophisticated puns with a metaphysical flavor. Christ's moments of human weakness especially moved her. "I rose—because He sank— / I thought it would be opposite— / But when his power dropped— / My Soul grew straight," begins one enigmatic deathbed poem describing how the speaker "cheered my fainting Prince" with "firm—even—Chants" (#616). Reminding him that "Best—must pass / Through this low Arch of Flesh," she infuses her despondent Prince with her own strong faith: "And so with Thews of Hymn— / And Sinew from within— / And ways I knew not that I knew—till then— / I lifted Him." The closing homonymic rhyme turns confusion of genders and religious roles into seeming fusion as by lifting a hymn she lifts him to salvation.[13]

Homonyms with different meanings point to an idea that Webster stressed in the Preface to his *American Dictionary:* the antithetical senses of primal words. "*For* in English, in the sentence, 'He that is not *for* us is against us,' denotes *in favor of*," he noted. "But in the phrase 'for all that' it denotes opposition" (p. xiv). Why? he wondered. Likewise, the Hebrew *barak* could mean both to *bless* and to *curse.* Rummaging through Semitic tongues, he found evidence that "to *bless* and to *curse* have the same radical sense, . . . to send or pour out words, to drive or to strain out the voice." Moreover, "it is also the same word as the English *pray*" and "the Greek βραχω, βρυχω . . . to *bray*" (pp. xxiii-xxiv). Antithetical ideas like praying and braying could be reconciled by finding "the primary action expressed by the root." Likewise, "the Latin *arceo* signifies to drive off . . . or keep from departing or escaping: two senses directly opposite. This is extremely natural; for *arceo* signifies to thrust off, repel, drive back. . . . The act of straining or holding produces both effects; to repel or stop what advances to assault, and protect what is enclosed or assaulted" (p. xxxv).

Webster's model for linguistic origins therefore revolved cloudily around a limited number of germinal terms for motion or physical force. "I am persuaded the primary sense of all the verbs in any language, may be expressed by thirty or forty words," he argued, offering a sample list of radical concepts like *go, set, rub, break, seize,* etc. (pp. xxxv–xxxvi). These thirty-four basic kinds of motion or action could in turn be reduced to very few words, for "the English words to *send, throw, thrust, strain, stretch, draw, drive, urge, press,* embrace the primary sense of a great part of all the verbs in every language which I have examined." Court de Gébelin's notions about primal nouns he dismissed contemptuously. As befits an expansive nation, our American vocabulary derives from basic manifestations of physical force. Its contradictory elements invite philological resolution in terms of Newtonian dynamic principles like action and reaction. Aspects of Webster's thinking vaguely resemble desynonymization, and the American's presentation is hardly more systematic than Coleridge's. Like many of his etymologies, it gains in imposing mystery from references to his "Synopsis of Words in Twenty Languages," an unpublished manuscript like Whiter's that now reposes in the bowels of the New York Public Library. In his dictionary its invisible authority is regularly invoked to fill lacunae in his sketch of linguistic evolution.

Did that theory help shape the poet's thought? Certainly she shares his respect for the verb as the driving engine of language. She uses more than 25 percent fewer adjectives and better than 25 percent more verbs than representative American poets of the 1840s.[14] "Cherish Power," she told her sister-in-law. "Remember that stands in the Bible between the Kingdom and the Glory, because it is wilder than either of them" (2:631).

More important, Webster encouraged Dickinson to think of words as bundles of polarized energy, poised but always threatening to split apart. The notion of antithetical primal meanings must have intrigued a poet who was fascinated by antitheses. Like the haunting lyric "It was not death, for I stood up" (#510), many of her definition poems define their subjects through negation.[15] Her imagination dwells on opposed but complementary states of being. "Should ever these exploring Hands / Chance Sovereign on a Mine— / Or in the long—uneven term / To win, become their turn— / How fitter they will be—for Want— / Enlightening so well— / I know not which, Desire, or Grant— / Be wholly beautiful" (#801). A series of poems exploring the paradoxical tension between desire and fulfillment makes this point obsessively. "Impossibility, like Wine / Exhilarates the Man / Who tastes it; Possibility / Is Flavorless— Combine / A Chance's faintest Tincture / And in the former Dram / Enchantment makes ingredient / As certainly as Doom" (#838). Add just a touch of the possible to fortify an impossible dream, shake well, and the result is the intoxicating, lethal cocktail of hope. For Dickinson enjoyment depends on its precariousness: "Uncertain lease—develops lustre / On Time" (#857). Pleasure and pain seem inextricably intertwined at their source. Reworking the most celebrated couplet from Thomas Campbell's *Pleasures of Hope* (1798), she insists that "Delight—becomes pictorial— / When viewed through Pain— / More fair—because impossible / That any gain— / The Mountain—at a given distance— / In Amber—lies— / Approached—the Amber flits—a little— / And That's—the Skies" (#572). Absence makes the heart grow fonder, so the surest way to kill desire is to fulfill it:

> Undue significance a starving man attaches
> To Food—
> Far off—He sighs—and therefore—Hopeless—
> And therefore—Good—
>
> Partaken—it relieves—indeed—
> But proves us
> That Spices fly
> In the Receipt—It was the Distance—
> Was Savory— (#439)

Pushed to extremes, the conviction that there is necessarily "an Austere trait in Pleasure" suggests that death is the spice of life (#807). One poem shows Dickinson pondering such questions in the light of contradictory meanings derived from the same verbal root. "Satisfaction—is the Agent / Of Satiety— / Want—a quiet Commissary / For Infinity," she claims. "To possess, is past the instant / We achieve the Joy— / Immortality contented / Were Anomaly" (#1036). Denoting opposed states of mind, *satisfaction* and *satiety* suggest how words might spring from a bipolar root (represented here by the Latin *satis* = enough) that balances forces complementarily in reciprocal attraction and repulsion. Webster explained that *sate* was akin to *set,* for "the primary sense is, to stuff, to fill, from crowding, driving" (s.v.). Extrapolating from this mistaken etymology, Dickinson could conclude that *satiety* absorbs force in static fixity while the dynamism of the primal root still powers true *satisfac-*

tion, a thrusting drive for infinity, Romantic *Strebung nach dem Unendliche.*

Similar wordplay underlies a lyric enclosed with a flower in a letter to friends:

> By a flower—By a letter—
> By a nimble love—
> If I weld the Rivet faster—
> Final fast—above—
>
> Never mind my breathless Anvil!
> Never mind Repose!
> Never mind the sooty faces
> Tugging at the Forge! (#109)

Dickinson admired Samuel Bowles. Corresponding lavishly with him and his wife, she sent more missives than they could always answer. "My cheek is red with shame because I write so often," she confessed (2:358). Her poetic apology for speedy replies revolves around two opposed senses of *fast:* firmly fixed and quickly moving. In the first stanza her ready pen strives to cement their friendship. If I weld it more firmly now, she argues, the final result will hold fast above. To this eternal steadfastness she playfully opposes her own nimble writing. With its sense of temporal bustle, the second stanza draws out the pun implicit in "faster" by dramatizing the hurry with which she is replying.

If she turned for enlightenment to her lexicon, she would have found the adjective *fast* given two separate entries. Its opposed meanings Webster attributed to "the same root . . . with a different application," which his "Synopsis" characterized by linking the ideas *press firm* and *press on.* Except for casting his net too widely for cognates, he was not far from the truth, for in the Teutonic family the meaning *speedy* did develop from the root meaning *steady* via the adverb. To run fast is to run hard, firmly, or steadily. By contrast, a modern *Webster's Third International* avoids Noah's etymological gaffes in this entry but gives no sense of how the two opposed meanings of *fast* developed. Like Noah, the poet who described a bluebird as "last to adhere when Summer cleaves away" was obviously intrigued by the antithetical meanings of such words as *cleave* (#1395).

"Could mortal lip divine / The undeveloped Freight / Of a delivered syllable / 'Twould crumble with the weight" (#1409). Webster's theory of antithetical primal meanings certainly warranted that conclusion. In reading the most ancient text she knew Dickinson responded to words in this spirit. Genesis 5:24 describes the end of Methusaleh's father Enoch as follows: "And Enoch walked with God: and he was not; for God took him."

Explicating this possibly corrupt verse in the light of the Septuagint and Jewish tradition, Paul claimed that "by faith Enoch was translated that he should not see death" (Heb. 11:5). About a year after the death of her father Dickinson jotted down her reaction to the cryptic verse:

> "Was not" was all the Statement.
> The Unpretension stuns—
> Perhaps—the Comprehension—
> They wore no Lexicons—
>
> But lest our Speculation
> In inanition die
> Because "God took him" mention—
> That was Philology— (#1342)

Reflecting her own quizzical struggles with faith, Dickinson's musing response registers awe at the way the suggestive parataxis of Scripture implies alternative meanings. Was Enoch translated, or did he simply disappear? Like Herder, she sees the sentence as sublimely poetic. In the absence of lexicons the dense resonance of the Hebrews' language confirms their "Philology," for the root meaning of that term is "love of the word." Was Genesis ardently glorifying Enoch or sadly mourning him? Perhaps both at once, for "a little overflowing word / That any, hearing, had inferred / For Ardor or for Tears, / Though Generations pass away, / Traditions ripen and decay, / As eloquent appears" (#1467).

The potency of speech is a favorite theme. "A word is dead / When it is said, / Some say," she notes, cocking an ear at the ironic contradiction involved. "I say it just / Begins to live / That day" (#1212). While she burlesqued poor sermons, she was rocked by good ones. One poem is often interpreted as her reaction to the preaching of the Reverend Charles Wadsworth. The description squares with what we know of his pulpit manner, but she had heard other spellbinding orators.[16] Whether or not the specific identification holds, these lines suggest how she could be overwhelmed by a skilled speaker's crescendo:

> He fumbles at your Soul
> As Players at the Keys
> Before they drop full Music on—
> He stuns you by degrees—
> Prepares your brittle Nature
> For the Etherial Blow
> By fainter Hammers—further heard—
> Then nearer—Then so slow
> Your Breath has time to straighten—
> Your Brain—to bubble Cool—

Deals—One—imperial—Thunderbolt—
That scalps your naked Soul— (#315)

The musical analogies are not casual, for Dickinson was a fair pianist noted for her impromptus, fond of Robert Burns's songs, and peculiarly sensitive to vocal timbre. Many rhetorics analyzed oratory in musical terms. Wadsworth's voice impressed her and others. When he called on her in 1880 after an interval of twenty years, her sister Lavinia announced, "The gentleman with the deep voice wants to see you, Emily" (3:901). Hearing Bowles made her think, "The Voice is the Palace of all of us" (2:540). Judge Lord's voice could also thrum on her heartstrings. "A group of students passed the House—one of them said Oh no, like you—the same vagabond Sweetness," she wrote in a draft fragment probably addressed to him. "I followed the voice ... You know I have a vice for voices" (3:914).

At times her vice for voices led her to decry silence. "Silence is all we dread. / There's Ransom in a Voice— / But Silence is infinity. / Himself have not a face" (#1251). Even gabble could seem preferable:

> I fear a Man of frugal Speech—
> I fear a Silent Man—
> Haranguer—I can overtake—
> Or Babbler—entertain—
>
> But He who weigheth—While the Rest—
> Expend their furthest pound—
> Of this Man—I am wary—
> I fear that He is Grand— (#543)

Her reserved father loomed grandly in her imagination. In poems like these the ominousness of silence is linked with inscrutable authority. One result could be a forbiddingly cold vision of eternity as a place where "Great Streets of silence led away / To Neighborhoods of Pause— / Here was no Notice—no Dissent / No Universe—no Laws" (#1159).

But for all her mistrust of silence, she also mistrusted speech. "The words the happy say / Are paltry melody / But those the silent feel / Are beautiful," she avers (#1750). "Eloquence is when the Heart / Has not a Voice to spare" (#1268). Tapping the primal language of inspiration, she knew moments when "I put my pleasure all abroad— / I dealt a word of Gold / To every Creature—that I met— / And Dowered—all the world." But such Edenic language could evaporate, leaving her groping for diction, feeling the "Wilderness roll back / Along my Golden lines." So bereft of inspiration, she finds herself naked, wondering "where my moment of Brocade— / My drop—of India?"

(#430). Like Adamic naming, India ink suggests the power of primal words by hinting at Bopp's notions about Sanskrit. In the absence of primal language,

> To tell the Beauty would decrease
> To state the Spell demean
> There is a syllable-less Sea
> Of which it is the sign
> My will endeavors for it's word
> And fails, but entertains
> A Rapture as of Legacies—
> Of introspective Mines— (#1700)

In such moods she could perceive words as not just futile but a positive threat to her feelings. "The Treason of an Accent / Might vilify the Joy— / To breathe—corrode the rapture / Of Sanctity to be" (#1358). Or the failure to find integrative primal language might attest to the ambitious scope of her vision. "If I could tell how glad I was / I should not be so glad— / But when I cannot make the Force / Nor mould it into Word / I know it is a sign / That new Dilemma be / From mathematics further off / Than from Eternity" (#1668).

Ordinary language was inadequate beside the awesome power of the creative Word. The Incarnation fused flesh and spirit at enormous cost hard to sustain. "Your thoughts don't have words every day / They come a single time / Like signal esoteric sips / Of the communion wine / Which while you taste so native seems / So easy so to be / You cannot comprehend its price / Nor it's infrequency" (#1452). Elsewhere the model is God's Fiat:

> You'll know it—as you know 'tis Noon—
> By Glory—
> As you do the Sun—
> By Glory—
> As you will in Heaven—
> Know God the Father—and the Son
>
> By intuition, Mightiest Things
> Assert themselves—and not by terms—
> "I'm Midnight"—need the Midnight say—
> "I'm Sunrise"—Need the Majesty?
>
> Omnipotence—had not a Tongue—
> His lisp—is Lightning—and the Sun—
> His conversation—with the Sea—
> "How shall you know"?
> Consult your Eye! (#420)

Convinced that the heavens declare the glory of God, King James's translators relied on Vulgate interpolations to claim, "Day unto day uttereth speech, and night unto night sheweth knowledge. *There* is no speech or knowledge *where* their voice is not heard" (Ps. 19:1-3). Transcendentalism agreed with that doctrine of correspondence. For Dickinson, however—like the Hebrew Psalmist—there seems no room left for speech when this sublime dumbshow appears.[17] The divine Word fusing speech, object, and action eclipses human speech—even poetic speech. Correctly deriving *intuition* from the Latin *intueor,* Webster defined it as "a looking on; a sight or view; *but restricted to mental view or perception."* Fond though she was of his tutelage in terms, she preferred ocular tuition in the Language of Nature.

Enclosing a flower in a letter, Dickinson accompanied it with a self-deprecating lyric: "All the letters I can write / Are not so fair as this— / Syllables of Velvet— / Sentences of Plush, / Depths of Ruby, undrained, / Hid, Lip for Thee— / Play it were a Humming Bird— / And just sipped me" (#334). Like an adolescent girl signing a love letter with a lip print, she craves words with the tangible reality of natural objects but is keenly aware of the gap between them. "The Veins of other Flowers / The Scarlet Flowers are / Till Nature leisure has for Terms / As 'Branch,' and 'Jugular,'" she writes elsewhere, comparing botanic classification to our normal use of words. "We pass and she abides. / We conjugate Her Skill / While She creates and federates / Without a syllable" (#811). Etymologically *terms* are *boundaries* or *limits—terminations.* We normally segment reality into individual words of different classes, just as a botanist anatomizes a flower into components. But Nature creates not parts but wholes, so that the veins of blossoms seem scarlet flowers in their own right—as well as being *flow*-ers. The seamless integrity of natural thing-events lies beyond our delimiting language of discrete terms, which can only be conjugated rather than federated. *Federate,* Webster mistakenly informed her, derived from a Semitic root meaning "to pledge," while "the primary sense of create and of cry is the same" (s.v.). Though without artificial subdivisions like syllables, Nature thus remains expansively linguistic for Dickinson, in a way calculated to put human terminology to shame. "These last thoughts are fictions—vain imaginations to lead astray foolish young women," she exclaims ironically in one letter, shattering an elaborate fantasy spun for a friend. "They are flowers of speech, they both make, and tell deliberate falsehoods, avoid them as the snake" (1:88). Her acute awareness that flowers of speech were not flowers drove her to express herself through Romantic irony.

Little Emily's Romantic Ironies

"Perception of an object costs / Precise the Object's loss— / Perception is itself a Gain / Replying to it's Price— / The Object Absolute—is nought— / Perception sets it fair / And then upbraids a Perfectness / That situates so far" (#1071). These lines versify Schlegel's solution to the Kantian predicament. The Absolute resists perception and formulation. Efforts to grasp it within the phenomenal realm are valuable, but they also distort it. Like perception, then, the artist may make visible a perfect beauty, but it does not correspond to the dynamic beauty he can imagine. Its perfection is too perfected, too remote from the fluid Absolute. He can restore his creative vision only by rending his own visible creation.

We can glimpse one stage in that ongoing, oscillating process of Romantic irony as Dickinson described herself trying to compose.

> Shall I take thee, the Poet said
> To the propounded word?
> Be stationed with the Candidates
> Till I have finer tried—
>
> The Poet searched Philology
> And was about to ring
> for the suspended Candidate
> There came unsummoned in—
>
> That portion of the Vision
> The Word applied to fill
> Not unto nomination
> The Cherubim reveal— (#1126)

Evidence that she was describing her own mode of writing litters her manuscripts. Some list a dozen alternatives for a single epithet, with none preferred. Here a possible word applies for a job and is jotted down beside other candidates as the poet ransacks Webster. It seems the best choice. But just as she is about to inscribe it in the line, her painstaking philological scrutiny triggers a renewed sense of what she would like to say but cannot. That flashing angelic insight comes unbidden. It is not vouchsafed to "nomination," for her candidate is rejected and no words can name her vision. These sprightly lines describe a failed poem. Indeed, perhaps they *are* a failed poem, for the wrenched syntax of the second stanza seems pointless (substituting *as* for *was* would be better) while the last two lines are clotted and awkward. We might "upbraid" them. But the poet hardly cares, for she is experiencing what she describes in "The tint I cannot take—is best," as one of those "Moments of Dominion / That happen on the Soul / And leave it with a Discontent / Too exquisite—to tell" (#627). This divine discontent is the high of Romantic irony. We cannot upbraid her verse any more than she does, for a sense of personal superiority to her own unfinished creations exhales from virtually all her unpublished oeuvre. "Whatever await us of Doom or Home, we are mentally permanent," she mused, but "'It is finished' can never be said of us" (2:613). Unlike Christ, we are always evolving, never perfected.

Like the primal words she sought, Dickinson's major themes are all two-sided. "Burglar! Banker—Father!" she cries to her God, encapsulating her ambivalent religious stance (#49). Poems of mock-drunken ecstasy with bees are punctuated by sobering encounters with snakes that inspire "tighter breathing / And Zero at the Bone" (#986). Peeping in the well, she glimpsed "an abyss's face." She remembered that "nature is a stranger yet" when romping in the Dickinsons' meadow (#1400). Her love poetry veers between fulfillment and frustration, each attitude enhancing the other. For all her protestations of eternal fidelity, she knew perfectly well that "We outgrow love, like other things / And put it in the Drawer— / Till it an Antique fashion shows— / Like Costumes Grandsires wore" (#887). In the long tradition of poetic melancholy hers are among the most powerful renditions of the state we call clinical depression, for this vernacular humorist believed that "Mirth is the Mail of Anguish" (#165). Her notion of language itself is polarized, as we have seen: words appear either omnipotent or impotent. It is hard to find a statement of hers that could not be offset by quoting her to the contrary. Probably that is what she had in mind when she contemplated "that polar privacy / A soul admitted to itself— / Finite Infinity" (#1695). Although her brief lyrics may appear impulsive efforts to crystallize a moment's feeling, her predilection for quasi-subjunctive verb forms can make even the most impassioned utterance seem conditional, tentative, abstract, as if part of her mind were always aware of antitheses. Hers is oddly impersonal personal poetry.

From her awareness of paradoxicality and contradictoriness she evolved an aesthetic of ambiguity. Riddles delighted her. In her letters enigmatic verse descriptions accompanied tokens like jewelweed, a cocoon, a pair of garters. Several notches above such *vers d'occasion* were her indirect verse descriptions of a snake, a locomotive, and— perhaps most spectacularly—a hummingbird that seems pure distilled energy.

A Route of Evanescence
With a revolving Wheel—
A Resonance of Emerald—
A Rush of Cochineal—
And every Blossom on the Bush
Adjusts it's tumbled Head—
The mail from Tunis, probably,
An easy Morning's Ride. (#1463)

This poem describes not the bird itself but the bird's appearance—and not so much its appearance, really, as its *disappearance,* the primary meaning Webster assigns to *evanescence.*

"Tell all the Truth but tell it slant" became her motto (#1129). To achieve gnomic utterance she condensed ruthlessly. "The riddle we can guess / We speedily despise," she felt, "Not anything is stale so long / As Yesterday's surprise" (#1222). Her Orphic manner differs from Emerson's in that syntax eludes her rather than synonyms. Connectives are suppressed, coordination and subordination vanish, punctuation violates grammar until her poems begin to resemble the word-heaps blurted out by aphasics with contiguity disorder.[18] Feckless indifference to grammar was part of her pose. To find "a gracious author sitting side by side with 'Murray'" in the village bookstore made her think of "Pegasus in the pound" (I, 144). Anything but tame, her Pegasus rattles the rails of its grammatical corral in the angry conviction that "True Poems flee" (#1472).

In that respect true poetry resembles life as experienced by one who could believe and disbelieve a hundred times a day. A striking number of her poems deal with such fleeting phenomena as thunderstorms, subtle shadings of light, the pivotal changes of seasons, the transitions of sunrise, noon, or sunset. Like the birds and insects that flit across her vision, these aspects of nature mirror a mind preoccupied with the fleetingness of inspiration, the elusiveness of fulfilled love, and those liminal moments on the verge between life and death. Many poems portray her pondering the aftermath of some crisis too rapid to be grasped as it was happening. "I would eat evanescence slowly," she proclaims (2:452). With Romantic irony her finest poems express her sense of life as incipient dissolution.

These are the days when Birds come back—
A very few—a Bird or two—
To take a backward look.

These are the days when skies resume
The old—old sophistries of June—
A blue and gold mistake.

Oh fraud that cannot cheat the Bee —
Almost thy plausibility
Induces my belief.

Till ranks of seeds their witness bear —
And softly thro' the altered air
Hurries a timid leaf.

Oh Sacrament of Summer days,
Oh Last Communion in the Haze —
Permit a child to join.

Thy sacred emblems to partake —
Thy consecrated bread to take
And thine immortal wine. (#130)

"These Indian-Summer Days with their peculiar peace remind me of those stillest things that no one can disturb," wrote Dickinson to a cousin. "I suppose we are all thinking of Immortality, at times so stimulatedly that we cannot sleep. . . . Speculate with all our might, we cannot ascertain" (2:463). Such musing underlies twenty or so lyrics that she wrote about the season, among them some of her choicest. Indian summer is the season of deception, christened from the same belief in the aborigines' hypocrisy that gave the American language the phrase "Indian giver." The opening line heralds a spring song. Only as the word *back* is echoed with new meaning in *backward* do we begin to suspect that not spring but fall is at hand. In a feat of legerdemain the flocks of "Birds" initially conjured up are replaced by "a very few," then by "a Bird" (well, maybe two at most — in point of fact no birds return for Indian summer). The poet is herself an Indian giver, taking back meanings that her words at first promise, summoning up springtime scenes only to puncture them as illusions. Any satisfaction we might feel at solving the riddle of the season in the second stanza is likewise punctured, for in this poem the deceptiveness of Indian summer is *not* contrasted with high summer. Instead, June is treated as a month of "sophistries" all too familiar to us in their own right. This Indian summer merely reprises them in one last, magnificent illusion that seems their quintessence. The poet locates us in a temporal world where it is hard to contrast illusion to truth, where at best we may simply compare one "blue and gold mistake" with another. Echoic repetitions of "old" and "These are the days" suggest the poet's sophisticated certainty that the more things change, the more they remain the same.

In the first line of the third stanza a harsh exclamation denouncing "fraud" modulates into a humorous, almost tender recognition of its inability to fool a bee. Yet the wise bee invoked seems less real than the season, seems hypothetical, for any bee smart enough to fathom the fraud cannot *be* there. The notion of the fraud's ineffectuality is itself promptly reversed in the next two lines by a confession of wistful near-belief on the poet's part. Then the sense of plausibility is punctured again with the details of the fourth stanza, yet punctured so gently by the oxymoron of the softly hurrying leaf that nature herself seems reluctant to challenge belief. The images of these two central stanzas alternately suggest and demolish the identity of Indian summer with summer. Yet even if that identity is a "mistake," to credit it may not be to be cheated by fraud but instead to indulge a wistful hope. If the leaf flutters fearfully and permanently to ground, in diction that is both legal and Christian the seeds "bear witness" not only to the fact of decay but to the possibility of rebirth.

The poem asks whether high summer and Indian summer are the same or different. With a slightly unorthodox rhyme, it also asks us to ponder the relation between *a leaf* and *belief*. The final syllables are the same in sound (hence an unconventional rhyme) yet different in spelling. Are they related in meaning? According to Webster, to believe was "in some cases, to have a full persuasion, approaching to certainty; in others, more doubt is implied." And his densely suggestive entry on the noun went on to explain that etymologically "*Belief* is from the root of *leave,* permission, assent. . . . See *Leave* and *Live.*"

Turning to the entry on the transitive verb LEAVE, Dickinson would have meandered through a forest of supposed Teutonic cognates: "Sax. . . *leofan,* to leave, to live. . . . *Belifan,* to remain or be left . . . *geleaf,* leave, license . . . faith or belief . . . ; *leof,* loved; *lufa,* love, also belief . . . *luflic,* lovely. The German has *leave* in *urlaub,* a furlow, and *belief* in *glaube; live* in *leben;* and *love* in *liebe, lieben,* the Latin *libet, lubet.* . . . These are a small part of the affinities of this word." The entry on the verb LIVE would also have informed her that "it coincides with leave. The primary sense probably is, to rest, remain, abide. If so, the root may be Ar[abic] . . . *labba,* to be, to abide. Class Lb, No. 1." The reference to etymological categories in Webster's unpublished "Synopsis" promised a wealth of further evidence. She could have explored it without consulting that, however. Running over the same Saxon and Latin roots, the entry on the verb LOVE added the Sanskrit "*loab,* love, desire. See *lief.* The sense is probably to be prompt, free . . . from leaning . . . or drawing forward." And the entry on the adverb LIEF would have informed her that "this word coincides with love, *lubet, libet,* and the primary sense is to be free, prompt, ready."

Webster's discussion mingled real insights with wild oversimplifications. Love and belief are indeed related, deriving from an Indo-European root *leubh-*, to love. We trust those whom we love, hence belief, and trust remains a crucial index of love. Marital infidelity can often be proven, but a beloved's fidelity cannot be proven—only believed. From the same root derive *lief* and the noun *leave*. To have people's leave to do something is to have their loving approval. Whatever you would as *lief* do is something desired.

But our verb *leave* comes from another root, *leip-*, to stick, to adhere as a fatty substance. Fat is what remains, what is *left*. From the same root comes our verb *live*. Life is essentially stick-to-itiveness, continuance—it is distantly related to *lipo*suction. Like any other *leaf*, however, *leaves* of fat come from a third root, *leup-*, to peel off, break off. By intriguing processes this root begat *libraries*, eytmologically repositories for dead foliage. It may also be related to a Germanic root for *sky* from which we get *lift, loft,* and *lofty.*

Such insights cannot be gleaned from a modern *Webster's.* Thanks, however, to old Noah's etymological bizarreries, Emily Dickinson dwelt in a fairer house than prose. She could dwell on the poetic possibility that living, loving, leaving, and believing were all aspects, however contradictory, of the same dynamic process observable in the growth and fall of a leaf. Belief included doubt, according to Webster, like her doubt that summer would linger or that a timid leaf would rise again.

Thus the last two stanzas begin with her exclamation "Oh Sacrament." Echoing her earlier exclamation "Oh fraud," she now embraces Indian summer for all that it is, both fraud and sacrament. Without the sophisticated knowingness of the opening stanzas, with their faintly world-weary repetitions, her choice involves all the awareness permitted by the haze. The lady who throughout her adult life did not attend church and never partook the Eucharist joins this ritual communion as a child might a game. An *emblem* was defined by Webster as "a picture representing one thing to the eye, and another to the understanding; a painted enigma." Would a childlike fondness for enigmas and riddles make her one of the little children to whom the Gospel promises the kingdom of heaven?

Quizzical yet fervent, the parodic nature sacrament of the last two stanzas is not so heretical as to bar Christian belief. The poem was among the few published during her lifetime with at least her tacit consent. In 1864 it appeared in *Drum Beat.* Devoted to raising money for medical aid to Union casualties, that newspaper was edited by a prominent Congregational minister who was a friend of the Dickinsons. Neither he nor she would have sanctioned its appearance had they understood the pantheistic communion ritual as critical of Christianity.[19] As the European Renaissance paralleled nature and grace, so the mid-Victorian sensibility was quite capable of imagining a subsidiary role for lesser deities.

> If "God is Love" as he admits
> We think that he must be
> Because he is a "jealous God"
> He tells us certainly
>
> If "All is possible with" him
> As he besides concedes
> He will refund us finally
> Our confiscated Gods— (#1260)

From the beginning Transcendentalism was rife with references to "the gods." But what shocked the orthodox in the 1830s was tame enough by the 1860s. Many welcomed a splash of polytheism to vie with Roman Catholicism and stave off encroaching atheism. Rather than being boldly iconoclastic, Dickinson's al fresco Eucharist is if anything chic.

Teetering between the unique grandeur of the Last Supper and the touching tiptoe pretension of a child's first communion, this natural sacrament avoids New England's sober middle ground, where children were not permitted to communicate. In Amherst the Eucharist was celebrated infrequently for those who had joined the church by making a mature declaration of faith after a conversion experience. "When a Child and fleeing from Sacrament I could hear the clergyman saying 'All who loved the Lord Jesus Christ—were asked to remain—'" she recalled. "My flight kept time to the Words" (2:524-25). Etymological echoes ("sacrament . . . sacred . . . consecrate") insist hypnotically on the holiness of her natural ritual. Yet perhaps the lady doth protest too much, for identical rhymes remind us that to partake may be to take part in a mistake. Indeed, the ambiguity of the entire ritual derives from an ambiguity of language. For the poet celebrates this "Last Communion in the Haze" at a table created out of thin air—out of "altered air." The airy altar at which Dickinson worships nature is no more than a pun, hewn by her in a moment's imaginative play from the shifting shapes of unstable language. The whole mock-ritual is spun from a pun. In fun.

Of course, the Unitarian Andrews Norton had argued that the Trinity was no more than a bad pun. And Horace Bushnell had countered by implying that even a bad pun might be quite good enough. Like that Transcendental minister, Dickinson delighted in paradox as a means of renewing stagnant forms. With Romantic irony she weaves her way through this enigmatic poem, where each stanza raises possibilities only to puncture them. The same oscillation between reality and illusion can be traced in many of her lyrics.

> Finding is the first Act
> The second, loss,
> Third, Expedition for
> The "Golden Fleece"
> Fourth, no Discovery—
> Fifth, no Crew—
> Finally, no Golden Fleece—
> Jason—sham—too. (#870)

Here we move from finding through loss to an apparent recovery that is at last unmasked as a fantasy. But whereas this would-be Jason is finally fleeced, the child-hero of "These are the days" is left enjoying an ambiguous triumph.

What faith if any does this poem express? In later gnomic quatrains Dickinson's feelings about religious faith crystallize in bewildering variety. She is serenely secure: "I never spoke with God / Nor visited in Heaven— / Yet certain am I of the spot / As if the Checks were given" (#1052). She is slyly cynical: "'Faith' is a fine invention / When Gentlemen can see— / But Microscopes are prudent / In an Emergency" (#185). She is heroically determined: "Too much of proof affronts belief" (#1228). She is defiantly skeptical: "That it will never come again / Is what makes life so sweet. / Believing what we don't believe / Does not exhilarate. / That if it be, it be at best / An ablative estate— / This instigates an appetite / Precisely opposite" (#1741). And she clings with wistful resolve to the usefulness of a sublime fraud: "The abdication of Belief / Makes the Behavior small— / Better an ignis fatuus / Than no illume at all" (#1551).

For all their epigrammatic bite, such postwar poems can seem shorthand abridgments of emotions explored more richly in her great poetry during the Civil War. A major poem like "These are the days when Birds come back" holds all these attitudes in solution at once, without allowing any to precipitate out—and its solution is Romantic irony. The poem is an expanded equivocation in its own right. A poet who experienced life as contradictory was well served by Webster's polyvalent primal words. With their aid she composed a poetry of flickering perspectives. "On subjects of which we know nothing, or should I say Beings," she wrote, "we both believe, and disbelieve a hundred times an Hour, which keeps Believing nimble" (3:728). That her quicksilver words indeed do. "Faith—is the Pierless Bridge," one poem punningly begins (#915). Without foundation but also without peer, it resembles the Romantic imagination with which she ironically explored ultimate questions.

11 /

Whitman's Experiments with Language

I charge you forever reject those who would expound me, for I cannot expound myself.
— (*LG*, p. 238)

The Allure of Native American Names

"Names are magic," declared Whitman. "One word can pour such a flood through the soul" (*Pr.*, p. 18). In this conviction he filled notebooks with pages of names. One long list with brief descriptions has been interpreted as a roll call of possible lovers. But however wistfully set down, these names also reflect a primal love of nomenclature. He was fascinated by the colorful nicknames of omnibus drivers like Brownie, Christmas Johnny, and Pretty Ike. "In words of names, the mouth and ear of the people show antipathy to titles, misters, handles. They love short first names abbreviated to their lips: Tom, Bill, Jack," he noted. "These are to enter into literature, and be voted for on political tickets for the great offices" (*Pr.*, p. 22). He himself did his mite to launch nicknames into literature. The 1855 edition of *Leaves of Grass* was copyrighted in the name of Walter Whitman. But in the 1856 edition the poem that became "Song of Myself" was titled "Poem of Walt Whitman, an American," fixing the author's identity for life. Sloughing his sputtering journalistic career, he drew on an explicit theory of demotic words to reinvent himself as a democratic bard.

His onomastic ideas were no more coherent than his thought in general.[1] "Give to infants the names of qualities—physical and mental attributes," this committed bachelor decided. "Do not name them, till they exhibit these markedly." How an anonymous Natty Bumppo should be called to dinner before shooting his first deer he blithely ignored. He was content to forestall delicate situations that might arise if his advice were uncharitably applied to problem children. "Always select, of course, the most favorable phases of character—or of natural things—as Day, Hope, Oak, Rocky, . . . Fisherman, Sweet-breath" (*DBN*, 3:701). He toyed with "Trout" as a name but had second thoughts. With no children of his own (save the bastards he invented to stave off suspicion of homosexuality) he could not enrich America with Sweet-breath Whitman. To honor his theories, Walt's favorite brother Jeff named a first daughter Mannahatta and put off naming a second for some time. "The new baby is immense, & I take to her in proportion," enthused her fond uncle. "I want her to be called California. She is fully worthy the name. She is large" (*Correspondence,* 1:183). Alas, despite his determined campaign to annex California, the family finally chose the more prosaic Jessie.

The state's name appealed to him more than those of its towns. "California is sown thick with the names of all the little and big saints," he complained in a spasm of anticlericalism. "Chase them away and substitute aboriginal names. . . . What do such names know of democracy,—of the hunt for the gold leads and the nugget or of the religion that is scorn and negation?" (*Pr.,* pp. 30, 35). He did not explain why aboriginal names were any better suited than Spanish piety to the desperado spirit of the Forty-niners who were merrily exterminating Native Americans. But he cherished a lifelong fondness for Amerindian nomenclature. "Monongahela—it rolls with venison richness on the palate" (*Pr.,* p. 30). Although its English name graphically describes Long Island, Whitman the journalist waged an unsuccessful newspaper campaign to rechristen it Paumanok. "It is far better to call a new inhabited island by the native word, than by its first discoverer, or to call it New anything," he argued. "All classic names are objectionable. How much better Ohio, Oregon, Missouri, Milwaukee, &c. . . . than New York, Ithaca, Naples, &c." (*DBN,* 3:705). Indignantly denouncing the Duke of York, later King James II of unhappy memory, Whitman wanted to rechristen his city and toyed with extending the term *Manhattan* to designate the entire state. Likewise, the aristocratic name of Lord Baltimore's city was "to be revolutionized" (*Pr.,* p. 31). The predominantly English names of the thirteen original colonies vexed him. "I would be in favor of changing West Virginia: yes, I am sure I would," he decided late in life, preferring to call it Kanawtha. "But Virginia I would let stand: it seems to have its own long reasons for being what it is."[2] English names sanctioned by long usage might be tolerable. Not so innovations. "Down in this country—right here, near us—there was a place called Longacoming," he recalled in his Camden retirement. "The name was fine, fine—the mere sound of it: yet they got it into their fat heads that the name was not satisfactory: they met, put the old name aside for a new name: changed Longacoming to Berlin: oh God!"[3]

Whitman's onomastic ideas sparked several poems. More than one was devoted to celebrating "My city's fit and noble name resumed, / Choice aboriginal name, with marvelous beauty, meaning, / A *rocky founded island—shores where ever gayly dash the coming, going, hurry-ing sea waves"* (*LG*, p. 507). The etymology of the name *Manhattan* is obscure. But if all those meanings lurk in the four-syllable Irvingesque version that furnished his title, in its three epigrammatic lines "Manna-hatta" implies a more devastating contrast between Indian terseness and his own expansive prolixity than any "fit" it ever suggests between mod-ern and Native American language. It celebrates a link that it simulta-neously belies.

Similar paradoxicality characterizes a longer poem of the same title that first appeared in 1860. "I was asking for something specific and per-fect for my city, and behold! here is the aboriginal name," Whitman began, then continued:

> Now I see what there is in a name, a word, liquid, sane, unruly, musical, self-sufficient,
> I see that the word of my city, is that word up there,
> Because I see that word nested in nests of water-bays, superb, with tall and wonderful spires,
> Rich, hemm'd thick all around with sailships and steamships—an island sixteen miles long, solid-founded,
> Numberless crowded streets—high growths of iron, slender, strong, light, splendidly uprising toward clear skies,
> Tides swift and ample, well-loved by me, toward sun-down,
> . . . .
> Immigrants arriving, fifteen or twenty thousand in a week;
> . . . .
> Trottoirs throng'd—vehicles—Broadway—the women—the shops and shows,
> The parades, processions, bugles playing, flags flying, drums beating;
> A million people—manners free and superb—open voices—hospitality—the most courageous and friendly young men:
> The free city! no slaves! no owners of slaves!
> The beautiful city, the city of hurried and sparkling waters! the city of spires and masts!
> The city nested in bays! my city!
> The city of such women, I am mad to be with them! I will return after death to be with them!
> The city of such young men, I swear I cannot live happy without I often go talk, walk, eat, drink, sleep, with them!   (1860 *LG*, *Variorum*)

Triggering the poem, the Indian name Mannahatta first wells up in his mind as audible energy, liquid, musical, and allegedly self-sufficient, reverberating orally through centuries. "Now I see what there is in a name" seems at first just a claim to sudden awareness of the potency of speech. But with the repetition of "I see" in the following line *see* can no longer mean just *understand,* for the poet fully understands the name of his city only by seeing "that word up there"—by physically seeing the word *Mannahatta* at the top of the page in a printed title no illiterate aborigine could have created. Does "Now" refer to the moment the word first occurs to him or the moment he writes it down? Do the doubled consonants and the single echoing vowel create a wave-like pattern in sound? Or does the shape of the type on the page (the poet set some type for the first edition of his book) alternating tall and short characters make this long printed word resemble a long island scalloped by bays?[4] The spoken word brings his view of the city into focus, yet his understanding of that word seems dependent on the very eyesight that it clarifies, on the print culture that allows him to learn an etymology otherwise obscure. That supposed etymology organizes his panorama. To "see that word nested" is concretely to imagine his island ringed by water as if in an aerial view but also to see his title stamped on that vista, as it were—and finally to *understand* how the printed "word" is related to a "name" transmitted orally by different means.

No sooner does the "original" etymological meaning of the name begin concretely to unfold before us than we confront flagrantly modern details no Indian could ever have beheld around his wave-girt Manhattan. This "rich" commercial city is "solid-founded" on prehistoric Manhattan schist, but it was also "solid-founded" historically by acquisitive Dutch burghers who bought it from the Indians for twenty-four dollars. The poet of *Leaves of Grass* proudly proclaims his descent from them, just as he proudly trots out European terms like *trottoirs* to describe his *quondam* Indian, *echt* American metropolis. The poem oscillates between various modes of seeing: philological, historical, and intellectual insight; specific photographic images of individual details like the printed title, Broadway, or "the city"; generic plurals that blur in cinematic montage—and prophetic vision. For in 1860 "owners of slaves" as well as immigrants enjoyed the hospitality of this bustling commercial city, with their valets still subject to the Fugitive Slave Act. In the closing lines Whitman envisions only what he wants to see, and the poem tails off in deliberately extravagant erotic fantasy. Alas, he could never sleep with as many "friendly young men" as he dreamed of. Peeping on tiptoe into this utopian future, he makes himself self-consciously silly, of course—an aging queen threatening to embrace the women of New York as a ghost! But he also makes "the city nested in bays . . . *my* city!" Following hard upon the original etymological meaning of his title, *my* caps twenty lines with which this poet takes possession of the island from the Indians as cannily as his Dutch ancestors ever did with twenty-odd dollars, while ostensibly deferring to prior rights. Indeed, the poem's title is a title.

"Still the present I raise aloft, still the future of the States I harbinge glad and sublime, / And for the past I pronounce what the air holds of the red aborigines." Paumanok, after all, was only a poetic starting point glimpsed over the shoulder.

> The red aborigines,
> Leaving natural breaths, sounds of rain and winds, calls as of birds and
>   animals in the woods, syllabled to us for names,
> Okonee, Koosa, Ottawa, Monongahela, Sauk, Natchez, Chattahoochee,
>   Kaqueta, Oronoco,
> Wabash, Miami, Saginaw, Chippewa, Oshkosh, Walla-Walla,
> Leaving such names to the States they depart, charging the water and the
>   land with names. (*LG*, p. 26)

Such passages suggest shamanic invocation of spirit powers, a placatory gesture to defeated enemies that seeks to neutralize their lurking power as *genii loci* by claiming them as ancestors. This grave and tender meditation was written by a poet who complained in his notebooks about the inaccuracy of calling Native Americans "Indians." He rarely used that term. His admiration for their tongues was not indiscriminate; he objected to naming the state of Wyoming with an Algonquian word properly designating a valley in Pennsylvania. As a clerk in the Bureau of Indian Affairs he neither romanticized Indians unduly nor condescended to them.[5] "Yet returning eastward, yet in the seaside State or in Maryland, / . . . Yet a true son either of Maine or of the Granite State, or the Narragansett Bay State, or the Empire State, / Yet sailing to other shores to annex the same, yet welcoming every new brother," the poet preferred the aboriginal names for states (*LG*, p. 25). These verses haphazardly substitute journalistic nicknames for Old World names of colonial states that displeased him. Yet the rechristening remains casually incomplete. Because it commemorates a frivolous Catholic queen with overtones of the Blessed Virgin, the name *Maryland* might seem more obnoxious to him than any he changed. As he well knew, the same holds for Maine, named after her French province. They survive as testimonials to linguistic hospitality, to the American melting pot, while his changes bespeak cultural annexation.

"What is the curious rapport of names?" Whitman asked himself in genuine puzzlement (*Pr.*, p. 31). If his sporadic attempts to answer that question seem ill-defined and contradictory, he at least sensed its complexity. His baffled efforts at analysis left him with the core conviction that using language was an occult, intuitive mystery. However shallow philosophically, that stance kept him from Lockean or Utilitarian complacency. It allowed him to evolve from his own fertile confusion a novel Transcendental poetic.[6]

"The right name . . . is a perpetual feast to the esthetic and moral nature," proclaims the *American Primer* (p. 34). But in his first version of this aperçu it was simply "a perpetual feast to the ear" (*DBN*, 3:756). Just what determined rightness? Right for what? Geographic names "should/must assimilate in sentiment and sound to something organic in the place, or identical with it" (*DBN*, 3:705). To some extent Whitman's ideas about language seem his garbled version of Emersonian correspondence theory. But in this sentence the key word is not *correspond* but *assimilate,* backed up by the vague term *organic,* by the epithet *identical,* and by evident uncertainty whether names can avoid assimilating ("should/must"). Fuzzy and sloppy though his diction could be, the push in this formulation toward actual fusion of word and object is worth noting.

"All aboriginal names sound good," Whitman proclaimed with gusto. "They are honest words—they give the true length, breadth, depth. They all fit" (*Pr.,* p. 18). But if a long word is fitted to give the true length of America's longest river, how does the four-letter word *Ohio* fit its stream? The word *Monongahela* is three times as long, yet that river is just a tributary of the Ohio. Perhaps the word *Ohio* "fits" simply by sounding good in musical terms. Its echoing long *o* makes it so singable that one can imagine Puccini scoring a barcarole for *La Fanciulla del Ohio.* But if the appropriacy of words lies in their operatic musicality, then *La Fanciulla del Connecticut* sounds less promising. Even orthography does not fit that word, for its silent *c* makes it a speller's nightmare—a dishonest word.

Whitman flirts with the idea that lengthy words suit long streams. He wonders if broad vowels like those in *Ottawa* are vocally pleasing, if long *o*'s make the mouth mimic the shape of the globe and so create orbic utterance.[7] He is sympathetic to phonetic spelling that reliably guides pronunciation. But perhaps the leading common denominator in the names of these rivers is that all repeat at least one sound internally, like the alternating *c*'s and *t*'s in *Connecticut,* which begins and ends on the same short vowel sound.

All these words echo themselves. By so doing, each creates a pattern, a crude rhythm—an incipient drumbeat. Their peculiar "fitness," then, is only partly correspondence to physical objects. That Emersonian view of language accommodates either metaphor or metonymy, draws heavily on both vision and print culture, fosters etymological speculation and a sense of history. But onomastic "fitness" for Whitman is also adaptation to the vocal/auditory needs of speakers hallooing over America's wide-open spaces. This oral conception of speech as transitory acoustic vibrations jibes with his declamatory and operatic interests. It shifts attention from analyzing fixed objects to feeling the body strain to project broad emotion via voice and gesture. And it points toward an even more basic sense of "fitness" in all these aboriginal names that fascinate Whitman: an internal harmony of parts that represents only musical repetition, creating a primitive, rhythmic, dancelike vortex that begins to draw world, speaker, and audience into itself. Echoing the eighteenth-century Englishman John Brown, Herder, A. W. Schlegel, and Wagner suggested that the sister arts of music, poetry, and dance were first fused in a primal, unitary language. In shamanic trances, driving auditory stimuli like drumming or chanting free the holistic-spatial right hemisphere of the brain from dominance by the linguistic-analytic left hemisphere, fostering oceanic out-of-body experiences and making logical antinomies seem harmoniously paradoxical.[8] The noun *fit* has diverse meanings, among them an arresting physical convulsion, a flight of inspiration, a division of a long oral poem, and a suitable match. All these meanings derive from an Anglo-Saxon root meaning *to marshal opposing forces in order.* They all coincide in a primitive bard's "poetic fit." "I am a dance—play up there! the fit is whirling me fast!" cries the poet in "The Sleepers," a haunting, eerie dream vision that corresponds in many points with shamanic ritual (*LG,* p. 426).

But if Whitman's quest for "fit" diction has a primitive side, we must note one further hallmark of all the Indian nomenclature he admires. For eyes and ears used to English morphemes and Indo-European roots, these names are all slightly shocking. Dragooned into the American vocabulary, they stress the novelty of our national experience. Since their exotic appeal depends precisely on *not* fitting into the language, their alleged "fitness" is also a matter of unfitness, of incongruity. Whitman was no literary sophisticate, but neither was he a primitive bard. Like parody and nonsense verse, his diction derives much of its effect from those linguistic and cultural conventions that it ostentatiously flouts.

Body Language and the Adamic Mystique of Voice

"The immense variety of languages—the points where they differ are not near as remarkable as where they resemble—all resemble," mused Whitman in an early draft for an unwritten poem about language. "The simple sounds— / Music" (*NB,* 4:1325). The poet of the first edition normally describes himself as singing or chanting, not as writing. Infatuation with sheer sound tempted him to treat it as a universal language. He liked being read to in French, Italian, and German, for despite his ignorance of those tongues he was convinced that "if everything else is present you do not need words" (*WWWC*, 1:217). "What do you hear Walt Whitman?" he asked himself in "Salut au Monde."

> I hear continual echoes from the Thames,
> I hear fierce French liberty songs,
> I hear the locusts in Syria as they strike the grain and grass with the showers of their terrible clouds,
> I hear the Coptic refrain toward sundown, pensively falling on the breast of the black venerable vast mother the Nile,
> I hear the chirp of the Mexican muleteer, and the bells of the mule.
>
> (*LG*, p. 138)

To be sure, there is a certain pretentiousness in his claim that as an Emersonian bard "he resolves all tongues into his own" (*LG*, p. 168). But his auditory mystique lets him identify sympathetically with strangers of all kinds, like the "Hottentot with clicking palate" (*LG*, p. 147). To his catholic ear such sounds were scarcely more outlandish than "Webster's sickish Boston pronunciation," which seemed a fatal defect in his dictionary (*DBN*, 3:718).

Blending into the diapason of human languages, the music of nature reveals Whitman's ear at its sharpest. He meditated a piece for recitation to be composed of native American calls: country children summoning cows at sundown with "Kush! Kush! Kush!" or decoying a fractious colt to the halter with an ear of corn and the murmur "Ku-juk"; whalers crying "There she blo-o-o-ws" from the masthead; "or the quail whistling . . . Phoo! Phoo! Phooet" (*NB*, 4:1385). "Don't attempt too close or vivid a rendering of the calls—a mere trick," he warned himself, "leave an easy margin—more poetical." The reporter who transcribed slang and foreign phrases with phonetic notation had an alert if uncertain ear. In *Specimen Days* he struggled to describe the noise of summer insects accurately: "Let me say more about the song of the locust, even to repetition; a long, chromatic, tremulous crescendo, like a brass disk whirling round and round, emitting wave after wave of notes, beginning with a certain moderate beat or measure, rapidly increasing in speed and emphasis, reaching a point of dropping down and out. Not the melody of the swinging-bird—far from it . . . but what a swing there is in that brassy drone, round and round, cymbaline—or like the whirling of brass quoits" (*Prose*, 1:130). In "Song of Myself" the poet is determined "to accrue what I hear into this song, to let sounds contribute toward it." Listening, "I hear bravuras of birds, bustle of growing wheat, gossip of flames, clack of sticks cooking my meals, / I hear all sounds running together, combined, fused or following . . ." (*LG*, p. 55). Culminating with the trained soprano, this famous catalog runs the gamut of Whitman's auditory sensitivity. But an acute ear informs many shorter passages, like the terrifying description of a battlefield operation unseen but not unheard: ". . . The hiss of the surgeon's knife, the gnawing teeth of his saw, / Wheeze, cluck, swash of falling blood, short wild scream, and long, dull, tapering groan" (*LG*, p. 58).

In a more correspondential mood Whitman read the Preface to Webster's *Dictionary*, which elevated the verb to primal status while criticizing Court de Gébelin. He demurred: "Me, W.W., I think with the Frenchman, that nouns begin the matter" (*DBN*, 3:715). Some catalogs are long lists of things, conjured performatively from a flux of activity for an instant: "See, steamers steaming through my poems, / See, in my poems immigrants continually coming and landing, / See, in arriere, the wigwam, the trail, the hunter's hut, the flat-boat, the maize-leaf, the claim, the rude fence and the backwoods village" (*LG*, p. 27). Images with the stiff clarity of Currier and Ives blur by like an animated cartoon. Such passages reflect the conviction articulated in *The American Primer* that "a perfect user of words uses things—they exude in power and beauty from him—miracles from his hands—miracles from his mouth—lilies, clouds, sunshine, woman, poured copiously—things, whirled like chain-shot rocks" (p. 14). "Pronunciation is the stamina of language," argued Whitman the elocutionist. "It is language." But in correspondential moods he was convinced that "the art of the use of words would be a stain, a smutch, but for the stamina of things" (*Pr.*, p. 21).

Such moods are scarcely the norm, however, for he proclaims with equal fervor, "Bodies are all spiritual.—All words are spiritual—nothing is more spiritual than words" (*Pr.*, p. 1). Etherealizing even concrete common nouns, he wants to know, "Whence are they? along how many thousands and tens of thousands of years have they come? those eluding, fluid, beautiful, fleshless, realities, Mother, Father, Water, Earth, Me?" If even the name of fleshy Walt Whitman is fleshless, how could "a perfect writer . . . make words sing, dance, kiss, do the male and female act, bear children, weep bleed . . . or do anything, that man or woman or the natural powers can do?" (*Pr.*, p. 16). Itching for verbal copulation, he toyed with new terminology like *lover/lovee* (*DBN*, 3:675). He was momentarily persuaded that in "clinch" he had found "*the word wanted* for the male and female act" (*DBN*, 3:682). Some phallic poems go to startling lengths to celebrate "this poem drooping shy and unseen that I always carry, and that all men carry" (*LG*, p. 103). But though he ends "Spontaneous Me" by equating his own lines with masturbatory ejaculate, there can be no perfect writer if one demands words that are not just seminal but literally semen. "Camerado, this is no book," he protests. But despite strident assertion he cannot make good his claim, "Who touches this touches a man" (*LG*, p. 505). Alas, that touching boast is not touch.

If words could not be things, perhaps things could be words. Love the earth, despise riches, give alms, hate tyrants, think for yourself, "and your very flesh shall be a great poem, and have the richest fluency, not only in its words, but in the silent lines of its lips and face, and between the lashes of your eyes, and in every motion and joint of your body" (*Prose*, 2:440-41). While both Condillac's language of nature and traditional rhetoric encouraged Whitman to treat our physique as an expressive medium, he drew heavily on phrenology for ideas about body language. Tapping Lavater's *Essays on Physiognomy* (1778) to found phrenology, Dr. Franz Joseph Gall added the concept of pathognomy. According to Webster's definition that Whitman copied into his notebooks, pathognomy was "the science of the signs by which the state of the passions is indicated—the natural language or operation of the mind, as indicated by the soft and mobile parts of the Body" (*DBN*, 3:815). In the 1850s physiognomy and pathognomy were popularized by American phrenologists such as Whitman's publisher Orson Fowler. "Even the movements of one's limbs, and the gestures of the hands . . . can fascinate," noted Whitman. These pseudo-sciences subtend his belief in "that charm, we don't know what it is, which goes with the mere face and body magnetism of some men and women and makes every body love them, wherever they go" (*DBN*, 3:777).

From his belief in the expressiveness of the body stem the famous portraits of the author prefixed to successive editions of *Leaves of Grass*. Hand on hip, the bearded rough engraved for the first edition conveys his nonchalance through pathognomy, just as the bewhiskered bard prefacing later editions hopes to magnetize readers with his face. "I would call the influence of these poems in a high, if not in the highest degree a physiological one," he allowed (*NB*, 4:1546). He was "chilled with the cold types and cylinder and wet paper between us," the reader is informed. "I pass so poorly with paper and types . . . I must pass with the contact of bodies and souls" (*Variorum*, 1:84). With the frontispieces as essential reference points, his book strains for physical communion between author and readers like the magnetism radiating from the old farmer he describes in "I Sing the Body Electric":

This man was of wonderful vigor, calmness, beauty of person,
The shape of his head, the pale yellow and white of his hair and beard, the
    immeasurable meaning of his black eyes, the richness and breadth
    of his manners,
These I used to go and visit him to see, he was wise also,
. . . .

When he went with his five sons and many grand-sons to hunt or fish, you
    would pick him out as the most beautiful and vigorous of the
    gang,
You would wish long and long to be with him, you would wish to sit by
    him in the boat that you and he might touch each other.

(LG, pp. 95-96)

The farmer's wisdom seems simply an afterthought that might be expressed in conventional language. Without being erotic, what he physically radiates transcends it. The "immeasurable meaning" of the body is likewise invoked as the ultimate answer to philosophic perplexity. "When the subtle air, the impalpable, the sense that words and reason hold not, surround us and pervade us," the handclasp of a friend suffices to charge the poet "with untold and untellable wisdom, I am silent, I require nothing further" (LG, p. 120).

"A Song of the Rolling Earth" expands the doctrine of body language into a mysterious vision of a language of things:

Were you thinking that those were the words, those upright lines? those
    curves, angles, dots?

No, those are not the words, the substantial words are in the ground and
    sea,
They are in the air, they are in you.
Were you thinking that those were the words, those delicious sounds out
    of your friends' mouths?
No, the real words are more delicious than they.
Human bodies are words, myriads of words
. . . .

Air, soil, water, fire—those are words,
I myself am a word with them—my qualities interpenetrate with theirs—
    my name is nothing to them,
Though it were told in the three thousand languages, what would air, soil,
    water, fire, know of my name?
A healthy presence, a friendly or commanding gesture, are words, sayings,
    meanings,
The charms that go with the mere looks of some men and women, are say-
    ings and meanings also.
The workmanship of souls is by those inaudible words of the earth,
The masters know the earth's words and use them more than audible
    words.   (LG, pp. 219-20)

It is tempting to interpret these lines as Whitman's reworking of Transcendental doctrine. "It is not words only that are emblematic; it is things which are emblematic," he had read in Emerson's *Nature*. "Every natural fact is a symbol of some spiritual fact" (*CW*, 1:18). But that formulation linked nature and language as emblems pointing beyond themselves to a transcendental ideal. Instead, Whitman insists that his language of things cannot be translated into written language. "The truths of the earth continually wait, they are not so concealed either," he says, but "they are calm, subtle, untransmissible by print / They are imbued through all things conveying themselves willingly." Emerson might legitimately call natural things true, for he held them truly to represent a transcendent realm elsewhere. What if anything Whitman's substantial earth-words refer to elsewhere remains obscure.

Whitman's idiosyncratic notions of language as self-propagating patterns of sound encouraged him to flirt with the idea of nonreferential words. "To me, each word . . . has its own meaning, and does not stand for anything but itself" (*DBN*, 3:736). Rather than seeking to nail words to primitive meanings, he often tries to dismiss words so that things can speak afresh for themselves. The waves of sound with which his poetry inundates the world do not simply purify things, they set them adrift. Despite his intermittent enthusiasm for etymological study, derivations did little to shape his poetry. In positive moods he warmed to the thought that "subtle living, entirely unbroken chains of succession back through the . . . Aryan mists with arriere-threads to all pre-history . . . though but breaths and vibrations of the invisible air" weld New Yorkers to vanished peoples of the past (*NB*, 5:1684-85). But at other times the idea dismayed him. "I think I am done with many of the words of the past hundred centuries," he proclaimed in the *American Primer*. "I am mad that their poems, bibles, words, still rule and represent the earth, and are not yet superseded" (*Pr.*, pp. 12-13). His earliest essays popularizing historical linguistics vigorously insisted, "*Language cannot be Traced to First Origins.*"[9] He was happiest with philology when it freed him to innovate without undue deference to early languages. "The English language, in its body or stock, is of just as great antiquity as the Greek, the Roman, or any of the languages of Asia," he noted exultantly. Lexicographers' claims that some English words are "derived" from similar words are worth no more than "the assertion that I am derived from my . . . father's side cousins . . . because we bear the same name" (*DBN*, 3:717). Even respect for his father stopped well short of ancestor worship. "Not . . . the invention but . . . the growth of an American English" was his focus in the *Primer* (*DBN*, 3:728). Too much attention to Murray's

Grammar "would make of the young men merely a correct and careful set of writers," he grumbled to himself. Murray "would deprive writing of its life—there would be nothing voluntary and insociant left"—not even the freedom to misspell *insouciant* (*DBN*, 3:667).

The "truths of the earth" mentioned in "Song of the Rolling Earth" might be simply its physical realities viewed as self-evident and self-sufficient. Perhaps to decode these "substantial words" we need only abandon our assumption that they form a code, a text to be interpreted. Referring to nothing elsewhere, they would not represent the truth but simply present it. Interpreted as presentational rather than representational, the language of nature resembles Adamic theories like those of Peter Chazotte and the Swedenborgian Sampson Reed. The latter's impact on Emerson was substantial. Our first parents "knew no language but their garden," Reed claimed. By means "not of words but of things" they could communicate for all prelapsarian purposes just by pointing at its objects.[10] On Reed's interpretation the Fall is a fall into speech. And much in "Song of the Rolling Earth" encourages such notions. But behind all the talk of substantial words lies a profound animus against writing, coupled with a fondness for sound. If earthly things are dumb signs in some Emersonian correspondential sense, representing ambiguously rather than presenting, at least reducing them to that status removes them from unfair competition with the poet, who must also use mute, ambiguous signs (i.e., writing) wistfully to suggest an audible presence. Originally titled "Poem of the Sayers of the Words of the Earth," these lines struggle to imagine an authentic role for oral, aural poetry. The poetic masters imagined seem sayers and singers rather than posturing pantomimists. What makes their use of language genuine?

By calling the earth's substantial words "inaudible" but not dumb, Whitman preserves the option of regarding the language of nature not as mute visual symbols or even as icons, but rather as sounds too faint to be heard by the normal ear. Paving stones "receive and return so many echoes" that there is "living and buried speech . . . always vibrating here" (*LG*, p. 36). Onomatopoetic theories like those of de Brosses and Kraitsir suggested the genesis of speech from sounds associated with natural objects. The linguistic primacy that Whiter accorded to muddy old Mother Earth left open the possibility that human language reverberates from a primal squelch. If all created objects, including man, are characterized by specific frequencies of vibration, then that innate pitch might account for the emergence of language. So argued Oken and Heyse, and this thesis was popularized for the nineteenth century by Max Müller, who christened it the "ding-dong theory" and flirted with it himself. The poet Gerard Manley Hopkins drew on it in formulating his notion of "inscape."[11] Whitman likewise was intrigued with the notion that every object was stamped with a peculiar structural pattern that served to identify it acoustically.

> The earth does not exhibit itself nor refuse to exhibit itself, possesses still
>   underneath,
> Underneath the ostensible sounds, the august chorus of heroes, the wail of
>   slaves,
> Persuasions of lovers, curses, gasps of the dying, laughter of young people,
>   accents of bargainers,
> Underneath these possessing words that never fail.

"Ostensible sounds" here contrast with deep, genuine sounds underlying them, pitched at a level of vibration below the normal range of the human ear, as it were. According to Whitman, the task of the masters is to detect and "echo the tones of souls and the phrases of souls, / (If they did not echo the phrases of souls what were they then?)" (*LG*, pp. 221-24.)

To echo a tone seems not to impose sound arbitrarily on a mute object but rather to amplify a tone already produced by the object until it becomes audible. "Song of Myself" memorably describes the primal tone produced by a soul. "I believe in you my soul," says the poet. "Loafe with me on the grass, loose the stop from your throat, / Not words, not music or rhyme I want, not custom or lecture, not even the best, / Only the lull I like, the hum of your valvéd voice" (*LG*, p. 33). In this famous vision of a mystical union where soul kisses the body's heart, the poet hears the soul's voice as a humming unbroken by articulation. Respite from ordinary sound makes audible a lulling, valved murmur like our physical heartbeat but still fainter. The soul's expression seems a kind of primal lallation, a pure vocalic stream unimpeded by consonants, nature's own utterance. Vaguely recalling the Pythagorean music of the spheres, Whitman's conception differs from that in the preeminence assigned the poet's voice as the receptor, amplifier, and transmitter of primal tones produced by physical bodies or spiritual entities (if that distinction is possible in his poetry).

His conception of vocal language seems persistently circular, an auditory loop. Sometimes he writes as if things produce sounds that the poet passively imitates or reproduces. Yet elsewhere the relation seems reciprocal. "Latent in a great user of words, must actually be all passions, crimes, trades, animals, stars, God, sex, the past, might, space metals, and the like," he insists, "because these are the words, and he who is not these, plays with a foreign tongue, turning helplessly to dictionaries and authorities" (*Pr.*, pp. 16-17). Microcosmically containing the universe, the poet often seems to project it into existence with his voice. "Dazzling and tremendous how quick the sun-rise would kill me," he claims, "if I could not now and always send sun-rise out of me."

> We also ascend dazzling and tremendous as the sun,
> We found our own O my soul in the calm and cool of the day-break.
> My voice goes after what my eyes cannot reach,
> With the twirl of my tongue I encompass worlds and volumes of worlds.
> Speech is the twin of my vision, it is unequal to measure itself,
> It provokes me forever, it says sarcastically,
> Walt you contain enough, why don't you let it out then?
> Come now I will not be tantalized, you conceive too much of articulation,
> Do you not know O speech how the buds beneath you are folded?
> Waiting in gloom, protected by frost
> The dirt receding before my prophetical screams . . .   (LG, pp. 54–55)

Like vision, articulate speech seems tauntingly inadequate to the poet's ambition. He relies on primitive feelings such as Rousseau postulated as the origin of language. His inarticulate screams germinate objects enfolded in the potential for words, his voice effusing itself as the creative force of the cosmos. Volumes of worlds (the word plays with the distinction between books and sound) can be absorbed in a concentric pattern of sympathetic vibrations that evokes the meanings of dead letters without even reading them.

At moments like these the powers that Whitman associates with the voice seem not just Adamic but divine. The conception of an omnipotent vocalism scarcely distinguished from the surrounding cosmos resembles infantile and shamanistic modes of thought. But his preoccupation with linguistic power rests on more than a belief in verbal magic. He intuited the distinction made familiar to our era by J. L. Austin between constative and performative utterances, between ordinary statements that merely describe acts and sentences that carry them out. "I celebrate myself and sing myself," his greatest poem begins. This locution is not just representational. The words refer us to no celebration in the real world beyond the poem, conjure up no image of the poet sporting a party hat. "Song of Myself" celebrates simply by employing the verb *celebrate* in the first person, so that this sentence thereby performs the very act it "describes." The poem's words themselves *are* their meaning.

Whitman's early poems abound in speech-acts like this, just as they abound in apostrophes. The peculiar power of this latter trope in his verse (he is arguably the world's supreme master of apostrophe) derives from its linkage to his quasi-magical ideas about language. When he apostrophizes speech itself in the lines above, he quietly animates an abstract category and fuses it concretely with his own specific words, just as when he addresses the reader or inhabitants of other countries he casually annihilates conventional limits of time and space. Indeed, as Tenney Nathanson observes, there is an essentially vocative dimension to much of the naming in Whitman's catalogs. He names the things of the world as if to invoke them, to summon them magically into his presence. The struggle to maintain this extraordinary belief in the creative power of the spoken word charges his greatest poetry with humor, pathos, and drama. But the imaginative strain of believing is great, and so is the temptation to formula. When the sense of magical urgency vanishes from his verse, invocations dwindle into tedious inventories.

The Mock Epic of the Elastic Self

To sing himself was to create himself—or at least to create a poet. The unique figure who creates and is created by the early poems dominates our experience of *Leaves of Grass*. Criticism has not always rendered that experience convincingly, for its novelty stretches conventional literary terminology. But any reader of "Song of Myself" will recall the eerie sensation of being guided by an author who seems to float through his world and rise off the page to accost us. "I see through the broadcloth and gingham whether or no," intones this spectre so insinuatingly that we may check our fly or our slip, "and am around, tenacious, acquisitive, tireless, and cannot be shaken away" (*LG*, p. 35). Oscillating between the particular and the generic, this speaker seems either an eccentric oddball or a being with no centered identity at all. "These tend inward to me, and I tend outward to them," he concludes one expansive catalog embracing some seventy-five different Americans in a dizzying series of parallel clauses, "And such as it is to be of these more or less I am, / And of these one and all I weave the song of myself" (*LG*, p. 44). His jaw-dropping claim to be related to all these people blends precise, skeptical reservation ("such as it is"), blandly evasive vagueness ("to be of these"), and comically casual assurance ("more or less I am").

In cataloging Americans, the poet seems to draw specific, concrete people toward his own body for affectionate fellowship and assimilation: "The old husband sleeps by his wife and the young husband sleeps by his wife." But as they tend inward he also tends outward, digesting and projecting them in his catalog as a stream of representative types, common nouns that his idealizing vision purifies of all the bodily particularity implied by the ostensive "the." Or rather the poet's voice makes/ reveals the type incarnate in the individual, so that the catalog seems both a list of people idealized into essences and a list of common nouns given the concrete particularity of proper names. The relentless, repetitive parallelism overrides the discrete categories that words normally imply. Magnetized by his speech, people converge on the poet, until their diverse activities begin to seem simply modes of the verbal energy by which he weaves his song. "I fly those flights of a fluid and swallowing soul," he proclaims. His orotund utterance sucks the universe toward him, then promises to inflate it to its proper dimensions. "You there, impotent, loose in the knees, / Open your scarf'd chops till I blow grit within you" (*LG*, p. 74). Like waves of sound he washes rhythmically over and around others: "I mind them or the . . . resonance of them—I come and I depart" (*LG*, p. 36). He even stands ready to reanimate the dying with the inspiration and respiration of his verse: "I dilate you with tremendous breath, I buoy you up" (*LG*, p. 74).

To dilate others the poet must dilate himself. The feat came naturally. "I cannot understand the mystery, but I am always conscious of myself as two—as my soul and I," he wrote in his earliest notebook before the gestation of *Leaves of Grass* (*NUP*, 1:63). This temperament went hand in hand with native humor in creating the shape-shifting, spasmodically gigantic "I" of "Song of Myself." Davy Crockett, Mike Fink, and other tall-tale heroes delighted in hyperbolic vaunts—comic bragging was the frontiersman's favorite form of verbal virtuosity. But Whitman's swelling persona also stems from the nation's schoolrooms, where there reigned confused speculation about personal pronouns like *I* and *you,* the first and last words of "Song of Myself." A modern linguist would call such words deictics. In a conversation between two parties they switch, applying alternately to A and B. Unlike nouns or proper names they are not linked to stable entities in the external world; they are relational, defined purely by reference to the discourse containing them.

Defining nouns as the names of things and pronouns as substitutes for nouns, most nineteenth-century grammars obscured this key fact. As a result, they purveyed a concept of grammatical *person* that was rather confusing.

> The *first person* denotes the speaker.
> The *second person* denotes the person or thing spoken to; as, "Listen, O *earth*!"
> The *third person* denotes the person or thing spoken of; as, "The *earth* thirsts."
> Nouns have but *two* persons, the second and third. When a man speaks, the *pronoun I* or *we* is always used; therefore nouns can never be in the *first* person. In examples like the following, some philologists suppose the noun to be in the *first* person:—"This may certify that I, *Jonas Taylor,* do hereby give and grant," &c. But it is evident that the speaker or

writer, in introducing his own name, speaks *of* himself; consequently the noun is of the *third person.*

   If you wish to understand the persons of nouns, a little sober thought is requisite.[12]

Most reading this passage would not grasp how equivocally the key term *person* is employed. Grammatical *person* denotes a grammatical *role* (cf. *dramatis personae* and the *persons* of the Trinity.) But talk of the "person spoken to" reifies that role and slides over into the notion of *person* as an actual human being. Terminological confusion like this bred a muddy scholastic debate about the personal pronouns. "That the pronouns of the first and second persons are sometimes masculine and sometimes feminine, is perfectly certain," opined Goold Brown, "but whether they can or cannot be neuter is a question difficult to be decided."[13]

   Whitman was no grammarian. In the 1850s, after years working as a teacher and journalist, he copied into his notebooks the standard definitions of orthography, etymology, syntax, and prosody as if they represented new information. One can imagine him pitching with eager curiosity upon grammatical conundrums like whether the earth could speak in the first person. In poems like "Song of the Rolling Earth" and "Song of Myself" that seems essentially what happens: "I harbor for good or bad, I permit to speak at every hazard, / Nature without check with original energy" (*LG,* p. 29). Refusing to treat *I* as just the origin of any given sentence, this cosmic speaker sounds like disembodied subjectivity detached from any particular individual yet retaining a categorical identity. If one tries to imagine the deictic *I* as a proper noun—hence capitalized—but also a common noun denoting a category of people, the result resembles the elastic Ego through which Whitman presumes to speak for America. "The pronoun *you,* though originally and properly plural, is now generally applied alike to one person or more," observed Goold Brown (p. 137). As our speech had individualized the meaning of *you,* so Whitman might pluralize *I* instead of employing the first-person plural *we,* which he rarely uses.[14] One may also see in the way deictic pronouns change reference in conversation a suggestive warrant for his claim that "every atom belonging to me as good as belongs to you" (*LG,* p. 28).

   Grammatical speculation fueled his desire to write like the first person in the cosmos.

   Early in the morning,
   Walking forth from the bower, refreshed with sleep,
   Behold me where I pass—hear my voice—approach,
   Touch me—touch the palm of your hand to my body as I pass,
   Be not afraid of my body.   (*Variorum,* 1860)

Whitman's later first line—"As Adam Early in the Morning"—weakens the poem by reducing to mere resemblance an audacious claim to identity. In these lines the first person is at once Adam leaving the bower to wander solitary through Eden, Walt Whitman soliciting contact from passers-by as he wanders the streets, and the poet's written words impersonating his voice to suggest his body touching a solitary reader whose hand cradles a book.

Spoken, the first-person pronoun expresses a physical presence. The written "I," however, is more shadowy, even ghostly. Encountered posthumously in a will, its effect can be eerie. Whitman's vocal mystique is of a piece with his body mysticism. The uncanny figure who presides over his early poetry is projected by writing that pretends to be a voice that pretends to be a body.

> The atmosphere is not a perfume, it has no taste of the distillation, it is odorless,
> It is for my mouth forever, I am in love with it,
> I will go to the bank by the wood and become undisguised and naked,
> I am mad for it to be contact with me.
> The smoke of my own breath,
> Echoes, ripples, buzz'd whispers, love-root, silk-thread, crotch and vine,
> My respiration and inspiration, the beating of my heart, the passing of blood and air through my lungs,
> The sniff of green leaves and dry leaves, and of the shore and dark-color'd sea-rocks, and of hay in the barn,
> The sound of the belch'd words of my voice loos'd to the eddies of the wind,
> A few light kisses, a few embraces, a reaching around of arms,
> The play of shine and shade on the trees as the supple boughs wag,
> The delight alone or in the rush of the streets, or along the fields and hillsides,
> The feeling of health, the full-noon trill, the song of me rising from bed and meeting the sun.
> Have you reckon'd a thousand acres much? have you reckon'd the earth much?
> Have you felt so proud to get at the meaning of poems?
> Stop this day and night with me and you shall possess the origin of all poems . . . [15]

These lines are a frontal assault on the way most poetry is read—as if "the meaning of poems" were some abstract generalization about a world lying elsewhere, some theme that the words of the poem long-windedly embroider. Meaning thus conceived is alienated from the poem much as writing sunders words from the speaker. For Whitman the origin of all poems is the pure pleasure of utterance as a creative act, the process of savoring words themselves—the process of savoring words *as* the self, fondling them autoerotically. The opening lines describe the poet communing with the universe by the air he breathes in and out. Wind washes over his body caressingly, bringing back to his own ears as sound the "belch'd words" that he launches upon it. Like the echoes and the soughing of the boughs, those words are part of the physical environment where they reverberate. Under the insistent drumbeat of the central catalog, which contains no finite verbs implying subject-object distinctions, voice and world become a closed loop. Sounds the poet breathes out mingle with scents he breathes in; tactile sensations blend into imagined erotic caresses; aspects of his body alternate haphazardly with aspects of natural objects. The division between self and world is blurred until it is hard to say whether the poet's voice enfolds or unfolds nature. His body seems fragmented, diffused among the objects of nature like sound waves. Indeed, with "the song of me rising from bed and meeting the sun," it becomes difficult to tell body from voice. Do the participles *rising* and *meeting* modify *song* or *me*? The poet seems to exist as an undulant voice that creates a body in its own fluid image. Shaped by a primal rhythm that pervades and defines space, this body-consciousness can merge with its surroundings like an infant's or shaman's until the world seems absorbed in its pulsating awareness.

The poems of the first two editions "announce the great individual, fluid as Nature" (*LG*, p. 505). To portray this hero Whitman sought a fluid style. His forays into popular philology convinced him that language was malleable. "Do not forget that what is now fixed was once floating and movable," he jotted down in his notebooks while reading one speculative treatise. "Individualism is a law in modern languages, and freedom also," he concluded from the gradual eclipse of inflected structure. "The words are not built in, but stand loose, and ready to go this way or that" (*DBN*, 3:720, 725).

"A popular method of obtaining new words in English, is the conversion of words from one part of speech to another," Whitman read in his copy of Schele de Vere's *Outlines of Comparative Philology* (New York: Putnam's, 1853). The paucity of inflections in English means that "the interchange can readily be made, and the convenience is so striking as to secure it almost invariable success."[16] One striking feature of Whitman's poetic diction in "Song of Myself" is his penchant for turning long-established English verbs into novel nouns with some shock value. Among the so-called deverbal nouns memorably deployed in the poem we encounter a sniff, a knit, a merge, a float, a suck, a sell, a pour, a dowse, a topple, a dangle, a soothe, a swash, a flaunt, a bask, a sidle, a blurt, and a yawp. Whereas English more often turns nouns into verbs, conversion of this sort results in nouns that retain much of the dynamic, temporal quality we normally associate with verbs.

> The *blab* of the pave, tires of carts, *sluff* of bootsoles, *talk* of the prome-
> naders,
> The heavy omnibus, the driver with his interrogating thumb, the *clank* of
> the shod horses on the granite floor,
> The snow-sleighs, clinking, shouted jokes, *pelts* of snow-balls,
> The *hurrahs* for popular favorites, the fury of rous'd mobs,
> The *flap* of the curtain'd litter, a sick man inside borne to the hospital . . .
> (*LG*, p. 36, emphasis added)

Three of the four main nouns in the first line derive from verbs, *blab* and *sluff* startlingly so. Together they tug upon more conventional nouns with which they are in apposition, inviting us to realize that the familiar substantive *talk* is likewise deverbal and denotes the activity of talking. The next line describes impressively solid bodies; but as the deverbal noun *clank* is echoed in *clinking* its verbal origin is stressed. Its "thing-ness" is half-dissolved, just as "pelts" of snowballs lack the substantial-ity of the fur pelts we may at first anticipate. Likewise we are urged to realize that the *flap* of the litter is not an object (which would be redun-dant with *curtain'd*) but a sound, a *flapping*. Sharing overtones of dynamic process rooted in the concept of sound as energy, in this pas-sage the deverbal nouns threaten to unsettle even the apparent fixity of heavy omnibus and granite floor.

Other deverbal nouns favored by Whitman involve suffixation. Sec-tion 15 of "Song of Myself" is a long catalog itemizing some seventy-five representative Americans (*LG*, pp. 41–44). Thirty of them are designated by nouns ending either in *-er* or *-or*: "The conductor beats time for the band and all the performers follow him." Like "the spinning-girl" and a few other figures whose names incorporate activity via a participle, the agential nouns in *-r* usually derive from dynamic verbs—verbs capable of forming the present progressive tense, unlike stative verbs like *know*. They can denote someone performing an action once or more regularly. If the action is habitual and common enough, the word may lose its dynamic verbal force and congeal as a common noun suggesting a fixed, static category. We may not think of a newspaper reporter as one who reports, a conductor as one who conducts, or performers as those who perform. In Whitman's catalog, however, "the duck-shooter walks by silent and cautious stretches," picking his way among quasi-occupational categories. He is out to shoot ducks. His carefully pondered muscular activity reminds us that the jour-printer is likewise engaged in printing, the dancers in dancing, and the paving-man in paving.

The catalog nears a crescendo in these lines:

> The floor-men are laying the floor, the tinners are tinning the roof, the
>   masons are calling for mortar,
> In single file each shouldering his hod pass onward the laborers;
> . . . .
> Seasons pursuing each other the plougher ploughs, the mower mows, and
>   the winter-grain falls in the ground;
> Off on the lakes the pike-fisher watches and waits by the hole in the frozen
>   surface,
> . . . .
> Coon-seekers go through the regions of the Red river or through those
>   drain'd by the Tennessee, or through those of the Arkansas . . .
> . . . .
> In walls of adobie, in canvas tents, rest hunters and trappers after their
>   day's sport,
> The city sleeps and the country sleeps,
> The living sleep for their time, the dead sleep for their time . . .

Like the pike-fisher, coon-seekers are not reified into professionals but are just people chasing raccoons. The hunters and trappers were also out for sport. Even construction workers seem defined by their activity rather than by an inert occupational category. Laborers labor because they are heavy-laden. Floormen and tinners are described with what would seem redundancy except for the poet's determination to root their identities in their activity. His tautological zeal climaxes as "the plougher ploughs, the mower mows." Under the wheeling seasons such apparently concrete nouns dissolve back into the temporal activity of which they are temporary concretions. The thrust of his rhetoric pulls other occupations along with them, until all specific figures begin to merge in the basic activities of living and sleeping. Like Whitman's greatest poetry, this catalog generates its power from a tug-of-war between a principle of stable identity embodied in the nouns designating the other forty-five Americans and a force that promises to dissolve all individuality into a sea of pure verbal energy like Schlegel's Abounding Fullness. In principle endless, the catalog's relentlessly repetitive structure threatens to overwhelm its finite elements with a sense of unboundedness.[17]

Whitman's fondness for agential nouns of this ilk sprinkled "Song of Myself" with plenty of odd ones: for example, *latherer, winder, vexer, buzzer, hummer, reacher, scooper, howler,* and *thruster.* "I am less the reminder of property or qualities, and more the reminder of life," he proclaimed in the first edition.[18] The word *reminder* itself exemplifies the rationale for such diction. Normally used as an inanimate noun for an object with a property or adjectival quality productive of remembrance, here it becomes an agential form of the verb—he who reminds—designating a living person engaged in the dynamic activity of reminding. "He most honors my style who learns under it to destroy the teacher," the poem suggests (*LG*, p. 84). For that occupational category conceived of as a common noun the poet has scant respect, so faithful disciples will continue to insist with him that people called teachers be demonstrably active and effective in teaching despite their high-souled opposition to competency testing.

Tension between noun and verb, fixity and fluidity, individuality and unboundedness charges the early poetry with quizzical humor. "Make no puns, funny remarks Double entendres 'witty' remarks ironies Sarcasms," Whitman had to warn himself as he began preparing the second edition of a book that he had titled with a pun (*NB*, 1:234). Emerson had rightly hailed it as an extraordinary piece of "wit and wisdom." In "Song of Myself" the extravagant claims to multiple identity are grandly comic. The opening lines register that with a pun: "What I assume you shall assume, / For every atom belonging to me as good as belongs to you" (*LG*, p. 28). Bodily assumption is a large assumption. Throughout the poem the very notion of bodily incarnation seems funny: "I dote on myself, there is that lot of me and all so luscious" (*LG*, p. 54). It yields a stream of jokes. "Having pried through the strata, analyzed to a hair, counsel'd with doctors and calculated close," quips our hero in a moment of finitude, "I find no sweeter fat than sticks to my own bones" (*LG*, p. 47).

But the cosmic Peeping Tom who cries, "Undrape!" or merges with the frustrated spinster spying on the twenty-eight men bathing is also comic (*LG*, p. 35). His prophetic ambition makes him "one of that centripetal and centrifugal gang," with slangy diction undercutting his own claims to prophetic authority (*LG*, p. 79). "Do you guess I have some intricate purpose?" he inquires jovially. "Well I have, for the Fourth-month showers have, and the mica on the side of a rock has"(*LG*, p. 46). His sympathetic communion with animals, who "do not lie awake in the dark and weep for their sins," masks the same sly social satirist who beholds "the little plentiful manikins skipping around in collars and tail'd coats, / I am aware who they are, (they are positively not worms or fleas,)" (*LG*, p. 77).

Irony intertwines with his most expansive proclamations:

> The supernatural of no account . . . . myself waiting my time to be one of
> the supremes,
> The day getting ready for me when I shall do as much good as the best,
> and be as prodigious,
> Guessing when I am it will not tickle me much to receive puffs out of pulpit or print;
> By my life-lumps! becoming already a creator!

Putting myself here and now to the ambushed womb of the shadows!
. . . . A call in the midst of the crowd,
My own voice, orotund, sweeping and final.

Come my children.   (*Variorum*, 1:65)

Swearing preposterously by his testicles (from Latin *testes* = witnesses),
he acknowledges the gap between physical and metaphysical intercourse
as he rapes the future. With delighted surprise he discovers the voice in
the crowd is his own, hearing it as if detached from his own utterance. In
fact, puffs from pulpit and press tickled Whitman so much that he wrote
several himself and carried Emerson's letter for weeks. The passage is
suffused with rueful amusement at the difficulty of begetting its own
desired audience through sheer vocal virility.

"I know perfectly well my own egotism," he can plausibly claim,
"Know my omnivorous lines and must not write any less" (*LG*, p. 77).
Inflating himself like a gigantic Thanksgiving Day balloon, he then pep-
pers the parade with an airgun. "Enough! enough! enough!" he cries, "I
discover myself on the verge of a usual mistake" (*LG*, p. 975). Expanding and contracting his identity like a concertina, "Song of Myself"
coaxes forth a blithe music, with epigrams that suggest Oscar Wilde at
times. "I resist any thing better than my own diversity," the poet blandly
announces, "Breathe the air but leave plenty after, / And am not stuck
up, and am in my place" (*LG*, p. 45). In the same sentence he poses as
modest spokesman for one and ironic spokesman for everyone.

What results from this oscillating self-inflation and self-spoofing is a
memorable comic hero who embodies the spirit of Romantic irony,
standing "amused, complacent, compassionating, idle, unitary, / . . . Looking with side-curved head curious what will come next, / Both in and out
of the game and watching and wondering at it" (*LG*, p. 32). Shuttling
between microcosm and macrocosm makes "Song of Myself" not so
much the epic of America as the greatest American mock epic. "I pride
myself on being a real humorist underneath everything else," the poet
could proclaim in old age. Warned he might go down in history as a
comedian, he replied that one "might easily end up worse."[19]

Ebbing Afflatus—and Unspeakable Ironies

After the first two editions, however, the comedy of the elastic self
dwindles. Recognizing his own homosexuality resulted in the *Calamus*
poems of 1860, which explicitly reject the representative pretenses of his
earlier pose. The cosmic lover became entangled in the frustrations and
fulfillments of an actual love affair. His beloved proved beyond his control.

Self-sufficiency exposed as a delusion, the poet could not easily muster belief in the magical powers of performative speech. Unlike "Song of Myself" the *Calamus* poems frankly avow their status as writing addressing future readers they can neither create nor specify.

"Out of the Cradle, Endlessly Rocking" also entered *Leaves of Grass* in the 1860 edition, there entitled "A Word Out of the Sea." Its structure is explicitly operatic: an overture, recitative narration alternating with the bird's italicized arias, a great trio for boy, bird, and sea, and a concluding coda for the mature bard. "The purport of this wild and plaintive song, well-enveloped, and eluding definition, is positive and unquestionable, like the effect of music," explained the editorial note accompanying the first printing (*LG*, pp. 246-53). With some plausibility, a hostile newspaper immediately charged that the poem was meaningless. It modulates from suggestive mimicry of warbling birdsong to lines where hypnotic repetition of single words like mantras washes out their semantic content, as if the poet's aim were to create a nonreferential language of pure feeling akin to music.[20]

But in fact the poem is a lament that no such primal language is possible. What the mockingbird's throat pours forth is no language of pure feeling, after all, but derivative strains borrowed from other birds. Like people, the bird must express its desire within alien linguistic conventions. As it imitates other fowl, so the boy imitates the bird. "Curiously peering, absorbing, translating," the boy is first lured to listen by the hope of fathoming its "hints." Were the bird's song the language of nature, its hints would not perplex and translation would be neither possible nor necessary. "*Do not be decoy'd elsewhere,*" cries the mockingbird to his missing mate, "*That is the whistle of the wind, it is not my voice.*" Neither bird nor boy is one with nature. The boy's effort to render "the aria's meaning" into English stems from his belief that it has referential "meanings which I of all men know." But however enlightening, such meanings remain profoundly unsatisfying. What bird and boy desperately crave is a language that does not merely represent objects but presents them. The bird wants his mate back; but all his eloquent invocation fails to produce her, for language here lacks the magical, performative, presentational powers with which Whitman's early poetry strove to endow it. As a result the mockingbird feels himself to be "*singing uselessly, uselessly all the night.*" Beautiful but futile, his song is a mockery.

The tragic mockery is full of meaning, however, for symbolic meaning is what is left when real presence evaporates from words. The very possibility of linguistic meaning seems rooted in loss, in the yawning gap between signifier and signified. If the bird's song were fulfilling, it would silence itself with the return of the she-bird. Denied the satisfaction of silence, the bird can only echo its anguish in notes that suggest others' pain but fail to relieve its own. "Is it indeed toward your mate you sing? or is it really to me?" asks the poet, betraying a lurking sense of the artificiality of the bird's art. Condemned to a fallen language of symbols, the poet suffers a similar fate: "O you singer solitary, singing by yourself, projecting me, / O solitary me listening, never more shall I cease perpetuating you, / Never more shall I escape, never more the reverberations, / Never more the cries of unsatisfied love be absent from me." To his request for a clue to the bird's ambiguous song, the sea "lisp'd to me the low and delicious word death." Speech provides neither a companion to talk to nor a lover for whom no words are necessary: here it merely describes their absence. Thus language seems hollow and arbitrary at the core in a way that belies Whitman's earlier confidence in the creative power of triumphant vocalism. Echoing endlessly, its conventional terms never terminate in an authoritative origin or a final word. The sublimations of art demand aesthetic pretense. The poet's destiny is determined as much by his audience as by his voice, and that realization is fatal to the insouciant, self-sufficient bard of the first two editions.

"As I Ebb'd with the Ocean of Life" (1860) offers the bitterest recognition of this impasse. The poet describes walking along the Long Island shore, "held by this electric self out of the pride of which I utter poems." He gazes out to sea for inspiration, then

> Fascinated, my eyes reverting from the south, dropt, to follow those slender windrows,
> Chaff, straw, splinters of wood, weeds, and the sea-gluten,
> Scum, scales from shining rocks, leaves of salt-lettuce, left by the tide,
> . . . .
> These you presented to me you fish-shaped island,
> As I wended the shores I know,
> As I walked with that electric self seeking types.   (LG, pp. 253-54)

Stranded by the ebb of his oceanic inspiration, he sees a horrifying correspondence between his life, his poems, and the sea-wrack littering the shore in rows.

> I too signify at the utmost a little washed-up drift,
> A few sands and sea leaves to gather,
> Gather and merge myself as part of the sands and drift.
> O baffled, balk'd, bent to the very earth,
> Oppress'd with myself that I have dared to open my mouth,
> Aware now that amid all that blab whose echoes recoil upon me I have not once had the least idea who or what I am,

But that before all my arrogant poems the real Me stands yet untouch'd,
    untold, altogether unreach'd,
Withdrawn far, mocking me with mock-congratulatory signs and bows,
With peals of distant ironical laughter at every word I have written,
Pointing in silence to these songs, and then to the sand beneath.
I perceive I have not really understood any thing, not a single object, and
    that no man ever can,
Nature here in sight of the sea taking advantage of me to dart upon me
    and sting me,
Because I have dared to open my mouth to sing at all.   (*LG*, p. 254)

The trails of debris are the lines of Whitman's earlier poetry, "all that blab" uttered in the arrogant pride of vocalism but now dead on the page when scanned as writing. *Leaves of Grass* now seems leaves of rotting seaweed. Instead of transcendental types, his book contains only printer's types. Having dared to sing open-mouthed, he must now watch his oral inspiration expire on the page. "See, from my dead lips the ooze exuding at last, / See, the prismatic colors glistening and rolling," he cries in lines rejected as too graphic for the *Atlantic Monthly*'s readers. Sickeningly his afflatus congeals. His living words become "loose windrows, little corpses," "tufts of straw, sands, fragments, / Buoy'd hither from many moods, one contradicting another." Instead of revealing the real Me (of whose nature the poem otherwise gives no hint) the dead language of print only obscures him. With savage disgust Whitman imagines his supernal alter ego gesticulating mockingly, fastidiously refusing to trust thought to speech, let alone to writing. Yet even the signs employed by the real Me are not self-explanatory. These ironic gestures scathingly travesty the notion that there could be an unambiguous language of nature founded on gesture, voice, or anything else.

The poem ends in despair with the poet prostrating himself on the sand like a corpse before "this phantom looking down where we lead, and following me and mine." Amalgamated into the detritus of the littoral that symbolized his poems,

Up just as much out of fathomless workings fermented and thrown,
A limp blossom or two, torn, just as much over waves floating, drifted at
    random,
Just as much for us that sobbing dirge of Nature,
Just as much whence we come that blare of cloud-trumpets,
We, capricious, brought hither we know not whence, spread out before you,
You up there, walking or sitting,
Whoever you are, we too lie in drifts at your feet.   (*LG*, p. 255)

With this shattering conclusion, the poet of "Song of Myself" renounces all knowledge of self and all sovereignty over his audience.

No longer able to mold hearers through omnipotent vocalism, he addresses a being like an alter ego, but so alienated as to be unrecognizable ("Whoever you are"). The self is apotheosized into a taunting divinity whom prayer scarcely moves. Under the supercilious scrutiny of the real Me, the poet is convicted of unavoidable linguistic hypocrisy. Trying to utter poems, he has also written them, and the fluid and evolutionary Me shuns confinement in fixed forms. In a devastating Romantic irony the poet himself is trapped by them. Like one more little corpse, he merges into the lines of desiccated debris that his verse becomes on the page when sundered from its creative afflatus. No longer self-defining, author and work lie at the mercy of the real Me, who pores over them like a critical reader rather than responding as the reflux of the poet's own breath. The alienated author merges with us hovering "up there" over his page and pondering for all he knows yet another academic study of Whitman.[21] Paralleling each other down the beach to a vanishing point, the tidelines reflect less their oceanic origin than each other, suggesting the maddening reflexivity of poetic discourse and the inconclusiveness of interpretation.

Whitman's horror at this fate was prescient, for after 1865 he was gradually frozen in the image of his words. As his poems became hopelessly prosaic, his personality grew ever more poetic, until the real Me decamped for good. Archaisms and genteel diction replaced slang. Forsaking the first person and performative speech-acts, shrinking his expansive catalogs into bald, circular epigrams, abandoning the comic drama of the questioning self for cosmic philosophy, the Good Gray Poet wrote a very gray poetry indeed. As the erotic rebel forgot his body, sublimated, and mellowed, his verse became a virtual death mask.

But even as the plaster hardened over his features, he could still protest. Skepticism about language tinged *Leaves of Grass* from the beginning. "Words are finite organs of the infinite mind," Emerson had warned in *Nature*. "They cannot cover the dimensions of what is in truth. They break, chop, and impoverish it" (*CW*, 1:44–45). Whitman worried about language's stranglehold on feeling. "Expression of speech!" he snorted in "Great Are the Myths." "In what is written or said, forget not that Silence is also expressive, / That anguish as hot as the hottest, and contempt as cold as the coldest, may be without words, / That true adoration is likewise without words, and without kneeling" (*LG*, p. 586). By 1856 silence could seem preferable to speech. "I swear I see what is better than to tell the best," he proclaimed, "It is always to leave the best untold" (*LG*, p. 224). "Silence silence silence silence," he counseled himself in his notebooks, "laconic taciturn" (*NB*, 1:234).

In old age his advocacy of silence became positively shrill. "I get humors—they come over me . . . against words," the exasperated bard confessed to Traubel. "God damn them, words: even the words I myself utter!" (*WWWC*, 4:13-14). "There's something better than to write: that's not to write," his faithful acolyte was advised: "Writing is a disease" (*WWWC*, 3:358). Throughout the 1880s he was struggling to diagnose it. "*Make a poem . . . the central theme of which should be* [?] The *Untellable*," he counseled himself. "That which can not be put in fine words, / Nor in any words or statement or essay or poem" (*NB*, 4:1411). This feeling crystallized in a brief, unmemorable lyric like "A Clear Midnight":

> This is thy hour O Soul, thy free flight into the wordless,
> Away from books, away from art, the day erased, the lesson done,
> Thee fully forth emerging, silent, gazing, pondering the themes thou lovest
>   best,
> Night, sleep, death and the stars.   (*LG*, p. 487)

These late, lax efforts to versify the ineffable were unrewarding, of course, so they had to be repeated. At the end of *Leaves of Grass,* on the page preceding "Good-bye My Fancy," the poet was still grappling with the subject of "The Unexpress'd." "How dare one say it?" that poem begins with commendable caution. Alas, valor gets the better of discretion. The poem proceeds to express the vague suspicion that despite the best efforts of Homer, Shakespeare, and Whitman, there is "still something not yet told in poesy's voice or print—something lacking, / . . . Who knows? the best yet unexpress'd and lacking" (*LG*, p. 556). Whether the unexpressed is untellable seems to be among the questions words fail to explain.

Whitman's war with words and his yearning for the ineffable shaped his sense of literary structure. Echoing Rush's technical term from *Philosophy of the Human Voice,* he proclaimed "the words of my book nothing, the drift of it every thing" (*LG*, p. 13). Insofar as terms are terminations, he deeply mistrusted them. "Let others finish specimens, I never finish specimens," he boasted, "I start them by exhaustless laws as Nature does, fresh and modern continually" (*LG*, p. 237). Whitman insists that "the words of the true poems are not the finish but the outset, / They bring none to his or her terminus or to be be content and full" (*LG*, p. 170). The freedom he wished to bestow on his countrymen included freedom from constricting verbal definition. "Thou wonder world yet undefined unform'd, neither do I define thee, / How can I pierce the impenetrable blank of the future?" he candidly confessed. "I do not undertake to define thee, hardly to comprehend thee, / I but thee name, thee prophesy, as now, / I merely thee ejaculate" (*LG*, pp. 458-59). Uncomprehending enthusiasm rarely appeals to academic interpreters, but finality of critical interpretation was what Whitman wanted to avoid by blurring terms with relentless iteration. "I charge that there be no theory or school founded out of me," he wrote, "I charge you to leave all free, as I have left all free" (*LG*, p. 238).

To meet that aim he supplemented verbal vagueness with deliberate disorganization. One sprawling line frankly states the principle on which most of *Leaves of Grass* was composed. "O lands! all so dear to me— what you are, (whatever that is,) I putting it at random in these songs, become a part of that, whatever it is" (*LG*, p. 175). But if this claim seems naive to the point of self-parody, fine poems like "Spontaneous Me" can properly pride themselves as composed of "beautiful dripping fragments, the negligent list of one after another as I happen to call them to me or think of them" (*LG*, p. 103).

Specimen Days rationalizes its own haphazard composition quite charmingly.

> Incongruous and full of skips and jumps as is the huddle of diary-jottings, war-memoranda of 1862-'65, Nature-notes of 1877-'81, with Western and Canadian observations afterwards, all bundled up and tied by a big string, the resolution and indeed mandate comes to me this day, this hour,—(and what a day! what an hour just passing! the luxury of riant grass and blowing breeze, with all the shows of sun and sky and perfect temperature, never before me filling me body and soul)—to go home, untie the bundle, reel out diary-scraps and memoranda, just as they are, large or small, one after another, into print-pages, and let the melange's lackings and wants of connection take care of themselves. . . . At any rate I obey my happy hour's command, which seems curiously imperative. May-be, if I don't do anything else, I shall send out the most wayward, spontaneous, fragmentary book ever printed. (*Prose*, 1:1)

That nature would harmonize any faithful rendering of details was a cherished tenet of Transcendental aesthetics. Emerson's notion that whimsy fosters organic form contributed largely to the frolic architecture of longer works like "Song of Myself." In the first edition of *Leaves of Grass* that poem appears as one sprawling whole composed of well over three hundred verse paragraphs, mostly short. The fifty-two numbered sections into which it was later divided are an authorial afterthought. Interpretations that see in them elaborate structural patterning are unconvincing. While the poem has a beginning and an end, the middle sections could be scrambled in various ways without spoiling its effect on the reader.

A similar imposition of ex post facto "structure" marks *Leaves of Grass* as a whole. Whitman devoted considerable energy to revamping the book's organization as his corpus grew, creating new sequences and shifting poems from one section to another. "I consider 'Leaves of Grass' and its theory experimental," he wrote, "as, in the deepest sense, I consider our American republic itself to be, with its theory" (*Prose*, 2:713). But all the classification did little to shape the way his poems were written. When his scheme petrified in the deathbed edition of 1891–92, it became a major barrier to the appreciation of his poetry, embalming works of genius in masses of flaccid verse. Ambitious to record the growth of a nineteenth-century consciousness, he might have been better served by strict chronological organization. He tinkered constantly with his texts, making his Variorum edition a bonanza for scholarly editors. But his changes often fail to improve the poems; much of the time they weaken them. "This subject of language interests me—interests me: I never quite get it out of my mind," he confided to Traubel. "I sometimes think the Leaves is only a language experiment" (*Pr.*, p. viii). With no clear rationale for what he wanted his book to become, his impulse to revise often seems aimless experiment, just a wish to disturb what he had written, to roil the waters of language to keep words from freezing over him in print.

Words were magic for Whitman. But he could not always believe in their magical power. When belief fails him, afflatus goes flat, and we get versified prose or make-believe. In the 1855 Preface he claims that the poet freely uses "the power to destroy or remould . . . but never the power of attack" (*LG*, p. 713). Over the years what began as an effort to destroy social institutions and remold himself also became an effort to destroy and remold his book. Encyclopedic in scope yet ostentatiously provisional, *Leaves of Grass* shares with satiric anatomies like those by Rabelais, Burton, Swift, Irving, Melville, and Joyce such features as gigantesque characters, utopian settings, catalogs run wild, bogus philosophy, scatological imagery, a merging of prose and verse, fanciful last testaments, and medley structure. Originally the word *satire* denoted a Roman smorgasbord.

The casual, ever-shifting, self-canceling organization of Whitman's works reflects an underlying temperament of Romantic irony.

> This day before dawn I ascended a hill and look'd at the crowded heaven,
> And I said to my spirit *When we become the enfolders of those orbs, and*
>> *the pleasure and knowledge of every thing in them, shall we be*
>> *fill'd and satisfied then,*
> And my spirit said *No, we but level that lift to pass and continue beyond.*
> You also are asking me questions and I hear you,
> I answer that I cannot answer, you must find out for yourself. (*LG*, p. 84)

These lines from "Song of Myself" frame the myth of the open road that governs so much of Whitman's poetry. The exaltation of process and the denial of any terminus committed him to the paradoxical subversion of his own authority. The devotee who takes shelter in *Leaves of Grass* is warned, "You must not stay sleeping and dallying there in the house, though you built it, or though it has been built for you" (*LG,* p. 157). Alas, such Emersonian advice proved easier for the poet to give than to follow. But from his preoccupation with linguistic fixity and fluidity this uncouth Romantic ironist distilled an utterly original rhetoric. In his greatest poetry it retains a unique ability to unsettle the most sophisticated reader. Exasperating in their pretensions, dazzling in their imaginative leaps, his masterpieces are the act of a poetic ventriloquist whom P. T. Barnum might have ballyhooed. Under the spell of his voice we are struck dumb. In our glassy eyes the world turns to glass. As he wiggles the lever that moves our gaping jaws, we feel the dear old fraud's arm round our shoulder.

12 /

Thoreau and the Sounds of Silence

> Everything in nature has a correspondence to something in the soul of man. This correspondence a deep and earnest soul not only sees, but feels; and every feeling has its melody, thus every object has its music.
> — *Dwight's Journal of Music*, 17 July 1852

Harvard Harkens to the Music of a Sphere

As Boylston Professor of Rhetoric and Oratory from 1819 to 1851, E. T. Channing had to mend the vernacular of Harvard students. Alas, his faithful labors in the rhetorical vineyard were hampered by his inadequacies as a public speaker. In 1829, therefore, Harvard appointed Dr. Jonathan Barber to teach elocution at an annual salary of $400, while Channing was paid $1,500 to focus loftily on composition and literature. His new coadjutor proved zealous but "pompous and fantastic in mien, speech, and manners."[1] Like his mentor Dr. James Rush, Barber was a medico who brought to the nascent elocutionary movement a strong physiological bias. Rush's *Philosophy of the Human Voice* (1827) neglected gesture, so Barber developed that topic in his own books, including *A Practical Treatise of Gesture . . . Adapted to the Use of Students . . . in Harvard University* (Cambridge: Hilliard & Brown, 1831) and *A Grammar of Elocution* (New Haven: Maltby, 1832).

No freshman was allowed to begin sawing the air, however, until "distinctness of utterance is insured by repeated exercises." Articulating elementary sounds to Barber's satisfaction was no mean task, Harvard underclassmen soon discovered.

> In pronouncing the word MAN the lips are first intentionally brought together and pressed in a certain way against each other, and air being at the same time forcibly impelled from the throat, a sound is heard which somewhat resembles the lowing of an ox. The lips which before were held in somewhat forcible contact are now separated, the mouth is opened and its cavity is put into a particular shape; and air being again impelled from the throat during this position of the mouth, the sound A is heard as that letter is pronounced in the word *a-t*. Finally this last sound being completed, the tip of the tongue is carried upwards from the lower part of the mouth, and air issuing from the throat in a forcible manner during this state of the parts, the peculiar sound appropriate to the letter N is heard.

In order to obtain a *demonstration* of the particulars of this description, let the word MAN be pronounced in a drawling manner, and let the process of articulation be carefully attended to during its continuance. Let the position which the lips first adopt be maintained for some time while the murmur, by which the sound M is produced, is continued from the throat; avoiding at the same time to proceed to sound A: then ceasing to sound the M, let the A be next sounded alone, observing the particular shape which the mouth assumes during the sound. . . . After the three sounds of the word have thus been separately pronounced, let MAN be slowly uttered, so that each separate sound and the coalescence of them with each other, may be distinctly perceived at the same time.[2]

Drilled in drawling until the proper Harvard accent was obtained, Barber's students were then required to utter each sound *"with the suddenness of the report of fire-arms,"* for there was no other method to "gain strength of voice . . . than by exploding the elements" (*Grammar,* p. 32). Practicing their elements in this way "may be thought by the indolent somewhat irksome," Barber conceded, but lowing like cattle, then popping off like musketry, would familiarize the diligent student with "the real sounds of his language" (p. 44).

Before ascending the podium, therefore, Harvard students convened regularly in small groups to ruminate on the word *man.* They also conned troublesome tongue-twisters like *troubl'd'st* that spellers might not have readied them to pronounce. Barber's exercises in orthoepy bade fair to convert Harvard Yard into kindergarten. If enunciating words was serious business, stringing them together struck him as positively perilous. "It is to be recollected that by the *measured* action of the heart, a certain *quantity* of blood is brought at each pulsation . . . to the lungs, for the purpose of coming into contact with the inspired air," he explained. "But as during speech, there can be no inspiration, speech must be so regulated, as not to interfere with the fluids described, or it must be . . . injurious to respiration and health." Since the voice is voluntary but the circulation is not, there was grave risk they might get out of sync. The orator had to cultivate a measured rhythm that would "not disturb the influx and efflux of air required, at *stated intervals,* to renovate the vital fluid." Breathing only at punctuation marks was dangerous; the orator needed more frequent pauses. Arguing that simplicity in thought and expression is not natural, he rebuffed those worried lest such measured delivery prove ponderous and artificial. "The fine arts do not look to what is *natural* but to what is *agreeable,*" he insisted, defiantly aware that Channing's required textbook stressed naturalness as the key to rhetoric. "Their principle is founded on the habits of taste not on the habits of the multitude" (*Grammar,* pp. 141–43).

After learning to masticate words methodically while breathing like metronomes, Harvard students were ready for the rostrum. To initiate them into the mysteries of rhetorical gesture Barber devised an ingenious apparatus like a bamboo cage (see fig. 12). The student stood inside four equal vertical hoops, each angled at forty-five degrees from the others. Around these meridians ran three horizontal great circles, so seven hoops encircled a student. Constituting a hollow globe over six feet in diameter, the hoops divided its surface into thirty-two different apertures. The student could thrust his hands into various openings in front of him. The postures so defined corresponded to "fifteen fundamental or systematic positions" that the orator's arms might assume while speaking, each associated by Barber with a specific emotion (*Treatise,* pp. 12–13). To master eloquence, all Harvard students were marched into this bathosphere and required to declaim under his watchful eye, thrusting their hands through designated slats at appropriate points in the text.

More beloved by its inventor than by its victims, the bamboo sphere was found one morning dangling from a Cambridge *barber* pole. Waggish undergraduates did more than lynch elocution with a visual pun. Barber's stepson and son-in-law was appointed a tutor in Greek for 1833–34. His even more bizarre personality soon sparked the penultimate Harvard rebellion. Nearly all the sophomore class were suspended.

After the fall semester of 1834 Barber left Harvard suddenly for greener pastures as a strolling lecturer on phrenology, but not before Thoreau had come within his sphere. Thoreau's reaction to this rhetorical mechanic is not on record, but from contemptuous references in later years to rigid grammarians and "posture-makers" we may surmise it was not enthusiastic (2 Jan. 1859). "The brave man is a perfect sphere . . . equally strong every way," his early essay "The Service" argued, whereas "the coward is wretchedly spheroidal at best, too much educated or drawn out on one side and depressed on the other, or may be likened to a hollow sphere." Memories of Barber's armillary apparatus led him to conclude that only by obedience to an inner law of gravity could we "acquire a perfect sphericity" (*Papers,* p. 3). Rambling in Concord's groves, he travestied the elocutionist by grading each tree on the "attitudes, which give it character. In its infinite postures I see my own erectness, or humbleness . . . I am posture-master to the wood" (16 Dec. 1840). Yet he admitted that "sometimes I have listened so attentively . . . to the whole expression of a man that I did not hear one word he was saying" (*PJ,* 2:68–69).

When Thoreau was examined in rhetoric at the end of his sophomore year, the more moderate elocutionist W. H. Simmons had replaced

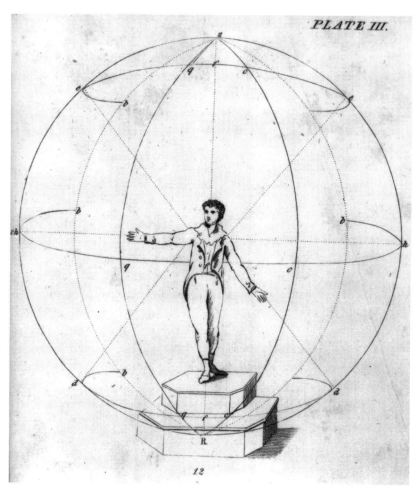

Fig. 12. Jonathan Barber, *A Practical Treatise of Gesture* (1829; Cambridge, Mass.: Hilliard & Brown, 1831), Plate III. Courtesy, Haverford College Library.

Barber as Channing's assistant. Upon that worthy devolved the task of coaching students speaking at Commencement. Simmons pleaded with the overseers for a more suitable classroom than the low dining hall under the college chapel, where the merest whisper easily carried. To this ennervating environment he ascribed the fact that most Harvard seniors participating in the outdoor Commencement ceremonies not only lacked eloquence but were scarcely audible. Illness forced Simmons to resign early in 1837. Filling his place temporarily, his brother George coached Harvard honors seniors, including Thoreau, for their parts in that summer's Commencement.

The discourse "The Commercial Spirit of Modern Times" that Thoreau delivered there on 30 August 1837 reflects no grateful pupil. Lumping together "buying and selling, money-changing and speech-making," he patronizingly dismissed all such activities (*Essays,* pp. 116-227). When he assured his audience that Truth "makes herself to be heard above the din and bustle of commerce," did he make himself heard above the bustling crowd?

Next day Emerson made history by declaiming "The American Scholar." But worn out with orations, Thoreau had apparently decamped for Concord the previous day after delivering his own. In his distaste for declamation he resembled Hawthorne rather than Emerson or Whitman. The most noteworthy orators discussed in his college essays were the devils in Milton's *Paradise Lost.* Sometimes Thoreau was to speak powerfully, especially when slavery tapped his deepest convictions. "In speech he was deliberate and positive," noted one friendly observer in 1861. "The emphatic words seemed to hang fire or to be held back for an instant as if to gather force and weight."[3] But more commonly he ignored Barber's counsels, trilling the letter *r* with a slight speech defect, mumbling, communing with his manuscript rather than his audience—then blaming them as uncooperative listeners. As a lecturer he would enjoy only limited success. Invitations tapered off as his themes grew more Transcendental, his humor more subtle, and his impatience with the podium more marked.

A Mediocre Lecturer Flirts with Acoustic Mysticism

A few months after graduating from Harvard Thoreau began his journal. Within a year he delivered the lecture "Society" at the Concord Lyceum. Like his Commencement address, that first lecture ironizes his own platform performance by describing a habitual impulse "to take himself out of sight and hearing of the orator, lest he lose his own identity in the non-entities around him" (*PJ,* 1:36). True society, he argued, is approached only through silence, while "conversation is only a refuge from the encounter of men." With such paradoxes he tried to prod neighborly nonentities beyond the mob psychology encouraged by oratory. His audience responded by electing him to act in their behalf as secretary and curator of the Lyceum. He planned a second lecture titled "Sound and Silence." But though he mulled the topic over for several years, he could not control its ironies to his satisfaction. There seemed nothing to do but remain silent about sound and silence.

Ruminations on the subject stud his early journals, however. "Why is it that thought flows with so deep and sparkling a current when the sound of distant music strikes the ear?" he wondered. Concord fosters thought, discordant noise disturbs it. "Nature makes no noise. The

howling storm—the rustling leaf—the pattering rain—are no distur-
bance, there is an essential and unexplored harmony in them" (18 Nov.
1837). Like Poe, he composed onomatopoetic verses to capture the
sound of bells heard at a distance.

> For they ring out their peals in a mingled throng,
> And the breezes waft the loud ding-dong along:
> And the metal goes round at a single bound,
> A-lulling the fields with measured sound,
> Till the tired tongue falls with a lengthened boom,
> As solemn and loud as the crack of doom.[4]

Gifted with a keen ear but fewer opportunities to gratify it than Whitman, Thoreau responded to stray strains of melody with an intensity one
might not expect of a man whose musical library consisted solely of the
Liberty and Anti-Slavery Song Book (1842). Indeed, song emancipated
him. "Nothing is so bounded and obedient to law as music," he mused,
"yet nothing so surely breaks all petty and narrow bonds" (5 Feb.
1854). Music "is God's voice—the divine breath audible" (28 June
1840). He fancied that "in a world of peace and love music would be the
universal language" (*RP,* pp. 9–10).

Since sound was sound, it could ravish one into health. "I who have
been sick hear cattle low in the street, with such a healthy ear as prophe-
cies my cure," Thoreau wrote during one early episode of illness. "If I
were a physician I would try my patients thus—I would wheel them to a
window and let Nature feel their pulse—It will soon appear if their sensuous existence is sound" (26 Feb. 1840). He seems not merely to have
heard sound but to have felt it, as if vibrations shook him. A synaesthetic
connoisseur, he extolled sounds heard with "all my senses" (Sept. 1851).
Because of lurking etymological correspondences the sound of wind in the
woods could also have a medicinal effect. Its sibilance helped him "suddenly recover my spirits—my spirituality, through my hearing" (17 Aug.
1851). During one illness the thrumming of a guitar downstairs seemed an
elixir, prompting him to hope for renewed health. As he lay on his deathbed an organ-grinder passed on the street. "Give him some money," he
urged, tears springing to his eyes, "give him some money" (*Days,* p. 463).

But too artful harmony aroused mistrust. "One will lose no music by
not attending the oratorios & operas," he felt (8 Aug. 1851). His disciple the American composer Charles Ives would applaud his disdain for
concert-going.[5] Improvising on an instrument learned from his father
pleased Thoreau more. "My music was a tinkling stream which meandered with the river," he observed after a night spent sailing and fluting.
"I did not hear the strains after they had issued from the flute, but before

they were breathed into it—for the original strain precedes the sound—by as much as the echo follows after." Heard or memorized melodies might distract from imaginary music reflecting more truly "the current of our thought" (18 Aug. 1841). In poetry, too, sound's charm enthralls us first but is soon lost, so "the fame of the poet must rest on the music of the sense. A great philosophical and moral poet would give permanence to the language by making the best sound convey the best sense" (13 Dec. 1841).

Lacking a human language of true, lasting sound, he was drawn to silence. Speech is fractional, silence integral, he decided (16 Dec. 1840). "Not only must men talk," he lamented, "but for the most part must talk about talk—even about books or dead and buried talk" (*PJ*, 1:68). Mastery over men never came from speech but rather from "eloquently refraining from it" (10 Apr. 1841). Walls and masonry bred the halloo. "The whisper is fittest for the depths of the wood," he declared, "but silence is best adapted to the acoustics of space" (Dec. 1838). He courted it with quiet ferocity. It was the natural condition of a pine forest, and his own silence was just as inhuman, he warned one would-be disciple eager for letters. Tuning his mind for birdsong required silence (and indulgent friends). "I have been breaking silence these twenty-three years and have hardly made a rent in it," he observed Delphically. "Silence has no end, speech is but the beginning of it. My friend thinks I *keep* silence who am only choked with letting it out so fast. Does he forget that new mines of secresy are constantly opening in me?" (9 Feb. 1841). A friend curious about his solitude was told how he got the world by the nape of the neck, "held it under in the tide of its own events, till it was drowned, and then I let it go downstream like a dead dog. Vast hollow chambers of silence stretched away on every side, and my being expanded in proportion, and filled them. Then first could I appreciate sound, and find it musical" (*W*, 6:231).

Cleansing the palate of an ear dulled by human speech, silence renewed appreciation of what he heard. A slight sound at evening could lift him by the ears and make life seem inexpressibly serene and grand: "It may be in Uranus—or it may be in the shutter.—It is the original sound of which all literature is but the echo" (10 July 1841). The cricket, the wood thrush, the locomotive whistle, the vibrating telegraph wire became audible icons, triggering regular acoustic epiphanies. "I would be drunk, drunk, drunk, dead drunk to this world with it forever," he exulted. "The contact of sound with a human ear . . . is coincident with an ecstasy. Sugar is not so sweet to the palate as sound to the healthy ear" (31 Dec. 1853).

Yet even as silence revealed sweeter sounds, they would dissolve again into deeper stillness. "I listened to the ancient, familiar, immortal, dear cricket sound under all others, hearing at first some distinct chirps; but when these ceased I was aware of the general earth-song, which my hearing had not heard," he observed on one moonlit walk. "I wondered if behind or beneath this there was not some other chant yet more universal" (13 June 1851). There was, and he learned to hear it too. "To ears that are expanded what a harp this world is!" he cried in triumph (21 July 1851). Purged of speech, a finely tuned ear might hope to catch the earth singing to herself in tones pitched beyond the normal range of hearing.

His aspiration to hear the earth-song resembles Whitman's auditory mystique. On one winter walk, at least, Thoreau was able to eavesdrop directly on subterranean tones when he heard an odd buzzing coming from the ground, just like a fly or a bee in a spider's web. Fearing that he might be stung by an insect, he searched for the source with a stick. By poking he traced it to a few spires of dead grass. "When I bent these one side it produced a duller and baser tone. It was a sound issuing from the earth, and as I stopped over it, the thought came over me that it might be the first puling infantine cry of an earthquake, which would ere long ingulf me" (13 Jan. 1854). He speculated that air trapped under frozen ground and released by an expansive thaw might be hissing through a hollow grass stem. But he was unable to explain the hum to his satisfaction. Such an episode lent plausibility to Whiter's theory that the earth itself could speak. As the sandbank confirmed, "the very soil can fabulate as well as you or I" (5 Feb. 1854).

In a world where sounds masked other sounds, silence was a strategy for tuning in to the music of the spheres. Reception was best on evening strolls. Cold nights made for marked acoustic clarity, he observed, letting him tiptoe gingerly through the galaxy.

> As I walk the railroad causeway I am, as the last two months, disturbed by the sound of my steps on the frozen ground. I wish to hear the silence of the night, for the silence is something positive and to be heard. I cannot walk with my ears covered. I must stand still and listen with open ears, far from the noises of the village, that the night may make its impression on me. A fertile and eloquent silence. Sometimes the silence is merely negative, an arid and barren waste in which I shudder, where no ambrosia grows. I must hear the whispering of a myriad voices. Silence alone is worthy to be heard. Silence is of various depth and fertility, like soil. Now it is a mere Sahara, where men perish of hunger and thirst, now a fertile bottom, or prairie, of the West. As I leave the village, drawing nearer to the woods, I listen from time to time to hear the hounds of Silence baying the

Moon,—to know if they are on the track of any game. If there's no Diana in the night, what is it worth? I hark the goddess Diana. The silence rings; it is musical and thrills me. A night in which the silence was audible. I hear the unspeakable. (21 Jan. 1853)

With all its Romantic self-consciousness this passage records a fragile epiphany—a moonlight sonata in prose by a connoisseur of quiet.

But a pathétique strain also echoes in the contrast with merely negative silence. Thoreau wants to be far from village noises—but not too far. Silence frequents no distant glens, only favorite dells, "and we dream not that she is then imported into them, when we wend thither," he could argue. "Where man is, there is silence" (*PJ*, 1:60). To hear myriad voices whispering he needs fertile silence to *cultivate,* as the agricultural metaphor suggests. By contrast, the ominous negative silence recalls his experience climbing Katahdin in 1846, when he shuddered to confront the inhuman loneliness of a radically material universe. "There is a two-fold *Silence,*" Poe had written in his sonnet of that title. In newly deserted places that resonate with human memories we may encounter "the corporate Silence: dread him not!" Such silence lurks within language, his name's "No More." It is only his "nameless" shadow haunting "the lone regions where hath trod / No foot of man" that need inspire fear in us (*Works*, 1:327). Walking a railroad track that rings daily with noise, Thoreau pays homage to Diana of the crossties. Here a well-trained pack of hounds in the service of Poe's corporate Silence helps him hunt the unspeakable.

"Writing may be either the record of a deed or a deed," Thoreau speculated. "It is nobler when it is a deed" (7 Jan. 1844). By aspiring to the status of action, language verged on silence. But unlike Emerson, who ravished audiences rhetorically, unlike Whitman, whose performatives oozed power, he remained ambivalent about the relation between language and action. Too often words were not deeds but only descriptions. Even the noblest, most dynamic words could seem distinctly inferior to physical actions—and rhetorical action as taught by Barber was a tawdry similacrum that hardly bridged the gap. "The word which is best said came very near not being spoken at all," Thoreau felt, "for it is cousin to a deed which would have been better done" (*Essays*, p. 212).

Yet even heroic feats could disappoint. "The hugest and most effective deed may have no sensible result at all on earth," he warned. "When in rare moments our whole being strives with one consent, which we name a yearning, we may not hope that our work will stand in any artist's gallery on earth. The bravest deed, which for the most part is quite left out of history, . . . is the life of a great man. To perform exploits is to be temporarily bold . . . but the exploit of a brave life consists in its momentary completeness" (*RP,* p. 16). Like the Aristotelian superman to whom Emerson compared Thoreau, like those Renaissance heroes whom Aristotle inspired, this hero may possess a soul so grand that no action can express his magnanimity. Whatever he does must fall ludicrously short of what he is. In the seventeenth century this heroic ideal helped beget a mock-heroic spirit.[6] In the nineteenth it made Thoreau playfully aware that his projects might seem absurdly inadequate to account for his earnest involvement in them. Emerson criticized him as the contented captain of a huckleberry party when he might have engineered for America. Thoreau cultivated that pose with comic brio because he doubted that either activity could express who he was. "As for Doing-good, that is one of the professions which are full," he argues in *Walden.* "I should say rather, set about being good" (p. 73). Words might be inferior to deeds, but concrete deeds were inferior to the spirit in which they were performed. If even the language of action fell short of his ideal, what resort was left to the writer but Romantic irony?

Thoreau's rhetorical heroes are men of action like Sir Walter Raleigh and John Brown. The authenticity of their speech is grounded less in what *it* accomplishes than in what it suggests *they* have accomplished personally. The crucial accomplishment of these martyrs, however, is not shaping history like Carlyle's heroes but shaping themselves. The Transcendental ethic of sincerity led Thoreau to conclude that "a man addresses effectually in another only himself still, and what he himself does and is, alone can he prompt the other to do and to become" (*Essays,* pp. 251-52). For such suasion language is nearly superfluous. Indeed, neither persuasion nor proof seems a central goal of this eloquence; it convinces by incarnating action and insight in the person of an exemplary heroic speaker.[7] But the platform can scarcely accommodate the optimal amount of lived experience. Rhetoric so conceived naturally issues not in oratory but in written autobiographical narrative.

Floating from Concord to the Heart of Silence

Thus Thoreau's lecture "Sound and Silence" was never delivered but finally found its place in his first book. In 1842 his brother John died in his arms from tetanus. Thoreau was devastated. For a week after the funeral he sat passively saying nothing, to his family's alarm. Then he himself suddenly fell victim to what appeared to be lockjaw, exhibiting all his brother's symptoms. The doctor despaired of his life. After three days this psychosomatic reaction gradually abated. He was confined to his bedroom for a month, however, and for long after remained quiet and depressed. "Why does God not make some mistake to show us that time is a delusion. Why did I invent time but to destroy it," he scribbled wearily in his journal. "Is it not a satire—to say that life is organic? . . . Where is my heart gone—they say men cannot part with it and live" (26 Mar. 1842). For years he absolutely refused to sing with his family. His brother's death literally silenced his voice.

Anniversaries of that death brought recurrent nightmares—but also a determination not to yield his brother quietly to the grave. The volume that he planned to commemorate their camping trip of 1839 would unlock both death's jaws and his own. He would reinvent time but to destroy it; in a hodgepodge tinged with satire he would say that life is organic. That might reclaim his heart. But it was hard to get started amid the bustle of the Thoreau household, the clatter of the pencil factory, the din of family dinners. In 1845 he moved to Walden Pond and began *A Week on the Concord and Merrimack Rivers* (1849). A hundred-page draft was finished within a year. The rhetorical occasion of the book was John's death, its source a journal the two brothers kept on the trip. But the book owes much of its impetus to Thoreau's meditations on sound and silence. Incorporating chunks from his unfinished lecture at pivotal points, it hints at what can and cannot be said about the river of time on which the brothers are voyaging. In a tacit concession to death, John is nowhere named or quoted directly, although the book is obliquely dedicated to him. Yet it tries to make his memory resonate as part of Thoreau's own windy bid for literary immortality.

Once the two brothers are launched on the Concord, "the village murmur subsided, and we seemed to be embarked on the placid current of our dreams, floating from past to future." The last neighbor they see is a quiet fisherman, "and we silently through him bade adieu to our friends." Saturday's voyage starts them drifting in a hush toward the meaning of stillness. Its votaries are taciturn fishermen like one old soul Thoreau can barely remember, who haunted the river "full of incommunicable thoughts." Unnoticed by the village then and forgotten now, this compleat angler's sport seems in retrospect "a sort of solemn sacrament and withdrawal from the world" (*Week,* pp. 19-25). When the brothers pitch their tent that first night, the novelty of their situation keeps them awake listening to sounds—foxes treading dead leaves, a muskrat nosing their provisions, a dreaming sparrow's abortive song, an owl's throttled cry, the breathing of the wind bearing fire alarms from distant Lowell like tinkling music. But after each sound "there was a sudden pause, and deeper and more conscious silence." Most noticeable were the house dogs, which they heard every night. With a full gamut of accents from mastiff's to terrier's, their barking was "at first loud and rapid, then faint and slow, to be limited only in a whisper: wow-wow-wow-wow—wo—wo—w—w." Like mantras such pure sounds provoke meditation. They attest to "nature's health or *sound* state. Such is the never failing beauty and accuracy of language." But the chapter ends with a very different sign of sound health—the lapse of language that occurred when "all sounds were denied entrance to our ears" by terminal drowsiness (pp. 40-42).

"Saturday" sets the pattern for *A Week*. Each day's voyage begins concretely, meanders like the river through vaguely related topics, and ends with the brothers' drifting asleep while pondering sounds in lieu of prayers. "Sunday," the most notorious chapter, is devoted to critical reflections on Christianity and language. Entering the Merrimack and beginning to ascend it, they must row hard, breaking the Sabbath; but in focusing attention on things of this world manual labor removes "palaver and sentimentality out of one's style" (p. 105). Preferring "the liberal divinities of Greece" to America's God, Thoreau knows some will be shocked to hear Christ named beside Buddha, "yet I am sure that I am willing that they should love their Christ more than my Buddha, for the love is the main thing, and I like him too." But he finds the ethic of Christianity too otherworldly, its mythus simply a reworking of older materials. The timelessness of mythology appeals to him. Polyvalent like puns, myths approach "that universal language which men have sought in vain." Christianity's effort "to fable of the ineffable" is undercut by presumptuous claims to historical exclusivity, whereas expressing variable truths makes true myths "hieroglyphics to address men unborn." Narcissus, Endymion, or Memnon son of morning are "representative of all promising youths who have died a premature death, and whose memory is melodiously prolonged to the latest morning." In such beautiful stories "we seem to hear the music of a thought, and care not if the understanding be not gratified" (pp. 58-70). From their trip Thoreau tries to distill a like myth of his brother that will transcend the dogma intruded when "at a third of a mile over the water we heard distinctly some children repeating their catechism in a cottage near the shore, while in the broad shallows between, a herd of cows stood lashing their sides, and waging war with the flies" (p. 80). After being kept awake that night by some railroad laborers cavorting rowdily on their day off, Thoreau falls asleep to troubled dreams. But untainted by theological rancor, John slept serenely. Reassuring his brother in the morning, he is discreetly elevated at chapter's end to the role of Good Genius.

Monday finds the voyagers again at odds with society. Now the world labors while they are on holiday. In their thoughts commercial bustle is interwoven with martial incidents from local history. Both suggest the active virtues with which the first settlers displaced the Indians. Thoreau's mood swings between epic and mock-heroic, between waking and dreaming. "To one who habitually endeavors to contemplate the true state of things, the political state can hardly be said to have any existence whatever," he hazards. While in Germany "philological industry is indirectly serving the cause of philosophy and poetry" by taking us back to India, the annals of history are delusive insofar as "the *past* cannot be *presented;* we cannot know what we are not" (pp. 148–56). Yet he is also skeptical of those caste-conscious eastern sages who "sat contemplating Brahm, uttering in silence the mystic 'Om,' being absorbed into the essence of the Supreme Being, never going out of themselves, but subsiding further and deeper within; so infinitely wise, yet infinitely stagnant." As an energetic gospel of brotherhood, practical morality, and social reform, the New Testament now appeals to him more, though Christianity's neglect of contemplative technique still means that a buzzing fly can disturb a Western mind's superficial meditations (pp. 129–38).

After fifty pages comparing Western and Eastern religions in such terms, the brothers camp for the night. Drifting asleep, they hear someone at a distance "beating a drum incessantly, in preparation for a country muster." Jarring though this tyro's awkward practice might seem, it triggers an audible epiphany, not disgust.

> These simple sounds related us to the stars. Aye, there was a logic in them so convincing that the combined sense of mankind could never make me doubt their conclusions. I stop my habitual thinking, as if the plow had suddenly run deeper in its furrow through the crust of the world. How can I go on, who have just stepped over such a bottomless skylight in the bog of my life. Suddenly old Time winked at me,—Ah you know me, you rogue,—and news had come that IT was well. That ancient universe is in such capital health, I think undoubtedly it will never die. Heal yourselves, doctors; by God I live.

Including passages from his unfinished lecture, Thoreau spends six pages elaborating the meaning of the nocturnal music that permits him "to hear beyond the range of sound." Under this relentless drumbeat, thinking stops, trance begins. It synthesizes the chapter's conflicting values of action and contemplation. Reminiscent of a passage of the Vedas, music suggests "the idea of infinite remoteness, as well as of beauty and serenity." But it also reminds him that "the hero is the sole patron of music. That harmony which exists naturally between the hero's moods and the universe the soldier would fain imitate with drum and trumpet." There may be a melancholy note, "perchance because we that hear are not one with that which is heard" (pp. 172–78). But any sadness is ours, not the music's. We can tip old time a wink of our own. Although his brother is dead, the universe will never die. With a casual allusion to Scripture he dismisses physicians and insouciantly proclaims his desire to live on with a pun that teeters between piety and profanity.

"When I would muse . . . an irregular-discordant drumming is intolerable," the youthful Thoreau had found (18 Nov. 1837). But later a child beating a tin pan came to seem the purest musician, for tiny ears could detect the melody in noise. Nostalgically envying "the infant drummer" who could make the heavens his sounding board, he wished that he too "could unfailingly draw music from a quart pot" (9 June 1852). On the Merrimack he learned to do that, in effect—and felt an ecstatic harmony with the cosmos.

But if music "is the flower of language," able to express the noblest ideas beyond speech, its harmonies are transient. The remainder of the trip increasingly suggests the difficulty of capturing meaning in writing. None of the authors who figure in his critical meditations seem to command his complete approval. When a passing hunter hails and asks if they had killed anything, "we shouted after him that we had shot a *buoy*, and could see him for a long while scratching his head in vain, to know if he had heard aright" (p. 201). Certain puns make speech uncertain. "The language of friendship is not words but meanings," the lengthy disquisition on that topic suggests.[8] The brothers' destination is Mount Agiocochook, but to reach it they must leave the river of time, and the climactic ascent is summarized in one bald sentence. Evidently the ineffable baffles words. "Unfortunately many things have been omitted which should have been recorded in our journal, for though we made it a rule to set down all our experiences therein, yet such a resolution is very hard to keep, for the important experience rarely allows us to remember such obligations, and so indifferent things get recorded," Thoreau coyly explains. "It is not easy to write in a journal what interests us at any time, because to write it is not what interests us" (p. 332).

Returning in autumnal weather on the last day, he develops this theme further:

> The true poem is not that which the public read. There is always a poem not printed on paper, coincident with the production of this, stereotyped in the poet's life. It is *what he has become through his work*. Not how is the idea expressed in stone, or on canvass or paper, is the question, but how far it has obtained form and expression in the life of the artist. . . .

> My life has been the poem I would have writ,
> But I could not both live and utter it. (p. 343)

Even this fine epigram belies its subject. With memorable finality it prefers action as the supreme expression, celebrating the lapse of language into life. Yet on *A Week*'s symbolic river journey the life celebrated is also lapsing; it survives for us only as written expression. Musing on language, Thoreau speculates that "our present senses are but the rudiments of what they are destined to become. We are comparatively deaf and dumb." But though the ears were made to hear celestial sounds, he despairs of our ever using them properly, for "where is the instructed teacher?" Where indeed? Not ensconced in the Boylston Chair at Harvard, one may surmise, or out on the phrenological hustings with Dr. Jonathan Barber. Thoreau wanted to hear the music of the spheres, not strains from the bamboo sphere. Whether or not his brother would have agreed that "we need pray for no higher heaven than the pure senses can furnish, a *purely* sensuous life," alas, that very belief means that John is not available for further pedagogical duty. And even if Thoreau thought himself qualified for the job, by what form of discourse could he teach us? Evidently his book alone cannot.

So their voyage ends with a stirring paean to Silence, the mistress of all sounds. They are "but bubbles on her surface, which straightway burst, an evidence of the strength and prolificness of the under-current." The five grandiloquent paragraphs that constitute this famous set piece were levied from his undelivered lecture, in the conviction that "the orator puts off his individuality, and is then most eloquent when most silent." Yet this riddling conclusion also reflects his belief that we overrate climactic conclusions. "Have you any *last* words?" readers may ask a friendly author on parting. "Alas, it is only the word of words, which you have so long sought and found not; you have not a *first* word yet" (p. 273). Death seems final, yet in the flow of time aesthetic closure is a fiction.

The paradoxical relation between sound and silence figures the relation between time and eternity—the relation that Theodore Parker described in his classic Transcendental sermon "The Transient and the Permanent in Christianity." With altered emphasis, the paradox also suggests Schlegel's dualism of flux and identity. Schlegel's absolute is flux, Parker's perhaps permanence, and Thoreau may seem tempted to cast his lot with the latter. But sound has become "so far akin to Silence" that he can scarcely disentangle the two. They coalesce, so that he meditates as a punning pundit upon an equivocal silence that may be either God's voice or nothingness—the ultimate double entendre. "A good book is the plectrum with which our else silent lyres are struck. We not unfrequently refer the interest which belongs to our own unwritten sequel to the written and comparatively lifeless body of the work. Of all books this sequel is the most indispensable part. It should be the author's aim to say once and emphatically, 'He said,' ἔφη,' 'ἔ.' This is the most the book maker can attain to. If he make his volume a mole whereon the waves of silence may break, it is well" (pp. 392–93). The Greek tags are Homeric formulae that conclude speeches. "In all epics, when, after breathless attention, we come to the significant words 'he said,'" Thoreau argued in his lecture draft, "then especially our inmost man is addressed" (*PJ*, 1:63–64). Why? Because the eloquent words that held us enthralled are not just punctuated but lightly punctured, and heroes must proceed to the epic test of action. "He said" makes us ask what he *did*. Like Schlegel, Thoreau relishes those moments when an author punctures the authority of his own words—hence the derogatory allusion to his own lifeless book. Etymological puns, like his claim floating downstream that "this portion of time is but the current hour," belie that criticism by wittily contrasting transient and permanent meanings (p. 331). Like Parker, he is committed to action, though his reforming zeal is directed less at society than at the self. The result is a conclusion that tempers Transcendental earnestness with Romantic irony.

Unraveling the Rhetoric of *Walden*'s "Reading"

"There was a time when the beauty and the music were all within, and I sat and listened to my thoughts, and there was a song in them. I sat for hours on rocks and wrestled with the melody which possessed me." In the aftermath of wrestling with the proof sheets of *Walden* Thoreau recalled his lost fervor. That book sought to express his inner music, but with what result? Now his vision seemed dominated by dead fish floating on the river. The fault must be his own, he thought, for no wholly extraneous object could preoccupy him. Longing for the days "when you were an organ of which the world was but one poor broken pipe," he sensed something fishy in his muse. "We soon get through with Nature," he speculated. "She excites an expectation which she cannot satisfy" (23 May 1854).

Ambivalence about his inspiration is writ large in "Reading" and "Sounds," the paired chapters of *Walden* focused on language. After the first two chapters introduce an antisocial Thoreau, we suppose that he is urging studious reading and celebrating the sounds of nature. So he is, but his attitude is more complicated than that.

"Men sometimes speak as if the study of the classics would at length make way for more modern and practical studies," he observes, "but the adventurous student will always study classics, in whatever language they may be written and however ancient they may be." In a spirit of adventure, then, we should note that while opposing speech to writing this sentence equivocates lightly on the word *classics*. "They are the only oracles which are not decayed, and there are such answers to the most modern inquiry in them as Delphi and Dodona never gave." The classical oracles were famous for equivocation. But here Thoreau invokes their manner to dismiss their authority. His defense of classical studies implies that *Walden* itself may be such a classic, although written in English of the current hour.

His contrast between *written* classics and what men *say* about them cuts deep. Native knowledge of the original languages is not enough, for "there is a memorable interval between the spoken and the written language, the language heard and the language read. The one is commonly transitory, a sound, a tongue, a dialect merely, almost brutish, and we learn it unconsciously, like the brutes, of our mothers. The other is the maturity and experience of that; if that is our mother tongue, this is our father tongue, a reserved and select expression, too significant to be heard by the ear, which we must be born again in order to speak." Though the next chapter praises brute sounds, here Thoreau staunchly rejects linguistic tutelage from Mother Nature. "The select language of literature" that he values is paternal, a stern initiation into maturity and cultural experience. Silently wrestling with written classics is a male puberty ritual for aspiring heroes that weans them from "daily colloquies and vaporous breath." Despite fluency in Greek and Latin, Greco-Roman audiences could not appreciate their own writers, he avers, for they could not hear them. Since "eloquence in the forum is commonly found to be rhetoric in the study," he denies it an educational role, for the noblest writing is "commonly far behind or above the fleeting spoken language." Rhetorical occasions tempt speakers to indulge their passions rather than display the exemplary integrity of their lives. "The orator yields to the inspiration of a transient occasion, and speaks to the mob before him, to those who can *hear* him; but the writer, whose more equable life is his occasion, and who would be distracted by the event and the crowd which inspire the orator, speaks to the intellect and heart of mankind, to all in any age who can *understand* him."

Harvard's elocutionists seem to have wasted their labors on Thoreau. He prefers books because, unlike orators, "they have no cause of their own to plead." Even a smattering of a dead language like Latin seems better than the "trivialness of the street," for it may equip a farmer to realize that street-corner conversation is the definition of *trivi-*

ality (from Latin *tres viae* = three roads). Indeed, as "the work of art nearest to life itself," a written word seems to take priority for Thoreau over oral expression. "Translated into every language . . . not only . . . read but breathed from all human lips . . . carved out of the breath of life itself," as if God gave Adam lessons in penmanship, here writing almost seems the origin of speech.

Did Thoreau prefer a work of art to living language? In an era that must weigh the competing claims of audiovisual media and literature would he unhesitatingly opt for the latter? Not necessarily. He does not share our cultural bias, often reinforced by poor readers' defensiveness, that treats any reading as virtuous. Most reading he views with the same contempt as speech. Though most have learned to read, "of reading as a noble intellectual exercise they know little or nothing." The appetite for ephemeral journalism strikes him as a ludicrous desire to cling to our primers, "forever repeating our a-b-abs and words of one syllable, in the fourth or fifth classes, sitting on the lowest and foremost form all our lives." A novel addict approaches his reading as "some little four-year-old bencher his two-cent gilt-covered edition of Cinderella,—without any improvement, that I can see, in the pronunciation, or accent, or emphasis, or any more skill in extracting or inserting the moral."

To be sure, his satire of naive reading ties it to the oral rituals of the classroom or to the Victorian custom of reading monthly installments of novels aloud in the family. Yet as the chapter proceeds there are hints that classic literature too has oral roots. "Shall I hear the name of Plato and never read his book?" Thoreau asks rhetorically. Surprisingly, the answer is yes. "His Dialogues, which contain what was immortal in him, lie on the next shelf, and yet I never read them." Rejecting hard distinctions between fellow townsmen who are functionally or just culturally illiterate, he includes himself in the latter group. Acting "as if Plato were my townsman" is impossible, after all, a grammatical condition contrary to fact. His Dialogues are no longer dialogue. Indeed, Thoreau's entire discussion of reading begins by admitting that his first active summer at Walden he read only "one or two shallow books of travel." Although he left Homer's *Iliad* lying on his table, it never tempted him. Like many a modern subscriber to the Classics Book Club, he hankered to read the classics in some leisured future. What postponed that pleasure for him was less the lack of a leather armchair than the fact that anyone who reads a Greek or Latin classic in the original, "whose praises are familiar even to the so called illiterate . . . will find nobody at all to speak to, but must keep silence about it." Here scholarly literacy seems incomplete without speech, and conventional scorn for illiteracy appears questionable. Classical scholars seem mere grammarians, for hardly any college professor has mastered "the wit and poetry of a Greek poet, and has any sympathy to impart to the alert and heroic reader." Apparently that reader still craves enlightening oral discourse.

He may also crave social cachet—and properly so. That is the startling conclusion suggested by Thoreau's example of the "illiterate and perhaps scornful trader" who makes a fortune only to be haunted by his unfamiliarity with books whose "authors are a natural and irresistible aristocracy in every society. . . . Admitted to the circles of wealth and fashion, he turns inevitably at last to those still higher but yet inaccessible circles of intellect and genius, and is sensible only of the imperfection of his culture." Enabling one to converse in the best society, here the classics serve the same need as Book-of-the-Month Club and *Reader's Digest*. If the parvenu must content himself with the latter, he "further proves his good sense" by securing for his children the intellectual culture he so keenly misses. Thoreau's ambitious parents sent him to Harvard from motives much like this. Would he be troubled to find *Walden* recommended today as a book that it was embarrassing not to have read? He was not always a snob about snobbery. Far more pragmatic than most realize, his Transcendental ethic is grounded in social awareness.

For that reason his chapter on reading culminates with a long paragraph at several removes from the stance of the lonely, bookish intellectual with which it began.

> But consider how little this village does for its own culture. I do not wish to flatter my townsmen, nor be flattered by them, for that will not advance either of us. We need to be provoked,—goaded like oxen, as we are, into a trot. We have a comparatively decent system of common schools, schools for infants only; but excepting the half-starved Lyceum in the winter, and latterly the puny beginning of a library suggested by the state, no school for ourselves. We spend more on almost any article of bodily aliment or ailment than on our mental aliment. It is time that we had uncommon schools, that we did not leave off our education when we begin to be men and women. It is time that villages were universities, and their elder inhabitants the fellows of universities, with leisure—if they are indeed so well off—to pursue liberal studies the rest of their lives. (pp. 108-9)

With this ambiguous first-person plural Thoreau cocks one eye at Concord, one at America. The eye pun on *aliment/ailment* goes better in writing as part of his effort to prod a national audience into awareness. But the writer who does not wish to flatter his townsmen, or to be flattered by them, is emphatically part of his own village.

Indeed, he seems hardly a writer, for the flattering response that he tries to head off presumes a forum like the lyceums, where he tried out many sections of *Walden* and where a lecture might be followed by dialogue. Thoreau shares with that audience his experience of not reading Plato in Greek; for that task perhaps he too needs to be provoked "into a trot." Rhetorical turns like the contrast between common and uncommon schools suggest public address. In summoning citizens to be fellows of Concord *qua* university he does not forget that they are also his *fellow* townsmen. The Lyceum was an independently funded organization, and in this paragraph its quondam curator seems to be appealing for public support. Evidently his own self-culture needs social encouragement. It is salutary to realize that a figure famous for refusing to pay taxes is here pleading for a tax increase to fund adult education. "To act collectively is according to the spirit of our institutions," he urges, shelving his former mistrust of rhetoric's mass appeal. Patronage of the arts was formerly the prerogative of noblemen; now the town should undertake it. "Instead of noblemen, let us have noble villages of men," he concludes. "If it is necessary, omit one bridge over the river, go round a little there, and throw one arch at least over the darker gulf of ignorance which surrounds us." By the end of "Reading" the author who extolled books with chiseled scorn for oratory is exhorting a town meeting to purchase them. Defer municipal maintenance of bridges, his peroration pleads, vote funds for a community college.

The Social Reverberations of *Walden*'s "Sounds"

By the end of "Reading" the disciplined and permanent language of literature half-dissolves into the passionate eloquence of a speech. The beginning of "Sounds" takes this process a step further. "But while we are confined to books, though the most select and classic, and read only particular written languages, which are themselves but dialects and provincial, we are in danger of forgetting the language which all things and events speak without metaphor, which alone is copious and standard." For understanding the language of nature "no method or discipline can supersede the necessity of being always on the alert." Yet no sooner is such a language opposed to that of classical literature than the distinction is undermined. Interpreting nature does require a discipline, it turns out—not grammatical paradigms and conjugations but "the discipline of looking always at what is to be seen. . . . Will you be a reader, a student merely, or a seer?"

"I did not read books that first summer; I hoed beans," begins the second paragraph. Then once again discipline suddenly goes by the board.

Nay, I often did better than this. There were times when I could not afford to sacrifice the bloom of the present moment to any work, whether of the head or hands. I love a broad margin to my life. Sometimes, in a summer morning, having taken my accustomed bath, I sat in my sunny doorway from sunrise till noon, rapt in a revery, amidst the pines and hickories and sumachs, in undisturbed solitude and stillness, while the birds sang around or flitted noiseless through the house, until by the sun falling in at my west window, or the noise of some traveller's wagon on the distant highway, I was reminded of the lapse of time. I grew in those seasons like corn in the night, and they were far better than any work of the hands would have been. . . . I realized what the Orientals mean by contemplation and the forsaking of works. . . . The day advanced as if to light some work of mine; it was morning, and lo, now it is evening, and nothing memorable is accomplished. Instead of singing like the birds, I silently smiled at my incessant good fortune. As the sparrow had its trill, sitting on the hickory before my door, so had I my chuckle or suppressed warble which he might hear out of my nest. My days were not days of the week, bearing the stamp of any heathen deity, nor were they minced into hours and fretted by the ticking of a clock; for I lived like the Puri Indians, of whom it is said that "for yesterday, to-day, and to-morrow they have only one word, and they express the variety of meaning by pointing backward for yesterday, forward for to-morrow, and overhead for the passing day." (pp. 111-12)

Often taken as the record of a mystical experience, this paragraph is powerfully evocative. But the attitude expressed is more complex than appears, nor is it necessarily the attitude described. The author who renounces book-learning to proclaim his oneness with nature retains "a broad margin" to his life as if that were a printed page. Does he scan it? After his talk of becoming a "seer," he claims to pass the time hardly seeing what is around him, for noontide takes him by surprise. Alternately musical and noiseless, the birds accentuate a stillness that seems to enfold him solemnly, "rapt in a revery." But this revery is not really reverential. It is the experience of a punning nudist who after taking his morning bath would sit in his "sunny doorway" to dry himself off, *wrapped* only in a revery. This coy joke must make us wonder just how rapt Thoreau was. As a prim Victorian he would have been alert to the approach of any woman who might threaten to catch him naked, one suspects. To relish an "undisturbed solitude" is to be aware of possible disturbances. Likewise, to realize that "nothing memorable is accomplished" is to be aware of the moral responsibilities that weigh upon the alert and heroic reader—and also to be aware of the ironic echo from the Creation story in Genesis. His silent smile becomes an audible chuckle as he thinks of the song-sparrow. The sound that wells up does not merely express ecstatic well-being and oneness with nature. Surely what amuses him here is partly the incongruity between himself and the bird. His dedication to "the language which all things and events speak without metaphor" means that he knows his hut is no nest, he knows he cannot really warble, he knows these are merely an author's conceits. He knows that whatever he harkened to at the time, sound or silence, he is not now writing the same language of nature. His experience of timelessness was temporary. He must render it in words saturated with time, even as the names for our days of the week bear the stamp of past heathen divinities. This etymological nudist claims to have lived like a Puri Indian relying on a gestural language of nature. But that very claim takes the form of ostentatious quotation from a book, and Thoreau was drilled in such "natural" gestures by Dr. Jonathan Barber.

Here puns and etymology register resistance to incorporation in a world of natural sounds. Yet that world exercises a powerful pull. When he sets his writing table outside to clean house, his books, pen, and ink seem glad, "unwilling to be brought in." Yet they lend his al fresco experience a literary element, so that his life seems "a drama of many scenes." From his window he sees hawks stirring up wild pigeons who give "a voice to the air," while along the shore a mink preys on frogs. Blending with the activity of these predators is "the rattle of railroad cars, now dying away and then reviving like the beat of a partridge."

Nine paragraphs devoted to the railroad dominate the chapter. He has more to say about its noises than about any natural sounds, and what he has to say is by no means unfavorable. Its whistle is "like the scream of a hawk." There is something grand about the iron horse that suggests the need for a new mythology. Even if its servitors are not always heroic, its barbarous energy compels Thoreau's respect. Its smoke blends into nature, "the train of clouds stretching far behind and rising higher and higher, going to heaven while the cars are going to Boston." Despite that wry antithesis between the train of clouds and the train of cars, he concedes the steady and cheerful valor of the crews. The author who began the chapter celebrating a life lived without the ticking of a clock now praises the railroad for encouraging punctuality in men. "Commerce is unexpectedly confident and serene, alert, adventurous, and unwearied," he admits. "It is very natural in its methods withal." With amused interest he scans it as a text. "This car-load of torn sails is more legible and interesting now than if they should be wrought into paper and printed books. Who can write so graphically the history of the storms they have weathered as these rents have done? They are proof-sheets which need no correction." He seems less troubled by industrial noise pollution than by the threat mass production poses to the literary sensibility. Sending timber to urban factories, "with such huge and lumbering civility the country hands a chair to the city." Specialization threatens all concerned. Forgoing crude, handmade furniture like his own writing table means that men are less likely to see the twofold meaning in words like *lumbering*. "Up come the books, but down goes the wit that writes them," he frets.

But not unduly. Drovers rattled by with a carload of sheep, "still clinging to their useless sticks as their badge of office," suggesting that the pastoral world may also be governed by inertia and herd instinct. Their failure to adapt to new economic circumstances seems sheeplike. Despite his disdain for the locomotive's hissing when it crowds him off the tracks, Thoreau's ears do adapt, to the point that he can dismiss it tolerantly with his verses, "What's the railroad to me? / I never go to see / Where it ends."

To its occasional rumbling he owes a renewed sense of stillness that leaves him "more alone than ever" with his meditations. With a favorable wind on Sundays, church bells penetrate the woods, "a faint, sweet, and, as it were, natural melody, worth importing into the wilderness." Like the railroad's business of importing, this man-made noise merges with nature to be revealed as important.

> At a sufficient distance over the woods this sound acquires a certain vibratory hum, as if the pine needles in the horizon were strings of a harp which it swept. All sound heard at the greatest possible distance produces one and the same effect, a vibration of the universal lyre, just as the intervening atmosphere makes a distant ridge of earth interesting to our eyes by the azure tint it imparts to it. There came to me in this case a melody which the air had strained, and which had conversed with every leaf and needle of the wood, that portion of the sound which the elements had taken up and modulated and echoed from vale to vale. The echo is, to some extent, an original sound, and therein is the magic and charm of it. It is not merely a repetition of what was worth repeating in the bell, but partly the voice of the wood; the same trivial words and notes sung by a wood-nymph. (p. 123)

Distance makes human beings trivial—and triviality beautiful. The universal harmony that he hears is a duet between man and nature, not an aria for the latter. *Conversing* with natural objects, the bells hold a dialogue in which their pure tones reemerge as "words."

Ostensibly natural, all the following sounds in the chapter figure likewise as dialogue. Wandering at night, the rowdy youths whose singing resembles the cheap and natural music of the cow are not satirized, Thoreau insists, for if "they were at length one articulation of Nature," then cows are just as truly strolling minstrels. Whippoorwills chant their vespers with "as much precision as a clock." Wise midnight hags, the owls seem "fallen souls that once in human shape nightwalked the earth." Their hooting is "the most melancholy sound in Nature, as if she meant by this to stereotype and make permanent in her choir the dying moans of a human being." Nature is evidently the proprietress of a print shop vending linguistic permanence, and the most melancholy sound she affords is a literary stereotype drawn from human behavior. "It is a sound admirably suited to swamps and twilight woods which no day illustrates," Thoreau claims, "suggesting a vast and undeveloped nature which men have not recognized." Yet even as he tries to imagine a purely nonhuman nature his diction jarringly obtrudes human history, for *illustrate* must be understood etymologically in terms of its archaic meaning *illumine*. In timeless swamps that no day illustrates, Nature is printing her illustrated daily, and owls are dragged hooting dolefully into service as moral illustrations. "Let them do the idiotic and manical hooting for men" is the editorial.

If Thoreau's owls are subcontractors in a thoroughly human enterprise, so too are baying dogs and distant wagons. Their rumbling over bridges travels further than any other sound at night, he observes. Walden's frogs furnish one of the book's comic set pieces, the marvelous description of the aldermanic drinking party that ends at dawn with all but one "under the pond ... vainly bellowing *troonk* from time to time." Evidently in the language of nature inebriated frogs can't quite articulate the word *drunk*. To judge from this drollery, Thoreau's hut might as well have adjoined the village tavern.

The chapter ends with a paragraph devoted to the most remarkable note of all—one that "would soon become the most famous sound in our woods" if it ever penetrated there. But it does not. Thoreau rhapsodizes about it at length while mentioning that at Walden he never heard a cockcrow. Though he professes to relish the absence of domestic sounds from churn, kettle, and spinning wheel, he is distinctly nostalgic for brave Chanticleer. Linking the concept of cause = *weil* to the idea of an egg = *ei,* the nineteenth-century German scholar Voightmann wanted to derive all language from the notes of cuckoos and roosters, the former's song representing the element of change, the latter's the principle of permanence. In the subdued quiet of his clearing Thoreau finds himself wondering whether he should keep a cock for music alone, like a singing bird. He gives himself over to a delighted fantasy of what the woods would sound like if cockerels still roamed wild. "It would put nations on the alert," he thinks. Although "its shrill sound never roused me from my slumbers," his enthusiasm for it is not just ironic. If sound tempts him to step out of time, it also calls him back in. The silence at

Walden lets hushed sounds be heard. But it also reverberates with an imaginary clarion, always audible to a man who proposed on his title page "to brag as lustily as chanticleer in the morning . . . if only to wake my neighbors up." Melodies heard beside Walden resound sweetly, but this unheard melody sounds sweetest of all.

Beginning as a meditation on literature and action, "Reading" moves paradoxically toward society by subsuming the idea of writing in speech. Beginning with the universal language that everything speaks without metaphor, "Sounds" moves paradoxically from silent meditation toward communication by crystallizing sound in metaphors drawn from writing. To read these chapters sensitively is to participate in a process in which sound and silence, action and contemplation, speech and writing, self and society, define themselves in opposition to each other. Yet the contradictions between these forms of human expression always seem about to dissolve. Bowing to their partners, words and ideas join hands to dance. So subtle is the counterpointing, so graceful the conceptual poetry, that these two chapters alone span the attitudes toward language explored at greater length in *A Week*.

13 /

Walden's Antic Dialectic between Self and Society

> Yes and No are lies—a true answer will not aim to establish anything, but rather to set all well afloat.
>
> — Thoreau (22 June 1840)

Fusing Polarities with Coleridgean Imagination

Like "Reading" and "Sounds," later chapters of *Walden* are paired contrastingly. "Solitude" is followed by "Visitors," "The Bean-Field" by "The Village," "Higher Laws" by "Brute Neighbors." This ordering reflects Thoreau's love of antithesis and contradiction. "Say—not so—and you will outcircle the philosophers," he believed (26 June 1840). "There seem to be two sides to this world presented us at different times—as we see things in growth or dissolution—in life or death," he meditated after John died. "If we see nature as pausing immediately all mortifies and decays—but seen as progressing she is beautiful" (12 Mar. 1842). The doubleness of experience might be matched by a doubleness of style. "There are two sides to every sentence; the one is contiguous to me, but the other faces the gods, and no man ever fronted it. . . . Consequently it demands a godlike insight—a fronting view, to read what was greatly written" (13 Jan. 1841). Straightforward factual writing could seem "crude, and one-idea'd, like a schoolboy's theme" (*Week*, p. 185). But "truth is always paradoxical" (26 June 1840). Approaching it in that spirit, "poetry *implies* the whole truth," whereas "philosophy *expresses* a particle of it" (26 Jan. 1852).

Much of this recalls the Schlegels, and with good reason, for Thoreau had read the elder brother's *Lectures on the History of Literature* as a Harvard senior.[1] But many currents in European Romanticism encouraged him to interpret the world as the dynamic union of conflicting opposites. Renaissance thinkers like Cusanus, Paracelsus, and Bruno carried on the Heraclitan tradition. Their doctrines were subsumed by the great seventeenth-century apostle of contrariety Jacob Boehme, whose direct impact on Emersonian Transcendentalism was substantial. "Without Contraries is no progression," proclaimed Blake in *The Marriage of Heaven and Hell,* acknowledging his own indebtedness to Boehme.[2] With the discovery of electrical polarity, that became a major model for the *Natürphilosophie* of Schelling and his disciples. "Keine Welt ohne polare Kraft," concluded Oken—no world without polarized force.[3] J. B. Wilbrand took wing from electricity and magnetism to trace polar principles through chemistry, biology, geology, and astronomy. His analysis of seasonal alternation was typical in treating it as a dance of complementary opposites stemming from a self-contradictory *Weltgeist.* Thirty years earlier Goethe had embodied a similar insight in his *Metamorphosis of Plants* (1790), which resolved organic entities into plural federations. And Hegel made polarization the key to his dialectic, where theses spawn antitheses only to recombine and transcend themselves in higher syntheses.

Nearer to hand, however, was Coleridge, the Transcendentalists' main pipeline to German idealism. Like most in the movement, Thoreau knew the *Aids to Reflection* and probably the *Biographia Literaria.* But his interest went further. Immediately upon their posthumous publication he copied into a notebook passages on polarity from Coleridge's *Hints toward the Formation of a More Comprehensive Theory of Life* (1848). Under the heading "Coleridge's Idea of Life" Thoreau transcribed this obiter dictum: "Thus in the identity of the two counter powers life *sub*sists; in their strife, it *con*sists; and in their reconciliation it at once dies and is 'born again' into a new form &c." He noted that Coleridge considered "life, then . . . as the copula, as the unity of thesis and antithesis."[4] Unlike logical opposites, which remain contradictory, Coleridge's polarities attract one another like electrical forces. Neither can exist alone, any more than one pole of a magnet can exist without the other. Both organic life and mental activity involve a process like desynonymization, where an original unity constantly projects itself through subdivision and reamalgamation, manifesting at once "the tendency . . . to individuate and to connect, to detach, but so as either to retain or to reproduce attachment."[5] This polar unity is hard to define in strictly logical terms, for grasping the reciprocal action that both generates and resolves dualities is the main function that Coleridge assigns to the primary imagination. This power "reveals itself in the balance or reconciliation of opposite or discordant qualities," he claims, "of sameness, with difference; of the general, with the concrete; the idea, with the image; the individual, with the representative." The ideal poet deploys such dichotomies only to overcome them by diffusing "a tone and spirit of unity, that blends, and (as it were) *fuses,* each into each, by that synthetic and magical power . . . imagination."[6]

While revising *Walden,* Thoreau found himself paying rapt attention to a raptor.

> Saw a large hawk circling over a pine wood below me—and screaming apparently that he might discover his prey by their flight- Travelling ever by wider circles What a symbol of the thoughts now soaring now descending—taking larger and larger circles or smaller and smaller circles like a courtier of the skies No such noble progress—how it comes round as with a wider sweep of thought— But the majesty is in the imagination of beholder for the bird is intent on its prey. Circling & ever circling you cannot divine which way it will incline—till perchance it dives down straight as an arrow to its mark. It rises higher above where I stand and I see with beautiful distinctness its wings against the sky—primaries & secondaries and the rich tracery of the outline of the latter? its inner wings within the outer—like a great moth seen against the sky. A Will-o-'the wind. . . . the poetry of motion—not as preferring one place to another but enjoying each as long as possible. Most gracefully so surveys new scenes & revisits the old. As if that hawk were made to be the symbol of my thought how bravely he came round over those parts of the wood which he had not surveyed—taking in a new segment.- annexing new territories
>
> Without heave yo! it trims its sail,— It goes about without the creaking of a block- That America Yacht of the air that never makes a tack—though it rounds the globe itself—takes in and shakes out its reefs without a flutter. . . . If there are two concentrically circling, it is such a regatta as South hampton waters never witnessed.
>
> Flights of imagination—Coleridgean thoughts. So a man is said to soar in his thought— Ever to fresh woods & pastures new. Rises as in thought.
>
> (20 Dec. 1851)

The bird's oscillating progress mirrors the movement of the mind in Coleridgean terms. Rhapsodic identification with the hawk as a noble symbol of the thoughts breeds scientific determination to define it *distinctly.* The more Thoreau feels himself drawn to the bird, the more he recognizes that "the majesty is in the imagination of the beholder for the bird is intent on its prey." He sees its wings silhouetted against the sky "with beautiful distinctness," almost like a specimen mounted in a case. But precise observation trails off with a question mark, and his mind keeps circling round the bird so that "you cannot divine which way it will incline." He contemplates it "as if that hawk were made to be the symbol of my thought" while his subjunctive emphasizes that it was not. Yet he seems tempted to reclaim the bird he has so carefully distinguished by establishing poetic kinship on a higher plane. Then, when the hawk's aerial survey nearly reconnects it to the surveyor watching below, suddenly Thoreau veers off on a fresh tack in the second paragraph. Annexing new territory rather than the hawk, the fanciful yachting comparison gives new meaning to the bird's lazy poetry of motion but does so while dramatizing the witty superiority of the observer. In the third paragraph the hawk vanishes as Thoreau's mind rounds on its own words and on itself. In Coleridgean terms, his imagination has generated a new synthetic category by detaching itself from the hawk while trying to overcome that detachment.

The Duplicity of Solitude

Walden embodies a similar process in "Solitude," among other chapters. "I go and come with a strange liberty in Nature, a part of herself," the opening paragraph proclaims. Yet the sounds of the previous chapter reverberate on the wind so that repose is never complete. Invaded in absentia by visitors who leave calling cards, his hut seems a tenuous haven for a hermit who says he can detect a passerby on the highway sixty rods off by the smoke from a pipe. The solitude that he enjoys by detaching himself from people is persistently treated as a form of reattachment. It demonstrates that "the most innocent and encouraging society may be found in any natural object." The antidote to "a vulgar sadness" is "the friendship of the seasons." His one attack of rainy-day blues after moving to the pond was dispelled by the conviction that "every little pine needle expanded and swelled with sympathy and befriended me." Beneath this exaggeration lurks a pun: sympathetic action is a scientific concept, and by swelling with moisture the pine needles befriended him with a denser canopy for shelter. Does the ironic hyperbole of such rhetoric express the satisfaction of solitude? or a desire to provoke a response? Indeed, a good bit of the chapter is devoted to actual or imaginary arguments with people who question what he finds in solitude. "Why should I feel lonely? is not our planet in the Milky Way?" he replies with deliberate outrageousness. "This which you put seems to me not to be the most important question."

Such mocking dialogue reaches beyond his proclaimed solitude to suggest that his relation with nature remains strange indeed. Midway through the chapter he becomes his own interlocutor, detaching himself not only from nature but from his own centered identity.

> With thinking we may be beside ourselves in a sane sense. By a conscious effort of the mind we can stand aloof from actions and their consequences; and all things, good and bad, go by us like a torrent. We are not wholly involved in nature. I may be either the drift-wood in the stream or Indra in the sky looking down on it. I *may* be affected by a theatrical exhibition; on the other hand, I *may not* be affected by an actual event which appears to concern me much more. I only know myself as a human entity; the scene, so to speak, of thoughts and affections; and am sensible of a certain dou-

bleness by which I can stand as remote from myself as from another. However intense my experience, I am conscious of the presence and criticism of a part of me, which, as it were, is not a part of me, but spectator, sharing no experience, but taking note of it; and that is no more I than it is you. (pp. 134–35)

He concludes that "this doubleness may easily make us poor neighbors and friends sometimes." But as he says so, he shifts back to the first-person plural as if craving neighborly solidarity. The reader whom he addresses seems no more alien than this internal alter ego. Much of *Walden,* after all, was written from a middle-aged near-failure's perspective foreign to the young author who boldly went to the pond to write *A Week.*

The sort of split personality here elaborated lent itself not only to standoffishness but to humor. In Whitman the sense of being "both in and out of the game, and watching and wondering at it" generated the comedy of the elastic self, crystallizing in poems like "That Shadow My Likeness." Indeed, the stance is basic to Romantic irony. "In my consciousness it is always as if I were doubled; as if there were two I's in me. Within I hear myself talking," confessed Jean Paul. The humorist "brings upon his comic stage his personal conditions, but only to annihilate them poetically. For he is himself his own fool and the comic quartet of Italian masks, himself the manager and the director."[7] Thoreau's "certain doubleness" corresponds to the spate of double entendres in his prose. Like the underlying theatrical metaphor, his pun about being *"beside ourselves* in a sane sense" grounds meditative self-transcendence in social slang. The "human entity" that he scrutinizes is a plurality, decomposing into the masks of his dramatis personae. He is his own manager and director; indeed, projecting and then reattaching himself, he becomes the audience applauding his own performance. Like Jean Paul, he embraces the absurdity involved. His paragraph ends by threatening to pull the rug from beneath its own argument. "When the play, it may be the tragedy, of life is over, the spectator goes his way. It was a kind of fiction, a work of the imagination only." If his life seems an imaginary play, then *Walden* too is only a kind of fiction in which a detached aesthetic perspective turns tragedy into comedy. In urging the seriousness of solitude it borders on laughter.

Toward social laughter the chapter inexorably moves. The central paradox of "Solitude" is that it is impossible. A man dying of famine in the woods "was relieved by the grotesque visions with which, owing to bodily weakness, his diseased imagination surrounded him, and which he believed to be real. So also, owing to bodily and mental health and strength, we may be continually cheered by a like but more normal and natural society, and come to know we are never alone." Communion with nature is here raised to the level of smiling nightmare. Since we have just been asked to pity factory girls, "never alone, hardly in their dreams," how are we now to take this vision of a wilderness thronged with nature spirits making privacy impossible like so many nosy neighbors?

In such hyperboles self-parody verges on travesty. "I have a great deal of company in my house; especially in the morning when nobody calls," proclaims this deadpan joker. "I am no more lonely than the loon in the pond that laughs so loud, or than Walden Pond itself. What company has that lonely lake, I pray? And yet it has not the blue devils, but the blue angels in it." Festooned with loony wordplay, this denial of depression has a manic quality that also tinges the defiant catalog that closes the paragraph: "I am no more lonely than a single mullein or dandelion in a pasture . . . or a horse-fly, or a humble-bee. I am no more lonely than the Mill Brook, or a weathercock, or the northstar, or the south wind . . . or the first spider in a new house." But self-sufficiency is qualified by the fact that mulleins and dandelions normally propagate in colonies, horseflies crave horses, and bees are social insects. The pasture, weathercock, and Mill Brook presuppose a social environment, while the north star at the hub of the universe has a polar relation to the south wind. Even the spider in the new house appears to be awaiting company.[8] Thoreau's flaunting catalog surrounds him with a crowd of fellow hermits by necessity. To be no more lonely than these neither rules out loneliness nor expresses a wish for complete isolation.

The vaunted sympathy of the elements dwindles under inspection. "All nature would be affected, and the sun's brightness fade, and the winds would sigh humanely, and the clouds rain tears, and the woods shed their leaves and put on mourning in midsummer, if any man should ever for a just cause grieve," Thoreau proclaims. But undergirding this trope is not the pathetic fallacy but the Stoic's cosmos. The imagined events are *adynata,* rhetorical impossibilities; they can never happen because there is never just cause for human grief. When he proceeds to ask, "Shall I not have intelligence with the earth?" an equivocation allows us to wonder whether he actually communicated with it or simply accepts the prospect of rejoining it. As Walden Pond's "original proprietor," God (or his stand-in Pan) is coyly reported to pay Thoreau occasional visits on winter evenings. But what this "most wise and humorous friend" offers is not sympathy but entertainment. "Between us we manage to pass a cheerful evening with social mirth and pleasant views of things" (p. 137).

If their soirées lacked apples and cider, they surely included puns. "Solitude" teems with them. Kept indoors by a gentle rain that waters his beans, he compares his lot to other men's: "It seems as if I were more favored by the gods than they, beyond any deserts that I am conscious of." By no means always brilliant, the punning is often so convoluted as to seem scarcely worth exhuming. "Some came from the village to fish for pouts,—they plainly fished much more in the Walden Pond of their own natures, and baited their hooks with darkness,—but they soon retreated, usually with light baskets, . . . and the black kernel of the night was never profaned by any human neighborhood" (p. 130). That these evening fishermen are sullen souls with pouty dispositions, who baited their hooks not only at dark but *with* dark, and so left disappointed with *light* baskets, is grudgingly acknowledged. More satisfying is the chapter's final resolution to eschew patent medicine in favor of "a draught of undiluted morning air. Morning air! If men will not drink of this at the fountain-head of the day, why, then, we must even bottle some up and sell it in the shops" (p. 138). Teased out at length over the last paragraph to provide a conclusion to the chapter, this pleasant whimsy owes its existence to the equivocation on *draught*. Hawking his nostrum humorously to all who will listen, our punning hermit is not so aloof as he seems.

Clowning for Visitors

"I think that I love society as much as most," Thoreau begins his next chapter, "Visitors." "I am naturally no hermit." He blandly lays claim to a deeper sociability than the villagers practice. His main habitué is the French-Canadian woodchopper. Thoreau values his spontaneity, his mirthfulness, his lack of sophistication. "In him the animal man chiefly was developed," he concludes. But when he draws him out, quizzing him as a philosophe might interrogate a savage, the virtue that most impressed him was "a certain positive originality, however slight, . . . and I occasionally observed that he was thinking for himself, a phenomenon so rare that I would any day walk ten miles to observe it, and it amounted to the re-origination of many of the institutions of society." The woodchopper ably defends the utility of money by reimagining how the Latin root for livestock gave rise to the word *pecunia*. Philosophical dialogue with this primitive man yields the surprising conclusion that society is genuinely natural, that man is indeed a political animal.

Thoreau vastly prefers this calm acceptance of the social status quo to the zeal of reformers hoping to find a kindred spirit at the pond. Whiny complainers about the world "appeal, not to your hospitality, but to your *hospitalality,*" he felt. They were "men of ideas instead of legs, a sort of intellectual centipede that made you crawl all over." Timidly conventional visitors and reforming zealots seemed two sides of the same coin. Both overrated the importance of society because they lived entirely within it, whereas the woodchopper tolerated it easily because it did not contain him. He experienced it as one pole of a healthy continuum with nature, so he could pun unwittingly about the birds pecking at his lunches as nice "little *fellers*" (p. 146). Swayed by a dubious derivation, conventional folk believed that "the village was literally a *community,* a league for mutual defence." Worrying about the dangers of the woods, they ignored the ubiquity of danger and forgot that "a man sits as many risks as he runs." The reformers were the greatest bores of all, trying to enlist Thoreau in collective schemes either as master or disciple and so missing the point of his experiment. "I did not fear the hen-harriers, for I kept no chickens," he remarks, "but I feared the men-harriers rather." Many honest pilgrims to the woods, who neither fled the village disgruntled nor insisted on replicating it there, he "was ready to greet with, —'Welcome, Englishmen! welcome, Englishmen!' for I had had communication with that race" (pp. 153–54).

With this closing flourish Thoreau wraps up the chapter by wrapping himself in the mantle of Samoset, the Indian whose greeting to the Pilgrims at Plymouth Rock became legendary. As adults Thoreau and his brother John still enjoyed playing Indian. Both had Indian nicknames and conversed with each other in improvised Cooperesque dialogue. As his notebooks testify, Thoreau's interest in Indians was deep and genuine. Playing the Indian was serious business for him. But it was also quite frankly a silly game. When he welcomes "honest pilgrims" to the new world of Walden by wrapping himself in Samoset's blanket, he conjures up the absurd image of a bearded brave offering visitors a fistful of cigars.

Walden's early chapters end in similar comic posturing. "Reading" closes with his playing the role of concerned citizen in town meeting, while "Sounds" fades out with an image of him as dauntless homesteader and frontiersman, sporting his coonskin cap within earshot of the pike to Boston. The mock spiel of a patent medicine salesman brings "Solitude" to a climax as amusing as that triggered by the thought of Thoreau in a feathered headdress. Such impersonations are the stuff and substance of *Walden.* "Economy" introduces Thoreau to us in various guises: gadfly author, hometown lecturer, insult comedian, earnest social reformer, thermodynamic scientist, idealistic nature lover, inept town crank, businessman, fashion designer, Carlylean clothes philosopher, architect, local historian, amateur carpenter, barbecue chef, Roman baker, accountant fixated on halfpence and farthings, proto-Marxist champion of oppressed workers, gentleman farmer, cabinetmaker, theologian, antiphilanthropist, Yankee misanthrope, and Persian sage. Accents shift, tocque yields to turban. Like Whitman's, his spinning Rolodex of roles turns the elastic self into a comic hero. One pose unsettles another, making all his bragging only half-serious.

Such a result is just what one would expect from his method of composition. *Walden* accumulated over seven long drafts, a mosaic pieced together from passages scattered throughout his journals. The chief effort of academic criticism has been to find and extol its supposed unity while pretending autobiography has nothing to do with biography. So far as the text itself is concerned, there has been no Dr. Johnson to stress that the special praise of this book is variety. Unity the book has, to be sure—but not seamless unity. Rather, Thoreau's strategy is to exploit the shifting perspectives of his mélange for Romantic irony. Like Emerson's *Essays,* like *Tales of the Grotesque and Arabesque,* like *The Scarlet Letter,* like *Moby-Dick,* this book is a variety show, a kaleidoscope. Instead of a certain doubleness, he might have claimed a definite multiplicity.

Contemporary reviewers were often readier to see the antic in the mantic than we are. They relished *Walden*'s "playful humor" or "ingenious pleasantry." "He has Sir Thomas Browne's love of pregnant paradox and stupendous joke," enthused the *New York Enquirer,* "and utters his paradoxes and his jokes with a mysterious phlegm." "The eccentricity of his mode of life, as he relates it, is laughable," observed the *New York Morning Express.* Another paper called humor and satire "the pepper and salt to the entertainment that Mr. Thoreau serves up." So amusing was Thoreau's book that "many have smiled and turned away their heads as they would at a clown," lamented the *Worcester Palladium.* The *New York Times* was a notable case in point. "As a contribution to the Comic Literature of America, *Walden* is worthy some attention," it judged, "but in no other respect."9

Parody of other discourses and genres looms large in *Walden.* There was a vogue for hermits in the 1840s that this book both exploits and travesties. Its subtitle takes a slap at an essay called "Life in the Woods" that appeared in the *Dial,* while its first chapter inverts many (but not all) assumptions underlying Catharine Beecher's *Treatise on Domestic Economy,* the popular housekeeping manual of the era. Casting a jaundiced eye on publicity blurbs for novels like Cooper's *The Wept of Wish-ton-Wish,* Thoreau concocted his own: "The Skip of the Tip-Toe-Hop, a Romance of the Middle Ages, by the celebrated author of 'Tittle-Tol-Tan,' to appear in monthly parts; a great rush; don't all come together" (p. 105). By glancing at the American Scott, this generic travesty hints at the complex motives for resorting to parody, for there is good reason to suspect that as a schoolboy he read Cooper's novel. It was from romances like *The Wept of Wish-ton-Wish* that he and his brother John drew the Ossianic dialogue that they affected in their long-running Indian masquerade.

The ambivalence of parody can ally it to Romantic irony, especially when self-parody is involved. Parody and punning are also akin. Both involve a word or words given a fixed meaning by context. Distortion substitutes another meaning without quite displacing the first. Getting the joke requires acknowledging two meanings at once. Like parodies, puns may seem attacks on fixed meanings; but like puns, parodies may also genuflect toward what they seem to reject. In Coleridgean terms, puns and parodies both let a speaker separate polarized meanings from each other yet keep them attached.

Biblical allusions are the most common form of parody in *Walden*. There are some 275, about one a page. Thoreau resorted to them increasingly as he took his manuscript through successive revisions.[10] "Men labor under a mistake," he puns early in "Economy." "They are employed, as it says in an old book, laying up treasures which moth and rust will corrupt and thieves break through and steal. It is a fool's life, as they will find when they get to the end of it, if not before" (p. 5). Like the pun on *labor,* the allusion to Matthew 6:19-21 is two-edged. *A Week* had made Thoreau notorious in Concord for viewing Holy Writ as simply another of the "ethnic scriptures," and not necessarily his favorite. Here he mockingly detaches himself from his community's sacred text by calling it merely an old book, yet at the same time he seems to value it more than they. His quotation wrests the words from their eschatological context, giving Christ's advice a worldly twist, yet it invokes Christ's authority in setting up as a rival prophet in his own right.

The texts in Thoreau's parodic sermon are mischievously employed, in the manner of much traditional American wordplay.[11] "Evil communications corrupt good manners," claimed St. Paul (1 Cor. 15:33). "Our manners have been corrupted by communication with the saints," suggests Thoreau in the peroration to "Economy" (p. 78). The equivocation on *saints* makes the orthodox wonder whether he is criticizing Paul as well as them, yet the barb attaches Thoreau firmly to his targets insofar as a common reference is necessary to understand the insult fully. Thoreau's allusions imply that the Bible, like the Hindu scriptures or *Walden,* is a cabalistic tangle of puns, full of double meanings that should be pondered more carefully by the pious reader. "While yet it is cold January, and the snow and ice are thick and solid, the prudent land-lord comes from the village to get ice to cool his summer drink: impres-sively, even pathetically wise, to foresee the heat and thirst of July now in January,—wearing a thick coat and mittens! . . . It may be that he lays up no treasures in this world which will cool his summer drink in the next" (pp. 293–94). In one breath Thoreau coolly distances himself from hellfire Christianity yet also suggests that its sanctions are ignored at their peril by the lukewarm and those committed to such interpretations of Scriptural texts. His attitude toward the prudent landlord shows both Christ's familiarity with tavern-keepers and Christ-like awareness of what drives the publicans' benevolence.

Bean-Field or Battlefield?

Another strand in the densely twisted parodies that are spun into *Walden* is mock-heroic.[12] "What was the meaning of this so steady and self-respecting, this small Herculean labor, I knew not," Thoreau observes about hoeing beans. "They attached me to the earth, and so I got strength like Antaeus. But why should I raise them? Only Heaven knows. This was my curious labor all summer." Plentiful as candidates for the title of world's largest midget, small Herculean labors abound in our daily life. They make it fabulous. Wrestling with beans, Thoreau seems on the verge of being thrown; he is both Hercules and his antago-nist Antaeus. But raise them from the ground he does with a triumphant equivocation, while an etymological pun invites us to realize that pains-taking manual labor can be an intellectual stimulus too (the Latin tag *labor curiosus* denotes *hard labor,* and *idle curiosity* is etymologically a contradiction in terms). Heaven indeed knows the purpose of these labors, for by making him "attached" to the earth their purpose is to purify a hero for heaven—fit Hercules to join the immortals. In this arduous struggle "my auxiliaries are the dews and rains . . . my enemies are worms, cool days, and most of all woodchucks."

Teasing wordplay both creates and undermines the mythological parallels. But as the chapter proceeds, Thoreau's claims to grandeur seem increasingly genuine. "As I drew a still fresher soil about the rows with my hoe, I disturbed the ashes of unchronicled nations who in pri-meval years lived under the heavens, and their small implements of war and hunting were brought to the light of this modern day." As a cultiva-tor of the soil he displaces the hunter-gatherers while inheriting their rel-ics and virtues. "Every field is a battle field to the mower—a pitched battle too," he had punningly observed in his journal (17 Aug. 1851). Now "when my hoe tinkled against the stones, that music echoed to the woods and the sky, and was an accompaniment to my labor which yielded an instant and immeasurable crop. It was no longer beans that I hoed, nor I that hoed beans; and I remembered with as much pity as pride, if I remembered at all, my acquaintances who had gone to the city to attend the oratorios." Sentences like these expand his identity to gigantic proportions, until he becomes a transparent eyeball. The music of nature seems to liberate a cosmic ego like Emerson's or Whitman's. He can sport transcendentally with the first-person pronoun, then soar up with the hawks overhead. Condescendingly aware yet unaware of his neighbors, he trumps their piddling culture jaunt to Boston with an imaginative tour of the Middle East via etymology and natural history, routing from beneath a stump "a sluggish portentous and *outlandish* spotted salamander, a trace of Egypt and the Nile, yet our contemporary" (emphasis added).

From his bean-field Thoreau hears salutes when the town fires its great guns on gala days. They echo like popguns to the woods "as if a puff ball had burst." Distant militia drills make the horizon itch uneasily till the companies disband for military whoopee. "I felt proud to know that the liberties of Massachusetts and of our fatherland were in such safe keeping," he avers, and resumes hoeing with effusive trust in the future.

> But sometimes it was a really noble and inspiring strain that reached these woods, and the trumpet that sings of fame, and I felt as if I could spit a Mexican with a good relish,—for why should we always stand for trifles?—and looked round for a woodchuck or a skunk to exercise my chivalry upon. These martial strains seemed as far away as Palestine, and reminded me of a march of crusaders in the horizon, with a slight tantivy and tremulous motion of the elm-tree tops which overhang the village. This was one of the *great* days; though the sky had from my clearing only the same everlastingly great look that it wears daily, and I saw no difference in it.
>
> It was a singular experience that long acquaintance which I cultivated with beans, what with planting, and hoeing, and harvesting, and threshing, and picking over, and selling them,—the last was the hardest of all,—I might add eating, for I did taste. I was determined to know beans. . . . Consider the intimate and curious acquaintance one makes with various kinds of weeds,—it will bear some iteration in the account, for there was no little iteration in the labor,—disturbing their delicate organizations so ruthlessly, and making such invidious distinctions with his hoe, levelling whole ranks of one species, and sedulously cultivating another. That's Roman wormwood,—that's pigweed . . . have at him, chop him up, turn his roots upward to the sun, don't let him have a fibre in the shade, if you do he'll turn himself t'other side up and be as green as a leek in two days. A long war, not with cranes, but with weeds, those Trojans who had sun and rain and dews on their side. Daily the beans saw me come to their res-

cue armed with a hoe, and thin the ranks of their enemies, filling up the
trenches with weedy dead. Many a lusty crest-waving Hector, that tow-
ered a whole foot above his crowding comrades, fell before my weapon
and rolled in the dust. (pp. 160-62)

Wit and vision go hand in hand in this passage—appropriately enough,
since the two terms derive from the same Indo-European root. The ridicule of jingoism is delicious, of course, but this satirist is no simple
pacifist. Like Dryden and Pope, he uses heroic comparisons not just to
topple cultural icons but to exalt the ordinary. While the Mexican War is
mocked as less than epic, our hero himself emerges as truly Homeric.
Admiring Homer, he detaches himself from conventional heroism only
to reincorporate it on a higher plane.

His truculent search for a hostile woodchuck is ludicrous but also
attests to a savage streak that keeps him from viewing martial heroism as
alien. "Men have made war from a deeper instinct than peace," he could
journalize. "War is but the compelling of peace" (*PJ*, 1:94). Like the
heroes of republican Rome or Concord's own Minutemen, in a good
cause he could turn from bean-field to battlefield in a trice. A grotesque
pun asks us to wonder whether this man would barbecue a Mexican. But
at Walden he slaughtered one woodchuck and ate him, he relates; his
friend the woodchopper dined on them regularly. A grotesque battle
between pygmies and cranes is mentioned in the *Iliad;* but like Homer's
epic similes drawn from agriculture, that battle serves less to travesty the
heroic worldview than to delimit it.[13] A string of radical puns on words
like *singular, cultivated, curious, iteration,* and *invidious distinctions* asks
us to realize that abstractions have concrete physical cores. So too heroes,
and Thoreau is just as determined to know heroism as he is to "know
beans." Literalizing our cliché, that joke does not reject the meanings
society attaches to words but extends them. The figure who wages war on
weeds is not waging war on society. Rather, he dwarfs society by projecting himself so as to reincorporate it and transcend it. His theme song
might be a cheeky rendition of "Anything You Can Do I Can Do Better."

Mythicizing his experience in the bean-field, he swells into an agricultural Paul Bunyan. By parading dubious derivations from Varro, this
mediocre farmer persuades us that hoeing beans with him and whistling
would be more entertaining and wholesome than parading or concert-
going with anyone else in Concord. Visionary humor and etymological
insight make good his claim that this was one of the *great* days. Nothing
had changed except for his synthesizing Coleridgean imagination. That
allowed him to live the town's military holiday as he wished to live every
day—as a *holy day.* "Husbandry was once a sacred art," the chapter

concludes, but it will not regain that status until the farmer learns to live by "sacrificing in his mind not only his first but his last fruits also" (p. 166). By relinquishing our first fruits we may yet keep our last fruits by learning to see them as holy (*sacrifice* = relinquish/sanctify, from Latin *sacer facere,* make holy.)

A World Reintegrated in Transcendental Sport

"Referred to the world's standard—the hero, the discoverer—is insane" (*PJ,* 3:67). Referred to his standard, of course, the world may be. Thoreau mounts regular expeditions to the village in the guise of an intrepid traveler exploring darkest Concord with gun and camera. "As I walked in the woods to see the birds and squirrels, so I walked in the village to see the men and boys. . . . as curious to me as if they had been prairie dogs, each sitting at the mouth of its burrow, or running over to a neighbor's to gossip." The pose of scientific observer intent on collecting data about the village as "a great news room" makes for memorable satire, especially when our hero boldly runs the gossip gauntlet in pursuit of cultural insight. But the villagers' ludicrous curiosity is mirrored in his own, and he too behaves ridiculously, singing loudly like Orpheus while thinking high thoughts or eluding fancied dangers by bolting gracelessly through gaps in fences. When he finally escapes to the woods again after gleaning from familiar houses "the kernels and the very last sieve-ful of news," that mixed metaphor mingles botanic detail with the paraphernalia of village kitchens to fuse a naturalist's perspective with a demented sociologist's.

One passage cut from "The Village" shows how keenly Thoreau eyed its denizens:

> How often in years gone by have I seen a country man come into town a-shopping, in a high-set wagon, whose clothes looked as if they were made before the last war by a maiden sister. . . . His coat hung so high that you could see the whole of his waistcoat pockets beneath it; while the scant coat-tail hastened to a speedy conclusion, like a frog couchant on a bank; the funnel-shaped sleeves halting at a respectful distance from his victorious palms, and the collar, hard-rolled and round like a boa-constrictor, prompting you to run to his rescue,—or as if crisped by an agony of heat. His waistcoat striped like the zebra's skin,—a kind of coarse grating or gridiron over the furnace of his heart; his "pants" straight and round like a stove-pipe, into which his boots fitted smoke tight, at a height which preserved them "guiltless of his country's mud," and his narrow-brimmed hat towering straight and round, like a column, to meet the sun in his rising,—of equal diameter throughout,—the torso of a shaft, or maybe a cenotaph to his brains,—with a nap as soft as a pussy, across which the dimpling shadows fly, as over a field of grain in autumn.[14]

This sketch is a merciless rendition of regalia sported by New England yokels like Jack Downing, whom Thomas Nast drew upon to create our image of Uncle Sam. Festooned with wordplay (made/maiden, victorious palms/palms of victory, mud/blood) in keeping with its Dickensian fancifulness, such a caricature may surprise us coming from an author who proclaimed indifference to fashion. But Thoreau could view country cousins from Boxboro with the eyes of a sophisticated suburbanite. Few realize that sartorial taste led him to a pioneering preference for corduroy. Though the passage does not appear in the final version, "The Village" begins as broadly *social* satire that also pokes fun at the satirist himself.

His inherently social habits are the burden of the second paragraph, which describes how on the darkest night he could navigate absentmindedly between Concord and his hut in a virtual trance while thinking high thoughts. Getting lost in the dark he extols as a Transcendental virtue, but oddly enough his neighbors seem more skilled at that than he is, so firmly fixed is his social and geographical template. Only the last paragraph staunchly rejects social ties in briefly describing how he was jailed for nonpayment of taxes. "Wherever a man goes, men will pursue and paw him with their dirty institutions, and, if they can, constrain him to belong to their desperate odd-fellow society," he observes with marked disgust. Still the chapter trails off with this citizen of the woods queuing up behind Confucius to advise civic leaders on the best policy for administering justice.

As "The Village" portrays Thoreau shuttling between the poles of hut and hamlet, so "The Ponds" portrays Walden as "intermediate in its nature between land and sky" (pp. 188–89). Linking heaven and earth, its vitreous greenish blue "partakes of the color of both." Fishing meditatively at midnight, Thoreau describes how queer it was "when your thoughts had wandered to vast and cosmogonal themes in other spheres, to feel this faint jerk, which came to interrupt your dreams and link you to Nature again. It seemed as if I might cast my line upward into the air, as well as downward" (p. 175). So he caught two fishes with one hook. On occasion he was partnered by a taciturn old man hard of hearing, who hummed psalms, "which harmonized well enough with my philosophy." When floating alone he deliberately raised echoes by smacking the side of his boat with a paddle or charmed schools of perch by playing his flute. The pond seems the locus for resolved polarities: earth and heaven, sound and silence, self and society, depth and surface—and work and play.[15]

As a boy he came to Walden to sport adventurously, he explains— but now he was trying to make a living there. Fishing was both work and play. No mere amusement, it supplied his table but recreated his spirit while doing so. Unlike many disappointed visitors to the pond, this hermit did not belong to "the ancient and honorable sect of Coenobites" whom he mocks with a grotesque pun (*see-no-bites*, p. 173). In boyhood, he recalled, "I have experienced such simple joy in the trivial matters of fishing and sporting . . . as might inspire the muse of Homer or Shakespeare" (7 July 1840). Because he finally rejects fishing and hunting in "Higher Laws," modern environmentalists see him as an opponent of blood sports.[16] But though he sold his own gun before going to Walden, he still preferred hunters and loafers to farmers for company. As a naturalist he welcomed specimens from them. "I hear these guns going today," he wrote late in life, "and I must confess they are to me a spring-like and exhilarating sound like the cock-crowing, though each one may report the death of a musquash." The cheery equivocation on *report* stresses his belief that "this is the best sort of glorifying of God and enjoying him that at all prevails here today" (22 Jan. 1859).

Thus in *Walden* he describes being tempted to seize and devour the occasional woodchuck raw, urges blood sports as the best education for boys, and doubts that adults ever substitute equally valuable pastimes. After momentary qualms, his fishing expedition to Baker Farm resumes with a transfiguring vision. "As I ran down the hill toward the reddening west, with the rainbow over my shoulder," punningly slung like an Indian's weapon, his Good Genius reassures him about the legitimacy of his quest:

> Go fish and hunt far and wide day by day,—farther and wider,—and rest thee by many brooks and hearth-sides without misgiving. Remember thy Creator in the days of thy youth. Rise free from care before the dawn, and seek adventures. . . . There are no larger fields than these, no worthier games than may here be played. Grow wild according to thy nature, like these sedges and brakes, which will never become English hay. Let the thunder rumble; what if it threaten ruin to farmers' crops? that is not its errand to thee. . . . Let not to get a living be thy trade, but thy sport. (p. 207)

The book's fishing interludes show how supporting ourselves "is not a hardship but a pastime, if we will live simply and wisely; as the pursuits of the simpler nations are still the sports of the more artificial" (p. 71). Like afternoon swims in Walden to cleanse himself after hoeing all morning, fishing is a solemn ritual that transcends our conventional dualism of work and play. So are experimental house-building, hoeing beans Homerically, and flute-playing in imitation of Krishna. Like his friend Rice "he plays at house-building," so vocational versatility makes for a poetic life (8 Mar. 1857). The woodchopper also knew how to amuse himself at work, hewing trees with artistic "flourishes and ornaments" that might be termed lumbering puns (p. 146). Warming Thoreau twice, the exercise of splitting wood for fuel was "pleasing work" for him too whenever he "played about the stumps" with an ax.

What is at stake for Thoreau is not the alternation of hard work and play that muscular Christians like Teddy Roosevelt came to value. That coarser late Victorian ethic is still very much with us, of course, preached by modern beer commercials where hard-driving yuppies are shown disporting themselves strenuously in scanty swimwear. Instead, like his disciple Robert Frost, Thoreau's object in living is "to unite / My avocation and my vocation / As my two eyes make one in sight." His ideal of play was not purely autotelic, for it had a goal. As his great essay "Walking" explained, the true *saunterer* is not one of the medieval beggars cadging money under pretense of going *à la Sainte Terre*. "They who never go to the Holy Land in their walks, as they pretend, are indeed mere idlers and vagabonds, but they who do go there are saunterers in the good sense, such as I mean" (*W,* 5:205).

"Brute Neighbors" offers a memorable instance of Transcendental sport. Loons visit the pond in the fall, stirring Concord sportsmen into comically frenzied efforts to shoot them—alas, often successful. Thoreau relates how once he hunted a loon differently, playing hide-and-seek with it for an hour in his boat. "It was a pretty game, played on the smooth surface of the pond, a man against a loon. Suddenly your adversary's checker disappears beneath the board, and the problem is to place yours nearest to where his will appear again." Efforts to guess the loon's intent never place him closer than a hundred feet when it surfaces, for the bird could not be driven from the widest part of the pond. Yet despite its evident desire to evade Thoreau, its wild cry immediately draws attention when it surfaces. Why, Thoreau wonders. "He was indeed a silly loon, I thought."

The goal of his sojourn at the pond, he had claimed, was "to drive life into a corner, and reduce it to its lowest terms, and, if it proved to be mean, why then to get the whole and genuine meanness of it and publish its meanness to the world; or if it were sublime, to know it by experience, and be able to give a true account of it in my next excursion" (p. 91). But the loon cannot be cornered or quite accounted for. Its "demoniac laughter" resists easy categorization as either silly or sublime. "This was his looning, perhaps the wildest sound that is ever heard here, making the woods ring far and wide. I concluded that he laughed in derision of my efforts, confident of his own resources." But not entirely so either. One final prolonged howl "as if calling on the god of loons to aid him" provokes a squall of misty rain, "and I was impressed as if it were the prayer of the loon answered, and his god was angry with me; and so I left him disappearing far away on the tumultuous surface."

Thoreau's attitude toward the bird's divinity is grammatically ambiguous, with the subjunctive of a condition contrary to fact yielding to the indicative. The Algonquin Indians regarded the loon as a sacred messenger. Thoreau too evidently imagined its savage *deus absconditus* as best approached through a sportive mock hunt. Pursued in a spirit of grotesque humor, the loon proves *pretty game* indeed. Like the narrator of Poe's "The Raven," Thoreau is keenly aware that his determined efforts to invest the bird with meaning border on the ludicrous. Yet he cannot shirk them. Even attempts to mythicize the god of loons may spark the anger of a cocky trickster who can resort to fowl play. Thus *Walden*'s myth-making always teeters on the verge of ironic self-transcendence, with a hero who—reincorporating society's foibles on a higher plane— still seems confessedly a bit loony.

14 /

Scatology and Eschatology
The Heroic Dimensions of Thoreau's Wordplay

> That boy yonder told me yesterday he thought the pinelog was God, &
> that God was in the jakes. What can Spinoza tell the boy?
> — Emerson of Thoreau ca. 1844-45 (*JMN*, 9:104)

Thoreau's Excremental Cosmology

"I will only hint at some of the enterprises which I have cherished," Thoreau writes early in *Walden*. After his famously obscure parable about losing a hound, a horse, and a dove, he describes the daily routine that rousted him from bed before dawn.

> It is true, I never assisted the sun materially in his rising, but, doubt not, it was of the last importance only to be present at it.
>
> So many autumn, ay, and winter days, spent outside the town, trying to hear what was in the wind, to hear and carry it express! I well-nigh sunk all my capital in it, and lost my own breath into the bargain, running in the face of it. If it had concerned either of the political parties, depend upon it, it would have appeared in the Gazette with the earliest intelligence. At other times watching from the observatory of some cliff or tree, to telegraph any new arrival; or waiting at evening on the hill-tops for the sky to fall, that I might catch something, though I never caught much, and that, manna-wise, would dissolve again in the sun.
>
> For a long time I was reporter to a journal, of no very wide circulation, whose editor has never yet seen fit to print the bulk of my contributions, and, as is too common with writers, I got only my labor for my pains. However, in this case my pains were their own reward. . . .
>
> I have looked after the wild stock of the town, which give a faithful herdsman a good deal of trouble by leaping fences; and I have had an eye to the unfrequented nooks and corners of the farm; though I did not always know whether Jonas or Solomon worked in a particular field to-day; that was none of my business. I have watered the red huckleberry, the sand cherry and the nettle tree, the red pine and the black ash, the white grape and the yellow violet, which might have withered else in dry seasons. (pp. 16-18)

Underlying the whimsical mystification with which he cloaks his activities are puns designed to show how a writer's trade secrets are "not

445

voluntarily kept" but inhere in the very nature of good writing. Thus we get riddling double entendres like being "reporter to a journal of no very wide circulation," that is, keeping a diary. Sunrise becomes a punning ritual when Thoreau participates in the levée of *le roi soleil,* never actually helping to robe that monarch but priding himself as a gentleman of the bedchamber on attending his majesty's "rising." His effort "to hear what was in the wind" literalizes a dead metaphor, for unlike his news-obsessed, cliché-ridden townsmen Thoreau actually listens to the soughing of the physical wind. The financial *capital* that he sinks into the effort is no more than his own head (Latin *caput*), sunk forward into a chilly breeze as he patrols the outskirts of Concord. Likewise, "watching from the observatory of some cliff or tree, to *telegraph* any new arrival" is simply this witty naturalist's way of saying etymologically that he recorded what he observed by *writing it down at a distance* in his field notebook (Greek *telegraphein* = distant writing). The amusing tableau of Thoreau "waiting at evening . . . for the sky to fall, that I might catch something, though I never caught much," might tempt his townsmen to suppose that this crackpot was emulating Chicken Little. But the discerning reader may recognize that he was simply playing around with words like *nightfall,* so what later dissolved in the sun manna-wise was simply a *chill* that in another dead metaphor he *caught.*

Liable to misunderstanding by people too stolid to recognize the physical world embedded in their own words, these self-appointed duties dramatize Concord's blinkered vision. Even sympathetic readers can be duped. Few notice precisely what Thoreau's insouciant claim to doing his "business" in out-of-the-way corners of Concord farms amounts to. Most are reluctant to realize that Thoreau did not spend summers scurrying around toting water in his hat to parched plants. When he claims to have watered a host of shrubs, he was actually less concerned to relieve withering vegetation than to relieve himself. He is playing on the reader's stock misconception of him as a crank nature lover, of course, while slyly asserting that, like an animal marking territory, he has urinated widely in Concord.

His discussion of shelter in "Economy" is similarly at the reader's expense: "As for a habitat, if I were not permitted still to squat, I might purchase one acre [as cheaply as the land which I cultivated]. . . . But as it was, I considered that I enhanced the value of the land by squatting on it" (p. 64). Very few readers catch the joke—that Thoreau's privy, genteelly neglected in *Walden*'s account of his construction projects, was not always used, and that squatter's rites of any sort served to manure and so improve Emerson's woodlot.

In a fragmentary but stimulating discussion of Thoreau's puns as subversive attacks on gentility, Richard Poirier links them with the "excremental vision" he finds in *Walden*.[1] Although this aspect of the book has received some slight attention, the issue has largely been avoided. At stake is not merely a taste for occasionally fanciful figurative language, such as the bizarre description in "Winter Animals" of noisily icebound Walden as "my great bedfellow... troubled with flatulency" (p. 272). This scatological metaphor is part of a larger pattern of meanings in the book that calls for inspection. There is, for instance, an obvious connection with Thoreau's complaint at the end of "Higher Laws" that "we are so degraded that we cannot speak simply of the necessary functions of human nature." There he praises the Hindu lawgiver who "teaches how to eat, drink, cohabit, void excrement and urine, and the like, elevating what is mean" (p. 221). But before we conclude that these two puns simply aim at undermining gentility, we must ask why subversion should be so self-effacing, so willingly foredoomed. As Poirier remarks, Thoreau's "best jokes occur... precisely where he sounds most harmless, most idiomatically familiar," and these he "was apparently willing to go to the grave without having anyone recognize" (pp. 86–87). Although dirty jokes constitute only a tiny fraction of Thoreau's covert wordplay, they are central to our understanding of the man and his greatest book.

In the decade preceding *Walden* Thoreau scrawled a fair amount of verse. Existing in several manuscript versions, fragmentary drafts of some lines show him struggling to express a curious concept of inspiration.

> It is a real place,
> Boston, I tell it to your face.
> And no dream of mine
> To ornament a line
> I can not come nearer to God & Heaven
> Than I live to Walden even.
> It is a part of me which I have not prophaned
> I live by the shore of me detained.
> Laden with my dregs
> I stand on my legs,
> While all my pure wine
> I to nature consign. (HM 924:D)
>
> . . . .
>
> Is consigned to the nine.
> I am but the jakes of myself.
> Without inlet it lies
> without outlet it flows
> From & to the skies

It comes and it goes
I am its source —
& my life is its course
I am its stoney shore,
& the gale that passes oer
In the hollow of my hand
Are its water and its sand;
Its deepest resort
Lies high in my thought. (MA 1302:9)[2]

Some of these lines reappear in *Walden*'s chapter "The Ponds." But in abridging his verses for that paean to purity, Thoreau excised all the scatological imagery that complicates his drafts. The manuscript lines present an author whose desire to tell Boston off to its face takes the form of indecent exposure. In this gesture defiance mingles oddly with lingering shame. As he voids his bladder, his fluids seem to circulate with Walden's. The poet imagines himself pouring pure wine in a libation to the Muses. But at the same time the libation consists of his "dregs." Did he ever piss in Walden — or would that prophane it?

Thoreau's scatological puns reflect more than a robust private sense of humor, more than simple fear of Mrs. Grundy. Despite his nostalgia, he is temperamentally estranged from those earlier Hindu ages "when every function was reverently spoken of and regulated by law" (p. 221). He agrees with the *Laws of Menu* in finding unclean "all excretions, that fall from the body. . . . Oily exudations, seminal fluids, blood, dandruff, urine, feces, earwax, nail parings, phlegm, tears, concretions on the eyes, and sweat, are the twelve impurities of the human frame."[3] But lacking the confidence in ritual purification that permits pious Hindus to drink their own urine, Thoreau remains haunted by a profound ambivalence toward the body and toward those excremental processes that he explicitly defends in "Higher Laws." Unlike Whitman, whose phrenological ardor begat hymns to the body electric, Thoreau could not project a convincing vision of "the bowels sweet and clean" (*LG*, p. 100). When he and Alcott first visited Whitman in Brooklyn, nothing bothered them more than being received in Walt's bedroom with the chamber pot clearly visible beneath the bed — a fact that Alcott stressed with exasperation. Although both puns cited above deal with excretion in what seems a benign natural context, fertilizing growth, Thoreau's instinct is still to conceal it.

By contrast, the triumphant conclusion of "Spring" depends precisely on his assurance, prompted by the dead horse in the hollow, that similar uncleanliness is purified through reabsorption into nature in the larger process of rebirth. "We are cheered when we observe the vulture feeding on the carrion which disgusts and disheartens us and deriving health and strength from the repast. . . . The impression made on a wise man is that of universal innocence. Poison is not poisonous after all" (p. 318). Thoreau is reluctant to treat excrement similarly. The writer who could note in his journal that sunset "is pinkish, even like the old cow-droppings found in pastures," then wryly add, "So universally does Nature blush at last," was not always inspired by a vision of universal innocence (8 Nov. 1858). His references to manure in *Walden* all remain faintly pejorative.

In "The Bean-Field" Thoreau quotes John Evelyn as an agricultural authority who disparages "all dungings and other sordid temperings" in raising crops (p. 162). Similar ideas were held by Dr. William Alcott, Bronson's cousin, whose dietary ideals intrigued Transcendentalists. His advocacy of vegetarianism in *The Young House-Keeper* (1838) probably influenced Thoreau. In that book Alcott deplores watermelons "raised by the aid of the most offensive manures of which the imagination can well conceive." He warns that the effects of "strong fresh manures . . . according to the observations of Dr. Whitlaw and others, are very unfavorable. In some instances they render [vegetables] actually poisonous."[4] These ideas lie behind Thoreau's repeated statement in "The Bean-Field" that despite advice from passersby he "did not give it any manure" (p. 156).

Such ideas clarify the startling outburst in "The Ponds," where Walden's purity is opposed to the impurity of Flint's Pond. This impurity is explained as a corruption derived from the avaricious and mean-spirited farming on its shore. In *A Week* Thoreau had recoiled from cultivated fertility, finding "something vulgar and foul" in the gardener's "closeness to his mistress" (p. 56). *Walden* expands the notion into a punning tirade.

> Farmers are respectable and interesting to me in proportion as they are poor,—poor farmers. A model farm! where the house stands like a fungus in a muckheap, chambers for men, horses, oxen, and swine, cleansed and uncleansed, all contiguous to one another! Stocked with men! A great grease-spot, redolent of manures and buttermilk! Under a high state of cultivation, being manured with the hearts and brains of men! As if you were to raise your potatoes in the churchyard! Such is a model farm. (pp. 196-97)

Exclamations and the lack of syntactic subordination suggest that this passage taps powerful feelings, but its imaginative and logical density is not so obvious. Like Indian philosophy, it invites us to see most human beings locked into a vicious cycle of the senses. They have no comprehension of the means for escape or even of the need for escape. True transmigration of souls is not involved, but Thoreau does confront us with a similar vision of dead generations poisoning the living. More horribly yet, the living poison themselves by consuming produce raised on their own offal mixed with that of beasts. Their "high" state of cultivation is punningly viewed as putrescence. To slaughter the beasts is made part of the larger process of devouring death. It is hardly distinguishable from ingesting their manure. One result of both acts is man's imbrutement. But the most terrifying consequence, the ultimate horror, is that living and dead become nearly indistinguishable. Life, feeding on its own waste, both bodily and spiritual, becomes fungoid. The word *fungus* reveals through its cognates how such parasitic life, always horrible for Thoreau, battens on the bodily *functions* and the *defunct*.[5] "Shall I become insensible as a fungus?" he asked himself (1 Dec. 1856). "Sometimes . . . a man is pasture for fungi . . . he being partly rotten" (14 Nov. 1853). "A sort of excrement they are" (14 Aug. 1853).

Here and elsewhere in Thoreau's work we are dealing with a homespun fecal cosmology created from his readings in agronomy and food faddism, from powerful anal drives, from his characteristic morbidity, and from the influence of those Hindu works he loved so well. For when he cut loose from traditional Christianity's emphasis on God's transcendence and attempted to stress immanence, like the Hindu he was naturally bothered by the problem of contamination. His militant sense of evil permitted little Emersonian serenity on this subject. How to preserve an immanent divinity from pollution is a recurring preoccupation in *Walden* and the journal, though often obscured by a more orthodox concern for heightening the spiritual side of life. His excremental mythology flowers in two lengthy journal entries where these representative passages occur:

> It is remarkable what a curse seems to attach to any place which has long been inhabited by man. . . . If, as here, an ancient cellar is uncovered, there springs up at once a crop of rank and noxious weeds, evidence of a certain unwholesome fertility—by which perchance the earth relieves herself of the poisonous qualities which have been imparted to her. As if what was foul, baleful, grovelling, or obscene in the inhabitants had sunk into the earth and infected it. Certain qualities are there in excess in the soil, and the proper equilibrium will not be attained until after the sun and air have purified the spot. The very shade breeds saltpetre. (22 Sept. 1859)
>
> Not only foul and poisonous weeds grow in our tracks, but our vileness and luxuriance make simple and wholesome plants rank and weed-like. All that I ever got a premium for was a monstrous squash, so coarse that nobody could eat. "The evil that men do lives after them." The corn and potatoes produced by excessive manuring may be said to have, not only a coarse, but a poisonous quality. They are made food [for] hogs and oxen too. What creatures is the grain raised on the cornfield of Waterloo for, unless it be for such as prey on men? Who cuts the grass in the graveyard?

> I can detect the site of the shanties that have stood all along the rail-roads by the ranker vegetation. I do not go there for delicate wild-flowers.
>
> It is important, then, that we should air our lives from time to time by removals, and excursions into the fields and woods,—starve our vices. Do not sit so long over any cellar hole as to tempt your neighbor to bid for the privilege of digging saltpetre there.
>
> So live that only the most beautiful wild-flowers will spring up where you have dwelt,—harebells, violets, and blue-eyed grass. (23 Sept. 1859)

Nebulous human effluvia and exudations have inescapably physical effects. The ascetic harshness of this notion is palliated by a loose symbolic equation with man's moral vices. It becomes a version of that familiar American myth, the curse conferred on an innocent continent by human society. We note the hallmarks of Thoreau's vision: dietary scrupulosity about the noxious effects of "excessive manuring," the morbidity that associates all offal with carrion, the veiled equations between excremental pollution and "what was . . . obscene" in former inhabitants, like their quasi-sexual "vileness and luxuriance" (cf. Thoreau's punning objection to sexual impurity as "the *luxury* of affection," *W,* 6:207). At last a corrupted nature shows a corresponding tendency to "relieve herself" in "unwholesome fertility" by breeding saltpeter, that grotesque and lethal parody of healthy organic life.

In "Economy" Thoreau criticizes ordinary houses as coffins, but this passage suggests that an even more important model shaped his thinking about conventional New England architecture. As the injunction not to sit too "long over any cellar hole" hints, Thoreau could conceive of houses as basically outhouses. "Going by the shanty," he noted on 11 July 1851, "I smell the excrements of its inhabitants." Roses in Concord front yards "do not atone for the sink and pigsty and cow-yard and jakes in the rear" (23 June 1852). Their dangerous miasma invites a crusade against most of our troubles, which "are literally domestic and originate in the house" (26 Apr. 1857). These ideas lend rather more plausibility to Poirier's conjecture that when Thoreau punningly remarks, "What is a house but a *sedes,* a seat?—better if a country seat," the word *seat* includes the notion of a privy (*Walden,* p. 88).

More important, these ideas undergird one of *Walden*'s most beautifully achieved chapters, "Former Inhabitants; and Winter Visitors." In narrating the short and simple annals of the poor people who were his predecessors near the pond, Thoreau manages, much like Gray's "Elegy," to combine real tenderness with a complete lack of sentimentality. There is pathos in the encounter with the revenant at Breed's hut, set in the desolate landscape with its panorama of deserted cellar holes now slowly closing over. The erasure of these trivial domestic relics by nature lends them a momentary dignity that touches us deeply. But Robert Frost, who perhaps better than anyone else has caught Thoreau's vision in this chapter, was right to epitomize such a scene in "Directive" with the cry, "Weep for what little things could make them glad." There is tragedy in Thoreau's account of Cato Ingraham, Brister Freeman, Colonel Quoil, and the rest, but it is the tragedy of stunted lives, and we are not allowed to forget that essential fact about the rude forefathers of the hamlet.

At one point Thoreau voices a musing wonder that commerce never throve here "where Wyman the potter squatted." But the question answers itself, for there is a principle of decay inherent in the nascent "stablebroom, matmaking . . . and pottery business." Thoreau himself, of course, deliberately rejected a doormat as a dirtcatcher and shunned the victuals to which his histories of the former inhabitants frequently advert, from the witchlike Zilpha's pot of gurgling bones to Quoil's fondness for tobacco and liquor—more important to the Irishman than nearby Brister's spring, which he never even bothered to locate. "Alas! how little does the memory of these human inhabitants enhance the beauty of the landscape!" While despite the sterile soil, berries and goldenrod grow "luxuriantly" around these cellar holes, profusions of Roman wormwood also spring up, together with that venomous family the sumachs, to exemplify the underlying theme of poison that reaches articulate statement only at the end of his meditation: "Deliver me from a city built on the site of a more ancient city, whose materials are ruins, whose gardens cemeteries. The soil is blanched and accursed there, and before that becomes necessary the earth itself will be destroyed." And further to point the moral we are given the anecdote of the vivacious lilac by the door, playfully planted long ago near the house by two innocent children and daily watered, "blossoming as fair, and smelling as sweet, as in that first spring" (pp. 257-64). Rather like Norman Mailer in our day, Thoreau purported to believe that "all odor is . . . advertisement of a moral quality" (16 June 1854). Echoing his favorite lines by James Shirley completes the lesson and reminds us that Christianity too had elements that lent themselves to his symbolic system: "Only the ashes of the just / Smell sweet and blossom in their dust."[6]

If an excremental vision illuminates the apexes of Thoreau's artistic achievement, it also betrays him to the nadirs. There is no more unpleasant chapter in *Walden* than "Baker Farm." Not even "Higher Laws" exceeds it in unholy devotion to Spirit, and the results of this fanaticism seem more dangerous in "Baker Farm" insofar as they threaten other human beings and not just Thoreau himself. The Yankee animus against philanthropy that sparked some of his most brilliant and truthful pages in "Economy" functions well in the abstract, but this theme resists dramatic treatment. Poor John Field—that "hard-working, but shiftless man plainly" (p. 204), not lazy but not getting on—should have inspired more than the probable double pun for not wearing an undershirt.[7] What may be a creditable revulsion from the charity of the welfare state as it seeks to embrace our selves becomes less attractive when the state of ourselves and others is involved. The sight of the celibate Thoreau airily patronizing Field and his family in the name of philosophy, urging him to drop his job, change their diet, and go a-huckleberrying, is as unsettling and vaguely repellent as it would be to see Socrates persuading Phaedo and company to commit suicide.

Thoreau's attitude is explained if not excused by the degree to which John Field is reduced to a merely symbolic entity. His last name is significant. Thoreau fails to see John Field in human terms because he is so determined to treat him as an allegorical John Farmer before his regeneration at the end of "Higher Laws." "Why should they eat their sixty acres, when man is condemned to eat only his peck of dirt?" Thoreau had inquired about farmers in "Economy" (p. 5). In his eyes Field becomes as dehumanized as his "too humanized" chickens—man and beast pecking at dirt because unable to transcend feeling peckish. Or, to cite another pun from "Economy," which Thoreau liked well enough to use twice, the Irishman serves as an example of a life dedicated to the "grossest of groceries" (p. 64). All the food in his diet, meticulously described—indeed, ultimately all food—is viewed by Thoreau as *grossery* (cf. French *gros,* fat; *graisse,* grease), unctuously fattening and spiritually repugnant. This is especially true of Field, who worked "bogging" for a neighboring farmer, "turning up a meadow with a spade or bog hoe at the rate of ten dollars an acre and the use of the land with manure" (pp. 204-6).

To lure him from this life, Thoreau opposes his own. "I did not use tea, nor coffee, nor butter, nor milk, nor fresh meat, and so did not have to work to get them; again, as I did not work hard, I did not have to eat hard," whereas when Field had worked hard to pay for his groceries, "he had to eat hard again to repair *the waste of his system*" (emphasis added). This double pun implies that Thoreau regards Field's system of living as inefficent, destructive of his physical system, and dedicated simply to replenishing his bodily wastes. When in the next breath he tells us that Field "wasted his life," we should sense not only the obvious meaning but a process that converts life to excrement. His excessive requirements, from the dietary habits that make him happy to catch a "mess" of fish to the need for stout clothing and thick boots for his "poor bogtrotting feet," depend on the fact that "he worked so hard at bogging." We are meant to catch the obscene meaning of the verb *bog* common in the nineteenth century. He views the Irishman as self-employed at defecation. Under the pressure of relentless punning on forms of the word *bog*, repeated seven times in the account of the Irishman, bogtrotting John Field is symbolically assimilated to the boggy field in which he wallows. The bogtrotter becomes not only a clod but virtually an ambulatory turd (except that the word *trots* suggests diarrhea), the culture of whom, according to his Socratic interlocutor, requires "a sort of moral bog hoe" that Thoreau evidently did not possess.

He highlights his description of the Fields with a noteworthy display of punning pyrotechnics. A running exegesis of the multiple meanings in the pasage is tedious but does suggest the extent of Thoreau's verbal skill, metaphoric vigor, and imaginative perversity:

> John heaved [*breathed/dug up*] a sigh at this, and his wife stared with arms a-kimbo [*regarded me with hands on hips/regarded John without sharing his labor*], and both appeared to be wondering if they had capital [*financial resources/heads*] enough to begin such a course [*of action/of studies/of navigation*] with, or arithmetic [*bookkeeping skill/reckoning longitude*] enough to carry it through. It was sailing by dead reckoning [*navigation/their dead minds*] to them, and they saw not clearly how to make their port so [*reach harbor/earn liquor?*]; therefore I suppose they still take life bravely [*bear up courageously/slaughter animals*], after their fashion [*in their way/in pursuit of clothing*], face to face [*head on/facing each other across the table/confronting the chickens' "too humanized' stare as they behead them?*], giving it tooth and nail [*fighting all out/tearing apart roasted chicken with fingernails and gnawing it/tooling it with sawteeth and hammered nails*], not having skill to split its massive columns [*military formations/pillars*] with any fine entering wedge [*V-shaped squadron/tool*], and rout it [*put to flight/groove with a routing tool*] in detail [*squad by squad/with fine handiwork*]—thinking to deal with it roughly, as one should handle a thistle [*slight opposition/vegetable life* (only)]. But they fight at an overwhelming disadvantage,—living, John Field, alas! without arithmetic [*mathematics/reckoning* (hence *recklessly*)] and failing so [*flunking/going bankrupt/declining physically*].

Men, Women, and the Pollution of Sympathy

Besides noting the greater hostility to the wife, who may not fully share her husband's momentary glimmer of understanding, we should remark the covert denunciation of the Fields as murderers—of animals and so of themselves. Transcendental feelings ran high on this score. At Bronson Alcott's Fruitlands two food faddists came to blows when one poured cream on his oatmeal and deprived an innocent calf of its mother's milk. A lady at one commune died from jealous devotion to beans. Thoreau himself reportedly never traversed the Emersons' kitchen without blushing as if at indecency. Although the cruelty involved was Alcott's main objection to eating flesh, Thoreau was driven less by fear of being unkind than by desire to avoid getting dirty—a rather less amiable motive.[8] "There is something essentially unclean about this diet and all flesh," his next chapter roundly proclaims (p. 214).

Even healthy living flesh bothers Thoreau, as his compulsive bathing might suggest. "There is nothing so strange to me as my own body—I love any other piece of nature, almost, better," he confessed (21 Feb. 1842). Because of "the bog in our brain and bowels" (30 Aug. 1856), "we are made the very sewers the cloacae of nature" (*PJ,* 3:65). The journal records his zealous cleanliness. "I find it difficult to get *wet* through—I would fain be the channel of a mountain brook. I bathe, and in a few hours I bathe again, not remembering. . . . I would fain take rivers in my walks endwise" (*W,* 8:335). What we sense here is not simply desire to beat the summer heat. Underlying this striking image is apparently the wish to forge upstream mouth agape, athletically flushing out the intestines and so cleansing the body's Augean stables. "If I am to be a thoroughfare," he punned, "I prefer that it be of the mountain-brooks, the Parnassian streams, and not the town sewers" (*Papers,* p. 172).

Walking was a central symbolic ritual for Thoreau, one magnificently described in his posthumous essay on the subject, where he claims for the Walker "the chivalric and heroic spirit which once belonged to the Rider" (*W,* 5:206). His productivity as a writer depended intimately on his daily walks. They gave "a true march to the sentence" (*PJ,* 2:118). Without them he felt imaginatively constipated. Authors' thoughts may be "the consequence of something they have eaten," although no one who picks up a book "wishes for the report of the clogged bowels" (21 Dec. 1851). Zeal for daily constitutionals was natural in a writer who felt that his prose closely reflected all his movements. Just as his typical paragraph follows the pattern of an excursion, so he saw himself returning from a day's study in some field like a "farmer driving into his barnyard with a load of muck" for fertilizer— except that "my barnyard is my journal" (20 Jan. 1852). Walking is also linked to fastidiousness by his loathing for fungi, mildew, and other parasites. Condemning these "lowest forms of vegetable life" as "the definition of dirt," he revealingly adds, "Cleanliness is by activity not to give any quiet shelf for the seeds of parasitic plants to take root in" (29 Jan. 1852).[9]

We should now be sufficiently sensitized to Thoreau's style to wonder about his rhetorical question concerning Walden's "wonderful
purity" in "The Ponds": "Who would not regret that the comparatively
impure waters of Flint's Pond should be mingled with it, or itself should
ever go to waste its sweetness in the ocean wave?" (p. 194). Since he is
considering the possibility that the "more elevated" Flint's Pond be can-
alized to *pass water* to Walden, the concept of bodily waste may be in his
mind as well as Gray's "Elegy." And this raises the possibility that, like
Tooke, he is connecting the word *mingle* with the Latin *mingere,* to
piss.[10] This possibility increases when we recall the common scriptural
tag-phrase for a male, "one that pisseth against a wall." Is Thoreau
recoiling from a situation in which a Flint's Pond pisseth against a
Walden?

If a male is scripturally defined by the fact that he pisses against
walls, a woman conventionally houses herself for such activity. Perhaps
we should consider the previously explained metamorphosis of "country
seat" into privy in light of the hostility displayed toward Mrs. Field and
other women throughout Thoreau's writing. Despite prudishness about
sex, he was capable of relishing "Rabelaisean" language, as his encounter with the salty Wellfleet oysterman in *Cape Cod* shows. The drunken
obscenities of a Dutch fisherman impressed him as the "happy repartee"
of an "illuminated swine," "the earthiest, slimiest wit I ever heard" (*PJ,*
3:100). The Journal records his rueful amusement at outhouse graffiti:
"The poetry of the Jakes,—it flows as perennially as the gutter" (30 Jan.
1852). Although I would not care to place undue weight on the following interpretation, Thoreau himself is my authority for any audacity:
"My friend will be bold to conjecture, he will guess bravely at the
significance of my words" (26 Oct. 1851). So I diffidently suggest that
when he rather obscurely demands, "What is a house but a *sedes,* a
seat?—better if a country seat," he has in mind the Shakespearean double entendre where *country* is a fanciful English plural in *-ry* like *poultry.*
What is a house but the *housewife*'s domain, her world, the poultry shed
where she hatches, raises, and henpecks her brood, the privy where
women perch to lay their *ova,* the waste products associated with men-
struation? Indeed, as Emerson's copy of Whiter's *Etymologicon Magnum* stressed, in many languages, like Spanish, "to be married is . . . to
be *Housed*" (pp. 54–55). Thoreau is thus mocking the cliché that no
house is complete without a woman in it. He probably endorsed
Whiter's explanation that etymologically a *husband* is *house-bound.*

Such an attitude would not be uncharacteristic of a man raised, as
Thoreau was, in a household increasingly dominated by women. "In the

east women religiously conceal that they have faces—in the west that they have legs," he remarked tartly. "In both cases it is evident that they have but little brains" (31 Jan. 1852). Because of his frequently expressed admiration for specimens of athletic manhood, Thoreau's misogyny has been plausibly interpreted as latent homosexuality.[11] But it may stem more directly from the feeling that whereas all sexuality is dirty, biology renders woman intrinsically more unclean than man and apparently sicklier and less independent to boot.

This common masculine attitude was specifically reinforced by Thoreau's ascetic philosophy. Porphyry's Abstinence from Animal Food, for example, claimed that "venereal connections are attended with defilement."[12] Seeking to limit even marital intercourse to once per month, dietary reformers like Sylvester Graham waxed perfervid in warning young men that sexual indulgence exposed them to discharges involving "great quantities of foetid, loathsome pus."[13] That Thoreau's recoil from women is part of a larger disgust with the general filth of the body is suggested by a striking antifeminine diatribe deploring women as more animalistic than men and hence less inclined to vegetarianism (28 Nov. 1850). Like his ready equation of the menstrual flow with mildew (18 Feb. 1857), his repugnance at the process of childbearing involves a specific distaste for messy fertility: "Birth and death are offensive and unclean things" (14 Dec. 1840). Strolling with a friend, he kicked a skunk cabbage and exclaimed, "There, marriage is like that."[14] Four months pregnant at the time of their wedding, his mother had perhaps trapped his father sexually. Following Whiter's lead, the entry "MOTHER" in Thoreau's copy of Webster's American Dictionary linked it etymologically with matter and matrix, then dredged up a slew of nasty connections between the womb and "a sink or sewer" linked to "mud," "mold," "hysterics," "the thick slimy concretion in vinegar," "purulent running . . . matter, pus" (s.v.). Feelings of this kind underlie the climax of "Economy," where Thoreau makes the cypress tree that bears no fruit the type of all spiritual freedom in being exempt from the cycle of generation. And they surface at the climax of "Solitude" in the revealing characterization of the parthenogenetically conceived goddess Hebe as "probably the only thoroughly sound-conditioned, healthy, and robust young lady that ever walked the globe" (p. 139).

Living in a family of women in Victorian Concord, Thoreau might well have thought that female sexuality consisted chiefly in quaffing patent medicine to dispel the megrims. But the man who welcomed death by "dry rot" as at least a relief from "the superfluous juices of the body" was no more lenient to his own sexuality (14 Dec. 1840). He shared the grave concern expressed in tracts like Lallemand's *Practical Treatise on the Causes, Symptoms, and Cure of Spermatorrhoea* (1839). This manual saw half a dozen American editions before 1860 as well as an adaptation peddled by M. E. Lazarus, an associationist gadabout often at Brook Farm. "Higher Laws" records Thoreau's complaint: "All sensuality is one, though it takes many forms; all purity is one. It is the same whether a man eat, or drink, or cohabit, or sleep sensually" (p. 220). From his personal experiences he concluded "that a man's seed was the direct tax of his race." No aunt's generosity could nullify his characteristic refusal to pay it. This ascetic gesture fostered self-improvement better than the town jail, for "when the brain chiefly is nourished, and not the affections, the seed becomes merely excremental" (28 Aug. 1854). With this rationale he was barely able to tolerate the occasional wet dream, which left him disgusted with his body as "a scuttle full of dirt—such a thoroughfare only as the street & the kennel" (26 Oct. 1851). Any homoerotism in a man so squeamish about expending himself involved no enthusiasm for genital sexuality in the male. "I love men with the same distinction I love woman—as if my friend were of some third sex," he claimed, and regularly deplored the "trivial titillation of the vulgar sense that calls man into life" (*PJ*, 2:245, 324). Like the strategy for artistic sublimation that eroticized his contact with nature, his reverence for chastity was oft expressed and quite sincere.

Indeed, rather than harboring like Whitman an undeniably physical attraction toward men, for the most part Thoreau simply displays an inhibited capacity for affection. The cult of friendship practiced in Concord's intellectual circles encouraged hothouse relationships, to be sure—but so highly idealized as almost to guarantee disappointment, frustration, and eventual recoil. Thoreau's dissatisfaction with actual friends prompted ethereal dreams of perfect friendship, but too often these served as a rationale for further standoffishness on his part. Perhaps no friend could be allowed to take the place of his lost brother.

His recoil from affectionate human contact goes deeper than the customs of the village salons, however. It has roots in his symbology. In his journal for 11 November 1851 he analyzes emotion in the following terms:

> When I have been confined to my chamber for the greater part of several days . . . by the ague . . . I have been conscious of a certain softness to which I am otherwise & commonly a stranger—in which the gates were loosened to some emotions— And if I were to become a confirmed invalid I see how some sympathy with mankind & society might spring up
>
> Yet what is my softness good for even to tears— It is not I but nature in me. I laughed at myself the other day to think that I cried while reading a

> pathetic story. I was no more affected in spirit than I frequently am methinks—the tears were merely a phenomenon of the bowels—& I felt that that expression of my sympathy so unusual with me was something mean—& such as I should be ashamed to have the subject of it understand. . . . I found that I had some bowels—but then it was because my bowels were out of order.

His equation of feeling with sickness and shame is only less remarkable than his revealing connection between tears and the bowels. Traditional biblical physiology located the affections in the bowels. But Thoreau's peculiar attitudes toward appetite and excrement colored this ancient concept unconventionally.

We begin to grasp just how thoroughly he was influenced when we reflect—as he himself undoubtedly did—on the fact that to cry is, in common parlance, to *blubber*. A like conception of sympathy oozing from the fat stored in the digestive process underlies his recoil upon meeting the reformers Foss, Moody, and Wright:

> Though Foss was a stranger to the others, you would have thought them old and familiar cronies. . . . They addressed each other constantly by their Christian names, and rubbed you continually with the greasy cheeks of their kindness. They would not keep their distance, but cuddle up and lie spoon-fashion with you, no matter how hot the weather nor how narrow the bed. . . . I was awfully pestered with his benignity; feared I should get greased all over with it past restoration. . . . It was difficult to keep clear of his slimy benignity, with which he sought to cover you before he swallowed you and took you fairly into his bowels. . . . I do not wish to get any nearer to a man's bowels than usual. They lick you as a cow her calf. They would fain wrap you about with their bowels. —— addressed me as "Henry" within one minute from the time I first laid eyes on him, and when I spoke, he said with drawling, sultry sympathy, "Henry, I know all you would say . . ." and to another, "I am going to dive into Henry's inmost depths." I said, "I trust you will not strike your head against the bottom." I do not like the men who come so near me with their bowels. It is the most disagreeable kind of snare to be caught in. Men's bowels are far more slimy than their brains. They must be ascetic indeed who approach you by this side. What a relief to have heard the ring of one healthy reserved tone! (17 June 1853)

Thoreau's contempt for greasy kindness and slimy benignity shows that he construed unctuousness physically—and that he saw it as a sweaty lubricant secreted in most social contact. Like tears, moreover, such oily exudations are clearly a by-product of the bowels.

In *Walden* Thoreau's sense of the potentially rancid nature of all love lies behind the striking denunciation of philanthropy that closes "Economy." "There is no odor so bad as that which arises from goodness

tainted. It is human, it is divine, carrion." He there portrays the philan-
thropist enveloping mankind in his own sorrow and calling it sympathy.
"If anything ail a man, so that he does not perform his functions, if he
have a pain in his bowels even,—for that is the seat of sympathy,—he
forthwith sets about reforming—the world." Compassion betokens diarrhea, and the remedy for this "dyspepsia" is to avoid green apples (pp.
74-77). In "The Pond in Winter" similar attitudes prompt him to
answer the question, "Why is it that a bucket of water soon becomes
putrid, but frozen remains sweet forever?" with the claim that "this is
the difference between the affections and the intellect" (p. 297). The four
winter chapters that follow "Higher Laws" represent a season of snowy
purity, of enforced emotional austerity that Thoreau rather welcomes.

Ascetic Heroism against Dirt, Disease, and Death

Despite Thoreau's reputation as the patron saint of civil disobedience,
Walden's skeptical view of social reform was less congenial to his 1960s
disciples than many imagined. It was natural enough that an author
whose "pages are . . . particularly addressed to poor students" (p. 4)
should be rather ineptly interpreted, especially behind campus barricades. But this is a pity, for his main objection to charity—that "we
should impart our courage, and not our despair, our health and ease,
and not our disease"—is founded on values more enduring than the
orthodox liberal imagination acknowledges. Believing that "this sickly
preaching of love, and . . . sympathy . . . is the dyspepsia of the soul,"
Thoreau attacks all forms of softness in an effort to reanimate the heroic
ethos of classical antiquity (31 Dec. 1840). No major English writer
since Milton and Pope has more assiduously sought to adapt the Greco-
Roman ideal of nobility to modern culture.

It was for a similar effort that Thoreau valued Carlyle. As he noted
approvingly, all the Scotsman's works seemed essentially one, "On
Heroes, Hero-Worship, and the Heroic in History." From his early
unpublished essay "The Service: Qualities of the Recruit," Thoreau envisioned life lived heroically. But this heroic moralist differs from those
other nineteenth-century figures whom Eric Bentley christened Heroic
Vitalists. His fundamentally democratic egalitarianism and individualism are opposed to Carlyle's and Nietzsche's emphasis on charismatic
leadership. The journals are full of Thoreau's insistence that *every* man is
potentially his own hero, his theater of action his daily life. "There are in
each the seeds of a heroic ardor . . . which need only to be stirred in with
the *soil where they lie,* by an inspired voice or pen, to bear fruit of a
divine flavor" (13 June 1838).

To this vision his great book gives magnificent form, confronting life, daring to live it beyond daring, making our ordinary existence into an epic. The central plot of *Walden* is the archetypal myth of a hero's retreat from society, initiation, and triumphal return. Mallet's *Northern Antiquities* taught Thoreau that the Scandinavian root of his surname, *thor*, meant *audacity*, and he punned gleefully on the heroic Norse origins of his own identity.[15] The man who could hoe beans heroically or hail a mosquito as genuinely Homeric has much to give an age with our fondness for almost any existential posturing, the more absurd the better.

The ascetic strain in Thoreau may strike us as oddly discordant with his epic of the self. "Higher Laws" confronts us with an author whose response to a tureen of turtle soup or to a preserve pot is a nervous revulsion from "this slimy, beastly life, eating and drinking" (p. 218). His abhorrence seems less courageous than eccentric and unhealthy. Thoreau himself was tempted to believe that "the hero . . . is the very opposite . . . of the ascetic" (*Essays*, p. 218). But opposites attract, so the anorexic's effort to control diet is actually a perverse quest for power and autonomy. Nor is *all* asceticism so perverse as modern consumer culture imagines. Our society of superfluity has detached desires from the healthy animal needs they arose to serve in a world that naturally curbed them. As the Transcendentalists foresaw, spiraling wishes will beget mass frustration unless kept in check by "artificial" self-restraints.[16] We should remember William James's shrewd defense of the ascetic impulse in religion as symbolic of "the belief that there is an element of real wrongness in this world, which is neither to be ignored nor evaded, but which must be squarely met and overcome by an appeal to the soul's heroic resources." James shares with Thoreau the conviction that "in heroism . . . life's supreme mystery is hidden"—hence our respect for anyone whose "highhearted indifference to life" lets him fling it away like a flower while we cling fearfully to it: "The metaphysical mystery thus recognized by common sense, that he who feeds on death that feeds on men possesses life supereminently and excellently, and meets best the secret demands of the universe, is the truth of which asceticism has been the faithful champion."[17]

As James can help us discern behind the faintly ridiculous ascetic the aspiring hero, so we may also come to understand just how literally Thoreau fed on death. His symbology explains why all eating required of him a truly heroic resolve. In his journal for 9 April 1856 he described sitting by the sandbank in the railroad cut, where "I remarked how many old people died off at the approach of the present spring. It is said that when the sap begins to flow in the trees our diseases become more violent." The sap that supports life also saps and destroys it. With dogged honesty his vision affirms the difficulty of distinguishing between the forces of life and death. "Is not disease the rule of existence? . . . Every shrub and tree has its gall . . . hardly to be distinguished from the fruit" (1 Sept. 1851). His mind revolved this theme in an effort to master it. "Man begins by quarreling with the animal in him, and the result is immediate disease" (3 Sept. 1851). Our aliments, as he puns in *Walden,* are our ailments. "Disease is in fact the rule of our terrestrial life" (3 Sept. 1851).

Therefore, to live—when living is conceived of as the process of dying—always requires courage. And it required special courage of Thoreau. Illness dogged him from youth. At twenty-four we find him musing thus in his journal: "How much of my well-being think you depends on the condition of my lungs and stomach—such cheap pieces of nature as they which indeed she is every day reproducing with prodigality— Is the arrow indeed fatal which wrankles in the breast of the bird on the bough—in whose eye all this fair landscape is reflected—and whose voice still echoes through the wood?" (15 Dec. 1841).

Yes, the arrow was fatal, even for a romantic poet-naturalist seeking literary immortality through creative observation. Thoreau was too shrewd an observer not to connect his own bouts of "bronchitis" with the history of early death in his tubercular family. "The whole duty of man may be expressed in one line," he had earlier decided—"Make to yourself a perfect body" (21 June 1840). The Journal records his preoccupation with his health, his interest in such unconventional remedies for phthisic as skunk secretion and rattlesnake broth, his concern for whether relatives had strong lungs. He shared the nineteenth century's fascination with the sinister epidemic deemed responsible for nearly half all adult deaths.[18] Fresh-air fanatics like Dr. William Alcott traced it to human effluvia, for there seemed "scarcely . . . a more subtle and poisonous agent than the gas . . . which is expelled from our bodies."[19] Some thought the new airtight stoves helped spread the plague, and on outings Thoreau eagerly gulped down chilly air "as a panacea" (29 Mar. 1855). Playing the flute was especially recommended to strengthen the lungs. Others, linking the disease with sexual passion or unrequited love, counseled chastity and cold bathing. One medico who lectured throughout Massachusetts in the 1840s luridly describes the fear gripping those whose family background was consumptive. "No state of mind is more distressing than to live for years, from earliest recollection, in the constant apprehension and expectation of dying of pulmonary consumption," observed Samuel Sheldon Fitch. "This horrible phantom, by night and day, follows many. . . . All pleasures are marred by its horrid apparition. It haunts them in their dreams, and terrifies them in their waking hours. Never do they see a notice of death by consumption, than they experience a thrill of horror through every nerve; and a cough . . . and their minds are filled with the deepest distress and despair."[20]

To combat this inheritance, Fitch counseled an ascetic regimen much like Thoreau's. As the offshoot of civilization, consumption resulted chiefly from "effeminacy" (p. 38). It might be forestalled through plain living, avoidance of animal diet, daily walks, exercise, and regular cold bathing. Deliberate cheerfulness was a necessary strategy, for "*mental emotions* . . . incline to depress all . . . the system . . . in which the lungs must suffer" (p. 50). Dusty occupations (like the Thoreau family pencil factory) were especially risky.

But most important of all, those predisposed by heredity to tuberculosis should beware "the BAD EFFECTS OF COSTIVENESS" (p. 291). Together with the lungs, kidneys, and sweat glands, the bowels purge the body of excrementitious poisons. When constipation interrupts this function, an extra burden is thrown on the lungs. Thus the potential consumptive must wear light clothing to facilitate perspiration, maintain a "free flow of urine" (p. 59)—and, above all, avoid costive dyspepsia, since in "the commencement of disease of the lungs, costiveness is almost always present" (p. 282). Nothing should ever discourage one from obeying a call of nature immediately, so as part of his campaign against tuberculosis Fitch calls for the construction of more comfortable outhouses.

Such ideas were widely diffused. During Thoreau's life Fitch's bestseller went through some forty printings, and it was still selling at century's end. Like Fitch, most physicians regarded phthisis as a disease of plethora caused by a surfeit of bodily wastes.[21] Under the classification *catarrh* a consumptive's handbook might group both bronchitis and diarrhea.[22] Patent medicines like Brandreth's Pills filled newspapers with clamorous advertising tracing consumption (and most other human ills) to constipation.[23] "Never ignore an impulse to stool," William James cautioned his brother Henry, who heeded this fraternal advice and fletcherized as well.[24] Considering this mystique, no wonder digestion should haunt Thoreau, that he should hate food and try to avoid *consumption* by limiting his nutritional intake and living frugally.[25] Alas, he did not know that reducing his protein intake to unhealthy levels may have abetted his illness. He believed in the theoretical prophylaxis for lung disease implicit in the analogy between fire and the vital heat that he picked up from Liebig. "Man's body is a stove, and food the fuel which keeps up the internal combustion in the lungs," he explains early in *Walden*. "The animal heat is the result of a slow combustion, and disease and death take place when this is too rapid" (p. 13).

A superstition first recorded in Pliny's *Natural History* suggests that the same reasoning underlay Thoreau's aversion to human contact. According to the Roman writer, "there are a sort of people . . . whose sweat if it chance to touch a man's body, presently he falleth into a phthisic or consumption of the lungs." Pliny links this contagiousness with a habit of feeding "upon the bowels and flesh."[26] There was a sanatorium for consumptives in nearby Lexington dedicated to the proposition that "Christ died to save us from dyspepsia." Its proprietor was convinced that tuberculosis resulted from "effete and poisonous matter" exuded by the skin and allowed to remain there.[27] He cautioned persons predisposed to phthisis to avoid contact with other consumptives (who supposedly made up nearly half the adult population). Well might Thoreau insist in *Walden*'s "Solitude" that "the value of a man is not in his skin, that we should touch him" (p. 136).

Such feelings are crucial in the grand description of the thawing sandbank—as manifold as Melville's doubloon—that is the focal symbol of *Walden*'s "Spring." To be sure, the passage can be partially explained as a conventional vision of evolution and rebirth, where such social excrescences as the railroad are suddenly revealed as transient modes through which nature fulfills herself—the circulatory system of industrial society rebegetting those of organic life. Or we may regard it less congenially as a metaphor of the spirit sluicing away the body in order to percolate through the universe in a wild realization of the American dream of freedom. But such encapsulation neglects Thoreau's insistence that the hillside illustrated "*all* the operations of Nature" (emphasis added). Despite its centrality in *Walden*, the sandbank is never mentioned in the journal until well after his departure from the pond. Most references to it there occur after a powder-mill explosion in nearby Acton scattered bodies across a landscape, confronting him with the unsettling vision of "some limbs and bowels here and there, and a head at a distance from its trunk" (8 Jan. 1853). The mills of the gods too grind slow but sure, without much concern for employee safety.

If the slope is the creation of an hour by "the Artist who made the world and me," this Artist occupies no studio, but a scientific "laboratory." The energy that manifests itself in fresh designs creates, yes, but in a charnel house where "the forms of sappy leaves or vines . . . of pulpy sprays . . . of some lichens . . . of coral, leopards' paws or birds' feet, of brains or lungs or bowels, and excrements of all kinds" are indiscriminately strewn about. As he confronts his own decadent lungs mirrored in the sand, Thoreau faces and accepts the harsh truth that freedom from the body's excrement will involve more than a "purgative" for "winter fumes and indigestions." To be truly free is to be disemboweled. The "excrementitious" phenomenon makes him pun wryly "that Nature has some bowels, and there again is mother of humanity" (pp. 231-33). But simultaneously another pun forces upon us a bleaker vision of human nature, the Augustinian *inter urinas et faeces nascimur.* Thoreau's vision of vernal rebirth is based on a scene that is actually destined to sandy sterility.

One might argue that the rigor of Thoreau's view is softened by the promise of immortality. Although, as one scholar asserts, "Thoreau never articulated a complete eschatology," the passage does show him groping for an eternal principle.[28] Kraitsir and Whiter encouraged him to conceive of language as the mode of man's immortality—hence the philological comparisons that stud the description of the flowing sand. The pulpy heaps of discarded organs are joints and appendages that an essentially linguistic *Weltgeist* may outgrow as it presses ever forward in an effort to *articulate* itself more satisfactorily. Like an outmoded grammar, the human body may eventually be superseded by purer spiritual forms. But for any comfort afforded by such immortality Thoreau unflinchingly pays the full price: the forfeiture of all the human individuality guaranteed by Christianity—terrifyingly suggested when he imagines the dissolving face of thawing clay—and the frank admission that compared to earth's great central life, "all animal and vegetable life is merely parasitic."

These are staggering retrenchments of his ruling ideals, and they cost Thoreau dearly. The notion of the world as a single organism may yield Stoic serenity, Berkeleyan irony, environmental ecstasy, or the leveling pantheism that Tocqueville found so congenial to American democracy. But it may also issue in the nightmare vision of Poe's "Fall of the House of Usher."[29] What blossoms on the sandbank, Thoreau insists with a wary etymological pun, is "a truly *grotesque* vegetation" (the Italian *grotto* derives from Latin *crypta* = crypt). Thus even in the serenity of his final flirtations with a fairer world, he contemplated with horrified fascination "the wasting away of his body, the going forth of his lungs . . . to Henry an inexplicably foreign event," according to his deathbed companion Ellery Channing Jr. And when "words could no longer express these inexplicable conditions of his existence," there was "that dream he had of being a railroad cut, where they were digging through and laying down the rails—the place being in his lungs."[30]

Heroic Language Games: Romantic Irony, Art, and the Play of Life

Thoreau has been criticized for evading death by turning it into a joke. He anticipated this charge by claiming that "a great cheerfulness indeed have all great wits and heroes possessed—almost a prophane levity—to such as understood them not" (15 Mar. 1841). The most sublime bravery, he felt, would show itself chiefly in "its superfluous cheerfulness . . . and its infinite humor and wantonness" (27 July 1840). He believed, indeed, that "the most serious events have their ludicrous aspect, such as death; but we cannot excuse ourselves when we have taken this view of them only" (19 Mar. 1858). To understand the thawing sandbank in its proper symbolic dimensions is surely to exonerate him from frivolity. He is neither Stubb nor Ahab but Ishmael. What is the passage but an unblinking vision of the interdependence of life and death, hard-earned in human terms and fully achieved artistically?

True, some of the wordplay that we have been examining seems evasive. We might be tempted to interpret such wordplay as a bid for absolution by private confession, as a way of flaunting before an audience whose approval he could neither forgo nor accept, feelings of enough ambivalence to be embarrassing: "I hesitate to say these things, but it is not because of the subject—I care not how obscene my *words* are— but because I cannot speak of them without betraying my impurity" (p. 221). As another episode dramatizing the return of the repressed in nineteenth-century literature the puns would then embody a mild obsessiveness like the covert and claustrophobic sexual allegory in Melville's "The Tartarus of Maids" or the tired jocularity of Twain's long-suppressed scatological sketch *1601*.

But Thoreau's excremental wordplay is primarily neither evasive nor subversive. It is in the radical sense *elusive*. As he himself hinted, "You will pardon some obscurities, for there are more secrets in my trade than most men's, and yet not voluntarily kept, but inseparable from its very nature" (p. 17). *Walden* wages war against "the brain-rot, which prevails so . . . widely and fatally," by teasing us with obscurity while inviting us to fathom verbal and conceptual riddles (p. 325). Making them obvious would leave our minds unexercised. Hence the book relies heavily on paradox and covert wordplay. The unnoticed puns demonstrate that it is not Thoreau but his readers who duck the realities of life and death. And this defective sensibility underlying our "lives of quiet desperation" Thoreau, drawing on Trench's etymological discussion of *amusement,* would relate directly to our stunted capacity for real fun. "A stereotyped but unconscious despair is concealed even under what are called the games and amusements of mankind," he insists. "There is no play in them, for this comes after work"—as the *play* in a rope comes from its *working.*[31]

If a major theme of *Walden* is our need for rebirth, its natural corollary is the importance of genuine *re-creation.* "The child plays continually, if you will let it, and all its life is a sort of practical humor of a very pure kind, often of so fine and ethereal a nature, that its parents, its uncles and cousins, can in no wise participate in it, but must stand aloof in silent admiration, and reverence even" (*Essays,* p. 237). Although few townsmen reverenced Thoreau for it, he could nonetheless insist, "I can see nothing so proper as unrelaxed play and frolic in this bower God has built for us" (29 Dec. 1841). The best portal to true wisdom is "childlike mirthfulness," he felt. "If you would know aught, be gay before it" (23 June 1840).

Not *obsessive* but fundamentally liberating, his wordplay is just that, *play,* the stylistic expression of a spirit that learned to cope with its isolation by imitating (albeit mainly in the medium of language) that supremely contented hawk who appears soaring over the marsh at the end of *Walden.* "Sporting there alone" in a gay war with gravity, it keeps feigning descent to the swamp with a "free and beautiful fall," accompanying all its feints with a "strange chuckle" (pp. 316-17). That Thoreau experienced this grand epiphany while standing uncertainly on "quaking" boggy ground watching a male marsh hawk play with itself, reinforces the symbolic structure of the book. His more morbid puns reflect the playful Demiurge in the railroad cut, who, while "sporting on the bank," could sacrifice myriads of "tender organizations" to be "serenely squashed out of existence like pulp" (pp. 306, 318).

First and foremost a reflection of his temperament, Thoreau's philosophy of play is also a pastiche of various thinkers, like Trench, whom he absorbed into the final version of *Walden.* One Hindu myth assumes that nothing could motivate an all-sufficient divinity to create the world—except sport. The same notion lurks in such Hebrew texts as Psalms 104:27, which may be translated, "There is that Leviathan, which you have made for the sport of it." Jonathan Edwards brought American Puritanism to the verge of such a conclusion. Significantly, when Thoreau coyly alludes to the Deity as "an old settler and original proprietor, who is reported to have dug Walden Pond," he calls him a "humorous friend" and stresses the "social mirth" of his occasional visits (p. 137). His conception of God is not unlike the myth of Vishnu playing hide-and-seek with himself by entering into the roles of his creatures. The concept of life as a game was also stressed by Victor Cousin, whose *History of Philosophy* Thoreau read in the Harvard Library. With his dilute

Hegelianism, Cousin, who enjoyed a considerable vogue in Transcendental circles, was given to pronouncements like "History is a game in which all are losers, except humanity: which gains by all,—by the discomfiture of one, as by the victory of another."[32] Like Schiller's seminal concept of the *Spieltrieb*, Friedrich Schlegel's version of Fichtean idealism put the same metaphor to aesthetic purposes in stressing that "all holy plays of art are only distant imitations of the infinite play of the world, of the eternally self-creating work of art."[33]

In America Emerson and Bushnell followed suit. "We love to see life in its feeling and activity, separated from its labors and historic results," Bushnell had declaimed in his Harvard Phi Beta Kappa oration. "Could we see all human changes transpire poetically or creatively, that is, in play, letting our soul play with them as they pass, then it were only poetry to live. Then to admire, love, laugh,—then to abhor, pity, weep,—all alike were grateful to us" (*Work and Play,* p. 22). It is this sense of experiencing life as detached drama that Thoreau elaborates in "Solitude" when he puns about "being beside ourselves in a sane sense" with thinking. Such wordplay enacts stylistically "that certain doubleness by which I can stand as remote from myself as from another," so that "when the play, it may be the tragedy of life is over, the spectator goes his way." As the theatrical metaphor that underpins this famous passage encapsulates the stance of the Romantic ironist, so the paragraphs that wryly celebrate his own erasure by the flowing sand are *Walden*'s most sustained and ambitious attempt at ironic self-transcendence. The last two chapters of the book use the first-person pronoun only half as often as the opening chapters.[34] The sandbank highlights the collapse of personal identity by letting Thoreau imagine his own death as if he were indeed "Indra in the sky looking down on it" (p. 135).

Like Schlegel's Abounding Fullness, the sandbank collapses normally opposed categories.[35] Solid yet fluid, natural yet social, lethal yet vital, by turns masculine, feminine, and neuter, the sand foliage seems "truly *grotesque*"—an unsettling game of Twenty Questions where the riddle can scarcely be defined as animal, vegetable, or mineral. The passage draws on Oken's ideas about the mutation of plants into animals.[36] Ordure undoes order, yet there are hints of a fourth category: spiritual. While playful philology suggests an original language of nature, a form beneath the flux, the clash of primary categories here (like clashing meanings in puns and clashing genres throughout the book as a whole) dramatizes our distortion in wresting from the flow of experience the stable percepts fixed and polarized by words. What we take to be things are revealed as events. In describing the sandbank, Thoreau juggles science, humor, the macabre, and the visionary so nimbly that genres blur, and the sportive author towers triumphantly above his self-destructive verbal recreation.

But we cannot fully understand the significance of play for Thoreau without some familiarity with the book that he acknowledged as an artistic precursor of *Walden,* James John Garth Wilkinson's *The Human Body and Its Connection with Man, Illustrated by the Principal Organs* (Philadelphia: Lippincott, 1851). Although Thoreau declared while revising *Walden* that "Wilkinson's book to some extent realizes what I have dreamed of," its importance as an influence on his thought has been neglected. The author of this odd volume, dedicated to Henry James Sr., was extolled by Emerson as a philosopher whose discourses "throw all the contemporary philosophy of England into the shade." He "has brought to metaphysics and to physiology a native vigor, with a catholic perception of relations, equal to the highest attempts, and a rhetoric like the armory of the invincible knights old."37 Henry James Jr. was to find him too metaphysical a physician, but to Thoreau Wilkinson represented at last "a *home* for the imagination" (5 Sept. 1851).

The Human Body is a Swedenborgian homeopath's effort to draw moral and spiritual analogies from a popular but fairly detailed account of human anatomy. Wilkinson's philosophic aims are paramount, however, so one may leaf through over four hundred pages without becoming aware that the human body possesses a reproductive system. Dividing the body into five spheres—brain, lungs, digestive organs, heart, and skin— he pays nominal tribute to the brain as the apex of human development, but his most ardent affection is reserved for the lungs. "The secret of the brains is the open lesson of the lungs," he avers. "The brains give us the free principles of life, and the lungs, its free play in nature. It is this *idea* of *the play of life* which is the principal point in our just knowledge of the lungs" (p. 83).

Throughout the book "the doctrine we are combating . . . belongs to the muscular department of truth, or that which has both ends closed, and is a solid body. Its spiritual correspondent is 'earnestness,' spasmodic vigor, upon which so many and such famous men rely for the salvation of the time" (p. 54). In this proto-Arnoldian polemic the lungs become the embodiment of Wilkinson's central human values, with an importance like that Descartes attached to the pineal gland. They control "inspiration, or the drawing in of the breath" (p. 86). "The use of breathing is to communicate motion to the body" (p. 98). All "life is spiritual motion," so in their elastic expansion and contraction the lungs are the chief repository of the vital principle. Overeating is dangerous because it "is a tyrant against motion. It impedes the play, not only of the lungs, but of the other members" (pp. 106-8).

According to Wilkinson, the lungs "introduce . . . transcendent representation, and the moral virtues that inhabit this order of intelligence commune with the organs through their means. . . . They emancipate the mind from the stimulus of the passions" (p. 117). By exhaling carbonic acid they dispose of the "excrements of the blood," which may receive injuries from "the passions of the mind" (pp. 88-90). Elaborations of the midcentury medical lore surrounding tuberculosis, these doctrines remain among the murkier tenets of Wilkinson's physiology. But in general we may say that emotion occupies no very high place in his scheme of things. Like Thoreau, he particularly connects feeling with the bowels. "The piteous and sentimental . . . act upon our intestine tenderness," he explains, and "women especially have such experiences" (pp. 233, 226). Not that the intestinal tube is without value: "It stands at the bottom, or it could not have the poor and needy for its objects" (p. 227). Nonetheless, we may feel that the quality of mercy is somewhat strained by the rectum. It is difficult to escape his implication that most passions, emotions, and feelings are better eliminated, according to what he terms "the prime law of excrementitious rejection." This fertile theme needs another volume to exhibit "its rationale in our Saviour's casting out of the devils" (p. 154). On a higher level, the lungs apparently perform this function for the heart, an inferior organ that is insulated from "the immediate play of the mind" (pp. 173-74).

As Thoreau was quick to note, Wilkinson firmly believed that "it is good to look to the ordinary language of mankind, not only for the attestation of natural truths, but for their suggestion." The primary role of the lungs is confirmed by the fact that "most of the words expressive of life, are borrowed by analogy, either from the atmosphere, or its organ the lungs." He notes that the words *animal* and *animation,* the Latin *anima,* soul, and *animus,* mind, all derive etymologically from a root meaning *breath;* likewise, our *inspirations* and *aspirations* have made us *spirits,* ever since "the breath of life . . . was breathed into the nostrils of our first parents, and man became a living soul." He thus concludes that "life cannot be imaged save in words borrowed from the lungs and their august ministration." Particular importance attaches to the following linguistic fact: "The vulgar call the lungs *lights,* and so they are; for the belly gives us gravity and links us to the ground, but the lungs give us levity, and lift us towards the air" (pp. 126-28). Common speech thus attests to their peculiar role in purging the emotions and gaily fostering *the play of life.*

In *The Friend* Coleridge had echoed German idealism by calling "mythology the apex and complement of all genuine physiology."[38] Wilkinson's book encouraged Thoreau to develop a similar view: "The poet writes the history of his body" (29 Sept. 1851). During 1852 when he undertook his major revision of the manuscript that became *Walden,* he was pondering Wilkinson's ideas about the lungs. The Journal shows that his own uncertain health was also much on his mind. Comparison with the earlier versions suggests that most of the puns entered *Walden* at this time. As one might expect, they are an essentially reflexive product of the unusually long process of composition, expansion, and revision from which the book emerged. And on some level they represent Thoreau's therapy for the vital principle of levity imperiled in his failing lungs. Wordplay is an effort to help that faltering organ sustain *the play of life* in Wilkinsonian terms. Likewise, the trancelike states of mind that Thoreau cultivates in "Solitude" may have therapeutic significance, for, like Whiter, Wilkinson believed that "in these conditions of suspended animation the chemical laws do not persist, but like the rest are *suspended. . . .* The tissues, particles and fluids, and the wind in the lungs, are entranced; the body is absent from chemical corrosions" (p. 116).

Why was Thoreau not more explicit about these efforts at self-therapy? He journalizes constantly about his health without ever asking himself directly, "Do I have consumption?" But such defenses are common among consumptives. In Stendhal's *Armance* Madame de Malivert worries constantly about her son but carefully avoids mentioning the word *phthisis* lest it hasten his disease. Believing that "but for fear, death itself is an impossibility," Thoreau too had reason to avoid naming his dread (*W,* 6:408). He justified such denial aesthetically. Carlyle's tough and brawny humor embodied the vigor of an old Norse hero, Thoreau felt, but a grotesque and ailing one, for its obviousness and straining after effect only dramatized the difficulty of his conflict. In contrast, Thoreau formulated a prescription for triumphantly self-occluding wit. "The poet will maintain serenity in spite of all disappointments. He is expected to preserve an unconcerned and healthy outlook over the world, while he lives," he wrote. "For that other, *Oratoris est celare artem,* we might read *Herois est celare pugnam,*—the hero will conceal his struggles" (*Essays,* p. 249). And conceal them the deft words do. No wonder that sometimes this hero seemed to himself more like a spineless squid writhing hidden behind his own ink: "Like cuttlefish we conceal ourselves, we darken the element in which we move; we are not transparent" (24 Aug. 1852).

Puns flourished in the Nazi death camps, and compulsive punsters of the nineteenth century display similar configurations of feeling.

Like Hawthorne's Hester Prynne, Irving, Melville, and Dickinson all cultivated the humor of heartbreak that Emerson's essay "The Comic" and Coleridge's criticism incisively analyze. The wordplay of Oliver Wendell Holmes was a relief from the strains of medical practice. Like the jestbooks, he himself pointed the connection by defining the pun as verbicide and equating *man's laughter* with *manslaughter*. In the bleak fall of 1820 the same impulse moved the dying Keats, who reported that he "summoned up more puns, in a sort of desperation, in one week than in any year of my life."[39] The painful spasms of gout that confined James Russell Lowell intermittently to his bed also stimulated his propensity for wordplay, allowing him to explain in one pun-filled letter that the disease was so named because the sufferer could not *go out*.[40] The English master punster Thomas Hood, a self-diagnosed consumptive, wisecracked sardonically about himself that "no gentleman alive has written so much Comic and spitten so much blood."[41] Poe's knowing diagnosis of Hood's punning remains valid. Physical misfortune or infirmity is the staple theme of Hood's humor, suggesting to one modern critic "morbid self-involvement," and the coruscating wordplay seems to express obliquely "a terror of mortality, and in its very frequency an unhealthy fascination with sickness."[42] Freud found that his patients' wordplay usually revolved around some body part. Racked with diseases real and fancied, Nietzsche made Zarathustra pun indefatigably against his arch-foe, "the Spirit of gravity." Zarathustra's wordplay mirrors the ecstatic dance of life that he envisions: "Whoever climbs the highest mountains laughs at all tragic plays and tragic seriousness."[43] Yet the vitality of this stylistic habit is undercut by Nietzsche's conviction that "the characteristic of all *literary décadence* . . . is that life no longer resides in the whole. The word gets the upper hand and jumps out of the sentence."[44]

As Eric Bentley has suggested, many Heroic Vitalists like Nietzsche were weak or sickly authors reacting against their own pronounced physical malaise. Decadence haunted them from within. Thus Carlyle compensated for his dyspeptic impotence by juggling words humorously while dreaming of heroes like Frederick the Great who had "strength . . . to wrestle with the mud-elements."[45] Less a creed than a faith rooted in despair, no two exemplars of Heroic Vitalism represent exactly the same complex of attitudes. But we can point to certain characteristics that recur often in such mud-wrestling hero-worshipers as Carlyle and Nietzsche, Wagner and Spengler, Lawrence and Shaw, Stefan George and Yeats.

Estranged from his lower-class or petty bourgeois origins, the Heroic Vitalist feels divided against himself, a fact that he sometimes elaborates into a doctrine of double personality. This split is augmented by an apparent dichotomy in his perceived world. He hungers to embrace the universe in its totality but would rather accept its differences than sacrifice any for metaphysical unity. Balked of a conventional religious belief, he borrows orthodox tropes and tries to elaborate a new mythology from evolutionary nature. The abstract pieties of an egalitarian and commercially minded liberalism, passionless except for its greedy fear of all genuine excellence, strike him not only as contemptible but as historically and psychologically naive. Instead, he cultivates an aristocratic radicalism. Facing up to the concrete realities of the body and brute fact, he learns almost to relish their tyranny. He is something of a misogynist, and his watchword remains courage rather than compassion. Though revering men of action, he views history and politics fundamentally as aesthetic performances. His sense of time is cyclical in the extreme. Obsessed with diurnal and seasonal metaphors, the Heroic Vitalist worships the sun, hails the twilight of the gods as prophesying a new dawn in human affairs, and yearns to be reborn in the spring like a phoenix. Often such rebirth is spasmodic, so evolution seems saltatory rather than regular. Sometimes this temporal flux is too much and he longs for escape, either by moments of mystic insight into eternity or by recourse to some jerry-built doctrine of immortality.

In the pragmatism of William James many positive features of Heroic Vitalism are fused with democratic ideology, and much the same may be said for Thoreau. But if the prophet of "Civil Disobedience" appears mainly to have influenced Tolstoy, Gandhi, and Martin Luther King in the twentieth century, similar premises made many Heroic Vitalists especially congenial to fascists. Joel Porte has justly noted some features that align Thoreau's aestheticism with that of Walter Pater, and perhaps it behooves us to pay more attention to a strain of decadence in Thoreau. "Is not Art itself a gall?" he inquired, while cherishing the lovely disease nonetheless (4 Sept. 1854). If he finally preferred the art of life to the life of art, he did so as a Yankee Doodle Dandy, the Poe of New England, a provincial American anticipation of such figures as Stevenson and Wilde, Flaubert and Huysman. As Emerson wisely observed in his obituary tribute, though Thoreau scoffed at conventional elegance, "he had many elegancies of his own."[46] While at times Emerson's young friend reminded him of the Aristotelian superman, in other contexts he shrewdly noted an odd resemblance to Beau Brummel. Fastidiously cultivating his senses, Thoreau could not abide the grit of gravel beneath his feet when walking. On evening strolls his nostrils picked up the odor of every dwelling house, each tainting the night air like an abattoir. The flowers of evil that Baudelaire plucked from Parisian bordellos Thoreau found growing in Concord's swamps. The fungus known as Devil's Phallus was only one of many decadent growths that fascinated him. Poison dogwood was "beautiful as satan" (21 Dec. 1851). Wading in bogholes to contemplate its lurid berries, Thoreau could feel a "certain excitement" like the Baudelairean *frisson* of evil, the aesthete's ultimate sensation (6 Jan. 1858). The pond lily became his central emblem of ethereal loveliness rooted in muck. Yet from another angle this icon of triumphant purity appears curiously like the Divine Artist's floral portrait of Dorian Gray.

This connoisseur of katydids possessed a side that his own legend has obscured. Too many Americans base their view of the man on such saccharine mass-culture treatments as Jerome Lawrence's popular play *The Night Thoreau Spent in Jail* (1971). Burnishing the legend so artfully created by Thoreau fills the coffers of the Sierra Club and yields a new coffee-table book every other year. But in making Thoreau into the prophet required by environmentalists and adolescents, hagiography and political partisanship have done him a disservice. By ignoring his weaknesses we do violence to what is strongest in the man, forgetting what he himself finely said: "Every judgment and action of a man qualifies every other, i.e., corrects our estimate of every other. . . . For in this sense a man is awfully consistent, above his own consciousness. All a man's strength and all a man's weakness go to make up the authority of any particular opinion which he may utter. He is strong and weak with all his strength and weakness combined. If he is your friend, you may have to consider that he loves you, but perchance he also loves gingerbread" (16 Feb. 1854).

How, then, shall we consider the gingerbread architecture of our friend's wordplay? If he is consumptive, alas, we must remember that during the nineteenth-century epidemic terminal stages of the disease were widely believed to promote *spes phthisica* or hectic gaiety. So far no neurological mechanism has been discovered to explain this venerable tradition, and it may be no more than a medical myth. But modern medicine has not absolutely ruled out the possibility that toxins released by the tubercle bacillus might in some cases trigger auto-intoxication capable of affecting those frontal-lobe centers of the brain implicated in punning. Defensive jocularity has been observed in many twentieth-century tuberculosis patients, while brain tumors, manic-depressive disorder, schizophrenia, and Tourette's syndrome can all trigger diseased wordplay.⁴⁷ More than willful denial of illness might just conceivably be at stake in this symptom. Whether or not Thoreau's puns were biologically grounded, readers should at least weigh the resemblance between this stylistic mannerism and a pathological tic.

Dying comes easiest to those with identities defined largely through membership in extended families, communal tribes, religious groups, or military organizations. It is normally hardest for people like Thoreau whose cultures let them develop a highly idiosyncratic sense of self. One of the most appealing aspects of his legend is the equanimity with which this arch-individualist strove to meet death. Cheerful to the last, he said he found the future "just as uninteresting as ever." He turned aside further questions with the remark, "One world at a time." Asked if he had made his peace with God, he quipped, "I did not know we had ever quarreled" (*Days,* pp. 456–65). On his deathbed he revised for publication the last lecture he ever gave. He had composed "Autumnal Tints" three years earlier during the final illness of his septuagenarian father, whose funeral postponed its first delivery. Now as he readied manuscripts for posthumous appearance in the *Atlantic,* he "rubbed out the more humorous part of those articles," telling Channing, "I cannot bear the levity I find."⁴⁸ The joke now came closer to home, and dying in one's forties seemed less funny.

Channing urged him to spare some humor, and enough puns remain to distinguish this essay from conventionally funereal treatments of the season like Poe's "Ulalume." Without quite being manic or morbid, it is a high-spirited meditation on dying in the guise of a nature essay celebrating the peculiarly American splendor of fall foliage. Viewing leaves as vital organs, Oken and other naturalists pressed the human analogy, explaining that annually every plant becomes "clothed with a beautiful foliage of lungs (every leaf being a distinct lung in itself) for the respiration of the rising brood."⁴⁹ But though *Walden* often suggests that beauty is functional and presupposes usefulness, "Autumnal Tints" forthrightly adopts a fin-de-siècle aesthete's stance in arguing that nature "keeps use and beauty distinct." The charm of these vegetable lungs lies precisely in their decadence. Ripe harvest fruits are destined "to a rather ignoble end" dictated by our appetites, whereas useless leaves "on an infinitely grander scale . . . address our taste for beauty alone."

Acquiring a bright tint just before it falls, every ripe fruit "commences a more independent and individual existence, requiring less nourishment . . . and that not so much from the earth through its stem as from the sun and air," declares Thoreau (*W,* 5:250–51). Airy levity makes his treatment of dying sunny. "What is the late greenness of the English Elm, like a cucumber out of season, which does not know when to have done, compared with the early and golden maturity of the American tree?" High colors bespeak "exuberance of spirits." The early demise of the red maple, *acer rubrum*, is nothing to regret, for "we may now read its title, or *rubric*, clear. Its *virtues*, not its sins, are as scarlet" (*W*, 5:261-63; Latin *acer = maple/clear*). Red vegetation "speaks to our blood." August pokeweed bespeaks "a successful life concluded by a death not premature, which is an ornament to Nature. What if we were to mature as perfectly, root and branch, glowing in the midst of our decay!"

He contemplated a book of leaf paintings illustrating all the brightest hues of fall foliage so that "you would only need to turn over its leaves to take a ramble through the autumn woods whenever you pleased" (*W*, 5:251-55). Instead of calling colors after foreign ores and oxides that few Americans ever see, like Naples yellow or raw Sienna, better to name them after our own landscapes. "Have we not an *earth* under our feet,—ay, and a sky over our heads? Or is the last *all* ultramarine?" The topmost leaves of scarlet oaks especially struck him. "Lifted higher and higher, and sublimated more and more, putting off some earthiness and cultivating more intimacy with the light each year, they have at length the least possible amount of earthy matter, and the greatest spread and grasp of skyey influences. There they dance, arm in arm with the light,— tripping it on fantastic points. . . . So intimately mingled are they with it, that . . . you can hardly tell at last what in the dance is leaf and what is light" (*W*, 5:274-79).

So too in his own dancing words we can hardly tell what is life and what is death. Their levity makes light of the world. Tracing the contours of foliage, "the eye rests with equal delight on what is not leaf and what is leaf," so perhaps a trained eye can take pleasure in what is lief and what is not lief (*W*, 5:279). Light and frisky, leaves "merrily . . . go scampering over the earth," seeking their graves so beautifully and contentedly that "they teach us how to die. One wonders if the time will ever come when men, with their boasted faith in immortality, will lie down as gracefully and as ripe,—with such an Indian-summer serenity will shed their bodies, as they do their hair and nails." Fall makes the world "a cemetery pleasant to walk in," with "no lying or vain epitaphs," for "this is the beautiful way in which Nature gets her muck." "Though you own no lot at Mount Auburn," here on earth "your lot is surely cast somewhere" (*W*, 5:269-70). Autumn trees are burning bushes we should turn aside to behold, for "if such a phenomenon occurred but once, it would be handed down by tradition to posterity, and get into the mythology at last" (*W*, 5:259).

Because of "the joy and exhilaration which these colored leaves excite," fall foliage suggests a holiday, for nature "holds her annual fair in October." Like a happy harvest festival celebrating all souls' liberation, "man's spirits should rise as high as Nature's . . . and the routine of his life be interrupted by an analogous expression of joy and hilarity" (W, 5:274-75). Although our Halloween was hardly celebrated in his era, that modern American holiday, climaxing an October when ritualized viewing of fall foliage is now encouraged, catches some of the spirit of Thoreau's essay. "The word 'ripe' is . . . derived from the verb 'to reap'," he had noted correctly, so celebration of harvest tends to mock the Grim Reaper (12 Nov. 1858). Like grimacing jack-o'-lanterns, his essay's silly puns embody the ambivalence about dying that lurks in our word *silly*, which formerly meant both *pitiable* and *blessed*. It stems from the same Indo-European root as do our words *hilarity* and *consolation*.

How, then, shall we consider Thoreau's wordplay? Not just an American's attempt to nationalize the language, not just an individual's attempt to transcend collective language, not just an invalid's attempt to flee from life to language—though all these interpretations ring true. "Talk about reading!—a good reader!" he exclaimed. "It takes two at least for this game, as for love, and they must cooperate" (5 Mar. 1859). The punster is the man who described his "peculiar love" for Ellen Sewall as a form of "sober play," teasing his meager feelings out into sentimental verse—the same man who journalized apropos of Mary Russell, "It is not easy to find one brave enough to play the game of love."[50] But the frustrated dandy who yearned for "a better opportunity to play life" (26 Oct. 1855) also wrote in his great book that we "should not *play* life, or *study* it merely, while the community supports . . . this expensive game, but earnestly *live* it from beginning to end" (p. 37).

In a seminal passage Plato punningly endorses a complex interplay between gaiety and seriousness that illuminates Thoreau's stance.

> I say that a man must be serious with the serious. God alone is worthy of supreme seriousness, but man is made God's plaything, and that is the best part of him. Therefore every man and woman should live life accordingly, and play the noblest games and be of another mind from what they are at present. . . . For they deem war a serious thing, though in war there is neither play nor culture worthy the name [*out' oun paidia . . . out' au paideia*], which are the things *we* deem most serious. Hence all must live in peace as well as they possibly can. What, then, is the right way of living? Life must be lived as play, playing certain games, making sacrifices, singing and dancing, and then a man will be able to propitiate the gods, and defend himself against his enemies, and win in the contest.[51]

Yeats, like Thoreau, began as an aesthete. His poem "Lapis Lazuli" stems like *Walden* from a concern for the heroic individual, for the artifact of a shaped self, and for the value of art as ritual. The old Chinamen it describes, who stare with Oriental delight "on all the tragic scene," might serve as a symbol of the identity that Thoreau strove to forge for himself through wordplay. His scatological jokes are the quintessential embodiment in style of a life lived at its best and worst moments (though not always) as a heroic game, in Yeats's intense conviction that "Hamlet and Lear are gay, / Gaiety transfiguring all that dread."[52] To a degree paralleled in English only by Shakespeare, Milton, and Joyce, he made the pun a vehicle for literary genius. What informs his approach to life, as Oriard suggests, is a Transcendental ethic of sober play. Bridging the gaps in a polarized universe, that ironic stance allowed Thoreau to go huckleberrying and Bunburying intensely while proclaiming the importance of being earnest about the art of living as well as the art of dying.

Concluding Unscientific Postscript

Like Ishmael and the pale usher of *Moby-Dick,* many antebellum grammarians and their pupils were aware that their efforts to classify linguistic chaos might seem laughable. Romantic irony was a natural outgrowth of Romantic philology. Wandering in a wilderness of words haunted by correspondences but governed by laws that resisted codification could breed jocular mistrust of language and book-learning. With puns people used what they picked up in school for a folksy critique of pure reason. Like the mock-heroic forms dear to the Enlightenment, Romantic literary wordplay genuflects toward the authority of the classroom while subversively undermining it.

Satirists have always favored scatology. Thoreau's dirty jokes laugh at facts of life that polite speech will not name. And for all our taboos against excrement, the fact of life that triggers perhaps the most euphemism is death. Is it coincidence that scatology tinges the work of Berkeley, Tooke, Whiter, and Carlyle, provides food for thought to Emerson and Whitman, surfaces jocularly in Irving, Poe, Melville, and Dickinson? The moon of idealism has its dark side, and the philosophical idealist often worries lest it moon him. Tuberculosis was the dark side for Thoreau. Like Whitman's, his family was diseased. Family pathology marks the lives of other Romantics. Like Coleridge and Byron, several major American punsters may have suffered from manic-depressive mood disorders—notably Lowell, Twain, Poe, Melville, and Dickinson.[53]

If personal instability powered the humor of some punsters, social and political instability helps explain the American vogue of etymology.

The upheavals of Jacksonian democracy, the westward drift of the popu-lace, the sectional and constitutional debates prefacing the Civil War all bred uneasiness. "We hear much, in political life, of recurrence to first principles," noted George P. Marsh, author of *Lectures on the English Language* (1860). "With equal truth, and greater sincerity, we may say that, in language and in literature, nothing can save us from ceaseless revolution but a frequent recourse to the primitive authorities." As civil war loomed, he urged the historical study of language as "the strongest bond of union in a homogeneous people, the surest holding ground against the shifting currents . . . of opinion and taste." Etymological researches seemed admirably calculated to counterbalance a prevailing "rootlessness" bred by "French principles of philosophy." He recom-mended "the *conservatism* of such studies" with self-conscious aware-ness of the radical meaning of that term "abused both by those who rally under it as a watchword of party and by those to whom it is a token of offense."[54]

Like the European philological sages reacting against Enlightenment skepticism, Thoreau and his fellow American Romantics were surpris-ingly conservative at heart. More often than not their ambiguous oracu-lar stances sought to conserve health, conserve sanity, conserve sanctity, conserve national unity. With Romantic irony our transcendental pun-sters tried to transcend antinomies that threatened to tear them and their country apart. Were they alive today to witness the partisan dogmatism with which literary academia invokes their names, few, one suspects, would be entirely pleased. But the spectacle would no doubt amuse them as hugely as did the pretensions of antebellum pedagogues.

Notes

Preface

1. *Times and Seasons,* 4 (15 May 1843), in Fawn M. Brodie, *No Man Knows My History: The Life of Joseph Smith the Mormon Prophet* (New York: Knopf, 1945), p. 276.

2. *The Cambridge Encyclopedia of Language,* ed. David Crystal (New York: Cambridge University Press, 1987), pp. 63–64.

3. See Stuart Sim, "Deconstructing the Pun," *British Journal of Aesthetics* 27 (1987): 326–34. For a less academic approach to punning, recent issues of the International Save the Pun Foundation's newsletter, *The Pundit,* may be consulted at their website, <HTTP://WWW.PUNPUNPUN.COM> (5 Nov. 1999).

Chapter 1

1. Noah Webster, *American Spelling Book,* ed. Henry Steele Commager, Classics in Education No. 17 (New York: Columbia University Teachers College, 1962), p. 11.

2. In Benjamin T. Spencer, *The Quest for Nationality: An American Literary Campaign* (Syracuse, N.Y.: Syracuse University Press, 1957), p. 184; cf. pp. 90–91, 150.

3. Walter Channing, "Essay on American Language and Literature," in *The American Literary Revolution, 1783–1837,* ed. Robert E. Spiller (Garden City, N.Y.: Doubleday, 1967), p. 113.

4. James Ruggles, *A Universal Language, Formed on Philosophical and Analogical Principles* (Cincinnati: M'Calla, 1829), pp. viii–ix.

5. On this classification of universal languages, see Albert Leon Guérard, *A Short History of the International Language Movement* (New York: Boni and Liveright, 1921), and Petr Evstaf'evic Stojan, *Bibliografio de Internacia Lingvo Kun bibliografia aldono de Reinhard Haupenthal* (Hildesheim: Georg Olms Verlag, 1973).

6. In Denis E. Baron, *Grammar and Good Taste: Reforming the American Language* (New Haven: Yale University Press, 1982), p. 19.

7. Edward Eggleston, *The Hoosier School-Master* (New York: Orange, 1871), pp. 24–25.

8. *The American Spelling Book, Containing the Rudiments of the English Language* (Brattleboro, Vt.: Holbrook, 1821), p. v.

9. Noah Webster, *The Elementary Spelling Book, Being an Improvement on the American Spelling Book* (1829; Montpelier, Vt.: Walton, 1839), p. 7.

10. Walt Whitman, *An American Primer*, ed. Horace Traubel (Boston: Small, 1904), pp. 13–14; hereafter *Pr.*

11. See esp. Walter J. Ong, S.J., "Latin Language Study as a Renaissance Puberty Rite," *SP* 56 (1959): 103–24.

12. In Ervin C. Shoemaker, *Noah Webster: Pioneer of Learning* (New York: Columbia University Press, 1936), p. 106.

13. "The Artful Devices," in Eric Partridge, *Comic Alphabets: Their Origin, Development, Nature* (London: Routledge, 1961), p. 50. For another American example, see [Edwin M. Snow], *The Comic English Grammar: A New and Facetious Introduction to the English Tongue* (New York: Wilson, 1845), pp. 10-11.

14. In Joseph H. Friend, *The Development of American Lexicography, 1798-1864* (The Hague: Mouton, 1967), pp. 85, 93.

15. James Russell Lowell, *Atlantic Monthly* 4 (1860): 633-34.

16. In David Simpson, *The Politics of American English, 1776-1850* (New York: Oxford University Press, 1986), p. 173.

17. "Introduction," in Eva May Burkett, *American Dictionaries of the English Language before 1861* (Metuchen, N.J.: Scarecrow Press, 1979), p. 96.

18. *First and Last Journeys of Thoreau*, ed. Franklin Benjamin Sanborn (Boston: Bibliophile Society, 1905), p. 81.

19. William Brotherhead, "New Americanisms," *AN&Q* 1 (Jan. 1, 1857): 75, in Michael G. Crowell, "John Russell Bartlett's *Dictionary of Americanisms*," *AQ* 24 (1972): 237.

20. *Paul Pry*, 25 April 1840, in Allen Walker Read, "The First Stage in the History of 'O.K.,'" *American Speech* 38 (February 1965): 24.

21. In Read, "First Stage," p. 11.

22. Ibid., pp. 22-23.

23. B. J. Whiting, "American Wellerisms of the Golden Age," *American Speech* 20 (1945): 4; see p. 8 for the specimen from *Yankee Notions* 1 (1852): 71.

24. In C. Grant Loomis, "Traditional American Wordplay: The Conundrum," *Western Folklore* 8 (1949): 245.

25. In Walter Blair and Hamlin Hill, *America's Humor* (New York: Oxford University Press, 1978), pp. 160-61, and see further pp. 276-91.

26. Willis Gaylord Clark, *Literary Remains,* ed. Lewis Gaylord Clark (New York: Burgess, Stringer, 1844), pp. 34-36.

27. *Life and Letters of Thomas Gold Appleton,* ed. Susan Hale (New York: Appleton, 1885), p. 58.

28. T. G. Appleton, *A Sheaf of Papers* (Boston: Roberts, 1874), pp. 37-38.

29. "The Ponder-Book of a Bachelor of Arts," *New York Literary Gazette and Phi Beta Kappa Repository* 1 (13 Feb. 1826): 329-30.

30. B. P. Shillaber, *Life and Sayings of Mrs. Partington* (New York: Derby & Jackson, 1860), p. 203.

31. Lewis Gaylord Clark, *Knick-Knacks from an Editor's Table* (New York: Appleton, 1852), pp. 77-78.

32. In Read, "First Stage," p. 26.

33. Mortimer Thompson, *Doesticks What He Says* (New York: Livermore, 1855), p. 18.

34. Oliver Wendell Holmes, *The Autocrat of the Breakfast Table* (1858; Boston: Houghton Mifflin, 1891), p. 11.

35. George Prentice, *Prenticeana; or Wit and Humor in Paragraphs* (New York: Derby & Jackson, 1860), p. 32.

36. In John James Piatt, ed., "Biographical Sketch," *Poems of George D. Prentice,* 5th ed. (Cincinnati: Clarke, 1887), p. xx.

37. Mary Scrugham, "George D. Prentice," *Register of the Kentucky State Historical Society* 13 (Sept. 1915): 21.

38. Charles G. Shanks, "George D. Prentice," *Lippincott's Magazine* 4 (Nov. 1869): 555.

39. *Dr. Valentine and Yankee Hill's Metamorphosis* (New York: Burgess, 1850), n.p.

40. Henry James, *Hawthorne* (London: Macmillan, 1879), pp. 43-44.

41. T. G. Appleton, *Checquer-Work* (Boston: Roberts, 1879), p. 211.

42. "The Comic" (1843), in *Complete Works of Ralph Waldo Emerson,* ed. Edward Waldo Emerson (Boston: Houghton Mifflin, 1904), 8: 157-74, 395-96n.

43. E. P. Whipple, "Wit and Humor" (1845), in *Lectures on . . . Literature and Life* (1849; Boston: Houghton Mifflin, 1899), p. 119.

44. In *Lowell: Essays, Poems and Letters,* ed. William Smith Clark II (New York: Odyssey, 1948), p. xxviii.

45. J. H. Anderson, ed., *The Brains of Boston . . . at Tremont Temple . . . Oct. 11, 1861* (Boston: Redding, 1861), p. 5.

46. Julia Ward Howe, *Reminiscences, 1819-1899* (Boston: Houghton Mifflin, 1899), pp. 270-71.

47. *Lincoln Talks: A Biography in Anecdote,* ed. Emanuel Hertz (New York: Viking, 1939), p. 224.

48. *The Story-Life of Lincoln,* ed. Wayne Whipple (Philadelphia: Winston, 1908), p. 482.

Chapter 2

1. *Walden,* pp. 244-45. On Thoreau's pervasive etymological wordplay, see esp. David Skwire, "A Check List of Wordplays in *Walden,*" *AL* 31 (1959): 282-89; Joseph Moldenhauer, "The Rhetoric of *Walden*" (Ph.D. diss., Columbia University, 1967); Donald Ross Jr., "Verbal Wit and *Walden,*" *ATQ* 11 (1971): 38-44; and Kevin J. Dettmar, "Ransacking the Root Cellar: The Appeal to/of Etymology in *Walden,*" *Strategies: A Journal of Theory, Criticism, and Politics* 1 (1988): 182-201. Tabulating wordplay is complicated by the difficulty of defining it adequately; see Walter Redfern, *Puns* (Oxford: Blackwell, 1984), p. 5. Moldenhauer's ambitious list of ca. four hundred instances, for example, misses a number that I would argue for, contains others that strike me as dubious, and includes a good many that seem borderline or unremarkable. Since myriads of words involve a root that differs significantly from a derived meaning, deciding just when Thoreau was aware of this fact—and wished to call the reader's attention to it—is not easy, especially when his wordplay becomes less a rhetorical device than a private game. Any list that tries to be comprehensive (like Moldenhauer, I have drafted my own checklist for *Walden* but have grown discontented with it) almost inevitably shades over, by imperceptible degrees, into implausible, unintentional, or insignificant wordplay. If the reader is often left in a quandary whether a pun was intended, that was one unsettling aim of Thoreau's style: thus in this pasage one must wonder inconclusively whether he jibes at table talk by implying that it is "only the parable of a dinner, commonly"—only the discourse of somebody making a din. Like other Romantics he was quite aware, *pace* Dettmar, that puns and etymology can tug in different directions. Granted the inadequacy of all pun taxonomies, Ross's article is useful

in stressing Thoreau's relative lack of interest in the homophonic punning that delighted Lamb; but even that generalization is risky insofar as Ross ignores such apparent examples as *Coenobites/see-no-bites, wrapped/rapt,* etc.

2. E. P. Whipple, "The Use and Misuse of Words," *North American Review* 79 (1854): 144.

3. John Locke, *An Essay Concerning Human Understanding,* ed. Alexander Campbell Fraser (1894; rpt. New York: Dover, 1959), III.i.5.

4. *Alciphron,* VII.5, in *Works of George Berkeley,* ed. A. A. Luce and T. E. Jessop (1948; rpt. London: Nelson, 1964). Berkeley's works are cited from this edition.

5. See esp. Nina Baym, "Thoreau's View of Science," *JHI* 26 (1965): 221–34. As a senior in college Thoreau studied philosophy under Francis Bowen, who was soon to publish *Berkeley and His Philosophy* (1838), so Thoreau probably read Berkeley as a required text in Bowen's course focused on Locke and his critics; see Kenneth Walter Cameron, *Thoreau's Harvard Years* (Hartford: Transcendental Books, 1966), p. 17.

6. See Ernst Cassirer, *The Philosophy of Symbolic Forms,* trans. Ralph Manheim (New Haven: Yale University Press, 1953), 1:139, on whom I draw heavily here. In emphasizing Berkeley's excremental preoccupations my interpretation of the *Siris* also owes much to John Oulton Wisdom, *The Unconscious Origin of Berkeley's Philosophy* (London: Hogarth, 1953).

7. Hugh Blair, *Lectures on Rhetoric and Belles Lettres,* ed. Harold F. Harding (Carbondale: Southern Illinois University Press, 1965), p. 102n. Harvard Library records show Thoreau definitely reading other works by De Brosses in his senior year; see Kenneth Walter Cameron, *Emerson the Essayist* (1945; Hartford: Transcendental Books, 1972), 2:200.

8. Pierpont Morgan MS MA.594, reprinted in *The Transcendentalists and Minerva,* ed. Kenneth Walter Cameron (Hartford: Transcendental Books, 1958), 1:165–66. For more on this subject see my "Thoreau and the Language Theories of the French Enlightenment," *ELH* 51 (1984): 747–70.

9. *Walden,* p. 19. On Thoreau's punning with this word, see Richard Poirier, *A World Elsewhere: The Place of Style in American Literature* (New York: Oxford University Press, 1966), pp. 85–88.

10. *Diversions of Purley* (London: Tegg, 1857), p. 14.

11. In Hans Aarsleff, *The Study of Language in England, 1780–1860* (Princeton: Princeton University Press, 1967), p. 171.

12. W. Hamilton Reid, as reprinted in *Analectic Magazine* 1 (Feb. 1813): 99–104.

13. *Elements,* III.11.3, in *Collected Works of Dugald Stewart Esq.,* ed. Sir William Hamilton (1854–60; facs. rpt. Farnborough, Eng.: Gregg, 1971), 4:191. I cite this edition.

14. Stephen Land, *From Signs to Propositions: The Concept of Form in Eighteenth-Century Semantic Theory* (London: Longman, 1974), pp. 121–22.

15. J. G. Herder, *Essay on the Origin of Language,* trans. Alexander Gode (New York: Ungar, 1966), p. 151.

16. In James A. Marchand, "Herder: Precursor of Humboldt, Whorf, and Modern Language Philosophy," in *Johann Gottfried Herder: Innovator through the Ages,* ed. Wulf Koepke and Samson B. Knoll (Bonn: Bouvier, 1982), p. 27.

17. *Athenaeum Fragments* 93, in *Kritische Ausgabe,* ed. Ernst Behler et al. (Munich: Schoningh, 1958-), 2:179, hereafter *KA.* Translations from Schlegel not otherwise acknowledged are mine.

18. In Anne K. Mellor, *English Romantic Irony* (Cambridge, Mass.: Harvard University Press, 1980), p. 7. My sketch of Schlegel's philosophical background draws heavily on Mellor's account but seeks to correct her misinterpretations as noted by Steven E. Alford, *Irony and the Logic of the Romantic Imagination* (New York: Lang, 1984), pp. 26-28, 105-7.

19. "On Incomprehensibility," in *Aesthetic and Miscellaneous Works,* trans. E. H. Millington (London: Bohn, 1849), p. 208 (*KA,* 2:370).

20. Trans. Lillian R. Furst, *Fictions of Romantic Irony* (Cambridge, Mass.: Harvard University Press, 1984), p. 28.

21. *KA,* 2:152, trans. Leon Chai, *The Romantic Foundations of the American Renaissance* (Ithaca, N.Y.: Cornell University Press, 1987), p. 319.

22. Peter C. Simpson, "The Critique of Wordplay during Early German Romanticism: Critical Construction of a Literary Style" (Ph.D. diss., Cornell University, 1985; Ann Arbor, Mich.: Univ. Microfilm Intl., pp. 229, 18-19. To this fine dissertation I owe many insights on German Romantic wordplay.

23. August Ferdinand Bernhardi, *Sprachlehre* (1801-3; rpt. Hildesheim: Olms, 1973), 2:397.

24. *KA,* 18:230; *Literary Notebooks,* ed. Hans Eichner (London: Athlone, 1957), p. 121, hereafter *LN.* If not otherwise acknowledged, translations from Schlegel are mine.

25. "Popular Fallacies IX," *Last Essays of Elia,* in *Works,* ed. E. V. Lucas (London: Methuen, 1903), 2:258.

26. *Werke,* Vol. 5, ed. Norbert Miller (Munich: Hanser, 1963), p. 193, my trans.

27. See Perry Miller, *The Raven and the Whale* (New York: Harbrace, 1956), pp. 73-74.

28. Samuel Taylor Coleridge, *Notebooks,* ed. Kathleen Coburn (London: Routledge, 1957-73), 2:2354.

29. Samuel Taylor Coleridge, *Poetical Works,* ed. E. H. Coleridge (1912; Oxford: Oxford University Press, 1968), 1:150; hereafter *PW.*

30. In Michael Kent Haven, "Coleridge on the Evolution of Language," *Studies in Romanticism* 20 (1981): 165. I draw heavily on Haven's account of desynonymization.

31. Samuel Taylor Coleridge, *Biographia Literaria,* ed. J. Shawcross (Oxford: Clarendon, 1907), 1:164.

32. In H. J. Jackson, "Coleridge, Etymology, and Etymologic," *JHI* 44 (1983): 81, on whom I draw freely.

33. Samuel Taylor Coleridge, *Collected Letters,* ed. E. L. Griggs (Oxford: Clarendon, 1956-71), 6:630; hereafter *CL.*

34. Samuel Taylor Coleridge, *Anima Poetae,* ed. Ernest Hartley Coleridge (London: Heinemann, 1895), p. 123; hereafter *AP.*

35. Samuel Taylor Coleridge, *Marginalia,* ed. George Whalley (London: Routledge, 1980-), 1:610.

36. Samuel Taylor Coleridge, *Unpublished Letters,* ed. Earl Leslie Griggs (London: Constable, 1932), 2:280. Hereafter *UL.*

37. James Holly Hanford, "Coleridge as Philologian," *MP* 16 (1919): 129. On the philological sage as a European figure, see Hans Aarsleff, *From Locke to Saussure: Essays on the Study of Language and Intellectual History* (Minneapolis: University of Minnesota Press, 1982), esp. pp. 35-41.

38. Samuel Taylor Coleridge, *Table Talk,* ed. T. Ashe (London: Bell, 1884), p. 41; hereafter *TT.*

39. In Alice D. Snyder, *Coleridge on Logic and Learning* (New Haven: Yale University Press, 1929), p. 57.

40. Samuel Taylor Coleridge, *Aids to Reflection,* ed. Thomas Fenby (Edinburgh: Grant, 1905), p. 42n.

41. In Michael Moran, "Coleridge," *Encyclopedia of Philosophy,* 2:135.

42. See esp. James R. McKusick, *Coleridge's Philosophy of Language* (New Haven: Yale University Press, 1986), pp. 134-35.

43. Samuel Taylor Coleridge, *Logic,* ed. J. R. de J. Jackson (London: Routledge, 1981), p. lvi.

44. In Joshua H. Neumann, "Coleridge on the English Language," *PMLA* 63 (1948): 647.

45. Samuel Taylor Coleridge, *Omniana* (1812), in *Notebooks,* 2:2751n.

46. See Daniel Zalewski, "Coleridge Regained," *Lingua Franca* 5 (May-June 1995): 70-73.

47. Marjorie Hope Nicolson, "James Marsh and the Vermont Transcendentalists," *Philosophical Review* 34 (1925): 31.

Chapter 3

1. For an admittedly partial list of printings of Murray, see R. C. Alston, *A Bibliography of the English Language* (Leeds: Author, 1965-), 1:92-96, 99-102. With the advent of stereotyping, the bibliographical distinction between separate printings and separate editions is not always easy to maintain. Nineteenth-century textbook publishers often blithely ignored it, denominating their reprintings new "editions." I have generally followed their lead.

2. Samuel Barnard, *A Polyglot Grammar of the Hebrew, Chaldee, Syriac, Greek, Latin, English, French, Italian, Spanish, and German Languages Reduced to the Common Rule of Syntax* (Philadelphia: Small, 1825), p. xiii.

3. Lindley Murray, *English Grammar* (Hallowell: Goodale, 1823), p. 11.

4. In Rollo Laverne Lyman, *English Grammar in American Public Schools before 1850,* Department of the Interior, Bureau of Education Bulletin, 1921, No. 12 (Washington, D.C.: U.S. Government Printing Office, 1922), p. 131.

5. Gertrude Stein, *Lectures in America* (New York: Random House, 1935), pp. 210-11.

6. Dudley Leavitt, *Complete Directions for Parsing the English Language . . . Designed as a Supplement to Lindley Murray's Grammar* (Concord, N.H.: Moore, 1826), pp. 9-10.

7. *Elements of English Grammar* (1826; Windsor, Vt., 1828), p. xxx.

8. John Sherman, *The Philosophy of Language Illustrated: An Entirely New System of Grammar; Wholly Divested of Scholastic Rubbish, of Traditionary Falsehood and Absurdity, and Reduced to the Principles of Fact and Com-*

mon Sense . . . *Designed for Colleges, Academies, and District Schools* (Trenton Falls, N.Y.: Dauby & Maynard, 1826), pp. 229-30.

9. "Descriptive Journal of a Jaunt up the Grand Canal," *Atheneum Magazine* 1 (Oct. 1825): 385-86.

10. James Brown, *An Appeal from the Present Popular Systems of English Philology to Common Sense, Designed to Aid the Introduction of the American System of English Grammar* (Carlisle, Pa.: The "Herald" Office, 1828), pp. 104, xii-xiii.

11. James Brown, *An Exegesis of English Syntax* (Philadelphia: May, 1840), p. 30.

12. James Brown, *Second Book of the Rational System of English Grammar* (Philadelphia: Author, 1853), p. 2.

13. Ian Michael, *English Grammatical Categories and the Tradition to 1800* (Cambridge, Eng.: Cambridge University Press, 1970), p. 490.

14. James Brown, *An English Syntascope, Developing the Constructive Principles of the English Phrenod, or Language* (Philadelphia: James Kay, 1839), pp. 6, 96.

15. James Brown, *An English Syntithology,* Book II (Philadelphia: Grubb, 1840), n.p.

16. James Brown, *Appeal from the Old Theory of English Grammar* (Philadelphia: Grubb & Reazor, 1845), foldout.

17. James Brown, *Brown's English Syntax Institution* (Philadelphia: Author, 1839), pp. 3-4.

18. Goold Brown, *Grammar of Grammars* (1851; New York: Wood, 1860), pp. 34, xiii.

19. James Brown, *The Grammatical Reader: A Class Book of Criticism on the Old Theory of English Grammar* (Philadelphia: Griffee, 1856), Preface, n.p.

20. See Jan Ziolkowski, ed., *On Philology* (University Park: Pennsylvania State University Press, 1990), pp. 8-9.

Chapter 4

1. *New York Literary Gazette and Phi Beta Kappa Repository,* No. 18 (7 Jan. 1826, misdated 1825): 286.

2. William B. Fowle, *The True English Grammar: Being an Attempt to Form a Grammar of the English Language* (Boston: Munroe & Francis, 1827), pp. 169-70; *The True English Grammar . . . Being the Second Part of an Attempt to Form a Grammar of the English Language* (Boston: Hilliard, 1829), p. 14.

3. Joshua Jones, *English Grammar in Two Parts. The First, A Brief Analysis of the English Language. The Second, A Practical System of Etymology and Syntax* (West-Chester, Pa.: Siegfried, 1833), p. 21.

4. N. Vernon, *An Essay on the Origins and Structure of Language, with a Concise System of English Grammar* (Frederic City, Md.: Schley, 1847), pp. iii-6.

5. See P. B. Salmon, "The Beginnings of Morphology: Linguistic Botanizing in the Eighteeenth Century," *Historiographia linguistica* 1 (1974): 313-39; Susan Jeffords, "The Knowledge of Words: The Evolution in Language and Biology in Nineteenth-Century Thought," *Centennial Review* 31 (1987): 66-83.

6. In Robert A. Ferguson, *Law and Letters in American Culture* (Cambridge, Mass.: Harvard University Press, 1984), p. 73.

7. Jonathan Badgley, *Principles of English Grammar in Familiar Lectures; Accompanied by Amusing Dialogues* (Whitesboro, N.Y.: Office of the Friend of Man, 1837), p. 13.

8. *Grammar of Grammars* (1851; New York: Wood, 1860), p. 56.

9. William S. McFeely, *Grant: A Biography* (New York: Norton, 1981), p. 517.

10. William Hall, *Encyclopedia of English Grammar* (1849; Columbus, Ohio: Scott, 1850), p. vi.

11. Gladys Hosmer, "Phineas Allen, Thoreau's Preceptor," *TSB* 59 (Spring 1957): 1.

12. In Hubert H. Hoeltje, "Thoreau and the Concord Academy," *NEQ* 21 (1948): 106-7.

13. Compare the brief essay on the Four Seasons sandwiched between sections on puns in Rensselaer Bentley's *Pictorial Spelling Book* (New York: Pratt, 1845), pp. 122-23. A similar theme appears in B. D. Emerson's *National Spelling Book* (1828), which claimed hundreds of printings, one of which figured in Emily Dickinson's household library.

14. Walter Harding, *The Days of Henry Thoreau* (New York: Knopf, 1965), p. 41.

15. Kenneth Walter Cameron, *The Transcendentalists and Minerva* (Hartford: Transcendental Books, 1958), 1:204-5.

16. *Correspondence,* ed. Walter B. Harding and Carl Bode (New York: New York University Press, 1958), pp. 19-20.

17. Orestes Brownson, *The Spirit-Rapper: An Autobiography* (Boston: Little, Brown, 1854), p. 320.

18. R. G. Parker, *Progressive Exercises in English Composition* (Boston: Lincoln, 1832), p. 68.

19. *New England Grammar . . . with an Essay on English Grammar Designed as an Introduction,* 2d ed. (1839; Boston: Lewis & Sampson, 1843), pp. 6-7.

20. John Goldsbury, *New Theories of Grammar: A Brief Review of Four Different Theories of English Grammar Opposed to That of Murray* (Boston: Munroe, 1846), pp. iv-vi.

21. In Rollo Laverne Lyman, *English Grammar in American Public Schools before 1850,* Department of the Interior, Bureau of Education Bulletin, 1921, No. 12 (Washington, D.C.: U.S. Government Printing Office, 1922), pp. 89-93.

22. *English Grammatical Categories and the Tradition to 1800* (Cambridge, Eng.: Cambridge University Press, 1970), p. 517.

23. In Charlton Laird, *Language in America* (New York: World, 1970), pp. 299-301.

24. In *Pittsburgh: The Story of an American City,* ed. Stefan Lorant (Garden City, N.Y.: Doubleday, 1964), pp. 92-93.

25. J. H. Newton, *History of the Pan-Handle* (Wheeling: Caldwell, 1879), 1:232.

26. See Richard Hildreth, "Hildreth," *New England Historical and Genealogical Record* 2 (1857): 10.

Chapter 5

1. F. McReady, *The Art of English Grammar in Verse,* 2d ed. (Philadelphia: Probasco, 1820), p. 143.

2. Alexis de Tocqueville, *Democracy in America,* trans. Henry Reeve et al., ed. Phillips Bradley (New York: Knopf, 1945), 2:66.

3. Noah Webster, *The Teacher; A Supplement to the Elementary Spelling Book* (New Haven: Babcock, 1836), p. 5.

4. William Smeaton, *An Etymological Manual of the English and French Languages* (New Haven: Hurt, 1843), pp. iii–v.

5. Samuel Austin Allibone, *Critical Dictionary of English Literature and British and American Authors* (London: Lippincott, 1884), s.v. "Lynd."

6. In Denis E. Baron, *Going Native: The Regeneration of Saxon English,* Publication of the American Dialect Society No. 69 (University, Ala.: University of Alabama Press, 1982), p. 28. But the best guide to this movement remains John Elwyn Bernbrock, "Walt Whitman and Anglo-Saxonism" (Ph.D. diss., University of North Carolina, 1961), of which Baron seems unaware. Baron ignores several textbooks published by A Literary Association; his discussion of that group is seriously flawed and quite unreliable. For the different editions of A Literary Association's textbooks consult both Bernbrock's list and the *National Union Catalogue*'s; neither is complete.

7. *A Hand-Book of Anglo-Saxon Root-Words* (1853; New York: Appleton, 1854), pp. v–vi.

8. *Handbook of Anglo-Saxon Derivatives, on the Basis of the Hand-book of Anglo-Saxon Root-Words* (New York: Appleton, 1854), pp. viii, x.

9. William Grimshaw, *An Etymological Dictionary of the English Language,* 3d ed. (Philadelphia: Grigg, 1848), p. vii.

10. Walter Harding's conjecture in "A New Checklist of the Books in Henry David Thoreau's Library," *SAR 1983,* s.v., that Thoreau's was a British edition, seems unlikely. His invaluable checklist should also be updated to indicate that Thoreau's copy of Oswald's *Etymological Dictionary* is now in the Concord Free Public Library.

11. *Thesaurus of English Words and Phrases . . . Enlarged and Improved,* ed. John Lewis Roget (1852; New York: Crowell, 1879), p. xvi.

12. David Booth, *An Analytical Dictionary of the English Language, in Which the Words Are Explained in the Order of Their Natural Affinity, Independent of Alphabetical Arrangement, and the Signification of Each Is Traced from Its Etymology . . . the Whole Exhibiting in One Continued Narrative, the Origin, History, and Modern Usage of . . . the English Tongue* (London: Cochrane, 1835), p. 2.

13. C. M. L. Wiseman, *Centennial History of Lancaster, Ohio* (Lancaster: Wiseman, 1898), pp. 150–51.

14. John Williams, *The Readable Dictionary, or Topical and Synonymic Lexicon: Containing Several Thousands of the More Useful Terms of the English Language, Classified by Subjects, and Arranged according to Their Affinities of Meaning; with Accompanying Etymologies, Definitions, and Illustrations. To Which Are Added . . . an Alphabetical List of Latin and Greek Roots . . . Derivatives* (Columbus: Follett, 1860), pp. iv–v.

15. In Gordon V. Boudreau, "Thoreau and Richard C. Trench: Conjectures on the Pickerel Passage of *Walden*," *ESQ* 20 (1974): 120, on whom I draw here.

16. So the London editions of 1878 and 1876, pp. 35n. and 227 respectively.

17. *Autobiography of Samuel K. Hoshour*, A.M., intro. Isaac Erret (St. Louis: Burns, 1884), pp. 70-72. In discussing Hoshour as "more an archaist than a Saxonist," Denis E. Baron, *Going Native*, p. 26, notably misunderstands Hoshour's humorous aims.

18. *Memoirs of Wayne County and the City of Richmond, Indiana*, ed. Henry Clay Fox (Madison, Wisc.: Western History Association, 1912), p. 422.

19. Samuel K. Hoshour, *Letters to Esq. Pedant, in the East, by Lorenzo Altisonaat, an Emigrant to the West* (Cambridge City, Ind.: Winder, 1844), pp. iii-iv.

20. In C. Carroll Hollis, "Whitman and William Swinton," *AL* 30 (1959): 432. My entire discussion of Swinton is deeply indebted to Hollis's pioneering article; see further references in Sherry G. Southard, "Whitman and Language: An Annotated Bibliography," *WWR* 2 (Fall 1984): 31-49.

21. *Letters of Ralph Waldo Emerson*, ed. Ralph Rusk (New York: Columbia University Press, 1939), 5:33.

22. *Journals of Bronson Alcott*, ed. Odell Shephard (Boston: Little, Brown, 1938), pp. 287-91.

23. "Walt Whitman and His Poems," *United States Review* n.s., 5 (Sept. 1855): 206.

24. *New York Dissected*, ed. Emory Holloway and Ralph Adiman (New York: Wilson, 1936), p. 55.

25. In Michael Rowan Dressman, "Walt Whitman's Plan for the Perfect Dictionary," *SAR 1979*, p. 468.

26. In Hollis, "Whitman and William Swinton," p. 436.

27. *Whitman's Manuscripts: Leaves of Grass (1860), a Parallel Text*, ed. Fredson Bowers (Chicago: University of Chicago Press, 1955), p. 70. See Bowers's discussion, pp. lxii-lxxiii.

28. See Michael Rowan Dressman, "Whitman, Chaucer, and French Words," *WWR* 23 (1977): 77-82.

29. In C. Carroll Hollis, *Language and Style in* Leaves of Grass (Baton Rouge: Louisiana State University Press, 1983), pp. 4-12. I draw heavily on this fine book, esp. the excellent analysis of the sinister growth of Whitman's Romance vocabulary, pp. 212-24, 255-56. But Hollis's skepticism about Whitman's oratorical ability should be qualified by Larry D. Griffin, "Whitman's Voice," *WWQR* n.s., 9 (1992): 125-33.

Chapter 6

1. See *Letters of Elizabeth Palmer Peabody, American Renaissance Woman*, ed. Bruce A. Ronda (Middletown, Conn.: Wesleyan University Press, 1984), p. 264. Since Kraitsir was still in Virginia in 1843, Ronda's tentative dating of this letter to Mary Moody Emerson is wrong; Peabody probably wrote it late in 1845 or early in 1846, before formally affiliated with his school. Ronda's editing of the original letter in the American Antiquarian Society is thoroughly unreliable. I am indebted to Barbara Trippel Simmons, formerly curator of manuscripts there, for a more accurate transcription. Likewise, the unidentifiable volume to which

Peabody refers as "Boff's Comparative grammar" in the letter on page 305 (if Ronda's transcription may be trusted) is undoubtedly E. B. Bostwick's translation of Franz Bopp's *Comparative Grammar of the Sanscrit, Zend, Greek, Latin, Lithuanian, Gothic, German, & Slavonic Languages,* of which several London editions appeared beginning in 1843. For ampler treatment of Kraitsir, see my "Charles Kraitsir's Influence upon Thoreau's Theory of Language," *ESQ* 19 (1973): 262-74.

2. Philip F. Gura has argued energetically that Thoreau was so committed to glossology that he structured his own prose in the sandbank passage on Kraitsir's triad of phonetic values; for his most recent version of this thesis, see his "Henry Thoreau and the Wisdom of Words," in *Critical Essays on Thoreau's Walden,* ed. Joel Myerson (Boston: G. K. Hall, 1988), pp. 203-19. In *The Roots of Walden and the Tree of Life* (Nashville, Tenn.: Vanderbilt University Press, 1990), pp. 196-99, Gordon V. Boudreau tries to supply statistical evidence for this claim. This evidence strikes me as unconvincing. One finds etymological connections like Kraitsir's in Noah Webster's *American Dictionary* of 1844: "A cion or banch, is precisely the Celtic word for arm; Irish *braie,* or *raigh* . . . whence . . . the Latin *brachium* . . . whence the French *bras,* whence the English *brace.* The arm is a shoot, a branch, and *branch* is from this root. . . . On this word . . . are formed, with the prefix *s,* the German *sprechen,* to speak . . . and the Swedish *spricka,* to *break.* . . . The same word with *n* casual is seen in *spring,* the breaking of winter" (p. xxiv). Neglecting parallel linguistic thinkers with whom Thoreau was acquainted like Webster, Gardner, Whiter, Court de Gébelin, and De Brosses, Gura's and Boudreau's theory exalts Kraitsir into Thoreau's supreme philological authority and ignores the playful Goethean irony with which *Walden* develops such speculations.

3. James Gilchrist, *Philosophic Etymology, or Rational Grammar* (London: Hunter, 1816), pp. 77-78. Another very similar etymological metaphysician with intriguing parallels to Thoreau is the American Jacob Wilson, author of the labyrinthine *Phrasis: A Treatise on the History and Structure of the Different Languages of the World* (Albany: Munsell, 1864) and other works. Both tried teaching and tired of it. Each idealized village culture but was contentiously antisentimental. Both mistrusted marriage, urged Stoic control of the emotions, and preached self-reliance. Each dreamed of deriving a new religious mythology from evolutionary nature. In both Wilson and Thoreau a rebellious temper blossomed into a full-blown philosophy of civil disobedience. And like Thoreau, Wilson's flirtations with a universal language drove him into the embrace of Romantic irony.

4. *A Specimen of a Commentary on Shakespeare,* ed. Alan Over and Mary Bell (London: Methuen, 1967), p. xlv. For ampler treatment of some parallels, see my "*Walden*'s Dirty Language: Thoreau and Walter Whiter's Geocentric Etymological Theories," *Harvard Library Bulletin* 22 (1974): 117-28.

5. *Lavengro; The Scholar—The Gypsy—The Priest* (New York: Harper, 1851), p. 59.

6. See esp. Philip F. Gura's remarks in *The Wisdom of Words: Language, Theology, and Literature in the New England Renaissance* (Middletown, Conn.: Wesleyan University Press, 1981), pp. 119-23, along with his "Thoreau and John Josselyn," *NEQ* 48 (1975): 505-18, and "Thoreau's Maine Woods Indians: More Representative Men," *AL* 49 (1977): 366-84.

7. This observation is from Martin Bickman, *Walden: Volatile Truths* (New York: Twayne, 1992), p. 69, who corroborates my own sense of the meanings at play in this passage.

Chapter 7

1. The main source for Johnson's life is his unpublished autobiography, heavily quoted by his biographers. I cite it here from Charles L. Todd and Robert Sonkin, *Alexander Bryan Johnson, Philosophical Banker* (Syracuse: Syracuse University Press, 1977), p. 23; hereafter *PB*.

2. Sidney Werthimer Jr., "Alexander Bryan Johnson: Businessman, Banker, and Author of 'A Treatise on Banking,'" in *Language and Value: Proceedings of the Centennial Conference on the Life and Works of Alexander Bryan Johnson,* ed. Charles L. Todd and Russell T. Blackwood (New York: Greenwood, 1969), p. 143; hereafter *LV*.

3. In Robert Sonkin, "Alexander Bryan Johnson's Plan for a 'Collated Dictionary,'" *LV*, p. 100. But Sonkin misinterprets the passage by assuming that Johnson refers to historical rather than grammatical etymology when he is actually confessing ignorance of the parts of speech. References to Johnson's *A Method of Acquiring a Full Knowledge of the English Language* (Utica, 1831) rely on Sonkin's citations.

4. *A Treatise on Language,* ed. David Rynin (Berkeley: University of California Press, 1947), p. 36. I cite both editions without distinction as *Tr.* from this synoptic edition, the most readily accessible, and often draw on Rynin's appended "Critical Essay."

5. Here I follow Lars Gustafson, "A Note on the Concepts of 'Verbal Significance' and 'Sensible Significance' in Alexander Bryan Johnson's *Treatise on Language,*" *LV*, pp. 68-70.

6. Max Black, "Johnson's Language Theories in Modern Perspective," *LV*, pp. 49-66, stresses his atomism and failure to account for organizational principles in the mind and the world. Black sees him as groping naively toward Kantian answers, but Gustafson wisely defends his right to philosophize without settling such questions. On this Johnsonian inconsistency and others, see further *LV*, pp. 80-89, and Rynin, "Critical Essay," *Tr.*, esp. pp. 357-430. I have not developed Johnson's philosophical shortcomings in much detail because until his strengths are more generally appreciated his weaknesses seem of secondary importance.

7. To the evidence of Johnson's limited influence discussed by Russell T. Blackwood, "Nineteenth-Century Appraisals of Alexander Bryan Johnson," *LV*, pp. 16-21, should be added the borrowings by Joel Chapin, *An Analytic and Philosophical Grammar* (Springfield, Mass.: Wood, 1842), pp. 45-51. Chapin quotes with acknowledgment five pages of Johnson's examples, then concludes that "the ambiguity of language is very extensive, and we shall have occasion from time to time as we proceed, to further point it out" (p. 51). Probably other "philosophical grammarians" also borrowed from Johnson without acknowledgment.

8. Rynin, "Alexander Bryan Johnson's Treatise on Morality," *LV*, p. 45. David Simpson, *The Politics of the American Language* (New York: Oxford University Press, 1986), pp. 255-57, astutely compares Johnson's aims with Feni-

more Cooper's. But in making them both sticks to beat Transcendentalism over the head with, he too readily ignores Johnson's own contradictory, paradoxical dimensions, as does Philip Gura, "Language and Meaning: An American Tradition," *AL* 53 (1981): 5–11.

9. In David M. Ellis, "Alexander Bryan Johnson: Reform and Religion," *LV*, p. 177.

10. *Statement of Reasons*, 12th ed. (Boston: American Unitarian Association, 1880), p. 138.

11. *Essay on Language and Other Papers*, ed. E. P. Peabody (Boston: Phillips, Sampson, 1857), p. 52.

12. In *The Transcendentalists*, ed. Perry Miller (Cambridge, Mass.: Harvard University Press, 1950), pp. 114, 85; hereafter *TR*.

13. In Mary Bushnell Cheney, *Life and Letters of Horace Bushnell* (New York: Harper, 1880), p. 199.

14. *JMN*, 11:20. Editorially misglossed as alluding to an earlier work of Bushnell's, Emerson's reference here is surely to *Work and Play*, for its publication in pamphlet form in late 1848 corresponded with the appearance of Thoreau's *Ascent of Katahdin* also mentioned.

15. *Work and Play, or Literary Varieties* (1864; New York: Scribner's, 1912), p. 28.

16. *God in Christ* (Hartford: Brown & Parsons, 1849), pp. 35–36, hereafter *GC*. In interpreting Bushnell I owe much to Donald A. Crosby, *Horace Bushnell's Theory of Language in the Context of Other Nineteenth-Century Philosophies of Language* (The Hague: Mouton, 1975).

17. *Christ in Theology* (Hartford: Brown & Parsons, 1851), p. 33.

18. Philip F. Gura, *The Wisdom of Words: Language, Theology, and Literature in the New England Renaissance* (Middletown, Conn.: Wesleyan University Press, 1981), pp. 75–105, provides a fine account of Emerson's evolving ideas on this topic; this book offers a perceptive sketch of their background in Unitarian Scriptural exegesis and the work of Marsh and Bushnell.

19. See Crosby, *Horace Bushnell's Theory of Language*, pp. 225, 21, 66, and 160. Gura, "Language and Meaning," p. 13, links Bushnell's emphasis on self-canceling rhetoric to Humboldt's doctrine that all understanding is simultaneously a misunderstanding and proclaims that "Bushnell's familiarity with Humboldt's writings on language opens for exploration a whole new area in American critical theory." But in adhering to a mechanical theory of language origins Bushnell managed to miss the main point of Humboldt's organic theory, and his espousal of self-canceling rhetoric can just as easily be traced to Johnson, Stewart, Coleridge, or Schlegel. As David L. Smith wisely observes in *Symbolism and Growth: The Religious Thought of Horace Bushnell*, American Academy of Religion Dissertation Series No. 36, ed. Wendell Dietrich (Chico, Calif.: Scholars Press, 1981), "it is distressingly difficult to pin down any specific lines of influence between Bushnell and documents of romantic philosophy, critical theory, or even literature." Despite evidence that he read at least snippets from Humboldt, Schleiermacher, Schlegel, Cousin, and a few other continental thinkers, there is no sign he ever read Kant; and despite the frequent similarity of their ideas, "the likelihoood seems to be not that he absorbed them from the romantics proper, but that his ideas grew out of the same soil as theirs" (pp. 23–24).

20. R. W. B. Lewis, *The American Adam: Innocence, Tragedy, and Tradition in the Nineteenth Century* (Chicago: University of Chicago Press, 1955), p. 7. Though Lewis largely ignores Bushnell's language theory, see pages 66-73 for an illuminating discusion of the ironic stance that Bushnell's persistent efforts at intellectual mediation fostered.

Chapter 8

1. In Charles Feidelson Jr., *Symbolism and American Literature* (Chicago: University of Chicago Press, 1953), p. 119. Interpreting Emerson, I owe perhaps most to Richard Poirier's *The Renewal of Literature: Emersonian Reflections* (New York: Random House, 1987).

2. John Dryden, *Works,* ed. Edward Niles Hooker et al. (Berkeley: University of California Press, 1961-89), 4:84, and Warren Chernaik, ibid., 580-81n.

3. In Porte, *Representative Man: Ralph Waldo Emerson in His Times* (New York: Oxford University Press, 1979), p. 239. See his entire chapter on this tendency in the aging Emerson.

4. In Catherine Albanese, *Corresponding Motion: Transcendental Religion and the New America* (Philadelphia: Temple University Press, 1977), p. 100.

5. *Topical Notebooks of Ralph Waldo Emerson,* ed. Susan Stanton Smith (Columbia: University of Missouri Press, 1990), 1:237; hereafter *TN.*

6. For skeptical scrutiny of Miller's "From Edwards to Emerson," see Lawrence Buell, "The Literary Significance of the Unitarian Movement," *ESQ* 33 (1987): 212-33.

7. Philip F. Gura, *The Wisdom of Words: Language, Theology, and Literature in the New England Renaissance* (Middletown, Conn.: Wesleyan University Press, 1981), p. 105.

8. *Emerson's* Nature: *Origin, Growth, Meaning,* ed. Merton M. Sealts Jr. and Alfred R. Ferguson (New York: Dodd, Mead, 1969), pp. 81, 84, 79.

9. Reprinted in Kenneth Walter Cameron, *Emerson the Essayist* (Raleigh, N.C.: Thistle Press, 1945), 2:86.

10. See esp. Eric Wilson, "Weaving: Breathing: Thinking: The Poetics of Emerson's *Nature,*" *ATQ* 10 (1996): 11 and passim.

11. *Poetry,* ed. Edward Connery Latham (New York: Holt, 1969), pp. 377-79.

12. *Works,* Vol. 8, ed. Walter Blair et al. (Berkeley: University of California Press, 1988), pp. 59-60.

13. Wilhelm von Humboldt, *On Language: The Diversity of Human Language-Structure and Its Influence on the Mental Development of Mankind,* trans. Peter Heath, intro. Hans Aarsleff (Cambridge, Eng.: Cambridge University Press, 1988), p. 49.

14. See David Shimkin, "Emerson's Playful Habit of Mind," *ATQ* No. 62 (Dec. 1986): 1-17.

15. J. R. Lowell, "Emerson the Lecturer," in Milton R. Konvitz, *The Recognition of Ralph Waldo Emerson* (Ann Arbor: University of Michigan Press, 1972), p. 48.

16. David Simpson, *The Politics of American English, 1776-1850* (New York: Oxford University Press, 1986), p. 242.

17. Oliver Wendell Holmes, *Ralph Waldo Emerson* (Cambridge, Mass.: Riverside, 1885), p. 348.

18. Ralph L. Rusk, *The Life of Ralph Waldo Emerson* (New York: Scribner's, 1949), p. 507.

19. Roman Jakobson, "Two Types of Language and Two Types of Aphasic Disturbances," in *Fundamentals of Language,* ed. Jakobson and Morris Halle (The Hague: Mouton, 1956), p. 66.

20. A. B. Paulson, "Emerson and Aphasia," *Language and Style* 14 (1981): 159. To this brilliant article I owe most of my observations about Emerson's aphasia. Consult it for further poignant examples. My main reservation concerns Paulson's suggestion, p. 170, that the correspondence theory of *Nature* was radically metonymic rather than metaphoric and represents Emerson's deepest conviction about language.

21. James Elliot Cabot, *A Memoir of Ralph Waldo Emerson* (Cambridge, Mass.: Riverside, 1887), 2:651.

22. *Correspondence of Emerson and Carlyle,* ed. Joseph Slater (New York: Columbia University Press, 1964), p. 185.

23. Martin Bickman, "'The Turn of His Sentences': The Open Form of Emerson's *Essays: First Series,*" *ESQ* 34 (1988): 73.

Chapter 9

1. *History of New York* (New York: Inskeep, 1809), 2:207. For a recent study of Irving's scatological humor, see Jonathan Cook, "Prodigious Poop: Comic Context and Psychological Subtext in Irving's *Knickerbocker History,*" *Nineteenth-Century Fiction* 49 (1995): 483-512.

2. In William T. Hedges, *Washington Irving: An American Study, 1802-1832* (1965; rpt. New York: Greenwood, 1980), pp. 192-93n.

3. *Early Critical Essays,* ed. James F. Beard Jr. (Gainesville: University of Florida Press, 1955), p. 139.

4. *The American Democrat,* ed. H. L. Mencken and Robert E. Spiller (New York: Vintage, 1956), p. 116.

5. Alexis de Tocqueville, *Democracy in America,* trans. Henry Reeve et al., ed. Phillips Bradley (New York: Knopf, 1945), 2:66-67.

6. David Simpson, *The Politics of American English, 1776-1850* (New York: Oxford University Press, 1986), p. 221. See his chapters 5-6 for a fine survey of Cooper's attitudes toward language, but note the reservations expressed by Julie Tetel Andresen, *Linguistics in America, 1769-1924: A Critical History* (London: Routledge, 1990), p. 91.

7. In Kenneth Silverman, *Edgar A. Poe: Mournful and Never-Ending Remembrance* (New York: Harper Collins, 1991), p. 203. I am pervasively indebted to this handsome biography (hereafter *EAP*). But I find Poe's humor more pivotal and amusing than Silverman allows.

8. Clarence S. Brigham, *Edgar Allan Poe's Contributions to Alexander's Weekly Messenger* (Worcester, Mass.: American Antiquarian Society, 1943), pp. 15-16.

9. See esp. Gregg Camfield, *Necessary Madness: The Humor of Domesticity in Nineteenth-Century American Literature* (New York: Oxford University Press, 1997), p. 51.

10. See esp. G. R. Thompson, *Poe's Fiction: Romantic Irony in the Gothic Tales* (Madison: University of Wisconsin, 1973), together with his subsequent studies of Romantic irony in American Romanticism.

11. *Works*, 2:397-417, and see also Mabbott 393-95.

12. In Alexander H. Fraser, ed., John Locke, *An Essay Concerning Human Understanding* (1894; rpt. New York: Dover, 1959), 1:448. See further Kevin M. McCarthy, "Another Source for 'The Raven': Locke's Essay Concerning Human Understanding," *Poe Newsletter* 1 (April 1968): 29.

13. *Works,* 1:364-69, and *Essays,* pp. 13-25.

14. T. D. English, in *Works,* 2:395.

15. See esp. Alexander Hammond, "Edgar Allan Poe's *Tales of the Folio Club*: The Evolution of a Lost Work," in *Poe at Work: Seven Textual Studies,* ed. Benjamin Franklin Fisher IV (Baltimore: Poe Society, 1978) pp. 13-43; David Galloway, ed., *The Other Poe* (London: Penguin, 1983), 7-22; Paul Lewis, "Poe's Humor: A Psychological Analysis," *SSF* 26 (1989): 531-46.

16. See esp. Pollin, *CW,* 1:4-16; also "Poe's Life through the Sources of *Pym*," in *Poe's* Pym: *Critical Explorations,* ed. Richard Kopley (Durham, N.C.: Duke University Press, 1992), pp. 95-103. I cite *Pym* from this edition.

17. See Christopher Newfield, "Controlling the Voice: Emerson's Early Theory of Language," *ESQ* 38 (1992): 17.

18. T. D. English, in *Works,* 3:799. See also Marc Shell, *Money, Language, and Thought* (Berkeley: University of California Press, 1982), chap. 1.

19. In *Works,* 1:413, and see Mabbott on Poe's pronunciation of *Ulalume,* 419n. On the poem as satire, see Richard M. Fletcher, *The Stylistic Development of Edgar Allan Poe* (The Hague: Mouton, 1973), pp. 182-83.

20. *Poetry and Tales,* ed. Patrick F. Quinn (New York: Library of America, 1984), p. 1342.

21. In Richard Harter Fogle, "Weird Mockery: An Element of Hawthorne's Style," *Style* 1 (1968): 194.

22. See Rose Hawthorne Lathrop, *Memories of Hawthorne* (Boston: Houghton Mifflin, 1898), pp. 12, 31.

23. "To Sophia Peabody, 3 July 1839," 15:322-23.

24. *Hawthorne's Lost Notebook, 1835-41,* ed. Barbara S. Mouffe (University Park: Pennsylvania State University Press, 1978), p. 84; hereafter *LN*.

25. *Tales and Sketches,* ed. Roy Harvey Pearce (New York: Library of America, 1982), pp. 1149, 35.

26. *Elements of Mental Philosophy* (Boston, 1831), 1:320, in John Franzosa, "Locke's Kinsman, William Molyneux: The Philosophical Context of Hawthorne's Early Tales," *ESQ* 29 (1983): 5.

27. James Rush, *Philosophy of the Human Voice,* 2d ed. (Philadelphia: Grigg, 1833), p. 329.

28. Patricia M. Roger, "Taking a Perspective: Hawthorne's Concept of Language and Nineteenth-Century Language Theory," *Nineteenth-Century Fiction* 51 (1997): 433-54, places Hawthorne's views on language midway between Bushnell's and A. B. Johnson's.

29. Here I draw on Sacvan Bercovitch, *The Office of the Scarlet Letter* (Baltimore: Johns Hopkins University Press, 1991), esp. chap. 1.

30. *Elements of Mental Philosophy,* 1:384-85, in Franzosa, p. 3.

31. *The Melville Log,* ed. Jay Leyda (New York: Harcourt, 1951), 1:35.

32. Ibid., 72-73, *sic.* See S. Foster Damon, "Why Ishmael Went to Sea," *AL* 2 (1930): 281-83.

33. See Edward H. Rosenberry, *Melville and the Comic Spirit* (Cambridge, Mass.: Harvard University Press, 1955), p. 43. To this fine study—still the best book on Melville's humor—I owe much in my treatment of Melville's punning. See also his "Melville's Comedy and Tragedy," in *A Companion to Melville Studies,* ed. John Bryant (New York: Greenwood, 1986), pp. 603-24; and Shawn F. Gerety, "The Play's the Thing: Melville's Art of Punning in *Moby Dick*," *Thalia* 16 (1996): 53-63.

34. For other examples, see Robert Shulman, "The Serious Function of Melville's Phallic Jokes," *AL* 33 (1961): 179-94.

35. Besides Rosenberry, *Melville,* chaps. 5 and 6, see Joseph Jones, "Humor in *Moby-Dick*," *Studies in English* (Austin: University of Texas Press, 1946), pp. 51-71.

36. In Mark Bauerlein, "Grammar and Etymology in *Moby-Dick*," *Arizona Quarterly* 46 (1990): 22, to whose argument I owe much.

37. Here I follow Gayle L. Smith, "The Word and the Thing: *Moby-Dick* and the Limits of Language," *ESQ* 31 (1985): 260-71.

38. See esp. Rosenberry, *Melville,* pp. 115, 123, and Smith, "The Word and the Thing," p. 267.

39. *Principles of English Grammar,* 16th ed. (1834; New York: Pratt, Woodford, 1846), p. 118.

40. See esp. Nina Baym, "Melville's Quarrrel with Fiction," *PMLA* 94 (1979): 909-23.

41. *Billy Budd, Sailor,* ed. Harrison Hayford and Merton M. Sealts Jr. (Chicago: University of Chicago Press, 1962), p. 49; hereafter *BB.* On its interpretive history, see Sealts, "Innocence and Infamy: Billy Budd, Sailor," in *A Companion,* pp. 407-30.

42. On subdued thematic punning in Melville's last work, see esp. Walter Redfern, "Between the Lines of *Billy Budd*," *Journal of American Studies* 17 (1983): 357-65.

43. See Merton M. Sealts Jr., *Melville's Reading,* rev. ed. (Columbia: University of South Carolina Press, 1988), p. 152.

44. *BB,* pp. 131-32. See Paul Brodtkorb, "The Definitive *Billy Budd:* 'But Aren't It All Sham?'" *PMLA* 82 (1967): 600-612.

45. See Neal Schleifer, "Melville as Lexicographer: Linguistics and Symbolism in *Moby Dick*," *Melville Society Extracts* 98 (Sept. 1994): 1-6.

Chapter 10

1. *The Years and Hours of Emily Dickinson,* ed. Jay Leyda (New Haven: Yale University Press, 1960), 2:30.

2. In Richard Sewall, *The Life of Emily Dickinson* (New York: Farrar, 1974), 2:423.

3. See Richard B. Sewall, "Science and the Poet: Emily Dickinson's Herbarium and 'The Clue Divine,'" *Harvard Library Bulletin* n.s. 3 (Spring 1992): 11-26; also William Howard, "Emily Dickinson's Poetic Vocabulary," *PMLA* 72 (1957): 225-48.

4. Noah Webster, *An American Dictionary of the English Language* (Amherst: Adams, 1844), s.v. "Glory."

5. See Jerome McGann, "Emily Dickinson's Visible Language," in *Emily Dickinson: A Collection of Critical Essays*, ed. Judith Farr (Upper Saddle River, N.J.: Prentice, 1996), 255–56.

6. See Brita Lindberg-Seyerstedt, *The Voice of the Poet: Aspects of Style in the Poetry of Emily Dickinson* (Uppsala: Almqvist & Wiksells, 1968), pp. 102; also Cristanne Miller, *Emily Dickinson: A Poet's Grammar* (Cambridge, Mass.: Harvard University Press, 1987), pp. 39–44.

7. In George Frisbie Whicher, *This Was a Poet* (New York: Scribner's, 1929), p. 176; see further pp. 170–88.

8. See Martha Winburn England, "Emily Dickinson and Isaac Watts: Puritan Hymnodists," *BNYPL* 69 (1965): 88 and passim anent Dickinson's witty allusiveness.

9. Though implausible in hypothesizing a full-blown affair culminating in illegitimate pregnancy, persuasive arguments for the centrality of one man in Dickinson's poetry are offered by William H. Shurr, *The Marriage of Emily Dickinson: A Study of the Fascicles* (Lexington: University of Kentucky Press, 1983). But note also the thesis advanced by Cynthia Griffin Wolff in *Emily Dickinson* (New York: Knopf, 1986), who argues that Dickinson could never have committed herself wholeheartedly to any man or woman. Conjecture in this area is risky, refracting the poet's image in the critic's until we are lost in a hall of mirrors with Camille Paglia. One recent lesbian study deduces the poet's preoccupation with her clitoris from the number of small round objects she describes, including not only peas but bees! "I hope you whip them Susie," she wrote fervently to her schoolmistress sister-in-law, and leather-loving readers will admire her candid confession, "So I may Come— / What Thou dost—is Delight— / Bondage as Play—be sweet" (1:145; #725). The transsexual Dickinson has not yet made her critical debut but no doubt soon will, flaunting her hope of a sex-change operation: "No matter—now—Sweet— / But when I'm Earl— / Wont you wish you'd spoken / To that dull Girl?" (#704). For a biographical reading that tactfully balances heterosexual and homosexual impulses in Dickinson, see Judith Farr, *The Passion of Emily Dickinson* (Cambridge, Mass.: Harvard University Press, 1992).

10. With Clark Griffith, *The Long Shadow: Emily Dickinson's Tragic Poetry* (Princeton: Princeton University Press, 1966), pp. 228–32, cf. Johnson, ed. *Poems*, 2:816. More plausible is David Porter, "The Crucial Experience in Dickinson's Poetry," *ESQ* 20 (1974): 285. On other wordplay involved, see Judy Jo Small, *Positive as Sound: Emily Dickinson's Rhyme* (Athens: University of Georgia Press, 1990), pp. 156–59.

11. Perhaps the most comprehensive survey of her punning is Bernhard Frank's "Wiles of Words: Ambiguity in Emily Dickinson's Poetry" (Ph.D. diss., University of Pittsburgh, 1965).

12. In her provocative "Recycling Language: Emily Dickinson's Religious Wordplay," *ESQ* 32 (1986): 232–52, Linda Munk notes these puns in the poem and suggests another that seems far-fetched but just possible. I am also indebted to her observations on punning in #1543 and #561; see her for further specimens.

13. Besides Wolff, *Emily Dickinson*, pp. 454–56, see Small, *Positive as*

Sound, on homonymic rhyme, pp. 140-73; also Dorothy Huff Oberhaus, "Tender Pioneer: Emily Dickinson's Poems on the Life of Christ," in *Emily Dickinson,* ed. Farr, pp. 105-18.

14. See Howard, "Emily Dickinson's Poetic Vocabulary," p. 242.

15. See Martha O'Keefe, "Primal Thought," *Dickinson Studies* No. 35 (1979): 8-11, for evidence that Dickinson structured her own manuscript gatherings of poems around paired oppositions reflecting an interest in primal words. On negation in Dickinson's poetry, see Miller, *A Poet's Grammar,* pp. 98-104.

16. See Jane D. Eberwein, "Emily Dickinson and Edwards Amasa Park: 'The Loveliest Sermon,'" *ATQ* n.s. 1 (1987): 311-22.

17. On the biblical roots of the Book-of-Nature tradition and the ambiguity in Psalm 19 smoothed over by the King James version, see Walter Hesford, "Coming Down the Page of Nature: Thoreau on Language and Nature," *Essays in Literature* (Macomb, Ill.) 12:1 (1988): 85-95. Cf. Wolff, *Emily Dickinson,* on the primacy of visual over verbal language for Dickinson, pp. 36-65. My discussion of #430 and #334 owes much to Cristanne Miller, "Terms and Golden Words: Alternatives of Control in Dickinson's Poetry," *ESQ* 28 (1982): 48-62.

18. See Sharon Cameron, "Naming as History: Dickinson's Poems of Definition," *Critical Inquiry* 5 (1978): 230-32; Miller, *A Poet's Grammar,* pp. 24-39, 44-88; Margarita Ardanaz, "Emily Dickinson's Poetry: On Translating Silence," *Emily Dickinson Journal* 5 (1996): 256-57.

19. See Karen Dandurand, "New Dickinson Civil War Publications," *AL* 56 (1984): 17-27.

Chapter 11

1. See esp. C. Carroll Hollis, "Names in *Leaves of Grass,*" *Names* 5 (1957): 134-35; Michael R. Dressman, "'Names Are Magic': Walt Whitman's Laws of Geographic Nomenclature," *Names* 26 (1978): 68-79.

2. Horace Traubel, *With Walt Whitman in Camden,* 4 (Philadelphia: University of Pennsylvania Press, 1953), 324; hereafter *WWWC,* 4.

3. Horace Traubel, *With Walt Whitman in Camden,* 3 (1914; rpt. New York: Rowman & Littlefield, 1961), 123; hereafter *WWWC,* 3.

4. For this suggestion, see Alan D. Hodder, "'Wonderful Indirections' and Whitman's Rocking Cradle," *ESQ* 31 (1989): 119-20.

5. Besides Dressman, "Names Are Magic," p. 74, see esp. Allen Walker Read, "Walt Whitman's Attraction to Indian Place Names," *Literary Onomastic Studies* 7 (1980): 189-203.

6. Besides work listed in Southard's 1984 bibliography, recent years have seen the publication of several important studies of Whitman's linguistic thought. Tenney Nathanson's *Whitman's Presence: Body, Voice and Writing in Leaves of Grass* (New York: New York University Press, 1992) has done most to shape my argument. Though Whitman's mistrust of language strikes me as greater than it does Nathanson, my indebtedness to this fine book exceeds the reach of footnotes. Also helpful have been James Perrin Warren, *Walt Whitman's Language Experiment* (University Park: Pennsylvania State University Press, 1990); and Mark Bauerlein, *Whitman and the American Idiom* (Baton Rouge: Louisiana State University Press, 1991).

7. See James Olney, *The Languages of Poetry: Walt Whitman, Emily Dickinson, G. M. Hopkins* (Athens: University of Georgia Press, 1993), p. 120.

8. See George B. Hutchinson, *The Ecstatic Whitman: Literary Shamanism and the Crisis of the Union* (Columbus: Ohio State University Press, 1985).

9. *New York Dissected*, ed. Emory Holloway (New York: Wilson, 1936), p. 56.

10. In Nathanson, *Whitman's Presence*, p. 212. Such doctrines were by no means confined to the Transcendental environs of Boston; see Peter S. Chazotte's similar formulation in *An Essay on the Best Method of Teaching Foreign Languages; To Which Is Prefixed a Discourse on the Origin and Progress of Languages* (Philadelphia: Earle, 1817), pp. 11-12. My discussion of "Song of the Rolling Earth" owes much to Nathanson, pp. 224-28.

11. See James H. Stam, *Inquiries into the Origin of Language: The Fate of a Question* (New York: Harper & Row, 1976), p. 243; James Milroy, *The Language of Gerard Manley Hopkins* (London: André Deutsch, 1977), pp. 65-66. David Hartley's *Observations on Man* (1749) was a fountainhead of speculation about primal vibrations.

12. Samuel Kirkham, *English Grammar in Familiar Lectures* (New York: Collins, ca. 1829), pp. 37-38. My discussion of Whitman's deictics owes much to Mitchell Robert Breitwieser, "Who Speaks in Whitman's Poems?" in *The American Renaissance: New Directions*, ed. Harry R. Garvin and Peter C. Carafiol (Lewisburg, Pa.: Bucknell University Press, 1983), pp. 121-43.

13. *Institutes of English Grammar* (New York: Wood, 1845), p. 48n.

14. In addition to Erik Ingvar Thurin, *Whitman between Impressionism and Expressionism: Language of the Body, Language of the Soul* (Lewisburg, Pa.: Bucknell University Press, 1995), p. 153, see esp. Stephen Railton, "The Performance of Whitman's Poetry," in *The Cambridge Companion to Walt Whitman*, ed. Ezra Greenspan (New York: Cambridge University Press, 1995), pp. 7-26.

15. *LG*, pp. 29-30. My analysis of this passage draws heavily on Nathanson, *Whitman's Presence*, pp. 47-49.

16. In Warren, *Language Experiment*, p. 45. I owe much both to chapter 2 and to his "The 'Real Grammar': Deverbal Style in 'Song of Myself,'" *AL* 56 (1984): 1-16.

17. See Carmine Sarracino, "Figures of Transcendence in Whitman's Poetry," *WWQR* 5 (1987): 1-11.

18. *Variorum*, 1:31. See Warren, *Language Experiment*, p. 54.

19. In Richard Chase, *Walt Whitman Reconsidered* (New York: William Sloane, 1955), p. 73.

20. On the musical structure, see Robert D. Faner, *Walt Whitman & Opera* (Philadelphia: University of Pennsylvania Press, 1951), esp. pp. 173-77. In its main outlines my interpretation coincides with that of Bauerlein, *American Idiom*, pp. 131-52; but see also Nathanson, *Whitman's Presence*, pp. 444-68.

21. See esp. C. Carroll Hollis, "Linguistic Features of Song of Myself," in *Approaches to Teaching Whitman's Leaves of Grass*, ed. Donald D. Kummings (New York: Modern Language Association, 1990), pp. 49-55.

Chapter 12

1. Andrew Preston Peabody, *Harvard Reminiscences* (Boston: Ticknor & Fields, 1888), p. 90.
2. *Grammar*, pp. 17-18. Besides Dillman, "Thoreau's Harvard Education," see Kenneth Walter Cameron, *Thoreau's Harvard Years* (Hartford: Transcendental Books, 1966), pp. 5-10.
3. *The Thoreau Log*, ed. Raymond R. Borst (New York: G. K. Hall, 1992), p. 580. See further Walter Harding, "Thoreau on the Lecture Platform," *NEQ* 24 (1951): 365-74.
4. Ms. 931, in *The Annotated Walden*, ed. Philip Van Doren Stern (New York: Crown, 1970), 254n.
5. See esp. Kenneth W. Rhoads, "Thoreau: The Ear and the Music," *AL* 46 (1974): 313-28.
6. See my "Dryden and the Disintegration of Renaissance Heroic Ideals," *Costerus* 7 (1973): 193-222.
7. See esp. J. L. Campbell, "'It Is as If a Green Bough Were Laid across the Page': Thoreau on Eloquence," *Rhetorical Society Quarterly* 70 (1990): 61-70.
8. *A Week*, p. 273. See esp. David B. Suchoff, "'A More Conscious Silence': Friendship and Language in Thoreau's *A Week*," *ELH* 49 (1982): 673-88; also Ted Billy, "Check-List of Wordplays in Thoreau's *A Week*," *Concord Saunterer* 14, No. 5 (1979): 14-19.

Chapter 13

1. See Kenneth Walter Cameron, *A Companion to Thoreau's Correspondence* (Hartford: Transcendental Books, 1964), p. 287.
2. *Complete Writings*, ed. Geoffrey Keynes (Oxford: Oxford University Press, 1979), p. 149.
3. In Thomas McFarland, *Romanticism and the Forms of Ruin* (Princeton : Princeton University Press, 1981), p. 298; see chapter 5 on this nineteenth-century intellectual tradition.
4. *Thoreau's Literary Notebook*, facs. ed. Kenneth Walter Cameron (Hartford: Transcendental Books, 1964), pp. 359-60.
5. Coleridge, *Theory of Life*, p. 578, in William C. Johnson Jr., *What Thoreau Said: Walden and the Unsayable* (Moscow, Ida.: University of Idaho Press, 1991), p. 57. His study offers a detailed if humorless treatment of this theme in Thoreau.
6. *Biographia Literaria*, 2:12, in McFarland, *Romanticism*, p. 331. With Thoreau's Coleridgean treatment of the hawk, cf. his description of the mouse in "Brute Neighbors," which also scientizes and humanizes simultaneously, as Lawrence Buell argues in *The Environmental Imagination: Thoreau, Nature Writing, and the Formation of American Culture* (Cambridge, Mass.: Harvard University Press, 1995), pp. 95-96.
7. In Alan Reynolds Thompson, *The Dry Mock: A Study of Irony in Drama* (Berkeley: University of California Press, 1948), pp. 66-67.
8. See Henry Golemba, *Thoreau's Wild Rhetoric* (New York: New York

University Press, 1990), p. 195. In stressing that Thoreau was less an Emerson-ian Yea-sayer or a Melvillean Nay-sayer than an Un-sayer, Golemba supports my emphasis on his Romantic irony.

9. *Emerson and Thoreau: The Contemporary Reviews,* ed. Joel Myerson (New York: Cambridge University Press, 1992), pp. 376–89. As Buell observes, *Environmental Imagination,* p. 168, modern readings of *Walden* neglect "the instability of the persona" that generates the humor relished in the American Renaissance.

10. See Larry R. Long, "The Bible and the Composition of *Walden,*" *SAR 1979,* pp. 309–54.

11. See C. Grant Loomis, "Traditional American Wordplay: The Epigram and the Perverted Proverb," *Western Folklore* 8 (1949):348–57.

12. See esp. Raymond Adams, "Thoreau's Mock-Heroics and the American Natural History Writers," *SP* 52 (1955): 86–97.

13. See my "Homer's *Iliad* and the Genesis of Mock-Heroic," *Cithara* 21 (1981): 3–22.

14. *The Annotated Walden,* ed. Philip Van Doren Stern (New York: Crown, 1970), pp. 297–98n.

15. On the dialectic of work and play see Michael Daher, "Leisure, Play and Labor in Thoreau," in *Play as Context,* ed. Alyce T. Cheska (West Point, N.Y.: AASP, 1981), pp. 159–67; Nicholas K. Bromell, *By the Sweat of the Brow: Literature and Labor in Antebellum America* (Chicago: University of Chicago Press, 1993), chap. 11; and esp. Michael Oriard, *Sporting with the Gods: The Rhetoric of Play and Game in American Culture* (New York: Cambridge University Press, 1991), pp. 373–78.

16. See esp. Thomas L. Altherr, "'Chaplain to the Hunters': Henry David Thoreau's Attitude toward Hunting," *AL* 56 (1984): 345–61; also Gordon V. Boudreau, "Transcendental Sport: Hunting, Fishing, and Trapping in *Walden,*" *Thought* 67 (1992): 74–87.

Chapter 14

1. *A World Elsewhere: The Place of Style in American Literature* (New York: Oxford University Press, 1966), p. 88. But Michael Ackland, "Thoreau's *Walden:* In Praise of Mental Perception," *ATQ* No. 49 (Winter 1981): 55–71, like many Thoreauvians, rejects earlier efforts to explore this issue.

2. Conflating two drafts, I rely on transcriptions of manuscripts now in the Huntington and Morgan Libraries provided by Elizabeth Witherell, "An Editor's Nightmare: 'It Is No Dream of Mine' in the Princeton Edition of Thoreau's Poetry," *Concord Saunterer* 12 (Fall 1977): 5–9.

3. In Charles R. Anderson, *The Magic Circle of Walden* (New York: Holt, Rinehart & Winston, 1968), p. 166.

4. In Joseph Jones, "Transcendental Grocery Bills: Thoreau's *Walden* and Some Aspects of American Vegetarianism," *University of Texas Studies in English* 36 (1957): 146.

5. On Thoreau's attitude toward fungi and death, see esp. Joel Porte, *Emerson and Thoreau: Transcendentalists in Conflict* (Middletown: Wesleyan University Press, 1965), pp. 181–90.

6. Thoreau transcribed these lines from Percy's *Reliques* into his poetical copybook, now in the Library of Congress, in 1842. See Ann Whaling, "Studies in Thoreau's Reading of English Poetry and Prose, 1340-1660" (Ph.D. diss., Yale University, 1946), pp. 101-2.

7. Describing a bogtrotter's typically ragged attire, William Carleton stressed the same detail in his *Traits and Stories of the Irish Peasantry* (1830), rpt. in *An Anthology of Irish Literature,* ed. David H. Greene (New York: Random House, 1954), p. 322. Carleton's similar sketch of a shanty family supports Thoreau's complaint that the Fields lived in a "derivative old country mode" (p. 208).

8. See Taylor Stoehr, *Nay-Saying in Concord* (Hamden, Conn.: Archon, 1979), pp. 115-42.

9. See Jeffrey E. Simpson, "Thoreau: The Walking Muse," *ESQ* 37 (1991): 1-33; John C. Broderick, "The Movement of Thoreau's Prose," *AL* 33 (1961): 133-42; David C. Smith, "Walking as Spiritual Discovery," *Soundings* 74 (1991): 129-40. Lorenz Oken's *Elements of Physiophilosophy,* trans. Tulk (1847), had much to say about the menace of lurking infusoria.

10. Discussing *muck* and *mixen* s.v., Tooke connects them respectively with *mingere* and *miscere.* Although he distinguishes these words, explaining *mix* etymologically as *to digest,* he cites Junius and Skinner as authorities for linking both meanings in a way that would have encouraged Thoreau to derive *mingle* from *mingere.* For Thoreau's reliance on Tooke see *PJ,* 2:189 (23 Dec. 1845).

11. Walter Harding, *The Days of Henry Thoreau* (New York: Knopf, 1965), pp. 77-78, considered and rejected this interpretation but later elaborated it in "Thoreau's Sexuality," *Journal of Homosexuality* 21, No. 3 (1991): 23-45; see also Michael Warner, "Thoreau's Bottom," *Raritan* 11 (1992): 53-79.

12. In Anderson, *Magic Circle,* p. 165. On the psychological basis of misogyny, see esp. G. J. Barker-Benfield, *The Horrors of the Half-Known Life: Male Attitudes toward Women and Sexuality in Nineteenth-Century America* (New York: Harper & Row, 1976). In "Thoreau, Womankind, and Sexuality," *ESQ* 22 (1976): 122-48, Mary Elkins Moller shows that Thoreau's misogyny was by no means total, but she cannot exempt him from the trait.

13. In James Armstrong, "Thoreau, Chastity, and the Reformers," in *Thoreau's Psychology: Eight Essays,* ed. Raymond Dante Gozzi (Lanham, Md.: University Press of America, 1983), p. 133.

14. In Harding, "Thoreau's Sexuality," p. 24.

15. For Thoreau's indebtedness to Mallet, see journal entries for 15 and 16 February 1852 as well as *Cape Cod,* p. 151. On his heroic ideals see esp. Linck C. Johnson, "Contexts of Bravery: Thoreau's Revisions of 'The Service' for *A Week,*" *SAR 1983,* pp. 281-96. But these need the intellectual context best sketched by Eric Russell Bentley, *A Century of Hero-Worship: A Study of the Idea of Heroism in Carlyle and Nietzsche with Notes on Other Hero-Worshippers of Modern Times* (Philadelphia: Lippincott, 1944), indispensable for understanding Thoreau.

16. See Stoehr, *Nay-Saying,* pp. 155-56, for a shrewd defense of Transcendental asceticism.

17. William James, *The Varieties of Religious Experience,* ed. Joseph Ratner (New York: University Books, 1963), pp. 363-64, and cf. his essay "The Moral

Equivalent of War." On other links between James and Thoreau, see Martha Banta, "American Apocalypses: Excrement and Ennui," *Studies in the Literary Imagination* 7 (1974): 1-30.

18. See Lawrence Willson, "Thoreau's Medical Vagaries," *Journal of the History of Medicine and Allied Sciences* 15 (1960): 64-74; Walter Harding, "Thoreau and Tuberculosis," *TSB* No. 186 (Winter 1989): 1-2.

19. *How to Prevent Consumption* (Boston: Light, 1839), p. 13.

20. *Six Lectures on the Uses of the Lungs; and Causes, Prevention, and Cure of Pulmonary Consumption* (New York: Carlisle, 1847), p. 76.

21. See Nan Marie McMurry, "'And I? I Am in a Consumption': The Tuberculosis Patient, 1780-1930" (Ph.D. diss., Duke University, 1985; Ann Arbor, Mich.: University Microfilms, 1985), pp. 64-70, 79.

22. See J. Hamilton Potter, M.D., *The Consumptive's Guide to Health*, 2d ed. (New York: Redfield, 1851), pp. 102-3, 113.

23. See James Harvey Young, *The Toadstool Millionaires: A Social History of Patent Medicines in America before Federal Regulation* (Princeton: Princeton University Press, 1961), pp. 79, 38.

24. *Correspondence of William James*, ed. Ignas K. Skrupskelis and Elizabeth M. Berkeley (Charlottesville: University Press of Virginia, 1992), 1:119.

25. For the influence on Thoreau of Say's pejorative treatment of economic consumption, see Robert D. Richardson, *Henry Thoreau: A Life of the Mind* (Berkeley: University of California Press, 1986), pp. 414-15n.

26. *Pliny's Natural History*, trans. Philemon Holland, ed. Paul Turner (Carbondale: Southern Illinois University Press, 1962), p. 75.

27. Dio Lewis, *Weak Lungs and How to Make Them Strong, or Diseases of the Organs of the Chest, with Their Home Treatment by the Movement Cure*, 28th ed. (1863; rpt. Boston: Ticknor & Fields, 1881), pp. 118, 205; see also pp. 184, 188, 217.

28. Arthur Christy, *The Orient in American Transcendentalism* (New York: Columbia University Press, 1932), p. 214.

29. See Herbert F. Smith, "Usher's Madness and Poe's Organicism," *AL* 39 (1967): 379-89.

30. *Thoreau, The Poet-Naturalist* (Boston: Roberts, 1873), pp. 321-22.

31. *Walden*, p. 8. Cf. Richard Chenevix Trench, *On the Study of Words* (1851; New York: Redfield, 1852), p. 219, and Aristotle, *Nicomachean Ethics*, 10.6.

32. *Introduction to the History of Philosophy*, trans. Henning Gottfried Linberg (Boston: Hilliard, 1832), p. 137. See Cameron, *Emerson the Essayist* (1945; Hartford: Transcendental Books, 1972), 1:303-19.

33. In René Wellek, *A History of Modern Criticism* (New Haven: Yale University Press, 1955), 2:17.

34. Lawrence Buell, *The Environmental Imagination: Thoreau, Nature Writing, and the Formation of American Culture* (Cambridge, Mass.: Harvard University Press, 1995), p. 122.

35. See esp. Robert E. Abrams, "Image, Object, and Perception in Thoreau's Landscapes: The Development of Anti-Geography," *Nineteenth-Century Literature* 46 (1991): 245-62; also Henry Golemba, "Unreading Thoreau," *AL* 60 (1988): 385-401.

36. See Thoreau's transcriptions from Oken in *The Transcendendalists and Minerva,* ed. Kenneth Walter Cameron (Hartford: Transcendental Books, 1958), 1:295.

37. *Representative Men,* in *Works,* 4:108; *English Traits,* ibid., 5:237-38.

38. In Wellek, *Modern Criticism,* 2:175. On Thoreau's revisions, see Ronald Clapper, "The Development of *Walden:* A Genetic Text" (Ph.D. diss., UCLA, 1967).

39. In Sylvan Barnet, "Coleridge on Puns: A Note to his Shakespeare Criticism," *JEGP* 56 (1957): 606n. On concentration camp punning, see Steven Lipman, *Laughter in Hell* (Northvale, N.J.: Aronson, 1991).

40. See Kathryn Anderson McEuen, "Lowell's Puns," *American Speech* 22 (1947): 24-33.

41. In John Clubbe, *Victorian Forerunner: The Later Career of Thomas Hood* (Durham, N.C.: Duke University Press, 1968), p. 34.

42. J. C. Reid, *Thomas Hood* (London: Routledge, 1963), pp. 235-37.

43. *The Portable Nietzsche,* ed. and trans. Walter Kaufmann (New York: Viking, 1969), pp. 152-53; see further Kaufmann's comments, pp. 106-11.

44. *The Case of Wagner,* trans. Thomas Common, in Nietzsche's *Works,* ed. Alexander Tille (New York: Macmillan, 1896), 11:24-25.

45. Thomas Carlyle, *History of Friedrich II of Prussia,* ed. John Clive (1858-65; Chicago: University of Chicago Press, 1969), p. 16.

46. "Thoreau," in *Works,* 10:448. Since the aesthetic interpretation of Thoreau has been vigorously challenged, most recently by Gary Borjesson, "A Sounding of *Walden*'s Philosophical Depth," *Philosophy and Literature* 18 (1994): 287-308, its origin in Emerson's own perceptions is worth noting. In *Language and Decadence in the Victorian Fin de Siecle* (Princeton: Princeton University Press, 1986), Linda Dowling suggests how nineteenth-century philology fostered the emergence of the decadent sensibility in figures like Swinburne and Pater.

47. In *A Psychiatrist Looks at Tuberculosis* (London: National Association for the Prevention of Tuberculosis, 1949), pp. 27-30, 40-41, Eric Wittkower finds that a syndrome of defensive jocularity marks 12 percent of tuberculosis patients, usually linked to conflicts over aggressiveness and independence. On pathogenic and psychogenic wordplay, see esp. Walter Redfern, *Puns* (Oxford: Blackwell, 1984), chap. 6.

48. *Thoreau, The Poet-Naturalist,* p. 34. See Bernard Rosenthal, "Thoreau's Book of Leaves," *ESQ* 56, No. 3 (1969): 7-11, for further examples of the punning in this essay; also Gordon Boudreau, *The Roots of Walden and the Tree of Life* (Nashville, Tenn.: Vanderbilt University Press, 1990), pp. 169-73.

49. John Mason Good, *The Book of Nature* (Boston: Wells, 1826), pp. 134-35. See Richard Grusin, "Thoreau, Extravagance, and the Economy of Nature," *American Literary History* 5 (1993): 30-50.

50. In Harding, *Days,* pp. 102, 109. On the trope of love as play, see Michael Oriard, *Sporting with the Gods: The Rhetoric of Play and Game in American Culture* (New York: Cambridge University Press, 1991), chap. 3.

51. In Johan Huizinga, *Homo Ludens: A Study of the Play-Element in Culture* (Boston: Beacon: 1955), pp. 18-19. See esp. his chapters 3-4 on the affiliations of play with heroism, which Oriard neglects in dichotomizing the two.

52. William Butler Yeats, *Collected Poems* (New York: Macmillan, 1955), pp. 292-93.

53. Kay Redfield Jamison, *Touched with Fire: Manic-Depressive Illness and the Artistic Temperament* (New York: Free Press, 1993), pp. 36-37, 216-19, 267-69, makes these plausible diagnoses. On less convincing evidence she also finds Whitman manic-depressive, while her claim that Emerson exhibited the syndrome seems highly dubious.

54. In Kenneth Cmiel, *Democratic Eloquence: The Fight over Popular Speech in Nineteenth-Century America* (New York: Morrow, 1990), p. 114. Though Cmiel's quotation is misattributed, I rely on his assurance in personal correspondence that it is from a like work by Marsh that he cannot now identify. See also Thomas Gustafson, *Representative Words: Politics, Literature, and the American Language, 1776-1865* (New York: Cambridge University Press, 1992).

Index

Page numbers in italics refer to illustrations.

Aarsleff, Hans, 273
Abernethy, Lunenberg G., *Laughable Anecdotes*, 24
Abounding Fullness, 52-54, 57, 270, 325, 391, 468
Adams, Frederic A., 241
Adams, John, 72
Adams, John Quincy, 94, 219, 228; letter to Johnson, 222; letter to Ruggles, 2
Alcott, Bronson, 42, 265, 448, 454-55; *Journal*, 171-72
Alcott, William: on consumption, 462; *The Young House-Keeper*, 449
Alexander's Weekly Messenger, Poe writing in, 304
Allen, Phineas, 126, 127, 140
almanacs, comic. *See* comic almanacs
American Academy of Belles Lettres, 72
American Democrat, The, Cooper writing in, 296, 298
American Indians: languages of, 46, 205, 297-98; rendered by Cooper, 297-98, 300, 301; Whitman's interest in nomenclature of, 370-76
American Notes and Queries, 13
American Renaissance, 13, 15; etymological study during, 156; grammars in use during, 135
Amherst Academy, Dickinson at, 344
Andover Theological Seminary, 238, 241
Anglo-Saxon roots, 147-55, 158; vs. Greco-Roman roots, 155-56
anima mundi, 31, 200
anthropomorphism, 41-42; Trinitarian doctrine and, 245-46
Anti-Bell-Ringing Society, 14
aphasia, Emerson afflicted with, 279-83
Appleton, Thomas Gold, as punster, 17-19, 25
architectural theory, Thoreau's, 39-42, 451
Aristotelian identity principle, 52, 230
Arnold, George, 14
Arp, Bill, 213
asceticism, Thoreau's, 460-65
Atlantic Monthly, 175, 351, 396
Austin, Gilbert, *Chironomia*, 332
A was an archer, or, A new amusing alphabet for children, 9

Bacon, Francis, 177
Bacon, Leonard, 241
Badgley, Jonathan, 115-16, 117
Bailey, Nathan, *Universal Etymological English Dictionary*, 164
Bailey, Rufus W., 155-56
Baker Farm, 442
Balch, William S., 134; *Inductive Grammar*, 118-20; *Lectures on Language*, 118
Bancroft, George, and Round Hill School, 17-18
Bank of Utica, 221
Barber, Jonathan, 402-6, 423; *A Grammar of Elocution*, 402-3
Barnes, Daniel H., 118
Barnes, William, 147
Bartlett, John, *Dictionary of Americanisms*, 12-13, 174
Bartol, Cyrus, on Bushnell, 242, 247, 249
Bauerlein, Mark, on *Moby-Dick*, 328-29
Beecher, Catharine, *Treatise on Domestic Economy*, 435
Bentham, Jeremy, 45
Bentley, Eric, on Heroic Vitalists, 460, 472
Berkeley, George, 49, 224; influence on Coleridge, 60, 65; *A New Theory of Vision*, 29-30; *Siris*, 31-32
Biblical Repository, 241-42
Billings, Josh, 213
Black, John, translation of A. W. Schlegel, 56
Blackwood's, on Irving, 294
Blair, David, 116; *Rhetoric*, 127
Blair, Hugh, 66; *Lectures on Rhetoric and Belles Lettres*, 32; *Rhetoric*, 46-47
Blake, William, *The Marriage of Heaven and Hell*, 427-28
Blanchard, Rufus, *The Grammatical Tree*, 136-37, *138*
Boehme, Jacob: influence on Coleridge, 60; influence on Transcendentalism, 427-28; and nature as language, 30
Booth, David, 161
Borrow, George, 196
Boston Courier, 15
Boston Evening Transcript, on Poe, 305
Boston Morning Post, 14
Boston Quarterly Review, 130
botanical language. *See* language, botanical; language, organic

bowels, Thoreau's obsession with, 445-79 passim

Bowen, Francis, 262, 268

Bowles, Samuel, 357, 359

Brace, Charles L., 249

Brackenridge, Hugh Henry, *Law Miscellanies,* 114

Brains of Boston Conundrum Contest, 25-26

Breckinridge, Robert, controversy with J. Brown, 95, 106

Bristol's Free Almanac, 24

Broad Grins, 21

Bronson, Cotesworth P., 313-14

Brosses, Charles de: influence on Kraitsir, 185; and onomatopoeia, 32-33, 382; summarized by Stewart, 49; theory on primitive language, 32-33; Tooke on, 44

Brown, Goold, 107; *Grammar of Grammars,* 116; on pronouns, 387

Brown, James, 91-109, 132, 134; *An American Grammar,* 72, 92; *American System of English Grammar,* 94, 95; controversy with Croes, 95; and definers, 92-93; English Syntax Institution, 105; failure of, 102-3; focus on syntax, 91, 93, 101, 108; success of, 106-7; teaching of syntax, 103-5; *A Treatise on the Nature and Reasons of the English Grammar,* 91, 94; tree metaphor for syntax, 96-97, 98, 99, 137

Browne, Daniel J., *The Etymological Encyclopedia of Technical Terms and Phrases,* 159

Brownson, Orestes, 129-30, 240, 266

Bryant, Jacob, 306; *Analysis of Ancient Mythology,* 42

Bryant, William Cullen, *U.S. Review and Literary Gazette,* 110

Bumppo, Natty, 296-303

Bungtown, 212-13

Bushnell, Horace, 67, 76, 242-50, 368, 468; *Christ in Theology,* 243; and Emerson, 247; *God in Christ,* 242, 248, 249, 250; influenced by Coleridge, 246-47; influenced by Johnson, 243-44, 248; and influence of Humboldt, 244-45, 493 n. 19; on Johnson's *Treatise,* 228; on Scripture, 245-46; on verbs and nouns, 243

Butler, Noble, *Practical Grammar,* 121

Butter, Henry, *Etymological Spelling Book and Expositor,* 155

Byron, George Gordon, Lord, 27; *Don Juan,* 56

Campbell, Thomas, *Pleasures of Hope,* 356

Cardell, William, 72-79; and *to be* (verb), 77-78; *Elements of English Grammar,* 73-74, 113; *Essay on Language,* 72-73, 74; and etymology, 112-13; influence of, 110-20; Johnson compared with, 231; *Philosophic Grammar of the English Language,* 74, 86-87; and "philosophic parsing," 72, 74-75; Sherman on, 86-87, 95

Carlyle, Thomas, 27, 159, 178, 250, 472; influence on Thoreau, 207-8, 460, 471; and philology, 62; *Sartor Resartus,* 41, 56

Channing, E. T., 402-3, 405

Channing, Edward Tyrell: as Thoreau's teacher, 129; as Thoreau's colleague, 402

Channing, Walter, "Essay on American Language and Literature," 1

Channing, William Ellery, 73

Channing, William Ellery Jr, as punster, 16

Chapman, John Liddell, 153

Chaucer, Geoffrey: influence on Dickinson, 343; influence on Whitman, 178-79; *rime riche* in, 354; Thoreau on, 128

Chazotte, Peter, 382; *An Introductory Lecture on the Metaphysics and Philosophy of Language,* 69-70

Chingachgook, 300-301

Christ: in Dickinson's poetry, 352-53; in *Walden,* 436-37

Cincinnati, Ohio, 2, 121, 162; *Type of the Times,* 5

Clark, Willis Gaylord, on puns, 17

Clinton, DeWitt, 95; on J. Brown, 94; and Walworth, 114

Clough, A. H., 25

Colebrooke, Henry, *Vocabulary of the Sanskrit Language,* 160

Coleridge, Hartley, 3-6, 59

Coleridge, Samuel Taylor, 57-67, 254; *Aids to Reflection,* 59, 63, 64, 65, 66, 246, 428; "Apology for Paronomasy," 61; *Biographia Literaria,* 64, 428; and desynonymization, 63-64; *The Friend,* 471; *Hints toward the Formation of a More Comprehensive Theory,* 428; influence on Bushnell, 246-47; influence on Cardell, 77; influence on Thoreau, 427-30; *Logic,* 62-63; *Notebooks,* 63; penchant for neologisms, 60; on punning, 61; Reason vs. Understanding, 64; on Shakespeare, 66; and Tooke's influence, 59-60

colloquialisms, of New England, 12-13
Columbus, Ohio, 117
comedy, and tragedy. *See* tragic/comic
dichotomy
comic almanacs, 15-16, 19
comic songs, 19
Concord Academy, 140; Thoreau as headmaster, 130-31; Thoreau at, 126-27
Concord Freeman, 16
Condillac, Étienne Bonnot de, 32, 46, 136,
237; *Essai sur l'origine des connaissances humaines,* 29; summarized by
Stewart, 49
Congregationalists: Andover Theological
Seminary, 238, 241; feud with Unitarians, 57, 238-42; reaction to Bushnell,
243
conjunctions, 43-44
Constitution. *See* U.S. Constitution
construing, 102, 109
consumption, 478; humor and, 24; medical
theories of, 462-64
Cooper, James Fenimore, 296-303; *The
Deerslayer,* 298; landscapes, 302-3; *The
Pioneers,* 300, 302; *The Prairie,* 297,
299; *The Wept of Wish-ton-Wish,* 435-
36
correspondence theory of nature, 259-67
Cousin, Victor, *History of Philosophy,* 467-
68
Crabb, George: on courage, 341; *English
Synonymes Explained,* 165-66, 336
Cranch, Christopher, 274, *275,* 276
Croes, John, controversy with J. Brown, 95

Darwinism, 152
Davy, Charles, *Conjectural Observations,*
318
definers, 92-93
Dennie, Joseph, 292
De Quincey, Thomas, 214
desynonymization, 63-64, 180, 355
diagramming sentences, 70
Dial, 258, 435
dialect humor, 19-20
Dickens, Charles: on Pittsburgh, 137; and
Wellerisms, 15
Dickinson, Emily, xiii, 334-69; at Amherst
Academy, 344; and the Bible, 347, 350,
352, 355, 357-58; and Bowles, 357,
359; and Christ, 352-53; fascination
with dictionaries, 334-44; and God as
Cosmic Joker, 352-53; and Gould, 346-
47; influenced by Chaucer, 343; influenced by Shakespeare, 344; influenced

by Webster, 354-55; and Lord, 338-39,
340, 359; at Mount Holyoke, 345; published in *Springfield Daily Republican,*
346; study of botany, 337; on tragic/
comic dichotomy, 25; use of puns, 344-
54; use of *rime riche,* 354; use of
Romantic irony, 361, 362-69; on Webster's *American Dictionary,* 10. Poems:
#3, 345-46; #48, 341; #109, 357; #130,
364-65; #243, 350; #249, 339; #276,
341-42; #315, 358-59; #324, 352;
#338, 353; #371, 338; #375, 348-49;
#420, 360; #439, 356; #459, 353; #543,
359; #572, 356; #709, 340; #801, 355-
56; #824, 269; #838, 356; #870, 369;
#1126, 362; #1167, 347-48; #1260,
368; #1307, 343; #1342, 358; #1347,
336; #1463, 364; #1554, 337; #1638;
#1700, 360
dictionaries, 10-12
die Fülle. See Abounding Fullness
Ding-an-sich, 51, 52, 183
Doesticks, Philander Q. Z., 213; Phunny
Phellows, 21-22
double negatives, in *Moby-Dick,* 330
Dryden, John, *Discourse on Satire,* 255
Du Ponceau, Peter, 222
Durrett, Reuben, duel with Prentice, 23
Duyckinck, Evert, 59
Dwight, Benjamin W., *Modern Philology,*
173

earth, as origin of language, 190-93
Eggleston, Edward, 113; on spelling, 3-4
Egyptian hieroglyphics. *See* hieroglyphics
Ellins, Charles, *The American Comic Almanac,* 15, 16
Ells, B. F., 111; Cardell's influence on, 112-
13; *Dialogue Grammar,* 112
elocution training, at Harvard, 402-6; influence on Poe, 314
Emerson, B. D.: *National Spelling Book,* 8
Emerson, Ralph Waldo, xii-xiii, 17, 84, 101,
251-90 passim, 468; afflicted with
aphasia, 279-83; "The American
Scholar," 251, 278, 283-90, 406; and
Anglo-Saxon English, 148; and Bushnell, 242, 247; "The Comic," 472; correspondence theory of nature, 259-67;
English Traits, 148; *Essays,* 435; and
games metaphor, 258; influenced by
Humboldt, 273; influenced by Reed,
382; influenced by Tooke, 254, 259;
influence of travel on, 210; influence on
Thoreau, 164-65, 194; influence on

Trench, 164; and intellectual fear, 286–87; "Language," 194, 252; letter to Fuller, 271–72; *Literary Ethics*, 256; *Nature*, 45, 81, 86–87, 136, 194, 233, 235, 247, 252, 259–67, 381, 397; obituary for Thoreau, 473; "The Poet," 6, 41, 164, 247, 259, 270, 273; and Poet as Primal Namer, 8, 252, 259; and power of verbs, 265; and self-consciousness, 79; on swearing, 13; on tragic/comic dichotomy, 25; and Unitarianism, 240–41; and Whitman's self-promotion, 171–72
English, T. D., 305
Enlightenment philosophers, 48, 50; Romanticism and, 51; scientists, 30
Episcopalianism, 241
Esperanto, 3
Essay Concerning Human Understanding (Locke), 28–29, 43
etymology: books on, 141–82 passim; in Cardell, 112–13; Coleridge on, 60, 61; vs. grammar battle, 79–91 passim; isolated from syntax, 71–72; in Murray's grammar, 68–69
Evelyn, John, 210–11; quoted in "The Bean-Field," 449; *Sylva*, 203
excrement: as creative product, 193–94; importance to American Romantics, 445–79 passim

Fern, Fanny, 305
Fichte, Johann, 51, 176; influence on F. Schlegel, 51–52, 468
Fisher's Comic Almanac, 15, 20
Fitch, Samuel Sheldon, on consumption, 462–63
Flint, Timothy, 228
Fowle, William B.: on Cardell, 110; *Common School Speller*, 142
Fowler, Orson, 379
Fowler, William Chauncy, 334
Francis, Convers, 121
Franklin, Benjamin, 34, 53, 292
Fredonia, 1
French, D'Arcy A., 116
Frost, Robert, "Directive," 270, 452
Fuller, Allen, *Grammatical Exercises*, 71–72
Fuller, Margaret, letter from Emerson, 271–72

Galena, Ill., 116–17
Gall, Franz Joseph, 379
games, as metaphor for Emerson, 258
Gardner, C. K., 2
Gardner, William, *The Music of Nature*, 186

Gébelin, Antoine Court de: *Dictionnaire étymologique de la langue Latine*, 195; *Dictionnaire étymologique François-Celte*, 35; *Grammaire Universelle*, 40; influence on de Brosses, 34; influence on Kraitsir, 185; influence on Thoreau, 35, 38, 194; influence on Vernon, 113–14; and letters as pictographs, 38–39; *Monde primitif analisé et comparé avec le monde moderne*, 34, 64, 128, 195, 222; on nouns, 378; *Origine du langage et de l'écriture*, 36, 37, 42; and primal nouns, 355; summarized by Stewart, 49
Genesis, 51; in Thoreau, 422
Gérando, Baron de, 42, 45, 161, 162
Germanic Higher Criticism, 239, 241
German Romantics, love of puns, 54–56
German roots. See Anglo-Saxon roots
Germany, Romantic irony in, 50–57
Gibbs, Josiah Willard, 243
Gilchrist, James, *Philosophic Etymology*, 195–96
Goethe, Johann von: *Metamorphosis of Plants*, 186, 428; as punster, 56
Goldsbury, John, 133–34
Goodenow, Smith B., 134; Etymology City, 132, *133*
Gould, George, and Dickinson, 346–47
Graham, George Frederick, *English Synonyms Classified and Explained*, 159
grammar: defined by Murray, 68–69, 74; vs. etymology battle, 79–91 passim; in Ohio, 117, 121; in Pennsylvania, 135; universal, 88
Grant, Ulysses S.: and Swinton, 175; as a verb, 117
Graves, John, 334
Greco-Roman roots, vs. Anglo-Saxon roots, 155–56
Greek language study, as male rite, 6
Greeley, Horace, and spelling bee, 4
Green, Richard W., *The Scholar's Companion*, 155–56
Greene, Samuel, *Treatise of the Structure of the English Language*, 131
Greenough, Horatio, 42
Griffith, Henry Wharton, *A Lift for the Lazy*, 168, 175
Grimshaw, William, 157–59; *Etymological Dictionary*, 158
Gummere, Samuel, *The Progressive Spelling Book*, 142
Gura, Philip, 259; on Emerson, 259, 261

Hall, William, 117–18

Hamann, J. G., *Kreuzzüge des Philologen*, 50-51

Harris, James: contrasted with Coleridge, 62-63, 65; *Hermes*, 42; Tooke on, 44

Hartford Wits, 10

Harvard University, 13; Anglo-Saxon English at, 147; elocution training at, 402-6; Hollis Chair of Divinity, 238, 242; J. Sherman allied with, 80; Thoreau at, 127-30, 402-6; and Unitarian ministers, 238

Hawthorne, Nathaniel, xiii, 315-23; and anthropomorphism, 41; "The Custom-House," 320-21, 322; and hieroglyphics, 318-19; and punning language, 316-17; *The Scarlet Letter*, 317-23, 435; and slavery, 322

Hazard, Rowland Gibson, *Language*, 240

Hazlitt, William, on Tooke, 45

Hebrew, 40, 51; Balch on, 118; botanical terms in, 58; and Cardell's verb *to be*, 77; Coleridge's belief in, 62; Herder on, 57-59

Hecker, Isaac, 130

Hedge, F. H., 1

Herder, Johann von, 190; *Älteste Urkunde des Menschengeschlects*, 51; on Hebrew, 57-59; influence on Bushnell, 244; influence on Cardell, 77; *The Spirit of Hebrew Poetry*, 57; *Über den Ursprung der Sprache*, 51

hermeneutics, 120-25; biblical, 238-39

Heroic Vitalists, 460, 472-73

hieroglyphics, xii, 39, 187, 318, 319

Higginson, T. W., 340; letters from Dickinson, 335

Hildreth, Ezekiel, 121-25, 193; *Logopolis, or City of Words*, 122, 139, 195; verbs and power, 122; in Wheeling, 137, 139-40

Hildreth, Richard, 140

Hill, A. S.: on punning, 17, 19; "Puns and Punsters," 10

Hollis, C. Carroll, on Whitman, 175

Holmes, Oliver Wendell, 12; "The Deacon's Masterpiece," 351; on Emerson, 277, 279, 280; and humor as therapy, 23-24; on pun as weapon, 22, 472; as punster, 16-17

Hone, Philip, 84, 90

Hood, Thomas (Tom), 27; Poe on, 304, 472

Hoosier irony, 170

Hopkins, Gerard Manley, and notion of inscape, 383

Hoshour, Samuel K., 169-71; *Autobiogra-phy*, 170-71; Grammar City, 169; *Letters to Esq. Pedant, in the East*, 169-70

hostility, of jestbook humor, 16

Howe, Julia Ward, 26

Howitt, William, *Book of the Seasons*, 128

Humboldt, Wilhelm von, 187, 197; influence on Bushnell, 244-45, 493 n. 19; possible influence on Emerson, 273

Hume, David, 224, 225

humor: dialect, 19-20; Johnson's ambiguity about, 235; as therapy, 23-24, 25, 471-72; Thoreau's hydraulic theory of, 197-200, 208

Humorist's Own Book, The, 16

Hutchins, Joseph, *Abstract of the First Principles of English Grammar*, 141

identity: Johnson on concept of, 233-34; Norton on, 239

Illinois, grammar in, 116-17

Indiana: etymology in, 112; importance of spelling, 3-4

infinity: F. Schlegel and, 52-53; Norton on, 239

Irving, Washington, xiv, 11, 291-96; *History of New York*, 292-95; "The Legend of Sleepy Hollow," 295; as punster, 17; "Rip Van Winkle," 295; *Salmagundi*, 291-92; use of puns, 295-96

Ives, Charles, 407

Jackson, Andrew, 75-76, 220-21

Jacksonian democracy, xi, 143-44, 219, 479

Jakobson, Roman, 279

James, Henry, 17, 24, 463, 469; on Hawthorne, 315-16

James, William: on ascetic impulse, 461; and Heroic Vitalism, 473; on stooling impulse, 463

Jefferson, Thomas, xi; and Anglo-Saxon English, 147-48; and *neology*, 3; on proposal for American academy, 72

Jerrold, Douglas, 23, 344-45

jestbooks, 15-16, 19-23, 25; and humor as therapy, 24

Jews, as romantic primitives, 57-58

Johnson, Abigail Adams, 221; death of, 230

Johnson, Alexander Bryan, 219-38; and abolition, 235; and ambiguity of language, 224-25; on concept of identity, 233-24; and death of Abigail, 230-31; *Deep Sea Soundings*, 223, 231; depression and, 230-31; and economics, 229; "The Effects of Language on the Speaker

and Hearer," 234; influence on Bushnell, 243-44, 248; *An Inquiry into the Nature and Value of Capital*, 220; Jewish background of, 227, 232; on Locke, 224; *The Meaning of Words*, 223; meets Abigail Adams, 221; and moral utilitarianism, 228; *The Philosophical Emperor*, 220; *Religion and Its Relation to the Present Life*, 228, 234; religious experience of, 227-28; *A Treatise on Language*, 223, 226-30, 248; use of Romantic irony, 236; and Utica Insurance Co., 221; on verbal unity, 232-34
Johnson, Samuel: dictionary, 11; on *saunter*, 168; Tooke on, 44
jokes, in comic almanacs, 19
Jones, Joshua, Cardell's influence on, 110

Kant, Immanuel: *Ding-an-sich*, 51, 52; Hamann's criticism of, 50; influence on Coleridge, 64
Kauy-a-hoo-ra, 80, 82, 84, 89, 90, 110
Keagy, J. M., 156
Keats, John: "Ode on a Grecian Urn," 264; wordplay while dying, 472
Kentucky, 24; in Civil War, 22-23; and *Louisville Daily Journal*, 22
Kierkegaard, Søren, 50
Kirkham, Samuel, 131, 136
Knickerbocker, Diedrich, 292-94
Know-Nothing party, 23
Kraitsir, Charles, 183-89, 195; definition of language, 187; *Glossology*, 183-84; and onomatopoeia, 382; *The Significance of the Alphabet* (with Peabody), 183; Thoreau and, 184-86, 465; and word as God, 187-88

Lamb, Charles, 17, 23, 27, 250; on puns, 55
Lancaster, Ohio, 161-62
language: of action, 29; ambiguity of, 224-25; botanical, 48, 58, 96-97, 205; dirt as origin of, 190-93; from earth, 206-11; Emerson on, 252; as fossil poetry, 194; mathematics and, 48-49; nonverbal, 66; organic, 197-200; philosophy of (*see* philosophy of language); and physical reality, 28-29; primal unity of, 63; primitive (*see* primitive language); scientific, 48; universal, 30-31, 32-33, 160-61
Latin language study, as male rite, 6
laughing, as therapy, 23-24; 321
Lawrence, Jerome, *The Night Thoreau Spent in Jail*, 474
Leatherstocking Tales, 296-303

Leaves of Grass (Whitman), 171-82, 370-401 passim; as tribute to Webster, 9; Variorum edition, 400
Leavitt, Dudley, *Complete Directions for Parsing the English Language*, 70-71
Lee, Robert E., 26
Lewis, John, *Analytical Outlines of the English Language*, 120-21
Life Illustrated, Whitman in, 173
Lincoln, Abraham, 19, 26; and Prentice, 22
linguistic development, Webster's theory of, 10-11, 354-55
Linnaean classification, 201-2, 205
Literary Association, A, 148-55; "The American System of Education," 149-50, 153; *The Hand-Book of Anglo-Saxon Derivatives*, 152; *Hand-Book of Anglo-Saxon Root-Words*, 148-55; *A Hand-Book of English Orthography*, 153; *Hand-Book of the Engrafted Words of the English Language*, 152, 153-54; influence on Whitman, 153-55, 173, 181
Locke, John, 46, 47, 49, 224; *Essay Concerning Human Understanding*, 28-29, 43; philosophical grammarians and, 136
Longfellow, Henry Wadsworth, 17; "Anglo-Saxon Literature," 128
Lord, Judge Otis, 338, 340, 359
Louisville, Ky., 22-23
Louisville Courier, 23
Louisville Daily Journal, 22-23
Lowell, James Russell: on Emerson, 277, 282; on etymologies, 12; and tragic/comic dichotomy, 25; and wordplay as therapy, 472
lyceum movement, 116
Lynd, James, 146-47, 156; *Class-Book of Etymology*, 146; *First Book of Etymology*, 146-47

Madison, James, 72
malapropisms, 19-20, 27
Mann, Horace, 5, 159; and educational reform in Mass., 130-31
Marsh, George Perkins: *The Goths in New England*, 148; *Lectures on the English Language*, 479
Marsh, James: edition of Coleridge's *Aids*, 59, 67; translation of Herder, 57; and University of Vermont, 66-67
Marshall, John, 72
Marx Brothers, 1
Massachusetts: Board of Education, 5; comic almanacs in, 15; congregational

feuding in, 57; educational reform in, 130-31
mathematics, and language, 48-49
Mather, Cotton, Thoreau on, 205
Mathews, Cornelius, 59
May, Amasa, *The Etymological Reader* (with Epes Sargent), 156
McClellan, George B., 26
McElligott, James Napoleon, 145-47; *American Debater*, 146
McReady, F., *Art of English Grammar in Verse*, 141
Melville, Herman, xii-xiii, 53, 272, 323-33; and anthropomorphism, 41; *Billy Budd*, 331-33; *The Confidence-Man*, 331; and double negatives in *Moby-Dick*, 330; "I and My Chimney," 268; *Israel Potter*, 59; *Mardi*, 324; *Moby-Dick*, 324, 325-31, 435; *Omoo*, 324; puns enumerated, 324, 325; *Redburn*, 324; "The Tartarus of Maids," 466; *Typee*, 324; *White-Jacket*, 324
Mencken, H. L., 120
Merriam-Webster *New American Dictionary*, 11
Michael, Ian, 102; on British grammars, 135
Mill, James, 45
Miller, Perry, 260
misogyny, Thoreau and, 456-57
Mitchill, Samuel Latham, 1
Moby-Dick (Melville), 324, 325-31, 435; double negatives in, 330; Ishmael's rhetoric in, 330-31; number of puns in, 325; scatological humor in, 325-26
mock-heroic: in Dickinson, 344; in Hoshour, 170; in Irving, 292-93; in *Walden*, 437-40; in Whitman, 393
moral utilitarianism, 228
morphology, 69
Mothers Magazine, 230
Mount Holyoke College, Dickinson at, 345
Müller, Max, 254; and "ding-dong theory," 382
Murray, Alexander, *History of the European Languages*, 49
Murray, Lindley, 23, 84, 85, 96; classification of verbs, 78; *English Grammar*, 68-72, 75; Sherman on, 80

Nasby, Petroleum V., 213
Native Americans. *See* American Indians
neologisms: Coleridge's penchant for, 60; Poe's penchant for, 303-4; in newspapers, 14-15
neology, 3

Neo-Platonists, 31; and nature as language, 30
New Criticism/New Critics, 260
New Orleans Weekly Picayune, 15
newspapers: neologisms in, 14-15; wordplay in, 13-14; wordplay in, Thoreau unamused by, 213
New System of Grammar, 84
Newton, Isaac, and "grammar of Nature," 30
Newtonian physics, and verbs, 76-77
New York Literary Gazette, 18-19, 110
New York Times, on *Walden*, 435
North American Review, 1, 72, 121, 128
Norton, Andrews, 238-40, 250, 368; *Statement of Reasons for Not Believing the Doctrines of Trinitarians*, 238
nouns, 43-44, 254, 264; Bushnell on, 243; in *Moby-Dick*, 330-31; into verbs, 389-90; Whitman and, 378, 386-87, 389-90

Oegger, Guillaume, 194, 259; *Le Vrai Messie*, 263
Ohio: grammar in, 117, 121; home of Ruggles, 2-3; home of Williams, 161-62
okay/OK, 13-14
Oken, Lorenz, 176, 382, 428, 468, 475
Old Testament, 46; punning in, 58
One God in One Person Only, 80
onomatopoeia: in de Brosses's language theory, 32-33; and primal languages, 243; Thoreau's use of, 407; theories of, 382; in Whitman, 375-76
oratory: Barber's textbooks on, 402-4; Emerson's interest in, 276-78; Hawthorne's attitude toward, 316, 322; Melville's youthful, 323, 330; Thoreau's attitude toward, 404-6, 418-19, 421; Whitman's interest in, 181-82
organic principles, to define language, 96-97, 257
Orphic poetry/Orphic Poet, 261, 263, 265-68, 269-70, 364
orthography, 6, 68; displaced by etymology, 69-70
Oswald, John, 157; *Etymological Dictionary of the English Language*, 146, 156

Park, Edwards, 241
Parker, Theodore, 265; "The Transient and the Permanent in Christianity," 416-17
paronomasia, 58, 61
parsing: "philosophic," 72, 74-75; of sentences, 70-71, 89
Pasigraphie, 160

Pater, Walter, 473
Paulson, A. B., 280
Peabody, Elizabeth Palmer, 183, 186, 194, 263
Peabody, Sophia, 316
Peirce, Oliver, Goldsbury on, 134
penny press, 27
Philadelphia, 95; Irving on, 291-92; J. Brown in, 91, 105-6
Philological Society, Webster's, 3
philology, x; Coleridge on, 62; Schlegels and, 52; Thoreau's interest in, 34; Whitman's study of, 172-74, 177
"philosophic parsing," 72, 74-75
philosophy of language: Locke's influence on, 29; Roget on, 160-61
phrenology, 379
Phunny Phellows, 21-22, 213
pictographs, letters as, 38-39
Pittsburgh: Dickens on, 137; Hildreth and, 137, 139-40; Presbyterian savants in, 143
plagiarism, 145-46; root of, 175
Plato, 31-32, 477; *Cratylus*, 46-47
play, importance: to Dickinson, 347; to Emerson, 257-58; to Thoreau, 466-78
Pliny, *Natural History*, 205, 464
Poe, Edgar Allan, xii-xiii, 158, 268, 303-15; and anthropomorphism, 41; "Berenice," 307; "The Cask of Amontillado," 314-15; "Enigmatical and Conundrumical," 304; *Eureka*, 315; "The Fall of the House of Usher," 307-8, 310, 465; "The Gold-Bug," 312-13; on Hood, 304, 472; "How to Write a Blackwood Article," 310; influenced by Schlegels, 307; *Marginalia*, 304, 306; "The Masque of the Red Death," 310; *The Narrative of Arthur Gordon Pym*, 311-12; "The Philosophy of Composition," 308-9; *Pinakidia*, 306; "The Pit and the Pendulum," 310; "The Raven," 308-10; and silence, 410; "A Tale of Jerusalem," 307; *Tales of the Grotesque and Arabesque*, 56, 435; "Ulalume," 314, 475
Poirier, Richard, 272; on excremental vision in *Walden*, 447
polarity/polarization, 468; Thoreau on, 427-30
Pond, Enoch, 75-76, 131
Porte, Joel, 473; on Emerson, 256
Prentice, George: *Prenticeana*, 22; and pun as weapon, 22-23
prepositions, 43-44

Primal Namer, Emerson's Poet as, 8, 252, 259
primitive language: de Brosses's theory on, 32-33; Hebrew as original, 62; Thoreau's interest in, 39
pronouns: degendered, 117-18; deictic, 386-87
prosody, 68
Protestantism, American, 242-50
Prynne, Hester, 317-22
punning: Coleridge on, 61; Elizabethan, 57; Melville's use of, 331; in Old Testament, 58; and spelling pedagogy, 20-21; as therapy, 471-72; Thoreau's, analyzed, 211-18
puns: in *The Confidence-Man*, 331; Dickinson's use of, 344-54; English cult of, 27; German Romantics' love of, 54-56; homonymic, 55; Irving's use of, 295-96; in *Moby-Dick*, 325, 331; and Philadelphians, 291-92; Poe's use of, 303-15; as pointed words, 218; as vehicle for genius, 478; as weapon, 22-23, 56, 472
Putnam's Magazine, 17, 171; "Puns and Punsters" (Hill), 10; Swinton in, 171, 175

Quarterly Review, on Tooke, 46
Quimby, Phineas Parkhurst, 271-72

Reed, Henry, 159
Reed, Sampson, 247, 253, 259; influence on Emerson, 382
Reid, Thomas, 46, 66
Rhode Island Republican, 15
Richardson, Charles, 175
Richter, Jean Paul, 51, 52, 431; *Vorschule der Aesthetik*, 55
rime riche, in Dickinson's poetry, 354
Ripley, George, 240, 265
Robbins, Manasseh, *Rudimental Lessons in Etymology and Syntax*, 72
Roche, Martin, controversy with Brown, 95
Roget, Peter Mark, *Thesaurus of English Words and Phrases*, 159-61
Romantic irony, x, 50-57, 66, 478-79; Bushnell and, 249; in Cooper, 302-3; Dickinson's use of, 361, 362-69; Emerson and, 282-83; Hawthorne's use of, 322-23; Irving's use of, 296; Johnson's use of, 236; in Melville, 331; puns as weapon of, 56; in Thoreau, 431, 435; in Whitman, 393, 400-401
Romantics: American, 27-67 passim; German, 50-57

Round Hill School, 17-18
Rousseau, Jean-Jacques, 46; and origin of language, 69, 190, 384
Ruggles, James, universal language of, 1-3
Rush, James, *Philosophy of the Human Voice,* 316, 320, 398, 402
Ruskin, John, and philology, 62

Sage, W. L., 249
Sand, George, *Mauprat,* 348
Sanders, Charles W., *Analysis of English Words,* 147
San Francisco Golden Era, 15
Sanskrit, Schlegels' study of, 52
Sapir-Whorf hypothesis, 88
Sargent, Epes, *The Etymological Reader* (with Amasa May), 156
Saturday Museum, Poe writing in, 304
Saunterer's pose, 168
Scarlet Letter, The (Hawthorne), 317-23
scatological humor, 445-79 passim; in *Moby-Dick,* 325-26
Schiller, Johann von, 51; concept of *Spieltrieb,* 52-53, 242, 468; *Letters on the Aesthetic Education of Man,* 52
Schlegel, A. W., 51-57, 308; *A Course of Lectures on Dramatic Art and Literature,* 56-57
Schlegel, Friedrich, x, 248, 270-71, 416; *Abounding Fullness,* 52-54, 57, 270, 325, 391, 468; influence on Thoreau, 427, 468; *Lectures on the History of Literature, Ancient and Modern,* 56, 427; *Lucinde,* 55; "Of Incomprehensibility," 53; "On the Limits of the Beautiful," 52; and philology, 62; *Philosophy of Language,* 249; and Romantic irony, 51-57
Schleyer, Johann, Volapuk, 3
scientific language. *See* language, scientific
Scott, James, 153
Scottish commonsense philosophy, 46-50, 121, 249
Scriblerians, 27
Scripture: Bushnell on, 245-46; Dickinson's reactions to, 357-58; as literature, 57, 228; naming in, 91; Norton's interpretation of, 238-40; Trinitarian passages in, 89, 238-40; Unitarian position and, 89
Sears, Barnas, 159
sensationalist theory, 28-32
sentence structure, 70
sexual identity: Dickinson's, 496 n. 9; Irving's, xiv; Thoreau's, 457-58; Whitman's, 177-78
sexuality: in comic almanacs, 15; in Emer-

son's and Thoreau's view of language, 198-99, 277-78
Shakespeare, William, 27; A. W. Schlegel on, 56-57; Coleridge on, 66; influence on Dickinson, 344
Shattuck, Samuel, 125
Sherman, John, 79-91; on Cardell, 86-87, 95; *A Description of Trenton Falls,* 80; interpretation of Scripture, 89; Johnson compared with, 231; Kauy-a-hoo-ra, 80, 82, 84, 89, 90, 110; on Murray, 80; *The Philosophy of Language Illustrated: An Entirely New System of Grammar,* 79-80, 84, 110; on Tooke, 84-85, 95; as Unitarian minister, 80; and universal grammar, 88, 90
Sherman, Roger, 1, 80
Shillaber, B. P., and Mrs. Partington, 10-20, 344
silence: Dickinson on, 359; Emerson on, 252-53; Peabody on, 183; Thoreau and, 408-26 passim
Silverman, Kenneth, 306
Simmons, W. H., 404-5
Sivry, Poisinet de, 190
slang, 13-14
Smeaton, William, 144-45
Smith, Adam, 220, 229; *Dissertation on Language,* 42-43; and origin of language, 69; summarized by Stewart, 49
Smith, E., *Philosophical Grammar of the English Language,* 110
Smith, Gayle, on double negatives in *Moby-Dick,* 330
Smith, Horace, 307
Smith, Roswell, 131
Smith, Sydney, 23
Society for the Diffusion of Useful Knowledge, 159, 161
Socrates, 53
solitude, Thoreau and, 430-33
South Hanover, Ind., 112
Spectator, The, 27
spellers, 3-10, 135, 141-47 passim
spelling: in Pennsylvania, 135; as source for punning, 20-21; 19th century obsession with, 3-4, 7-8; Whitman on, 5
spelling bee, 4, 69
Springfield, Ill., 117
Springfield Daily Republican, Dickinson published in, 346
Stein, Gertrude, on diagramming sentences, 70
Stewart, Dugald, 121, 248-49, 308, 318; *Elements of the Philosophy of the Human Mind,* 47-50

Stuart, Moses, 241
swearing: Emerson and Thoreau on, 13; Thoreau's attitude toward, 456
Swedenborgianism, 247; Emerson and, 259; and nature as language, 30
Swinton, William, 171-82; influenced by Trench, 175; influence on Whitman, 172-73, 177-79; *Rambles among Words*, 175, 177-79, 182; "Rambles over the Realms of Verbs and Substantives," 171
synonyms/synonymies, 165-66
syntascope, 103-4
syntax, 68; Brown's focus on, 91, 93, 101, 108; Brown's tree comparison, 96-97, 98, 99; Elizabethan, 201; isolated from etymology, 71-72; teaching of, 103-5
syntithology, 104

teaching, influence: on Melville, 323-24; on Thoreau, 130-31; on Whitman, 387
Ten Commandments, 318
terra firma. *See* earth
textbooks: on etymology, 141-47; on grammar, 73-74, 79-102, 110-25, 130-40; on spelling, 3-10, 141-43
therapy: humor as, 23-24, 25; wordplay as, 471-72
Thomas, Joseph, 147, 156
Thompson, Mortimer, *Doesticks What He Says*, 213
Thoreau, Henry David, xiii, 171-82; and American speech, 12-13; architectural theory, 39-42, 451; asceticism, 460-65; "Autumnal Tints," 475; aversion to human contact, 458, 464; "Baker Farm," 452-53; "The Bean-Field," 437-40, 449; Biblical allusions in *Walden*, 436-37; bowel obsession, 445-79 passim; "Brute Neighbors," 443-44; and career as naturalist, 30; as Channing's student, 129; on Chaucer, 128; and Christ, 436-37; "Civil Disobedience," 473; Commencement address, 405-6; and consumption, 462-64; on disease, 462; "Economy," 434-35, 436, 446, 451, 453, 457, 459-60; educational experiences, 125-30; enthusiasm for Tooke, 45; excremental vision of, 445-54; "Former Inhabitants; and Winter Visitors," 451-52; and Genesis, 422; at Harvard, 127-30, 402-6; "Higher Laws," 198-99, 447, 448, 452-53, 458, 460, 461; hydraulic psychology, 199-200, 208; and importance of play, 466-

78; influenced by Coleridge, 427-30; influenced by Emerson, 164-65; influenced by F. Schlegel, 427, 468; influenced by Trench, 466-67; influenced by Whiter, 465; influenced by Wilkinson, 469-71; influence of Carlyle, 207-8, 460, 471; influence of Gébelin, 35, 38; interest in philology, 34; Journal, 402-26 passim, 437-38, 450-51, 455, 456, 458-59, 460, 462, 464, 473-74, 477; and Kraitsir, 184-86, 465; misogyny of, 456-57; mistrust of punning, 216; moves to Walden Pond, 130, 412; and *OK*, 14; and organic language, 197-200, 206-11; and "playing Indian," 434, 436; on polarity, 427-30; "The Pond in Winter," 460; "The Ponds," 441-43, 448, 456; punning analyzed, 211-18; "Reading," 417-21, 434; Romantic irony in, 431, 435; and Samoset, 434; and Saunterer's pose, 168; as self-styled economist, 39; "The Service," 460; sexual identity, 457-58; and silence, 408-26 passim; "Society," 406; "Solitude," 430-33, 434, 457, 464, 468; "Sounds," 421-26, 434; "Spring," 185-86, 188, 448-49, 464; on swearing, 13; as teacher, 129-30; on tears and bowels, 459; "Thomas Carlyle and His Works," 207; translation of Gérando, 42; on trees, 203-4; use of mock-heroic, 437-40; use of onomatopoeia, 407; and vegetarianism, 449, 455; "The Village," 440-41; "Visitors," 433-37; *Walden, or Life in the Woods*, xi, 27-28, 31, 47-48, 50, 156, 165, 184-86, 184-218 passim, 268, 411, 417-79 passim; and walking as ritual, 455; *A Week on the Concord and Merrimack Rivers*, 38, 128, 197, 412-17; "Winter Animals," 447; and "Young America," 59
Thoreau, John, 130; death of, 411-12
Ticknor, Almon, *Columbian Spelling-Book*, 142
to be (verb): in Cardell's system, 77-78; and Cooper's Indians, 297-98; in Gébelin's system, 40; in Hildreth's system, 122; Williams on, 163
Tocqueville, Alexis de, x, 11
Tooke, John Horne, 3, 11, 64, 66, 121, 176; *Diversions of Purley*, 42-46, 68, 116, 127-28, 136, 252; influence on Cardell, 75, 77-78; influence on Coleridge, 59-60; influence on Emerson, 254, 259; influence on Grimshaw, 158; influence

on Thoreau, 127–28; influence on Vernon, 113; and origin of language, 69; Sherman on, 84–85, 95; summarized by Stewart, 49

Topsell, Edward, *History of Four-Footed Beasts*, 201

Town, Salem: *An Analysis of the Derivative Words in the English Language*, 143–44; charges McElligott with plagiarism, 145–46; *Spelling, and Defining, Book*, 144

tragic/comic dichotomy, 25

trees: Blanchard's grammatical, 136–37, *138*; as Brown's metaphor for syntax, 96–97, *98, 99*; Thoreau on, 203–4

Trench, Richard Chenevix, 163–67; influence on Swinton, 175; influence on Thoreau, 466–67; influence on Whitman, 176–77; *On the Study of Words*, 163–64

Trenton, N.Y., Unitarian church in, 80

Trinitarian doctrine, 239–40; and anthropomorphism, 245–46

Trumbull, John, 72

tuberculosis. *See* consumption

Turner, Sharon, *History of the Anglo-Saxons*, 128

Twain, Mark, *Huckleberry Finn*, 270, 271–72

Type of the Times, 5

Unitarians: Boston, xii, 57, 80, 240–41; British, 59; feud with Congregationalists, 57, 238–42; and silence, 253

Universalchemie, 55

universal grammar, 88

universal language: Roget on, 160–61; Ruggles's proposal for, 1–3

Universal Language of Nature, Berkeley's doctrine of, 30–31

University of Vermont, 66–67

Upham, Thomas, 318

U.S. Constitution: Brown's offer to clarify, 94; Webster and ratification of, 3

U.S. Literary Gazette, on Irving, 296

Utica, N.Y., 219–38 passim; Bank of Utica, 221; cholera epidemic of 1832, 234

Utica Insurance Company, A. B. Johnson and, 221

Utilitarianism, 45

Valentine, William: *Budget of Wit and Humor, A*, 24; on laughing as therapy, 23–24

Van Buren, Martin, 14, 220–21

Vandalia Free Press, 15

vegetarianism, Thoreau and, 449, 455

verbal conceits, 58–59

verbs, 43–44; Bushnell on, 243; Dickinson and, 356; Emerson and, 254–55, 264–65, 280; energy of, 264–65, 391; importance in Hebrew, 57–58; in *Moby-Dick*, 331; Murray's classification of, 78; Newtonian physics and, 76–77; into nouns, 389–90; and power, 122, 140, 265; Whitman and, 378, 389–90

Vere, Maximilian Schele de, *Outlines of Comparative Philology*, 172, 389

Vermont: Transcendentalism in, 57, 67; University of, 66–67

Vernon, N., Cardell's influence on, 113–14

violence, in comic almanacs, 15

vocalism: Dickinson's sensitivity to, 359; in Whitman, 376–85 passim, 395, 397

Wadsworth, Charles, 338, 347, 358

Walden, or Life in the Woods (Thoreau), xi, 27–28, 47–48, 50, 184–86, 184–218 passim, 268, 411, 417–79 passim; Biblical allusions in, 436–37; Christ in, 436–37; excremental vision in, 445–79 passim; on living earth, 31; mock-heroic in, 437–40; publication of, 156, 165, 211; reviews of, 435

walking, as ritual for Thoreau, 455

Walworth, Reuben Hyde: Cardell's influence on, 114; *Hyde Genealogy*, 115; *Rules and Orders*, 114–15

Ward, Artemus, 19, 26, 213

War of the Dictionaries, 11–12

Webster, Noah, 334–35, 342; *American Dictionary*, 10–12, 354–55, 378, 457; *American Spelling Book*, 3, 4, 5–6, 142–43; and Anglo-Saxon English, 147–48; Bowdlerized Bible, 9; *Elementary Spelling Book*, 6–7, 21; influence on Dickinson, 354–55; *International Dictionary*, 12; Merriam-Webster *New American Dictionary*, 11; *Philosophical and Practical Grammar of the English Language*, 68; *The Teacher*, 144, 156; theory of linguistic development, 10–11, 355; and U.S. Constitution, 3

Wellerisms, 15

Western Messenger, 262

Wheeler, Charles Stearns, 127

Wheeling, Va., 137, 139–40

Whig party, *Louisville Daily Journal* and, 23

Whipple, E. P., 25

Whiter, Walter, 189–96; *Dissertation on the Disorder of Death*, 196; *Etymologicon*

Magnum, 189–90, 456; *Etymologicon Universale,* 190–93, 195, 196; influence on Thoreau, 465; *A Specimen of a Commentary on Shakespeare,* 196; theory of language from dirt, 190–93, 382

Whitman, Sarah Power, 305

Whitman, Walt, xiii, 101, 147–54, 171–82, 268, 370–401; *The American Primer,* 8–9, 174, 375, 378, 381; "America's Mightiest Inheritance," 154–55, 173, 178; and Amerindian nomenclature, 370–76; and Anglo-Saxon roots, 147–55; "Apostrophe," 173–74; "Calamus," 177; *Calamus* poems, 393–94; "City of Ships," 176–77; "A Clear Midnight," 398; and doctrine of body language, 376–85 passim; "Good-bye My Fancy," 398; on "Indians," 374; influenced by A Literary Association, 153–55, 173, 181; influenced by Chaucer, 178–79; influenced by Swinton, 172–73, 177–79; influenced by Trench, 176–77; "I Sing the Body Electric," 379–80; *Leaves of Grass,* 9, 153, 171–82, 370–401 passim; lectures, 181–82; and Manhattan, 371–73; on nouns, 386–87; on nouns vs. verbs, 378; and onomatopoeia, 375–76, 382–83; "Out of the Cradle, Endlessly Rocking," 394; "Passage to India," 179; "Salut au Monde," 377; "Scented Herbage of My Breast," 177–78; self-promotion of, 171–72; and sexual identity, 177–78; "Slang in America," 174; "The Sleepers," 376; "Song of Myself," 370–401 passim; "Song of the Broad-Axe," 153; "A Song of the Rolling Earth," 176, 380–81, 382; and sound, 376–78; *Spec-* *imen Days,* 377, 399; on spelling, 5; "Spontaneous Me," 379; study of philology, 172–74, 177; on swearing, 13; "That Shadow My Likeness," 431; "There Was a Child Went Forth," 154; "The Unexpress'd," 398; Variorum edition of *Leaves of Grass,* 400; and verbs into nouns, 389–90; vocalism in, 376–85 passim, 395, 397; "A Word Out of the Sea," 394

Whitney, William Dwight, 334

Wilbrand, J. B., 428

Wilkins, Bishop, 2; *Essay towards a Real Character and a Philosophical Language,* 160

Wilkinson, James John Garth, *The Human Body,* 469–71

Williams, John, 161–63; *The Readable Dictionary,* 162–63

Willis, N. P., 305, 314

Wilson, Jacob, *Phrasis,* 196

Wirt, William, 2

Worcester, Joseph Emerson, 11–12, 165; as Hawthorne's teacher, 316; *Universal Dictionary,* 11

Worcester Palladium, on *Walden,* 435

word: as God, 187–88; as semen, 198–99

wordplay, xiv–xv; as heart of Romantic irony, 54; as therapy, 471–72

Wordsworth, William, 65, 200

Wortspiel, German Romantics and, 54. *See also* puns

Wright, Frank Lloyd, on Thoreau, 40

Yankee Doodle, Melville writing in, 324

Yeats, William Butler, "Lapis Lazuli," 478

"Young America," 59, 324